ROGET'S THESAURUS

OF
ENGLISH WORDS AND PHRASES

FACSIMILE OF THE FIRST EDITION 1852

Bloomsbury Books
London

Peter Mark Roget
Thesaurus of English Words and Phrases
Original Edition 1852

This edition published by Bloomsbury Books, an imprint of
Godfrey Cave Associates, 42 Bloomsbury Street, London WC1B 3QJ.
under licence from Banson 1992

© Banson Marketing Ltd (this Edition and this design) 1992.
Introduction © 1987 Laurence Urdang

ISBN 1 85471 076 1

Printed in England by
BPCC Hazell Books
Aylesbury, Bucks, England
Member of BPCC Ltd.

INTRODUCTION

Although the name of Peter Mark Roget is known to us today
almost entirely as that of the creator of the *Thesaurus of
English Words & Phrases*, the man was quite remarkable in
other respects, as well. Born in 1779, Roget trained as a doctor
and practised medicine in London from 1808 to 1840. In 1824,
he wrote *The Persistence of Vision with Regard to Moving
Objects*, a document setting out the principle that the eye
retains an image of the continuation of movement for a time
after the stimulus of watching a body in motion. The
significance of this thesis was not lost on resourceful inventors
of the day, who at once set about developing a variety of devices
that we today regard as the forerunners of the motion-picture
projector: the Zoëtrope, the Stroboscope, and the Praxino-
scope.

Roget began making notes for the system of verbal
classification later employed in his *Thesaurus* in 1805; but it
was not until after his retirement, in 1840 at age 61, that he
started to work on the synonym book in earnest. The *First
Edition*, a facsimile copy of which you are holding, was
published by Longman in 1852, when Roget was 73 years of age.
Subsequent editions, which were numerous, were worked on
by him and, later, by his son. There is no known bibliography
of all the editions of the *Thesaurus*, which have been published
in both England and America for many years, there is no telling
exactly how many have been published to date, but the number
is quite large.

Comparison between this *First Edition* and a modern edition
the latest was published in June 1987 – reveals many
differences: much more science and technology, which did not

exist in Roget's day, is reflected in the recent editions; however, although some categories have been added: Roget's original work still had over 1,000. The 1987 edition is claimed by the publishers (still Longman) to contains '11,000 new words and phrases' not included in the previous edition, published in 1982. These additions are the result not only of the expansion of the language by its persistent, continued acquisition of words and phrases from other languages (many of which have become totally assimilated), but also of the propensity of English for new coinages and, far from least, of its energetic capacity for 'internal' expansion by means of productive metaphor. Today, the word stock of English is probably greater than that of any other language on earth – past or present – and up-to-date editions of *Roget's Thesaurus* confirm this burgeoning of meaning.

The unique feature of *Roget's Thesaurus* is the hierarchical arrangement of categories. Today, some of those classifications may strike the user of the book as curious; but it must be remembered that they result from an early nineteenth-century philosophical view of the universe. We know too little about Roget to comment sensibly on him personally – his social, psychological, religious, philosophical views – except insofar as the classifications themselves offer evidence of his attempt at creating a cogent structure out of those views. It must be borne in mind that while he attempted a classification that was 'scientific', the science of his day was, by modern standards, quite primitive, coming towards the end of centuries of Neo-Platonism. Classification systems prevalent at the time were those of the positivistic methods set forth by Linnaeus: there remained in the minds of even the most forward-thinking people of the day the notion of a metaphysical 'truth'. This was seen in the works not only of Linnaeus but of Erasmus Darwin, John Stuart Mill, and Lamarck, culminating in the struggles of Hegel to impose order on the chaos of the universe. The methods of empirical science had yet to evolve, and, in the sense that Roget was very much a product of his time, his *Thesaurus* represents a latter-day manifestation of the notions set by the eighteenth-century French encyclopedists and exemplified by Cudworth's *The True Intellectual System of the Universe*.

Later on in the nineteenth century, such a priori structuring became anathema, and modern observers find it interesting that the structure devised by Roget persists to this day. From our observation, it appears that few people actually use the structure of the *Thesaurus*: invariably, one uses the Index to find the word for which a synonym (or antonym) is required in order to be referred to the section where that set of words and phrases is grouped. In practice, users only infrequently refer to the hierarchical classification system, carefully outlined in precis form in the front matter of the book. On the other hand, the subsystem, in which the notions set out in the classifications are set as opposites to one another, where the words associated with good are contrasted with those for bad or evil – that subsystem does work. It is unfortunate that, for reasons of space, some modern editions have had to lose Roget's careful positioning of synonyms adjacent to their antonyms which was one of the cornerstones of the structure of this first edition of the *Thesaurus*. *Roget's Thesaurus* survives as one of the most frequently used systems of its kind. Perhaps that is so because we still have so much to learn about the English language.

Laurence Urdang

June 1987
Aylesbury, Buckinghamshire

THESAURUS

OF

ENGLISH WORDS AND PHRASES,

CLASSIFIED AND ARRANGED

SO AS

TO FACILITATE THE EXPRESSION OF IDEAS

AND ASSIST IN

LITERARY COMPOSITION.

BY PETER MARK ROGET, M.D., F.R.S., F.R.A.S., F.G.S.

FELLOW OF THE ROYAL COLLEGE OF PHYSICIANS;

MEMBER OF THE SENATE OF THE UNIVERSITY OF LONDON;

OF THE LITERARY AND PHILOSOPHICAL SOCIETIES ETC. OF MANCHESTER, LIVERPOOL,
BRISTOL, QUEBEC, NEW YORK, HAARLEM, TURIN, AND STOCKHOLM.

AUTHOR OF

THE "BRIDGEWATER TREATISE ON ANIMAL AND VEGETABLE PHYSIOLOGY,"
ETC.

"It is impossible we should thoroughly understand the nature of the SIGNS, unless
we first properly consider and arrange the THINGS SIGNIFIED."—Ἔπεα Πτερόεντα.

LONDON:

LONGMAN, BROWN, GREEN, AND LONGMANS.

1852.

London:
Spottiswoodes and Shaw
New-street-Square.

PREFACE.

It is now nearly fifty years since I first projected a system of verbal classification similar to that on which the present Work is founded. Conceiving that such a compilation might help to supply my own deficiencies, I had, in the year 1805, completed a classed catalogue of words on a small scale, but on the same principle, and nearly in the same form, as the Thesaurus now published. I had often, during that long interval, found this little collection, scanty and imperfect as it was, of much use to me in literary composition, and often contemplated its extension and improvement; but a sense of the magnitude of the task, amidst a multitude of other avocations, deterred me from the attempt. Since my retirement from the duties of Secretary of the Royal Society, however, finding myself possessed of more leisure, and believing that a repertory, of which I had myself experienced the advantage, might, when amplified, prove useful to others, I resolved to embark in an undertaking, which, for the last three or four years, has given me incessant occupation, and has, indeed, imposed upon me an amount of labour very much greater than I had anticipated. Notwithstanding all the pains I have bestowed on its execution, I am fully aware of its numerous deficiencies and imperfections, and of its falling far short of the degree of excellence that might be attained. But, in a work of this nature, where perfection is placed at so great a distance, I have thought it best to limit my ambition to that moderate share of merit which it may claim in its present form; trusting to the indulgence of those for whose benefit it is intended, and to the candour of critics, who, while they find it easy to detect faults, can, at the same time, duly appreciate difficulties.

P. M. ROGET.

Upper Bedford Place, London.
April 29th, 1852.

INTRODUCTION.

THE present Work is intended to supply, with respect to the English language, a desideratum hitherto unsupplied in any language; namely, a collection of the words it contains and of the idiomatic combinations peculiar to it, arranged, not in alphabetical order, as they are in a Dictionary, but according to the *ideas* which they express. The purpose of an ordinary dictionary is simply to explain the meaning of words; and the problem of which it professes to furnish the solution may be stated thus:—The word being given, to find its signification, or the idea it is intended to convey. The object aimed at in the present undertaking is exactly the converse of this; namely,—The idea being given, to find the word, or words, by which that idea may be most fitly and aptly expressed. For this purpose, the words and phrases of the language are here classed, not according to their sound or their orthography, but strictly according to their *signification*.

The communication of our thoughts by means of language, whether spoken or written, like every other object of mental exertion, constitutes a peculiar art, which, like other arts, cannot be acquired in any perfection but by long and continued practice. Some, indeed, there are, more highly gifted than others with a facility of expression, and naturally endowed with the power of eloquence; but to none is it at all times an easy process to embody in exact and appropriate language the various trains of ideas that are passing through the mind, or to depict in their true colours and proportions the diversified and nicer shades of feeling which accompany them. To those who are unpractised in the art of composition, or unused to extempore speaking, these difficulties present themselves in their most formidable aspect. However distinct may be our views, however vivid our conceptions, or however fervent our emotions, we cannot but be often conscious that the phraseology we have at our command is inadequate to do them justice. We seek in vain the words we need, and strive ineffectually to devise forms of expression which shall faithfully portray our thoughts and sentiments. The appropriate terms, notwithstanding our utmost efforts, cannot be conjured up at will. Like " spirits from the vasty deep," they come not when we call; and we are driven to the employment of a set of words and phrases either too general or too limited, too strong or too feeble, which suit not the occasion, which hit not the mark we aim at; and the result of our prolonged exertion is a style at once laboured and obscure, vapid and redundant, or vitiated by the still graver faults of affectation or ambiguity.

It is to those who are thus painfully groping their way and struggling with the difficulties of composition, that this Work professes to hold out a helping hand. The assistance it gives is that of furnishing on every topic a copious store of words and phrases, adapted to express all the recognizable shades and modifications of the general idea under which those words and phrases are arranged. The inquirer can readily select, out of the ample collection spread out before his eyes in the following pages, those expressions which are best suited to his purpose, and which might not have occurred to him without such assistance. In order to make this selection, he scarcely ever need engage in any elaborate or critical study of the subtle distinctions existing between synonymous terms; for if the materials set before him be sufficiently abundant, an instinctive tact will rarely fail to lead him to the proper choice. Even while glancing over the columns of this work, his eye may chance to light upon a particular term, which may save the cost of a clumsy paraphrase, or spare the labour of a tortuous circumlocution. Some felicitous turn of expression thus introduced will frequently open to the mind of the reader a whole vista of collateral ideas, which could not, without an extended and obtrusive episode, have been unfolded to his view; and often will the judicious insertion of a happy epithet, like a beam of sunshine in a landscape, illumine and adorn the subject which it touches, imparting new grace, and giving life and spirit to the picture.

Every workman in the exercise of his art should be provided with proper implements. For the fabrication of complicated and curious pieces of mechanism, the artisan requires a corresponding assortment of various tools and instruments. For giving proper effect to the fictions of the drama, the actor should have at his disposal a well-furnished wardrobe, supplying the costumes best suited to the personages he is to represent. For the perfect delineation of the beauties of nature, the painter should have within reach of his pencil every variety and combination of hues and tints. Now the writer, as well as the orator, employs for the accomplishment of his purposes the instrumentality of words; it is in words that he clothes his thoughts; it is by means of words that he depicts his feelings. It is therefore essential to his success that he be provided with a copious vocabulary, and that he possess an entire command of all the resources and appliances of his language. To the acquisition of this power no procedure appears more directly conducive than the study of a methodized system such as that now offered to his use.

The utility of the present Work will be appreciated more especially by those who are engaged in the arduous process of translating into English a work written in another language. Simple as the operation may appear, on a superficial view, of rendering into English each of its sentences, the task of transfusing, with perfect exactness, the sense of the original, preserving at the same time the style and character of its composition, and reflecting with fidelity the mind and the spirit of the author, is a task of extreme difficulty. The cultivation of this useful department of literature was in ancient times strongly recommended both by Cicero and by Quinctilian, as essential to the formation of a good writer and accomplished orator. Regarded simply as a mental exercise, the practice of translation is the best training for the attainment of that mastery of language and felicity of diction, which are the sources of the highest oratory, and are requisite for the possession of a graceful and persuasive eloquence. By rendering ourselves the faithful interpreters of the thoughts and feelings of others, we are rewarded with the acquisition of greater readiness and facility in correctly expressing our own ; as he, who has best learned to execute the orders of a commander, becomes himself best qualified to command.

In the earliest periods of civilization, translators have been the agents for propagating knowledge from nation to nation, and the value of their labours has been inestimable ; but, in the present age, when so many different languages have become the depositories of the vast treasures of literature and of science which have been accumulating for centuries, the utility of accurate translations has greatly increased, and it has become a more important object to attain perfection in the art.

The use of language is not confined to its being the medium through which we communicate our ideas to one another; it fulfils a no less important function as an *instrument of thought*, not being merely its vehicle, but giving it wings for flight. Metaphysicians are agreed that scarcely any of our intellectual operations could be carried on to any considerable extent without the agency of words. None but those who are conversant with the philosophy of mental phenomena can be aware of the immense influence that is exercised by language in promoting the development of our ideas, in fixing them in the mind, and detaining them for steady contemplation. In every process of reasoning, language enters as an essential element. Words are the instruments by which we form all our abstractions, by which we fashion and embody our ideas, and by which we are enabled to glide along a series of premises and conclusions with a rapidity so great, as to leave in the memory no trace of the successive steps of the process; and we remain unconscious how much we owe to this potent auxiliary of the reasoning faculty. It is on this ground, also, that the present Work founds a claim to utility. The review of a catalogue of words of analogous signification will often suggest by association other trains of thought, which, presenting the subject under new and varied aspects, will vastly expand the sphere of our mental vision. Amidst the many objects thus brought within the range of our contemplation, some striking similitude or appropriate image, some excursive flight or brilliant conception, may flash on the mind, giving point and force to our arguments, awakening a responsive chord in the imagination or sensibility of the reader, and procuring for our reasonings a more ready access both to his understanding and to his heart.

It is of the utmost consequence that strict accuracy should regulate our use of language, and that every one should acquire the power and the habit of expressing his thoughts with perspicuity and correctness. Few, indeed, can appreciate the real extent and importance of that influence which language has always exercised on human affairs, or can be aware how often these are determined by causes much slighter than are apparent to a superficial observer. False logic, disguised under specious phraseology, too often gains the assent of the unthinking multitude, disseminating far and wide the seeds of prejudice and error. Truisms pass current, and wear the semblance of profound wisdom, when dressed up in the tinsel garb of antithetical phrases, or set off by an imposing pomp of paradox. By a confused jargon of involved and mystical sentences, the imagination is easily inveigled into a transcendental region of clouds, and the understanding beguiled into the belief that it is acquiring knowledge and approaching truth. A misapplied or misapprehended term is sufficient to give rise to fierce and interminable disputes: a misnomer has turned the tide of popular opinion; a verbal sophism has decided a party question; an artful watchword, thrown among combustible materials, has kindled the flames of deadly warfare, and changed the destiny of an empire.

In constructing the following system of classification of the ideas which are expressible by language, my chief aim has been to obtain the greatest amount of practical utility. I have accordingly adopted such principles of arrangement as appeared to me to be the simplest and most natural, and which would not require, either for their comprehension or application, any disciplined acumen, or depth of metaphysical or antiquarian lore. Eschewing all needless refinements and subtleties, I have taken as my guide the more obvious characters of the ideas for which expressions were to be tabulated, arranging them under such classes and categories as reflection and experience had taught me would conduct the inquirer most readily and quickly to the object of his search. Commencing with the ideas expressing mere abstract relations, I proceed to those which relate to the phenomena of the material world, and lastly to those in which the mind is concerned, and which comprehend intellect, volition, and feeling; thus establishing six primary Classes of Categories.

1. The first of these classes comprehends ideas derived from the more general and ABSTRACT RELATIONS among things, such as *Existence*, *Resemblance*, *Quantity*, *Order*, *Number*, *Time*, *Power*.

2. The second class refers to SPACE and its various relations, including *Motion*, or change of place.

3. The third class includes all ideas that relate to the MATERIAL WORLD; namely, the *Properties of Matter*, such as *Solidity*, *Fluidity*, *Heat*, *Sound*, *Light*, and the *Phenomena*

they present, as well as the simple *Perceptions* to which they give rise.

4. The fourth class embraces all ideas of phenomena relating to the INTELLECT and its operations; comprising the *Acquisition*, the *Retention*, and the *Communication of Ideas*.

5. The fifth class includes the ideas derived from the exercise of VOLITION; embracing the phenomena and results of our *Voluntary and Active Powers;* such as *Choice, Intention, Utility, Action, Antagonism, Authority, Compact, Property,* &c.

6. The sixth, and last class, comprehends all ideas derived from the operation of our SENTIENT AND MORAL POWERS; including our *Feelings, Emotions, Passions,* and *Moral and Religious Sentiments.**

The further subdivisions and minuter details will be best understood from an inspection of the Tabular Synopsis of Categories prefixed to the work, in which are specified the several *topics* or *heads of signification*, under which the words have been arranged. By the aid of this table, the reader will, with a little practice, readily discover the place which the particular topic he is in search of occupies in the series; and on turning to the page in the body of the work which contains it, he will find the group of expressions he requires, out of which he may cull those that are most appropriate to his purpose. For the convenience of reference, I have designated each separate group or heading by a particular number; so that if, during the search, any doubt or difficulty should occur, recourse may be had to the copious alphabetical

---

* It must necessarily happen in every system of classification framed with this view, that ideas and expressions arranged under one class must include also ideas relating to another class; for the operations of the *Intellect* generally involve also those of the *Will*, and *vice versâ;* and our *Affections* and *Emotions*, in like manner, generally imply the agency both of the *Intellect* and of the *Will*. All that can be effected, therefore, is to arrange the words according to the principal or dominant idea they convey. *Teaching*, for example, although a Voluntary act, relates primarily to the Communication of Ideas, and is accordingly placed at No. 537, under Class IV. Division II. On the other hand, *Choice, Conduct, Skill*, &c., although implying the co-operation of Voluntary with Intellectual acts, relate principally to the former, and are therefore arranged under Class V.

Index of words at the end of the volume, which will at once indicate the number of the required group.*

The object I have proposed to myself in this Work would have been but imperfectly attained if I had confined myself to a mere catalogue of words, and had omitted the numerous phrases and forms of expression, composed of several words, which are of such frequent use as to entitle them to rank among the constituent parts of the language.† Very few of these verbal combinations, so essential to the knowledge of our native tongue, and so profusely abounding in its daily use, are to be met with in ordinary dictionaries. These phrases and forms of expression I have endeavoured diligently to collect and to insert in their proper places, under the general ideas they are designed to convey. Some of these conventional forms, indeed, partake of the nature of proverbial expressions; but actual proverbs, as such, being wholly of a didactic character, do not come within the scope of the present Work; and the reader must therefore not expect to find them here inserted.

For the purpose of exhibiting with greater distinctness the relations between words expressing opposite and correlative ideas, I have, whenever the subject admitted of such an arrangement, placed them in two parallel columns in the same page, so that each group of expressions may be readily contrasted with those which occupy the adjacent column, and constitute their antitheses. By carrying the eye from

---

* It often happens that the same word admits of various applications, or may be used in different senses. In consulting the Index the reader will be guided to the number of the heading under which that word, in each particular acceptation, will be found, by means of *supplementary words*, printed in Italics; which words, however, are not to be understood as explaining the meaning of the word to which they are annexed, but only as assisting in the required reference. I have also, for shortness sake, generally omitted words immediately derived from the primary one inserted, which sufficiently represents the whole group of correlative words referable to the same heading. Thus the number affixed to *Beauty* applies to all its derivatives, such as *Beautiful, Beauteous, Beautify, Beautifulness, Beautifully*, &c., the insertion of which was therefore needless.

† For example :—To take time by the forelock,—to turn over a new leaf,—to show the white feather,—to have a finger in the pie,—to let the cat out of the bag,—to take care of number one,—to kill two birds with one stone, &c. &c.

the one to the other, the inquirer may often discover forms of expression, of which he may avail himself advantageously, to diversify and infuse vigour into his phraseology. Rhetoricians, indeed, are well aware of the power derived from the skilful introduction of antitheses in giving point to an argument, and imparting force and brilliancy to the diction. A too frequent and indiscreet employment of this figure of rhetoric, may, it is true, give rise to a vicious and affected style; but it is unreasonable to condemn indiscriminately the occasional and moderate use of a practice on account of its possible abuse.

The study of correlative terms existing in a particular language may often throw valuable light on the manners and customs of the nations using it. Thus, Hume has drawn important inferences with regard to the state of society among the ancient Romans, from certain deficiencies which he remarked in the Latin language.*

In many cases, two ideas, which are completely opposed to each other, admit of an intermediate or neutral idea, equi-

* "It is an universal observation," he remarks, "which we may form upon language, that where two related parts of a whole bear any proportion to each other, in numbers, rank, or consideration, there are always correlative terms invented, which answer to both the parts, and express their mutual relation. If they bear no proportion to each other, the term is only invented for the less, and marks its distinction from the whole. Thus, *man* and *woman, master* and *servant, father* and *son, prince* and *subject, stranger* and *citizen,* are correlative terms. But the words *seaman, carpenter, smith, tailor,* &c. have no correspondent terms, which express those who are no seamen, no carpenters, &c. Languages differ very much with regard to the particular words where this distinction obtains; and may thence afford very strong inferences concerning the manners and customs of different nations. The military government of the Roman emperors had exalted the soldiery so high, that they balanced all the other orders of the state: hence *miles* and *paganus* became relative terms; a thing, till then, unknown to ancient, and still so to modern languages."—"The term for a slave, born and bred in the family, was *verna.* As *servus* was the name of the genus, and *verna* of the species without any correlative, this forms a strong presumption that the latter were by far the least numerous: and from the same principles I infer that if the number of slaves brought by the Romans from foreign countries had not extremely exceeded those which were bred at home, *verna* would have had a correlative, which would have expressed the former species of slaves. But these, it would seem, composed the main body of the ancient slaves, and the latter were but a few exceptions."—HUME, *Essay on the Populousness of Ancient Nations.*

distant from both : all these being expressible by corresponding definite terms. Thus, in the following examples, the
words in the first and third columns, which express opposite
ideas, admit of the intermediate terms contained in the middle
column, having a neutral sense with reference to the former.

Identity,	*Difference,*	*Contrariety.*
Beginning,	*Middle,*	*End.*
Past,	*Present,*	*Future.*

In other cases, the intermediate word is simply the negative to each of two opposite positions ; as, for example, —

Convexity,	*Flatness,*	*Concavity.*
Desire,	*Indifference,*	*Aversion.*

Sometimes the intermediate word is properly the standard
with which each of the extremes is compared ; as in the
case of

Insufficiency,	*Sufficiency,*	*Redundance ;*

for here the middle term, *Sufficiency,* is equally opposed, on
the one hand to *Insufficiency,* and on the other to *Redundance.*

These forms of correlative expressions would suggest the
use of triple, instead of double, columns, for tabulating this
threefold order of words ; but the practical inconvenience
attending such an arrangement would probably overbalance
its advantages.

It often happens that the same word has several correlative
terms, according to the different relations in which it is considered. Thus, to the word *Giving* are opposed both *Receiving* and *Taking ;* the former correlation having reference to
the *persons* concerned in the transfer, while the latter relates
to the *mode* of transfer. *Old* has for opposite both *New* and
Young, according as it is applied to *things* or to *living beings.*
Attack and *Defence* are correlative terms ; as are also *Attack*
and *Resistance. Resistance,* again, has for its other correlative *Submission. Truth in the abstract* is opposed to *Error ;*
but the opposite of *Truth communicated* is *Falsehood. Acquisition* is contrasted both with *Deprivation* and with *Loss.*

Refusal is the counterpart both of *Offer* and of *Consent*. *Disuse* and *Misuse* may either of them be considered as the correlative of *Use*. *Teaching*, with reference to what is taught, is opposed to *Misteaching;* but with reference to the act itself, its proper reciprocal is *Learning*.

Words contrasted in form do not always bear the same contrast in their meaning. The word *Malefactor*, for example, would, from its derivation, appear to be exactly the opposite of *Benefactor ;* but the ideas attached to these two words are far from being directly opposed ; for while the latter expresses one who confers a benefit, the former denotes one who has violated the laws.

Independently of the immediate practical uses derivable from the arrangement of words in double columns, many considerations, interesting in a philosophical point of view, are presented by the study of correlative expressions. It will be found, on strict examination, that there seldom exists an exact opposition between two words which may at first sight appear to be the counterparts of one another ; for, in general, the one will be found to possess in reality more force or extent of meaning than the other with which it is contrasted. The correlative term sometimes assumes the form of a mere negative, although it is really en-dowed with a considerable positive force. Thus *Disrespect* is not merely the absence of *Respect;* its signification trenches on the opposite idea, namely, *Contempt*. In like manner, *Untruth* is not merely the negative of *Truth;* it involves a degree of *Falsehood*. *Irreligion*, which is properly *the want of Religion*, is understood as being nearly synonymous with *Impiety*. For these reasons, the reader must not expect that all the words which stand side by side in the two columns shall be the precise correlatives of each other ; for the nature of the subject, as well as the imperfections of language, renders it impossible always to preserve such an exactness of correlation.

There exist comparatively few words of a general cha-racter to which no correlative term, either of negation or of opposition, can be assigned, and which therefore require no corresponding second column. The correlative idea, especially that which constitutes a sense negative to the primary one, may, indeed, be formed or conceived; but, from its occurring rarely, no word has been framed to represent it; for in language, as in other matters, the supply fails when there is no probability of a demand. Occasionally we find this deficiency provided for by the contrivance of prefixing the syllable *non*; as, for instance, the negatives of *existence, performance, payment,* &c., are expressed by the compound words, *non-existence, non-performance, non-payment,* &c. Functions of a similar kind are performed by the prefixes *dis-*, anti-, contra-, mis-, in-,* and *un-.†* With respect to all these, and especially the last, great latitude is allowed according to the necessities of the case; a latitude which is limited only by the taste and discretion of the author.

On the other hand, it is hardly possible to find two words having in all respects the same meaning, and being therefore interchangeable; that is, admitting of being employed indiscriminately, the one or the other, in all their applications. The investigation of the distinctions to be drawn between words apparently synonymous, forms a separate branch of inquiry, which I have not presumed here to enter upon; for the subject has already occupied the attention of much abler critics than myself, and its complete exhaustion would require the devotion of a whole life. The purpose of this work, it must be borne in mind, is not to explain the signification of words, but simply to classify and arrange them according to the sense in which they are now used, and which I presume to be already known to the reader. I enter into no inquiry into the changes of meaning they may have undergone in the

---

* The word *disannul*, however, has the same meaning as *annul*.

† In the case of adjectives, the addition to a substantive of the terminal syllable *less*, gives it a negative meaning: as *taste, tasteless; care, careless; hope, hopeless; friend, friendless; fault, faultless;* &c.

course of time. I am content to accept them at the value of their present currency, and have no concern with their etymologies, or with the history of their transformations; far less do I venture to thrid the mazes of the vast labyrinth into which I should be led by any attempt at a general discrimination of synonyms. The difficulties I have had to contend with have already been sufficiently great without this addition to my labours.

The most cursory glance over the pages of a Dictionary will show that a great number of words are used in various senses, sometimes distinguished by slight shades of difference, but often diverging widely from their primary signification, and even, in some cases, bearing to it no perceptible relation. It may even happen that the very same word has two significations quite opposite to one another. This is the case with the verb *to cleave*, which means *to adhere tenaciously*, and also *to separate by a blow*. *To propugn* sometimes expresses *to attack;* at other times, *to defend.* *To ravel* means both *to entangle* and *to disentangle*. The alphabetical Index at the end of this Work sufficiently shows the multiplicity of uses to which, by the elasticity of language, the meaning of words has been stretched, so as to adapt them to a great variety of modified significations in subservience to the nicer shades of thought, which, under peculiarity of circumstances, require corresponding expression. Words thus admitting of different meanings have therefore to be arranged under each of the respective heads corresponding to these various acceptations. There are many words, again, which express ideas compounded of two elementary ideas belonging to different classes. It is therefore necessary to place these words respectively under each of the generic heads to which they relate. The necessity of these repetitions is increased by the circumstance, that ideas included under one class are often connected by relations of the same kind as the ideas which belong to another class. Thus we find the same relations of *order* and of *quantity* existing among the ideas of *Time* as well as those of *Space*.

Sequence in the one is denoted by the same terms as sequence in the other; and the measures of time also express the measures of space. The cause and the effect are often designated by the same word. The word *Sound*, for instance, denotes both the impression made upon the ear by sonorous vibrations, and also the vibrations themselves, which are the cause or source of that impression. *Mixture* is used for the act of mixing, as well as for the product of that operation. *Taste* and *Smell* express both the sensations and the qualities of material bodies giving rise to them. *Thought* is the act of thinking; but the same word denotes also the idea resulting from that act. *Judgment* is the act of deciding, and also the decision come to. *Purchase* is the acquisition of a thing by payment, as well as the thing itself so acquired. *Speech* is both the act of speaking and the words spoken; and so on with regard to an endless multiplicity of words. Mind is essentially distinct from Matter; and yet, in all languages, the attributes of the one are metaphorically transferred to those of the other. Matter, in all its forms, is endowed by the figurative genius of every language with the functions which pertain to intellect; and we perpetually talk of its phenomena and of its powers as if they resulted from the voluntary influence of one body on another, acting and reacting, impelling and being impelled, controlling and being controlled, as if animated by spontaneous energies and guided by specific intentions. On the other hand, expressions, of which the primary signification refers exclusively to the properties and actions of matter, are metaphorically applied to the phenomena of thought and volition, and even to the feelings and passions of the soul; and in speaking of a *ray of hope*, a *shade of doubt*, a *flight of fancy*, a *flash of wit*, the *warmth of emotion*, or the *ebullitions of anger*, we are scarcely conscious that we are employing metaphors which have this material origin.

As a general rule, I have deemed it incumbent on me to place words and phrases, which appertain more especially to one head, also under the other heads to which they have a

relation, whenever it appeared to me that this repetition would suit the convenience of the inquirer, and spare him the trouble of turning to other parts of the work; for I have always preferred to subject myself to the imputation of redundance, rather than incur the reproach of insufficiency.*
When, however, the divergence of the associated from the primary idea is sufficiently marked, I have contented myself with making a reference to the place where the modified signification will be found. But in order to prevent needless extension, I have, in general, omitted *conjugate words*† which are so obviously derivable from those that are given in the same place, that the reader may safely be left to form them for himself. This is the case with adverbs derived from adjectives by the simple addition of the terminal syllable *-ly;* such as *closely, carefully, safely,* &c., from *close, careful, safe,* &c., and also with adjectives or participles immediately derived from the verbs which are already given. In all such cases, an " &c. " indicates that reference is understood to be made to these roots. I have observed the same rule in compiling the Index ; retaining only the primary or more simple word, and omitting the conjugate words obviously derived from them. Thus I assume the word *short* as the representative of its immediate derivatives *shortness, shorten, shortening, shortened, shorter, shortly,* which would have had the same references, and which the reader can readily supply.

The same verb is frequently used indiscriminately either in

---

* Frequent repetitions of the same series of expressions, accordingly, will be met with under various headings. For example, the word *Relinquishment,* with its synonyms, occurs as a heading at No. 624., where it applies to *intention,* and also at No. 782., where it refers to *property.* The word *Chance* has two significations, distinct from one another : the one implying the *absence of an assignable cause;* in which case it comes under the category of the relation of Causation, and occupies the No. 156. : the other, the *absence of design,* in which latter sense it ranks under the operations of the Will, and has assigned to it the place No. 621. I have, in like manner, distinguished *Sensibility, Pleasure, Pain, Taste, &c.,* according as they relate to *Physical,* or to *Moral Affections;* the former being found at Nos. 375, 377, 378, 390, &c., and the latter at Nos. 822, 827, 828, 850, &c.

† By "*conjugate* or *paronymous* words is meant, correctly speaking, different "parts of speech from the same root, which exactly correspond in point of "meaning." — *A Selection of English Synonyms,* edited by Archbishop Whately.

the active or transitive, or in the neuter or intransitive sense. In these cases, I have generally not thought it worth while to increase the bulk of the Work by the needless repetition of that word; for the reader, whom I suppose to understand the use of the words, must also be presumed to be competent to apply them correctly.

There are a multitude of words of a specific character, which, although they properly occupy places in the columns of a dictionary, yet, having no relation to general ideas, do not come within the scope of this compilation, and are consequently omitted. The names of objects in Natural History, and technical terms belonging exclusively to Science or to Art, or relating to particular operations, and of which the signification is restricted to those specific objects, come under this category. Exceptions must, however, be made in favour of such words as admit of metaphorical application to general subjects, with which custom has associated them, and of which they may be cited as being typical or illustrative. Thus, the word *Lion* will find a place under the head of *Courage*, of which it is regarded as the type. *Anchor*, being emblematic of *Hope*, is introduced among the words expressing that emotion; and, in like manner, *butterfly* and *weathercock*, which are suggestive of fickleness, are included in the category of *Irresolution*.

With regard to the admission of many words and expressions, which the classical reader might be disposed to condemn as vulgarisms, or which he, perhaps, might stigmatize as pertaining rather to the slang than to the legitimate language of the day, I would beg to observe, that, having due regard to the uses to which this Work was to be adapted, I did not feel myself justified in excluding them solely on that ground, if they possessed an acknowledged currency in general intercourse. It is obvious, that, with respect to degrees of conventionality, I could not have attempted to draw any strict lines of demarcation; and far less could I have presumed to erect any absolute standard of purity. My object, be it remembered, is not to regulate the use of words, but simply to supply and to suggest such as may be wanted on occasion, leaving the proper selection entirely to the discretion and taste of the employer. If a novelist or a dramatist, for example, proposed to delineate some vulgar personage, he would wish to have the power of putting into the mouth of the speaker expressions that would accord with his character; just as the actor, to revert to a former comparison, who had to personate a peasant, would choose for his attire the most homely garb, and would have just reason to complain if the theatrical wardrobe furnished him with no suitable costume.

Words which have, in process of time, become obsolete, are of course rejected from this collection. On the other hand, I have admitted a considerable number of words and phrases borrowed from other languages, chiefly the French and Latin, some of which may be considered as already naturalized; while others, though avowedly foreign, are frequently introduced in English composition, particularly in familiar style, on account of their being peculiary expressive, and because we have no corresponding words of equal force in our own language.* The rapid advances which are being made in scientific knowledge, and consequent improvement in all the arts of life, and the extension of those arts and sciences to so many new purposes and objects, create a continual demand for the formation of new terms to express new agencies, new wants, and new combinations. Such terms, from being at first merely technical, are rendered, by more general use, familiar to the multitude, and having a well-defined acceptation, are eventually incorporated into the language, which they contribute to enlarge and to enrich. *Neologies* of this kind are perfectly legitimate, and highly advantageous; and they necessarily introduce those gradual and progressive changes which every language is destined to undergo.† Some modern writers, however, have indulged in

* All these words and phrases are printed in Italics.

† Thus in framing the present classification, I have frequently felt the want of substantive terms corresponding to abstract qualities or ideas denoted by certain

a habit of arbitrarily fabricating new words and a new-fangled phraseology, without any necessity, and with manifest injury to the purity of the language. This vicious practice, the offspring of indolence or conceit, implies an ignorance or neglect of the riches in which the English language already abounds, and which would have supplied them with words of recognized legitimacy, conveying precisely the same meaning as those they so recklessly coin in the illegal mint of their own fancy.

A work constructed on the plan of classification I have proposed might, if ably executed, be of great value in tending to limit the fluctuations to which language has always been subject, by establishing an authoritative standard for its regulation. Future historians, philologists, and lexicographers, when investigating the period when new words were introduced, or discussing the import given at the present time to the old, might find their labours lightened by being enabled to appeal to such a standard, instead of having to search for data among the scattered writings of the age. Nor would its utility be confined to a single language; for the principles of its construction are universally applicable to all languages, whether living or dead. On the same plan of classification there might be formed a French, a German, a Latin, or a Greek Thesaurus, possessing, in their respective spheres, the same advantages as those of the English model. Still more useful would be a conjunction of these methodized compilations in two languages, the French and the English, for instance; the columns of each being placed in parallel juxtaposition. No means yet devised would so greatly facilitate the acquisition of the one language by those who are acquainted with the other: none would afford such ample assistance to the translator in either language; and none

adjectives; and have been often tempted to invent words that might express these abstractions: but I have yielded to this temptation only in the four following instances; having framed from the adjectives *irrelative, amorphous, sinistral,* and *gaseous,* the abstract nouns *irrelation, amorphism, sinistrality,* and *gaseity.* I have ventured also to introduce the adjective *intersocial* to express the active voluntary relations between man and man.

would supply such ready and effectual means of instituting an accurate comparison between them, and of fairly appreciating their respective merits and defects. In a still higher degree would all those advantages be combined and multiplied in a *Polyglot Lexicon* constructed on this system.

Metaphysicians engaged in the more profound investigation of the Philosophy of Language will be materially assisted by having the ground thus prepared for them, in a previous analysis and classification of our ideas; for such classification of ideas is the true basis on which words, which are their symbols, should be classified.* It is by such analysis alone that we can arrive at a clear perception of the relation which these symbols bear to their corresponding ideas, or can obtain a correct knowledge of the elements which enter into the formation of compound ideas, and of the exclusions by which we arrive at the abstractions so perpetually resorted to in the process of reasoning, and in the communication of our thoughts.

Lastly, such analyses alone can determine the principles on which a strictly *Philosophical Language* might be constructed. The probable result of the construction of such a language would be its eventual adoption by every civilized nation; thus realizing that splendid aspiration of philanthropists, — the establishment of a Universal Language. However utopian such a project may appear to the present generation, and however abortive may have been the former endeavours of Bishop Wilkins and others to realize it†, its accomplishment is surely not beset with greater difficulties than have impeded the progress to many other beneficial

* The process of verbal classification is similar in principle to that which is employed in the various departments of Natural History. Thus the sectional divisions I have formed, correspond to Natural Families in Botany and Zoology, and the filiation of words presents a net-work analogous to the natural filiation of plants or animals.

† "The Languages," observes Horne Tooke, "which are commonly used "throughout the world, are much more simple and easy, convenient and philoso-"phical, than Wilkins's scheme for a *real character*; or than any other scheme that "has been at any other time imagined or proposed for the purpose."—Ἔπεα Πτερόεντα, p. 125.

objects, which in former times appeared to be no less visionary, and which yet were successfully achieved, in later ages,
by the continued and persevering exertions of the human
intellect. Is there at the present day, then, any ground for
despair, that at some future stage of that higher civilization
to which we trust the world is gradually tending, some new
and bolder effort of genius towards the solution of this great
problem may be crowned with success, and compass an object
of such vast and paramount utility? Nothing, indeed, would
conduce more directly to bring about a golden age of union
and harmony among the several nations and races of mankind, than the removal of that barrier to the interchange of
thought and mutual good understanding between man and
man, which is now interposed by the diversity of their respective languages.

PLAN OF CLASSIFICATION.

TABULAR SYNOPSIS OF CATEGORIES.

Class I. ABSTRACT RELATIONS.

I. EXISTENCE.

1°. Abstract	1. Existence.	2. Inexistence.
2°. Concrete	3. Substantiality.	4. Unsubstantiality.
3°. Formal	*Internal.*	*External.*
	5. Intrinsicality.	6. Extrinsicality.
4°. Modal	*Absolute.*	*Relative.*
	7. State.	8. Circumstance.

II. RELATION.

1°. Absolute	9. Relation.	10. Irrelation.
	11. Consanguinity.	
	12. Reciprocality.	
	13. Identity.	14. Contrariety.
		15. Difference.
2°. Continuous	16. Uniformity.	
3°. Partial	17. Similarity.	18. Dissimilarity.
	19. Imitation.	20. { Non-imitation. Variation.
	21. Copy.	22. Prototype.
4°. General	23. Agreement.	24. Disagreement.

III. QUANTITY.

1°. Simple	*Absolute.*	*Relative.*
	25. Quantity.	26. Degree.
2°. Comparative	27. Equality.	28. Inequality.
	29. Mean.	
	30. Compensation.	
	By comparison with a Standard.	
	31. Greatness.	32. Smallness.
	By comparison with a similar Object.	
	33. Superiority.	34. Inferiority.
	Changes in Quantity.	
	35. Increase.	36. Decrease.
3°. Conjunctive	37. Addition.	38. { Non-addition. Subduction.
	39. Adjunct.	40. Remainder.
	41. Mixture.	42. Simpleness.
	43. Junction.	44. Disjunction.
	45. Vinculum.	
	46. Coherence.	47. Incoherence.
	48. Combination.	49. Decomposition.

VII. CHANGE.

1°. SIMPLE	140. Change.	
	141. Cessation.	142. Permanence.
		143. Continuance.
	144. Conversion.	145. Reversion.
	146. Revolution.	
	147. Substitution.	148. Interchange.

2°. COMPLEX	149. Mutability.	150. Immutability.
	Present.	*Future.*
	151. Eventuality.	152. Destiny.

VIII. CAUSATION.

1°. CONSTANCY OF SE-QUENCE	153. { *Constant Ante-cedent.* Cause.	154. { *Constant Sequent.* Effect.
	155. { *Assignment of Cause.* Attribution.	156. { *Absence of As-signment.* Chance.

2°. CONNECTION BETWEEN CAUSE AND EFFECT	157. Power.	158. Impotence.
	Degrees of Power.	
	159. Strength.	160. Weakness.

3°. POWER IN OPERATION	161. Production.	162. Destruction.
	163. Reproduction.	
	164. Producer.	165. Destroyer.
	166. Paternity.	167. Posterity.
	168. Productiveness.	169. Unproductiveness.
	170. Agency.	
	171. Energy.	172. Inertness.
	173. Violence.	174. Moderation.

4°. INDIRECT POWER	175. Influence.	
	176. Tendency.	177. Liability.

5°. COMBINATIONS OF CAUSES	178. Concurrence.	179. Counteraction.

CLASS II. SPACE.

I. SPACE IN GENERAL.

1°. ABSTRACT SPACE	180. { *Indefinite.* Space.	181. { *Definite.* Region.
		182. { *Limited.* Place.

2°. RELATIVE SPACE	183. Situation.	
	184. Location.	185. Displacement.

3°. EXISTENCE IN SPACE	186. Presence.	187. Absence.
	188. Inhabitant.	189. Abode.
	190. Contents.	191. Receptacle.

II. DIMENSIONS.

1°. GENERAL	192. Size.	193. Littleness.
	194. Expansion.	195. Contraction.
	196. Distance.	197. Nearness.
	198. Interval.	199. Contiguity.

2°. LINEAR	200. Length.	201. Shortness.
	202. { Breadth. Thickness.	203. { Narrowness. Thinness.
	204. Layer.	205. Filament.
	206. Height.	207. Lowness.
	208. Depth.	209. Shallowness.

2°. LINEAR — *continued*.....

210. Summit.	211. Base.
212. Verticality.	213. Horizontality.
214. Pendency.	215. Support.
216. Parallelism.	217. Obliquity.
218. Inversion.	219. Crossing.

3°. CENTRICAL

General

220. Exteriority.	221. Interiority.
222. Covering.	223. Centrality.
	224. Lining.
225. Investment.	226. Divestment.
227. Circumjacence.	228. Interjacence.
229. Outline.	
230. Edge.	
231. Circumscription.	
232. Inclosure.	
233. Limit.	

Special ...

234. Front.	235. Rear.
236. Laterality.	237. Anteposition.
238. Dextrality.	239. Sinistrality.

III. FORM.

1°. GENERAL ....

240. Form.	241. Amorphism.
242. Symmetry.	243. Distortion.

2°. SPECIAL ....

244. Angularity.	
245. Curvature.	246. Straightness.
247. Circularity.	248. Convolution.
249. Rotundity.	

3°. SUPERFICIAL ....

250. Convexity.	251. Flatness.
	252. Concavity.
253. Sharpness.	254. Bluntness.
255. Smoothness.	256. Roughness.
257. Notch.	
258. Fold.	
259. Furrow.	
260. Opening.	261. Closure.
262. Perforator.	263. Stopper.

IV. MOTION.

1°. MOTION IN GENERAL

264. Motion.	265. Quiescence.
266. Journey.	267. Navigation.
268. Traveller.	269. Mariner.
270. Transference.	
271. Carrier.	
272. Vehicle.	273. Ship.

2°. DEGREES OF MOTION.

274. Velocity.	275. Slowness.

3°. CONJOINED WITH FORCE................

276. Impulse.	277. Recoil.

4°. WITH REFERENCE TO DIRECTION. ....

278. Direction.	279. Deviation.
280. Precession.	281. Sequence.
282. Progression.	283. Regression.
284. Propulsion.	285. Traction.
286. Recession.	287. Approach.
288. Repulsion.	289. Attraction.
290. Divergence.	291. Convergence
292. Departure.	293. Arrival.
294. Egress.	295. Ingress.
296. Ejection.	297. Reception.
298. Excretion.	299. Food.
300. Extraction.	301. Insertion.

2°. SENSATION.

(1) General
- 375. Sensibility. 376. Insensibility.
- 377. Pleasure. 378. Pain.

(2) Special

1. Touch
- 379. Touch.
- 380. { Perceptions of Touch. 381. Numbness.

2. Heat
- 382. Heat. 383. Cold.
- 384. Calefaction. 385. Frigefaction.
- 386. Furnace. 387. Refrigeratory.
- 388. Fuel.
- 389. Thermometer.

3. Taste
- 390. Taste. 391. Insipidity.
- 392. Pungency.
- 393. Condiment.
- 394. Savoriness. 395. Unsavoriness.
- 396. Sweetness. 397. Sourness.

4. Odour
- 398. Odour. 399. Inodorousness.
- 400. Fragrance. 401. Fœtor.

5. Sound

1. Sound in General.
- 402. Sound. 403. Silence.
- 404. Loudness. 405. Faintness.

2. Specific Sounds.
- 406. Snap. 407. Roll.
- 408. Resonance. 409. Sibilation.
- 410. Stridor.
- 411. Cry. 412. Ululation.

3. Musical Sounds.
- 413. Harmony. 414. Discord.
- 415. Music.
- 416. Musician.
- 417. Musical Instruments.

4. Perception of Sound.
- 418. Hearing. 419. Deafness.

6. Light

1. Light in General.
- 420. Light. 421. Darkness.
- 422. Dimness.
- 423. Luminary. 424. Shade.
- 425. Transparency. 426. Opacity.
- 427. Semitransparency.

2. Specific Light.
- 428. Colour. 429. Achromatism.
- 430. Whiteness. 431. Blackness.
- 432. Gray. 433. Brown.
- 434. Redness. 435. Greenness.
- 436. Yellowness. 437. Purple.
- 438. Blueness. 439. Orange.
- 440. Variegation.

3. Perceptions of Light.
- 441. Vision. 442. Blindness.
- 443. Dimsightedness.
- 444. Spectator.
- 445. Optical Instruments.
- 446. Visibility. 447. Invisibility.
- 448. Appearance. 449. Disappearance.

Class IV. INTELLECT.

Division I. Formation of Ideas.

Division II. COMMUNICATION OF IDEAS.

I. NATURE OF IDEAS COMMUNICATED ....
- 516. Meaning.
- 517. Unmeaningness.
- 518. Intelligibility.
- 519. Unintelligibility.
- 520. Equivocalness.
- 521. Metaphor.
- 522. Interpretation.
- 523. Misinterpretation.
- 524. Interpreter.

II. MODES OF COMMUNICATION...
- 525. Manifestation.
- 526. Latency.
- 527. Information.
- 528. Concealment.
- 529. Disclosure.
- 530. Ambush.
- 531. Publication.
- 532. News.
- 533. Secret.
- 534. Messenger.
- 535. Affirmation.
- 536. Negation.
- 537. Teaching.
- 538. Misteaching.
- 539. Learning.
- 540. Teacher.
- 541. Learner.
- 542. School.
- 543. Veracity.
- 544. Falsehood.
- 545. Deception.
- 546. Untruth.
- 547. Dupe.
- 548. Deceiver.
- 549. Exaggeration.

III. MEANS OF COMMUNICATION.

1°. *Natural Means*............
- 550. Indication.
- 551. Record.
- 552. Obliteration.
- 553. Recorder.
- 554. Representation.
- 555. Misrepresentation.
- 556. Painting.
- 557. Sculpture.
- 558. Engraving.
- 559. Artist.

2°. *Conventional Means.*

   1. *Language generally*
- 560. Language.
- 561. Letter.
- 562. Word.
- 563. Neology.
- 564. Nomenclature.
- 565. Misnomer.
- 566. Phrase.
- 567. Grammar.
- 568. Solecism.
- 569. Style.

Qualities of Style.
- 570. Perspicuity.
- 571. Obscurity.
- 572. Conciseness.
- 573. Diffuseness.
- 574. Vigour.
- 575. Feebleness.
- 576. Plainness.
- 577. Ornament.
- 578. Elegance.
- 579. Inelegance.

   2. *Spoken Language*.....
- 580. Voice.
- 581. Aphony.
- 582. Speech.
- 583. Stammering.
- 584. Loquacity.
- 585. Taciturnity.
- 586. Allocution.
- 587. Response.
- 588. Interlocution.
- 589. Soliloquy.

   3. *Written Language*
- 590. Writing.
- 591. Printing.
- 592. Correspondence.
- 593. Book.
- 594. Description.
- 595. Dissertation.
- 596. Compendium.
- 597. Poetry.
- 598. Prose.
- 599. The Drama.

Class V. VOLITION.

Division I. Individual Volition.

III. ACTION	1°. *Simple*	680. Action.	681. Inaction.
		682. Activity.	683. Inactivity.
		684. Haste.	685. Leisure.
		686. Exertion.	687. Repose.
		688. Fatigue.	689. Refreshment.
		690. Agent.	
		691. Workshop.	
	2°. *Complex*	692. Conduct.	
		693. Direction.	
		694. Director.	
		695. Advice.	
		696. Council.	
		697. Precept.	
		698. Skill.	699. Unskilfulness.
		700. Proficient.	701. Bungler.
		702. Cunning.	703. Artlessness.
IV. ANTAGONISM	1°. *Conditional*	704. Difficulty.	705. Facility.
		706. Hindrance.	707. Aid.
		708. Opposition.	709. Co-operation.
		710. Opponent.	711. Auxiliary.
		712. Party.	
		713. Discord.	714. Concord.
		715. Defiance.	
		716. Attack.	717. Defence.
	2°. *Active*	718. Retaliation.	719. Resistance.
		720. Contention.	721. Peace.
		722. Warfare.	723. Pacification.
		724. Mediation.	
		725. Submission.	
		726. Combatant.	
		727. Arms.	
		728. Arena.	
V. RESULTS OF ACTION		729. Completion.	730. Non-completion.
		731. Success.	732. Failure.
		733. Trophy.	
		734. Prosperity.	735. Adversity.
		736. Mediocrity.	

Division II. INTERSOCIAL VOLITION.

I. GENERAL	737. Authority.	738. Laxity.
	739. Severity.	740. Lenity.
	741. Command.	
	742. Disobedience.	743. Obedience.
	744. Compulsion.	
	745. Master.	746. Servant.
	747. Sceptre.	
	748. Freedom.	749. Subjection.
	750. Liberation.	751. Restraint.
		752. Prison.
	753. Keeper.	754. Prisoner.
	755. Commission.	756. Abrogation.
		757. Resignation.
	758. Consignee.	
	759. Deputy.	

II. SPECIAL ....
- 760. Permission.   761. Prohibition.
- 762. Consent.
- 763. Offer.   764. Refusal.
- 765. Request.   766. Deprecation.
- 767. Petitioner.

III. CONDITIONAL ....
- 768. Promise.   768a. Release.
- 769. Compact.
- 770. Conditions.
- 771. Security.
- 772. Observance.   773. Non-observance.
- 774. Compromise.

IV. POSSESSIVE RELATIONS.

1°. *Property in General* ......
- 775. Acquisition.   776. Loss.
- 777. Possession.   778. Participation.
- 779. Possessor.
- 780. Property.
- 781. Retention.   782. Relinquishment.

2°. *Transfer of Property* ....
- 783. Transfer.
- 784. Giving.   785. Receiving.
- 786. Apportionment.
- 787. Lending.   788. Borrowing.
- 789. Taking.   790. Restitution.
- 791. Stealing.
- 792. Thief.
- 793. Booty.

3°. *Interchange of Property*
- 794. Barter.
- 795. Purchase.   796. Sale.
- 797. Merchant.
- 798. Merchandise.
- 799. Mart.

4°. *Monetary Relations* ......
- 800. Money.
- 801. Treasurer.
- 802. Treasury.
- 803. Wealth.   804. Poverty.
- 805. Credit.   806. Debt.
- 807. Payment.   808. Non-payment.
- 809. Expenditure.   810. Receipt.
- 811. Accounts.
- 812. Price.   813. Discount.
- 814. Dearness.   815. Cheapness.
- 816. Liberality.   817. Economy.
- 818. Prodigality.   819. Parsimony.

CLASS VI. AFFECTIONS.

I. AFFECTIONS GENE-RALLY ....
- 820. Affections.
- 821. Feeling.
- 822. Sensibility.   823. Insensibility.
- 824. Excitation.
- 825. Excitability.   826. Inexcitability.

II. PERSONAL.

	827. Pleasure.	828. Pain.
	829. Pleasurableness.	830. Painfulness.
	831. Content.	832. Discontent.
		833. Regret.
1°. PASSIVE	834. Relief.	835. Aggravation.
	836. Cheerfulness.	837. Dejection.
	838. Rejoicing.	839. Lamentation.
	840. Amusement.	841. Weariness.
	842. Wit.	843. Dulness.
	844. Humourist.	
	845. Beauty.	846. Ugliness.
	847. Ornament.	848. Blemish.
		849. Simplicity.
	850. Taste.	851. Vulgarity.
2°. DISCRIMINATIVE	852. Fashion.	853. Ridiculousness.
		854. Fop.
		855. Affectation.
		856. Ridicule.
		857. Laughing-stock.
	858. Hope.	859. Hopelessness.
		860. Fear.
	861. Courage.	862. Cowardice.
	863. Rashness.	864. Caution.
3°. PROSPECTIVE	865. Desire.	866. Indifference.
		867. Dislike.
		868. Fastidiousness.
		869. Satiety.
4°. CONTEMPLATIVE	870. Wonder.	871. Expectance.
	872. Prodigy.	
	873. Repute.	874. Disrepute.
	875. Nobility.	876. Commonalty.
	877. Title.	
	878. Pride.	879. Humility.
	880. Vanity.	881. Modesty.
5°. EXTRINSIC	882. Ostentation.	
	883. Celebration.	
	884. Boasting.	
	885. Insolence.	886. Servility.
	887. Blusterer.	

III. SYMPATHETIC.

	888. Friendship.	889. Enmity.
	890. Friend.	891. Enemy.
	892. Sociality.	893. Seclusion.
	894. Courtesy.	895. Discourtesy.
	896. Congratulation.	
1°. SOCIAL	897. Love.	898. Hate.
	899. Favourite.	
		900. Resentment.
		901. Irascibility.
	902. Endearment.	
	903. Marriage.	904. Celibacy.
		905. Divorce.
	906. Benevolence.	907. Malevolence.
		908. Malediction.
2°. DIFFUSIVE		909. Threat.
	910. Philanthropy.	911. Misanthropy.
	912. Benefactor.	913. Evil doer.

ABBREVIATIONS.

Adj. Adjectives, Participles, and Words having the power of Adjectives.
Adv. Adverbs, and adverbial expressions.
Ep. Epithets.
Int. Interjections.
Phr. Phrases.
V. Verbs.

THESAURUS

OF

ENGLISH WORDS AND PHRASES.

CLASS I.

WORDS EXPRESSING ABSTRACT RELATIONS.

SECTION I. EXISTENCE.

1°. BEING, IN THE ABSTRACT.

(1) EXISTENCE, being, entity, *ens*, subsistence:—coexistence (120).

Reality, actuality, positiveness, absoluteness, fact, matter of fact; *see* Truth (494).

Science of existence, Ontology.

Existence in space; *see* (186).

V. To be, to exist, have being, subsist, live, breathe, stand, obtain, occur, prevail,—to consist in, lie in.

To come into existence, to arise, come out, come forth, appear (448).

To bring into existence, produce, &c. (161).

Adj. Existing, being, subsisting, in being, in existence, extant, living, breathing, obtaining, prevailing, current, prevalent.

Real, actual, positive, absolute, virtual, substantial, self-existing, self-existent, undestroyed,— not ideal, unideal, not imagined, not supposititious, not potential, true (494).

Phr. The sober reality.

(2) INEXISTENCE, non-existence, nonentity, no such thing, *nil,*—vacuity (4), negativeness.

Annihilation, abeyance, extinction, *see* Destruction (162), and Disappearance (449).

V. Not to be, not to exist, &c., to have no existence.

To cease to be, pass away, vanish, fade, dissolve, melt away, perish, disappear (449), to be annihilated, extinct, &c., to die (360).

Phr. To leave not a rack behind.

Adj. Inexistent, non-existent, non-existing, &c., negative, blank.

Unreal, potential, virtual, baseless, unsubstantial (4), imaginary, ideal, vain, supposititious, shadowy.

Unborn, uncreated, unbegotten.

Annihilated, destroyed, extinct, gone, lost, perished, melted, dissolved, faded, exhausted, vanished, missing, disappeared, departed, defunct (360).

1

Adv. Actually, really, absolutely, positively, &c., in fact, in reality, *ipso facto.*

Absence (187), removal (185).
Adv. Negatively, virtually, &c.

2°. BEING, IN THE CONCRETE.

(3) SUBSTANTIALITY, *hypostasis,* thing, something, a being, an existence, a body, substance, object, article, creature, matter, material, stuff (316), *substratum, plenum.*
Totality of existences, *see* World (318).
Adj. Substantive, substantial, bodily, material, objective, hypostatic.
Adv. Substantially, &c., essentially.

(4) UNSUBSTANTIALITY, nothingness, nihility, nothing, naught, *nil,* zero, nothing at all; nothing whatever, nothing on earth;—Nobody, *see* (187); a desert.
A shadow, phantom, phantasm, dream, air, thin air.
Void, vacuum, vacuity, vacancy, voidness, vacuousness, inanity, emptiness, hollowness, blank, chasm, gap, hiatus, &c. (198).
Adj. Unsubstantial, void, vacuous, blank, null, inane, vacant, hollow.

3°. FORMAL EXISTENCE.

Internal conditions.
(5) INTRINSICALITY, inbeing, inherence, inhesion, essence, essentialness, essential part, quintessence, quiddity, gist, pith, marrow, incarnation.
Nature, constitution, character, quality (157), crasis, temperament, temper, spirit, humour, grain, endowment, capacity, capability, moods, declensions, features, aspects, specialities, particularities, peculiarities (79), idiosyncrasy, idiocrasy, diagnostics.
Adj. Derived from within; intrinsic, intrinsical, inherent, essential, natural, internal, innate, inborn, inbred, instinctive, ingrained, inherited, immanent, congenital, congenite, in the grain, bred in the bone.
Characteristic, peculiar, special, diagnostic (79).
Adv. Intrinsically, &c.

External conditions.
(6) EXTRINSICALITY, extraneousness, accident.
Adj. Derived from without; extrinsic, extrinsical, extraneous, modal, adventitious, adscititious, (or ascititious), incidental, accidental, nonessential, objective.
Implanted, ingrafted.
Adv. Extrinsically, &c.

4°. MODAL EXISTENCE.

Absolute.
(7) STATE, condition, category, estate, case, constitution, diathesis.
Frame, fabric, structure, texture, contexture (329), conformation.
Mode, modality, schesis, form, shape, figure, cut, cast, mould, stamp, set, fit, tone, tenor, turn, trim, guise, fashion, aspect, complexion, character.
V. To be in a state, condition, &c.,

Relative.
(8) CIRCUMSTANCE, situation, phase, position, posture, attitude, place, point, terms, fare, *régime,* footing, standing, *status,* predicament, contingency, occasion, juncture, conjuncture, emergence, emergency, exigency, crisis, pass, push, pinch, pickle, plight.
Adj. Circumstantial,—given, conditional, provisional, critical, contingent, incidental (6, 151).

2

—to fare; to have, possess, enjoy, &c., a state, &c.

To bring into a state, &c. (144).

Adj. Conditional, modal, formal, structural, textural.

Phr. As the matter stands.

Adv. Conditionally, &c.

Adv. In, or under the circumstances, conditions, &c. — Thus, being so, such being the case, since, sith, accordingly, seeing that, as matters stand, as things go.

Conditionally, provided, if, if so, if so be, if it be so; if it so happen, or turn out, provisionally, unless, without.

According to circumstances, as it may happen, or turn out.

Phr. Pro re natâ, cæteris paribus; according as the wind blows.

Section II. RELATION.

1°. Absolute Relation.

(9) RELATION, bearing, reference, concern, cognation, correlation, analogy, affinity, homology, alliance, homogeneity, association, approximation, filiation, &c. (166), interest, habitude.

Relevancy, pertinency, fitness, &c. (646).

Aspect, point of view, comparison (464), — ratio, proportion.

V. To be related, have a relation, &c.; to relate to, refer to, bear upon, regard, concern, touch, to have to do with, pertain to, belong to, appertain to, answer to, interest.

To bring into relation with, connect, link (43), approximate, bring together, bring near (197), to bring to bear upon.

Adj. Relative, correlative, agnate, relating to, relative to, relevant, in relation with, referable (or referrible) to, pertinent, germane, pat, to the point, apposite, to the purpose, à propos, ad rem, in loco, just the thing; quite the thing; belonging, pertaining, or appertaining to; — implicated, associated, connected.

Approximative, approximating, proportional, proportionate, proportionable.

Adv. Relatively, thereof, as to,

(10) Want, or absence of relation.

IRRELATION, disconnection, inconnection, dissociation, misrelation, independence, isolation (44), disproportion; — incommensurability, irrelevancy; — heterogeneity, irreconcileableness (24), impertinence.

V. To have no relation, &c. to; to have nothing to do with; not to concern, &c.

To isolate, separate, detach, segregate (44).

Adj. Irrelative, irrespective, unrelated, without reference &c. to; arbitrary, episodic, remote, out of place, mal à propos, irrelevant, foreign to, alien, impertinent, extraneous to, stranger to, independent, outlandish, exotic, unallied, unconnected, disconnected, adrift, isolated, insular.

Not comparable, incommensurable, irreconcileable, heterogeneous.

Phr. Foreign to the purpose, nothing to the purpose, neither here nor there; beside the mark: à propos de bottes.

Adv. Parenthetically, by the way, by the bye, en passant, incidentally, head and shoulders.

about, concerning, touching, anent, as relates to, with relation to, relating to; as respects, with respect to, in respect of, respecting;

3

as regards, with regard to, regarding, with reference to, in connexion with, in as much as, in point of, as far as, on the part of,
quoad hoc: pertinently, &c.

In various ways, in all manner of ways, under the head, category,
class, &c. of (75).

(11) Relations of kindred.

CONSANGUINITY, relationship, kindred, parentage, filiation, lineage, agnation, connexion, alliance, family connexion, family tie; *see* Paternity (166).

A kinsman, kinsfolk, kith and kin, relation, relative, connexion, sib,
cousin, brother, sister, &c. &c.; — a near relation, a distant relation.

Family, fraternity, brotherhood, sisterhood, &c.; — race, generation,
sept, &c.

Adj. Related, akin, consanguineous, family, allied, collateral, sib, fraternal &c., nearly or closely related, remotely or distantly related.

(12) Double relation.

RECIPROCALNESS, reciprocity, mutuality, correlation, correlativeness, in-
terdependence, interchange, &c. (148), interchangeableness (149).

V. To reciprocate, alternate, interchange, exchange, counterchange.

Adj. Reciprocal, mutual, commutual, correlative, alternate.

International, interchangeable.

(13) IDENTITY, sameness, coincidence, coalescence, convertibility;
selfness, self, oneself, *alter ego*, number one; identification.

V. To be identical; to be the
same, &c., to coincide, coalesce.

To render the same; to identify.

To recognise the identity of; to
identify; *see* to compare (464).

Adj. Identical, same, self, very
same, self-same, no other, ilk, one
and the same, unaltered, coincident,
coinciding, coalescing, coalescent,
indistinguishable, equivalent, equipollent, convertible.

Adv. All one, all the same, iden-
tically, &c.

(14) Non-coincidence.

CONTRARIETY, contrast, antithesis,
contradiction, opposition, opposite-
ness, antagonism (708), inversion,
reversion (218).

The opposite, the reverse, inverse,
converse, antipodes (237).

V. To be contrary, opposite, &c.,
to contrast with, contradict, contravene, oppose, antagonize, invert, reverse.

Adj. Contrary, opposite, counter,
converse, reverse, diametrically opposite, opposed, antipodean, antagonistic, opposing, inconsistent, contradictory, contrarious.

Phr. Differing *toto cœlo;* As opposite as black and white; — as light
and darkness; — as fire and water.

Adv. Contrarily, contrariously, contrariwise, *per contra*, oppo-
sitely, on the contrary, *tout au contraire*, quite the contrary.

(15) DIFFERENCE, variance, variation, variety, diversity, modification,
shade of difference, *nuance;* deviation, divergence, divarication (290), disagreement (24).

Distinction, discrimination, contradistinction. A nice, fine, or subtle
distinction (465).

V. To be different, &c.; to differ, vary, ablude, mismatch, contrast.

To render different, &c., to vary, change, modify, &c. (140).

To distinguish, severalize (465), split hairs.

Adj. Different, differing, disparate, heterogeneous, varying, distinguish-
able, discriminative, varied, modified, diversified, deviating, diverging, de-

vious, disagreeing (24), various, divers, all manner of, multifarious, multiform, &c. (81).

Other, another, not the same, widely apart, changed (140).

Phr. As different as chalk is from cheese.

Adv. Differently, variously, &c., otherwise.

2°. Continuous Relation.

(16) UNIFORMITY, homogeneity, consistency, conformity (82), connaturality, connaturalness; accordance, *see* Agreement (23), and Regularity (82).

V. To be uniform, &c., to accord with.

To become uniform, to conform to.

To render uniform, to assimilate, level, smooth, &c. (255).

Adj. Uniform, homogeneous, homologous, of a piece, consistent, connatural.

Adv. Uniformly, uniformly with, conformably, consistently with, in unison with, in conformity with, according to (23).

Absence or want of uniformity, *see* (83).

—————

3°. Partial Relation.

(17) SIMILARITY, resemblance, likeness, similitude, semblance, approximation, parallelism (216), analogy, analogicalness, connaturalness, connaturality, brotherhood, family likeness; alliteration, repetition (104).

An analogue, match, *pendant,* fellow, pair, mate, twin, parallel, counterpart, brother, sister; simile, parable (521).

Phr. One's second self; *arcades ambo;* birds of a feather.

V. To be similar, like, resembling, &c.; to resemble, bear resemblance, approximate, parallel, match, imitate (19), represent, simulate, personate.

To render similar, assimilate, approximate, connaturalize, bring near, &c.

Adj. Similar, like, alike, resembling, twin, analogous, analogical, allied to, of a piece, such as, connatural, congener, matching.

Near, something like, mock, *pseudo,* simulating, representing, approximating.

Exact, accurate, true, faithful, close, speaking, true to nature, to the life, the very image.

Phr. As like as two peas; for all the world like; *comme deux gouttes d'eau;* as like as it can stare; *Ex uno disce omnes.*

Adv. As if, so to speak, as it were, *quasi,* as if it were.

(18) DISSIMILARITY, unlikeness, dissimilitude, diversity; novelty (123), originality (515).

V. To be alike, &c., to vary (20), to ablude.

To render unlike, to diversify, vary, &c., to strike out something new.

Adj. Dissimilar, unlike, disparate, of a different kind, class, &c. (75); diversified, cast in a different mould; novel, new, unmatched (123).

—————

(19) IMITATION, assimilation, copying, transcribing, transcription, repetition (104), duplication, reduplication, quotation, reproduction.

(20) NON-IMITATION.

Adj. Unimitated, uncopied, unmatched, unparalleled, inimitable (648).

5

Mockery, mocking, mimickry, echoing, simulation, counterfeiting, acting, personation, representation, parody, *travestie*.

Result of imitation, *see* Copy (21).

An imitator, echo, cuckoo, parrot, ape, monkey, mocking bird.

Phr. Imitatores servum pecus.

V. To imitate, copy, repeat (104), echo, re-echo, transcribe, match, parallel; to take, or catch a likeness; take off, hit off.

To mock, mimic, simulate, personate (554), act, represent, adumbrate, counterfeit, parody, travesty, caricature, burlesque.

To take after, do like, follow, tread in the steps of, follow in the wake of, follow the footsteps, take a leaf out of, model after, strike in with, emulate.

Adj. Imitated, copied, matched, repeated, paralleled, mimic, parodied, &c., modelled after, moulded on, paraphrastic, imitative, second-hand, imitable.

Adv. Literally, *verbatim, literatim, sic, totidem verbis,* word for word, *mot à mot* (562).

Variation, alteration, modification, *see* Difference (15), Change (140), Deviation (279), Divergence (280); moods and tenses.

V. To vary, modify, diversify, change &c. (140).

Adj. Varied, modified, diversified, &c.

---

(21) Result of imitation.

COPY, fac-simile, counterpart, effigies, form, likeness, similitude, semblance, cast, ectype, imitation, representation (554), adumbration.

Duplicate, transcript, repetition, reflexion of, second edition, a twice-told tale, *réchauffé,* a chip of the old block.

Rough copy, rough cast, *ébauche,* draught, proof, *brouillon,* protoplast, reprint, apograph.

Counterfeit, parody, caricature, burlesque, *travesti.*

(22) Thing copied.

PROTOTYPE, original, model, pattern, type, archetype, protoplast, antitype, module, exemplar, example, ensample, paradigm, fugleman.

Text, copy, design; key-note.

Mould, matrix, last, plasm, proplasm, mint.

4°. GENERAL RELATION.

(23) AGREEMENT, accord, accordance, unison, harmony, union, concord, concordance (714), cognation, conformity, consonance, consentaneousness, consistency, congruity, congruence, congeniality, correspondence, parallelism.

Fitness, pertinence, suitableness, adaptation, sortance, meetness, patness, relevancy, aptitude, coaptation, propriety, appositeness, reconcileableness, applicability, applicableness, admissibility, commensurability, compatibility.

Adaptation, adjustment, graduation, accommodation, reconciliation.

(24) DISAGREEMENT, discord, discordance, dissonance, dissidence, discrepancy, unconformity, disconformity, non-conformity, incongruity, incongruence, *mésalliance,* discongruity, jarring, clashing, jostling (713), inconsistency, disparity, disproportion, disproportionateness, variance, *concordia discors.*

Unfitness, repugnance, unsuitableness, unaptness, inaptitude, inaptness, impropriety, inapplicability, inadmissibility, irreconcileableness, incommensurability, inconcinnity, incompatibility, interference, intrusion; —*see* Irrelation (10).

V. To be accordant, to agree, accord, correspond, tally, respond, harmonize, fall in with, chime in with, square with, quadrate with, comport with, dovetail, assimilate, unite with.

To render accordant; to fit, suit, adapt, accommodate, adjust, reconcile, fadge, dovetail, square, regulate, accord, comport, graduate.

Adj. Agreeing, accordant, concordant, consonant, congruous, consentaneous, corresponding, correspondent, harmonizing, harmonious with, tallying with, conformable with, in harmony with, in unison with, in keeping with, squaring with, falling in with, consistent with, compatible, reconcileable with.

Apt, apposite, pertinent, pat, to the purpose, to the point, *ad rem*, bearing upon (9); applicable, relevant, fit, fitting, suitable, proper, meet, *à propos*, appropriate, suiting, befitting, sortable, deft, accommodating.

Phr. Rem acu tetigisti.

V. To disagree, clash, jar, oppose (708), interfere, jostle, intrude, have no business there.

Phr. To bring, or lug in, head and shoulders.

Adj. Disagreeing, discordant, discrepant, at variance, clashing, repugnant, incompatible, irreconcileable, inconsistent with, unconformable, incongruous, disproportionate, unproportioned, unharmonious, out of keeping, unconsonant, unconformable, incommensurable.

Unapt, inappropriate, improper, unsuited, unsuitable, inapposite, inapplicable, irrelevant, not pertinent, impertinent, out of place, ill-timed, intrusive, unfit, unfitting, unbefitting, unbecoming, *mal à propos*, out of season, forced, unseasonable, farfetched, inadmissible, uncongenial, unaccommodating, irreducible.

Phr. Neither here nor there.

Adv. At variance with, in defiance of, in contempt of, in spite of.

Section III. QUANTITY.

1°. Simple Quantity.

(25) Absolute Quantity.

Quantity, magnitude (192), amplitude, mass, amount, *quantum*, measure, handful, mouthful, &c.

Science of quantity; mathematics.

(26) Relative quantity.

Degree, grade, extent, measure, stint, standard, height, pitch, reach, amplitude, range, scope, gradation, shade, tenor, compass, sphere, rank, standing, rate, way, sort.

Point, mark, stage, step, peg; term (71).

Intensity, might, fulness, *see* Conversion (144), and Limit (233).

Adj. Comparative, gradual.
Adv. By degrees, gradually, inasmuch, *pro tanto*, however, howsoever, step by step, little by little, by inches.

2°. Comparative Quantity.

(27) Sameness of quantity or degree.

Equality, parity, co-extension, evenness, level, balance, equivalence, equipollence, equipoise, equilibrium, poise, equiponderance, par, quits, tie;

(28) Difference of quantity or degree.

Inequality, disparity, imparity, odds, difference (15), unevenness.

Preponderance, preponderation, inclination of the balance, advantage,

Equalization, equation, equilibration, coordination, adjustment.

A match, peer, compeer, mate, fellow, brother.

V. To be equal, &c.; to equal, match, come up to, come to, amount to, be or lie on a level with, to balance, to cope with.

To render equal, equalize, level, balance, equate, trim, adjust, poise; to strike a balance, to establish or restore equality, to readjust.

Phr. To stretch on the bed of Procrustes.

Adj. Equal, even, level, coequal, coordinate, on a par with, on a level with, equivalent, tantamount, much at one, as broad as long, as good as, up to the mark, equipollent, equiponderant, equiponderous.

prevalence, partiality;—superiority (33).

Short coming, *see* (304).

V. To be unequal, &c., to preponderate, outweigh, outbalance, overbalance, prevail, predominate, overmatch, to have or give the advantage.

Phr. To turn the scale, to kick the beam.

To fall short of, to want (304), not to come up to.

Adj. Unequal, uneven, disparate, unbalanced, overbalanced, preponderating, prevailing, &c., above or below par.

Adv. Haud passibus æquis.

———

Rendered equal, equalized, equated, poised, levelled, balanced, trimmed, &c.

Adv. Pari passu, equally, &c., *ad eundem, cæteris paribus.*

(29) MEAN, medium, intermedium, average, middle (68), the golden mean, *juste milieu,* αριστον μετρον.—Taking the one with the other, taking all things together, taking all in all, neutrality, middle course (628).

V. To split the difference, take the average, reduce to a mean.

Adj. Mean, intermediate, middle, average.

Adv. On an average, in the long run, half way.

One year with another, *communibus annis.*

(30) COMPENSATION, equation, indemnification, neutralization, counteraction.

A set-off, make weight, casting weight, counterpoise, amends, a *quid pro quo. See* Counteraction (179), Recoil (277), Atonement (952).

V. To compensate, compense, indemnify, countervail, counterpoise, balance, out-balance, over-balance, counter-balance, set off, countervail, make up for, cover, fill up, redeem, make amends, neutralize.

Adj. Compensating, compensatory, countervailing, &c., in the opposite scale, equipollent.

Phr. As broad as it's long;—It is an ill wind that blows nobody good.

QUANTITY BY COMPARISON WITH A STANDARD.

(31) GREATNESS, largeness, magnitude, size (192), fulness, vastness, immensity, enormity, infinity (105), intensity (26).

A large quantity, deal, power, world, mass, heap (72), pile, sight, peck, load, cart-load, cargo, ship-load, flood or spring tide, abundance (639), wholesale.

V. To be great, &c., run high,

(32) SMALLNESS, littleness, minuteness (193), tenuity, scantness, scantiness, slenderness, meanness, mediocrity.

A small quantity, *modicum,* atom, particle, molecule, corpuscle, jot, iota, dot, speck, ace, *minutiæ,* thought, idea, *soupçon,* whit, tittle, shade, shadow, the shadow of a shade, touch, cast, grain, spice, sprinkling, dash,

soar, tower, transcend, rise, or carry to a great height, &c. (305).

Adj. Great, large, considerable, big, huge, ample, full, plenary, extensive, goodly, heavy, precious, mighty (157), sad, arrant, downright, utter, cross, arch, consummate, rank, thorough-paced, sovereign, above par, unparalleled, unapproached.

Vast, immense, enormous, towering, inordinate, excessive, extravagant, outrageous, preposterous, swinging, monstrous, over-grown, stupendous, prodigious, astonishing (870), incredible, marvellous, transcendent, incomparable, tremendous.

Indefinite, boundless, unbounded, unlimited, incalculable, illimited, illimitable, immeasurable, infinite, unapproachable, unutterable, unspeakable, inexpressible, beyond expression, unconscionable.

Undiminished, unabated, unreduced, unrestricted.

Absolute, positive, decided, unequivocal, serious, essential, perfect, abundant (639).

Adv. In a great degree; much, well, considerably, largely, greatly, very, very much, a deal, not a little, pretty, pretty well, enough, to a large or great extent, ever so, ever so much, insomuch, wholesale, in all conscience.

In a positive degree; truly (494), positively, verily, really, indeed, actually, in fact, fairly, assuredly, decidedly, unequivocally, absolutely, seriously, essentially, downright.

In a comparative degree; comparatively.

In a complete degree; altogether, quite, wholly, totally, *in toto, toto cœlo,* utterly, thoroughly, out and out, completely, outright, clean, to the full, in every respect, in all respects, *sous tous les rapports,* on all accounts, nicely, perfectly, fully, amply, richly, abundantly, consummately, widely, as .... as .... can be, every inch, *à fonds, de fond en comble,* far and wide.

smack, scantling, scantlet, dole, scrap, mite, bit, morsel, crumb, shaving, trifle, spoonful, mouthful; *see* (51).

Finiteness, a finite quantity.

V. To be small, &c., to run low, shrink.

Phr. To lie in a nutshell.

Adj. Small, little, inconsiderable, diminutive, minute (193), tiny, puny, petty, miserable, paltry (643), weak (160), slender, feeble, faint, slight, scanty, trifling, moderate, mean, *mediocre,* passable, passing, light, sparing, at a low ebb.

Below par, below the mark, under the mark, imperfect (651), inappreciable, evanescent, infinitesimal, atomic.

Mere, simple, stark, bare.

Adv. In a small degree; somethir.g, somewhat, next to nothing, little, inconsiderably, slightly, minutely, faintly, feebly, lightly, imperfectly, moderately, scantily, miserably, sparingly, tolerably, passing, passably, weakly, pretty well, slenderly, modestly.

In a limited degree; in a certain degree, to a certain degree or extent, some, somewhat, rather, in some degree, in some measure, something, simply, purely, merely, in a manner, at the most, at least, at the least, at most, ever so little, as little as may be, *tant soit peu,* to say the least, next to nothing, in ever so small a degree.

Almost, nearly, well nigh, all but, short of, not quite, *peu s'en faut,* near the mark.

In an uncertain degree; about, thereabouts, scarcely, hardly, barely, somewhere about, nearly.

In no degree; not at all, not in the least, not a bit, not a bit of it, not a whit, not a jot, by no means, nowise, in nowise, in no respect, by no manner of means, on no account, at no hand.

In a greater degree; even, yea, *à fortiori,* still more.

In a high degree; highly, deeply, strongly, mighty, mightily, powerfully (157), profoundly, superlatively, extremely, exceedingly, excessively, sorely, intensely, exquisitely, acutely, soundly, vastly, hugely, immensely, enormously, stupendously, supremely, beyond measure, immoderately, inordinately, over head and ears, exorbitantly, indefinitely, immeasurably, unspeakably, inexpressibly, ineffably, unutterably, incalculably, infinitely.

In a marked degree; particularly, remarkably, singularly, peculiarly, notably, *par excellence*, signally, prominently, emphatically, κατ' εξοχην, strangely, wonderfully, amazingly, surprisingly, astonishingly, monstrously, incredibly, marvellously, shockingly, frightfully, dreadfully, fearfully, terribly, horribly, awfully, stupendously;

In a violent degree; violently, furiously, desperately, tremendously, outrageously, extravagantly, confoundedly, deucedly, devilishly, with a vengeance, *à toute outrance.*

In a painful degree; sadly, grievously, woefully, lamentably.

QUANTITY BY COMPARISON WITH A SIMILAR OBJECT.

(33) SUPERIORITY, majority, supremacy, advantage.

Maximum, acme, climax, zenith, summit, utmost height, culminating point (210), the height of.

V. To be superior, &c.; to exceed, excel, outweigh, pass, surpass, top, overtop, o'ertop, cap, beat, cut out, override, out-Herod, kick the beam, outbalance, overbalance (30), overweigh.

Adj. Superior, greater, major, higher, exceeding, excelling, passing, surpassing, ultra, vaulting, transcending, unequalled.

Supreme, greatest, utmost, paramount, pre-eminent, culminating, superlative, topmost, highest.

(34) INFERIORITY, minority, subordinacy, shortcoming (304);

Minimum.

V. To be less, inferior, &c.; to fall, or come short of; not to pass (304).

Phr. To hide its diminished head.

Adj. Inferior, smaller, minor, less, lesser, lower, subordinate, subaltern;

Least, smallest, minutest, &c. (193); lowest.

Adv. Less; under or below the mark; below par; at the bottom of the scale; at a low ebb.

Adv. Beyond; over or above the mark; above par, over and above; at the top of the scale.

In a superior degree; eminently, egregiously, pre-eminently, prominently, superlatively, supremely, above all, principally, especially, particularly, peculiarly, &c.

CHANGES IN QUANTITY.

(35) INCREASE, augmentation, enlargement, extension, dilatation, *see* (194), development, growth, swell, swelling, aggrandisement, aggravation, rise, exacerbation, spread, diffusion (73), increment, flood tide; accession.

V. To increase, augment, enlarge, amplify, extend, dilate, swell, ex-

(36) NON-INCREASE.

DECREASE, diminution, lessening, reduction, abatement, bating, declension, falling off, dwindling, contraction (195), shrinking, attenuation, extenuation, abridgment, curtailment (201), coarctation, narrowing.

Subsidence, wane, ebb, decrement.

V. To decrease, diminish, lessen,

10

pand, grow, stretch, shoot up, rise, run up, sprout, advance, spread, aggrandise, add, raise, heighten, strengthen, exalt, enhance, magnify, redouble, aggravate, exaggerate, exasperate, exacerbate.

Phr. To add fuel to the flame ; *oleum addere camino.*

Adj. Increased, augmented, enlarged, &c., undiminished.

Adv. Crescendo.

dwindle, shrink, contract, shrivel, fall away, waste, wane, ebb, decline, wear off.

To abridge, reduce, curtail, cut down, pare down, cut short, dock, &c. (201), bate, abate, dequantitate, extenuate, lower, weaken, dwarf; to mitigate, &c. (174).

Phr. To hide its diminished head.

Adj. Unincreased, decreased, diminished, lessened, &c., shorn, short by.

3°. CONJUNCTIVE QUANTITY.

(37) ADDITION, annexation, adjection, superposition, superaddition, subjunction, accession, superfœtation, supplement, accompaniment (88), sprinkling, spargefaction.

V. To add, annex, superadd, subjoin, superpose, clap on, tack to, append, tag, ingraft, saddle with, sprinkle.

To become added, to accrue, advene.

Adj. Added, annexed, &c., additional, supplementary, suppletory, subjunctive, adjectitious, adscititious (or ascititious).

Adv. In addition, more, *plus, extra.*

And, also, likewise, too, furthermore, item, and also, and eke, else, besides, to boot, *et cætera,* and so forth, into the bargain, *cum multis aliis,* over and above, moreover.

With, together with, withal, along with, including, inclusive, as well as ; not to mention ; conjointly (43).

(39) Thing added.

ADJUNCT, additament, addition, *additum,* affix, appendage, suffix, augment, increment, augmentation, accessory, garnish, sauce, supplement, adjective, *addendum,* complement, corollary.

Sequel, postscript, codicil, rider, heel-piece, skirt, flap, lappet, tail, *queue,* train, suite, *cortège,* accompaniment (88).

(38) NON-ADDITION, SUBDUCTION, subtraction, deduction, deducement, retrenchment, removal, ablation, curtailment, &c. (36), garbling, mutilation, truncation, abscission, excision, amputation, sublation. *See* (789).

V. To subduct, deduct, subtract, retrench, remove, withdraw, bate, detract, deduce, take away, deprive of, curtail, &c. (36), garble, truncate, mutilate, amputate, cut off, cut out, dock, lop, prune, pare, clip, thin, shear, decimate, geld.

Adj. Subtracted, deducted, &c.

Adv. In deduction, &c., less, *minus,* without, except, excepting, with the exception of, barring, save, exclusive of, save and except (83).

(40) Thing remaining.

REMAINDER, residue, remains, remnant, the rest, relic, leavings, heeltap, odds and ends, cheese-parings, off-scourings, orts.

Residuum, caput mortuum, ashes, cinders, slay, sediment, silt, *alluvium,* stubble ; *exuviæ,* result, educt.

Surplus, overplus, superfluity, excess (641), balance, complement, fag-end, wreck.

V. To remain, be left, be left behind, exceed.

Adj. Remaining, left, left behind, residual, residuary, out-standing, odd, unconsumed.

Superfluous, over and above, exceeding, redundant, supernumary.

(41) Forming a whole without coherence.

MIXTURE, admixture, commixture, admixtion, commixion, commixtion, mixtion, intermixture.

Impregnation, infusion, diffusion, suffusion, interspersion, transfusion, seasoning, sprinkling, interlarding, interpolation, interposition (228), intrusion,—adulteration, sophistication.

Thing mixed. A touch, spice, tinge, tincture, dash, smack, sprinkling, seasoning, infusion, &c., *soupçon*.

Compound resulting from mixture. Alloy, amalgam, *mélange*, *tertium quid*, miscellany, medley, *pasticcio*, patchwork, odds and ends: — farrago, jumble (59), mess, salad, sauce, hash, hodgepodge, (hodgepotch, or hotchpot), mash, mishmash, *omnium gatherum*, gallimaufry, *olla podrida*, salmagundi, *pot-pourri*, Noah's ark, mosaic (440).

V. To mix, commix, immix, intermix, mingle, commingle, intermingle, bemingle, interlard, intersperse, interpolate ; shuffle together, hash up, huddle together, deal, pound together, stir up, knead, brew, jumble (59).

To instil, imbue, infuse, infiltrate, dash, tinge, tincture, season, sprinkle, besprinkle, suffuse, transfuse, attemper, medicate, blend, alloy, amalgamate, compound (48), adulterate, sophisticate.

Adj. Mixed, mingled, intermixed, &c. ; implex, composite, mixed up with, half and half, linsey-wolsey, hybrid, mongrel, heterogeneous, miscible.

(42) Freedom from mixture.

SIMPLENESS, singleness, purity, clearness, homogeneity.

Purification (652), elimination, sifting, winnowing.

V. To render simple, simplify, sift, winnow, eliminate; to separate, disjoin (44).

To purify (652).

Adj. Simple, uniform, of a piece, homogeneous, single, pure, clear, sheer, neat, elementary :—unmixed, unmingled, untinged, unblended, uncombined, uncompounded, undecomposed, unadulterated, unsophisticated.

Free from, exempt from.

---

(43) JUNCTION, joining, connexion, connecting, conjunction, conjugation, annexion, annexation, annexment, attachment, compagination, astriction, alligation, fastening, linking, coupling, matrimony (903), grafting; inosculation, anastomosis, association (72), communication, approach (197).

Joint, joining, juncture, suture, articulation, commissure, seam, stitch, meeting, reunion, mortoise, scar, cicatrix.

Closeness, firmness, tightness, compactness.

V. To join, conjoin, connect, associate, embody, re-embody, hold together, pack, fix together, attach,

(44) DISJUNCTION, disconnection, disunity, disunion, disassociation, disengagement, inconnexion, abstractedness, isolation, insularity, separateness, severalness, severality.

Separation, parting, detachment, sejunction, seposition, diduction, discerption, elision, division, subdivision, dismemberment, disintegration, dislocation, laxation, severance, disseverance, severing, scission, rescission, abscission, laceration, dilaceration, wrenching, disruption, avulsion, divulsion, tearing asunder, section, cutting, resection, cleavage, fissure, breach, rent, split, crack, slit, dispersion (73), dissection, anatomy.

affix, fasten, bind, secure, make fast, tie, string, strap, sew, lace, string, stitch, tack, knit, button, buckle, hitch, lash, truss, bandage, braid, splice, swathe, gird, tether, picket, harness.

Chain, enchain, shackle, pinion, manacle, handcuff, lock, latch, belay, clap together, leash, couple, link, yoke, bracket, hang together, pin, nail, bolt, hasp, clasp, clamp, screw, rivet, impact, wedge, rabbet, mortoise, jam, dovetail, enchase, engraft, interlink, inosculate, entwine, interlace, intertwine, intertwist, interweave.

Adj. Joined, conjoined, coupled, &c., bound up together, conjunct, corporate, compact.

Firm, fast, close, tight, secure, set, impacted, jammed, locked, &c., intervolved, inseparable, indissoluble.

Adv. Conjointly, jointly, &c.

With, along with, together with, in conjunction with.

Fast, firmly, closely, &c.

V. To be disjoined, separated, &c.

To disjoin, disconnect, disunite, dispart, detach, separate, sepose, dispair, dissociate, isolate, disengage, set apart, loose, set free, unloose, unfasten, untie, unbind, unfix, unlace, unclasp, undo, unbuckle, unchain, unfetter, untack, unharness, ungird, unlatch, unlock, unlink, uncouple, unpin, unclinch, unscrew, unhook, unrivet, untwist, unshackle, unyoke, unknit, unravel, disentangle, unglue.

Sunder, divide, dissever, abscind, cut, incide, incise, snip, cleave, rive, slit, split, splinter, chip, crack, snap, rend, break, or tear asunder, shiver, chop, cut up, hack, hew, slash, whittle, hackle, discind, tear, lacerate, mangle, gash, hash.

Dissect, anatomize; take, pull, or pick to pieces; tear to tatters; dismember, disbranch, dislocate, disjoint, mince, break up, crunch, gride.

Adj. Disjoined, disconnected, &c., abstract, disjunctive, isolated, separate, discrete, apart, asunder, loose, disengaged, free, liberated, disengaged, unattached, unannexed, distinct, unassociated, adrift, straggling, dispersed.

Cut off, &c., rift, reft.

Capable of being cut, scissile.

Adv. Separately, &c., apart, adrift; in the abstract, abstractedly.

(45) Connecting medium.

VINCULUM, link, connective, copula, intermedium, hyphen, bridge, stepping-stone, isthmus.

Bond, filament, fibre (205), hair, cordage, cord, thread, strings, packthread, twine, twist, tape, line, ribbon, rope, cable, hawser, wire, chain.

Fastening, tie, ligament, ligature, strap, tackle, rigging, traces, harness, band, brace, bandage, fillet, thong, braid, girder, girth, cestus, garter, halter, noose, lasso, surcingle, knot, running-knot.

Pin, corking-pin, nail, brad, skewer, staple, clamp, cramp, screw, button, clasp, hasp, latch, latchet, tag, hook, tooth, hook and eye, lock, locket, padlock, rivet, grappling-iron, trennel, stake, post, shackle, &c. (752).

Cement, glue, gum, paste, size, solder, lute, putty, birdlime, mortar, stucco, plaster, grout.

(46) COHERENCE, cohesion, adherence, adhesion, accretion, concretion, agglutination, conglutination, aggregation, consolidation, cementation, soldering, welding.

(47) Want of adhesion, non-adhesion.

INCOHERENCE, looseness, laxity, slackness, relaxation, freedom.

Phr. A rope of sand.

Sticking, clinging, adhesiveness, stickiness, gumminess, gummosity, glutinousness, glutinosity, cohesiveness, density (321), inseparability, inseparableness.

Clot, concrete, cake, lump, solid, conglomerate (321).

V. To cohere, adhere, stick, cling, cleave, hold, take hold of, hold fast, hug, grow or hang together, twine round.

To concrete, curdle, cake.

Phr. To stick like a leech;—to cling like ivy;—to cling like bur.

To glue, agglutinate, conglutinate, consolidate, solidify (321), cement, lute, paste, gum, glue, solder, weld.

Adj. Cohesive, adhesive, cohering, &c., sticky, glutinous, gluey, gummy, viscous (352).

United, unseparated.

V. To loosen, slacken, relax, unglue, unsolder, &c., detach, untwist, unravel, unroll, &c. (44, 313).

Adj. Incoherent, detached, nonadhesive, loose, slack, lax, relaxed.

Segregated, flapping, streaming, dishevelled, unincorporated, unconsolidated, uncombined, &c., like grains of sand.

(48) COMBINATION, union, synthesis, incorporation, amalgamation, coalescence, *crasis,* fusion, blending, centralization.

Compound, amalgam, impregnation.

V. To combine, unite, incorporate, amalgamate, embody (or imbody), re-embody, blend, merge, fuse, melt into one, coalesce, centralize, to impregnate, to put together.

Adj. Combined, &c., impregnated with, ingrained.

(49) DECOMPOSITION, analysis, resolution, dissolution.

V. To decompose, analyze, decompound, resolve, take to pieces, separate into its elements, dissect, unravel, &c., break up.

Adj. Decomposed, &c.

4°. CONCRETE QUANTITY.

(50) WHOLE, totality, integrity, totalness, *ensemble,* collectiveness, individuality, unity (87), indivisibility, indiscerptibility, indissolvableness;—integration.

All, total, aggregate, integer, gross, amount, sum, sum total, *tout ensemble,* upshot, root and branch, head and shoulders, neck and heels, trunk, skeleton, hulk, lump, heap (72).

The principal part, bulk, mass, staple, body, compages, the main, the greater part, major part, essential part, best part, the lion's share;—marrow, soul of, pith.

V. To form, or constitute a whole, to integrate, embody, aggregate, amass (72).

(51) PART, portion, division, subdivision, section, sector, segment, fraction, fragment, frustum, detachment, piece, bit, scrap, whit, ought, morsel, mouthful, scantling, cantle, cantlet, slip, crumb, fritter, rag, tag, tatter, splinter, snatch, flitter, cut, cutting, snip, snick, collop, slice, shiver, sliver, driblet, clipping, *débris,* odds and ends, oddments, *detritus,* scale, lamina, *excerpta,* shadow;

Part and parcel, share, dividend, particular, article, chapter, clause, count, paragraph.

Member, limb, lobe, lobule, arm, branch, bough, joint, link, ramification, twig, bush, spray, sprig, leaf, leaflet, stump.

14

Adj. Whole, total, integral, entire, one, unbroken, uncut, undivided, individual, unsevered, unclipped, uncropped, unshorn, undiminished, undemolished, undissolved, unbruised, undestroyed, indivisible, indissoluble, indissolvable, indiscerptible.

Wholesale, sweeping.

Adv. Wholly, altogether, totally, entirely, all, all in all, wholesale, in the mass, *en masse,* on the whole, *in toto,* in the gross, *in extenso,* to the full, throughout, every inch, in the long run, in the main.

Phr. The long and the short; nearly, or almost all.

(52) COMPLETENESS, entirety, fulness, completion (729), perfection (650), solidity, filling up, integration, absoluteness.

Complement, supplement (39).

V. To be complete, &c.

To render complete, or whole, to complete, perfect, finish, make up, make good, piece out, eke out, give the last finish, supply deficiences, to go the whole length.

Adj. Complete, entire, perfect, full, plenary, solid, undivided, with all its parts, supplementary, adscititious, — thorough.

Phr. Full as an egg; full as a vetch.

Adv. Completely, entirely, to the full, thoroughly.

(54) COMPOSITION, constitution, *crasis.*

Inclusion, admission, comprehension, reception.

Inclusion in a class (76).

V. To be composed of, to consist of, be made of, formed of, made up of, be resolved into.

To contain, include, hold, comprehend, take in, admit, embrace, involve, implicate.

To compose, constitute, form, make, make up, build up, embody.

To enter into the composition of, to be, or form part of (51), to merge in, be merged in.

Adj. Comprehending, containing, including, comprising, &c.

Forming, constituting, composing,

15

V. To part, divide, sub-divide, break, &c. (44); to partition, parcel out, portion, apportion (786).

Adj. Part, fractional, fragmentary, sectional, aliquot, divided, multifid, partitioned, &c.

Adv. Partly, in part, partially, piecemeal, in detail, part by part, by driblets, bit by bit, by inches; inch by inch; foot by foot; drop by drop; in lots.

(53) INCOMPLETENESS, deficiency, defectiveness, failure, imperfection (651), hollowness.

Part wanting, defect, deficit, *caret.*

V. To be incomplete, &c., to fail, fall short (304).

Adj. Incomplete, imperfect, defective, deficient, wanting, failing, short by, hollow.

Mutilated, garbled, docked.

Phr. Cætera desunt.

(55) EXCLUSION, non-admission, exception, rejection, repudiation, exile, banishment, excommunication.

Separation, segregation, seposition.

Exclusion from a class (77).

V. To be excluded from, &c.

To exclude, shut out, bar, leave out, omit, reject, repudiate, neglect, blackball; lay, put, or set apart, or aside; segregate, pass over, throw overboard, slur over, neglect (460), excommunicate, banish, expatriate, ostracise, relegate.

To eliminate, weed, winnow, garble, bar, separate (44), strike off.

Adj. Excluding, omitting, &c., exclusive.

Excluded, omitted, &c., unrecounted, inadmissible.

&c., entering into, being or forming part of, &c., belonging to, appertaining to, inclusive.

(56) COMPONENT, component part, element, constituent, ingredient, member, limb (51), part and parcel, contents, appurtenance.

Adv. Exclusive of, barring, &c.

(57) EXTRANEOUSNESS, foreign body, alien, stranger, intruder, interloper, foreigner.

SECTION IV. ORDER.

1°. ORDER IN GENERAL.

(58) ORDER, regularity, orderliness, uniformity, even tenor, symmetry.

Gradation, progression, pedigree, subordination, course, array, routine.

Method, disposition, system, economy, discipline.

Rank, station, place, *status*, stand, scale, step, stage, term, footing; rank and file.

V. To be, or become in order, to form, fall in, arrange itself, place itself, range itself, fall into its place, fall into rank.

Adj. Orderly, regular, in order, arranged, &c. (60), in its proper place, *en règle*, well regulated, methodical, uniform, systematic, unconfused, tidy, undisturbed, untangled, unruffled, unravelled, still, &c. (265).

Phr. In apple-pie order; *lucidus ordo.*

Adv. Orderly, &c., in its turn.

Step by step, by regular steps, stages, periods, or intervals.

At stated periods, (138).

(59) Absence, or want of Order, &c.

DISORDER, irregularity, anomaly, confusion, confusedness, disarray, jumble, huddle, litter, lumber, *cahotage*, farrago, mess, hodge-podge, anarchy, anarchism, *imbroglio*, chaos, *omnium gatherum.*

Complexedness, complexity, complexness, complication, intricacy, intricateness, implication, perplexity, involution, ravelling, entanglement, knot, coil, skein, sleeve, Gordian knot.

Turmoil, tumult, ferment, fermentation, pudder, riot, rumpus, scramble, *fracas*, vortex, whirlpool, hurly-burly, bear-garden, Babel.

Tumultuousness, riotousness, inquietude (173).

Phr. Rudis indigestaque moles; confusion worse confounded; most admired disorder.

A pretty kettle of fish;—All the fat being in the fire;—*Le diable à quatre;*—The Devil to pay.

Derangement (61), inversion of order.

Topsy-turvy (218), hocus-pocus.

Phr. The cart before the horse, ὕστερον πρότερον.

V. To be out of order, irregular, disorderly, &c.

To put out of order (61).

Phr. To fish in troubled waters.

Adj. Disorderly, orderless, out of order, deranged (61), irregular, anomalous, untidy, unarranged, immethodical, unsymmetric, unsystematic, unmethodical, undigested, unsorted, unclassified, unclassed.

Disjointed, out of joint, confused, tangled, involved, fumbled, inextricable, irreducible.

Mixed, scattered, promiscuous, indiscriminate, straggling.

Tumultuous, turbulent, riotous, troublous, tumultuary (173).

Adv. Irregularly, &c., pell-mell ; higgledy-piggledy ; at sixes and sevens ; helter-skelter ; harum-scarum.

(60) Reduction to Order.

ARRANGEMENT, disposal, disposition, collocation, allocation, distribution, sorting, assortment, allotment, apportionment, marshalling, *taxis, syntaxis,* gradation, organization.

Analysis, sifting, classification.

Result of arrangement, digest, synopsis, analysis, *syntagma,* table, register (551).

Instrument for sorting : sieve, riddle, screen.

V. To reduce to order, bring into order, introduce order into.

To arrange, dispose, place, form ; to put, set, place, &c., in order ; to set out, collocate, pack, marshal, range, rank, group, parcel out, allot, assort, sort, sift, riddle ; to put or set to rights ; to assign places to.

To class, classify, file, string, tabulate.

To methodize, digest, regulate, graduate, organize, settle.

To unravel, disentangle, ravel, card, disembroil.

Adj. Arranged, methodical, &c., *see* (58).

(61) Subversion of Order, bringing into disorder.

DERANGEMENT, disarrangement, misarrangement, displacement, misplacement, discomposure, disturbance, disorganization, perturbation, shuffling, rumpling, embroilment, corrugation (258), inversion (218).

V. To derange, disarrange, misplace, mislay, discompose, disorder, unsettle, disturb, confuse, perturb, jumble, tumble, huddle, muddle, toss, fumble, riot ; bring, put, or throw into disorder, confusion, &c.

To unhinge, put out of joint, turn over, invert ; turn topsy-turvy ; turn inside out (218).

To complicate, involve, perplex, tangle, entangle, ravel, ruffle, rumple, dishevel, litter, scatter.

Adj. Deranged, &c., *see* (59).

___

2°. CONSECUTIVE ORDER.

(62) PRECEDENCE, coming before, antecedence, priority, anteriority, antecedency, *le pas.*

Superiority (33), Precession (280).

V. To precede, come before, introduce, usher in ; to have the *pas,* to lead, to get the start.

To place before ; to prefix, affix, premise, prelude, preface.

To prepare (673).

Adj. Preceding, precedent, antecedent, anterior, prior, previous, before, ahead of.

Former, foregoing ; coming or going before ; prevenient, preliminary, prefatory, introductory, prelusive, prelusory, proemial, preparatory.

Adv. In advance, ahead, &c., in front of, *see* (234).

(63) SEQUENCE, coming after, consecution, succession, posteriority, secondariness.

Continuation, order of succession, successiveness.

Subordination, inferiority (34).

Alternation (138).

V. To succeed, come after, follow, come next, ensue, come on, tread close upon ; to alternate.

Phr. To be in the wake, or trail of ; to tread on the heels of ; to step into the shoes of.

To place after, to suffix.

Adj. Succeeding, coming after, following, subsequent, ensuing, sequent, sequarious, consequent, next ; consecutive ; alternate.

Latter, posterior.

Adv. After, subsequently, since, behind, in the wake of, in the train of, at the tail of, in the rear of, *see* (235).

(64) PRECURSOR, antecedent, predecessor, forerunner, van-courier, outrider, *avant-courrier.*

Prelude, preamble, preface, prologue, *avant-propos, protasis, proemium,* prolusion, *preludium,* proem, prolepsis, prolegomena, prefix, introduction, frontispiece, groundwork (673).

(66) BEGINNING, commencement, outset, incipience, inception, inchoation, initiative, overture, *exordium,* symphony, inauguration, onset, *alpha.*

Origin, rise, birth, bud, embryo, rudiment, start, starting-point, starting-post, *see* Departure (292).

Van, vanguard, title-page, heading, front (234), fore part, head (210).

Dawn, morning (125).

Opening, entrance, entry, inlet, orifice, porch, portal, gateway, door, gate, postern, wicket, threshold, vestibule, mouth, chops, chaps, lips.

V. To begin, commence, inchoate, rise, arise, originate, initiate, open, dawn, set in, take its rise, enter upon, set out (292).

To lead off, lead the way, take the lead, or the initiative ; head, stand at the head, stand first ; broach, set on foot, set a-going, set abroach, launch, break ground, break the ice.

Adj. Beginning, commencing, arising, initial, initiatory, initiative, incipient, proemial, inaugural, inchoate, inchoative, primogenial, aboriginal, rudimental, nascent, opening, dawning, entering.

(65) SEQUEL, after-part, suffix, successor, tail, *queue,* train, wake, trail, rear, retinue, appendix (39), postscript, epilogue, after-piece, after-thought.

Phr. More last words.

(67) END, close, termination, desinence, conclusion, finish, *finis, finale,* period, term, *terminus,* last, *omega,* extreme, extremity, butt-end, fag-end, tail, after-part, rear (235), *colophon,* peroration, *bonne-bouche.*

Completion (729), winding-up, *dénouement,* catastrophe, consummation, finishing stroke, upshot.

Phr. Ne plus ultra.

V. To end, close, finish, terminate, conclude ; come, or draw, to an end, close or stop.

To bring to an end, close, &c., to put a period, &c., to ; to close, finish, &c., to wind up, complete, achieve (729), crown, determine.

Adj. Ending, closing, &c., final, terminal, desitive, definitive, crowning.

Last, ultimate, hindermost, rear, caudal, conterminate, conterminous, conterminable.

Ended, closed, terminated, &c.

Unbegun, fresh, uncommenced.

First, foremost, leading, heading, maiden (*ex. gr.* maiden speech).

Begun, commenced, &c.

Adv. At, or in the beginning ; first, in the first place, *imprimis,* first and foremost, *in limine,* in the bud.

From the beginning, *ab initio ; ab ovo ; ab incunabulis.*

(68) MIDDLE, mediety, mean, medium, middle term, centre (222), *mezzo termine, juste milieu,* half-way-house, nave, navel, nucleus, bisection (91).

Equidistance, midst, equator, diaphragm, midriff.

Intervenience, interjacence, intervention (228), mid-course (628).

Adj. Middle, medial, mean, mid, mediate, intermediate (29), intervenient, interjacent (228), central (222), equidistant, embosomed, merged.

Mediterranean, equatorial.

Adv. In the middle, mid-way, midships, half-way, in the thick of, *in medias res.*

18

(69) Uninterrupted sequence.

CONTINUITY, consecution, succession, suite, progression, series, train, chain, catenation, concatenation, scale, gradation, course, procession, column, retinue, *cortége*, ⌐avalcade, rank and file, line of battle, array, pedigree, genealogy, lineage, race.

File, line, row, range, tier, string, thread, team, suit, colonnade.

V. To follow in a series, &c. ; to form a series, &c. ; to fall in.

To arrange in a series, to marshal, &c. (60) ; to string together, file, graduate, tabulate.

Adj. Continuous, consecutive, serial, successive, continued, uninterrupted, unbroken, entire, linear, in a line, in a row, &c., gradual, unintermitting (110).

Adv. Continuously, consecutively, &c., *seriatim ;* in a line, in a row, series, &c., in succession, &c., running, gradually.

(70) Interrupted sequence.

DISCONTINUITY, interruption, break, interval, gap, chasm, *hiatus* (198), *cæsura*, rhapsody.

Intermission, alternation, *see* Periodicity (138).

V. To be discontinuous, &c. ; to alternate, intermit.

To interrupt, break, interpose (228) ; to break in upon, disconnect (44) ; to break or snap the thread.

Adj. Discontinuous, unsuccessive, broken, interrupted, desultory, *décousu*, disconnected, unconnected, rhapsodical.

Alternate, every other, intermitting, alternating (138).

Adv. At intervals, by snatches, *per saltum*, by fits and starts, *longo intervallo.*

(71) TERM, rank, station, stage, step, degree (26), remove, grade, place, point, *pas*, period, pitch, stand, standing, footing, range.

3°. COLLECTIVE ORDER.

(72) ASSEMBLAGE, collection, collocation, gathering, muster, colligation, contesseration, *attroupement*, association, concourse, conflux, meeting, assembly, congregation, *levée, réunion*, accumulation, cumulation.

Congress, convocation, *comitium*, quorum, conclave, synod, caucus, conventicle.

Miscellany, museum, menagery, Noah's ark, portfolio.

A multitude (102), crowd, throng, rabble, mob, press, crush, *cohue*, horde, posse, body, tribe, crew, gang, knot, band, party, bevy, covey, drove, corps, troop, squad, squadron, phalanx, platoon, company, regiment, battalion, legion, host, army, myrmidons.

Clan, brotherhood, sisterhood, party (712).

Volley, shower, storm, cloud, &c.

(73) NON-ASSEMBLAGE.

DISPERSION, scattering, dissemination, diffusion, dissipation, spreading, casting, distribution, sprinkling, respersion, circumfusion, interspersion, spargefaction.

V. To disperse, scatter, sow, disseminate, diffuse, shed, spread, disperse, disband, distribute, dispel, give, cast, or disperse to the winds, cast forth ; to sow broadcast, strew, sprinkle, issue, deal out, utter, resperse, intersperse, set abroach, circumfuse.

Adj. Unassembled, uncollected, dispersed, scattered, diffused, sparse, spread, cast, broadcast, &c., adrift, dishevelled, streaming, &c.

Adv. Sparsim, here and there.

19

Group, cluster, clump, set, batch, pencil, lot, pack, budget, assortment, bunch, parcel, packet, bundle, *fasciculus*, package, faggot, wisp, truss, tuft, shock, rick, fardel, stack, sheaf.

Accumulation, congeries, heap, lump, pile, *rouleau*, mass, pyramid, bale, drift, snow-ball, acervation, glomeration, agglomeration, conglobation, conglomeration, conglomerate, coacervation, coagmentation, aggregation, concentration, congestion, Pelion upon Ossa, *spicilegium, omnium gatherum.*

V. To assemble, collect, muster, meet, unite, cluster, flock, herd, crowd, throng, associate, congregate, rendezvous, resort, flock together, re-assemble.

To bring, or gather together, collect, draw together, group, convene, convocate, collocate, colligate, scrape together, rake up, dredge, bring into a focus, amass, accumulate, heap up, pile, pack, stack, truss, pack together, acervate, agglomerate, garner up, lump together.

Phr. To heap Pelion upon Ossa.

Adj. Assembled, collected, &c., unscattered, met together, closely packed, dense, crowded, huddled together, teeming, swarming, populous.

Phr. As thick as hops.

(74) Place of meeting.

Focus, point of convergence, corradiation, *rendezvous*, head-quarters, centre (222), gathering, place, resort, museum, repository, *depôt* (636).

4°. DISTRIBUTIVE ORDER.

(75) Class, division, category, *categorema*, head, order, section, department, province.

Kind, sort, genus, species, family, race, tribe, caste, sept, clan, breed, kit, sect, set, assortment, suit, range.

Gender, sex, kin, kidney, manner, description, denomination, designation, predicament.

(76) Inclusion, comprehension under a class, reference to a class.

Inclusion in a compound (54).

V. To be included in, to come under, to fall under, to range under; to belong, or pertain to; to range with, to merge in.

To include, comprise, comprehend, contain, admit, embrace, enumerate among, number among, refer to, place under, arrange under, or with.

Adj. Including, &c., inclusive, congener, congenerous, *et hoc genus omne*, of the same class, &c.

Included, merged, &c.

(77) Exclusion from a class*, rejection, &c., proscription, nobody.

Exclusion from a compound (55).

V. To be excluded from, &c.; to exclude, proscribe, &c.

Phr. To shut the door upon.

Adj. Exclusive, excluding, &c.

(78) Generality, universality, catholicism.

(79) Speciality, particularity, individuality, peculiarity, indivi-

* The same set of words are used to express *Exclusion from a class* and *Exclusion from a compound*. Reference is therefore here made to the former at (55). This identity does not occur with regard to *Inclusion*, which therefore required to be made a separate heading.

Miscellaneousness, miscellany, generalization, prevalence, drag-net.

V. To be general, &c., to prevail. To render general, to generalize.

Adj. General, generic, collective, comprehensive, sweeping, universal, catholical, catholic, common, œcumenical (or ecumenical), transcendental, prevalent, prevailing.

Every, every one, all, to a man. Unspecified, impersonal.

duity, personality, *propria persona,* characteristic, mannerism, idiosyncrasy, specificness, singularity (83).

Particulars, details, items, counts. I, myself, self; I myself, I.

V. To specify, particularize, individualize, realize, specialize, designate, determine, to descend to particulars, to enter into detail.

Adj. Special, particular, individual, specific, proper, personal, private, respective, definite, determinate, especial, certain, esoteric, endemic, partial, party, peculiar, characteristic, exclusive, *sui generis,* singular, exceptional (83).

Adv. Specially, specifically, &c., in particular, respectively, personally, *in propriâ personâ, ad hominem.*

Each, apiece, one by one, severally, *seriatim, videlicet.*

5°. ORDER AS REGARDS CATEGORIES.

(80) RULE, regularity, uniformity, constancy, standard, model, nature, the order of things, routine, prevalence, practice, usage, custom, use, habit (613), regulation.

Form, formula, law, canon, principle.

Type, pattern, precedent, *paradigma,* normal, natural, ordinary, model, state or condition, a standing dish.

(81) MULTIFORMITY, variety, diversity, multifariousness.

Adj. Multiform, multifold, manifold, multifarious, multigenerous, omnifarious, heterogeneous, motley, epicene, of all sorts and kinds, desultory, irregular, diversified, and what not?

Phr. Et hoc genus omne.

(82) CONFORMITY, conformance, observance, naturalization.

Example, instance, specimen, sample, ensample, *exemplar,* exemplification, illustration, case in point, quotation.

V. To conform to rule, be regular, &c., to follow, observe, go by, bend to, obey rules, to be regulated by; be wont, &c. (613), to naturalize.

To exemplify, illustrate, cite, quote, put a case, produce an instance, &c.

Adj. Conformable to rule, regular, uniform, constant, according to rule, *selon les règles,* normal, formal, canonical, strict, rigid, positive, uncompromising.

Phr. Regular as clockwork.

Adj. Ordinary, natural, usual, common, wonted, accustomed, habitual,

(83) UNCONFORMITY, informality, arbitrariness, abnormity, anomaly, anomalousness, lawlessness, peculiarity, exclusiveness, infraction, breach, violation, &c. of law, or rule, eccentricity, aberration, irregularity, singularity, exemption, salvo.

Exception, nondescript, monster, prodigy (872), *lusus naturæ, rara avis,* queer fish, mongrel, hybrid, mule, mulatto, *tertium quid,* hermaphrodite.

Phœnix, chimera, hydra, sphinx, minotaur, griffin, centaur, hippocentaur, sagittary, hippogriff, kraken, sea-serpent, mermaid, unicorn, &c.

V. To be unconformable to rule, to be exceptional, &c.

Phr. To beggar description, to be neither fish, flesh, nor foul, (nor a red herring).

21

every-day, current, prevailing, prevalent, established, received, acknowledged, recognized, hacknied, well-known, familiar, vernacular, commonplace, trite, of daily or every-day occurrence, in the order of things, naturalized.

Exemplary, illustrative, in point.

Adv. Conformably, by rule, regularly, &c., agreeably to.

Usually, generally, ordinarily, commonly, as usual, *ad instar.*

Of course, as a matter of course, *instar omnium.*

For example, for instance, *exempli gratiâ, inter alia,* to wit, namely, *videlicet,* that is to say.

Phr. Ex uno disce omnes; Cela va sans dire.

Adj. Unconformable, abnormal, abnormous, anomalous, anomalastic, out of order, irregular, arbitrary, informal, aberrant, stray, exceptional, peculiar, exclusive, unnatural, eccentric.

Unusual, unaccustomed, unwonted, uncommon, rare, singular, *unique,* curious, odd, extraordinary, strange, out of the way, unheard of, queer, quaint, nondescript, undescribed, none such, *sui generis,* unprecedented, unparalleled, unfamiliar, fantastic, new-fangled, grotesque, outlandish, exotic, preternatural, denaturalized.

Heterogeneous, heteroclite, amorphous, out of the pale of, mongrel, amphibious, epicene, half-blood, hybrid, androgynous, androgynal.

Phr. Unlike what the world ever saw.

Adv. Except, unless, save, barring, beside, without, save and except, let alone.

However, yet, but, unusually, &c.

Phr. Never was seen, or heard, or known the like.

Section V.   NUMBER.

1º. Number in the Abstract.

(84) Number, symbol, numeral, figure, cypher, digit, integer, counter, a round number, notation.

Sum, difference, complement, product, multiplicand, multiplier, multiplicator, coefficient, multiple, dividend, divisor, factor, quotient, fraction, numerator, denominator, decimal, circulating decimal, repetend, common measure, aliquot part, reciprocal, prime number, permutation, combination, election.

Ratio, proportion, progression, (arithmetical, geometrical, harmonical), figurate, pyramidal, and polygonal numbers.

Power, root, exponent, index, logarithm, antilogarithm;—differential, integral, fluxion, fluent.

Adj. Numeral, complementary, divisible, aliquot, reciprocal, prime, fractional, decimal, figurate, &c., fractional, mixed, incommensurable.

Proportional, series, exponential, logarithmic, logometric, differential, fluxional, integral.

Positive, negative, rational, irrational, surd, radical, real, imaginary, impossible.

(85) Numeration, numbering, counting, tale, telling, calling over, recension, enumeration, summation, reckoning, computation, supputation, calculation, calculus, algorithm.

Arithmetic, analysis, algebra, fluxions, differential and integral calculus.

22

Statistics; dead reckoning, muster, poll, census, capitation, roll call, muster-roll, account, score, recapitulation.

Operations; addition, subtraction, multiplication, division, reduction, involution, evolution, approximation, interpolation, differentiation, integration.

Instruments; abacus, swan-pan, logometer, sliding-rule, &c.

V. To number, count, tell, call over, take an account of, enumerate, muster, poll, run over, recite, recapitulate, — sum, sum up, tell off, score, compute, calculate, suppute,—add, subtract, &c.

Check, prove, demonstrate, balance, audit, overhaul.

Adj. Numerical, arithmetical, numeral, analytic, algebraic, statistical, computable, calculable, commensurable, incommensurate.

Phr. According to Cocker.

(86) List, catalogue, inventory, schedule, register, record (551), registry, syllabus, roll, terrier, file, muster-roll, calendar, index, table, book synopsis, *catalogue raisonné, tableau,* contents, invoice, bill of lading, red-book, *cadastre,* prospectus, programme.

Registration, &c. (551).

2°. Determinate Number.

(87) Unity, oneness, individuality, singleness, solitariness, solitude, isolation, abstraction.

One, unit, ace.

Some one, somebody, no other, none else, an individual.

V. To be one, to be alone, &c.; to isolate, insulate.

Adj. One, sole, single, individual, apart, alone, lone, isolated, solitary, lonely, lonesome, dreary, insular, insulated, disparate, discrete.

Unaccompanied, unattended, *solus,* singular, odd, unique, unrepeated, azygous.

Adv. Singly, &c., alone, by itself, *per se,* only, apart, in the singular number, in the abstract.

One and a half, *sesqui-.*

(88) Accompaniment, coexistence, concomitance, company, association, companionship, partnership, copartnership, coefficiency.

Concomitant, accessory, coefficient (39), companion, attendant, fellow, associate, consort, spouse, colleague, partner, copartner, satellite, escort, hanger on.

V. To accompany, coexist, attend, be associated with, hang on, wait on, go hand in hand with.

Adj. Accompanying, coexisting, attending, &c., concomitant, fellow, joint, associated with, accessory.

Adv. With, together with, along with, in company with, hand in hand, cheek by jowl, &c.; therewith, herewith.

(89) Duality, dualism, duplicity.

Two, deuce, couple, brace, pair, twins, Castor and Pollux, fellows, yoke, conjugation, polarity.

V. To unite in pairs, to pair, couple, bracket, yoke.

Adj. Two, twain, dual, binary, dualistic, duplex, twofold, bifold, biform, bifarious, duplicate, dyadic, binomial, twin, *tête-à-tête.*

Coupled, bracketed, paired, &c., conjugate.

Both, the one and the other.

(90) Duplication, doubling, gemination, reduplication, ingemination, repetition, iteration (104), renewal.

(91) Division into two parts.

Bisection, bipartition, dichotomy, halving, demidation, bifurcation, forking, branching, ramification, di-

23

V. To double, redouble, geminate, reduplicate, repeat, iterate, re-echo, renew.

Adj. Doubled, redoubled, &c.

Adv. Twice, once more, over again, *da capo, bis, encore,* anew, as much again, twofold (104, 136).

Secondly, in the second place, again.

varication, splitting, cleaving, fork, prong.

Half, moiety, semi-, demi-, hemi-.

V. To bisect, halve, divide, cut in two, demidate, dichotomize, to go halves.

To separate, fork, bifurcate, branch out, ramify, to split, cleave.

Adj. Bisected, halved, divided, &c., bipartite, bifid, bifurcous, bifurcate, cloven, cleft, split, &c.

(92) TRIALITY, trinity.*
Three, triad, triplet, trey, trio, ternion, trinomial, leash.
Third power, cube.
Adj. Three, triform, trinal, trinomial, tertiary.

(93) TRIPLICATION, triplicity, trebleness, trine.
V. To treble, triple, triplicate.
Adj. Treble, triple, tern, ternary, triplicate, threefold, trilogistic.
Adv. Three times, thrice, threefold, in the third place, thirdly.

(94) Division into three parts.
TRISECTION, tripartition, trichotomy ; third part, third.
V. To trisect, divide into three parts.
Adj. Trifid, trisected, tripartite, trichotomous, trisulcate.

(95) QUATERNITY, four, tetrad, quartet, quaternion, square, quadrature, quater.
V. To reduce to a square, to square.
Adj. Four, quaternary, quaternal, quadratic, quartile, tetractic.

(96) QUADRUPLICATION.
V. To multiply by four, quadruplicate, biquadrate.
Adj. Fourfold, quadruple, quadruplicate, quadrible.
Adv. Four times, in the fourth place, fourthly.

(97) Division into four parts.
QUADRISECTION, quadripartition, quartering, a fourth, a quarter.
V. To quarter, to divide into four parts, &c.
Adj. Quartered, &c., quadrifid, quadripartite.

(98) FIVE, cinque, quint.
Adj. Five, quinary, quintuple.
SIX.
Adj. Senary, sextuple.
TEN, a decade.
Adj. Decimal, denary, decuple.

TWELVE, a dozen.
Adj. Duodenary.
TWENTY, a score.
EIGHTY, fourscore.
HUNDRED, centenary, hecatomb, century.
Adj. Centuple, centuplicate, centennial, centenary.

(99) QUINQUESECTION, &c.
Adj. Quinquefid, quinquarticular, quinquepartite.

DECIMATION.
V. To decimate.
Adj. Decimal, tenth, tithe.
DUODECIMAL, twelfth.

HUNDREDTH, centesimal.

---

* *Trinity* is hardly ever used except in a theological sense, (976).

THOUSAND, chiliad.
MYRIAD, lack.
MILLION, billion, trillion, &c.

Millesimal, &c.

3°. INDETERMINATE NUMBER.

(100) More than one.
PLURALITY, a number, a certain number, a round number.
Adj. Plural, more than one, some, certain, some one, somebody.

(102) MULTITUDE, numerousness, numerosity, numerality, multiplicity, legion, host, a great, or large number, numbers, sight, army.
A shoal, swarm, draught, bevy, flock, herd, drove, covey, hive, brood, litter, teem, fry, nest, crowd, &c. (72).
Increase of number, multiplication.
V. To be numerous, &c., to swarm, teem, crowd, come thick upon, outnumber, multiply.
Adj. Many, several, sundry, divers, various, ever so many, numerous, numerose, manifold, multiplied, multitudinous, multiple, multinomial, endless (105).
Frequent, repeated, reiterated, outnumbering, thick, crowding.
Phr. Thick as hops; thick as hail.

(101) ZERO, nothing (4), naught, cypher, a solitude, a desert.
Adj. None, not one, not any, nobody, not a soul, *âme qui vive.*

(103) FEWNESS, paucity, a small number, scantiness, rareness, rarity, thinness.
Diminution of number, reduction, weeding, elimination, thinning.
V. To be few, &c.
To render few, reduce, diminish the number, weed, eliminate, thin, decimate.
Adj. Few, scanty, rare, thinly scattered, *rari nantes*, hardly or scarcely any, reduced, thinned, weeded, &c., unrepeated.

(104) REPETITION, iteration, reiteration, recurrence (136), battology, tautology, monotony, cuckoo-note, chimes, repetend, echo, burden of a song, *refrain*, renewal, rehearsal.
Cuckoo, mocking-bird.
Periodicity (138).
V. To repeat, iterate, reiterate, renew, reproduce, echo, re-echo, rehearse, redouble, battologize, do or say over again, ring the changes on, drum, to harp on the same string, to din in the ear, to conjugate in all its moods, tenses, and inflexions.
Adj. Repeated (136), repetitional, repetitionary, recurrent, recurring, reiterated, renewed, ever recurring, monotonous, harping, mocking, chiming, aforesaid.
Phr. Regular as clockwork.
Adv. Repeatedly, often (136), again, over again, afresh, again and again, over and over again, ding-dong, ditto, *encore, de novo*. *See* Twice (90).

(105) INFINITY, infinitude.
Adj. Infinite, numberless, innumerable, countless, sumless, untold, unnumbered, incalculable, unlimited, limitless, illimited, illimitable, immeasurable, unmeasured, unbounded, boundless, endless, interminable, unfathomable, exhaustless, termless, indefinite.
Phr. Numerous as the stars in the firmament; as the sands on the seashore; as the hairs on the head; their name is "Legion."
Adv. Infinitely, &c., without measure, limit, &c., *ad infinitum.*

25

SECTION VI. TIME.

1°. ABSOLUTE TIME.

(106) DURATION, period, term, space, span, spell, season, era.

Intermediate time, while, interval, *interim*, pendency, intervention, intermission, interregnum, interlude, intermittence, respite.

Long duration (110).

V. To continue, last, endure, remain, to take, take up, or occupy time, to persist, to intervene.

To pass, spend, employ, or consume time.

Adj. Continuing, lasting, enduring, remaining, persistent, permanent (150).

Adv. While, whilst, during, or pending, till, until, the time, or interval; the whole time, or period; all the time, in the long run, all along, throughout.

Phr. Ab ovo usque ad mala.

Pending, mean time, meanwhile, in the mean time, in the interim, *ad interim, pendente lite*, from day to day, *de die in diem*, for a time, for a season, for good.

(107) NEVERNESS*, absence of time, no time.

Short duration (111).

Adv. Never, ne'er, at no time, on no occasion, at no period, nevermore, *sine die, dies non.*

Phr. On Tib's eve; on the Greek Kalends.

---

(108) Definite duration, or portion of time.

PERIOD, second, minute, hour, day, week, month, quarter, year, *lustrum, quinquennium*, lifetime.

Century, age, millennium.

Adj. Hourly, horary; diurnal, quotidian; hebdomadal, menstrual, monthly, annual, secular.

Adv. From day to day, from hour to hour, &c., till, until, up to.

(109) Indefinite duration.

COURSE, progress, process, succession, lapse, flow, flux, stream, tract, current, tide, march, step, flight, &c. of time.

The scythe of time, the glass of time.

Indefinite time, aorist.

V. To elapse, lapse, flow, run, proceed, roll on, advance, pass, slide, press on, flit, fly, slip.

Adj. Elapsing, passing, &c., aoristic.

Adv. In course of time; in due time, or season; in process of time; in the fulness of time.

Phr. Traditur dies die.

(110) Long duration.

DIUTURNITY, a long time, an age, a century, an eternity.

Durableness, durability, persistence, lastingness, continuance, permanence (150), longevity, survival, survivance.

Protraction, extension, or prolongation of time (133).

(111) Short duration.

TRANSIENTNESS, transitoriness, evanescence, transitiveness, fugitiveness, fugacity, fugaciousness, caducity, mortality, span, one's days being numbered, shortness, brevity.

Quickness, promptness (132), suddenness, abruptness.

A *coup de main*, bubble, May-fly.

---

* A term introduced by Bishop Wilkins.

V. To last, endure, stand, &c.; linger, tarry, protract, prolong, outlast, outlive, survive ; spin out, draw out, eke out, linger, loiter, lounge, wait.

Adj. Durable, of long duration, permanent, enduring, chronic, intransient, intransmutable, lasting, persistent ; livelong, longeval, long-lived, diuturnal, perennial, unintermitting, unremitting.

Protracted, prolonged, spun out, long-winded, surviving, &c.

Adv. Long, a long time, all the day long, all the year round, the livelong day, *sine die.*

Phr. As the day is long.

(112) PERPETUITY, eternity, everness*, aye, sempiternity, immortality, athanasia, everlastingness.

V. To last, or endure for ever, to have no end, to eternize.

Adj. Perpetual, eternal, everlasting, sempiternal, coeternal ; endless, ceaseless, incessant, indesinent, unceasing, interminable, having no end, unfading, never fading, deathless, immortal, undying, never dying, imperishable.

Adv. Always, ever, evermore, aye, for ever, for aye, for evermore, still, perpetually, eternally, &c., in all ages, from age to age, to the end of time, every day, *in secula seculorum.*

Phr. For ever and a day.

(114) Estimation and measurement of time.

CHRONOMETRY, chronology, registry, date, epoch, style.

Almanac, calendar, ephemeris, chronicle, annals, register, journal, diary, chronogram.

V. To be transient, &c., to flit, fly, gallop, vanish, intromit.

Adj. Transitory, transient, passing, evanescent, fleeting, fugacious, fugitive, flitting, shifting, flying, temporary, provisional, temporal, cursory, galloping, vanishing, short-lived, ephemeral, deciduous.

Brief, sudden, quick, prompt, brisk, abrupt, extemporaneous, summary, hasty, precipitate.

Adv. Temporarily, &c., *pro tempore.*

In a short time, soon, awhile, anon, briefly, apace, eft, eftsoons, straight, straightway, quickly, speedily, promptly, *presto*, directly, immediately, incontinently, presently, straightforth, forthwith, *à vue d'œil*, by and bye.

Suddenly, *per saltum*, at one jump.

(113) Point of time.

INSTANTANEITY, instantaneousness, moment, instant, second, minute, twinkling, trice, flash, breath, span, jiffy, flash of lightning, stroke of time, epoch, the twinkling of an eye, suddenness, *see* (111).

V. To twinkle, flash, to be instantaneous, &c.

Adj. Instantaneous, momentary, extempore.

Phr. Quick as thought, quick as lightning, as electricity.

Adv. Instantly, momentarily, *subito*, *instanter*, suddenly, in a moment, in an instant, in a second, in no time, in a trice, in a twinkling, in a breath, extempore.

Phr. Before one can say "Jack Robinson;" between the cup and the lip ; on the spur of the moment ; on the spot.

(115) False estimate of time.

ANACHRONISM, prolepsis, metachronism, prochronism, parachronism, misdate, anticipation, antichronism.

V. To misdate, antedate, postdate, overdate, anticipate.

* Bishop Wilkins.

Instruments for the measurement of time; clock, watch, chronometer, time-piece, dial, sun-dial, horologe, pendulum, hour-glass, clepsydra.

Chronographer, chronologer, chronologist, annalist.

V. To fix or mark the time, date, register, &c., to bear date, to measure time, to beat time.

Adj. Chronological, chronometrical, chronogrammatical, &c.

Adj. Misdated, &c., undated.

2°. RELATIVE TIME.

1. *Time with reference to Succession.*

(116) PRIORITY, antecedence, anteriority, precedence, pre-existence.

Precursor, predecessor, prelude, forerunner, &c. (64), harbinger, dawn, introduction, prodrome.

V. To precede, come before, pre-exist, prelude, usher in, dawn, forerun, announce, &c. (511).

Adj. Prior, previous, preceding, anterior, antecedent, pre-existing, former, foregoing.

Precursory, prelusive, prelusory, preludious, proemial, introductory, prefatory, prodromous.

Adv. Before, prior to, previously, anteriorly, antecedently, afore, ere, ere now, before now, already, yet.

(117) POSTERIORITY, succession, sequence, subsequence, supervention, sequel, successor (65).

V. To follow, come or go after, succeed, supervene.

Phr. To tread on the heels of.

Adj. Subsequent, posterior, following, after, later, succeeding, postliminious, postnate, postdiluvial, postdiluvian, *puisné*, posthumous.

Adv. Subsequently, after, afterwards, since, later, next, in the sequel, close upon, thereafter, thereupon, upon which.

(118) The PRESENT TIME, the existing time, the time being, the present moment, juncture, the nonce, crisis, epoch, day, hour.

Adj. Present, actual, instant, current, existing, that is.

Adv. At this time, moment, &c., now, at present, at this time of day, at the present time, day, &c., to-day, now-a-days, already, even now, but now, just now, upon which, for the time being, for the nonce, *pro hâc vice*, on the nail, on the spot, on the spur of the occasion.

(119) Time different from the present.

DIFFERENT TIME, other time.

Indefinite time, aorist.

Adj. Aoristic.

Adv. At that time, moment, &c., then, at which time, &c., on that occasion.

When, whenever, whensoever, upon which, on which occasions, at another or a different time, &c., at various times, ever and anon.

(120) SYNCHRONISM, coexistence, coincidence, simultaneousness, contemporaneousness, concurrence, concomitance, contemporariness.

Having equal times, isochronism.

A contemporary, coetanian.

V. To coexist, concur, accompany.

Adj. Synchronous, synchronal, synchronical, synchronistical, simultaneous, coexisting, coincident, concomitant, concurrent, coeval, coevous, cotemporary, coetaneous, contemporaneous, coeternal, isochronous.

Adv. At the same time, simultaneously, &c., together, during the same time, &c., in the same breath, *pari passu*, meantime (106).

(121) Prospective time.

FUTURITY, the future, futurition, hereafter, the time to come, after time, after age, the coming time, the morrow, after days, hours, years, &c., after life, millennium, doomsday, the day of judgment, the crack of doom.

The approach of time, advent, time drawing on, the womb of time.

Prospection, anticipation, prospect, perspective, expectation (507), horizon, heritage, heirs, posterity, descendants.

Future existence, future state, post-existence.

V. To look forwards, anticipate, have in prospect, keep in view, wait (133), expect, lie in wait for, to wait impatiently, kick one's heels, dance attendance.

To impend, hang over, lie over, approach, await, threaten, draw near, prepare.

Phr. To be in the wind.

Adj. Future, to come, coming, going to happen, approaching, impending, instant, at hand, about to be or happen, next, hanging, awaiting, forthcoming, near, near at hand, imminent, threatening, brewing, preparing, eventual, ulterior, in view, in prospect, prospective, in perspective, in the horizon, in the wind, on the cards, that will be.

Unborn, in embryo, in the womb of time.

Phr. All in good time.

Adv. Prospectively, hereafter, by and bye, anon, in future, to-morrow, in course of time, in process of time, sooner or later, *proximo, paulo post futurum.*

On the eve of, soon, ere long, on the point of, beforehand, against the time.

After a time, from this time, henceforth, henceforwards, thence, thenceforth, thenceforward, whereupon, upon which.

(122) Retrospective time.

PRETERITION, the past, past time, days of yore, time gone by, former times, old times, the olden time, ancient times, antiquity, antiqueness, the good old time, lang syne, time out of mind, time immemorial.

Archæology, paleology, archaism, retrospection, looking back.

Ancestry (166), pre-existence.

V. To pass, lapse, go by, elapse, run out, expire, blow over, to look back, cast the eyes back.

Adj. Past, gone, gone by, over, bygone, foregone, pristine, quondam, lapsed, preterlapsed, expired, run out, blown over, that has been.

Former, foregoing, late, last, latter, recent, overnight, preterperfect, preterpluperfect, forgotten, irrecoverable.

Looking back, retrospective, retroactive, *ex post facto.*

Pre-existing, pre-existent.

Adv. Formerly, of old, erst, whilom, erewhile, before now, time was, ago, over, in the olden time, anciently, in days of yore, long since, retrospectively, ere now, before now, till now, once, once upon a time, hitherto, heretofore, *ultimo.*

The other day, yesterday, just now, recently, lately, of late.

Long ago, a long while or time ago, some time ago, once upon a time, from time immemorial, in the memory of man, time out of mind.

Already, yet, at length, at last.

---

2. *Time with reference to a particular Period.*

(123) NEWNESS, novelty, recentness, recency, freshness, greenness, immaturity, rawness.

Innovation, renovation.

(124) OLDNESS, age, antiquity, primitiveness, maturity, decline, decay, seniority, first-born, eldest, eldership, primogeniture.

29

Adj. New, novel, recent, fresh, green, evergreen, raw, immature, bran new, spick and span new, untrodden, late, modern, neoteric, new-fangled, vernal, renovated.

Phr. Fresh as a rose ;—Fresh as a daisy ;—Fresh as paint.

Adv. Newly, recently, &c., afresh, anew.

Adj. Old, ancient, antique, after-age, antiquated, out of date, of long standing, time-honoured, primitive, diluvian, antediluvian, primeval, primordial, primordinate, primigenous, prime.

Immemorial, inveterate, rooted, mediæval.

Senior, elder, eldest, oldest, first-born.

Obsolete, stale, time-worn, faded, decayed, effete, declining, &c., crumbling, decrepit (128).

Phr. Nothing new under the sun ;—Old as the hills ;—Old as Methuselah ;—Old as Adam ; —*Nihil sub sole novi.*

(125) MORNING, morn, forenoon, prime, dawn, daybreak, peep of day, break of day, aurora, first blush of the morning, prime of the morning, twilight, crepuscule, sunrise, cock-crow.

Noon, noontide, meridian, noon-day, prime, spring.

Adj. Matutinal, vernal.

(126) EVENING, eve, e'en, decline of day, fall of day, eventide, night-fall, curfew, dusk, twilight, eleventh hour, sunset, afternoon, going down of the sun.

Midnight, the witching time of night, the dead of night, autumn.

Adj. Nocturnal, autumnal.

(127) YOUTH, infancy, babyhood, juvenility, childhood, boyism, youth-hood, juniority, minority, nonage, teens, tender age, bloom.

Cradle, nursery, leading strings, puberty, prime or flower of life.

Adj. Young, youthful, juvenile, sappy, *puisné*, beardless, under age, in one's teens, girlish.

(128) AGE, old age, senility, senescence, oldness, years, anility, decline of life, grey hairs, climacteric, decrepitude, hoary age, caducity, the sere and yellow leaf, wane of life, crow's feet, superannuation, dotage, vale of years, seniority, green old age, elder-ship, elders.

Adj. Aged, old, elderly, senile, matronly, anile, in years, advanced in life, or in years, stricken in years, ripe, mellow, grey, hoary, hoar, time-worn, declining, antiquated, *passé*, rusty, effete, decrepit, super-annuated, with one foot in the grave.

Patriarchal, ancestral, primitive, preadamite, antediluvian, diluvian.

Older, elder, senior, turned of.

Eldest, oldest, first-born, firstling.

(129) INFANT, babe, baby, nurse-ling, suckling, seedling, brat, chit, urchin, bantling, bratling, elf, scion, sapling, tendril, mushroom, nestling, chicken, larva, chrysalis, tadpole, whelp, cub, pullet, fry, callow, cod-ling, fœtus, calf, colt, pup, foal, kitten.

Child, bairn, little one, youth, boy, lad, stripling, youngster, younker,

(130) VETERAN, old man, seer, patriarch, greybeard, grandsire, grandam, matron, crone, sexage-narian, octogenarian, centenarian.

Preadamite, Methuselah.

Elders, forefathers, fathers, ancestors, ancestry.

whipster, whippersnapper, schoolboy, hobbardy-hoy, hobbledy-hoy, cadet, minor.

Girl, lass, lassie, wench, miss, damsel, maid, maiden, virgin.

Adj. Infantine, infantile, puerile, boyish, childish, baby, babyish, in leading strings, at the breast, in arms, unfledged, new fledged, kittenish, callow.

(131) ADOLESCENCE, majority, adultness, manhood, prime of life, virility, man's estate, flower of age, ripeness, maturity, meridian of life, years of discretion, *toga virilis.*

A man, adult (373), a woman, matron (374).

Adj. Adolescent, of age, out of one's teens, grown up, mature, middle-aged, manly, virile, adult.

Womanly, matronly.

3. *Time with reference to an Effect or Purpose.*

(132) EARLINESS, timeliness, punctuality, readiness, promptness, promptitude, expedition, quickness, haste, acceleration, hastening, hurry, bustle, precipitation, anticipation.

Suddenness, abruptness (111).

V. To be early, to be in time, &c., to keep time.

To anticipate, forestall.

To expedite, hasten, haste, quicken, press, dispatch, accelerate, precipitate, hurry, bustle.

Phr. To take time by the fore-lock;—to steal a march upon.

Adj. Early, prime, timely, punctual, matutinal, forward, ready, quick, expeditious, precipitate, summary, prompt, premature, precocious, prevenient, anticipatory.

Sudden, abrupt, unexpected (508), subitaneous, extempore.

Adv. Early, soon, anon, betimes, rath, apace, eft, eftsoons, in time, ere long, punctually, in good time, in pudding time, at sunrise, with the lark, extempore.

Beforehand, prematurely, before one's time, in anticipation.

Suddenly, abruptly, on the point of.

(134) OPPORTUNITY, occasion, opening, room, suitable or proper time, or season, high time, the nick of time, opportuneness, tempestivity, seasonableness, crisis, turn, juncture, conjuncture, golden opportunity,

(133) LATENESS, tardiness, slowness, delay, cunctation, procrastination, deferring, postponement, dilation, adjournment, prorogation, the Fabian policy, *La Médecine expectante.*

Protraction, prolongation, leeway.

Phr. An afternoon man.

V. To be late, &c., tarry, wait, stay, bide, take time, dally, dawdle, linger, loiter, bide one's time.

To stand over, lie over.

To put off, defer, delay, lay over, suspend, shift off, stave off, postpone, adjourn, procrastinate, prolong, protract, draw out, prorogue.

Adj. Late, tardy, slow, behindhand, postliminious, posthumous, backward, unpunctual.

Delayed, &c., suspended, in abeyance.

Adv. Late, after time, too late, *sine die.*

At length, at last, backward, at sunset.

Slowly, leisurely, deliberately.

Phr. Nonum prematur in annum; — A day after the fair; — At the eleventh hour.

(135) INTEMPESTIVITY, unsuitable time, improper time, unseasonableness, inopportuneness, evil hour, *contretemps.*

V. To be ill-timed, &c., to mistime, intrude.

mollia tempora, well-timed opportunity.

Spare time, leisure, holiday (685), spare moments, hours, &c., time on one's hands, the enemy.

V. To take the opportunity, to temporize, to time well.

To use, make use of, employ, profit by, avail oneself of, lay hold of, embrace, catch, seize, snatch, clutch, pounce upon, grasp, &c., the opportunity.

To give, offer, present, afford, &c., the opportunity.

To spend, or consume time.

Phr. To turn the occasion to account;— to strike the iron while it is hot;— to make hay while the sun shines;— *carpe diem;— occasionem cognosce.*

To lose, omit, let slip, let go, neglect, pretermit, allow, or suffer the opportunity or occasion to pass, slip, go by, escape, lapse, slip through the fingers, lose time (683), to fritter away time.

Adj. Ill-timed, untimely, intrusive, mistimed, unseasonable, out of season, unpunctual, inopportune, timeless, intrusive, too late (133), *mal à propos*, unlucky, inauspicious, unpropitious, unfortunate, unfavourable.

Adv. Inopportunely, &c.

Phr. As ill luck would have it; —in evil hour;—after meat mustard ;— after death the physician.

Adj. Opportune, timely, well-timed, timeful, seasonable, happy, lucky, fortunate, favourable, propitious, auspicious, critical.

Adv. Opportunely, &c., on the spot, in proper or due time or season, high time.

Phr. In the nick of time, in pudding time; between the cup and the lip ; on the spur of the moment (612).

By the way, by the bye, *en passant, à propos.*

Phr. Non semper erit æstas.

3°. RECURRENT TIME.

(136) FREQUENCY, oftness, recurrence, repetition (104), reiteration, iteration, run, reappearance, renewal, *ritornello*, burden.

V. To recur, revert, return, repeat, reiterate, reappear, renew, reword.

Adj. Frequent, many times, not rare, repeated, reiterated, thickcoming, recurring, recurrent, &c.

Adv. Often, oft, oft-times, frequently, oftentimes, many times, several times, a number of times,

(137) INFREQUENCY, rareness, variety, seldomness.

V. To be rare, &c.

Adj. Infrequent, rare, unfrequent.

Adv. Seldom, rarely, scarcely, hardly, ever; scarcely ever, hardly ever, not often, unfrequently, unoften.

Once, once for all, once in a way, *pro hâc vice.*

many a time, many a time and oft, repeatedly, not unfrequently.

Again, anew, afresh, ditto, over again, *da capo*, again and again, over and over, ever and anon, many times over, repeatedly (104).

Perpetually, continually, constantly.

Sometimes, occasionally, at times, now and then, there are times when, &c ,—*toties quoties.*

Most often, for the most part.

(138) REGULARITY of recurrence, punctuality.

PERIODICITY, intermittence, beat, alternation, alternity, pulsation, alternateness, alternativeness, bout, round, revolution, rotation, turn, routine.

Anniversary, centenary.

Regularity of return, rota, cycle, period, stated time.

V. To recur in regular order or succession, to come round, return, revolve, alternate, come in its turn, beat, pulsate, intermit.

Adj. Periodic, periodical, recurrent, cyclical, revolving, intermittent, remittent, alternate, alternating, steady, punctual, diurnal, quotidian, annual, &c.

Phr. Regular as clockwork.

Adv. Periodically, at regular intervals, at stated times, at fixed periods, punctually.

By turns, in turn, in rotation, alternately, off and on, ride and tie.

(139) IRREGULARITY of recurrence, uncertainty, &c.

Adj. Irregular, uncertain, unpunctual, capricious, desultory, fitful, flickering.

Adv. Irregularly, &c., by fits, by snatches, by starts, by catches, skippingly, by skips.

SECTION VII. CHANGE.

1°. SIMPLE CHANGE.

(140) Difference at different times.

CHANGE, alteration, mutation, permutation, variation, modification, modulation, mood, qualification, innovation, *metastasis*, deviation, turn, inversion, reversion, reversal, eversion, subversion, *bouleversement*, organic change, revolution.

Transformation, transmutation, transfiguration, metamorphosis, transmigration, transubstantiation, transanimation, metempsychosis, avatar.

Vicissitude, flux, unrest (149).

V. To change, alter, vary, modify, modulate, qualify, tamper with, turn, shift, veer, tack, chop, shuffle, swerve, warp, deviate, turn aside, turn topsy-turvy, invert, reverse, intervert, subvert, evert, turn inside out.

Form, fashion, mould, model, vamp, warp, work a change, superinduce, innovate, reform, remodel, refound, new model, revolutionize.

Transform, transume, transmute, transfigure, transmogrify, metamorphose, to ring the changes, pass to, leap to.

Phr. Nous avons changé tout cela.

Adj. Changed, altered, new fangled, warped, &c.

Adv. Mutatis mutandis ; quantum mutatus !

(141) Change from action to rest.

CESSATION, discontinuance, desistance, desinence.

Intermission, remission, suspension, interruption, stop, stoppage, pause, rest, respite, drop, interregnum.

Comma, colon, semicolon, &c.

V. To discontinue, cease, desist, break off, leave off, hold, stop, pause,

(142) PERMANENCE, persistence, endurance, *status quo ;* maintenance, preservation, conservation, truce, suspension, settledness (265).

Phr. The law of the Medes and Persians.

V. To remain, stay, stop, tarry, hold, last, endure, bide, abide, aby, maintain, keep, hold on, stand, subsist, live, stand still, outlive, survive.

33

rest, drop, give over, relinquish (624), stay one's hand, surcease.

Phr. To shut up shop.

To come to a stand, or stand-still, suspend, cut short, cast off, go out, be at an end; intromit, interrupt, interpel, intermit, remit; put an end or stop to.

To pass away, go off, pass off, die away, wear away, wear off, pass away like a shadow, or cloud.

Int. Hold! stop! enough! avast!

Adj. Persisting, &c., unchanged, unmodified, unrenewed, unaltered, fixed, settled, unvaried, intact, persistent, stagnant, rooted, monotonous, unreversed, conservative, undestroyed, unrepealed, unsuppressed, unfailing.

Adv. In statu quo, for good, finally, at a stand, at a stand still, *uti possidetis.*

(143) CONTINUANCE in action, continuation, perseverance, repetition (104), persistence, run.

V. To continue, persist, go on, keep on, abide, keep, pursue, hold on, run on, carry on, keep up, uphold, hold up, persevere, keep it up, maintain, maintain one's ground, harp upon, repeat (104), take root.

Phr. Stare super antiquas vias ; quieta non movere.

Adj. Continuing, &c., uninterrupted, inconvertible, unintermitting, unreversed, unstopped, unrevoked, unvaried, unshifting.

(144) Gradual change to something different.

CONVERSION, reduction, transmutation, resolution, assimilation; chemistry, alchemy ; growth, lapse.

Passage, transit, transition, transmigration, flux, shifting, sliding, running into, &c.; phase, conjugations; convertibility.

Laboratory, alembic, &c. (691).

V. To be converted into ; to become, to wax, come to, turn to, assume the form of, pass, slide, glide, lapse, shift, run, fall, merge, melt, grow, grow into, open into, resolve itself into, settle into, mature, mellow ; assume the form, shape, state, nature, character, &c. of, illapse.

To convert into, make, render, form, mould, reduce, resolve into ; transume (140), fashion, model, remodel, reorganize, shape, mould, modify ; assimilate to; reduce to ; bring to.

Adj. Converted into, become, &c., convertible.

Adv. Gradually, *gradatim*, by degrees, step by step, by inches, inch by inch, by little and little, by slow degrees, consecutively, *seriatim.*

(145) REVERSION, return, reconversion, relapse, reaction, recoil, rebound, *ricochet*, revulsion.

Reinstatement, re-establishment, &c. (660), undoing, the work of Penelope. Alternation (138), inversion.

V. To revert, return to, relapse, recoil, rebound, react ; to restore, &c. (660), to undo, unmake.

Phr. To turn the tables (719).

Adj. Reverting, &c., restored, &c., placed *in statu quo*, revulsive.

Int. As you were !

(146) Sudden or violent change.

REVOLUTION, counter-revolution, transilience, jump, leap, plunge, jerk, start, spasm, convulsion, throe, storm, earthquake, cataclysm (173).

Legerdemain, conjuration, sleight of hand, hocus-pocus, harlequinade, witchcraft, &c. (992).

Adv. Root and branch.

34

(147) Change of one thing for another.

SUBSTITUTION, commutation, metonymy, supplanting, synecdoche.

Thing substituted. Substitute (634), *succedaneum*, make shift, *locum tenens*, representative, proxy ; deputy (759), vice, double, dummy, changeling, stop-gap, jurymast, palimpsest.

V. To substitute, commute, supplant, change for.

To give place to ; to replace, serve as a substitute, &c., stand in the shoes of, take the place of, supersede.

Adj Substituted, &c., vicarious, subdititious.

Adv. Instead, in place of, in lieu of, in the room of, *mutato nomine ; mutatis mutandis.*

(148) Double and mutual change.

INTERCHANGE, exchange, commutation, reciprocation, transposition, permutation, shuffling, castling (at chess), hocus-pocus, interchangeableness.

Reciprocity (12), retaliation (719), barter (794).

Phr. A *quid pro quo.*

V. To interchange, exchange, bandy, transpose, shuffle, change hands, swap, permute, reciprocate, commute, counterchange.

Phr. To play at puss in the corner.

Adj. Interchanged, &c., reciprocal, mutual, commutative, interchangeable.

Phr. A Roland for an Oliver ; tit for tat ; *vice versâ.*

Adv. In exchange.

2°. COMPLEX CHANGES.

(149) MUTABILITY, changeableness, inconstancy, variableness, mobility, instability, unsteadiness, vacillation, unrest, restlessness, slipperiness, impermanence, fragility, fluctuation, vicissitude, alternation, vibration, oscillation (314), flux, ebbing and flowing, ebbs and flows, ups and downs, fidgets, fugitiveness, disquiet, disquietude.

A proteus, chameleon, quicksilver, weathercock, a harlequin.

Phr. The Cynthia of the minute.

Alternation, subalternation, the times being changed.

V. To fluctuate, vary, waver, flounder, vibrate, flicker, flitter, shuffle, shake, totter, tremble, ebb and flow, turn and turn about, change and change about.

To fade, pass away like a cloud, shadow, or dream.

Adj. Mutable, changeable, variable, everchanging, inconstant, unsteady, unstable, proteiform, unfixed, fluctuating, vacillating, versatile, restless, unsettled, mobile, fickle, wavering, flickering, flitting, flittering, fluttering, oscillating, vibratory,

(150) IMMUTABILITY, unchangeableness, constancy, permanence, persistence (106), invariableness, durability, steadiness, immobility, fixedness, stability, stableness, stabiliment, firmness, stiffness, anchylosis, solidity, *aplomb*, incommutability, insusceptibility, irrevocableness.

Phr. The law of the Medes and Persians.

Rock, pillar, tower, foundation.

V. To be permanent, &c. (265), to stand, remain.

To settle, establish, stablish, fix, set, stabilitate, retain, keep, hold, make sure, nail, clinch, rivet, fasten (43), settle down.

Adj. Immutable, unchangeable, unaltered, unalterable, not to be changed, constant, permanent, invariable, undeviating, stable, durable (265), perennial (110).

Fixed, steadfast, firm, fast, steady, immovable, irremovable, rooted, stablished, established, inconvertible, indeclinable, settled, &c., stationary, stagnant.

Moored, at anchor, on a rock.

vagrant, wayward, desultory, afloat, alternating, disquiet, alterable.

Frail, tottering, shaking, trembling, fugitive, ephemeral, transient (111), fading, fragile, deciduous, slippery, unsettled, irresolute (605).

Phr. Tempora mutantur, et nos mutamur in illis; changeable as the moon, as a weathercock.

Present events.

(151) EVENTUALITY, event, occurrence, incident, affair, transaction, proceeding, fact, matter of fact, phenomenon, advent.

Business, concern, circumstance, particular, casualty, accident, adventure, passage, crisis, pass, emergency, contingency, consequence.

The world, life, things, doings, course of things, the course, tide, stream, current, run, &c. of events, stirring events.

Phr. The ups and downs of life, the chapter of accidents, the cast of the die.

V. To happen, occur, take place, take effect, come, come of, become of, come about, pass, come to pass, fall, fall out, run, fall in, befall, betide, bechance, turn out, prove, eventuate, draw on, turn up, cast up, supervene, survene, issue, arrive, ensue, arise, spring, start, come into existence.

Pass off, wear off, blow over.

To experience, meet with, go through, endure (821), suffer, fare.

Adj. Happening, occurring, &c., current, incidental, eventful, stirring, bustling.

Phr. The plot thickening.

Adv. Eventually, in the event of, on foot, on the *tapis*, as it may happen, happen what may, at all events, sink or swim.

Phr. In the course of things; as the tree falls; as the cat jumps; as the world goes.

Indefeasible, irretrievable, intransmutable, irresoluble, irrevocable, irreversible, inextinguishable, irreducible, indissoluble, indissolvable, indestructible, undying, imperishable, indelible, indeciduous, insusceptible of change.

Phr. Without a shadow of turning.

Future events.

(152) DESTINY, fatality, fate, doom, destination, lot, fortune, star, stars, preordination, predestination, fatalism, inevitableness, *see* Futurity (121), and Necessity (601).

V. To impend, hang over, be in store, await, come on, approach, stare one in the face, fore-ordain, preordain, predestine, doom, must be.

Adj. About to happen, impending, coming, &c., inevitable, inexorable fate, doomed, devoted.

Phr. Che sarà sarà; the die being cast; "It is written."

SECTION VIII. CAUSATION.

1°. CONSTANCY OF SEQUENCE IN EVENTS.

(153) Constant antecedent.

CAUSE, origin, source, principle, occasioner, prime mover, *primum mobile*, spring, main spring, agent, seed, leaven, groundwork, fountain, well, font, fountain-head, springhead, element, *fons et origo.*

Pivot, hinge, turning-point, key, lever.

(154) Constant sequent.

EFFECT, consequence, product, result, resultant, resultance, issue, fruit, crop, harvest, development.

Production, produce, work, performance, creature, creation, fabric, first fruits, firstlings, *premices*, *dénouement.*

V. To be the effect, work, fruit,

Final cause, ground, reason, the reason why, the why and the wherefore, rationale, occasion, derivation.

Rudiment, germ, embryo, mushroom, root, *radix*, radical, etymon, nucleus, seed, stem, stock, trunk.

Nest, cradle, womb, *nidus*, birthplace, hot-bed.

Origination, production (161).

Phr. Behind the scenes, *Le dessous des cartes.*

V. To be the cause of, to originate, give origin to, cause, occasion, give rise to, kindle, suscitate, bring on, bring to pass, give occasion to, bring about, found, lay the foundation of, lie at the root of, procure, induce, realize, entail, develope.

To conduce, contribute, tend to (176).

Phr. To have a hand in, to have a finger in the pie, *see* Produce (161).

Adj. Caused, occasioned, &c., original, primary, primordial, having a common origin, connate, radical, embryonic, embryotic.

result, &c., of, to be owing to, originate in or from, rise from, to take its rise from, arise, spring, proceed, come of, emanate, come, grow, bud, sprout, issue, flow, result, follow, accrue, &c. from, come to, to come out of, be derived from, be caused by, depend upon, hinge upon, turn upon, result from, to be dependent upon, hang upon.

Adj. Owing to, resulting from, through &c., all along of, hereditary, derivative.

Adv. Of course, consequently, necessarily.

Phr. Cela va sans dire; thereby hangs a tale.

---

(155) Assignment of cause.

ATTRIBUTION, theory, ætiology, ascription, reference to, rationale, accounting for, palætiology *, imputation, derivation from, filiation, genealogy, pedigree, paternity, maternity.

V. To attribute, ascribe, impute, refer to, derive from, lay to, point to, charge on, invest with, assign as cause, trace to, father upon, lay to the door of, account for, theorize, point out the reason, ground, &c., to tell how it comes.

Phr. To put the saddle on the right horse.

Adj. Attributable, imputable, ascribable, referable (or referrible), owing to, derivable from, &c., trovable.

Putative, attributed, imputed, &c.,

Adv. Hence, thence, therefore, because, from that cause, for that reason, on that account, owing to, for as much as, whence.

Why? wherefore? whence? how

(156) Absence of assignable cause.

CHANCE †, indetermination, accident, fortune, hazard, hap, haphazard, chance, medley, random, lot, fate (152), casualty, contingence, adventure, venture, pot-luck, hit.

A lottery, toss up, game of chance, *sortes,* the turn or hazard of the die or cards, the chapter of accidents, a cast, or throw of the dice, bat, *rouge et noir,* heads or tails, &c.

Possibility, contingency, odds, long odds.

V. To chance, hap, to fall to one's lot, to be one's fate, &c. (152).

To take one's chance, to game, gamble, cast lots, toss up for, raffle, play for, stand the hazard of the die, light upon.

Adj. Casual, fortuitous, random, accidental, adventitious, causeless, incidental, contingent, uncaused, undetermined, indeterminate, possible (470).

Adv. By chance, by accident, perchance, peradventure, perhaps, may be, mayhap, haply, possibly.

---

* Whewell, Indications of a Creator.

† The word *Chance* has two distinct meanings; the first, the absence of assignable *cause*, as above; and the second, the absence of *design* : for the latter *see* (621).

comes it? how is it? how happens it? how does it happen?

In some way, somehow, somehow or other.

Casually, &c., at random, at a venture, as it may be, as it may chance, as it may turn up, as it may happen, as chance, luck, fortune, &c., would have it.

Phr. Jacta est alea.

2°. CONNECTION BETWEEN CAUSE AND EFFECT.

(157) POWER, potentiality, potency, prepotency, prepollence, puissance, might, force, metal, dint, right hand, ascendancy, sway, control, allmightiness, ability, competency, efficiency, effectiveness, efficacy, efficaciousness, validity, cogency, enablement, agency (170).

Capability, capacity, faculty, quality, attribute, endowment, virtue, gift, property.

V. To be powerful, &c., to exercise power, sway, &c., to constrain.

To be the property, virtue, attribute, &c. of, to belong to, pertain to.

To give or confer power, to empower, enable, invest, indue, endow, arm, &c., *see* Strengthen (159).

To gain power, to take root.

Adj. Powerful, potent, puissant, potential, capable, able, cogent, forcible, valid, effective, effectual, efficient, efficacious, adequate, competent.

Forcible, energetic, vigorous, vivid, sturdy, all-powerful, resistless, irresistible, inextinguishable, sovereign, invincible, unconquerable.

Adv. Powerfully, &c.

(159) Degree of power.

STRENGTH, energy (171), vigour, force, main force, physical force, brute force, spring, elasticity, tone, tension, tonicity.

Stoutness, sturdiness, lustihood, stamina, nerve, muscle, thews and sinews, pith, pithiness.

Adamant, steel, iron, oak, heart of oak.

An athlete, an Atlas, a Hercules, an Antæus, a Sampson.

A giant refreshed, a tower of strength.

Strengthening, invigoration, brac-

(158) IMPOTENCE, inability, disability, disablement, impuissance, imbecility, inaptitude, incapacity, incapability, invalidity, inefficacy, inefficiency, inefficaciousness, ineffectualness, disqualification, helplessness, incompetence.

Tele imbellum ; — sine ictu.

V. To be impotent, powerless, &c.

To render powerless, &c., to deprive of power, disable, disenable, incapacitate, disqualify, invalidate, deaden, cripple, cramp, paralyze, muzzle, hamstring, clip the wings of, put *hors de combat,* break the neck of, break the back. *See* Weaken (160).

Adj. Powerless, impotent, unable, incapable, incompetent, inadequate, unequal to, inefficient, inefficacious, ineffectual, ineffective, incapacitated, imbecile, disqualified, disabled, armless, disarmed, unarmed, weaponless, defenceless, unnerved, paralyzed, nerveless, unendowed.

Phr. Laid on the shelf ; — Laid on one's back ; — *Hors de combat ;* — Not having a leg to stand on.

(160) WEAKNESS, feebleness, debility, atony, relaxation, languor, slackness, enervation, nervousness, faintness, faintishness, infirmity, emasculation, effeminacy, feminality, softness, defencelessness, orphan.

Declension, loss, failure, &c., of strength, invalidation, decrepitude, asthenia, palsy, paralysis, exhaustion, collapse, prostration, syncope, deliquium, apoplexy.

A reed, a thread, a house of cards.

V. To be weak, &c., to droop, fade, faint, swoon, languish, decline, fail, drop.

ing, recruiting, refreshment, refocillation (689). ·

Science of forces; Dynamics, Statics.

V. To be strong, &c., to be stronger, to overmatch.

To render strong, &c., to give strength, tone, &c., to strengthen, invigorate, brace, fortify, harden, caseharden, steel, gird, screw up, wind up, set up, set on one's legs.

To reinforce, refit, recruit, vivify, restore (660), refect, refocillate (689).

Adj. Strong, mighty, vigorous, robust, sturdy, powerful, puissant, able-bodied, athletic, Herculean, muscular, brawny, sinewy, made of iron, stalwart, gigantic.

Manly, manlike, masculine, male, virile, manful.

Unweakened, unallayed, unwithered, unshaken, unworn, unexhausted.

Phr. Strong as a lion;—as a horse;—as brandy;—sound as a roach.

Adv. Strongly, forcibly, &c., by main force, *vi et armis*, by might and main, tooth and nail.

To render weak, &c., to weaken, enfeeble, debilitate, deprive of strength, relax, enervate, unbrace, unman, emasculate, castrate, hamstring, disable, unhinge, cripple, cramp, paralyze, sprain, exhaust, prostrate, blunt the edge of, deaden.

Adj. Weak, feeble, debile, strengthless, nerveless, imbecile, unnerved, relaxed, unstrung, unbraced, enervated, nervous, sinewless, lustless, effeminate, feminine, womanly, unmanned, emasculated, castrated, crippled, maimed, lamed, shattered, broken, halting, shaken, crazy, shaky, paralyzed, palsied, paralytic, decrepit, drooping, languid, faint, sickly, flagging, dull, slack, evanid, spent, effete, weather-beaten, worn, seedy, exhausted, languishing, wasted, washy, vincible, untenable.

Unstrengthened, unsustained, unsupported, unaided, unassisted, unfortified, unfriended, fatherless, &c.

Phr. On one's last legs;—Weak as a child; as a baby; as a chicken; as a cat; as water; as water gruel; as gingerbread; as milk and water.

3°. POWER IN OPERATION.

(161) PRODUCTION, creation, formation, construction, fabrication, manufacture, building, architecture, edification, coinage, organization, putting together, performance (729), workmanship.

Development, genesis, generation, *epigenesis*, procreation, progeneration, propagation.

V. To produce, effect, perform, do, make, gar, form, construct, fabricate, frame, manufacture, weave, forge, coin, carve, chisel, build, raise, edify, rear, erect, run up, establish.

To constitute, compose, organize, work out, realize, bring to bear, bring to pass, accomplish.

To create, generate, engender, beget, bring into being, breed, bear, procreate, bring forth, hatch, develope, bring up, progenerate.

(162) Non-production.

DESTRUCTION, waste, dissolution, breaking up, consumption, disorganization, falling to pieces, crumbling, &c., erasion.

Fall, downfall, ruin, perdition, crash, smash, havoc, *délabrement*, desolation, *bouleversement*, wreck, shipwreck, cataclysm, extinction, annihilation; doom, destruction of life, *see* Death (360).

Demolition, demolishment, overthrow, subversion, suppression, dismantling, cutting up, corrosion, erosion, crushing, upsetting, abolition, abolishment, sacrifice, immolation, holocaust, dilapidation, devastation, *razzia*, extermination, eradication, extirpation, rooting out, averrucation, sweeping, &c., death-blow, *coup-de-grâce*.

To induce, superinduce, suscitate, *see* Cause (153).

Adj. Produced, &c., producing, productive of, &c.

(163) REPRODUCTION, renovation, revival, regeneration, revivification, resuscitation, reanimation, resurrection, reappearance, phœnix.

V. To reproduce, revive, renovate, regenerate, revivify, resuscitate, quicken ; come again into life, reappear.

Adj. Reproduced, &c., renascent, reappearing.

V. To be destroyed, &c., waste, fall to pieces, break up, crumble.

To destroy, do away with, demolish, overturn, upset, throw down, overthrow, overwhelm, subvert, put an end to, uproot, eradicate, extirpate, root out, grub up, break up, pull down, crumble, smash, crash, crush, quell, quash, squash, cut up, shatter, shiver, batter, tear, or shake to pieces, nip, tear to tatters, cut up root and branch, pick to pieces, put down, suppress, strike out, throw, or knock down, cut down, knock on the head, stifle, dispel, fell, sink, swamp, scuttle, engulph, corrode, erode, consume, sacrifice, immolate, burke, blow down, sweep away, erase, expunge, mow down.

To waste, lay waste, ravage, dilapidate, dismantle, disorganize, devour, swallow up, desolate, devastate, sap, mine, stifle, despatch, extinguish, quench, annihilate, kill (361), unroot, root out, rout out, averrucate.

Phr. To lay the axe to the root of, make a clean sweep of, to make mince meat of, to scatter to the winds.

Adj. Unproduced, unproductive, destroyed, &c., done for, dished, &c.

(164) PRODUCER, originator, author, founder, workman, doer, performer, &c., forger, agent (690), builder, architect.

(165) DESTROYER, extinguisher, exterminator, assassin (361), executioner (975), ravager, annihilator, subverter, &c.

(166) PATERNITY, parentage, parent, father, sire, dad ; mother, dam ; procreator, progenitor, ancestor, ancestry, forefathers, grandsire ; house, parent stem, trunk, stock, pedigree ; motherhood, maternity.

(167) POSTERITY, progeny, breed, issue, offspring, brood, seed, spawn, scion, offset, child, son, daughter, bantling, shoot, sprout, sprit, branch, line, lineage, filiation, offshoot, ramification, descendant.

Straight descent, sonship, primogeniture.

(168) PRODUCTIVENESS, fecundity, fruitfulness, fertility, prolificness.

Pregnancy, pullulation, fructification, multiplication, propagation, procreation.

A milch cow, a rabbit, a warren, a hydra.

V. To procreate, multiply, pullulate, fructify, generate.

Adj. Productive, prolific, teemful, fertile, fruitful, fecund, pregnant.

Procreant, procreative, generative, propagable, life-giving.

(169) UNPRODUCTIVENESS, infertility, barrenness, sterility, unfruitfulness, unprofitableness, infecundity, *see* Inutility (645), non-agency.

V. To be unproductive, &c.

Adj. Unproductive, inoperative, barren, addle, unfertile, unprolific, sterile, unfruitful, teemless, infecund, issueless, unprofitable (645).

(170) AGENCY, operation, force, working, strain, function, office, hand, intervention, exercise, work, swing, play.

Modus operandi, quickening power, maintaining power, home stroke.

V. To be in action, to operate, work, act, perform, play, support, sustain, strain, maintain, take effect, quicken, strike, strike hard, strike home.

Adj. Acting, operating, &c., operative, efficient, efficacious, effectual.

(171) Physical ENERGY, activity, keenness, intensity, sharpness, pungency, vigour, strength, acrimony, causticity, virulence, corrosiveness, poignancy, harshness, severity, edge, point, raciness, metal.

Seasoning, mordant, pepper, mustard, cayenne, caviar (392).

Mental energy, *see* (604), mental excitation (824).

Exertion, activity, stir, bustle, agitation, effervescence, fermentation, ferment, ebullition, splutter, perturbation, briskness, voluntary activity (682), quicksilver.

Adj. Strong, energetic, active, keen, vivid, intense, severe, sharp, acute, irritating, pungent, poignant, mordant, acrid, acrimonious, virulent, caustic, corrosive, racy, brisk, harsh, double-edged, drastic, escharotic.

V. To give energy, energize, stimulate, excite, exert (173).

Phr. Fortiter in re.

(172) Physical INERTNESS, inertia, passiveness, *vis inertiæ,* passiveness, inactivity (683), torpor, latency, torpidity, dulness, deadness, heaviness, flatness, slackness, tameness, slowness, languor, lentor, quiescence (265), sleep (683).

V. To be inert, inactive, passive, &c. ; to hang fire, to let alone.

Adj. Inert, inactive, passive, torpid, sluggish, dull, heavy, flat, slack, tame, slow, blunt, lifeless, &c.

Latent, dormant, smouldering, unexerted, unstrained, uninfluential.

---

(173) VIOLENCE, vehemence, might, impetuosity, boisterousness, abruptness, ebullition, turbulence, bluster, uproar, riot, rumpus, fierceness, rage, wildness, fury, heat, exacerbation, exasperation, malignity, fit, paroxysm, orgasm, force, brute force, *coup de main,* strain, shock, shog, spasm, convulsion, throe.

Outbreak, burst, desilience, discharge, volley, explosion, blow up, blast, detonation, eruption, displosion, torrent.

Turmoil, storm, tempest, squall, hurricane, tornado, earthquake, volcano, thunderstorm, typhoon.

A fury, dragon, demon, tiger, beldame, Tisiphone, Megæra, Alecto.

V. To be violent, &c., to run high, ferment, effervesce, run wild, run riot, rush, tear, rush headlong, bluster, rage, riot, storm, boil, fume, foam, wreak, bear down.

To break out, fly out, bounce, ex-

(174) MODERATION, gentleness, temperateness, calmness, mildness, softness, sobriety, slowness, tameness, quiet (740), reason.

Relaxation, remission, measure, mitigation, tranquillization, assuagement, soothing, allaying, &c., contemperation, pacification (723), restraint, check (751), lullaby, sedative, lenitive, demulcent, opiate, anodyne, milk, opium.

V. To be moderate, &c., to keep within bounds or within compass, to settle down, to keep the peace, to sober down, remit, relent.

To moderate, soften, soothe, mitigate, appease, temper, accoy, attemper, contemper, mollify, lenify, tame, dull, take off the edge, blunt, obtund, sheathe.

To tranquillize, assuage, appease, lull, smooth, compose, still, calm, quiet, hush, quell, sober, pacify, damp, lay, allay, rebate, slacken,

plode, displode, fly, detonate, blow up, flash, flare, burst, burst out, shock, shog, strain.

To render violent, sharpen, stir up, quicken, excite, incite, stimulate, kindle, lash, suscitate, urge, accelerate, foment, aggravate, exasperate, exacerbate, infuriate, madden, lash into fury, explode, let off, discharge.

Phr. To break the peace, to out-Herod Herod.

Adj. Violent, vehement, warm, acute, rough, rude, boisterous, impetuous, ungentle, abrupt, rampant, bluff, turbulent, blustering, riotous, thundering, obstreperous, uproarious, outrageous, frantic, headstrong.

Savage, fierce, ferocious, fiery, fuming, excited, unquelled, unquenched, unextinguished, unrepressed, boiling, boiling over, furious, raging, running riot, storming, hysteric, wild, running wild, ungovernable, unappeasable, unmitigable, uncontrollable, insuppressible, irrepressible, raging, desperate, mad, infuriate, exasperated.

Tempestuous, stormy, squally, spasmodic, convulsive, bursting, explosive, detonating, &c., volcanic, meteoric.

Phr. Fierce as a tiger.

Adv. Violently, &c., by force, by main force, &c., by might and main, tooth and nail, *vi et armis*, at the point of the sword.

Phr. At one fell swoop.

smooth, soften, alleviate, rock to sleep, deaden, check, restrain, slake, curb, bridle, rein in, hold in, repress, smother, counteract (179).

Phr. Mettre de l'eau dans son vin. To pour oil on the waves, pour balm into.

Adj. Moderate, gentle, mild, sober, temperate, reasonable, tempered, calm, unruffled, tranquil, smooth, untroubled, unirritating, soft, bland, oily, demulcent, lenitive, cool, quiet, anodyne, hypnotic, sedative, peaceful, peaceable, pacific, lenient, tame, halcyon.

Phr. Gentle as a lamb, mild as mother's milk.

Adv. Moderately, gently, softly, &c.

Phr. Suaviter in modo ; est modus in rebus.

4°. INDIRECT POWER.

(175) INFLUENCE, weight, pressure, prevalence, sway, predominance, predominancy, dominance, reign, ableness, capability, &c. (157).

Footing, hold, purchase, *point d'appui*, που στω, *locus standi*, leverage, vantage ground, ascendance, auspices.

Independence, voluntary influence (737).

V. To have influence, &c., to have a hold upon, &c., to gain a footing, work upon, take root, take hold, prevail, dominate, predominate, outweigh, overweigh, to bear upon, to be in the ascendant.

Adj. Influential, valid, weighty, prevailing, prevalent, dominant, regnant, predominating, predominant, in the ascendant, rife.

(176) TENDENCY, aptness, proneness, proclivity, conduciveness, bent, bias, quality, inclination, propensity, conducement, subservience (631).

V. To tend, contribute, conduce, lead, dispose, incline, verge, bend to, affect, carry, promote, redound to, subserve to (644), bid fair to.

Adj. Tending, contributing, conducing, conducive, working towards, calculated to, disposing, inclining,

Adj. Unconducing, unconducive, unconducting.

bending, leading, carrying to, subservient, subsidiary (644, 707), in a fair way to.

Adv. For, whither.

(177) LIABILITY, liableness, subjection to, dependence on, exposure to, contingency, *see* Chance (156), susceptivity, susceptibility, obnoxiousness.

V. To be liable, &c., incur, to lay oneself open to, lie under, expose oneself, &c., stand a chance, to open a door to.

Adj. Liable, subject, open to, incident to, exposed to, dependent on, obnoxious to.

Contingent, incidental, guardless (665), unexempt.

5°. COMBINATIONS OF CAUSES.

(178) CONCURRENCE, co-operation, union, agreement, pulling together, alliance.

Voluntary concurrence (709).

V. To concur, co-operate, conspire, agree, conduce, contribute, unite; to pull together, to join forces.

Phr. To be in the same boat; to go hand in hand (709).

Adj. Concurring, concurrent, co-operating, conspiring, agreeing, pulling together, &c., in alliance with.

(179) COUNTERACTION, opposition, antagonism, polarity, clashing, &c., collision, resistance, interference, friction.

Neutralization, nullification, compensation (30).

Reaction, retroaction (277), *contrecoup*, repercussion, rebound, recoil, *ricochet.*

Check, obstacle, hindrance (706).

Voluntary counteraction (708).

V. To counteract, oppose, contravene, antagonize, interfere with, clash, neutralize, nullify, render null, withstand, resist, hinder, &c. (706), repress, control, curb, check, rein in.

To react (277), countervail, counterpoise, &c. (30), overpoise.

Adj. Counteracting, opposing, &c., antagonistic, opposite, retroactive, cohibitive, counter, contrary (14).

Adv. Counter, notwithstanding, nevertheless, nathless, yet, still, although, though, albeit, howbeit, maugre.

But, even, however, *quoad minus, quand même,* in spite of, in defiance of, in the teeth of, in despite of, *non obstante,* against, *see* (708).

CLASS II.

WORDS RELATING TO SPACE.

~~~~~~~~~~~~~~~~

SECTION I. SPACE IN GENERAL.

1°. ABSTRACT SPACE.

(180) Indefinite space.

SPACE, extension, extent, expanse, room, scope, range, way, expansion, compass, sweep, play, latitude, field, swing, spread, spare room, headway, elbow-room, freedom, house-room, stowage, roomage.

Open space, void space, vacuity (2), opening, waste, wildness, moor, moorland.

Abyss, unlimited space, the four winds, *see* Infinity (105), Ubiquity (186).

Adj. Spacious, roomy, extensive, expansive, capacious, ample.

Boundless, unlimited, unbounded, limitless, infinite, ubiquitous, shoreless, trackless, pathless.

Adv. Extensively, &c., wherever, everywhere, far and near, far and wide, all over, all the world over, from China to Peru, in every quarter; in all quarters; in all lands; here, there, and everywhere; from pole to pole; throughout the world; under the sun.

(181) Definite space.

REGION, sphere ground, area, realm, quarter, district, orb, circuit, circle, compartment, domain, tract, department, territory, country, canton, county, shire, province, *arrondissement*, principality, duchy, kingdom.

Arena, precincts, *enceinte*, walk, patch, plot, paddock.

Clime, climate, zone.

Limited space, locality.

(182) PLACE, lieu, spot, point, nook, corner, recess, hole, niche, compartment, premises, precinct, station, venue, latitude and longitude, abode (189).

Adv. Somewhere.

————

2°. RELATIVE SPACE.

(183) SITUATION, position, locality, *status*, latitude and longitude, footing, standing, post, stage, bearings, aspect.

Place, site, station, seat, *venue*, the whereabouts, direction, azimuth, &c. (278).

Topography, geography, chorography.

A map, chart, plan (554).

Adj. Local, topical.

Adv. In situ, here and there, *passim*, whereabouts.

(184) LOCATION, localization, lodgment, deposition, reposition, stowage, establishment, fixation, grafting, in-

(185) DISPLACEMENT, elocation, amotion, dislodgment, ejectment (296), deportation, exile.

44

sertion (301), package, lading, encampment, installation.

A colony, settlement, cantonment.

A habitation, residence, dwelling, cohabitation (189).

V. To place, situate, locate, put, lay, set, seat, station, lodge, post, instal, house, stow, establish, fix, root, plant, graft, stick in, insert, wedge in, shelve, pitch, camp, deposit, reposit, cradle, encamp, moor, pack, tuck in, embed, vest.

To billet on, quarter upon.

To pocket, put up, bag.

To inhabit, reside (186), colonize.

Adj. Placed, located, &c., situate, situated, posited, nestled, embosomed, housed, moored, rooted, unremoved.

Removal, remotion, transposition, &c., relegation, *see* Transference (270), and Exhaustion (638).

V. To displace, dislodge, unkennel, break bulk, take off, eject, expel, &c. (296), exile, relegate, oust, ablegate, ostracise, remove, transfer, transpose (270), sweep off, sweep away, do away with, root out, unpeople, depopulate.

To vacate, leave.

Adj. Displaced, &c., unhoused, houseless.

3°. EXISTENCE IN SPACE.

(186) PRESENCE, occupancy, occupation, attendance, whereness.

Diffusion, permeation, pervasion, dissemination (73).

Ubiquity, ubiety, ubiquitariness, omnipresence.

V. To exist in space, to be present, attend.

To occur in a place, lie, stand, occupy.

To inhabit, dwell, reside, live, abide, lodge, nestle, perch, roost, put up at, squat, hive, burrow, camp, encamp, bivouac, anchor, settle, take up one's quarters, pitch one's tent, get a footing, frequent, haunt, tenant, take root, strike root, revisit.

To fill, pervade, permeate, be diffused through, be disseminated through, overspread.

Adj. Present, occupying, inhabiting, &c., moored, at anchor, resiant, resident, residentiary.

Ubiquitous, omnipresent.

Adv. Here, there, where? every where, aboard, on board, at home, afield, &c.

Phr. Here, there, and everywhere.

(187) Nullibiety.*

ABSENCE, non-existence (2), non-residence, non-attendance, absenteeism.

Void, *vacuum*, voidness, vacuity, vacancy, vacuousness.

An absentee, nobody, nobody on earth, *alibi.*

V. To be absent, not present, &c., to keep away, to keep out of the way, make oneself scarce, absent oneself, take oneself off, vacate.

Adj. Absent, not present, away, gone, from home, missing, non-president.

Phr. Nowhere to be found, *non est inventus*, not a soul, nobody present, *âme qui vive*, the bird being flown.

Vacant, untenanted, tenantless, empty, uninhabited, deserted, void, devoid, unoccupied, unhabitable.

Adv. Without, nowhere, elsewhere.

Phr. One's back being turned.

* Bishop Wilkins.

(188) INHABITANT, resident, residentiary, dweller, indweller, occupier, occupant, lodger, inmate, tenant, sojourner, commorant, settler, squatter, colonist, denizen, citizen, cit, townsman, burgess, villager, garrison, crew, population.

Native, indigene, aborigines, autochthones.

A colony, settlement.

Adj. Indigenous, native.

----

(189) Place of habitation.

ABODE, dwelling, lodging, domicile, residence, address, habitation, berth, seat, lap, sojourn, housing, quarters, head-quarters, resiance, throne, ark.

Nest, *nidus*, lair, haunt, eyry, den, hole, aerie, rookery, resort, retreat, nidification.

Bivouac, camp, encampment, cantonment, castramentation, tent, wigwam, awning.

Cave, cavern, cell, grove, grot, grotto, alcove, bower, arbour, cove, chamber, &c. (191).

Home, homestead, homestall, fireside, snuggery, hearth, *lares et penates*, household gods, roof, household, housing.

Building, structure, edifice, fabric, erection, pile, tenement, messuage, farm, grange.

Cot, cabin, hut, croft, shed, booth, stall, hovel, out-house, barn, bawn, hole, kennel, stye, dog-hole, coot, stable.

House, mansion, villa, cottage, box, lodge, bungalow, hermitage, folly, rotunda, tower, *chateau*, castle, pavilion, hotel, court, hall, palace.

Inn, hostel, hotel, tavern, caravansary, hospice, barrack, casemate.

Hamlet, village, thorp, kraal, borough, burgh, town, city, metropolis.

Street, place, terrace, parade, road, row, lane, alley, court, wynd, close, yard, passage, rents, — square, polygon, circus, crescent, mall, *piazza*.

Anchorage, roadstead, dock, basin, wharf, quay, port.

(190) Things contained.

CONTENTS, cargo, lading, freight, load, burden, ware (798).

(191) RECEPTACLE, recipient, receiver, reservatory, compartment.

Cell, cellule, hole, corner, niche, recess, nook, crypt, stall, dog-hole, pigeon-hole, lodging, *see* (189), bed, berth, &c. (215).

Capsule, vesicle, cyst, *cancelli*, utricle, bladder, utensil, alembic.

Stomach, paunch, ventricle, crop, craw, maw, gizzard, bread-basket.

Pocket, pouch, fob, sheath, scabbard, socket, bag, sac (or sack), saccule, wallet, scrip, poke, kit, knapsack, haversac, sachel, reticule.

Chest, box, hutch, coffer, case, casket, pyx (or pix), *caisson*, desk, bureau, cabinet, reliquary, trunk, portmanteau, band-box, *valise*, boot, imperial, *vache*.

Vessel, vase, bushel, barrel, canister, jar, can, pottle, basket, pannier, corbeille, hamper, dosser, dorser.

For liquids; cistern, tank, vat, caldron, barrel, cask, keg, rundlet, firkin, kilderkin, carboy, bottle, jar, decanter, ewer, cruise, crock, kit, canteen, flagon, flask, flasket, noggin, vial (or phial), cruet, caster, urn.

Tub, bucket, pail, pot, tankard, jug, pitcher, mug, noggin, pipkin, galipot (or gallipot), matrass, receiver, alembic, bolthead, capsule.

Bowl, basin, jorum, punch-bowl, cup, goblet, chalice, tumbler, glass,

46

horn, can, pan, dish, patera, calabash, porringer, saucepan, skillet, posnet, tureen, potager, saucer, platter, hod, scuttle, shovel, trowel, spoon, ladle, thimble.

Closet, commode, cupboard, cellaret, locker, bin, buffet, press, safe, sideboard, drawer, chest of drawers, till.

Chamber, story, apartment, room, cabin, bower, office, court, hall, saloon, parlour, state-room, presence chamber, drawing-room, gallery, cabinet, closet, boudoir, *adytum, sanctum,* lumber-room, dormitory, refectory.

Attic, loft, garret, cockloft, cellar, vault, hold, cockpit, ground-floor, *rez de chaussée,* basement, kitchen, pantry, scullery.

Portico, porch, veranda, lobby, court, hall, vestibule, corridor, passage, anteroom, antechamber.

Section II. DIMENSIONS.

1°. General Dimensions.

(192) Size, magnitude, dimension, bulk, volume, largeness, greatness (31), expanse, amplitude, mass, massiveness.

Capacity, capaciousness, tonnage or tunnage, calibre, scantling.

Turgidity, turgidness, expansion (194), corpulence, obesity, plumpness, *embonpoint,* stoutness, hypertrophy; corporation, flesh and blood, brawniness.

Hugeness, vastness, enormousness, enormity, immensity, monstrousness, monstrosity; infinity (105).

A giant, Brobdignagian, Antæus, monster, whale, leviathan, elephant, porpoise, colossus, tun, lump, bulk, block, mass, bushel.

A mountain, mound, heap (72).

V. To be large, &c., to become large, *see* Expansion (194).

Adj. Large, big, great, considerable, bulky, voluminous, ample, massive, massy, capacious.

Corpulent, stout, fat, plump, lusty, strapping, bouncing, portly, burly, brawny, fleshy, goodly, in good case, chapping, jolly, chubby, full grown, chubfaced, lubberly, hulky, unwieldy, lumpish, gaunt, stalwart, spanking.

Overgrown, bloated, tumid, turgid, hypertrophied, big-swoln, swag-bellied, puffy, distended, œdematous, dropsical.

(193) Littleness, smallness, minuteness, diminutiveness, exiguity, parvitude, parvity, puniness, dwarfishness, undersize, epitome, duodecimo, rudiment, microcosm.

Leanness, emaciation, thinness, macilency, flaccidity.

A dwarf, runt, pigmy, Lilliputian, chit, pigwidgeon, urchin, elf, doll, puppet, skeleton, shadow, Tom Thumb, manikin.

Animalcule, mite, insect, emmet, fly, gnat, shrimp, minnow, worm, grub, tit, tomtit, runt, mouse, small fry, mushroom, pollard, millet seed, mustard seed, grain of sand.

Atom, point, speck, dot, mote, ace, jot, iota, tittle, whit, thought, idea, look, particle, corpuscule, molecule, monad, granule, grain, crumb, globule, nutshell, minim, drop, droplet, mouthful, thimbleful, sprinkling, dash, minimum, powder (330), driblet, patch, scrap, chip, inch, mathematical point; *minutiæ.*

V. To be small, &c., to become small, *see* Contraction (195).

Adj. Little, small, minute, diminutive, inconsiderable, exiguous, puny, tiny, wee, petty, minikin, hop-o'-my-thumb, miniature, pigmy, undersized, dwarf, stunted, dwarfed, dwarfish, pollard, Lilliputian; pocket, portative, portable.

47

Squab, dumpy, squat, squabby, tumerous, pursy, blowsy.

Huge, immense, enormous, mighty, unbounded, vast, vasty, stupendous, inordinate, preposterous, monstrous, monster; gigantic, giant-like, colossal, Brobdignagian; indefinite, infinite.

Phr. Large as life; plump as a partridge; fat as a pig; fat as a quail; fat as butter; fat as brawn *; plump as a dumpling; fat as bacon.

(194) EXPANSION, enlargement, extension, augmentation, increase of size, amplification, ampliation, aggrandizement, spread, increment, growth, development, pullulation, swell, dilatation, rarefaction, turgescence, turgidity, dispansion, tumefaction, intumescence, swelling, *diastole*, distension, puffing, inflation.

Overgrowth, hypertrophy, overdistension, tympany.

Bulb, knot, knob (249).

Superiority of size.

V. To become larger, to expand, enlarge, extend, grow, increase, swell, deploy, dilate, stretch, spread, mantle, bud, shoot, spring up, sprout, germinate, vegetate, pullulate, open, burst forth, gather flesh, outgrow.

To render larger, to expand, aggrandize, &c., distend, develope, take open order, amplify, magnify, rarefy, inflate, puff, blow up, stuff, cram.

To be larger than, to surpass, exceed, be beyond, cap, o'ertop, *see* Height (206), and Superiority (33).

Adj. Expanded, enlarged, increased, &c., swelled out, bulbous; exaggerated, bloated, &c., full-blown, full-grown.

(196) DISTANCE, remoteness, farness, elongation, offing, removedness, parallax, reach, span.

Antipodes, outpost, outskirt, aphelion, horizon.

Phr. Ultima Thule, ne plus ultra, the uttermost parts of the earth.

Microscopic, evanescent, impalpable, imperceptible, invisible, inappreciable, infinitesimal, homœopathic, atomic, corpuscular, molecular, rudimentary, rudimental.

Lean, thin, meagre, emaciated, lank, macilent, fallen away, scrubby, reduced, shrunk, extenuated, shrivelled, limber, flaccid, starved, skinny, stunted.

Phr. Thin as a lath; worn to a shadow; skin and bone.

(195) CONTRACTION, reduction, diminution, or decrease of size, defalcation, lessening, decrement, shrinking, collapse, emaciation, attenuation, tabefaction, consumption, marasmus, atrophy, hour-glass.

Condensation, compression, squeezing, friction (331).

Inferiority of size.

Corrugation; contractility; astringency.

V. To become smaller, to lessen, diminish, decrease, dwindle, shrink, contract, shrivel, collapse, wither, lose flesh, wizen, fall away, decay, purse up, waste, wane, ebb, to grow less.

Phr. To grow "small by degrees, and beautifully less" (659).

To render smaller, to contract, lessen, &c., draw in, to condense, reduce, clip, compress, squeeze, attenuate, chip, dwarf, bedwarf, cut short (201), corrugate, pinch, tweak.

To be smaller than, to fall short of, not to come up to.

Phr. To hide its diminished head.

Adj. Contracting, &c., astringent, contracted, lessened, &c., stunted, waning, ebbing, &c., neap, condensed, *multum in parvo.*

Unexpanded, contractile, compressible.

(197) NEARNESS, nighness, propinquity, vicinity, vicinage, neighbourhood, adjacency, closeness; perihelion.

A short distance, a step, an earshot, close quarters, a stone's throw, a hair's breadth, a span, bowshot.

* Psalm cxix. v. 70.

Separation (44), transference (270). Diffusion, dispersion (73).

V. To be distant, &c.; to extend to, stretch to, reach to, spread to, go to, get to, stretch away to; outgo, outstep, to go great lengths.

To remain at a distance, keep away, stand off, keep off, stand aloof.

Adj. Distant, far, far off, remote, distal, wide of, yon, yonder, at arm's length, apart, asunder, ulterior, ultramontane, transmontane, transalpine, ultramundane, hyperborean.

Inaccessible, out of the way, unapproachable; incontiguous.

Adv. Far, away, far away, afar, off, a long way off, afar off, wide away, aloof, wide of, clear of, out of the way, a great way off, out of reach, abroad.

Phr. Far and near; far and wide, over the hills and far away; from end to end; from pole to pole; from China to Peru; from Dan to Beersheba; *à perte de vue.*

Apart, asunder.

Yonder, farther, beyond, *longo intervallo.*

(198) INTERVAL, interspace, *see* Discontinuity (70), break, gap, opening (260), chasm, *hiatus, cæsura,* interstice, cleft, foss, mesh, crevice, chink, creak, cranny, crack, slit, fissure, scissure, chap, rift, flaw, gash, cut, leak, dike, haha, fracture, solution of continuity, breach, rent, oscitation, gaping, yawning, pandiculation, insertion (301), gorge, defile, ravine, frith, furrow, *see* (259).

Thing interposed, a go-between, interjacence (228).

V. To separate (44), gape.

Purlieus, environs, *alentours,* suburbs, the whereabouts.

A bystander, neighbour.

Approach, approximation, appropinquation, appulse (287), junction (43), concentration.

Meeting, *rencontre.*

V. To be near, &c., to adjoin, hang about, trench on, border upon, stand by, approximate, tread on the heels of, cling to, clasp, hug, get near, &c., to approach (287), to meet.

To bring near, to crowd, pack, huddle together.

Adj. Near, nigh, close at hand, neighbouring, proximate, adjacent, adjoining, proximal, intimate, bordering upon, close upon, hard upon, trenching on, treading on the heels of, verging to, at hand, handy, near the mark, home.

Adv. Near, nigh, hard by, fast by, next door to, within call, within hearing, within an ace of, close upon, at hand, on the verge of, near the mark, in the environs, &c., at one's elbow, within pistol-shot, a stone's throw, &c., cheek by jole (or jowl), beside, alongside, at the heels of.

About, hereabouts, thereabouts, in the way, in presence of, in round numbers, approximatively.

(199) CONTIGUITY, contact, proximity, apposition, no interval, juxtaposition, touching, abutment, osculation, meeting (293), syzygy, coincidence, coexistence, adhesion (46).

Confine, frontier, demarcation (233).

V. To be contiguous, &c., to touch, meet, adhere (46), osculate, coincide, coexist, abut on, graze.

Adj. Contiguous, touching, meeting, in contact, conterminous, osculating, osculatory, hand to hand, proximate, in juxtaposition, apposition, &c.

2°. LINEAR DIMENSIONS.

(200) LENGTH, longitude, span.

A line, bar, rule, stripe, spoke, radius.

(201) SHORTNESS, brevity, briefness, a span, &c., *see* Smallness (193).

Lengthening, elongation, prolongation, production, producing, protraction, tension, stretching, tensure.

V. To be long, &c., to extend to, reach, stretch to.

To render long, lengthen, extend, elongate, prolong, produce, stretch, draw out, protract, spin out, drawl.

Phr. To drag its slow length along.

Adj. Long, longsome, lengthy, wiredrawn, outstretched, lengthened, produced, &c., Alexandrine, sesquipedalian, interminable, there being no end of.

Linear, longitudinal, oblong.

Phr. As long as my arm;—As long as to-day and to-morrow.

Adv. Lengthwise, longitudinally, in a line, along, from end to end, endwise, fore and aft, from head to foot, from top to toe.

(202) BREADTH, width, latitude, amplitude, diameter, bore, calibre, superficial extent, expanse.

THICKNESS, crassitude (192), expansion, dilatation, &c. (194).

V. To be broad, thick, &c.

To become broad, to render broad, to swell, dilate, expand, outspread, &c. (194), to incrassate.

Adj. Broad, wide, ample, extended, fan-like, outstretched, &c.

Thick, dumpy, squab, squat.

Phr. Wide as a church door;— Thick as a rope.

Shortening, abbreviation, abbreviature, abridgment, curtailment, decurtation, reduction, contraction, compression (195), retrenchment, elision, ellipsis, compendium (596), conciseness (in style) (572).

V. To be short, brief, &c.

To render short, to shorten, curtail, abridge, abbreviate, reduce, contract, compress, scrimp.

To retrench, cut short, cut down, pare down, clip, dock, lop, prune, crop, snub, truncate, cut, hack, hew, &c.; (in drawing) to foreshorten.

Adj. Short, brief, curt, compendious, compact, stubby, scrimp, stumpy, pug, oblate, elliptical, concise (572), summary.

(203) NARROWNESS, slenderness, closeness, scantiness, exility, lankness, incapaciousness.

A line (205), a hair's breadth, a finger's breadth.

THINNESS, tenuity, leanness, meagreness, *marcor.*

A shaving, a slip (205), a mere skeleton, a shadow.

A middle constriction, neck, waist, isthmus, wasp, hour-glass, ridge, ravine, defile, gorge, pass.

Narrowing, coarctation, angustation, tapering, compression, squeezing, &c. (195).

V. To be narrow, &c., to taper, contract, shrink.

To render narrow, &c., to narrow, contract, coarctate, attenuate, constrict, constringe, cramp, pinch, squeeze, compress, tweak, corrugate.

To shave, sheer, &c., *see* (195).

Adj. Narrow, slender, thin, fine, filiform, filamentous, fibrous, capillary, stringy, wiredrawn, fine-spun, anguilliform, taper, dapper, slim, scant, spare, delicate, unenlarged, incapacious.

Meagre, lean, macilent, emaciated, lank, starveling, attenuated, skinny, scraggy, gaunt, skin and bone, bare-bone, raw-boned, spindle-shanks.

Phr. Thin as a lath;—thin as a whipping-post;—lean as a rake;—thin as a thread-paper;—thin as a wafer;—thin as a shadow.

(204) LAYER, stratum, bed, zone, substratum, floor, flag, stage.

Plate, lamina, lamella, sheet, flake, scale, coat, pellicle, membrane, film, slice, shive, cut, shaving, rasher, board, plank, platter, trencher, spatula.

Stratification, scaliness, a nest of boxes, coats of an onion.

V. To slice, shave, &c.

Adj. Lamellar, scaly, filmy, membranous, flaky, foliated, foliaceous, stratified, stratiform, tabular.

(206) HEIGHT, altitude, elevation, eminence, pitch, loftiness, sublimity.

Stature, tallness, procerity, culmination, *see* Summit (210).

A giant, grenadier.

Alps, mountain, mount, hill, hillock, monticle, fell, moorland, hummock, knap, knoll, cape, headland, foreland, promontory, ridge, pike, uplands, rising ground, downs, mound, mole, steeps, bluff, cliff, craig, vantage ground.

Tower, pillar, column, obelisk, monument, steeple, spire, minaret, turret, cupola, pilaster.

Pole, pikestaff, maypole, flagstaff, topmast.

Ceiling, roof, awning, canopy, *see* (210), attic, loft, garret.

Growth, upgrowth (194).

V. To be high, &c., to tower, soar, ride, beetle, hover, cap, overtop, culminate, overhang, hang over, impend, bestride, mount, surmount, to cover (223).

To render high, to heighten, exalt, *see* Elevate (307), perch up, perk up.

To become high, grow, upgrow, soar, tower, rise (305).

Adj. High, elevated, eminent, exalted, lofty, supernal, tall, towering, beetling, soaring, stalwart, colossal, gigantic, Patagonian, culminating, raised, elevated, &c., perked up, hanging (gardens), crowning.

Upland, cloud-touching, heaven-kissing, cloud-topt, cloud-capt, alpine, aerial.

Upper, uppermost, top-gallant.

Overhanging, impending, incumbent, superincumbent, supernatant, superimposed, hovering, hilly, moorland.

Phr. Tall as a maypole ;—Tall as a steeple.

Adv. On high, high up, aloft, above, aloof, overhead, in the clouds, on tiptoe, on stilts, on the shoulders of.

Over, upwards, from top to bottom, from top to toe, from head to foot, *à capite ad calcem.*

(205) FILAMENT, line, fibre, fibril, hair, capillament, gossamer, wire, thread, cord, rope, yarn, &c., *see* (45).

Strip, shred, slip, spill, list, string, band, fillet, *fascia*, ribbon (or ribband) ; roll, lath, splinter, shiver, shaving ; arborescence, *see* (256).

(207) LOWNESS, lowlands, depression, a molehill, recumbency, prostration, *see* Horizontality (213).

A ground floor, *rez de chaussée* (191), hold.

V. To be low, &c., crouch, slouch, lie flat.

To lower, depress (306), take down a peg, prostrate, subvert.

Adj. Low, neap, debased, nether, prostrate, flat, level with the ground, grovelling, crouched, crouching, subjacent, underlying, squat.

Adv. Under, beneath, underneath, below, down, adown, over head and ears, downwards, underfoot, at the foot of, underground, at a low ebb.

(208) DEPTH, deepness, profundity, profoundness, depression, bathos, anticlimax, depth of water, draught.

A pit, shaft, well, crater, gulf, abyss, bottomless pit, hell.

Soundings, submersion, plunge, dive (310).

V. To be deep, &c.

To render deep, &c., to deepen, sink, submerge, plunge, dip, dive (310).

To dig, scoop out, hollow, sink, delve (252).

Adj. Deep, deep-seated, profound, sunk, buried, submerged, &c., subaqueous, submarine, subterranean, underground, subterrene.

Bottomless, soundless, fathomless, unfathomed, unfathomable.

Phr. Deep as a well; knee-deep.

Adv. Beyond one's depth, out of one's depth, underground.

Phr. Over head and ears.

(209) SHALLOWNESS, shoaliness, shoals.

Adj. Shallow, skin-deep, superficial, shoaly.

---

(210) SUMMIT, summity, top, vertex, apex, zenith, pinnacle, acme, climax, culminating point, pitch, meridian, sky.

Tip, tip-top, crest, peak, turning point, pole, head, crown, brow, nib, nob, noddle.

Capital, cornice, sconce, pediment, entablature, frieze.

Roof, ceiling, thatch, tiling, slating, awning, canopy, *see* Cover (223).

Adj. Top, topmost, uppermost, tip-top, culminating, meridian, capital, head, polar, supreme, crowning.

(211) BASE, basement, plinth, foundation, substratum, ground, earth, pavement, floor, paving, flag, ground floor, deck, substructure, footing, groundwork.

The bottom, nadir, foot, sole, toe, root, keel.

Adj. Bottom, undermost, nethermost, fundamental.

(212) VERTICALITY, erectness, uprightness, perpendicularity.

Wall, precipice, cliff.

Erection, raising, rearing.

V. To be vertical, &c., to stand up, to stand on end, to stand erect, to stand upright, to stick up.

To render vertical, to set up, stick up, erect, rear, raise up, cock up, raise on its legs.

Adj. Vertical, upright, erect, perpendicular, normal, straight, standing up, &c., up on end, bolt upright.

Adv. Up, vertically, &c., on end, up on end, *à plomb*, on its beam ends.

(213) HORIZONTALITY, a level, plane, dead level, flatness (251).

Recumbency, lying, lying down, reclination, decumbence, decumbency, discumbency, accubation, supination, resupination, prostration.

A plain, floor, platform, bowling-green, plateau, terrace, estrade, esplanade, offset, parterre, table-land.

V. To be horizontal, recumbent, &c., to lie, recline, lie down, sit down, squat, lie flat, lie prostrate, sprawl, loll.

To render horizontal, &c., to lay, lay down, level, flatten, prostrate, knock down, floor.

Adj. Horizontal, level, plane, flat, even.

Recumbent, decumbent, accumbent, lying, prone, supine, couchant, couching, jacent, prostrate, squat, squatting, on one's back, on all fours, sitting, reclining.

Adv. Horizontally, &c., on one's back, &c.

(214) PENDENCY, dependency, suspension, hanging.

A pedicle, peduncle, tail, flap, skirt.

A peg, knob, button, hook, nail, ring, staple, knot (45).

V. To be pendent, &c., to hang, swing, dangle, swag, daggle, flap, trail.

To suspend, hang, sling, hook up, hitch, fasten to.

Adj. Pendent, pendulous, pensile, hanging, swinging, &c., suspended, &c.

Having a peduncle, &c., pedunculate, tailed, caudate.

Adv. Dingle-dangle.

---

(215) SUPPORT, ground, foundation, base, basis, *terra firma*, fulcrum, *point d'appui*, που στω, *locus standi*, landing, landing-place, resting-place, groundwork, *substratum*, floor, bed, stall, berth.

A supporter, prop, stand, anvil, fulciment, stay, shore, truss, sleeper, staff, stick, crutch, stilts, alpenstock, *bâton*.

Post, pillar, shaft, column, pediment, pedicle, pedestal, plinth (211).

A frame, framework, scaffold, skeleton, beam, rafter, joist, travis, corner-stone, stanchion, girder, tie-beam (45), back-bone, key-stone.

A board, form, ledge, platform, shelf, hob, bracket, arbor, rack, mantel, counter, dresser, flange, table, trestle, shoulder, perch, truss, horse, easel, desk.

A seat, throne, dais, divan, musnud, chair, bench, sofa, settee, couch, *fauteuil*, stool, tripod, footstool, *tabouret*, trevit, woolsack, ottoman, settle, squab, hassock, cushion.

Bed, pillow, bolster, mattrass, shakedown, tester, pallet, hammock, crib, cradle.

Atlas, Caryatides, Hercules.

V. To be supported, &c., to lie, sit, recline, lean, abut, bear, rest, repose, &c. on, be based on.

To support, bear, carry, hold, sustain, shoulder, uphold, hold up, prop, underprop, shore up, underpin.

To give, furnish, afford, supply, lend, &c. support or foundations, to bottom, to found.

Adj. Supported, &c., astride on, astraddle, fundamental.

(216) PARALLELISM, coextension.

V. To be parallel, &c.

Adj. Parallel, coextensive.

Adv. Alongside, abreast, beside, side by side, cheek by jole (or jowl).

---

(217) OBLIQUITY, inclination, slope, slopeness, leaning, slant, crookedness, bias, bend, bevel, tilt, swag, cant.

Acclivity, uphill, rise, ascent, gradient, rising ground, bank.

Declivity, downhill, fall, devexity.

A gentle or rapid slope, easy ascent or descent, tower of Pisa.

Steepness, precipitousness, cliff, precipice, escarpment, measure of inclination, clinometer.

Diagonal, zigzag, distortion.

V. To be oblique, &c., to slope, slant, lean, incline, shelve, stoop, bend, sag, swag, seel, slouch, cant.

To render oblique, &c., to slope, tilt, bend, incline, &c., distort.

Adj. Oblique, inclined, clinal, sloping, shelving, skew, askew, slant, aslant, slanting, indirect, distorted, wry, awry, crooked, canted, tilted, biassed, swagging, bevel, slouched, slouching, &c.

Uphill, rising, ascending.

Downhill, falling, descending, declining, devex.

Steep, abrupt, precipitous, breakneck.

Diagonal, transverse, athwart, transversal, antiparallel.

Adv. Obliquely, &c., on one side, askew, askaunt, sideways, slope-wise.

(218) INVERSION, contraposition, overturn, somerset (somersault or summerset), *culbute*, subversion, retroversion, reversion, interversion, eversion, transposition, anastrophy, *metastasis*, pronation and supination, overturn, antipodes (237).

V. To be inverted, &c.

To render inverted, &c., to invert, reverse, upset, overset, overturn, turn over, upturn, subvert, retrovert, transpose, turn topsy-turvy, tilt over, *culbuter*, topple over, capsize.

Adj. Inverted, inverse, upside down, topsy-turvy, top heavy.

Adv. Inversely, topsy-turvy, &c.

Phr. The cart before the horse, head over heels, *hysteron proteron*.

(219) CROSSING, intersection, decussation, transversion.

Reticulation, network, inosculation, anastomosis, interweaving, twining, intertwining, matting, plaiting, interdigitation.

Net, *plexus*, web, mesh, twill, skein, felt, lace, wicker, trellis, lattice, grating, gridiron, tracery, fretwork, filigree.

Cross, chain, wreath, braid, cat's cradle, dove-tail, mortise, St. Andrew's cross.

V. To cross, intersect, decussate, interlace, intertwine, intertwist, entwine, weave, interweave, inweave, twine, twist, wreathe, interdigitate, anastomose, inosculate, dovetail.

To mat, plait, plat, braid, felt, twill, tangle, entangle, ravel, net, knot, dishevel.

Adj. Crossing, intersecting, &c., crossed, intersected, matted, &c., crucial, cruciform.

Retiform, reticulated, areolar, cancellated, grated, barred, streaked.

Adv. Across, thwart, athwart, transversely.

3°. CENTRICAL DIMENSIONS.*

1. *General.*

(220) EXTERIORITY, the outside, the exterior, surface, superficies, superstratum, excentricity.

Disc, face, facet, front (234).

V. To be exterior, &c.

To place exteriorly, or outwardly, to turn out.

Adj. Exterior, external, outer, outward, outlying, outside, superficial, skin-deep, frontal, discoid, extraregarding, excentric.

(221) INTERIORITY, the inside, interior, interspace, substratum, subsoil.

Vitals, viscera, pith, marrow, heart, bosom, breast, entrails, bowels, intestines, guts, womb, lap, backbone, *penetralia*, inmost recesses, cave, cavern, &c. (191).

V. To be interior, internal, within, &c.

To place or keep within, to enclose, circumscribe, *see* (231, 232).

* That is, Dimensions having reference to a centre.

Adv. Externally, &c., out, without, outwards, out of doors, *ab extra*, in the open air, *sub Jove, à la belle étoile, al fresco.*

Adj. Interior, internal, inner, inside, inward, intraregarding, inmost, innermost, deep-seated, intestine, intestinal, inland, insterstitial, subcutaneous.

Home, domestic, indoor.

Adv. Internally, inwards, inwardly, within, inly, therein, *ab intra*, withinside, in-doors, within doors, at home.

(222) COVERING, cover, roof, canopy, awning, tilt, tent, lid, covercle, *operculum* (263).

Integument, skin, tegument, pellicle, fleece, cuticle, scarfskin, *epidermis*, hide, pelt, peal, crust, bark, rind, *cortex*, husk, scale, shell, capsule, coat, tunic, tunicle, sheath, case, sheathing, wrapping, wrapper, envelope, veneer.

Superposition, coating, paint, varnish, anointing, inunction, incrustation, stucco.

V. To cover, superpose, overspread, wrap, lap, overlap, case, veneer.

To coat, paint, varnish, pay, daub, to lay it on thick, bedaub, encrust, stucco, dab, smear, anoint, do over, gild, japan, lacker (or lacquer).

Adj. Covering, &c., cutaneous, dermal, cortical, cuticular, tegumentary, skinny, scaly, squamous, imbricated.

(223) CENTRALITY, mediety (68), centricalness, centre, middle, focus, core, kernel, nucleus, nucleolus, heart, nave, *umbilicus*, concentration.

V. To be central, &c.

To render central, centralize, concentrate.

Adj. Central, centrical, middle, focal, umbilical, concentric.

Adv. Middle, midst, centrally, &c.

(224) LINING, coating, facing, internal incrustation, stalactite, stalagmite, wainscot, *parietes*, wall.

V. To line, incrust, face.

Adj. Lined, incrusted.

(225) INVESTMENT, dress, clothing, raiment, drapery, costume, attire, trim, habiliment, vesture, apparel, wardrobe, fancy dress, accoutrement, outfit, *trousseau*, uniform, regimentals, equipment, livery, gear, harness, turn out, caparison, suit, rigging, trappings, slops, frippery, dishabille, morning-dress, undress, rags.

Clothes, garment, garb, robe, tunic, habit, gown, coat, frock, stole, *blouse, toga,* haik, smockfrock, *surtout,* boddice.

Cloak, mantle, mantlet, shawl, wrapper, veil, tippet, kirtle, plaid, mantilla, bornouse (or burnoose), *roquelaure,* greatcoat, *surtout,* spencer, wrap-rascal, surplice, cassock, pallium, &c., mask, domino, cardinal, pelerine.

Jacket, vest, jerkin, waistcoat,

(226) DIVESTMENT, nudity, bareness, nakedness, baldness, undress, dishabille, threadbareness.

Denuding, nudation, denudation, stripping, uncovering, decortication, peeling, flaying, excoriation, desquammation, moulting, exfoliation.

V. To divest, uncover, denude, bare, strip, unclothe, undress, unrobe, disrobe, disapparel, disarray, take off, doff, cast off, peel, decorticate, uncoif, excoriate, skin, flay, expose, exfoliate, lay open, unroof, uncase, moult.

Adj. Bare, naked, nude, stripped, denuded, undressed, unclothed, uncovered, exposed, in dishabille, in buff, bald, threadbare, roofless.

Phr. In a state of nature, *in puris naturalibus,* bald as a coot.

doublet, gaberdine, stays, corselet, corset, cestus, petticoat, kilt, stomacher, kirtle.

Trousers, breeches, pantaloon, overalls, inexpressibles, smalls, tights.

Cap, hat, beaver, castor, bonnet, hood, headgear, headdress, kerchief, scarf, *coiffure*, coif, tartan, skull-cap, *calotte*, cowl, chapelet, capote, calash, pelt, wig, peruke, periwig, caftan, turban, fez, helmet.

Shirt, smock, shift, *chemise*, drawers, collar, cravat, neckcloth, stock, handkerchief.

Shoe, boot, jackboot, slipper, goloche, legging, buskin, greaves, mocassin, *gamache*, gambado, gaiter, stocking, sock, sandal.

Glove, gantlet (or gauntlet), mitten.

V. To invest, cover, envelope, lap, involve, inwrap (or enwrap), wrap up, lap up, sheathe, vest, clothe, array, enrobe, dress, dight, attire, apparel, accoutre, trick out, rig, fit out, invest, caparison, invest, don, put on, wear, huddle on, slip on, roll up in, muffle, perk, mantle, swathe, swaddle, circumvest, equip, harness.

Adj. Invested, clothed, arrayed, &c., clad, shod, &c.

(227) CIRCUMJACENCE, circumambiance, encompassment, atmosphere, medium, outpost, skirt, outskirts, suburbs, purlieus, precincts, *faubourgs, environs.*

V. To lie around, surround, beset, compass, encompass, environ, enclose, encircle, embrace, circumvent, lap, gird, begird, engird, skirt, twine round.

Adj. Circumjacent, circumambient, surrounding, &c., circumfluent, circumferential, suburban, land-locked, begirt, buried in (363), immersed in (301), embosomed, in the bosom of.

Adv. Around, about, without, on every side, on all sides, right and left.

(229) OUTLINE, circumference, perimeter, periphery, ambit, lines, *tournure,* contour, profile, *silhouette.*

Zone, belt, girth, belt, baldric, zodiac, *cordon.*

(230) EDGE, verge, brink, brow, brim, margin, border, skirt, rim, mouth, jaws, lip, muzzle, door, porch, portal (260).

Frame, flounce, frill, list, fringe, hem, selvedge, welt.

(228) INTERJACENCE, intervenience, interlocation, intervention, insertion, interposition, interdigitation, interpolation, interlineation, intercurrence, intrusion, obtrusion, insinuation, intercalation, insertion, interference, permeation, infiltration.

An intermedium, a go-between, bodkin, intruder, interloper, parenthesis, fly-leaf, *see* Mean (68), a partition, *septum,* diaphragm, party-wall.

V. To lie, come, or get between, intervene, intrude, slide in, permeate, to put between, interpose, interject, throw in, wedge in, thrust in, foist in, insert, intercalate, interpolate, interline, interleave, interlard, interdigitate, dovetail, worm in, insinuate, obtrude (301), intersperse, infiltrate.

Adj. Interjacent, intervening, &c., intermediate, intercalary, interstitial, parenthetical, mediterranean.

Adv. Between, betwixt, 'twixt, among, amongst, amid, amidst, midst.

(231) CIRCUMSCRIPTION, limitation, enclosure, confinement, shutting up, circumvallation, entombment.

Imprisonment, incarceration (751).

V. To circumscribe, limit, bound, confine, enclose, surround (227), compass about, impound, restrict, restrain (751), shut in, shut up, lock up, bottle up, hem in, hedge in, wall in, rail in, fence, picket, pen, enfold, coop, encage, cage, entomb, bury, immure, encase, pack up, seal up, wrap up (223), &c.

Adj. Circumscribed, &c., imprisoned, pent up (754).

(232) INCLOSURE, envelope, case, box, &c. (191), pen, penfold, pound, wall.

Barrier, bar, gate, door, barricade.

Dike (or dyke), ditch, foss, moat.

Fence, pale, paling, balustrade, rail, railing, palisade, battlement, &c. (717), circumvallation, contravallation.

(233) LIMIT, boundary, bounds, confine, term, bourn, kerb-stone, line of demarcation, termination, stint, frontier, precinct, marches, line of circumvallation, the pillars of Hercules, the Rubicon.

Adj. Definite, conterminate, conterminable.

2. *Special.*

(234) FRONT, face, anteriority, fore-rank, fore-ground, van, vanguard, advanced guard, outpost, *proscenium, façade,* frontispiece, disk.

Forehead, visage, physiognomy, phiz, countenance, mug, beak, rostrum, bow, stem, prow, prore.

(In a medal), the obverse.

V. To be in front, &c., to front, face, confront, bend forwards, &c.

Adj. Fore, anterior, front.

Adv. Before, in front, ahead, right ahead, in the van, foremost, *vis-à-vis,* in the foreground, face to face, before one's eyes, in the lee of.

(236) LATERALITY, side, flank, quarter, hand, cheek, jole, wing, profile, temple, loin, haunch, hip, broadside, lee-side.

V. To be on one side, &c., to flank, outflank, to sidle.

Adj. Lateral, sidelong, collateral, sideling, many-sided.

Adv. Sideways, side by side (216), abreast, alongside, aside, by the side of, to windward, or to leeward.

(238) DEXTRALITY, right, right hand, *dexter,* off side, starboard.

Adj. Dextral, right-handed, ambidextral.

(235) REAR, back, posteriority, the rear rank, the background, heels, tail, rump, croup, breech, *dorsum,* dorsal region, stern, poop, after-part.

(In a medal), the reverse.

V. To be in the rear, behind, &c., to fall astern, to bend backwards, turn the back upon.

Adj. Back, rear, postern, hind, hinder, hindermost, posterior, dorsal, after.

Adv. Behind, in the rear, in the background, behind one's back, at the heels of, at the tail of, at the back of, after, aft, abaft, astern, aback.

(237) ANTEPOSITION, opposite side, contraposition, reverse, inverse, antipodes, opposition, inversion (218).

V. To be opposite, &c.

Adj. Opposite, reverse, inverse, antipodal, sub-contrary.

Fronting, facing, diametrically opposite.

Adv. Over, over the way, over against, facing, against, fronting (234).

(239) SINISTRALITY, left, left hand, *sinister,* near side, larboard.

Adj. Sinistral, left-handed.

Section III. FORM.

1°. General Form.

(240) FORM, figure, shape, configuration, make, formation, frame, conformation, efformation, cut, set, trim, stamp, cast, mould, fashion.

Feature, lineament, phase, turn, attitude.

Science of form, Morphology.

Similarity of form, isomorphism.

Formation, figuration, efformation, sculpture.

V. To form, shape, figure, fashion, efform, carve, cut, chisel, hew, rough-hew, cast, rough-cast, hammer out, trim, lick into shape, mould, sculpture, cast, stamp.

Adj. Formed, &c., receiving form, plastic, fictile.

Giving form, plasmic.

(241) Absence of form.

AMORPHISM, disfigurement, defacement, mutilation, informity, *see* Deformity (846).

V. To destroy form, deface, disfigure, mutilate.

Adj. Shapeless, amorphous, formless, unhewn, rough, unfashioned, unshapen.

———

(242) Regularity of form.

SYMMETRY, shapeliness, uniformity, finish, *see* Beauty (845), arborescence, (256).

Adj. Symmetrical, regular, shapely, uniform, finished, &c., arborescent (256).

(243) Irregularity of form.

DISTORTION, twist, wryness, detortion, contortion, *see* Ugliness (846).

V. To distort, twist, wrest, writhe, contort.

Adj. Irregular, distorted, twisted, awry, askew, crooked, on one side.

Phr. All manner of ways.

2°. Special Form.

(244) ANGULARITY, angularness, angle, cusp, bend, elbow, knee, knuckle, groin, crinkle, aduncity, hook, crook, crotch, crutch, crane, fluke, scythe, sickle, zig-zag, kimbo, anfractuosity.

Fork, bifurcation, dichotomy.

A right angle, *see* Perpendicularity (212), salient and re-entering angles.

A polygon, square, triangle, &c., lozenge, diamond, rhomb, &c., wedge.

V. To bend, crook, hook, fork, bifurcate, crinkle.

Adj. Angular, bent, crooked, hooked, aduncous, aquiline, jagged, serrated, falcated, forked, bifurcate, zig-zag; dove-tailed, knock-kneed, crinkled, kimbo, geniculated, polygonal, &c., fusiform, wedge-shaped, cuneiform.

(245) CURVATURE, curvation, incurvity, incurvation, bend, flexure, flexion, bought, bending, deflexion, inflexion, arcuation, devexity, turn, deviation, *détour*, sweep, sinuosity, curl, curling, winding, recurvity, recurvation, flexibility (324).

A curve, arc, arch, vault, bow, crescent, half-moon, lunule, horseshoe, loop, crane-neck, conchoid, &c.

(246) STRAIGHTNESS, rectilinearity, directness.

A straight line, a right line, a direct line; inflexibility (324).

V. To be straight, &c.

To render straight, to straighten, rectify, unbend, unfold, uncurl, uncoil, unroll, unwind, unravel, untwist, unwreathe, unwrap.

Adj. Straight, rectilinear (or recti-

V. To be curved, &c., to decline, turn, trend, deviate, re-enter, sweep.

To render curved ; to bend, curve, incurvate, deflect, inflect, turn, arch, arcuate, bow, curl, recurve, frizzle.

Adj. Curved, bent, &c., curvilinear (or curvilineal), devex, recurved, recurvous, crump, bowed, crooked, arched, vaulted, arcuated, falcated, crescentic, semilunar, conchoidal, tenticular, reniform ; bow-kneed, knock-kneed, devious.

lineal), direct, even, right, in a line ; not inclining, bending, turning, or deviating to either side ; undeviating, unturned, undistorted, unswerving.

Phr. Straight as an arrow.

---

(247) Simple circularity.

CIRCULARITY, roundness.

A circle, circlet, ring, hoop, roundlet, *annulus*, annulet, bracelet, ringlet, eye, loop, wheel, cycle, orb, orbit, rundle, zone, belt, *cordon*, band, sash, girdle, cestus, cincture, baldric, fillet, fascia, wreath, garland, crown, corona, coronet, chaplet, necklace ; noose, lasso.

An ellipse, oval, ovule, ellipsoid, cycloid, epicycloid, epicycle, &c.

V. To encircle, environ, &c. (227).

Adj. Round, circular, annular, orbicular.

Oval, elliptical, elliptic, ovate, egg-shaped ; cycloidal, &c., moniliform.

(248) Complex circularity.

CONVOLUTION, winding, wave, undulation, circuit, tortuosity, anfractuosity, sinuosity, involution, sinuation, circumvolution, meandering, circumbendibus, twist, twirl, windings and turnings, *ambages*, inosculation.

A coil, spiral, helix, corkscrew, worm, volute, rundle, scollop (or scallop).

Serpent, eel, maze, labyrinth.

V. To be convoluted, &c.

To wind, twine, turn and twist, twirl, wave, undulate, meander, scallop, inosculate, entwine, twist together.

Adj. Convoluted, winding, twisting, contorted, waving, waved, wavy, undulating, undated, serpentine, anguilliform, mazy, tortuous, sinuous, flexuous, snaky, involved, sigmoidal, vermiform, vermicular, meandering ; scolloped (or scalloped), wreathed, wreathy, crisped, frizzled, ravelled, twisted, dishevelled.

Spiral, coiled, heliacal, turbinated.

Adv. In and out.

(249) ROTUNDITY ; cylindricity ; cylinder, barrel, drum, cylindroid, roll, roller, rouleau, column, rolling-pin, rundle.

Cone, conoid ; pear-shape, bell-shape.

Sphericity, spheroidity ; a sphere, globe, ball, spheroid, ellipsoid, drop, spherule, globule, vesicle, bulb, bullet, pellet, *pelote*, pill, clew, marble, pea, knob, pommel.

V. To form into a sphere, to sphere, to roll into a ball, give rotundity, &c.

Adj. Rotund, cylindric, cylindrical ; conic, conical.

Spherical, globular, globated, globous, globose, ovoid, egg-shaped, gibbous, bell-shaped, campaniliform, campaniform, campanulate.

Phr. Round as an apple ; round as a ball.

3°. SUPERFICIAL FORM.

(250) CONVEXITY, prominence, projection, swelling, gibbosity, bulge, protuberance, intumescence, tumor, tuberosity, tubercle, tooth, knob, excrescence, process, *apophysis*, condyle, bulb, node, nodule, nodosity, *dorsum*, hump, hunch, bunch, boss, embossment, bump, clump, sugar-loaf, point (253).

Pimple, wen, wheal, pustule, caruncle, corn, wart, furuncle, fungus, fungosity, *exostosis*, bleb, blister, blain.

Papilla, nipple, teat, pap, mammilla, proboscis, nose, neb, beak, snout, nozzle, back, shoulder, elbow, lip, flange.

Peg, button, stud, ridge, rib, jetty, jutty, snag, eaves; mole, cupola, dome, balcony.

Cameo, bas-relief, basso relievo, alto relievo.

Mount, hill, &c. (206); cape, promontory, foreland, headland, point of land.

V. To be prominent, &c., to project, bulge, jut out, to hang over, beetle, bend over, protrude, barrow, stand out, stick out, poke out, stick up, start up, cock up, shoot up, swell.

To render prominent; to raise, *see* (307).

Adj. Prominent, projecting, bulging, &c., bowed, bold, tuberous, bossed, bossy, embossed, gibbous, salient, mammiform.

(251) FLATNESS, plane; *see* Horizontality (213), Layer (204), and Smoothness (255).

V. To render flat, flatten, smooth, level.

Adj. Flat, plane, level, &c., flush, scutiform.

Phr. Flat as a pancake; flat as a board; flat as my hand.

(252) CONCAVITY, depression, hollow, hollowness, indentation, *intaglio*, cavity, dent, dint, dimple, follicle, pit, *sinus, alveolus, lacuna*, honeycomb, excavation, trough (259).

Cup, basin, crater, chalice, &c. (191), bowl.

Valley, vale, dale, dell, dingle, glade, glen, cave, cell, cavern, cove, grotto, alcove, gully, *cul-de-sac*.

V. To be depressed, &c., to retire.

To depress, hollow, scoop, dig, delve, excavate, dent, dint, mine, undermine, burrow, tunnel.

Adj. Depressed, concave, hollow, stove in, retiring, retreating, cavernous, honey-combed, alveolar, funnel-shaped, infundibuliform, bell-shaped, campaniliform.

---

(253) SHARPNESS, pointedness, acuteness, acuity, acumination, spinosity, prickliness.

A point, spike, spine, *spiculum*, needle, pin, prickle, prick, spear, bayonet, spur, rowel, barb, spit, cusp, horn, barb, snag, tag, thorn, briar, bramble, thistle, nib, tooth, tusk, spoke, cog, rachet, staple, bristle, beard, crag, *chevaux de frise*, crest, cone, spire, pyramid, steeple, porcupine, hedgehog.

Cutting edge, wedge, edge-tool, knife, razor, scalpel, axe, adze, &c.

V. To be sharp, &c., to taper to a point, to bristle with.

To render sharp, &c., to sharpen, point, aculeate, whet, barb, spiculate, bristle up.

(254) BLUNTNESS, obtuseness, dullness.

V. To be blunt, &c., to render blunt, &c., to obtund, dull, take off the point or edge, turn.

Adj. Blunt, obtuse, dull, bluff.

Adj. Sharp, pointed, acute, acicular, aculeated, spiked, spiky, ensiform, peaked, acuminated, salient, cusped, cornute, prickly, spiny, spinous, thorny, bristling, muricated, pectinated, studded, thistly, briary, cragged, craggy, snaggy, digitated, barbed, spurred, tapering, fusiform, denticulated, toothed, cutting.

Phr. Sharp as a needle ;— as a razor.

(255) SMOOTHNESS, evenness, level, &c. (213), polish, glassiness, sleekness, slipperiness, lubricity, lubrication, down, velvet.

V. To smooth, smoothen, plane, polish, burnish, calender, glaze, iron, file, lubricate.

Adj. Smooth, even, level, plane, sleek, polished, glazed, glossy, sleeky, silken, silky, velvety, glabrous, slippery, oily, soft, lubricated, unwrinkled.

Phr. Smooth as glass,— as velvet,— as oil; slippery as an eel.

(256) ROUGHNESS, unevenness, asperity, rugosity, ruggedness, scabrousness, salebrosity, scragginess, cragginess, craggedness, corrugation, nodosity, crispness, plumosity.

Bur, nap, shag, down, feather, plume, crest, tuft, *panache, byssus,* hair, wool, fur, mane, *cilia,* fringe, *fimbriæ,* tress, beard, moss, plush, velvet, arborescence.

V. To be rough, &c.

To render rough, to roughen, crisp, crumple, corrugate, rumple.

Adj. Rough, uneven, scabrous, rugged, rugose, rugous, salebrous, unsmooth, rough-hewn, craggy, cragged, scraggy.

Arborescent, dendriform.

Feathery, plumose, tufted, fimbriated, hairy, ciliated, hirsute, bushy, hispid, tomentous, downy, velvety, villous, bearded, pilous, shaggy.

Phr. Rough as a bear.

(257) NOTCH, dent, nick, indent, indentation, dimple.

Embrasure, battlement, saw, tooth.

V. To notch, nick, cut, dent, indent, jag.

Adj. Notched, &c., jagged, crenated, dented, denticulated, toothed, fimbriated, serrated.

(258) FOLD, plicature, plait, ply, crease, flexion, flexure, doubling, duplicature, gather, wrinkle, rimple, crinkle, crankle, crumple, rumple, rivel, ruck, ruffle, dog's-ear, corrugation, frounce, pucker.

V. To fold, double, plicate, plait, crease, wrinkle, crinkle, crankle, curl, cockle up, cocker, rimple, frizzle, rumple, frounce, rivel, twill, corrugate, pucker.

Adj. Folded, &c.

(259) FURROW, groove, rut, *sulcus,* scratch, streak, *striæ,* crack, score, rib.

Channel, gutter, trench, ditch, dike, foss, trough, kennel, chamfer, ravine, *see* (198).

V. To furrow, &c., flute, plough.

Adj. Furrowed, &c., ribbed, striated, sulcated, canaliculated, bisulcate, trisulcate, &c.

(260) OPENING, hole, *foramen,* perforation, window, eye, eyelet, key-hole, loop-hole, port-hole, mouse-hole, pigeon-hole, eye of a needle, pin-hole, puncture.

(261) CLOSURE, occlusion, blockade, shutting up, filling up, plugging, sealing, obstruction, infarction, impassableness, blocking up, blind alley, blind corner, *cul-de-sac.*

Aperture, apertness, hiation, yawning, ocsitancy, patefaction, pandiculation, *see* Interval (198).

Orifice, mouth, throat, inlet, muzzle, throat, gullet, wizen, nozzle, portal, porch, gate, gateway, door, *embouchure*, doorway.

Channel, passage, tube, pipe, vessel, tubule, canal, thoroughfare, gut, *fistula*, ajutage, chimney, flue, funnel, gully, tunnel, main, adit, shaft, gallery, alley, aisle, glade, bore, mine, calibre, pore, follicle, porousness, *lacunæ*.

Sieve, cullender, colander, cribble, riddle, screen.

Imperforation, imperviousness, impermeability.

V. To close, occlude, plug, block up, fill up, blockade, obstruct, stop, seal, plumb, cork up, shut up, choke, throttle, ram down, dam up, cram.

Adj. Closed, shut, unopened, occluded, &c., impervious, imperforate, unpassable, invious, pathless, untrodden, unpierced, unventilated, impermeable, imporous, operculated.

Phr. Hermetically sealed.

Apertion, perforation, piercing, boring, mining, terebration, drilling, &c., empalement, pertusion, puncture, acupuncture, penetration (302).

V. To open, gape, yawn.

To perforate, lay open, pierce, bore, mine, drill, scoop out, tunnel, transpierce, transfix, enfilade, empale, spike, spear, gore, stab, pink, stick, prick, riddle, punch.

To uncover, unrip, stave in.

Adj. Open, pierced, perforated, &c., perforate, wide open, unclosed, unstopped, patulous, oscitant, gaping, yawning, patent.

Tubular, fistulous, pervious, permeable, foraminous, follicular.

(262) PERFORATOR, borer, auger, gimlet, drill, wimble, awl, scoop, terrier, corkscrew, dibble, trepan, probe, bodkin, needle, stiletto, lancet, punch.

(263) STOPPER, stopple, plug, cork, bung, spigot, spike, spill, stopcock, tap, stop-gap, rammer, ramrod, piston, wadding, tompion.

Cover, lid, *operculum,* covering, covercle, door, &c. *see* (223), valve.

A janitor, doorkeeper, porter, beadle, Cerberus.

SECTION IV. MOTION.

1°. MOTION IN GENERAL.

(264) Successive change of place.*

MOTION, movement, transit, transition, move, going, &c., passage, course, stir.

Step, gait, post, footfall, carriage, transference (270), locomotion (266).

Mobility, restlessness, unrest, movableness, inquietude, flux.

V. To be moving, &c., to move,

(265) QUIESCENCE, rest, stillness, stagnation, stagnancy, fixedness, immobility, catalepsy, indisturbance.

Quiet, tranquillity, calm, calmness, sedentariness.

Pause, suspension, suspense, lull, stop, stoppage, interruption, stopping, stand, standstill, standing still, laying to, repose (687), respite.

* A thing cannot be said to *move* from one place to another unless it passes in succession through every intermediate place : hence motion is only such a change of place as is *successive*. "Rapid or swift as thought" are therefore incorrect expressions.

go, stir, hie, gang, budge, stir, pass, flit, shift, roll, roll on, flow (347, 348), sweep along, wander (279), change or shift one's place or quarters, dodge.

Adj. Moving, in motion, on the move.

Shifting, movable (270), mobile, restless, nomadic, wandering, vagrant, discursive, erratic (279), mercurial.

Lock, dead-lock, dead stop, embargo.

Resting-place, anchorage, post (189, 666), bed, pillow, &c. (215).

V. To be quiescent, &c., to remain, stand, stand still, [lay to], lie to, pull up, hold, halt, stop, stop short, rest, pause, repose.

To stay, tarry, sojourn, dwell (186), pitch one's tent, cast anchor, settle, bivouac, moor, tether, picket, plant oneself, alight, land, &c. (293), ride at anchor.

Phr. Not to stir a peg or step; go to bed.

To stop, suspend, arrest, avast, hold one's hand, interrupt, intermit, discontinue (142), put a stop to, lay an embargo on, quell, becalm.

Adj. Quiescent, still, motionless, moveless, at rest, stationary, untravelled, at a stand, stock-still, standing still, sedentary, undisturbed, unruffled, fast, stuck fast, rooted, moored, aground, at anchor, tethered, becalmed, stagnant, quiet, unmoved, immovable, restful, cataleptic, irremovable, stable, steady, steadfast.

Phr. Still as a statue; still as a post; quiet or still as a mouse.

Adv. At a stand, at a standstill, &c., *tout court.*

Int. Soho! stop! stay! avast!

(266) Locomotion by land.

JOURNEY, travel, travelling, excursion, expedition, tour, trip, circuit, peregrination, discursion, ramble, pilgrimage, course, ambulation, march, marching, walk, walking, promenade, stroll, saunter, stalk, perambulation, ride, equitation, drive, airing, jaunt.

Roving, vagrancy, flit, flitting, migration, emigration, immigration, intermigration, demigration.

Plan, itinerary, road book, guide.

Organs and instruments of locomotion; legs, feet, wings, pinions, pennon, oar, sail, paddle, locomotive, vehicle (272, 273).

V. To travel, journey, ramble, roam, rove, course, wander, stroll, straggle, expatiate, gad about; to go or take a walk, journey, tour, turn, trip, &c.; to prowl, stray, saunter, make a tour, emigrate, flit, migrate.

(267) Locomotion by water, or air.

NAVIGATION, voyage, sail, cruise, circumnavigation.

Natation, swimming, drifting.

Flight, volitation, aerostation, aeronautics, aerostatics.

V. To sail, make sail, warp, put to sea, navigate, take ship, get under weigh, spread sail, spread canvass, carry sail, plough the waves, plough the deep, walk the waters, scud, boom, drift, course, cruise, coast, circumnavigate.

To row, paddle, scull, steam.

To swim, float, buffet the waves, skim, *effleurer*, dive, wade.

To fly, be wafted, hover, soar.

Adj. Sailing, &c., under weigh, under sail, on the wing, volant, nautical, aerostatic.

To walk, march, step, tread, pace, wend, wend one's way, promenade, perambulate, circumambulate, take a walk, take the air, trudge, stalk, stride, strut, foot it, stump, peg on, bundle, toddle, shuffle on, tramp, traverse, bend one's steps, thread one's way, make one's way, find one's way, tread a path, take a course, defile, file off.

Ride, jog on, trot, amble, canter, gallop, take horse, prance, fisk, *caracoler.*

To drive, slide, glide, skim.

To go to, repair to, resort to.

Adj. Travelling, &c., ambulatory, itinerant, peripatetic, discursive, migratory, nomadic, on the wing, &c., circumforanian.

Adv. By the way, *chemin faisant,* on the road, *en passant.*

(268) TRAVELLER, wayfarer, voyager, itinerant, passenger, tourist, wanderer, rover, straggler, rambler, bird of passage, gad about, vagrant, tramp, vagabond, nomad, pilgrim, palmer, runner, courier, pedestrian, peripatetic, emigrant, fugitive.

Rider, horseman, equestrian, cavalier, jockey, postillion.

Mercury, Ariel, Comet.

(269) MARINER, navigator, seaman, sailor, seafarer, shipman, tar, bluejacket, marine, jolly, boatman, ferryman.

An aerial navigator, aeronaut.

(270) TRANSFERENCE, translocation, displacement, elocation, *metastasis, metathesis,* transposition (148), remotion, removal (185), relegation, deportation, extradition, conveyance, carriage, carrying, convection, conduction.

Transmission, passage, ferry, transport, portage, porterage, cartage, carting, shovelling, vectitation, vection, vecture, shipment, freight, wafture, transportation, transumption, transplantation, translation, shifting, dodging, dispersion (73), traction (285).

V. To transfer, convey, transmit, transport, carry, bear, carry over, remove, &c. (185), transpose, shift, convey, conduct, convoy, send, relegate, turn over to, deliver, waft, shovel, ladle, decant, empty, break bulk, ship, ferry over.

To bring, fetch, reach, draft.

To load, lade, charge.

Adj. Transferred, &c., movable, portable, portative.

Adv. From hand to hand.

(271) CARRIER, porter, bearer, coolly, conveyer, conductor.

Beast of burden, horse, steed, nag, palfry, galloway, charger, courser, racer, racehorse, hunter, jument, pony, filly, colt, barb, roan, jade, hack, *bidet,* pad, cob, tit, panch, roadster, goer, packhorse, drafthorse, carthorse, ketch, shelty, bayard, mare, stallion, gelding, stud.

Ass, donkey, jackass, mule, hinny, sumpter mule.

Camel, dromedary, llama, elephant, carrier-pigeon.

Pegasus, Bucephalus, Rozinante.

(272) VEHICLE, conveyance.

Carriage, caravan, van, waggon, stage-waggon, cariole, wain, dray, cart, sledge, sled, truck, tumbrel, barrow, wheelbarrow, handbarrow.

Equipage, carriage, coach, chariot, chaise, phaeton, curricle, whisky, landau, berlin, droschki, *désobligeant,* diligence, stage, stage-coach, car, omnibus, cabriolet, cab, calash, brougham, clarence, buggy, tandem, shan-

(273) SHIP, vessel, bottom, craft, shipping, marine, fleet, flotilla, squadron, armada, navy, H. M. S., man-of-war, ship of the line, first-rate, flag-ship, frigate, brig, schooner, sloop, cutter, corvette, yacht, skiff, yawl, ketch, smack, hoy, lugger, barge, bark, wherry, lighter, hulk, buss, packet.

Merchantman, fire-ship, transport, slaver, steamer, steam-boat, tug, col-

dredhan, kibitka, sedan chair, palan keen (or palanquin), litter, brancard, crate, hurdle, stretcher.

Shovel, spoon, ladle, hod.

lier, whaler, galley, galleyfoist, bilander, brigantine, dogger, clipper.

Argosy, galleon, galliot, polacca, tartane, junk, praam, saic, prahu, sampan, xebec.

Boat, long-boat, pinnace, shallop, jolly-boat, gig, funny, dingy, bumboat, fly-boat, cobble, cock-boat, punt, cog, kedge, catamaran, fishing-boat, coracle, life-boat, gondola, felucca, caique, canoe, raft.

Balloon, air-balloon, aerostat, Montgolfier, pilot-balloon, kite.

Adv. Afloat, aboard.

2°. DEGREES OF MOTION.

(274) VELOCITY, speed, celerity, swiftness, rapidity, fleetness, expedition, speediness, quickness, eagle-speed, nimbleness, briskness, agility, promptness, promptitude, dispatch, pernicity, acceleration.

Gallop, canter, trot, run, rush, scamper, hand-gallop, amble; flight, dart, bolt, spurt, flying, &c.

Haste, precipitation, post-haste, hurry, scurry, precipitancy, &c. (684), forced march, race, steeple-chase.

Rate, pace, step, gait, course, progress.

Lightning, light, cannon-ball, wind, rocket, arrow, dart, quicksilver, telegraph, express train.

An eagle, antelope, courser, race-horse, gazelle, greyhound, hare, squirrel.

Mercury, Ariel, Camilla, Harlequin.

V. To move quickly; to speed, haste, hie, hasten, press, press on, press forward, post, push on, whip, scamper, run, scud, scour, shoot, tear, whisk, sweep, skim, brush, glance, cut along, dash on, trot, gallop, amble, troll, rush, bound, bounce, flounce, bolt, flit, spring, fly off at a tangent, carry sail, crowd sail, take to one's heels, clap spurs to one's horse, to run like mad, ride hard, outstrip the wind, boom, scramble, haste, hurry, run a race.

To hasten, accelerate, expedite, urge, whip, forward, hurry, precipitate, quicken pace.

(275) SLOWNESS, tardiness, dilatoriness, slackness, lentor, languor, drawl, *see* Inactivity (683).

Hobbling, creeping, lounging, &c., shambling, claudication, halting, jog-trot, dog-trot, mincing steps.

A slow-goer, dawdle, lingerer, slow coach, drone, tortoise, snail, slug.

Retardation, slackening, lentor.

V. To move slowly, to creep, crawl, lag, slug, drawl, dawdle, linger, loiter, plod, trudge, flag, saunter, lounge, lumber, trail, grovel, glide, steal along, jog on, rub on, bundle on, toddle, waddle, shuffle, lose ground, halt, hobble, limp, claudicate, shamble, mince, falter, totter, stagger, hang fire.

Phr. To "drag its slow length along."

To retard, slacken, relax, check, rein in, curb, take in sail, strike sail, reef, put on the drag, apply the break, clip the wings.

Adj. Slow, slack, tardy, dilatory, easy, lazy, languid, drowsy, sleepy, heavy, drawling, leaden, sluggish, snail-like, creeping, crawling, &c., lumbering, hobbling, tardigrade.

Adv. Slowly, &c., gingerly, softly, leisurely, deliberately, gradually, &c. (144), *piano, adagio, largo,* lamely, &c.

Phr. Under easy sail; with mincing steps; with clipped wings; *haud passibus equis;* lamely, &c.

To keep up with, keep pace with, outrun, outstrip, gain ground.

Adj. Fast, speedy, swift, rapid, full drive, quick, fleet, nimble, agile, expeditious, prompt, brisk, frisky, hasty, hurried, flying, &c., light-footed, nimble-footed, winged, eagle-winged, mercurial, electric, telegraphic, light-legged.

Phr. Swift as an arrow, as a doe, as a lamplighter; off like a shot; quick as lightning; quick as thought.*

Adv. Swiftly, with speed, speedily, &c., apace, post-haste, *presto,* tantivy, by express, by telegraph, slap, slap-dash, headlong, hurry-skurry.

Phr. Under press of sail, or canvass; *velis et remis;* double quick time; with giant, or gigantic steps; *à pas de géant;* in seven league boots; whip and spur; *ventre à terre;* as fast as one's legs or heels will carry one; *sauve qui peut;* the devil take the hindmost; *vires acquirit eundo.*

3°. MOTION CONJOINED WITH FORCE.

(276) IMPULSE, momentum, impetus, push, impulsion, pulsion, thrust, shove, jog, jolt, brunt, booming, throw, volley.

Percussion, collision, concussion, clash, encounter, cannon, carambole, appulse, shock, bump.

Blow, stroke, knock, tap, fillip, pat, rap, dab, smack, slap, hit, cuff, bang, whack, thwack, squash, dowse, swap, punch, thump, pelt, kick, lunge, yerk, calcitration, recalcitration, *ruade,* arietation, beating (972), volley.

(277) RECOIL, retroaction, revulsion, reaction, rebound, repercussion, *ricochet,* rebuff, reverberation, reflux, springing back, &c., ducks and drakes.

A boomerang, spring, &c., *see* Elasticity (325).

V. To recoil, react, spring back, fly back, bound back, rebound, reverberate, repercuss.

Adj. Recoiling, &c., on the recoil, &c., refluent, repercussive.

———

Hammer, mallet, flail, cudgel, bludgeon, cane, stick, club, &c., ram, battering ram, monkey, catapult, balistes, rammer, sledge hammer; explosion (173).

Propulsion (284); Science of mechanic forces, Dynamics.

V. To impel, push, give impetus, &c., drive, urge, hurtle, boom, thrust, elbow, shoulder, jostle, justle, hustle, shove, jog, jolt, encounter, collide, clash, bump against, run foul of.

To strike, knock, tap, slap, dab, pat, pash, slam, hit, rap, cuff, smite, butt against, impinge, thump, beat, bang, punch, thwack, whack, swap, batter, dowse, baste, pummel, pelt, patter, drub, buffet, belabour, whip, &c., *see* (972), poke at, pink, lunge, kick, yerk, calcitrate.

To throw, &c., *see* Propel (284), shy.

Adj. Impelling, &c., impulsive, impellent, impelled, &c., booming.

* See Note on (264).

4°. MOTION WITH REFERENCE TO DIRECTION.

(278) DIRECTION, bearing, course, bent, inclination, drift, tenour, tendency, incidence, set, leaning, bending, trending, steerage, tack, steering, aim, collimation.

A line, path, road, aim, range, quarter, point of the compass, rhumb, azimuth, line of collimation.

V. To tend towards, go to, point to, or at; trend, verge, incline, conduct to.

To make for, or towards, aim at, take aim, level at, steer for, keep or hold a course, be bound for, bend one's steps towards, direct one's course.

To ascertain one's direction, *s'orienter.*

Adj. Directed, &c.

Adv. Towards, to, *versus*, thither, directly, straight, point blank, before the wind, near the wind, close to the wind, whither.

In all directions, *quaquaversum.*

(279) DEVIATION, swerving, aberration, *ambages*, warp, bending, sideling, straying, straggling, warping, &c., digression, circuit, *détour*, departure from, divergence (290), desultory motion.

V. To alter one's course, deviate, depart from, turn, bend, swerve, shift, warp, stray, straggle, sidle, diverge (290), tralineate, digress, wander, meander, veer, tack, turn aside, turn a corner, turn away from, face about, wheel, wheel about, steer clear of, ramble, rove, go astray, step aside.

Phr. To fly off at a tangent; to face to the right about.

Adj. Deviating, &c., aberrant, discursive, devious, desultory, erratic, vagrant, undirected, circuitous.

Adv. Astray, from.

Phr. To the right about; all manner of ways.

(280) Going before.

PRECESSION, leading.

Precedence in order (62).

V. To precede, lead, go in the van, take the lead, go ahead.

Adj. Preceding, leading, &c.

Adv. In advance, before (62).

(281) Going after.

SEQUENCE, following, pursuit, chase, hunt.

A follower, pursuer, attendant, shadow, satellite.

Sequence in order (63).

V. To follow, pursue, chase, hunt, hound, go after, go in the rear, or in the wake of, tread in the steps of, tread on the heels of, go after, fly after, to follow as a shadow, to lag behind.

Adj. Following, &c., in the wake of, in the rear of, on the heels of.

Adv. Behind, in the rear, &c., *see* (63).

(282) Motion forwards.

PROGRESSION, advance, progress, ongoing, progressiveness, progressive motion, floodtide, headway, advancing, &c., pursuit, steeplechase, *see* (622).

V. To advance, proceed, progress, go, move, bend or pass forwards, go on, pass on, get on, get along, jog on, push on, go one's way, go ahead, make head, make way, make head-

(283) Motion backwards.

REGRESSION, regress, recess, retrogression, retrogradation, crab-like motion, refluence, reflux, retroaction, return, reflexion, reflex, ebb, tergiversation, countermotion, countermarch, veering, recidivation, regurgitation.

V. To recede, retrograde, regrade, return, fall back, fall or drop astern, lose ground, put about, go back, turn

67

way, work one's way, press forward, get over the ground, gain ground, make progress, keep or hold on one's course, keep up with, get forward, distance.

Phr. To make up lee-way;—To go with the stream.

Adj. Advancing, &c., progressive, profluent, undeviating.

Adv. Forward, onward, forth, on, in advance, ahead, under weigh.

back, double, countermarch, turn tail, draw back, get back, retrace one's steps, regurgitate.

Adj. Receding, &c., retrograde, retrogressive, regressive, refluent, reflex, recidivous, crab-like.

Adv. Backwards, reflexively, to the right about, *à reculons, à rebours.*

(284) Motion given to an object in front.

PROPULSION, push, pushing, projection, jaculation, ejaculation, throw, fling, toss, shot, discharge, shy.

Things thrown; a missile, projectile, shot, ball, bolt, dart, arrow, bullet, stone, shaft, brickbat.

Bow, sling, catapult, &c. (727).

V. To propel, project, throw, fling, cast, pitch, chuck, toss, jerk, lance, ejaculate, hurl, bolt, drive, sling, flirt, shy at, dart, send, roll, send off, let off, discharge, fire off, shoot, launch, let fly.

Bowl, trundle, roll along (312).

To put in motion, start, give an impulse, impel (276), expel (296).

Phr. To carry off one's legs.

Adj. Propelling, &c., propulsive, projectile, &c.

(285) Motion given to an object behind.

TRACTION, drawing, draught, pull, pulling.

Phr. A long pull, a strong pull, and a pull all together.

V. To draw, pull, haul, lug, drag, tug, tow, trail, train, wrench, jerk, twitch, touse, to take in tow.

Adj. Drawing, &c., tractile.

———

(286) Motion from.

RECESSION, retirement, withdrawal, retreat, retrocession, *see* (283), departure (292), recoil (277), decampment, flight, reflexion.

A runaway, a fugitive.

V. To recede, go, move or fly from, retire, retreat, withdraw, come away, go or get away, draw back, shrink, move away.

To move off, stand off, fall back, turn tail, march off, decamp, sheer off, bolt, slip away, run away, pack off, fly, beat a retreat, remove, abscond, take to one's heels, sneak off, slink away.

Phr. To take French leave;—To cut and run;—To hop the twig;—*Sauve qui peut;*—the devil take the hindmost.

Adj. Receding, &c., fugitive, run away (671).

(287) Motion towards.

APPROACH, approximation, appropinquation, appulse, afflux, affluxion, pursuit (622), collision (276).

V. To approach, draw near, approximate, to near, drift, come, get, go, moor, &c., draw near, set in towards, make up to, gain upon, to tread on the heels of.

Adj. Approaching, &c., approximative.

———

(288) Motion from, actively.

REPULSION, push, driving from, repulse, abduction, *see* Impulse (276).

(289) Motion towards, actively.

ATTRACTION, drawing to, pulling towards, adduction, attractiveness.

V. To repel, push, drive, &c. from, retrude, abduce, abduct.

Adj. Repelling, &c., repellent, repulsive, abducent, abductive.

Int. Begone! &c. (292).

A loadstone, magnet.

V. To attract, draw, pull, drag, &c. towards, adduce.

Adj. Attracting, &c., adducent, attrahent, adductive, attractive.

Int. Come! come hither! approach!

(290) Motion farther off.

DIVERGENCE, aberration, divarication, radiation, separation (44), dispersion, diffusion, dissemination (73).

Oblique motion, sidling.

V. To diverge, divaricate, radiate, branch off, file off, draw aside.

To spread, disperse, scatter, distribute, diffuse, disseminate, shed, sow broadcast, sprinkle.

To sidle, swerve, heel.

To part, part company, turn away from.

Adj. Diverging, &c., divergent, radiant, aberring, aberrant, centrifugal.

Adv. Broadcast.

(291) Motion nearer to.

CONVERGENCE, appulse, meeting, confluence, concourse, conflux, congress, concurrence, concentration.

Resort, assemblage (72), focus (74), assymptote.

V. To converge, come together, unite, meet, fall or run foul of, fall in with, close in upon, centre in, enter in, to meet, come across.

To gather together, unite, concentrate, &c.

Adj. Converging, &c., convergent, confluent, concurring, concurrent, centripetal, assymptotical.

(292) Initial motion from.

DEPARTURE, outset, removal, exit, decampment, embarkation, flight.

Valediction, adieu, farewell.

A starting point or post, place of departure or embarkation.

Phr. The foot being in the stirrup.

V. To depart, go, set out, set off, start, start off, issue, go forth, sally, sally forth, set forward, be off, move off, pack off, begone, get off, sheer off.

To leave a place, quit, retire, withdraw, go one's way, take wing, flit, embark, go on board, set sail, put to sea, weigh anchor, slip cable, decamp (671).

To take leave, bid or take adieu, bid farewell.

Adj. Departing, &c., valedictory.

Adv. Whence, hence, thence.

Int. Go! begone! get you gone! go along! off with you! avaunt! go thy way! aroynt!

Farewell! adieu! good bye! bye! bye bye! *au revoir!* fare you well! God bless you!

(294) Motion out of.

EGRESS, exit, issue, emersion, emergence.

(293) Terminal motion at.

ARRIVAL, advent, reception, welcome, return, recursion, remigration.

Home, goal, resting-place, destination, harbour, haven, port, landing-place.

Meeting, rencontre, encounter.

V. To arrive, get to, come, come to, reach, attain, come up with, come up to, make, fetch, overtake.

To light, alight, land, disembark, debark, put in, put into, visit, cast anchor.

To come upon, light upon, pitch upon, hit, drop in, pop upon, bounce upon, plump upon, bump against, close with.

Phr. To be in at the death.

To come back, return.

To meet, encounter, rencounter, come in contact (199).

Adj. Arriving, &c., here, hither.

Int. Welcome! hail! all hail!

(295) Motion into.

INGRESS, entrance, entry, introgression, admission, intromission, in-

Exudation, extravasation, transudation (348), leakage, percolation, distillation, oozing, effluence, efflux, effusion, drain, dropping, dripping, dribbling, filtering, defluxion, gush, trickling, eruption.

Export, expatriation, emigration.

An outlet, vent, spout, flue, chimney, pore, drain, sewer (350).

V. To emerge, emanate, issue, go, come, move, pass, pour, flow, &c. out of, pass off.

To transude, leak, percolate, strain, distil, drain, ooze, filter, filtrate, dribble, trickle, drizzle, drip, gush, spout, run, flow out, effuse, extravasate, disembogue (348).

(296) Motion out of, actively.

EJECTION, emission, effusion, rejection, expulsion, proruption, detrusion, extrusion, trajection.

Discharge, ejection, evacuation, vomition.

Deportation, exile, banishment, relegation, extradition.

V. To be let out, &c., to ooze, percolate, fall out, to emit, eject, expel, reject, discharge, give out, let out, cast out, turn out, drive out, root out, pour out, shed, void, evacuate, disgorge, extrude, empty, detrude, throw off, spit, spirt, spill, slop.

To vomit, spew, puke, cast up, keck, retch, spatter, splutter, slobber, slaver, slabber, squirt, eructate, belch, give vent to, tap, open the sluices, heave out, bale out, shake off.

To unpack, unlade, unload.

To banish, exile, deport.

Adj. Emitting, &c., emitted, &c.

(298) EXCRETION, emanation, exhalation, exudation, secretion, extrusion, effusion, extravasation, ec-

troduction, insinuation, insertion (301), intrusion, inroad, incursion, influx, irruption, invasion, penetration, interpenetration, infiltration, import, immigration.

A mouth, door, &c., *see* Opening (260).

V. To enter, go into, come into, set foot in, intrude, invade, flow into, pop into, insinuate itself, penetrate, infiltrate, to put into, &c., bring in, insert, drive in, run in, wedge in, ram in (301), intromit, introduce, import, smuggle.

(297) Motion into, actively.

RECEPTION, admission, importation, immission, ingestion, imbibition, absorption, ingurgitation, inhalation.

Eating, swallowing, deglutition, devouring, gulp, gulping, gorging.

Drinking, potation, sipping, suction, sucking, draught, libation.

Mastication, manducation, chewing.

V. To admit, receive, intromit, import, ingest, absorb, imbibe, inhale, let in, take in, readmit, resorb, reabsorb, snuff up, suck in, swallow, take down, gulp, ingulp, bolt, ingurgitate, engulph.

To eat, fare, feed, devour, tuck in, pick, peck, gorge, engorge, fall to, stuff, cram, gobble, guttle, raven, eat heartily, do justice to.

To feed upon, live on, feast upon, carouse, batten upon, fatten upon, dine, &c., browse, graze, crop, chew, champ, munch, gnaw, nibble, cranch, royne, masticate, mumble.

To drink, quaff, guzzle, swill, swig, drench, sip, sup, lap, drain the cup.

Phr. To wet one's whistle.

Adj. Admitting, &c., admitted, &c., admissible.

(299) FOOD, *pabulum*, aliment, nutriment, sustenance, nurture, subsistence, provender, provision, prey,

chymosis, evacuation, fæces, excrement (653), perspiration, &c.

V. To emanate, exhale, excern, exude, effuse, secrete, extravasate, evacuate, discharge, &c. (296).

———

pasture, pasturage, keep, fare, diet, regimen.

Comestibles, eatables, victuals, prog, meat, bread, bread-stuffs, *cerealia*, viands, cates, delicacy, creature comforts, belly-timber, contents of the larder, dish, flesh-pots, pottage, pudding, *ragoût*.

Table, board, commons, good-cheer, bill of fare, commissariat, *table d'hôte*, ordinary, *cuisine*.

Meal, repast, feed, mess, course, regale, regalement, entertainment, feast, banquet, junket; breakfast, *déjeûné*, lunch, bever, luncheon, tiffin, refreshment, refection, dinner, supper, whet, bait, dessert, *entremet, hors d'œuvre*, pic-nic, snack.

Mouthful, bolus, gobbet, sip, sop.

Drink, beverage, liquor, broth, soups, &c., *symposium*.

Adj. Eatable, edible, esculent, comestible, alimentary, culinary, potable, potulent.

(300) Forcible egress.

EXTRACTION, taking out, removal, elimination, extrication, evulsion, avulsion, wrench.

Expression, squeezing.

V. To extract, take out, draw, draw out, pull out, tear out, pluck out, wrench, rake up, grub up, root up, dredge, remove, get out (185), elicit, extricate, eliminate.

To express, squeeze out.

Adj. Extracted, &c.

———

(301) Forcible ingress.

INSERTION, putting in, implantation, introduction, interjection, insinuation, planting, intercalation, injection, inoculation, importation, intervention (228), dovetailing, wedge.

Immersion, dip, plunge, bath, submersion, souse, duck, soak.

Interment, burying, burial, &c. (363).

V. To insert, introduce, put into, import, throw in, interlard, inject, interject, intercalate, infuse, instil, inoculate, impregnate, imbue, imbrue, graft, ingraft, bud, plant, implant, obtrude, foist in, worm in, thrust in, stick in, ram in, plough in, let in, dovetail, mortoise, insinuate, wedge in, press in, impact, drive in, run in, empierce (260).

To immerse, dip, steep, immerge, merge, submerge, bathe, plunge, drop in, souse, douse, soak, duck, drown.

To inter, bury, &c. (363).

Adj. Inserting, inserted, &c.

(302) Motion through.

PASSAGE, transmission, permeation, penetration, interpenetration, infiltration (295), endosmose, exosmose.

Terebration, empalement, &c. (260).

V. To pass, pass through, traverse, terebrate, pierce, empale, spear, spike, spit (260), penetrate, permeate, thread, thrid, enfilade, go through, go across, go over, pass over, cut across, pass and repass, work, thread or worm one's way, force a passage, to transmit.

Adj. Passing, intercurrent, &c.

(303) Motion beyond.

TRANSCURSION, transilience, trans-

———

(304) Motion short of.

SHORTCOMING, failure, falling short

gression, trespass, encroachment, infringement, extravagation, transcendence.

V. To transgress, overstep, surpass, overpass, overgo, outgo, outstep, overleap, outleap, pass, go by, strain, overshoot the mark, overjump, overskip, overlap, go beyond, transcend, encroach, exceed, trespass, infringe, trench upon.

Phr. To pass the Rubicon.

Adv. Beyond the mark.

(305) Motion upwards.

ASCENT, rise, ascension, upgrowth, leap (309).

A rocket, skyrocket, lark.

V. To ascend, rise, mount, arise, uprise, go up, get up, climb, clamber, scale, scramble, escalade, surmount, aspire, over-ride, over-reach, get up on one's hind legs, start up.

To tower, soar, hover, spire, plane, swim, float, surge.

To leap, jump, hop, skip, vault, bound, dance, bob, curvet, romp, caracole, caper, cut capers.

Adj. Rising, &c., scandent, buoyant, floating, supernatant, superfluitant, leaping, &c., saltatory, frisky.

Adv. Uphill.

(307) ELEVATION, raising, lifting, erection, lift, sublevation, sublimation.

V. To elevate, raise, lift, uplift, upraise, set up, erect, stick up, rear, uprear, upbear, upcast, hoist, uphoist, heave, upheave, weigh, exalt, give a lift, sublimate.

To drag up, fish up, dredge.

Adj. Elevated, &c.

Adv. On stilts, on the shoulders of.

(309) LEAP, jump, hop, spring, bound, vault, saltation.

(732), defalcation, lee-way, incompleteness (53).

V. To fall short of, not to reach, keep within bounds, keep within compass.

Adj. Unreached, deficient (53), short, *minus.*

Adv. Within the mark, within compass, within bounds, &c.

(306) Motion downwards.

DESCENT, fall, descension, declension, declination, drop, subsidence, lapse, downfall, tumble, tilt, toppling, trip, lurch, *culbute.*

Titubation, shambling, stumble.

An *avalanche, débâcle.*

The fate of Icarus.

V. To descend, go down, fall, sink, drop, drop down, droop, come down, dismount, alight, settle, slide.

To stoop, bend, bow, curtsey, bob, bend the head or knee, dip, crouch, cower.

To recline, lie, lie down, sit, sit down, couch, squat.

To tumble, slip, trip, stumble, lurch, swag, topple, topple over, swoop, tilt, sprawl, plump down.

To alight, dismount, get down.

Adj. Descending, &c., descendent.

Adv. Downhill.

(308) DEPRESSION, lowering, abasement, detrusion, reduction.

Overthrow, upset, prostration, subversion, overset, overturn, precipitation.

V. To depress, lower, let down, sink, debase, abase, reduce, detrude, let down, or take down a peg, let fall.

Overthrow, overturn, upset, overset, subvert, prostrate, level, fell; cast, take, throw, fling, dash, pull, cut, knock, hew &c. down, pull about one's ears (218).

Adj. Depressed, sunk, prostrate, &c.

(310) PLUNGE, dip, dive, ducking.

V. To plunge, dip, souse, duck,

Dance, caper, curvet, caracole, *gambade*, capriole; hop, skip and jump.

Kangaroo, jerboa.

dive, plump, submerge, submerse, squash, sink, engulph.

(311) Curvilinear motion.

CIRCUITION, turn, wind, circuit, curvet, *détour*, excursion, circumbendibus, circumvention, circumnavigation, north-west passage.

Turning, winding, twist, twisting, wrench, evolution, twining, coil, circumambulation, meandering.

V. To turn, bend, wheel, put about, heel, go round, or round about, turn a corner, double a point, wind, whisk, twirl, twist, twill, raddle.

Phr. To lead a pretty dance.

Adj. Turning, &c., circuitous, circumforaneous.

Adv. Round about.

(312) Motion in a continued circle.

ROTATION, revolution, gyration, roll, circumrotation, circumgyration, volutation, circination, *pirouette*, circumvolution, convolution, verticity, whirl, eddy, vortex, whirlpool, gurge, surge, a dizzy round.

A wheel, screw, whirligig, rolling stone, windmill.

Axis, spindle, pivot, pin, hinge, swivel, gimbals.

Science of rotatory motion, Trochilics.

V. To rotate, roll, revolve, spin, turn, turn round, circumvolve, gyre, gyrate, wheel, whirl, twirl, thrum, trundle, troll, twidle, boll (or bowl), roll up, furl, wallow, welter.

Phr. To box the compass.

Adj. Rotating, &c., rotatory, rotary, circumrotatory, trochilic, vertiginous, gyratory.

(313) Motion in a reverse circle.

EVOLUTION, unfolding, &c., development, introversion, reversion.

V. To evolve, unfold, unroll, unwind, uncoil, untwist, unfurl, develope, introvert, reverse.

Adj. Evolving, &c., evolved, &c.

_____

(314) Reciprocating motion, motion to and fro.

OSCILLATION, vibration, undulation, pulsation, libration, nutation, swing, beat, shake, seesaw, going and coming, wag, evolution, vibratiuncle.

Fluctuation, vacillation, dance, lurch, dodge, rolling, pitching, tossing, &c.

V. To oscillate, vibrate, undulate, librate, wave, rock, swing, pulsate, beat, wag, waggle, nod, bob, tick, play, wamble, wabble, dangle, swag.

To fluctuate, vacillate, dance, curvet, reel, quake, quaver, roll, top, pitch, flounder, stagger, totter, brandish, shake, flourish, move up and down, to and fro, backwards and forwards.

Adj. Oscillating, &c., oscillatory, vibratory, undulatory, pulsatory, pendulous.

Adv. To and fro, up and down, backwards and forwards, seesaw, zig-zag, wibble-wabble.

(315) Irregular motion.

AGITATION, stir, tremor, shake, ripple, jog, jolt, jar, succussion, trepidation, quiver, quaver, dance, jactitation, jactitancy, restlessness, twitter, flicker, flutter, bobbing.

Disturbance, perturbation, commotion, turmoil, turbulence, tumult, tumultuation, jerk, throe, convulsion, *subsultus,* staggers, epilepsy, writhing, ferment, fermentation, effervescence, hurly-burly, *cahotage;* ground swell.

V. To be agitated, to shake, tremble, quiver, quaver, shiver, twitter, twire, writhe, toss about, tumble, stagger, bob, reel, wag, waggle, dance, wriggle, stumble, flounder, shuffle, totter, flounce, flop, curvet, prance, throb, pulsate, beat, palpitate, go pit-a-pat, flutter, flitter, flicker, bicker.

Phr. To jump like a parched pea ; to shake like an aspen leaf.

To agitate, shake, toss, tumble, bandy, wield, brandish, flap, flourish, whisk, jerk, hitch, jolt, jog, joggle, jostle, hustle, disturb, shake up, churn, jounce, ferment, effervesce, boil, wallop.

Adj. Shaking, &c., agitated, tremulous, desultory, subsultory, shambling, giddypaced, saltatory.

Adv. By fits and starts ; subsultorily, *per saltum.*

CLASS III.

WORDS RELATING TO MATTER.

SECTION I.　MATTER IN GENERAL.

(316) MATERIALITY, corporeity, corporality, materialness, substantiality, physical condition.

Matter, body, substance, brute matter, stuff, element, principle, *parenchyma*, material, *substratum*, frame, stocks and stones.

Science of matter; Physics, Somatology, Somatics, Natural Philosophy, Physical Science, Experimental Philosophy, *Philosophie positive*.

Adj. Material, bodily, corporeal, physical, somatic, somatoscopic, sensible, tangible, ponderable.

(317) IMMATERIALITY, incorporeity, spirituality, spirit, &c. (450), immaterialness, inextension.

V. To disembody.

Adj. Immaterial, incorporeal, asomatous, immateriate, unextended, incorporal, unbodied, disembodied, spiritual, extramundane, unearthly.

(318) WORLD, nature, universe; earth, globe; the wide world, *cosmos*, macrocosm.

The heavens, sky, welkin, empyrean, starry heaven, firmament; the vault, or canopy of heaven; the celestial spaces, the starry host, the heavenly bodies, stars, asteroids, constellations, galaxy, milky-way, *via lactea*, nebulæ, &c.

Science of the heavenly bodies; Astronomy, uranography, uranology, cosmography, cosmogony, eidouranion, orrery.

An astronomer, star-gazer.

Adj. Cosmical, mundane, terrestrial, terraqueous, terrene, terreous, terrestrious, sublunary, under the sun, subastral.

Celestial, heavenly, sphery, starry, stellar, nebular, &c., sidereal, sideral, astral.

(319) GRAVITY, weight, heaviness, gravitation, ponderosity, ponderousness, pressure, load, burden, ballast, a lump.

Lead, a millstone, mountain, Pelion on Ossa.

Science of gravity, Statics.

V. To be heavy, to gravitate, weigh, press, cumber, load.

Adj. Weighty, heavy, ponderous, gravitating, weighing, &c., ponderable, lumpish, cumbersome, massive, unwieldy, incumbent, superincumbent.

Phr. Heavy as lead.

(320) LEVITY, lightness, imponderability, subtlety, buoyancy, airiness, portableness.

A feather, dust, mote, down, thistledown, flue, cobweb, gossamer, straw, cork, bubble; a float, buoy.

V. To be light, to float, swim, be buoyed up.

Adj. Light, subtile, airy, imponderous, weightless, imponderable, etherial, sublimated, floating, swimming, buoyant, portable, uncompressed.

Section II. INORGANIC MATTER.

1°. Solid Matter.

(321) DENSITY, solidity, solidness, impenetrability, incompressibility, cohesion, coherence, cohesiveness (46), imporosity, impermeability, closeness, compactness, constipation, consistence, spissitude, thickness.

Specific gravity ; hydrometer, areometer.

Condensation, consolidation, solidification, solidation, concretion, coagulation, petrifaction, lapidification, lapidescence, vitrification, crystallization, precipitation, inspissation, thickening, grittiness, knottiness, indivisibility, indiscerptibility, indissolvableness.

A solid body, mass, block, lump, concretion, concrete, cake, clot, stone, curd, coagulum.

V. To be dense, &c.

To become, or render solid; solidify, solidate, concrete, to take a set, consolidate, congeal, coagulate, curdle, curd, fix, clot, cake, cohere, crystallize, petrify, vitrify, condense, thicken, inspissate, compress, squeeze, ram down, constipate.

Adj. Dense, solid, solidified, consolidated, &c., coherent, cohesive, compact, close, substantial, massive, lumpish, impenetrable, incompressible, impermeable, imporous, constipated, concrete, crystalline, crystallizable, vitreous, coagulated, thick, incrassated, inspissated, curdled, clotted, grumous.

Undissolved, unmelted, unliquefied, unthawed.

Indivisible, indiscerptible, indissolvable, indissoluble.

(322) RARITY, tenuity, absence of solidity, subtility, sponginess, compressibility ; hollowness (252).

Rarefaction, expansion, dilatation, inflation, subtilization.

Ether, vapour, air, gas (334).

V. To rarefy, expand, dilate, subtilize.

Adj. Rare, subtile, thin, fine, tenuous, compressible.

Porous, cavernous, spongy, bibulous, spongious.

Rarefied, expanded, dilated, subtilized, unsubstantial, uncompact, uncompressed ; hollow (252).

---

(323) HARDNESS, rigidity, firmness, renitence, inflexibility, stiffness, starchness, starchedness, temper, callosity, durity, induration, petrifaction, &c. (321), ossification.

A stone, pebble, flint, marble, rock, granite, iron, steel, adamant.

Tenseness, stretching, tensure 200).

V. To render hard, harden, stiffen, indurate, petrify, temper, ossify.

Adj. Hard, rigid, stiff, firm, starch, stark, unbending, unyielding, inflexible, tense, indurate, indurated, gritty, &c., proof, adamantean.

Phr. Hard as iron, &c.;—Hard as a brick ;— Hard as a nail ;— Hard

(324) SOFTNESS, tenderness, flexibility, pliancy, pliableness, pliantness, litheness, pliability, suppleness, sequacity, ductility, malleability, tractility, extensibility, extendibility, plasticity, inelasticity, laxity.

Clay, wax, butter ; a cushion, pillow, featherbed, down.

Mollification, softening, &c.

V. To render soft, soften, mollify, relax, temper, mash, knead, squash.

To bend, yield, relent.

Adj. Soft, tender, supple, pliable, limber, flexible, flexile, lithe, pliant, plastic, ductile, tractile, tractable, malleable, extensile, sequacious.

Yielding, bending, flabby, floc-

as a deal board ;—Stiff as buckram; —Stiff as a poker.

(325) ELASTICITY, springiness, spring, resilience, renitency, contractility (195), compressibility, Indian rubber, caoutchouc.
V. To be elastic, &c., to spring back, fly back, rebound, recoil (277).
Adj. Elastic, tensile, springy, resilient, renitent, buoyant.

(327) TENACITY, toughness, strength, cohesion (46), sequacity, stubbornness.
V. To be tenacious, &c., to resist fracture.
Adj. Tenacious, tough, stubborn, cohesive, strong, resisting, coriaceous, sequacious.
Phr. Tough as leather.

culent, downy, flimsy, œdematous, doughy, argillaceous, mellow.
Phr. Soft as butter;— Soft as down.

(326) INELASTICITY, want or absence of elasticity, *see* (324).

(328) BRITTLENESS, fragility, crispness, friability, frangibility, fissility.
V. To be brittle, break, crack, snap, split, shiver, splinter, crumble, break short, fly.
Adj. Brittle, frangible, fragile, frail, gimcrack, shivery, fissile, splitting, splintery, crisp, crimp, short, crumbling.
Phr. Brittle as glass.

(329) TEXTURE, structure, organization, anatomy, frame, fabric, framework, architecture, *compages*, substance, *parenchyma*, constitution, intertexture, contexture, tissue, grain, web, woof, nap (256), fineness or coarseness of grain.
Science of textures, Histology.
Adj. Textural, structural, organic.
Fine, delicate, subtle.
Coarse, rough-grained.
Flimsy, unsubstantial, gossamery.

(330) PULVERULENCE, state of powder, dust, sand, sawdust, grit, meal, bran, flour, limature, filings, *débris, detritus*, scobs, magistery, crumb, flocculence, efflorescence, sandiness, friability.
Reduction to powder, pulverization, comminution, granulation, disintegration, subaction, contusion, trituration, levigation, abrasion, filing, &c. (331).
Instruments for pulverization ; a mill, grater, rasp, file, pestle and mortar.
V. To reduce to powder, to pulverize, comminute, granulate, triturate, levigate, file, abrade, rub down, grind, grate, rasp, pound, bray, contuse, contund, beat, crush, cranch, scranch, crumble, disintegrate.
Adj. Powdery, granular, mealy, floury, branny, furfuraceous, flocculent, dusty, sandy, sabulous, arenaceous, gritty, efflorescent, impalpable, pulverizable, pulverulent, friable, crumbly, shivery, pulverized, &c., attrite.

(331) FRICTION, attrition, affriction, rubbing, abrasion, contrition, rub, &c., scouring, limature, filing.
V. To rub, abrade, &c., scrape, scour, polish, rub out.

(332) Absence of friction.
LUBRICATION, prevention of friction.
V. To lubricate, smooth (255).
Adj. Lubricated, &c.

2°. FLUID MATTER.

1. *Fluids in general.*

(333) FLUIDITY, fluid, (including both inelastic and elastic fluids).

Inelastic fluid.

LIQUIDITY, liquidness, a liquid, liquor, lymph, humour, juice, sap, serum, serosity, gravy, rheum, ichor, sanies, solubility.

Science of liquids at rest; Hydrology, Hydrostatics.

V. To be fluid or liquid, to flow, run.

Adj. Liquid, fluid, fluent, running, flowing, serous, juicy, succulent, sappy.

Liquefied, uncongealed, melted, &c. (335).

(335) LIQUEFACTION, fusion, melting, colliquation, colliquefaction, thaw, deliquation.

Solution, dissolution, decoction, apoxem, lixivium, infusion, &c., liquescency.

V. To render liquid, to liquefy, run, melt, thaw, fuse, solve, dissolve, resolve, to hold in solution.

Adj. Liquefied, &c., molten, liquescent, liquefiable, deliquescent, soluble.

(334) Elastic fluid.

GASEITY, vaporousness, gas, air, vapour, ether, steam, fume, reek, effluvium.

Smoke, cloud.(353).

Science of elastic fluids; Pneumatics, Aerostatics, Pneumatostatics.

Adj. Gaseous, aeriform, etherial, aerial, airy, vaporous, volatile, evaporable.

(336) VAPORIZATION, volatilization, vaporation, evaporation, distillation, sublimation, exhalation, volatility.

V. To render gaseous, vaporize, volatilize, evaporate, exhale, distil, sublime.

Adj. Volatilized, &c., volatile, evaporable.

2. *Specific Fluids.*

(337) WATER, serum, lymph, rheum.

Dilution, immersion, maceration, humectation, infiltration, sprinkling, affusion, irrigation, *douche,* balneation, bath, inundation, deluge, *see* (348), a diluent.

V. To be watery, &c., to reek.

To add water, to water, wet, moisten (339), dilute, dip, immerse, plunge, merge, immerge, steep, souse, duck, submerge, drown, soak, macerate, pickle, wash, sprinkle, affuse, splash, swash, douse, drench, slop, slobber, irrigate, inundate, deluge.

(338) AIR, common air, atmospheric air.

The atmosphere, the sky, the open air, weather, climate.

Science of air; Aerology, Aeroscopy.

Exposure to the air or weather.

Adj. Containing air, windy, flatulent, effervescent.

Atmospheric, airy, aerial, aeriform.

Adv. In the open air, *à la belle étoile, al fresco, sub Jove.*

Adj. Watery, aqueous, wet, aquatic, lymphatic, diluted, &c., reeking, dripping, soaking, washy, sloppy, squashy, splashy, slobbery, diluent.

Phr. Wet as a rat;—Wet as a rag.

(339) MOISTURE, moistness, humidity, dampness, wetness, humectation, madefaction, dew, muddiness.

V. To be moist, &c.

To moisten, wet, humect, humectate, damp, bedew, imbue, infiltrate, imbrue.

Adj. Moist, damp, undried, humid, wet, dank, muggy, dewy, roral, rorid, roscid, juicy, wringing wet.

(340) DRYNESS, siccity, aridity, drought.

Exsiccation, desiccation, arefaction, dephlegmation, drainage.

V. To be dry, &c.

To render dry, to dry, dry up, exsiccate, desiccate, drain, parch.

Adj. Dry, anhydrous, arid, dried, &c., undamped, husky, waterproof, juiceless, sapless.

Phr. Dry as a bone;—Dry as dust ;—Dry as a stick ;—Dry as a mummy ; — Dry as a biscuit.

(341) OCEAN, sea, main, the deep, "the vasty deep," brine, salt water, tide, wave, surge, ooze, &c. (348).

Neptune, Thetis, trident.

Adj. Oceanic, marine, maritime, pelagic, pelagian.

(342) LAND, earth, ground, *terra firma*, continent, oasis, mainland, peninsula, tongue of land.

Coast, shore, seaboard, seaside, seabank, strand, beach, bank, lea, an iron-bound coast.

Cape, promontory, &c. (250), headland, point of land, highland.

Soil, glebe, clay, loam, marl, clod, clot, rock, crag, &c. (206), mould, subsoil.

Adj. Terrene, earthy, continental. Littoral, midland.

Adv. Ashore, on shore, on land.

(343) GULPH, bay, inlet, bight, estuary, arm of the sea, armlet, sound, frith, firth, lough, lagoon, indraught, cove, creek, strait, Euripus.

LAKE, loch, mere, tarn, plash, pond, pool, puddle, slab, well, standing water, dead water, a sheet of water.

Adj. Lacustrine.

(344) PLAIN, table land, open country, the face of the country, champagne country, basin, downs, waste, wild, steppe, pampas, "weary waste," savanna, prairie, heath, common, wold, moor, moorland.

Meadow, mead, pasturage, park, field, lawn, terrace, esplanade, sward, turf, sod, heather.

Adj. Campestrian, alluvial, champaign.

(345) MARSH, swamp, morass, moss, fen, bog, quagmire, slough, sump, wash.

Adj. Marshy, marish, swampy, boggy, plushy, poachy, paludal.

(346) ISLAND, isle, islet, holm, reef, breaker.

Adj. Insular.

3. *Fluids in Motion.*

(347) Fluid in motion.

STREAM, flow, current, jet, undercurrent.

V. To flow, stream, issue.

(348) Water in motion, corrivation.

RIVER, running water, jet, spirt, squirt, spout, splash, gush, water-

(349) Air in motion.

WIND, draught, *flatus, afflatus,* breath, air, breath of air, puff, whiff, zephyr, blow.

spout, sluice, waterfall, cascade, ca-tadupe, cataract, *débâcle, avalanche.*

Rain, shower, mizzle, drizzle, drip-ping, stillicideum, flux, flow, proflu-ence, effluence, efflux, effluxion, efflu-sion, defluxion.

Spring, fountain, rill, rivulet, gill, gullet, rillet, streamlet, runnel, sike, burn, beek, brook, stream, river, torrent, rapids, flush, flood, swash, tide, spring tide, high tide, fresh, current, indraught, eddy, gurge, whirlpool, regurgitation.

Wave, billow, surge, swell, ripple, ground swell, surf, breakers.

Inundation, cataclysm, *débâcle.*

Science of fluids in motion; Hy-draulics, Hydraulicostatics.

V. To flow, run, gush, spout, roll, jet, well, drop, drip, trickle, dribble, ooze (294), transcolate, distil, transude, stream, sweat, perspire (298), overflow, flow over, splash, swash, guggle, sputter, spurt, regurgitate.

To rain, rain hard, pour with rain, drizzle, spit, mizzle, set in.

To flow into, fall into, open into, discharge itself, disembogue, disgorge, meander.

Phr. To rain cats and dogs.

To cause a flow, to pour, drop, distil, splash, squirt, spill, drain, empty, discharge, pour out, open the sluices, or flood-gates ; shower down.

To stop a flow, to stanch, dam, dam up (261), intercept.

Adj. Fluent, profluent, affluent, tidal, flowing, &c., babbling, bub-bling, gurgling, meandering, meandry, meandrous.

Fluviatile, streamy, showery, rainy, pluvial, stillicidious.

Gust, blast, breeze, squall, gale, storm, tempest, hurricane, whirl-wind, tornado, simoom, samiel, har-mattan, monsoon, trade wind, sirocco, *bise,* a capful of wind, windiness, ventosity.

Insufflation, sufflation, perflation, blowing, fanning, ventilation, blow-ing up, inflation, afflation, sneezing, sternutation.

Eolus, Boreas, the cave of Eolus.

Bellows, fan, ventilator, punka.

V. To blow, blow hard, blow a hurricane, breathe, puff, whiff, whif-fle, wheeze, snuffle, sniffle, sneeze.

To fan, ventilate, inflate, perflate, blow up.

Phr. To blow great guns.

Adj. Blowing, &c., windy, breezy, gusty, squally, stormy, tempestuous, blustering.

---

(350) Channel for the passage of water.

CONDUIT, duct, watercourse, water-shed, race, adit, aqueduct, canal, sluice, dyke, main, gully, moat, ditch, trough, gutter, drain, sewer, culvert, cloaca, sough, kennel, siphon, pipe, emunctory, gully-hole, artery, pore, spout, scupper, ajutage, waste-pipe.

Floodgate, dam, watergate, lock, valve.

(351) Channel for the passage of air.

AIR-PIPE, air-tube, shaft, flue, chimney, vent, blow-hole, nostril, nozzle, throat, weasand, *trachea,* wind-pipe, spiracle, ventiduct.

3°. IMPERFECT FLUIDS.

(352) SEMILIQUIDITY, pulpiness, viscidity, viscosity, ropiness, slimi-ness, gumminess, siziness, clammi-

(353) Mixture of air and water.

BUBBLE, foam, froth, head, spume, lather, bleb, spray, surf, yeast, suds.

ness, mucosity, spissitude, lentor, thickness, crassitude.

Inspissation, thickening, incrassation.

V. To inspissate, thicken, incrassate, mash, squash, churn, beat up.

Adj. Semifluid, semiliquid, milky, emulsive, creamy, curdly, thick, pappy, pasty, pulpy, pultacious, succulent, grumous, doughy, squashy.

Gelatinous, albuminous, gummy, amylaceous, mucilaginous, glairy, slimy, ropy, clammy, glutinous (46), viscid, viscous, sticky, slab, slabby, sizy, lentous.

(354) PULPINESS, pulp, jelly, mucilage, gelatin, mucus, gum, albumen, size, milk, cream, emulsion, rob, jam.

Paste, dough, curd, pap, pudding, poultice, soup, squash, mud, slush.

Cloud, vapour, fog, mist, haze, scud, rack, cumulus, &c.

Science of clouds, Nephelognosy.

Effervescence, foaming, mantling, fermentation, frothing, &c.

V. To bubble, boil, foam, froth, mantle, sparkle, guggle, gurgle, effervesce, ferment.

Adj. Bubbling, &c., frothy, nappy, effervescent.

(355) UNCTUOUSNESS, unctuosity, oiliness, greasiness, slipperiness, lubricity.

Lubrication, anointment.

V. To oil, grease, anoint, wax, lubricate.

Adj. Unctuous, oily, oleaginous, adipose, sebaceous, fat, fatty, greasy, waxy, butyraceous, soapy, saponaceous, pinguid, lardaceous.

(356) OIL, fat, butter, cream, grease, tallow, suet, lard, blubber, pomatum, *pomade*, stearine, elaine, soap, wax, spermaceti, loam, unguent, liniment.

SECTION III. ORGANIC MATTER.

1°. VITALITY.

1. *Vitality in General.*

(357) ORGANIZATION, the organized world, organized nature, living nature, animated nature, living beings.

The science of living beings; Biology, Natural History*, Organic Chemistry.

(359) LIFE†, vitality, Archeus, animation, viability, the vital spark or flame.

Vivification, revivification.

The science of life; Physiology, the animal economy.

V. To be living, alive, &c., to

(358) INORGANIZATION, the mineral world or kingdom, unorganized, inorganic, brute or inanimate matter.

The science of the mineral kingdom; Mineralogy, Geognosy, Geology, Metallurgy, &c.

(360) DEATH, decease, dissolution, demise, departure, *obit*, expiration, termination, close or extinction of life, existence, &c., sideration, mortality, fall, doom, fate, release, rest, *quietus*, loss.

Last breath, last gasp, last agonies,

* The term *Natural History* is also used as relating to all the objects in Nature, whether organic or inorganic, and including therefore *Mineralogy*, *Geology*, and *Meteorology*.
† Including the life both of *plants* and *animals.*

live, breathe, fetch breath, respire, draw breath, to be born, to see the light, to come into the world.

To bring, restore, or recall to life, to vivify, revive, revivify.

Phr. To keep life and soul together.

Adj. Living, alive, in life, above ground.

Vital, vivifying, vivified, Promethean.

the death rattle, dying breath, agonies of death.

Phr. The ebb of life, the jaws of death, *Le chant du cygne.*

V. To die, expire, breathe one's last, cease to live, depart this life, be no more, go off, drop off, pop off, lose one's life, drop down dead, resign, relinquish, or surrender one's life, drop or sink into the grave, close one's eyes, break one's neck.

Phr. To give up the ghost; — To pay the debt to nature; — To take one's last sleep; — To shuffle off this mortal coil; — To go the way of all flesh; — To kick the bucket; — To hop the twig; — To cross the Stygian ferry; — To go to the wall; — To go off like the snuff of a candle; — To be numbered with the dead; — To make one's will.

Adj. Dead, lifeless, deceased, demised, gone, departed, defunct, exanimate, inanimate, out of the world, mortuary.

Dying, expiring, moribund, morient, *in articulo, in extremis,* in the agony of death, &c., going, life-ebbing, going off, life failing, *aux abois.*

Phr. Dead as a door-nail; — Dead as mutton; — as a door-post; as a herring; — as nits; — Launched into eternity; — Gathered to one's fathers; — Gone to Davy Jones's locker.

At death's door; — In the jaws of death; — Death staring one in the face; — One's days being numbered; — One foot in the grave; — On one's last legs; — Life hanging by a thread.

Adv. Post mortem, post obit.

(361) Destruction of life.

KILLING, homicide, murder, assassination, blood, bloodshed, slaughter, carnage, butchery, massacre, fusillade, Thuggism, Aceldama.

Suicide, *felo de se,* execution, *see* (972).

Destruction of animals, slaughtering, &c., Phthisozoics.*

Slaughter-house, shambles, *abattoir.*

A butcher, slayer, murderer, assassin, cutthroat, bravo, Thug, Moloch, executioner, *see* (975).

V. To kill, put to death, slay, murder, assassinate, slaughter, butcher, immolate, massacre, take away life, make away with, dispatch, burk.

To strangle, throttle, choak, stifle, suffocate, smother, asphyxiate, drown, hang, turn off.

To cut down, sabre, put to the sword, put to the edge of the sword, cut to pieces, cut off, cut the throat, run through the body, stab, shoot, blow the brains out, behead, decapitate, execute (972), to commit suicide, give the *coup de grâce.*

Adj. Killing, &c., murderous, slaughterous, bloodstained.

Mortal, fatal, deadly, lethal, internecine, mortiferous, suicidal.

(362) CORPSE, corse, carcass, bones, skeleton, carrion, defunct, relic, remains, ashes, earth, clay, mummy, food for worms.

Shade, ghost, *manes.*

* Bentham, Chrestomathia.

(363) INTERMENT, burial, sepulture, inhumation, obsequies, exequies, funeral, wake, pyre, funeral pile, cremation, obit, catafalque, *memento mori*, epitaph, *hic jacet.*

Knell, passing bell, tolling, dirge, requiem, epicedium.

A shroud, grave clothes, winding-sheet, pall, cerement, hearse, urn, coffin, bier.

Grave, pit, vault, sepulchre, sarcophagus, tomb, shrine, crypt, cenotaph, mausoleum, house of death, mortuary, cemetery, churchyard, grave-yard, burial-ground, burial-place, cromlech, barrow, tumulus, cairn, catacomb, ossuary, charnel-house, *la morgue.*

Exhumation, disinterment.

V. To inter, bury, lay in the grave, consign to the grave or tomb, entomb, intomb, inhume, lay out.

Phr. To be put to bed with a shovel.

To exhume, disinter.

Adj. Buried, &c., funereal, funebrial, mortuary, sepulchral.

2. *Special Vitality.*

(364) ANIMALITY, animal life, animation, breath, animalization.

(365) VEGETABILITY, vegetable life, vegetation.

(366) ANIMAL, the animal kingdom.

A beast, brute, creature; creeping or living thing; dumb creature; the beasts of the field; fowls of the air; denizens of the deep; flock, herd, flight.

Mammal, quadruped, bird, reptile, fish, mollusk, worm, insect, zoophyte, animalcule, &c., menagery, fossil remains.

Adj. Animal, zoological, piscatory, molluscous, vermicular, &c.

(367) PLANT, vegetable, the vegetable kingdom, fauna, herb, grass, creeper, shrub, bush.

Clump of trees, grove, glade, brake, thicket, underwood, copse, brushwood, jungle, weald, chase, frith, holt, hurst, park.

Tree, wood, forest, *parterre*, plantation, *arboretum*, foliage, &c.

Hortus siccus, herbarium, herbal.

Adj. Vegetable, vegetous, herbaceous, herbal, botanic, sylvan, woody, rural, verdant.

(368) The science of animals;

ZOOLOGY, Zoography, Anatomy, Zootomy, Comparative Anatomy, Animal or Comparative Physiology.

Oryctology, Palæontology.

(369) The science of plants;

BOTANY, Phytography, Phytology, Vegetable Physiology.

(370) The economy or management of animals.

CICURATION, Zohygiastics.*

(371) The economy or management of plants;

AGRICULTURE, cultivation, husbandry, Geoponics, georgics, tillage, gardening, horticulture, vintage, &c., arboriculture.

Vineyard, garden, nursery, *arboretum.*

A husbandman, horticulturalist, gardener, florist, agriculturalist, agricultor, farmer.

Adj. Agricultural, agrarian, arable, pastoral, bucolic.

* Bentham.

83

(372) MANKIND; the human race or species; man, human nature, humanity, mortality, flesh, generation.

The science of man; Anthropology, Ethnology, Ethnography, Anthropography.

People, persons, folk, population, public, world, community, nation, state, realm, commonwealth, republic, commonweal, nationality.

Phr. The lords of the creation.

Adj. National, civic, public.

(373) MAN, manhood, virility.

A human being, man, mortal, person, body, soul, individual, fellow creature, one, some one, somebody.

Personage, wight, swain, fellow, blade, chap, gaffer, sir, master, yeoman, citizen, denizen, burgess, cosmopolite.

Adj. Human, manly, virile, mortal, personal, individual, cosmopolitan.

(374) WOMAN, female, feminality, womanhood, muliebrity.

Womankind, the sex, the fair, the fair sex, the softer sex, the weaker vessel.

Dame, madam, *madame*, mistress, lady, *donna*, belle, matron, dowager, goody.

Damsel, girl, maid, maiden, *demoiselle*, nymph, wench.

Adj. Female, feminine, womanly, ladylike, matronly, maidenly, girlish.

2°. SENSATION.

(1.) *Sensation in general.*

(375) PHYSICAL SENSIBILITY, sensitiveness, feeling, perceptivity, æsthetics, acuteness, &c.

Sensation, impression, consciousness (490).

The external senses, sensation.

V. To be sensible of, to feel, perceive.

To render sensible, to sharpen.

To cause sensation, to impress, excite.

Adj. Sensible, conscious, sensitive, sensuous, æsthetic, perceptive.

Acute, keen, vivid, lively, impressive.

(376) PHYSICAL INSENSIBILITY, obtuseness, dulness, apathy, callousness (823), paralysis.

V. To be insensible, &c.

To render insensible, to blunt, dull, obtund, benumb, paralyze.

Adj. Insensible, unfeeling, senseless, impercipient, apathetic, obtuse, dull, anæsthetic, paralytic, &c., unaffected, untouched, &c.

(377) PHYSICAL PLEASURE, bodily enjoyment, gratification, luxury, voluptuousness.

A bed of roses, a bed of down, velvet, clover, *see* (827).

V. To feel, experience, receive, &c. pleasure, to enjoy, relish, luxuriate, revel, riot, bask.

To cause or give physical pleasure, to gratify, tickle, regale, &c., *see* (829).

(378) PHYSICAL PAIN, bodily pain, suffering, sufferance, dolour, ache, aching, smart, smarting, shoot, shooting, twinge, twitch, gripe, griping, headache, &c.

Spasm, cramp, night-mare, crick, *ephialtes,* convulsion, throe.

Pang, anguish, agony, torment, torture, rack, cruciation, crucifixion, martyrdom.

V. To feel, experience, suffer,

Adj. Enjoying, &c.

&c. pain; to suffer, ache, smart, bleed, tingle, gripe, shoot, twinge, lancinate, wince, writhe, twitch.

Phr. To sit on thorns; to sit on pins and needles.

To give pain; to pain, hurt, chafe, sting, bite, gnaw, pinch, grate, gall, fret, prick, pierce, &c., wring, torment, torture, rack, agonize, cruciate, break on the wheel, &c., convulse.

Adj. In pain, in a state of pain, &c., pained, &c.

Painful, aching, &c., sore, raw, agonizing, excruciating, &c.

(2.) *Special Sensation.*

1. *Touch.*

(379) Sensation of pressure.

Touch, tact, taction, tactility, feeling, palpation, manipulation, palpability.

V. To touch, feel, handle, finger, thumb, paw, fumble, grope, grabble; pass, or run the fingers over, manipulate.

Adj. Tactual, tangible, palpable, tactile.

(380) PERCEPTIONS OF TOUCH.

Itching, titillation, formication, &c., creeping, *aura*, tingling, thrilling.

V. To itch, tingle, creep, thrill; to tickle, titillate.

Adj. Itching, &c.

(381) Insensibility to touch.

NUMBNESS, deadness, *anæsthesia*.

V. To benumb, paralyze.

Adj. Numb, benumbed, intangible, impalpable.

2. *Heat.*

(382) HEAT, temperature, warmth, calidity, incalescence, glow, flush, fever, hectic.

Fire, spark, scintillation, flash, flame, blaze, firework, wildfire, pyrotechny, ignition (384).

Insolation, summer, dog-days, tropical or Bengal heat, sirocco, simoom.

V. To be hot, to glow, flush, sweat, swelter, bask, smoke, reek, stew, simmer, seethe, boil, burn, broil, blaze, smoulder; to be in a heat, in a glow, in a fever, in a blaze, &c.

Adj. Hot, warm, mild, unfrozen, genial, tepid, lukewarm, blood-hot, thermal, calorific, sunny, close, sultry, baking, boiling, broiling, torrid, tropical, canicular, glowing, piping, scalding, reeking, &c., on fire, afire, fervid, fervent, ardent, unquenched.

Phr. Hot as fire; warm as a toast; warm as wool.

(383) COLD, frigidity, coolness, gelidness, chilness, freshness, inclemency, *fresco*.

Frost, ice, snow, sleet, hail, hailstone, rime, hoar-frost, icicle, iceberg, glacier, winter, incombustibility.

Sensation of cold, chilliness, shivering, shuddering, goose-skin, horripilation, chattering of teeth, &c.

V. To be cold, &c., to shiver, quake, shake, tremble, shudder, didder, quiver.

Adj. Cold, cool, chill, gelid, frigid, bleak, raw, inclement, bitter, biting, cutting, nipping, piercing, clay-cold, fresh, algid, pinched, starved, shivering, &c., aguish, *transi de froid*, unthawed, unwarmed, incombustible.

Phr. Cold as a stone; cold as marble; cold as a frog; cold as charity; cold as Christmas; cool as a cucumber; cool as a custard.

85

Igneous, fiery, incandescent, red-hot, white-hot, incalescent, smoking, blazing, unextinguished, smouldering.

(384) CALEFACTION, increase of temperature, heating.

Melting, fusion, liquefaction, thaw, liquescence, liquation, estuation, incandescence.

Burning, ambustion, combustion, incension, accension, cremation, cautery, roasting, broiling, frying, torrefaction, scorification, branding, incineration, cineration.

Boiling, coction, ebullition, simmering, scalding, elixation, decoction, smelting, incineration.

Ignition, inflammation, setting fire to, adustion, flagration, deflagration, arson, conflagration, *auto da fé.*

Inflammability, combustibility.

Transmission of heat, Diathermancy, transcalency.

V. To heat, warm, chafe, stive, fire, set fire to, set on fire, kindle, enkindle, light, apply the match to, ignite.

Phr. To stir the fire, blow the fire, fan the flame.

To melt, thaw, fuse, liquefy.

To burn, inflame, roast, toast, broil, fry, grill, singe, parch, scorch, brand, scorify, torrify, bake, cauterize, sear, char, calcine, incinerate, smelt, reduce to ashes.

To boil, stew, cook, seethe, scald, parboil, simmer.

To take fire, catch fire.

Adj. Combustible, heating, &c.

Icy, glacial, frosty, freezing, wintry, brumal, hibernal, boreal, arctic, hyemal, hyperboreal, icebound.

Adv. Al fresco, à pierre fendre.

(385) REFRIGERATION, infrigidation, reduction of temperature, cooling, freezing, congealing, congelation, conglaciation.

V. To cool, refrigerate, congeal, freeze, glaciate, benumb, refresh, damp, slack, quench, put out, blow out, extinguish, starve, pinch, pierce, cut.

Adj. Cooled, frozen, benumbed, &c.

(386) FURNACE, stove, kiln, oven, bake-house, hot-house, conservatory, focus, fireplace, grate, reverberatory, athanor, fiery furnace, brasier, salamander, warming-pan, stew-pan, boiler, caldron, kettle, chafing-dish, gridiron, frying-pan, sudatory.

(387) REFRIGERATORY, ice-house, freezing mixture, cooler.

(388) FUEL, firing, coal, coke, charcoal, peat, combustible, tinder, touchwood, lucifer, ingle, brand, match, embers, faggot, firebrand, incendiary, port-fire.

(389) THERMOMETER, pyrometer, calorimeter, thermoscope.

3. *Taste.*

(390) TASTE, flavour, gust, *gusto,* savour, sapor, twang, smack, after-taste, smatch, sapidity.

Tasting, gustation, degustation.

Palate, tongue, tooth, stomach.

V. To taste, savour, smack, smatch, flavour, twang, smack the lips.

Adj. Sapid, gustable, gustatory, saporific.

(391) INSIPIDITY, tastelessness, insipidness, vapidness, mawkishness, mildness.

V. To be void of taste, tasteless, &c.

Adj. Insipid, tasteless, gustless, savourless, mawkish, flat, vapid, *fade,* wish-wash, mild, untasted.

(392) PUNGENCY, *haut-goût*, strong taste, twang, raciness, race, saltness, sharpness, roughness; caviar.

V. To be pungent, &c.

To render pungent, to season, spice, salt, pepper, pickle, devil.

Adj. Pungent, high-flavoured, *haut-goût*, sharp, piquant, racy, biting, mordant, spicy, seasoned, hot, peppery, vellicating, escharotic, high-seasoned, salt, saline, brackish.

Phr. Salt as brine; salt as a herring; salt as Lot's wife; hot as pepper.

(393) CONDIMENT, salt, mustard, pepper, cayenne, curry, seasoning, spice.

(394) SAVORINESS, palatableness, daintiness, delicacy, relish, zest.

A tit-bit, dainty, delicacy, ambrosia, nectar, *bonne-bouche.*

V. To be savoury, &c.

To render palatable, &c.

To relish, like, smack the lips.

Adj. Savoury, well-tasted, palatable, nice, dainty, delectable, toothsome, gustful, delicate, delicious, exquisite, rich, luscious, ambrosial.

(395) UNSAVORINESS, unpalatableness, bitterness, amaritude, acrimony, acritude, roughness, acerbity, austerity, gall and wormwood.

V. To be unpalatable, &c.

To sicken, disgust, nauseate, pall.

Adj. Unsavoury, unpalatable, ill-flavoured, bitter, acrid, acrimonious, unsweet, rough, austere, offensive, nasty, fulsome, sickening, nauseous, nauseating, disgusting, loathsome, palling.

Phr. Bitter as gall.

(396) SWEETNESS, sugar, syrup, treacle, molasses, honey, manna, confection, conserve, jam, julep, sugar-candy, plum, sugar plum, lollypop, *bon-bon*, comfit, sweetmeat, nectar, hydromel, honeysuckle.

Dulcification, dulcoration.

V. To be sweet, &c.

To render sweet, to sweeten, edulcorate, candy, dulcorate, dulcify.

Adj. Sweet, saccharine, sacchariferous, dulcet, candied, honied, lush, edulcorated, nectarious.

Phr. Sweet as a nut.

(397) SOURNESS, acid, acidity, tartness, crabbedness, hardness, roughness, the acetous fermentation.

Vinegar, verjuice, crab.

V. To be sour, &c., set the teeth on edge.

To render sour, turn sour, acidify, acidulate.

Adj. Sour, acid, acidulous, sourish, subacid, tart, crabbed, acetous, acetose, styptic, hard, rough.

Phr. Sour as vinegar.

4. *Odour.*

(398) ODOUR, smell, odorament, scent, effluvium, emanation, fume, exhalation, essence; trail, nidor.

The sense of smell, act of smelling.

V. To have an odour, to smell of, to exhale, to give out a smell, &c.

To smell, scent, snuff, sniff, nose.

Adj. Odorous, odoriferous, smelling, strong-scented, quick-scented, graveolent.

Relating to the sense of smell; olfactory.

(399) INODOROUSNESS, absence or want of smell.

V. To be inodorous, &c.

Adj. Inodorous, scentless, wanting smell, inodorate.

(400) FRAGRANCE, aroma, redolence, perfume, *bouquet.*

(401) FŒTOR, strong smell, *empyreuma*, stench, stink, mustiness,

Incense, musk, frankincense, ottar, balm, *pot-pourri*, pulvil, scent-bag, sachet, nosegay.

V. To perfume, embalm.

Adj. Fragrant, aromatic, redolent, balmy, scented, sweet smelling, sweet scented, perfumed, muscadine.

fustiness, rancidity, foulness, putrescence, putridity.

A pole-cat, skunk.

V. To smell, to stink.

Adj. Fœtid, strong-smelling, noisome, offensive, rank, rancid, reasty, mouldy, fusty, musty, foul, frouzy, olid, olidous, nidorous, fulsome, stinking, rotten, putrescent, putrid, putrefying, mephitic, empyreumatic.

5. *Sound.*

(1) SOUND IN GENERAL.

(402) SOUND, noise, strain, voice (580), accent, twang, intonation, resonance; sonorousness, audibleness.

Science of Sound; Acoustics (or Acustics), Phonics, Phonetics, Phonology.

V. To produce sound; to sound, make a noise, give out or emit sound.

Adj. Sonorous, sounding, sonorific, sonoriferous, resonant, audible.

(403) SILENCE, stillness, quiet, peace, calm, hush, lull; muteness (581).

V. To be silent, &c., to keep silence, to hold one's tongue, to hold one's peace.

To render silent, to silence, still, hush, stifle, muffle, muzzle.

Adj. Silent, still, noiseless, soundless, inaudible, hushed, &c., mute, mum, solemn, awful, deathlike.

Phr. Still as a mouse; deathlike silence.

Adv. Silently, softly, &c., *sub silentio.*

Int. Hush! silence! soft! mum! whist! tush! chut! tut!

(404) LOUDNESS, din, clangour, clang, roar, uproar, racket, hubbub, flourish of trumpets, *fanfare,* larum, *tintamare,* blast, echo, *fracas,* hullaballoo, chorus, clamour, hue and cry, whoop, *charivari,* vociferation, lungs, stentor.

Artillery, cannon, thunder.

V. To be loud, &c., to resound, echo, re-echo, peal, clang, boom, thunder, fulminate, roar, hoop, shout, *s'égosiller* (411), din in the ear, deafen, stun, pierce, split or rend the ears, or head.

Phr. To shout, or thunder at the pitch of one's breath, or at the top of one's voice; *faire le diable à quatre.*

Adj. Loud, resounding, &c., high-sounding, deep, full, clamorous, vo-

(405) FAINTNESS, lowness, faint sounds, whisper, undertone, breath, under breath, murmur, mutter, hum.

Hoarseness, huskiness, raucity.

V. To whisper, breathe, murmur, purl, hum, gurgle, ripple, babble, flow, steal on the ear, melt, float on the air.

Adj. Inaudible, scarcely audible, low, dull, stifled, muffled, hoarse, husky, gentle, breathed, &c., soft, floating, purling, &c., liquid, mellifluous, dulcet, flowing, soothing.

Adv. In a whisper, with bated breath, *sotto voce,* between the teeth, aside, *piano, pianissimo, à la sourdine.*

ciferous, stunning, piercing, splitting, rending, deafening, ear-deafening, ear-piercing, obstreperous, deep-mouthed, open-mouthed, trumpet-tongued, uproarious, stentorian, stentorophonic; in full cry.

Phr. Enough to split the head or ears.
Adv. Loudly, aloud, &c.
Phr. At the top of one's voice.

(2) Specific Sounds.

(406) Sudden and violent sounds.
Snap, knock, click, clash, slam, crack, crackling, crepitation, decrepitation, report, pop, bang, clap, burst, explosion, discharge, crash, detonation, firing, salvo.
Squib, cracker, gun, pop-gun.
V. To snap, knock, &c., brustle.
Adj. Snapping, &c.

(407) Repeated and protracted sounds.
Roll, rumble, rumbling, hum, humming, shake, trill, chime, tick, beat, toll, ticking, tattoo, ding-dong, drumming, rat-a-tat, quaver, cuckoo, clatter, clutter, rattle, racket, rub-a-dub.
V. To roll, beat, tick, toll, drum, &c., drum, or din in the ear.
Adj. Rolling, rumbling, &c.

(408) Resonance, ring, ringing, jingle (or gingle), chink, tinkle, tink, guggle, chime.
Reflection, reverberation, echo.
V. To resound, ring, jingle, clink, &c.
Adj. Resounding, resonant, tinnient, ringing, &c.
Base, low, bass, flat or grave note, deep-toned, hollow, sepulchral.

(409) Hissing sounds.
Sibilation, hiss, buzz, whiz, rustle, fizz, fizzle, wheeze, whistle, snuffle, sneeze, squash, sternutation.
V. To hiss, buzz, &c.
Adj. Sibilant, hissing, buzzing, &c.
High notes, *see* (410).

(410) Harsh sounds.
Stridor, jar, grating, creak, clank, twang, jangle, jarring, creaking, rustling, roughness, gruffness, sharpness.
High note, shrillness, acuteness, soprano, falsetto, treble, penny trumpet, *voce di testa.*
V. To creak, grate, jar, pipe, twang, jangle, rustle, clank, set the teeth on edge, *écorcher les oreilles.*
Adj. Stridulous, jarring, &c., harsh, hoarse, discordant, scrannel (414), cacophonous, rough, gruff, sepulchral.
Sharp, high, acute, shrill, piping, screaming.

(411) Human sounds, *see* Voice (580).
Cry, vociferation, outcry, roar, shout, bawl, brawl, halloo, hullaballoo, hoop, whoop, yell, cheer, hoot, howl, chorus, scream, screech, screak, shriek, squeak, squall, whine, pule, pipe, grumble, plaint, groan, snore, snort.
V. To vociferate, roar, shout, bawl, &c., raise or lift up the voice.
Adj. Vociferating, &c.

(412) Animal sounds.
Ululation, latration, cry, roar, bellow, reboation, bark, yelp, howl, bay, baying, yap, growl, grunt, gruntle, snort, neigh, bray, croak, snarl, howl, mew, mewl, purr, pule, bleat, low, caw (or kaw), coo, cackle, gobble, quack, gaggle, squeak, chuckle, chuck, cluck, clack, chirp, chirrup, crow, woodnote, twitter, caterwalling.
Insect cry, fritancy, drone.
Cuckoo, screech-owl.
V. To cry, bellow, rebellow, &c.
Phr. To bay the moon.
Adj. Crying, &c., blatant, remugient.

(3) MUSICAL SOUND.

(413) HARMONY, rhythm, melody, unison, unisonance, concord, concent, consonance, chime; harmonics.

Pitch, note, tone, *timbre*, treble, tenor, bass: high or low, acute or grave notes, *contralto*, soprano, baritone, *falsetto*.

Scale, interval, gamut, diatonic, chromatic and enharmonic scales; key (or clef), chords; modulation, temperament, *solfeggio*, syncopation.

Staff (or stave), lines, spaces, brace; bar, rest, appogiatura.

Notes of a scale; sharps, flats, naturals; breve, semibreve, minim, crotchet, quaver, semiquaver, demi-semiquaver, &c.

(414) DISCORD, discordance, dissonance, jar, jarring, cacophony.

Hoarseness, croaking, &c. (410).

Confused sounds; Babel, Dutch concert, marrow-bones and cleavers.

V. To be discordant, &c., to croak, jar.

Adj. Discordant, dissonant, out of tune, tuneless, absonant, unmusical, unharmonious, inharmonious, immelodious.

Cacophonous, harsh, hoarse, croaking, jarring, stridulous, &c. (410).

Tonic, supertonic, mediant, subdominant, dominant, submediant, octave, tetrachord, major and minor modes, &c., passage, &c.

Science of harmony; harmonics, thorough-bass, fundamental bass, counterpoint.

V. To harmonize, chime, symphonize.

Adj. Harmonious, harmonical, in concord, in unison, in tune, in concert, in harmony, unisonant, concentual, symphonizing.

Measured, rhythmical, diatonic, chromatic, enharmonic.

Melodious, musical, tuneful, tuneable, sweet, dulcet, mellow, mellifluous, silver-toned, euphonious, euphonic, euphonical, symphonious; enchanting, ravishing, &c.

(415) MUSIC, tune, air, aria, arietta, sonata, *rondo*, *pastorale*, fantasia, *concerto*, overture, symphony, accompaniment, *recititavo*, variations; fugue, march, pibroch, *minuetto*, *gavotta*, waltz, &c., serenade, jig, dithramb, opera, oratorio, &c.

Instrumental music, solo, duet, trio, quartet, &c.; full score, minstrelsy, band, orchestra.

Vocal music, chant (or chaunt), psalmody, psalm, hymn, song, sonnet, canticle, canzonet, *cantata*, *bravura*, lay, ballad, ditty, pastoral, recitative:— Solo, duet, trio, &c.; glee, catch, canon, madrigal, choir (or quire), chorus, antiphon.

Dirge, requiem, lullaby, knell, lament, coronach.

Performance, execution, touch, expression, roulade, cadence.

Composition, score:— Muses; Erato, Euterpe, Terpsichore, Apollo.

V. To play, pipe, fiddle, strike, strike up, thrum, strum, grind, touch, sound the trumpet, &c., execute, perform.

To compose, to set to music.

To sing, chaunt (or chant), hum, warble, carol, chirp, chirrup, purl, quaver, trill, shake, twitter, whistle.

To put in tune, to tune, attune.

Adj. Musical, harmonious, &c. (413), instrumental, vocal, choral, operatic, performing, playing, singing, &c.

Adv. Adagio, largo, *andante*, *andantino*, *larghetto*, *maestoso*, *moderato*, *allegretto, spirituoso, vivace, veloce, allegro, presto, prestissimo;* — *scherzo, scherzando, legato, staccato, crescendo, diminuendo, rallentando,* &c.

(416) MUSICIAN, performer, player, minstrel.

Organist, pianist, harper, violinist, fiddler, flutist, fifer, trumpeter, piper, drummer, &c.; band, orchestra, waits.

Vocalist, singer, songster, songstress, chaunter, chauntress, *cantatrice, improvisatore,* troubadour, minne-singer.

Chorus, choir, quire.

(417) MUSICAL INSTRUMENTS.

1. Stringed instruments; Monochord, polychord, harp, lyre, lute, mandolin, guitar, gittern, cithern, rebec, *bandurria,* &c.

Violin, fiddle, kit, *viola* (or tenor), cremona, violoncello, viol-d'amor, base-viol (or bass-viol), bassetto, doublebass, violone, psaltery, &c.

Pianoforte, harpsichord, *clavier,* clavichord, spinet, virginal, dulcimer, hurdy-gurdy (or *vielle*), Eolian harp, &c.

2. Wind instruments; Organ, syren, pipe, pitch-pipe, Pandean pipes, flute, fife, piccolo, clarionet, cornet, *cornet à piston,* clarion, flageolet, oboe (or hautboy), bassoon, serpent, horn, French-horn, basset-horn, bugle, trumpet, trombone, ophicleide, accordion, seraphina, concertina, bagpipe, whistle, humming-top, &c.

3. Vibrating surfaces: Cymbal, bell, gong, tabor, tambourine, drum, kettle-drum, (or tymbal), timbrel; castanet, musical glasses, musical stones, harmonica, sounding-board, &c.

4. Vibrating bars; reeds, tuning-fork, triangle, Jew's harp, musical boxes, &c.

(4) PERCEPTION OF SOUND.

(418) Sense of sound.

HEARING, audition, auscultation, listening, eavesdropping.

Acuteness, nicety, delicacy of ear.

Ear, acustic organs, auditory apparatus, ear-drum, tympanum.

A hearer, auditor, listener, eavesdropper, auditory, audience.

V. To hear, overhear, hark, listen, list, harken, give or lend an ear, prick up one's ears, give a hearing or audience to.

Phr. To hang upon the lips of.

To become audible, to catch the ear, to be heard.

Adj. Hearing, &c., auditory, auricular.

Int. Hark! list! hear! listen!

Adv. Arrectis auribus.

(419) DEAFNESS, hardness of hearing, surdity.

V. To be deaf, to shut, stop, or close one's ears.

To render deaf, to stun, to deafen.

Phr. To turn a deaf ear to.

Adj. Deaf, hard of hearing, earless, surd, dull of hearing, deaf-mute, stunned, deafened, having no ear.

Phr. Deaf as a post; — Deaf as a beetle; — Deaf as a trunkmaker.

6. *Light.*

(1) LIGHT IN GENERAL.

(420) LIGHT, ray, beam, stream, gleam, streak, pencil, sun-beam.

Day, daylight, sunshine, sunlight, the light of day, the light of heaven,

(421) DARKNESS, night, midnight, obscurity, dusk, duskiness, gloom, gloominess, shade, umbrage, shadiness, penumbra, Erebus.

noontide, noonday, noontide light, broad daylight.

Glimmer, glimmering, phosphorescence, lambent flame, play of light, flush, halo, glory.

Meteor, Northern lights, *aurora borealis*, fire-drake, *ignis fatuus*, jack-o'-lantern, Will-o'-the-wisp.

Spark, *scintilla*, sparkling, emication, scintillation, flame, flash, blaze, coruscation, fulguration, lightning, flood of light.

Lustre, shine, sheen, gloss, tinsel, spangle, brightness, brilliancy, refulgence, dazzlement, resplendence, luminousness, luminosity, lucidity, lucidness, nitency, renitency, radiance, transplendency, illumination, irradiation, glare, flare, glow, effulgence.

Science of light; Optics, Photology, Photometry.

V. To shine, glow, glitter, glisten, glister, twinkle, gleam, flare, glare, beam, irradiate, shoot beams, shimmer, sparkle, scintillate, coruscate, flash, blaze, fizzle, dazzle, bedazzle, hang out a light.

To illuminate, illume, illumine, lighten, enlighten, light, light up, irradiate, shine upon, cast lustre upon, cast, throw, or shed a light upon, brighten, clear.

Adj. Luminous, shining, glowing, &c., lambent, sheen, glossy, lucid, lucent, luculent, lustrous, lucific, glassy, clear, bright, scintillant, lightsome, unclouded, sunny, orient, noonday, noontide, beaming, beamy, vivid, splendent, radiant, radiating, cloudless, clear, unobscured.

Gairish (or garish), resplendent, transplendent, refulgent, fulgent, effulgent, in a blaze, relucent, splenid, blazing, ratilant, meteoric, burnished.

Phr. Bright as silver, as day, as noonday.

(423) Source of light, self-luminous body.

LUMINARY, sun, star, orb, meteor, galaxy, glow-worm, fire-fly.

Artificial light, flame, torch, candle, flambeau, link, light, taper, lamp, lantern (or lanthorn), rushlight, far-
92

Obscuration, adumbration, obumbration, obtenebration, offuscation, caligation, extinction, eclipse, gathering of the clouds, dimness (422).

V. To be dark, &c.

To darken, obscure, shade, dim, bedarken, overcast, overshadow, offuscate, obfuscate, obumbrade, adumbrate, cast in the shade, becloud, bedim, put out, extinguish.

To cast, throw, spread a shade or gloom.

Adj. Dark, unenlightened, obscure, darksome, tenebrious, rayless, beamless, sunless, lightless, pitch dark, pitchy, caliginous, stygian, Cimmerian.

Sombre, dusky, unilluminated, nocturnal, dingy, lurid, overcast, cloudy, murky, murksome, shady, umbrageous.

Phr. Dark as pitch, dark as Erebus, darkness visible, the palpable obscure.

(422) DIMNESS, paleness, glimmer, glimmering, owl's light, nebulousness, nebulosity, nebule, cloud, film, mist, haze, fog, smoke, haziness, eclipse, cloudiness, dawn, twilight, crepuscule, *demi-jour*.

V. To be dim, &c., to glimmer, loom, lower.

To grow dim, to pale, to render dim, to dim, obscure, pale.

Adj. Dim, dull, lack lustre, dingy, glassy, faint, confused, shorn of its beams.

Cloudy, misty, hazy, foggy, muggy, nebulous, lowering, overcast, crepuscular, muddy, lurid, looming.

(424) SHADE, screen, curtain, veil, mask, gauze, blind.

A shadow, *chiaro-scuro*.

Adj. Umbrageous, &c.

thing rushlight, fire-work, rocket, blue lights, fizgig, bude light, electric light.

Chandelier, candelabra, girandole, lustre, sconce.

Light-house, beacon, watch-fire.

(425) TRANSPARENCY, pellucidity, diaphaneity, lucidity, limpidity.

Glass, crystal, lymph.

V. To be transparent, &c., to transmit light.

Adj. Transparent, pellucid, diaphanous, translucent, tralucent, relucent, limpid, clear, crystalline, vitreous, transpicuous, glassy, hyaline.

Phr. Clear as crystal.

(426) OPACITY, thickness, opaqueness, turbidness, muddiness, cloud, film, haze.

V. To be opaque, &c., not to transmit, to obstruct the passage of light.

Adj. Opaque, turbid, thick, muddy, opacous, obfuscated, fuliginous, cloudy, hazy, misty, foggy.

(427) SEMITRANSPARENCY, opalescence, gauze, milkiness.

Adj. Semitransparent, opalescent, semipellucid, semidiaphanous, semiopacous, pearly, milky.

(2) SPECIFIC LIGHT.

(428) COLOUR, hue, tint, tinge, dye, complexion, shade, spectrum, tincture, cast, livery, coloration.

Science of colour, Chromatics.

A pigment, colouring matter, paint, dye, wash, stain, mordant.

V. To colour, dye, tinge, stain, tinct, paint, wash, illuminate, emblazon, bedizen, imbue.

Adj. Coloured, colorific, chromatic, prismatic, full coloured, lush, tingent.

Bright, florid, fresh, high coloured, unfaded, gay, showy, gaudy, gairish (or garish), flaunting, vivid, gorgeous, glaring, flaring, flashy.

(429) Absence of colour.

ACHROMATISM, decoloration, discoloration, paleness, pallidity, pallidness, etiolation.

A spot, blot, &c. (846).

V. To lose colour, to fade, fly, become colourless.

To deprive of colour, discolour, bleach, tarnish, achromatize.

Adj. Colourless, uncoloured, untinged, achromatic, aplanatic, hueless, undyed, pale, pallid, faint, faded, dull, wan, sallow, dead, dingy, ashy, cadaverous, glassy, lack-lustre, tarnished, bleached, discoloured.

Phr. Pale as death ; pale as ashes ; pale as a witch.

(430) WHITENESS, milkiness, hoariness.

Albification, etiolation.

Snow, paper, milk, lily, sheet, ivory, silver, alabaster.

V. To be white, &c.

To render white, whiten, bleach, whitewash, blanch, etiolate.

Adj. White, milk-white, snow-white, cream-coloured, hoary, hoar, silvery, argent, pearly, fair, blonde, etiolated.

Phr. White as the driven snow.

(431) BLACKNESS, swarthiness, swarthness, dinginess, lividity, inkiness, pitchiness.

Nigrification, infuscation.

Jet, ink, ebony, coal, pitch, charcoal, soot, sloe, smut, raven, negro, blackamoor.

V. To be black, &c.

To render black, to blacken, infuscate, denigrate, blot, blotch.

Adj. Black, sable, swarthy, sombre, inky, ebon, atramentous, livid, coal-black, fuliginous, dingy, Ethiopic, nocturnal, nigrescent.

Phr. Black as my hat ;—black as

a shoe;—Black as November;—Black as thunder.

(432) GRAY, dun, drab, dingy, sombre, tawny, mouse-coloured, ash, cinereous, cineritious, slate, stone, grizzly, grizzled.

(433) BROWN, bay, dapple, auburn, chesnut, nutbrown, fawn, russet, olive, hazle, tawny, fuscous, chocolate, liver-coloured, brinded, brindled, brunette, sallow.

Phr. Brown as a berry;—Brown as mahogany.

V. To render brown, to tan, &c.

Adj. Brown, &c.

Primitive Colours.

(434) REDNESS, scarlet, vermilion, crimson, pink, carnation, damask, ruby, rose, rubescence, rosiness, ruddiness, rubicundity, blush, colour, peach colour, flesh colour, gules, lobster.

Erubescence, rubification.

V. To become red, to blush, flush, mantle, redden, incarnadine.

To render red, redden, rouge, rubify.

Adj. Red, ruby, crimson, pink, &c., ruddy, florid, rosy, roseate, rose-coloured, blushing, mantling, &c., erubescent, blowsy, rubicund, stammel, blood-red, rubiform, murrey, carroty, sorrel.

Phr. Red as fire;—as blood;—as scarlet;—as a turkey-cock.

(435) GREENNESS, verdure, viridescence, emerald, jasper, verdantique, verdigris.

Adj. Green, verdant, pea-green, grass-green, apple-green, sea-green, olive-green, bottle-green, glaucous, virent, virescent.

Phr. Green as grass.

(436) YELLOWNESS, buff colour.

Adj. Yellow, citron, gold-coloured, aureate, flavous, citrine, fallow, fulvid, saffron, lemon, sulphur, amber, straw-coloured, sandy-coloured, lurid, Claude-tint.

Phr. Yellow as a quince;—Yellow as a guinea;—Yellow as a crow's foot.

(437) PURPLE, violet, plum, lavender, lilac, puce, gridelin, lividness, lividity.

(438) BLUENESS, bluishness, azure, indigo, ultramarine, bloom.

Adj. Blue, cerulean, sky-blue, sky-coloured, sky-dyed, watchet, azure, bluish, sapphire.

(439) ORANGE, golden, flame, copper, brass, apricot colour.

(440) VARIEGATION, dichroism, trichroism, iridescence, play of colours, variegatedness, patch-work, maculation, spottiness, marquetry.

A rainbow, iris, tulip, peacock, chameleon, tortoiseshell, leopard, zebra, harlequin, mother-of-pearl.

V. To be variegated, &c.

To variegate, speckle, stripe, streak, chequer, bespeckle, inlay.

Adj. Variegated, many-coloured, versicolor, many-hued, divers-coloured, party-coloured, polychromatic, tricolor.

Iridescent, nacreous, pearly, shot, *chatoyant*, all manner of colours, pied, piebald, motley, mottled, veined, marbled, paned, dappled, clouded.

Mosaic, inlaid, tesselated, chequered, tortoiseshell.

Dotted, spotted, bespotted, spotty, speckled, bespeckled, maculated, freckled, fleckered, studded.

Striped, striated, streaked, barred, veined, brinded, brindled, tabby, grizzled, listed.

(3) PERCEPTIONS OF LIGHT.

(441) VISION, sight, optics, eyesight, view, look, espial, glance, glimpse, peep, gaze, stare, leer, perlustration, contemplation, regard, survey, introspection, inspection, speculation, watch, *coup d'œil, espionage*, bopeep, ocular demonstration, autopsy.

A point of view, gazebo, vista, *visto*, loop-hole, *belvedere*, field of view, theatre, amphitheatre, horizon, arena, commanding view, periscope.

The organ of vision, eye, the naked or unassisted eye, optics.

Perspicacity, lynx, eagle, Argus.

V. To see, behold, discern, have in sight, descry, catch a sight, glance, or glimpse of, spy, espy.

To look, view, eye, open one's eyes, glance on, cast or set one's eyes on, look on or upon, turn or bend one's looks upon, turn the eyes to, peep, peer, pry, scan, survey, reconnoitre, inspect, recognize, mark, discover, distinguish, see through, speculate, to see sights, lionize.

(442) BLINDNESS, cecity, excecation, *amaurosis*, ablepsy, prestriction, nictitation, wink, blink.

V. To be blind, &c., not to see, to lose sight of.

Not to look, to close or shut the eyes, to look another way, to turn away or avert the eyes, to wink, blink, nictitate.

To render blind, &c., to put out the eyes, to blind, blindfold, hoodwink, dazzle.

Phr. To throw dust into the eyes; —*jetter de la poudre aux yeux.*

Adj. Blind, purblind, eyeless, sightless, dark, stone-blind, sandblind, stark-blind, mope-eyed, dazzled, hoodwinked, blindfolded, undiscerning.

Phr. Blind as a bat;—as a buzzard;—as a beetle;—as a mole.

Adv. Blindly, &c., blindfold.

To watch, have an eye upon, keep in sight, contemplate, regard, look about one, glance round.

To look intently, strain one's eyes, look full in the face, stare, gaze, pore over, gloat on, leer, to see with half an eye, to blink, ogle.

Adj. Visual, ocular, optic, optical.

Seeing, &c., the eyes being directed to, fixed, rivetted upon.

Sharp-sighted, quick-sighted, eagle-eyed, hawk-eyed, lynx-eyed, keen-eyed, Argus-eyed, piercing, penetrating.

Adv. Visibly, &c., at sight, in sight of, to one's face, before one's face, with one's eyes open.

Int. Look! behold! see! lo! mark! observe! lo and behold!

(443) Imperfect vision.

DIMSIGHTEDNESS, lippitude, confusion of vision, scotomy, failing sight, shortsightedness, *myopia*, nictitation, longsightedness, *presbyopia*, squint, strabism, cast of the eye, Albino.

Fallacies of vision; *deceptio visus*, refraction, false light, phantasm, *anamorphosis*, distortion, looming, *mirage*, the *Fata Morgana*, the spectre of the Brocken, *ignis fatuus*, dissolving views, &c.

V. To be dimsighted, &c., to see double, to squint, look askant, to see through a prism, wink, nictitate.

Adj. Dimsighted, half-sighted, short-sighted, myopic, long-sighted, presbyopic, moon-eyed, mope-eyed, blear-eyed, goggle-eyed, nictitating, winking.

Phr. *Nimium ne crede colori ; — Fronti nulla fides.*

(444) SPECTATOR, looker-on, bystander, inspector, spy, beholder, stargazer, &c.

(445) OPTICAL INSTRUMENTS, lens, magnifier, microscope, megascope, spectacles, glasses, barnacles, goggles, eye-glass, periscopic, telescope, spyglass, glass, tienoscope.

Mirror, reflector, speculum, looking-glass, pier-glass, kaleidoscope.

Prism, polyscope, camera lucida, camera obscura, magic lantern, phantasmagoria, thaumatrope, stereoscope, pseudoscope.

Photometer, polariscope, polemoscope, eriometer.

(446) VISIBILITY, perceptibility, conspicuousness, distinctness, conspicuity, appearance.

V. To be visible, &c., to appear, come in sight, come into view, heave in sight, open to the view, catch the eye, show its face, present itself, show itself, manifest itself, produce itself, discover itself, expose itself, come out, come to light, come forth, come forward, arise, peep out, peer out, start up, loom, burst forth, break through the clouds, glare, reveal itself, betray itself.

Phr. To show its colours ; to tell its own tale ; *cela saute aux yeux;* to stare one in the face.

Adj. Visible, perceptible, discernible, in sight, apparent, plain, manifest, patent, obvious, clear, distinct, definite, well-defined, well-marked, recognizable, autoptical, evident, unmistakeable, palpable, naked, bare, barefaced, ostensible, conspicuous, prominent, staring, staring one in the face, glaring, notable, notorious, overt, above board, exposed to view, periscopic, under one's nose, there is no mistaking.

Phr. Open as day; clear as day; plain as a pikestaff; plain as the nose in one's face.

Intelligible, &c., *see* (518).

(447) INVISIBILITY, indistinctness, imperceptibility, non-appearance, dilitescence, concealment, latitency (526).

V. To be invisible, &c., to lie hidden, concealed, &c., to be in, or under a cloud, in a mist, in a haze, &c.; to lurk, lie in ambush, skulk.

Not to see, &c., to be blind to.

To render invisible, to hide, conceal, &c. (528).

Adj. Invisible, imperceptible, unseen, unbeheld, undiscerned, viewless, undiscernible, indiscernible, sightless, unapparent, non-apparent, hid, hidden, concealed, &c. (528), covert.

Confused, dim, obscure, dark, misty, hazy, foggy, indistinct, ill-defined, indefinite, ill-marked, blurred, shadowy, nebulous, shaded, screened, veiled, masked.

Unintelligible, &c., *see* (519).

(448) APPEARANCE, phenomenon, sight, spectacle, show, premonstration, scene, species, view, *coup d'œil,* look out, prospect, vista, perspective, bird's-eye view, scenery, landscape, picture, *tableau,* display, pageant, raree-show, panorama, diorama, cos-

(449) DISAPPEARANCE, evanescence, eclipse, occultation.

V. To disappear, vanish, dissolve, fade, melt away, pass, avaunt, begone, be lost, &c.

To efface, blot, blot out, erase, rub out, expunge (552).

morama, georama, *spectacle, coup de théâtre, jeu de théâtre.*

Phantasm, phasma, phantom, *spectrum,* apparition, spectre, *mirage,* &c. (443).

Aspect, phase, *phasis,* seeming, guise, look, complexion, shape, mien, air, cast, carriage, port, demeanour, presence, expression, first blush.

Lineament, feature, *trait,* lines, outline, face, countenance, physiognomy, visage, phiz, profile, *tournure.*

V. To seem, look, appear; to present, wear, carry, have, bear, exhibit, take, take on, or assume the appearance of; to look like, to manifest, &c. (525).

Adj. Apparent, seeming, &c.

Adv. Apparently, &c., on the face of it, *primâ facie.*

Adj. Disappearing, &c., lost, vanishing, evanescent, missing.

Phr. Lost in the clouds.

Int. Begone! away! avaunt! vanish! disappear! *see* (292).

CLASS IV.

WORDS RELATING TO THE INTELLECTUAL FACULTIES.

~~~~~~~~~~

DIVISION I. FORMATION OF IDEAS.

Section I. OPERATIONS OF INTELLECT IN GENERAL.

(450) INTELLECT, mind, understanding, reason, thinking principle, nous, sense, common sense, consciousness, capacity, intelligence, percipience, intuition, instinct, conception, judgment, genius, parts, wit, wits, shrewdness, archness, intellectuality; *see* Skill (698), and Wisdom (498).

ABSENCE or want of intellect, *see* (499).

Soul, spirit, ghost, inner man, heart, breast, bosom, *penetralia mentis, divina particula auræ.*

Organ or seat of thought; *sensorium,* sensory, brain, head, headpiece, pate, noddle, skull, *pericranium, cerebrum, cranium.*

Science of mind; Metaphysics, Psychology, Psychics, Ideology, Idealism, Ideality, Pneumatology, Materialism.

Adj. Relating to intellect; intellectual, mental, spiritual, metaphysical, psychical, psychological, nooscopic, ghostly, immaterial (317), cerebral.

(451) THOUGHT, reflection, cogitation, consideration, meditation, study, lucubration, speculation, deliberation, pondering, head-work, application, attention (457), contemplation.

Abstraction, musing, reverie, Platonism; depth of thought, workings of the mind, inmost thoughts, self-counsel, self-communing, self-consultation ; succession, flow, train, current, &c. of thought, or of ideas.

After-thought, reconsideration, retrospection, retrospect (505), examination, *see* Inquiry (461).

Thoughtfulness, pensiveness, intentness, intentiveness.

V. To think, reflect, cogitate, excogitate, consider, deliberate, speculate, contemplate, meditate, ponder,

(452) Absence or want of thought.

INCOGITANCY, vacancy, inunderstanding, fatuity, *see* (499), thoughtlessness, *see* Inattention (458).

V. Not to think, to take no thought of, not to trouble oneself about, to put away thought; to dismiss, discard, or discharge from one's thoughts, or from the mind ; to drop the subject, set aside, turn aside, turn away from, turn one's attention from, abstract oneself, dream ; to indulge in reverie.

To unbend, relax, divert the mind.

Adj. Vacant, unintellectual, unideal (499), unoccupied, unthinking, inconsiderate, thoughtless, absent, *distrait,* inattentive (458), diverted, distracted, unbent, &c.

muse, ruminate, chew the cud upon, brood over, animadvert, revolve in the mind, turn or run over in the mind, con over, study, bend or apply the mind, digest, discuss, hammer at, weigh, perpend, take into account, take into consideration.

Phr. To take counsel; to commune with oneself; to collect one's thoughts, to advise with one's pillow.

To harbour, entertain, cherish, nurture, &c., an idea, or a thought, a notion, a view, &c.

To enter the mind, come into the head, occur, present itself, pass in the mind, suggest itself.

Phr. To flash on the mind; to flit across the view.

To fancy, trow, dream of, come uppermost, run in one's head.

To make an impression; to sink, or penetrate into the mind; fasten itself on the mind.

Adj. Thinking, &c., thoughtful, pensive, meditative, reflective, wistful, contemplative, speculative, deliberative, studious, abstracted, platonic.

Close, active, diligent, mature, deliberate, laboured, steadfast, deep, profound, intense, &c. thought, study, reflection, &c.

Intent, engrossed, absorbed, deep-musing, absorped, wrapped, rapt, abstracted; sedate.

Phr. Having the mind on the stretch; the mind, or head running upon.

Unthought of, unconsidered, incogitable, undreamed.

---

(453) Object of thought.

IDEA, notion, conception, thought, fancy, conceit, impression, perception, image, ειδωλον, sentiment, *see* Opinion (484), phantasy, flight of fancy.

Point of view, light, aspect, field of view.

(454) Subject of thought.

TOPIC, subject, matter, theme, thesis, text, subject-matter, point, proposition, business, affair, matter in hand, question, argument, motion, resolution, moot point (461), head, chapter; nice or subtle point, *quodlibet.*

Adv. In question, on the *tapis,* relative to, *see* (9).

Section II. PRECURSORY CONDITIONS AND OPERATIONS.

(455) The desire of knowledge.

CURIOSITY, curiousness, inquisitiveness.

A quidnunc, Paul Pry, bibliomaniac.

V. To be curious, &c., to take an interest in, to stare, gape.

Adj. Curious, inquisitive, inquiring, all agog, staring, gaping, agape.

Adv. With open mouth, on tiptoe, *arrectis auribus.*

(456) Absence of curiosity.

INCURIOSITY, incuriousness, *insouciance,* want of interest.

V. To be incurious, &c., to have no curiosity, take no interest in, &c., not to care, not to mind, &c.

Adj. Incurious, uninquisitive.

(457) ATTENTION, advertence, advertency, observance, observation, notice, heed, look, regard, view, remark, inspection, introspection, mindfulness, look out, watch, vigilance, circumspection, *surveillance*, revision, review, revise, particularity, *see* Care (459).

Close, intense, deep, profound, &c., attention, application, or study.

V. To be attentive, &c.; to attend, advert to, mind, observe, look, look at, see, view, look to, see to, remark, heed, notice, take heed, take notice, mark; give or pay attention to; give heed to, have an eye to; turn, apply, or direct the mind, the eye, or the attention to; look after, give a thought to, animadvert to, occupy oneself with, trouble one's head about, lend or incline an ear to.

To examine cursorily; to glance at, upon, or over; cast or pass the eyes over, run over, turn over the leaves, dip into, perstringe.

To examine closely or intently, consider, give one's mind to, overhaul, pore over, note, mark, inspect, review, have one's eyes open, fix the eye, mind, thoughts, or attention on, keep in view, contemplate, &c. (451).

Phr. To have one's eyes about one.

To fall under one's notice, observation, &c., to catch the eye; to catch, awaken, wake, invite, solicit, attract, claim, excite, engage, occupy, strike, arrest, fix, engross, absorb, rivet, &c. the attention, mind, or thoughts.

Adj. Attentive, mindful, heedful, regardful, alive to, bearing in mind, occupied with, engaged, taken up with, engrossed, wrapped or rapt in, absorbed.

Awake, watchful (459), broad awake, wide awake, intent on, with eyes fixed on, open-eyed, undistracted, with bated breath, upon the stretch.

Adv. Nota bene.

Int. See! look! mark! lo!

(458) INATTENTION, inconsideration, inconsiderateness, inadvertence, inadvertency, non-observance, disregard, regardlessness, unmindfulness, giddiness, respectlessness, thoughtlessness, *see* Neglect (460), *insouciance*, wandering, distracted, &c. attention.

Absence of mind, abstraction, preoccupation, *distraction,* reverie, brown study.

Phr. The wits going a-woolgathering.

V. To be inattentive, &c., to overlook, disregard, pass by, slur over, pass over, gloss over, blink, miss, skim, skim the surface, *effleurer* (460).

To call off, draw off, call away, divert, &c. the attention; to disconcert, put out, discompose, confuse, perplex, bewilder, moider, muddle, dazzle.

Adj. Inattentive, mindless, unobservant, unmindful, inadvertent, heedless, regardless, respectless, careless, *see* (460), unwatchful, listless, hand over head, cursory, blind, deaf, &c.

Absent, abstracted, *distrait,* lost, preoccupied, dreamy, napping, caught napping.

Disconcerted, put out, &c., dizzy, muzzy, *see* (460).

Adv. Inattentively, &c., cavalierly.

----

(459) CARE, caution, heed, heedfulness, wariness, prudence, discretion, captel, watch, watchfulness, vigilance, circumspection, watch and

(460) NEGLECT, negligence, omission, laches, heedlessness, carelessness, perfunctoriness, remissness, imprudence, secureness, indiscretion,

ward, deliberation, forethought, pre-deliberation, solicitude, precaution (673), scruple, scrupulousness, scrupulosity, particularity, *surveillance*.

Phr. The eyes of Argus; *l'œil du maître*.

V. To be careful, &c., to take care, have a care, look to it, heed, take heed, keep watch, keep watch and ward, look sharp, look about one, keep a sharp look out, set watch, take precautions.

Phr. To have all one's eyes about one; to mind one's P's and Q's; to speak by the card; to pick one's steps.

Adj. Careful, cautious, heedful, wary, guarded, on one's guard, on the alert, on the watch, watchful, on the look out, *aux aguets*, awake, vigilant, circumspect, broad awake, having the eyes open, Argus-eyed.

Phr. On the *qui-vive*.

Discreet, prudent, sure-footed, provident, scrupulous, particular.

Adv. Carefully, &c., with care, &c., gingerly.

Phr. Ne réveillez pas le chat qui dort.

étourderie, incautiousness, indiscrimination, rashness (863), recklessness, *nonchalance*; a slattern, slut.

(In rhetoric) Paralepsis.

V. To be negligent, &c., to neglect, pass over, omit, pretermit, set aside, cast or put aside.

To overlook, disregard, slight, pay no regard to, make light of, trifle with, blink, wink at, connive at; take or make no account of; gloss over, slur over, slip over, skip, jump over.

Phr. To give to the winds.

To render neglectful &c., to put, or throw off one's guard.

Adj. Neglecting, &c., unmindful, heedless, careless, negligent, neglectful, slovenly, remiss, perfunctory, thoughtless, uncircumspect (or incircumspect), off one's guard, unwary, incautious, unguarded, indiscreet, inconsiderate, imprudent, improvident, rash, headlong, reckless, heels over head, witless, hare-brained, giddy-brained, off-hand, cursory, brain-sick.

Neglected, unheeded, unperceived, unseen, unobserved, unnoticed, unnoted, unmarked, unattended to, unthought of, overlooked, unmissed, unexamined, unsearched, unscanned, unweighed, unsifted.

Phr. In an unguarded moment; buried in a napkin.

Adv. Negligently, &c., hand over head.

(461) INQUIRY, search, research, quest, pursuit, examination, scrutiny, investigation, indagation, perquisition, perscrutation, pervestigation, inquest, inquisition, exploration, exploitation, sifting, calculation, analysis, dissection, resolution, induction; the Baconian method; a searching inquiry; *scire facias*, *ad referendum*.

Questioning, asking, interrogation, interpellation, interrogatory, the Socratic method, examination, cross-examination, cross-questioning, catechism.

Reconnoitering, prying, spying, espionage, the lantern of Diogenes.

(462) ANSWER, response, reply, replication, *riposte*, rejoinder, rebutter, retort, repartee, rescript, antiphony, rescription, acknowledgment.

Explanation, solution, resolution, exposition, rationale, interpretation (522).

A key, master-key, open sesame, *passe partout*.

Œdipus, *see* Oracle (513).

V. To answer, respond, reply, rebut, retort, rejoin, return for answer, acknowledge, echo.

Phr. To turn the tables upon.

To explain, solve, resolve, expound, decipher, spell, interpret (522),

Subject of inquiry; QUESTION, moot-point, query, difficulty, problem, *desideratum*, point to be solved; point or matter in dispute; moot-point, question at issue, plain question, fair question, open question, knotty point.

Enigma, riddle, conundrum, a bone to pick, *quodlibet*, Gordian knot, *dignus vindice nodus*.

An inquirer, querist, quidnunc.

to unriddle, unlock, cut the knot, unravel, pick or open the lock, discover, fish up.

Adj. Answering, responding, &c., responsive, respondent.

Phr. Mutato nomine de te fabula narratur.

———

V. To inquire, seek, search, look for, look about for, look out for, cast about for, beat about, grope for, feel for, reconnoitre, explore, sound, rummage, ransack, pry, look round, look over, look through.

Phr. To look, peer, or pry into every hole and corner; to beat the bushes; to leave no stone unturned; to seek a needle in a pottle of hay.

To pursue, hunt, track, trail, mouse, dodge, trace.

To investigate, take up, follow up, institute, pursue, conduct, carry on, prosecute, &c. an inquiry, &c., to overhaul, to examine, study, consider, fathom, take into consideration, dip into, look into, calculate, pre-examine, dive into, to delve into, discuss, canvass, probe, fathom, sound, scrutinize, analyze, anatomize, dissect, sift, winnow, to grapple with a question, torture, resolve.

To subject to examination.

To undergo examination.

To ask, question, demand, put, propose, propound, moot, raise, stir, suggest, put forth, start, pop, &c. a question, interrogate, catechise, pump, cross-question, cross-examine, dodge, require an answer, *see* (765).

Adj. Inquiring, &c., inquisitive, requisitive, requisitory, catechetical, inquisitorial, analytic, in search of, in quest of, on the look out for.

Undetermined, untried, undecided, to be resolved &c., in question, in dispute, *sub judice*, moot.

Adv. Why? wherefore? whence? quere? how comes it? how happens it? how is it?

(463) EXPERIMENT, essay, trial, tentative method, *tâtonnement*, verification, probation, *experimentum crucis*, proof, criterion, test, touchstone, pix, assay, ordeal.—Empiricism.

A feeler, a pilot balloon, a messenger balloon; a straw to show the wind.

V. To essay, try, explore, grope, beat the bushes; feel, or grope one's way; to thread one's way; to make an experiment, make trial of.

To subject to trial &c., to experiment upon, give a trial to, put, bring, or submit to the test or proof; to prove, verify, test, touch, practise upon.

Adj. Experimental, tentative, probationary, empirical, *sub judice*.

Adv. A tâtons.

(464) COMPARISON, collation, contrast, identification,—a simile, metaphor, allegory.

V. To compare to or with; to collate; place side by side, or in juxtaposition, to draw a parallel, institute a comparison, contrast, identify.

Phr. **Parva componere magnis.**
Adj. Comparative, metaphorical, figurative, allegorical.

(465) DISCRIMINATION, distinction, perception or appreciation of difference, taste (850), judgment, nice perception, tact.
Phr. To split hairs.
V. To discriminate, distinguish, to separate, or winnow the chaff from the wheat.
Adj. Discriminating, &c., discriminative, distinctive.

(465 a) INDISCRIMINATION, indistinctness, indistinction (460).
Adj. Indiscriminate, undistinguished, undistinguishable, unmeasured.

(466) MEASUREMENT, admeasurement, mensuration, valuation, appraisement, assessment, assize, estimation, reckoning.
Geodetics, geodæsia, orthometry, gauging, altimetry, sounding, surveying, weighing, ponderation, trutination, dead reckoning.
A measure, standard, rule, compass, callipers, gage (or gauge), meter, line, rod, plummet, log, log-line, sound, check.
Scale, graduation, graduated scale, quadrant, theodolite, &c., balance, scales, steelyard, beam, weather-glass, barometer, areometer, altimeter, &c.
V. To measure, mete, value, assess, rate, appraise, estimate, form an estimate, set a value on, appreciate, span, pace, step, apply the compass, rule, scale &c., gauge, plumb, probe, sound, fathom, heave the log, survey, weigh, poise, balance, hold the scales, take an average, graduate, to place in the beam, to take into account.
Adj. Measuring, &c., metrical, ponderable, measurable.

Section III.   MATERIALS FOR REASONING.

(467) EVIDENCE on one side, premises, *data*, *præcognita*, indication (550).
Testimony, testimonial, deposition, attestation, testification, authority, warrant, warranty, surety, handwriting, autograph, signature, endorsement, seal, sigil, signet, superscription, entry.
Voucher, *pièce justificative*, credential, certificate, deed, indenture, probate, affidavit, attestation, diploma; admission, concession, allegation, deposition, citation, quotation.
Criterion, test, touchstone, check, prerogative fact, argument.
A witness, eye-witness, indicator, ear-witness, deponent, tell-tale, sponsor.
Assumption, presumption, show

(468) Evidence on the other side, on the other hand.
COUNTER-EVIDENCE, disproof, contradiction, rejoinder, answer (462), weak point, conflicting evidence, *see* Refutation (479).
Phr. A *tu quoque* argument.
V. To countervail, oppose, rebut, check, weaken, invalidate, contradict, contravene.
Adj. Countervailing &c., contradictory, unattested.
Adv. Although, though, but.
Phr. *Audi alteram partem.*

(469) QUALIFICATION, limitation, modification, allowance, grains of allowance, consideration, extenuating circumstance, condition, proviso, exception (83), assumption (514).
V. To qualify, limit, modify,

103

of reason, postulation, *postulatum, lemma.*

Reason, proof, *see* Demonstration (478).

Ex parte evidence, one-sided view. Confirmation, corroboration, support, comprobation, approval.

V. To be evidence, &c., to evince, show, indicate (550), imply, involve, argue, admit, allow, concede, certify, testify, attest, bear testimony, depose, witness, vouch for, sign, seal, set one's hand and seal to, endorse, confirm, corroborate, support, bear upon, bear out, to speak volumes.

To hold good, hold water.

To adduce, cite, quote, call, bring forward, produce, bring into court, confront witnesses, collect, bring together, rake up evidence.

To allege, plead, assume, postulate, presume.

Adj. Showing, &c., indicating, indicative, indicatory, following, deducible, consequential, consectary, corroborative, confirmatory; postulatory.

Sound, logical, strong, valid, cogent, persuasive, persuasory, demonstrative, irrefragable, irresistible, &c. (478).

Adv. According to; witness; *à fortiori;* still more, still less, &c.

allow for, make allowance for, take into account, introduce new conditions, admit exceptions, take exception.

Adj. Qualifying &c., conditional, exceptional (83).

Adv. Provided, if, unless, but, yet, according as, conditionally, admitting, supposing; on the supposition, assumption, presumption, allegation, hypothesis, &c. of; with the understanding, even, although, after all.

Phr. With grains of allowance, *cum grano salis.*

Degrees of Evidence.

(470) POSSIBILITY, potentiality, contingency, *see* Chance (156), what may be, what is possible, &c.

Practicability, feasibility (705), compatibility (23).

V. To be possible, &c., to admit of, to bear; may, may be, mayhap.

To render possible, &c., to put into the way of.

Adj. Possible, contingent, on the cards.

Practicable, feasible, achievable, attainable, obtainable, compatible.

Adv. Possibly, by possibility, may be, perhaps, *in posse.*

Phr. Wind and weather permitting; within the bounds of possibility.

(472) PROBABILITY, likelihood, verisimilitude, plausibility, credibility, reasonable chance, favourable chance, fair chance, presumptive evidence, circumstantial evidence, appearances being in favour of.

(471) IMPOSSIBILITY, what cannot be, what can never be, hopelessness (859), a dead lift.

Impracticability, incompatibility (704), incredibility.

V. To be impossible, &c., to have no chance whatever.

Phr. To wash a blackamoor white; to make a silk purse out of a sow's ear; *prendre la lune avec les dents.*

Adj. Impossible, contrary to reason, inconceivable, unreasonable, incredible, marvellous, desperate, hopeless, unheard of.

Impracticable, unattainable, unachievable, unfeasible, unobtainable.

(473) IMPROBABILITY, unlikelihood, unfavourable chances, small chance, &c., incredibility, increditableness.

V. To be improbable, &c., to have a small, little, poor, &c. chance.

Adj. Improbable, unlikely, con-

V. To be probable, &c., to bid fair, to stand fair for, to stand a good chance, to stand to reason.

Adj. Probable, likely, likely to happen, in a fair way, hopeful, well-founded.

Plausible, specious, ostensible, colourable, standing to reason, reasonable, credible, easy of belief, presumptive.

Adv. Probably, &c., belike, in all probability, or likelihood, apparently, to all appearance, *primâ facie.*

trary to all reasonable expectation; having scarcely a chance, &c.

———

(474) CERTAINTY, certitude, positiveness, a dead certainty, infallibleness, infallibility, gospel, scripture, surety, assurance, indisputableness, moral certainty, *see* Truth (494).

Fact, matter of fact, *fait accompli.*

V. To be certain, &c., to believe (454).

To render certain, &c., to ensure.

Adj. Certain, sure, assured, solid, absolute, positive, determinate, categorical, unequivocal, unavoidable, avoidless, unerring, infallible, indubitable, indubious, indisputable, undisputed, uncontested, incontestible, incontrovertible, undoubted, doubtless, without doubt, beyond a doubt, past dispute, unanswerable, decided, unquestionable, beyond all question, unquestioned, questionless, demonstrable (478).

Phr. Sure as fate; *à coup sûr;* sure as a gun; sure as death and taxes; *cela va sans dire.*

Adv. Certainly, assuredly, &c., for certain, *in esse,* sure, surely, sure enough, of course, as a matter of course, yes, *see* (488).

(475) UNCERTAINTY, incertitude, *see* Doubt (485), doubtfulness, dubiety, dubiousness, suspense, precariousness, indefiniteness, indetermination, slipperiness, fallibility, perplexity, ambiguity, hesitation, *équivoque.*

V. To be uncertain, &c.

To be in a state of uncertainty.

To render uncertain, &c., to perplex, embarrass, confuse, confound.

Phr. To tremble in the scale; to hang by a thread.

Adj. Uncertain, doubtful, dubious, precarious, casual, random, contingent, indecisive, dependent on circumstances, undecided, vague, indeterminate, indefinite, ambiguous, undefined, equivocal, undefinable, puzzling, enigmatic, questionable, apocryphal, problematical, controvertible, fallible, fallacious, suspicious, slippery, ticklish, debateable.

Unauthentic, unconfirmed, undemonstrated, undemonstrable.

Section IV. REASONING PROCESSES.

(476) REASONING, ratiocination, dialectics, induction, generalization.

Argumentation, discussion, controversy, polemics, debate, wrangling, logomachy, disputation.

The art of reasoning, logic, process, train, or chain of reasoning, argument, proposition, terms, premises, postulate, data, conclusion.

(477) The absence of reasoning.

INTUITION, instinct, presentiment.

False or vicious reasoning.

SOPHISTRY, paralogy, fallacy, perversion, casuistry, jesuitry, equivocation, evasion, chicanery, quiddity, mystification, *non sequitur, ignorantio elenchi.*

Syllogism, prosyllogism, enthymeme, sorites, dilemma, *perilepsis*, a comprehensive argument.

Correctness, soundness, force, validity, cogency, conclusiveness.

Phr. The horns of a dilemma.

A disputant, controversialist, controvertist, controverter, debater.

V. To reason, argue, discuss, debate, dispute, wrangle ; bandy words or arguments ; hold, or carry on an argument, controvert, contravene, comment upon, moralize upon, spiritualize.

To open a discussion, or case ; to moot, to join issue, to stir, agitate, torture, or ventilate a question.

Phr. To chop logic ; to try conclusions ; to impale on the horns of a dilemma.

Adj. Reasoning, &c., argumentative, controversial, dialectic, polemical, discursory, discursive, debateable, controvertible ; disputatious.

Ep. Correct, just, fair, sound, valid, cogent, logical, consectary, demonstrative (478), relevant, pertinent (9), to the point, to the purpose, *ad rem*, subtle, fine spun.

Phr. Rem acu tetigisti.

Adv. For, because, for that reason, forasmuch as, inasmuch as, whereas, considering, in consideration of, therefore, consequently, *ergo*, thus, accordingly, wherefore, *à fortiori*.

In conclusion, in fine, after all, *au bout du compte*, on the whole, taking one thing with another.

(478) DEMONSTRATION, proof, conclusiveness, *apodixis*, probation, comprobation, *experimentum crucis*, test, &c. (463).

V. To demonstrate, prove, establish, show, evince, verify, make good, set at rest, substantiate, settle the question, reduce to demonstration.

Adj. Demonstrating, &c., demonstrative, probative, demonstrable, unanswerable, conclusive, apodictic,

106

Phr. Begging the question, reasoning in a circle.

Misjudgment, miscalculation (481).

Sophism, solecism, paralogism, quibble, elench, fallacy, *quodlibet*, subterfuge.

Speciousness, plausibility, illusiveness, irrelevancy, invalidity.

Phr. The meshes or cobwebs of sophistry.

V. To judge intuitively, &c.

To reason ill, falsely, &c. To pervert, quibble, equivocate, mystify, evade, elude, gloss over, varnish, throw off the scent ; to beg the question, reason in a circle, misjudge, miscalculate (481).

To refine, subtilize.

Phr. To split hairs, to cut blocks with a razor.

Adj. Intuitive, instinctive, impulsive, independent of, or anterior to reason.

Sophistical, illogical, false, unsound, not following, inconsequent, unwarranted, untenable, inconclusive, incorrect, fallacious, groundless, fallible, unproved, deceptive, illusive, illusory, specious, plausible, irrelevant.

Ep. Weak, feeble, poor, flimsy, trivial, trumpery, trashy, puerile, childish, irrational, silly, foolish, imbecile, absurd, extravagant, farfetched.

Phr. Non constat, non sequitur : away from the point, foreign to the purpose or subject, having nothing to do with the matter, not bearing upon the point in question.

(479) CONFUTATION, refutation, disproof, conviction, redargution, invalidation, exposure, exposition ; demolition of an argument, a clincher.

Phr. Reductio ad absurdum ; a knock-down argument, a *tu quoque* argument.

V. To confute, refute, disprove, redargue, expose, show the fallacy of, rebut, defeat, overthrow, demolish, overturn, invalidate, silence, reduce to silence.

irrefutable, irrefragable, categorical.

Demonstrated, &c., unconfuted, unrefuted ; evident, self-evident, axiomatic.

Phr. Probatum est ; there being nothing more to be said ; *Q. E. D.*

Phr. To clinch an argument or question.

Adj. Confuting, &c., confuted, &c., capable of refutation, refutable, confutable, &c., exhaustive ; unproved, &c.

Phr. Having exhausted the subject ; at the end of one's tether ; *au bout de son latin ; cadit questio ; suo sibi gladio hunc jugulo.*

Section V.   Results of Reasoning.

(480) JUDGMENT, conclusion, determination, deduction, inference, illation, corollary.

Estimation, valuation, appreciation, dijudication, judication, arbitrament, arbitration, assessment, review.

Decision, sentence, verdict, moral, finding ; detection, discovery, estimate.

A judge, arbiter, arbitrator, assessor, censor, referee, reviewer.

V. To judge, deduce, conclude, draw a conclusion, infer, make a deduction, draw an inference ; come to, arrive or jump at a conclusion ; to derive, gather, collect.

To estimate, appreciate, value, count, assess, rate, account, regard, review, settle, pass an opinion, decide, pronounce, pass judgment, arbitrate, perpend, sit in judgment, hold the scales.

To ascertain, determine, find, find out, make out, detect, discover, elicit, recognize, trace, get at ; get, or arrive at the truth ; meet with, fall upon, light upon, hit upon, fall in with, stumble upon, pop upon, lay the finger on, smoke, solve, resolve, unravel, fish out, worm out, ferret out, root out, grub up, fish up, *see* Investigate (461).

Adj. Judging, &c., deducible (467), impartial, unbiassed, unprejudiced, unwarped, unbigoted, equitable, fair, sound, rational, judicious.

Int. Eureka !

(481) MISJUDGMENT, obliquity of judgment, *see* Error (495), presumption.

Prejudgment, prejudication, prejudice, pre-notion, prevention, preconception, prepossession, pre-apprehension, presentiment.

Bias, warp, twist, narrowmindedness, bigotry, dogmatism, intolerance, tenacity, obstinacy (606), blind side ; one-sided, partial, narrow, or confined views, ideas, conceptions, or notions, *idée fixe.*

V. To misjudge, misestimate, misconceive, misreckon, &c., *see* (495).

To prejudge, forejudge, prejudicate, dogmatize, have a bias, &c., presuppose, presume.

Phr. Jurare in verba magistri. To look only at one side of the shield ; to view with jaundiced eye.

To produce a bias, twist, &c. ; to bias, warp, twist, prejudice, &c.

Adj. Prejudging, &c., prejudiced, jaundiced, narrow-minded, dogmatic, besotted, *entêté,* positive, obstinate, tenacious, pig-headed, having a bias, twist, &c., warped, partial.

Phr. Wedded to an opinion.

(482) OVERESTIMATION, exaggeration.

V. To overestimate, overrate, overvalue, overprize, overweigh, outreckon; exaggerate, extol, make too much of, overstrain.

Adj. Overestimated, &c.

---

(483) DEPRECIATION, disparagement, detraction, underrating, underestimation, undervaluing, &c.

V. To depreciate, disparage, detract, underrate, underestimate, undervalue, underreckon, misprize, not to do justice to, make light of, slight; make little, or make nothing of, hold cheap, disregard, to care nothing for, set at naught, derogate, decry, avile, vilipend, run down (932).

To scout, deride, mock, scoff at, laugh at, whistle at, play with, trifle with, fribble, niggle (856).

Phr. To snap one's fingers at; throw into the shade; not to care a pin, rush, &c. for; *see* (643).

Adj. Depreciating, &c., derogatory, detractory, cynical.

Depreciated, &c., unvalued, unprized.

(484) BELIEF, credence, faith, trust, troth, confidence, credit, dependence on, reliance, assurance.

Opinion, notion, idea (453), conception, apprehension, impression, conceit, mind, view, persuasion, plerophory, conviction, convincement, sentiment, voice, judgment, estimation, self-conviction.

System of opinions, creed, doctrine, tenet, dogma, principle, way of thinking, popular belief, *vox populi*, public opinion.

Change of opinion, proselytism, propagandism (607).

V. To believe, credit, give faith to, give credit to, rely upon, make no doubt, doubt not, confide in, count upon, depend upon, calculate upon, take upon trust, swallow, gulp down, take one's word for, take upon credit.

To think, hold, take, look upon, take it, consider, esteem.

Phr. To pin one's faith upon; to take at one's word.

To be of opinion, to opine, to have, hold, possess, entertain, adopt, imbibe, embrace, foster, nurture, cherish, &c. a notion, idea, opinion, &c.; to think, look upon, view, consider, take, take it, hold, trow, ween, conceive, fancy, apprehend, regard, esteem, deem, account; meseems, methinks.

Phr. To take it into one's head.

108

---

(485) UNBELIEF, disbelief, misbelief, discredit, miscreance, scepticism.

DOUBT, dubitation, misgiving, demur, suspense; shade or shadow of doubt, distrust, mistrust, misdoubt, suspicion, shyness, embarrassment, hesitation, uncertainty (475), scruple, qualm, dilemma; casuistry; schism (489), incredulity (487).

V. To disbelieve, discredit, not to believe, refuse to admit, or believe, misbelieve, controvert; put, or set aside; join issue, dispute, &c.

To doubt, be doubtful, &c., diffide, distrust, mistrust, suspect, smoke; have, harbour, entertain, &c. doubts; demur, stick at, pause, hesitate, scruple, question, call in question.

Phr. Not to know what to make of; to smell a rat.

To cause, raise, suggest, or start a doubt; to pose, stagger, embarrass, puzzle; shake, or stagger one's faith or belief.

Adj. Unbelieving, &c., sceptical, shy of belief, at sea, at a loss (487).

Doubting, &c., doubtful, dubious, scrupulous, suspicious; *see* Uncertain (475).

Unworthy or undeserving of belief, hard to believe, doubtful, dubious, staggering, puzzling, &c., paradoxical, incredible, inconceivable.

Phr. With grains of allowance;

To cause to be believed, thought, or esteemed; to satisfy, persuade, assure, convince, convert, bring over, win over, indoctrinate ; *see* Teach (537).

Phr. To cram down the throat.

Adj. Believing, &c., impressed with, imbued with, wedded to, unsuspecting, unsuspicious, void of suspicion, &c., credulous (486), convinced, &c.

Believed, &c., credited, accredited, unsuspected, received, current, popular.

Worthy or deserving of belief, commanding belief, credible, *see* Probable (472), fiducial, fiduciary ; relating to belief, doctrinal.

Ep. Firm, implicit, steadfast, fixed, rooted, staunch, unshaken, inveterate ; — calm, sober, dispassionate, impartial.

cum grano salis; Fronti nulla fides; Nimium ne crede colori; Timeo Danaus et dona ferentes.

---

(486) CREDULITY, credulousness, gullibility, infatuation, self-delusion, *bonhommie*, superstition, gross credulity.

A credulous person, gull, *gobemouche ;* dupe (547).

V. To be credulous, &c., to follow implicitly, swallow, &c.

To impose upon, practise upon, palm upon, cajole, &c., *see* Deceive (545).

Phr. Jurare in verba magistri.

Adj. Credulous, gullible, easily deceived, cajoled, &c., superstitious, simple, suspectless, unsuspicious, &c. (484), soft, childish, silly, stupid.

(487) INCREDULITY, scepticism, pyrrhonism, suspicion, &c., *see* (485), suspiciousness, scrupulousness, scrupulosity.

An unbeliever, sceptic, misbeliever.*

V. To be incredulous, &c., to distrust, *see* (485).

Phr. Let those believe who may ; *Credat Judæus Apella.*

Adj. Incredulous, hard of belief, sceptical, unbelieving, inconvincible.

(488) ASSENT, acquiescence, admission, assentment, nod, consent, concession, accord, accordance, agreement, concordance, concurrence, ratification, confirmation, recognition, acknowledgment, granting, avowal, confession.

Unanimity, chorus; affirmation (535).

V. To assent, acquiesce, agree, yield assent, accord, concur, consent, nod assent, coincide, go with, go along with, chime in with, strike in with, say amen, close with, conform with, defer to ; say yes, &c.

To acknowledge, own, avow, confess, concede, subscribe to, admit, allow, recognize, grant.

(489) DISSENT, discordance, denial (536), dissonance; difference or diversity of opinion, recusancy, contradiction, non-conformity, schism ; protest, shake of the head, shrug of the shoulders.

A dissenter, non-conformist, recusant.

V. To dissent, deny, disagree, refuse assent, say no, &c., ignore, protest, contradict, shake the head, shrug the shoulders, give the lie ; secede.

Adj. Dissenting, &c., dissentient, discordant, protestant, recusant ; unconvinced, unconverted, unavowed, unacknowledged.

Unwilling, reluctant, extorted, &c.

---

* The word *miscreant*, which originally meant simply *misbeliever*, has now quite another meaning (949).

Adj. Assenting, &c., acquiescent, willing; agreed; uncontradicted, unquestioned, uncontroverted.

Adv. Affirmatively, in the affirmative (535).

Yes, yea, well, very well, even so, just so, to be sure, "thou hast said;" exactly, precisely, truly, certainly, certes, verily, very true (494), *ex concesse.*

Be it so, so be it, by all means, by all manner of means, *à la bonne heure*, amen, willingly, &c. (602).

Agreed, with one accord, *unâ voce*, unanimously, in chorus, to a man, *nem. con.* or *nemine contradicente, nemine dissentiente*, without a dissentient voice, one and all, on all hands.

Adv. Negatively, in the negative, (536).

No, nay, not, not so, not at all, nowise, not in the least, not a bit, not a whit, not a jot, by no means, by no manner of means, on no account, in no respect.

Phr. I am your humble servant; many men, many minds; *tant s'en faut; il s'en faut bien.*

Int. God forbid! Forbid it heaven!

---

(490) KNOWLEDGE, cognizance, cognition, cognoscence, acquaintance, privity, insight, familiarity, comprehension, understanding, recognition; discovery (480).

Intuition, consciousness, conscience, precognition, light, enlightenment, glimpse, inkling, glimmer, scent, suspicion; conception, notion, idea (453).

System, or body of knowledge; science, philosophy, pansophy, pandect, doctrine, theory, etiology, literature, *belles lettres.*

Erudition, learning, lore, scholarship, book-learning, bookishness, bibliomania, education, instruction, information, acquisitions, acquirements, accomplishments, proficiency; a liberal education, encyclopedical knowledge, omniscience.

Elements, rudiments, abecedary, cyclopædia, encyclopædia, school, &c.

Depth, extent, profoundness, profundity, stores, &c., solidity, accuracy, &c. of knowledge.

Phr. The march of intellect; the progress, advance, &c. of science; the schoolmaster being abroad.

V. To know, be aware of, ken, wot, ween, weet, trow, have, possess, conceive, apprehend, understand, comprehend, make out, recognize, be master of, know full well, possess

(491) IGNORANCE, nescience, unacquaintance, unconsciousness, darkness, blindness, incomprehension, inexperience, emptiness; *ignorance crasse; tabula rasa; terra incognita.*

Imperfect knowledge, smattering, sciolism, glimmering; bewilderment, perplexity; incapacity.

Affectation of knowledge, pedantry.

V. To be ignorant, &c., not to know, to know not, to know not what, not to be aware of, to be at a loss, to be at fault, to ignore, to be blind to, &c., not to understand, &c.

Phr. To be caught tripping; not to know what to make of, not to be able to make head or tail of; not to know a hawk from a handsaw.

Adj. Ignorant, unconscious, unaware, weetless, unwitting, unweeting, witless, a stranger to, unacquainted, unconversant, unenlightened, unversed, uncultivated, in the dark.

Uninformed, uninstructed, untaught, unapprized, untutored, unschooled, unguided.

Shallow, superficial, green, half-learned, illiterate, unread, uneducated, unlearned, unlettered, emptyheaded, rude, having a smattering, &c., pedantic.

Confused, puzzled, bewildered,

the knowledge of, experience, discern, perceive, see through, have in one's head.

Phr. Connaître le dessous des cartes.

Adj. Knowing, aware of, &c., cognizant of, acquainted with, privy to, conscious of, no stranger to, *au fait, au courant,* versed in, up to, alive to, conversant with, proficient in, read in, familiar with.

Phr. Behind the scenes.

Apprized of, made acquainted with, led into, informed of ; undeceived, unbenighted, unbigoted.

lost, benighted, belated, at sea, at fault, posed, blinded, abroad, distracted, in a maze, hoodwinked, in the dark, *désorienté,* caught tripping.

Phr. Having a film over the eyes.

Unknown, unapprehended, unexplained, unascertained, uninvestigated, unexplored, unheard of, unperceived.

Adv. Ignorantly, unwittingly, unawares ; for anything one knows ; for aught one knows.

Erudite, instructed, learned, well read, lettered, well informed, *savant,* bookish, scholastic, deep read ; self-taught, well grounded.

Known, &c., notorious, proverbial, familiar ; cognoscible.

Ep. Extensive, vast, encyclopedical, acroatic, deep, profound, accurate, solid.

(492) SCHOLAR, *savant,* pundit, schoolman, graduate, doctor, gownsman, philosopher, philomath, clerk.

Linguist, *literati, dilettanti, illuminati.*

Pedant, pedagogue, bookworm, bibliomaniac, blue-stocking, *basbleu,* bigwig.

(493) IGNORAMUS, sciolist, smatterer, novice, greenhorn, half-scholar, booby, dunce (501), bigot (481).

Adj. Bookless, shallow (499), ignorant, &c. (491).

(494) Object of knowledge.

TRUTH, verity, actual existence (1), reality, fact, matter of fact, actuality, nature, principle, orthodoxy, gospel ; substantialness, genuineness, authenticity.

Accuracy, exactness, exactitude, precision, preciseness, niceness, delicacy, fineness, strictness, rigour, punctuality.

Phr. The plain truth, the honest truth, the naked truth, the sober truth, the very thing ; a stubborn fact ; not a dream, fancy, illusion, &c. ; the exact truth, &c. ; the real Simon Pure.

V. To be true, real, &c., to hold good.

To render true, legitimatize, substantiate, to make good, establish.

To get at the truth, *see* (480).

Phr. Vitam impendere vero ; magna est veritas et prevalebit.

Adj. True, real, veritable, actual,

(495) Untruth, *see* (546).

ERROR, mistake, miss, fallacy, misconception, misapprehension, misunderstanding, inaccuracy, incorrectness, inexactness, misconstruction (523), miscomputation.

Fault, blunder, bull, *quiproquo,* slip of the tongue, *lapsus linguæ, équivoque,* cross purposes, oversight, misprint, erratum ; heresy, misstatement, misreport.

Illusion, delusion, self-deceit, self-deception, hallucination, monomania, aberration ; fable, dream, shadow, bubble, *fantasia,* false light, the mists of error, Will o' the wisp, Jack o' lantern, *ignis fatuus,* chimera.

V. To be erroneous, false, &c., to cause error, to mislead, lead astray, lead into error, delude, give a false impression, idea, &c., to falsify, misstate, misrepresent, deceive (545), beguile.

To be in error, to mistake, to re-

positive, absolute, existing (1), substantial, categorical; unrefuted, unconfuted.

Exact, accurate, definite, precise, just, correct, strict, rigid, rigorous, scrupulous, conscientious, religious, punctilious, nice, mathematical, axiomatic, demonstrable, scientific, unerring, faithful, *bonâ fide*, curious, delicate.

Genuine, authentic, legitimate, orthodox, pure, sound, sterling, unsophisticated, unadulterated, unvarnished; solid, substantial, undistorted, undisguised, unaffected, unexaggerated, unromantic.

Phr. Just the thing; neither more nor less.

Adv. Truly, verily, veritably, troth, certainly, certes, assuredly, in truth, in good truth, of a truth, really, indubitably, in sooth, forsooth, in reality, in fact, *de facto*, indeed, in effect, actually, *ipso facto*, positively, virtually.

Precisely, accurately, &c., mathematically, to a nicety, to a hair, to a T, to an inch; to the letter.

In every respect, in all respects, *sous tous les rapports*, at any rate, at all events, by all means.

Phr. Joking apart; in good earnest; in sober earnest; sooth to say; at the bottom of the well.

ceive a false impression; to lie, or labour under an error, mistake, &c., to blunder, be at fault, to misapprehend, misconceive, misunderstand, misconjecture, misreckon, miscount, misestimate, misjudge, misthink, flounder, trip.

Phr. To take the shadow for the substance; to go on a fool's errand.

Adj. Erroneous, untrue, false, unreal, unsubstantial, baseless, groundless, ungrounded.

Inexact, unexact, incorrect, illogical, partial, one-sided, unreasonable, absonous, absonant, indefinite, unscientific, inaccurate, aberrant.

In error, mistaken, &c., tripping, floundering, &c.

Illusive, illusory, ideal, fanciful, chimerical, visionary, shadowy, mock.

Spurious, illegitimate, *pseudo*, bastard, meretricious, deceitful, sophisticated, adulterated.

———

(496) MAXIM, aphorism, apothegm, *dictum*, saying, adage, saw, proverb, sentence, precept, rule, formula, code, motto, word, byeword, moral, sentiment, phylactery, conclusion, reflexion, thought, golden rule, *protasis*, axiom, theorem, scholium, truism.

Adj. Aphoristic, proverbial, phylacteric, axiomatic, conclusive.

Ep. Wise, sage, true, received, admitted, recognized; — common, hackneyed, trite, commonplace.

———

(497) ABSURDITY, absurdness, nonsense, folly, paradox, inconsistency, quibble, sophism (477), stultiloquy, stultiloquence, bull, Irishism, Hibernicism.

Jargon, gibberish, rigmarole, *galimathias*, fustian, rant, bombast, bathos, *amphigouri*, rhapsody, extravagance, rhodomontade, romance.

Twaddle, twattle, fudge, verbiage, trash, stuff, balderdash, slipslop, *bavardage*, palaver, *baragouin*, moonshine, fiddlestick, wishwash, *platitude, niaiserie*, flummery.

Vagary, tomfoolery, mummery, monkey trick, *boutade*, lark, *escapade*.

Phr. A cock and bull story; a mare's nest; a wild goose chase.

Adj. Absurd, nonsensical, foolish, &c., *see* (499), sophistical, inconsistent, extravagant, cock and bull, quibbling, trashy, washy, twaddling, &c.

(498) INTELLIGENCE, capacity, nous, parts, sagacity, sagaciousness, wit, mother wit, *esprit*, gumption, quick parts.

Acuteness, acumen, shrewdness, astuteness, arguteness, sharpness, quickness, subtlety, archness, penetration, perspicacity, perspicacy, perspicaciousness, clear-sightedness, discrimination, discernment.

Head, brains, head-piece, a long head.

WISDOM, sapience, sense, good sense, common sense, reason, reasonableness, judgment, judiciousness, solidity, depth, profoundness, enlarged views.

Genius, inspiration, the fire of genius.

Wisdom in action ; prudence, discretion, *aplomb* (698), sobriety, tact, ballast.

Phr. Discretion being the better part of valour.

V. To be intelligent, wise, &c., to reason (476), to discern (441), discriminate (465), to penetrate, to see far into.

Adj. (Applied to persons). Intelligent, long-headed, sagacious, quick, sharp, acute, shrewd, astute, sharpsighted, quick-sighted, quick-eyed, keen, keen-eyed, keen-sighted, keen-witted, penetrating, piercing, clearsighted, discerning.

Wise, sage, sapient, sagacious, reasonable, rational, sound, sensible, judicious, enlightened, impartial, unprejudiced, unbiassed, unprepossessed, undazzled, unperplexed.

Cool, cool-headed, long-headed, calculating, thoughtful, reflecting, oracular, heaven-directed.

Prudent, discreet, sober, staid, solid, considerate, provident, politic.

Phr. Wise as a serpent ; wise as Solomon ; wise as Solon.

(Applied to actions). Wise, sensible, reasonable, judicious, welljudged, well-advised, prudent, politic (646).

(499) IMBECILITY, incapacity, vacancy of mind, poverty of intellect, shallowness, dulness, stupidity, obtuseness, stolidity, hebitude, doltishness.

Silliness, simplicity, childishness, puerility, babyhood ; dotage, second childishness, fatuity, idiocy, idiotism (503).

FOLLY, absurdity, irrationality, senselessness, foolishness, inconsistency, lip-wisdom, conceit, giddiness, extravagance, oddity, eccentricity, ridiculousness.

Act of folly (497), imprudence (699).

Phr. The fool's paradise ; one's wits going a-woolgathering.

V. To be imbecile, foolish, &c., to trifle, drivel, ramble, *radoter.*

Phr. To play the fool ; to play the monkey ; to pursue a wild goose chase ; *battre la campagne ;* to reckon without one's host ; to quarrel with one's bread and butter ; *Semel insanavimus omnes.*

Adj. (Applied to persons). Unintelligent, unintellectual, witless, reasonless, imbecile, shallow, *borné,* weak, soft, sappy, weak-headed, weak-minded, feeble-minded, halfwitted, short-witted, shallow-brained, beetle-headed, dull, stupid, obtuse, stolid, doltish, asinine, dull-witted, blunt, silly, childish, infantine, infantile, babish, babyish, child-like.

Fatuous, idiotic, lack-brained, drivelling, blatant, brainless, bluntwitted, beef-witted, fat-witted, insulse, having no head or brains, thick-skulled, blockish, Bœotian, Bœotic.

Foolish, senseless, irrational, insensate, nonsensical, blunder-headed, puzzle-headed, muddle-headed, muddy-headed, ungifted, undiscerning, unenlightened, unphilosophical ; prejudiced, bigoted, narrow-minded, wrong-headed, crotchetty, conceited, self-opinionated, pig-headed, mulish, besotted, infatuated.

Wild, giddy, thoughtless, eccentric,

odd, extravagant, light-headed, rantipole, crack-brained, shatter-brained, shatter-pated, ridiculous.

(Applied to actions). Foolish, unwise, injudicious, imprudent, unreasonable, nonsensical, absurd, ridiculous, silly, stupid, asinine, ill-advised, ill-judged, ill-devised, inconsistent, irrational, unphiloso-phical, extravagant, preposterous, egregious, sleeveless, imprudent, indiscreet, improvident, impolitic, improper (645, 647).

(500) SAGE, wise man, *savant*, expert, luminary, adept, authority.

Oracle, a *Magnus Apollo*, a Solomon, a shining light, *esprit fort* (wiseacre), big-wig, philomath, school-man, Magi.

Ep. Venerable, reverenced, authoritative.

(501) FOOL, blockhead, wiseacre (ironically), simpleton, witling, ass, goose, ninny, dolt, booby, noodle, numskull, nizy, noddy, goose-cap, half-wit, *imbecille*, ninnyhammer, *badeau*, driveller, idiot ; natural, lackbrain, *niais*, child, infant, baby, innocent, greenhorn, zany, dunce, lout, loon, oaf, lown, dullard, dull-head, doodle, calf, colt, buzzard, block, put, stick, stock, numps, tony, clodpoll, clotpoll, clodhopper, clod, lubber, bull-calf, bullhead, thick-skull, dunderhead, dizzard, hoddydoddy, nonny, looby, nincompoop, a poor head, *un sot à triple étage*, loggerhead, sot, jolthead, beetle-head, jobbernowl, changeling, dotard, driveller, grasshead, mooncalf, giddyhead, *gobemouche*, rantipole, old woman, crone, April-fool.

Phr. One who would not set the Thames on fire ; one who did not invent gunpowder ; one who is no conjuror ; *qui n'a pas inventé la poudre.*

Men of Gotham ; men of Bœotia.

Measure of folly ; foolometer.

(502) SANITY, rationality, being in one's senses, in one's right mind, in one's sober senses ; sobriety, lucidity, lucid interval.

V. To be sane, &c., to retain one's senses, reason, &c.

To become sane, come to one's senses, sober down.

To render sane, bring to one's senses, to sober.

Adj. Sane, rational, reasonable, *compos*, in one's sober senses, in one's right mind, sober-minded.

Adv. Sanely, soberly, &c.

(503) INSANITY, lunacy, madness, derangement, alienation, aberration, demency, mania, calenture of the brain, phrenzy, frenzy, raving, mo-nomania, disordered intellect, inco-herence, wandering, delirium, hallu-cination, fantasia ; vertigo, dizziness, swimming, dementation : Bedlam.

V. To be, or become insane, &c., to lose one's senses, intellects, reason, faculties, &c., to run mad, rave, dote, ramble, wander, drivel.

Phr. Battre la campagne ; avoir le diable au corps.

To render, or drive mad ; to mad-den, dementate, turn the brain, addle the wits, turn one's head, befool, in-fatuate.

Adj. Insane, mad, lunatic, crazy, crazed, *non compos*, cracked, out of one's mind, bereft of reason, unsettled in one's mind, insensate, reasonless, beside oneself, demented, daft, possessed, maddened, moon-struck, mad-brained, maniacal, delirious, incoherent, rambling, doting, wandering, frantic, raving, corybantic, rabid, light-headed, giddy, vertiginous, wild, haggard, flighty, distracted, sleeveless, *écervelé*.

Phr. The head being turned; having a bee in one's bonnet; far gone; stark staring mad; mad as a March hare; the devil being in one; dizzy as a goose.

The wits going a-woolgathering, or a-bird's-nesting.

(504) MADMAN, lunatic, maniac, bedlamite, raver, monomaniac, dreamer, insane, a highflier.

Section VI.   EXTENSION OF THOUGHT.

1°. *To the Past.*

(505) MEMORY, remembrance, reminiscence, recognition, retention, retentiveness, readiness, tenacity.

Recurrence, recollection, retrospection, rememoration, retrospect, the tablets of the memory.

Suggestion, prompting, flapping (514).

Token of remembrance, memorial, *memento, souvenir,* keepsake, relic, reliquary, *memorandum,* remembrancer.

Things to be remembered, *memorabilia.*

Art of memory, artificial memory; Mnemonics, Mnemosyne.

V. To remember, retain, mind, bear or keep in mind, have or carry in the memory, know by heart or by rote, rememorate.

To be deeply impressed, to live, remain, or dwell in the memory, to be stored up, bottled up, to sink in the mind, to rankle, &c.

Phr. To have at one's fingers' ends; — *Manet altâ mente repostum;* — *Olim meminisse juvabit.*

(506) OBLIVION, forgetfulness, obliteration (552), a short memory, the memory failing, being in fault, or deserting one, the waters of Lethe, Napenthe, *tabula rasa.*

V. To forget, lose, unlearn, discharge from the memory.

To slip, escape, fade, die away from the memory, to sink into oblivion.

Phr. To cast behind one's back; to have a short memory; to have no head; to apply the spunge; *Non mi ricordo;* let bygones be bygones.

Adj. Forgotten, &c., lost, effaced, blotted out, obliterated, discharged, spunged over, buried or sunk in oblivion, clean out of one's head or recollection, past recollection, unremembered.

Forgetful, oblivious, mindless, out of mind.

To occur to the mind (514), recollect, call to mind, bethink oneself, recall, call up, retrace, carry one's thoughts back, look back, rake up, think upon, call to remembrance, tax the memory.

To suggest, prompt, hint, recall to mind, put in mind, remind, whisper, call up, summon up, rip up, renew, commend to, jog or refresh the memory.

Phr. To keep the memory alive; — To keep the wound green; — *Infandum renovare dolorem;* — *Tangere alcus.*

To say by heart, repeat by rote, say one's lesson, repeat as a parrot.

To commit to memory, get or learn by heart or rote, con, con over, repeat, to fix, imprint, impress, stamp, grave, engrave, store, treasure up, bottle up, embalm, enshrine &c. in the memory; to load, store, stuff, or burden the memory with.

Adj. Remembering, &c., mindful, remembered, &c., fresh, green, unforgotten, present to the mind, living in, being in, or within one's memory, indelible, green in remembrance, reminiscential.

Ep. The memory being retentive, ready, correct, exact, faithful, trustworthy, capacious.

Adv. By heart, by rote, *memoriter.*

2°. *To the Future.*

(507) EXPECTATION, expectance, anticipation, forestalling, foreseeing, reckoning, calculation.

Contemplation, prospect, perspective, hope, trust (858), abeyance, waiting, &c. (121).

V. To expect, look for, look out for, look forward to, anticipate, contemplate, flatter oneself, to dare to say, foresee (510), forestall, reckon upon, count upon, lay one's account to, to calculate upon, rely upon, build upon, make sure of, prepare oneself for.

Phr. To reckon one's chickens before they are hatched.

To wait, tarry, lie in wait, watch for, abide.

To raise or excite expectation, to bid fair, to promise, to augur, &c. (511), we shall see, *nous verrons.*

Adj. Expectant, expecting, &c., prepared for, gaping for, ready for.

Expected, anticipated, foreseen, &c., long expected.

Ep. Anxious, ardent, eager, breathless, sanguine.

Adv. With breathless expectation, on tenterhooks.

(508) INEXPECTATION, non-expectation, *see* Surprise (870).

V. Not to expect, not to look for, &c., to be taken by surprise, to come upon, to fall upon, not to bargain for.

Phr. To reckon without one's host.

To be unexpected, &c., to pop, to come unawares, suddenly, abruptly, like a thunderbolt, burst upon, bounce upon.

Phr. To drop from the clouds.

Adj. Non-expectant, unexpected, unlooked for, unhoped for, unforeseen, beyond expectation, abrupt, sudden.

Surprised, taken by surprise, unwarned, startled, &c., taken aback.

Adv. Suddenly, abruptly, unexpectedly, pop, *à l'improviste*, unawares, without notice or warning.

(509) Failure of expectation.

DISAPPOINTMENT, vain expectation, surprise, astonishment (870).

A balk, an afterclap, a miscalculation.

V. To be disappointed, &c., to look blue, to look aghast.

To disappoint, balk, dumfounder, miscalculate, dash one's hope (859).

Adj. Disappointed, aghast, blue.

Happening contrary to, or against expectation.

Phr. Rusticus expectat, &c.; — *Diis aliter visum.*

(510) FORESIGHT, prospiscience, prescience, foreknowledge, forethought, forecast, prevision, precognition, second-sight, *clairvoyance.*

Anticipation, foretaste, prenotion, presentiment, foregone conclusion, providence.

Announcement, programme.

V. To foresee, foreknow, forejudge, forecast, anticipate, look forwards or beyond, look, peep, or pry into the future.

Adj. Foreseeing, &c., prescient, weather-wise.

Ep. Rational, sagacious, perspicacious.

(511) PREDICTION, announcement, *prognosis*, prophecy, vaticination, mantology, prognostication, premonstration, haruspicy, auguration, bodement, omination, augury, abodement, aboding, horoscope, nativity, genethliacs, fortune-telling, sooth, ominousness.

Divination ;— By oracles ; Theomancy.

By the bible; Bibliomancy.

By the stars ; Astrology, Sideromancy, Horoscopy, Judicial Astrology.

By ghosts ; Psychomancy.

By shadows or manes ; Sciomancy.

By appearances in the air; Aeromancy, Chaomancy.

By winds ; Austromancy.

By sacrificial appearances ; Aruspicy (or Haruspicy), Hieromancy, Hieroscopy.

By the entrails of animals sacrificed; Ieromancy.

By the entrails of a human sacrifice ; Anthropomancy.

By the entrails of fishes ; Ichthyomancy.

By sacrificial fire; Pyromancy.

By smoke from the altar ; Capnomancy.

By mice ; Myomancy.

By birds ; Ornithomancy.

By herbs ; Botanomancy.

By water; Hydromancy.

By fountains; Pegomancy.

By a wand; Rhabdomancy.

By dough of cakes ; Crithomancy.

By meal ; Aleuromancy.

By salt; Alomancy.

By dice; Cleromancy.

By arrows ; Belomancy.

By a balanced hatchet; Axinomancy.

By a balanced sieve ; Coscinomancy.

By a suspended ring; Dactyliomancy.

By dots made at random on paper ; Geomancy.

By precious stones ; Lithomancy.

By nails reflecting the sun's rays ; Onychomancy.

By names; Onomancy.

By pebbles; Pessomancy.

By pebbles drawn from a heap ; Psephomancy.

By mirrors ; Catoptromancy.

By writings in ashes; Tephramancy.

By dreams; Oneiromancy.

By the hand ; Palmistry, Chiromancy.

By numbers; Arithmancy.

By the letters forming the name of the person ; Nomancy.

By the mode of laughing ; Geloscopy.

By walking in a circle ; Gyromancy.

By a cock picking up grains; Alectryomancy (or Alectoromancy).

Place of prediction ; *adytum.*

V. To predict, prognosticate, prophecy, vaticinate, presage, augur, bode, forebode, foretell, croak, soothsay, augurate.

To foretoken, betoken, prefigure, portend, foreshadow, forethrow, ominate, usher in, herald, signify, premise, announce, point to, lower, admonish, warn, forewarn, advise.

117

Adj. Predicting, &c., predictive, prophetic, fatidical, vaticinal, oracular, Sibylline.

Ominous, portentous, augurous, augurial, prescious, monitory, extipicious, premonitory, significant of, pregnant with, weatherwise.

Phr. " Coming events cast their shadows before."

(512) OMEN, portent, presage, prognostic, sign, forerunner, precursor (64), harbinger, herald, monitor, warning, *avant-courier*, pilot-balloon, handwriting on the wall, rise and fall of the barometer, a bird of ill omen.

(513) ORACLE, prophet, seer, soothsayer, fortune-teller, geomancer, Sibyl, Python, Pythoness, *Pythia*, Pythian oracle, witch, Monitor, Aruspex, Sphinx, Tiresias, Cassandra, Œdipus.

Section VII. Creative Thought.

(514) SUPPOSITION, conjecture, surmise, presurmise, guess, guess-work, divination, conceit, conjecturality ; assumption, hypothesis, pre-supposition, postulate, presumption, theory ; suggestion, allusion, proposition, motion, proposal.

V. To suppose, conjecture, surmise, guess, divine, give a guess, hazard a conjecture, throw out a conjecture, &c., presuppose, fancy, wis, take it, dare to say, take it into one's head, presume.

To suggest, hint, insinuate, put forth, propound, propose, start, allude to, prompt, put a case, move, make a motion.

To suggest itself, occur to one, come into one's head ; to run in the head ; to haunt (505).

Adj. Supposing, &c., supposed, supposititious, suppositive, suggestive, allusive, conjectural, presumptive, putative, hypothetical, theoretical.

Ep. Warranted, authorized, fair, reasonable, just, natural.

Unwarranted, gratuitous, baseless, wild, hazarded, rash, untenable, extravagant, unreasonable, unsatisfactory, loose, vague, unconnected.

Adv. If, if so be, an, may be, perhaps.

(515) IMAGINATION, fancy, conception, ideality, idealism, inspiration, dreaming, somnambulism, phrenzy, ecstacy, excogitation.

Phr. Flight of fancy ; fumes of fancy ; fine frenzy ; thickcoming fancies ; coinage of the brain ; the mind's eye.

Invention, originality, fertility, conceit, pigment, coinage, fiction, romance, novel, myth, the man in the moon, dream, day-dream, vapour, phantom, phantasy, whim, whimsy, vagary, rhapsody, *extravaganza*, air-drawn dagger, bug-bear, castle in the air, air-built castle, *château en Espagne*, Will o' the wisp, *ignus fatuus*, Jack-o'-lantern, *le pot au lait*, Utopia, millennium.

A visionary, romancer, rhapsodist, highflyer, enthusiast, dreamer, seer, fanatic, knight-errant, Don Quixote.

V. To imagine, fancy, conceive, idealize, realize ; fancy, or picture to oneself ; create, devise, invent, coin, fabricate.

Phr. To take into one's head ; to strain, or crack one's invention ; to strike out something new ; to give a loose to the fancy ; to give the reins to the imagination.

Adj. Imagining, imagined, &c. ; ideal, unreal, imaginary, *in nubibus*, fictitious, *ben trovato*, fanciful, air-drawn, air-built, original, fantastic, whimsical, high-flown.

118

Imaginative, inventive, creative, fertile, romantic, flighty, extravagant, fanatic, *romanesque*, enthusiastic, Utopian, Quixotic.

Ep. Warm, heated, excited, sanguine, ardent, fiery, boiling, wild, bold, daring ; playful, fertile, &c.

Division II. COMMUNICATION OF IDEAS.

Section I. Nature of Ideas Communicated.

(516) Idea to be conveyed.

Meaning, signification, sense, import, purport, significance, drift, acceptation, acceptance, acception, bearing, interpretation (522), reading, tenor, allusion, spirit, colouring, expression ; literal meaning, literality, obvious meaning, first blush, *primâ facie* meaning ; after acceptation.

Equivalent meaning, synonym.

Thing signified ; matter, substance, gist, pith, marrow, argument, text.

V. To mean, signify, express, import, purport, convey, breathe, imply, bespeak, bear a sense, involve, declare (527), insinuate, allude to, point to, drive at, to come to the point.

(517) Absence of meaning.

Unmeaningness, empty sound, a dead letter, inexpressiveness.

Nonsense, gibberish, empty babble, empty sound.

V. To mean nothing, to be unmeaning, &c.

Adj. Unmeaning, void of meaning, of sense, &c., senseless, not significant.

Inexpressible, undefinable, unmeant, unconceived.

Phr. Vox et præterea nihil. " A tale told by an idiot, full of sound and fury, signifying nothing."

To take, understand, receive, or accept in a particular sense.

Adj. Meaning, &c., significant, significative, significatory, pithy, full of meaning, pregnant with meaning.

Synonymous, equivalent, tantamount ; the same thing as.

Ep. Plain, simple, natural, *primâ facie*, obvious, explicit, precise, downright, definite, distinct, defined, literal, ostensible, overt, broad, naked, unstrained, undisguised, positive, formal, honest, emphatic, *bonâ fide*, true.

Implied, tacit, understood, implicit, inferred, latent.

Adv. Literally, &c.

Phr. Au pied de la lettre, so to speak, so to express oneself; as it were.

(518) Intelligibility, clearness, lucidity, perspicacity, explicitness, distinctness, plain speaking, expressiveness, legibleness.

Intelligence, comprehension, understanding, learning (539).

V. To be intelligible, &c.

(519) Unintelligibility, incomprehensibleness, inconceivableness, darkness (421), obscurity, confusion, indistinctness, indefiniteness, vagueness, ambiguity, looseness, uncertainty, mysteriousness (526), paradox, inexplicableness, spinosity.

To render intelligible, &c., to simplify.

Phr. Cela saute aux yeux ; he that
runs may read.

To understand, comprehend, take,
take in, catch, grasp, collect ; to come
to an understanding.

Adj. Intelligible, clear, lucid, explicit, expressive, significant, express, distinct, precise, definite, well-
defined, perspicuous, transpicuous,
plain, obvious, manifest, palpable,
glaring, transparent, above board,
unambiguous, unmistakeable, legible,
open, positive, unconfused, unequivocal, graphic.

Jargon, gibberish, rigmarole, rhodomontade, &c. (497).

High Dutch, Greek, Hebrew, &c.

V. To be unintelligible, &c.

To render unintelligible, &c., to
perplex, confuse, confound, bewilder,
darken, moider.

Not to understand, &c., to lose,
miss, &c., to lose the clue.

Phr. Not to know what to make
of ; not to be able to make either
head or tail of ; to play at cross purposes.

Adj. Unintelligible, incomprehensible, inconceivable, above or past
comprehension, inexplicable, illegible, undecipherable, inscrutable, beyond one's depth, paradoxical, insolvable.

Obscure, dark, confused, indistinct, indefinite, nebulous, undefined,
ill defined, perplexed, loose, vague, ambiguous, enigmatical, mysterious, mystic, mystical, intricate.

Hidden, recondite, abstruse, transcendental, farfetched, searchless,
unconceived.

(520) Having a double sense.

EQUIVOCALNESS, double meaning, *équivoque*, equivocation, *double entendre*, amphibology, prevarication, slip of the tongue, *lapsus linguæ*.

Having a doubtful meaning, ambiguity, *see* (475), homonymy.

Having a false meaning, *see* (544), *suggestio falsi*.

V. To be equivocal, &c., to have two senses, &c., to equivocate, prevaricate, palter to the understanding.

Adj. Equivocal, ambiguous, amphibolous, double-tongued.

(521) METAPHOR, figure, metonymy, trope, *catachresis, synecdoche*,
figure of speech, figurativeness, image, imagery, *metalepsis*, type (22).

Personification, *prosopopœia*, allegory, apologus, parable.

Implication, inference, allusion, adumbration.

V. To employ metaphor, &c., to personify, allegorize, adumbrate, shadow
forth, imply, understand, apply, allude to.

Adj. Metaphorical, figurative, catachrestical, typical, tralatitious, parabolic, allegorical, allusive, implied, inferential, implicit, understood.

Phr. Where more is meant than meets the ear.

(522) INTERPRETATION, *exegesis*,
explanation, explication, expound-
ing, exposition, rendition, reddition.

Translation, version, construction,
reading, spelling, restoration, metaphrase.

Comment, commentary, illustration, exemplification, definition,
éclaircissement, elucidation, dilucida-

(523) MISINTERPRETATION, misapprehension, misunderstanding, misacceptation, misconstruction, mis-
spelling, misapplication, *catachresis*,
mistake, cross reading, cross purposes.

Misrepresentation, perversion, falsification, misquotation, garbling,
exaggeration (549), false colouring,

tion, gloss, glossary, annotation, *scholium*, note, clue, key, master key, *dénouement*, answer (462).

Palæography, metaposcopy, dictionary, glossology, &c. (562).

V. To interpret, expound, explain, construe, translate, render, do into, turn into, transfuse the sense of.

To read, spell, make out, decipher, unfold, disentangle, elicit the meaning of, find the key of, unriddle, unravel, restore.

To elucidate, illustrate, exemplify, comment upon, define, unfold.

Adj. Explanatory, expository, explicatory, exegetical.

Paraphrastic, metaphrastic,— literal.

Adv. That is to say, *id est, videlicet*, in other words, in plain words, simply, in plain English.

Literally, *verbatim, au pied de la lettre*.

abuse of terms, parody, travesty, misstatement, &c. (544).

V. To misinterpret, misapprehend, misunderstand, misconceive, misspell, mistranslate, misconstrue, misapply, mistake (495).

To misstate, &c. (544); to pervert, falsify, distort, detort, stretch, strain, or wrest the sense or meaning ; to put a bad or false construction on ; to misquote, garble, belie, explain away.

Phr. To make neither head nor tail of ; to play at cross purposes.

Adj. Misinterpreted, &c., untranslated, untranslatable.

(524) Interpreter, expositor, scholiast, commentator, spokesman, speaker, mouthpiece, dragoman, *trucheman*, Œdipus (513).

Section II.　Modes of Communication.

(525) Manifestation, expression, showing, &c., indication, exposition, demonstration, exhibition, production, display, showing off, retection, premonstration.

Openness, frankness (543), publicity (531).

V. To manifest, show, express, indicate, point out, bring forth, bring forward, set forth, exhibit, expose, produce, bring into view, set before one, hold up to view, lay open, lay bare, expose to view, set before one's eyes, show up, shadow forth, bring to light, display, demonstrate, indigitate, to unroll, unveil, unmask, disclose, *see* (529), hold up the mirror, draw, lift up, raise or remove the curtain, elicit, educe, draw out, bring out, disinter.

To be manifested, &c., to appear, transpire, come to light, *see* Visibility (446), to come out.

Adj. Manifest, clear, apparent,

(526) Latency, latitency, latitation, secrecy, secretness, privacy, invisibility, *see* (447), occultness, darkness, reticence, silence, closeness, reserve, inexpression.

Retirement, delitescence, seclusion (893).

V. To be latent, &c., to keep back, reserve, suppress, keep close, keep secret, keep to oneself, keep snug, hush, hold one's tongue, hold one's peace, leave in the dark, hush up.

Phr. To keep one's own counsel ; — To seal the lips ;—not to breathe a syllable about.

Adj. Latent, secret, close, latitant, unapparent, unknown (491), delitescent, in the background, occult, snug, private, privy, *in petto*, anagogic, sequestered, dormant.

Unconspicuous, indiscoverable, unperceived, invisible (447), unseen, unwitnessed, impenetrable, unspied, unsuspected.

121

evident, visible (446), prominent, in the foreground, conspicuous, palpable, open.

Manifested, shown, expressed, &c., disclosed, *see* (529), frank, capable of being shown, producible.

Adv. Openly, before one's eyes, face to face, above board, in open court, in open daylight, in the open streets.

(527) INFORMATION, communication, intimation, notice, notification, enunciation, announcement, annunciation, statement, specification, report, advice, monition, mention, acquaintance, acquainting, &c., outpouring, communicativeness.

An informant, teller, intelligencer, messenger (534).

Hint, suggestion (514), wrinkle, insinuation, innuendo, wink, glance, leer, nod, shrug, gesture, whisper, implication, cue.

Phr. Verbum sapienti.

V. To inform, acquaint, tell, mention, express, intimate, communicate, apprize, make known, notify, signify to, let one know, advise, state, specify, give notice, announce, annunciate, report, set forth, bring word, send word, leave word, write word, declare, pronounce, explain, convey the knowledge of, give an account of.

To hint, give an inkling of, give, throw out, or drop a hint, insinuate, allude to, glance at, make allusion to, to wink, to tip the wink, glance, leer, nod, shrug, give the cue, wave, whisper, suggest, prompt, whisper in the ear.

To be informed, &c. of, made acquainted with, to hear of, to understand.

To come to one's ears, to come to one's knowledge, to reach one's ears, to hear of.

Adj. Informed, &c. of, made acquainted with, undeceived.

Reported, made known, bruited.

Expressive, significant, pregnant with meaning, &c., *see* (516), decla-

Untold, unpublished, unbreathed, untalked of, unsung, unpronounced, unreported, unexposed, unproclaimed, unexpressed, not expressed, tacit, implied, undeveloped, unsolved, unexplained, undiscovered, untracked, unexplored, uninvented.

Phr. No news being good news.

Adv. Secretly, &c., *sub silentio.*

(528) CONCEALMENT, hiding, &c., secrecy, stealth, stealthiness, slyness, disguise, *incognita,* masquerade, mystery, mystification, freemasonry, reservation, suppression, back stairs, reserve, uncommunicativeness : secret path.

A mask, vizor (or visor), ambush, &c., *see* (530), enigma, riddle, &c. (533).

V. To conceal, hide, secrete, cover, screen, cloak, veil, shroud, shade, muffle, mask, disguise, ensconce, eclipse.

To keep from, lock up, bury, sink, suppress, hush up, keep snug or close, &c.

Phr. To draw or close the curtain.

To keep in ignorance, blind, hoodwink, mystify, pose, puzzle, perplex, embarrass, bewilder, bamboozle, &c. (545).

To be concealed, &c., to lurk, skulk, smolder, lie hid, lie in ambush, lie *perdu,* sneak, retire, steal into, steal along.

To conceal oneself, put on a veil, mask, &c. (530).

Phr. To play at bo-peep, to play at hide and seek, to hide under a bushel, to throw dust into the eyes.

Adj. Concealed, hid, hidden, &c., secret, clandestine, close, furtive, surreptitious, stealthy, underhand, sly, sneaking, skulking, hide and seek, undivulged, unrevealed, undisclosed, mum.

Mysterious, mystic, mystical, enigmatical, problematical, anagogical, paradoxical, occult, recondite, abstruse, unexplained, impenetrable, indiscoverable, inexplicable, in a maze.

ratory, enunciative, nuncupatory, expository, communicatory, communicative.

Adv. Expressively, significantly, &c.

By post, courier, express, estafette, telegraph.

————

Covered, closed, shrouded, veiled, masked, screened, shaded, disguised, under cover, under a cloud, veil, &c., in a fog, haze, mist, &c., under an eclipse, inviolable.

Reserved, uncommunicative, buttoned up, taciturn (585).

Adv. Secretly, clandestinely, privily, in secret, mum, with closed doors, *à huis clos, à la dérobée*, under the rose, underhand, *en tapinois*, privately, in private, aside, on the sly, *sub silentio*, behind one's back, behind the curtain.

Confidentially, between ourselves, between you and me, *entre nous, inter nos*, in strict confidence.

Phr. Like a thief in the night; under the seal of secrecy;— *Davus sum, non Œdipus.*

(529) DISCLOSURE, revealment, revelation, deterration, exposition.

Acknowledgment, avowal, confession ; a tell tale, an *exposé.*

V. To disclose, open, lay open, divulge, reveal, unfold, let drop, let out, lay open, acknowledge, own, confess, avow, unburden or disburden one's mind, or one's conscience, to unbosom oneself, to open one's mind, unfold, unseal, unveil, unmask, unkennel.

(530) AMBUSH, hiding-place, retreat, cover, lurking-hole, secret place, recess, ambuscade, crypt, *adytum*, trap, gin, *see* (545).

A mask, veil, vizor (or visor), cloak, screen, curtain, shade, cover, disguise, masquerade dress, domino.

V. To lie in ambush, lurk, lie in wait for, lay or set a trap for.

To blab, peach, let out, tell tales, speak out, blur out.

To make public, publish, *see* (531).

To make no secret of, to disabuse, unbeguile.

Phr. To let into the secret ; to let the cat out of the bag ; to make a clean breast of it ; to tell tales out of school ; not to mince the matter.

To be disclosed, revealed, &c., to come out, to transpire, to ooze out, to creep out.

Phr. The murder will out.

Adj. Disclosed, revealed, divulged, laid open, &c., unriddled, &c.

Open, public, exoteric.

Int. Out with it !

(531) PUBLICATION, announcement, notification, enunciation, annunciation, advertisement, promulgation, circulation, propagation, indiction, edition, proclamation, hue and cry.

Publicity, notoriety, currency, cry, bruit, rumour, fame, report, *on dit*, flagrancy.

Notice, notification, manifesto, advertisement, placard, bill, *affiche*, newspapers, gazette.

V. To publish, make known, announce, notify, annunciate, set forth, give forth, give out, utter, advertise, placard, *afficher*, circulate, propagate, spread, spread abroad, edit, rumour, diffuse, disseminate, blaze about ; blaze, or noise abroad ; buzz, bandy, hawk about, trumpet, herald, give

123

tongue, raise a cry, raise a hue and cry, bring, lay or drag before the public, give currency to.

Phr. To proclaim at Charing Cross; to publish in the Gazette ; *Spargere auras per vulgum ambiguas;* with beat of drum.

To be published, &c., to become public, to go forth, to get abroad, to get wind, to take air, to get afloat, to acquire currency, to spread, to go the rounds, to buzz about, to blow about.

Phr. Virum volitare per auras.

Adj. Published, &c., made public, exoteric, rumoured, rife, current, afloat, notorious, flagrant, whispered, buzzed about, in every one's mouth, reported, trumpet-tongued, encyclical.

Phr. As the story runs.

Int. Oyez! O yes!

(532) NEWS, piece of information, intelligence, tidings, budget of news, word, advice, *aviso,* message, errand, embassy, despatch.

Report, rumour, hearsay, *on dit,* fame, talk, gossip, *oui-dire,* scandal, buzz, *bruit.*

Letters, mail, post (592).

Glad-tidings; old news, stale news, stale story, fresh news.

(533) SECRET, *arcanum,* profound secret, mystery, *arrière pensée,* problem, enigma, riddle, puzzle, conundrum, charade, rebus, logograph, monogram, paradox, maze, labyrinth, perplexity, chaos (528), the Hyrcynian wood ; *Terra incognita.*

Phr. The secrets of the prison-house.

(534) MESSENGER, envoy, nuncio, internuncio, herald, ambassador, legate, emissary, *corps diplomatique.*

Marshal, crier, trumpeter, pursuivant, *parlementaire,* courier, runner, Ariel, estafette, Mercury.

Narrator, &c., tale-bearer, spy, scout.

(535) AFFIRMATION, predication, assertion, declaration, word, averment, asseveration, protestation, swearing, protest, profession, deposition, avouchment, affirmance, assurance, allegation, acknowledgment, avowal, confession, confession of faith, oath.

Remark, observation, position, thesis, proposition, saying, *dictum,* theorem.

Positiveness, dogmatism, *ipse dixit.*

V. To assert, make an assertion, &c., say, affirm, predicate, declare, profess, aver, avouch, put forth, advance, allege, propose, propound, broach, set forth, maintain, contend, pronounce, pretend, pass an opinion, &c.

To vouch, assure, vow, swear, take oath, recognize, avow, acknowledge, own, confess, announce, hazard an opinion.

(536) NEGATION, abnegation, denial, disavowal, disclaimer, abjuration, contradiction, contravention, recusation, retraction, retractation, recantation, renunciation, palinody, palidoxy, recusancy.

Qualification, modification (469).

V. To deny, disown, contradict, negative, gainsay, contravene, disclaim, withdraw, eat one's words, recant, disavow, retract, revoke, abjure.

To dispute, impugn, question, call in question, give the lie to, rebut, belie.

Adj. Denying, &c., denied, &c., contradictory, recusant.

Adv. No, nay, not, *see* (489).

To dogmatize, lay down, lay down the law ; to call heaven to witness, protest, depose, warrant.

Phr. I doubt not ; I warrant you ; I'll engage ; depend upon it ! I'll be bound, I am sure, I have no doubt, sure enough, faith !

Adj. Asserting, &c., dogmatic, positive, emphatic, indeed, predicable, pronunciative, unretracted.

Positive, broad, round, express, explicit, pointed, marked, distinct, decided, formal, solemn, categorical, peremptory, emphatic.

Adv. Ex cathedrâ, positively, broadly, roundly, &c., so to speak ; ay, yes, indeed, &c., *see* (488).

(537) TEACHING, instruction, direction, guidance, tuition, inculcation, inoculation, indoctrination, *éclaircissement,* explanation.

Education, initiation, preparation, training, schooling, discipline, exercise, drill, exercitation, breaking in, taming, drilling, &c., preachment, persuasion, edification, proselytism, propagandism.

A lesson, lecture, prolusion, prelection, exercise, task ; *curriculum.*

Rudiments, elements, grammar, text-book, *vade-mecum,* school-book.

V. To teach, instruct, enlighten, edify, inculcate, indoctrinate, instil, imbue, inoculate, infuse, impregnate, graft, infix, ingraft, implant, sow the seeds of, infiltrate, give an idea of, put up to, sharpen the wit, beat into the head, cram, coach.

To explain, expound, lecture, hold forth, read a lecture or sermon, give a lesson, preach ; sermonize, moralize, point a moral.

To educate, train, discipline, school, form, ground, tutor, prepare, qualify, prime, drill, exercise, bring up, nurture, dry nurse, breed, break in, tame.

To direct, guide, put in the way of, preinstruct, proselytize, bring round to an opinion, bring over, win over, persuade, convince, convict, set right, enlighten, give one new ideas, put one up to.

Adj. Teaching, &c., taught, &c.

Didactic, academic, doctrinal, disciplinal, instructive, scholastic, persuasive.

(538) MISTEACHING, misdirection, misinformation, misguidance, misinstruction, perversion, false teaching, mispersuasion.

Indocility, incapacity, misintelligence, dulness.

V. To misinform, mislead, misdirect, misguide, miscorrect, pervert, lead into error, bewilder, mystify (528), throw off the scent ; to unteach.

Phr. Piscem natare doces ; obscurum per obscurius ; the blind leading the blind.

Adj. Misteaching, &c., unedifying.

(539) LEARNING, acquisition of knowledge, acquirement, attainment, scholarship, erudition, instruction, study, &c., *see* Knowledge (490), apprenticeship.

Docility, aptitude, aptness to be taught, persuasibleness, persuasibility, docibleness, capacity.

V. To learn ; to acquire, gain, catch, receive, imbibe, pick up, gather, collect, glean, &c., knowledge or information.

To hear, overhear, catch hold of, take in, fish up, drink in, run away with an idea, to make oneself acquainted with, master, read, spell, turn over the leaves, peruse, grind, cram, make oneself master of, go to school, to get up a subject.

To be taught, &c.

Adj. Docile, apt, teachable, persuasible, studious.

(540) TEACHER, instructor, apostle, master, director, tutor, preceptor, institutor, mentor, adviser, monitor, counsellor, expositor, Corypheus, dry nurse, coach, grinder, governor, bear leader, disciplinarian, martinet, guide, *cicerone*, pioneer, governess, duenna.

Orator, speaker, mouthpiece (582).

Professor, lecturer, reader, prælector, prolocutor, schoolmaster, usher, pedagogue.

Professorship, lectureship, chair, pulpit, rostrum.

(541) LEARNER, scholar, student, disciple, pupil, *élève*, schoolboy, beginner, tyro, abecedarian, novice, neophyte, inceptor, probationer, apprentice, condisciple, freshman, freshwater sailor.

Proselyte, convert, catechumen, sectator, class, form.

Pupillage, pupillarity, apprenticeship, novitiate, leading-strings, matriculation.

Phr. In statu pupillari.

(542) SCHOOL, academy, university, alma-mater, college, seminary, nursery, institute, institution, palæstra, gymnasium, hot-bed, class, propaganda.

Horn-book, rudiments, *vade-mecum*, abecedary.

Pulpit, chair, ambo, theatre, amphitheatre, forum, stage, rostrum, platform, hustings.

Adj. Scholastic, academic.

Adv. Ex cathedrâ.

(543) VERACITY, truthfulness, truth, sincerity, frankness, straightforwardness, ingenuousness, candour, honesty, fidelity, openness, unreservedness, bluntness, plainness, plain speaking, plain dealing, simplicity, *bonhommie, naïveté*, artlessness (703), love of truth.

Phr. Le palais de la vérité.

V. To speak the truth, speak one's mind, think aloud.

Phr. Not to mince the matter.

Adj. Truthful, true, veracious, sincere, candid, frank, open, free-spoken, openhearted, *ingénu*, honest, simple, simple-hearted, ingenuous, blunt, plainspoken, straightforward, fair, singleminded, artless, guileless, pure, natural, unaffected, simpleminded, undisguised, unfeigned, unflattering.

Adv. Truly, &c. (494), aboveboard, broadly.

Phr. In plain English ;—Without mincing the matter.

(544) FALSEHOOD, falseness, mendacity, falsification, perversion of truth, romance, forgery, prevarication, equivocation, shuffling, evasion, fencing, caption, duplicity, double dealing, unfairness, dishonesty, misrepresentation, *suggestio falsi, suppressio veri*, Punic faith, giving the go-by, disguise, disguisement, irony.

Insincerity, dissimulation, dissembling, hypocrisy, cant, humbug, jesuitry, mental reservation, simulation, acting, sham, malingering, pretending, &c., crocodile tears, meallymouthedness, false colouring, art, artfulness (702), perjury, deceiver, *see* (548).

V. To be false, &c., to speak falsely, lie, fib, tell a lie or untruth, &c. (546), to mistake, misreport, misrepresent, falsify, prevaricate, equivocate, palter, shuffle, fence, mince the truth.

To foreswear, swear false, perjure oneself, bear false witness.

To garble, gloss over, disguise, colour, varnish, cook, put a false colouring or construction upon (523).

To invent, fabricate, trump up, forge, romance.

To dissemble, dissimulate, feign, assume, act or play a part, simulate, pass off for, counterfeit, sham, malinger, make believe, cant, put on.

Phr. To play the hypocrite; to give the go-by; to play fast and loose; to blow hot and cold; to lie like a conjuror; — *Faire patte de velours;* to look as if butter would not melt in one's mouth.

Adj. False, dishonest, faithless, truthless, trothless, unfair, uncandid, disingenuous, hollow, insincere, canting, hypocritical, jesuitical, pharisaical, tartuffian, double, double-tongued, double-faced, smooth-spoken, smooth-tongued, plausible, mealy-mouthed.

Artful, insidious, sly, designing, diplomatic, Machiavelian.

Untrue, unfounded, fictitious, invented, *ben trovato*, forged, falsified, &c., counterfeit, spurious, bastard, sham, mock, *pseudo*, disguised, simulated, &c., artificial, supposititious, colourable, catchpenny, Brummagem, illusory, elusory, supposititious, surreptitious, ironical.

Phr. All is not gold that glitters ; — *Non e tutto oro quelle che luce ; — Parthis mendacior.*

Adv. Falsely, &c., *à la Tartuffe.*

(545) DECEPTION, fraud, deceit, imposition, artifice, juggle, juggling, sleight of hand, legerdemain, conjuration, hocus-pocus, *escamoterie*, jockeyship, trickery, coggery, fraudulence, imposture, *supercherie*, cozenage, circumvention, ingannation, prestigation, subreption, collusion, guile, gullery.

Quackery, charlatanism, charlatanry, empiricism, humbug, gammon, mummery.

Stratagem, trick, cheat, wile, artifice, fraud, deception, make believe, *ruse*, manœuvre, *finesse*, hoax, hum, bubble, fetch, catch, reach, go-by, abuse, hocus, dodge, bite, forgery, delusion, stalking-horse.

Snare, trap, pitfall, decoy, gin, springe, noose, springle, hook, bait, net, meshes, mouse-trap, trap-door, ambush, ambuscade, masked-battery, dupe *see* (547).

V. To deceive, mislead, cheat, impose upon, practise upon, circumvent, play upon, put upon, dupe, mystify, blind, hoodwink, outreach, trick, hoax, hum, hocus, juggle, trepan, nick, entrap, beguile, lure, inveigle, decoy, lime, insnare, entangle, lay a snare for, trip up, give the go-by.

To defraud, cheat, take in, jockey, do, cozen, diddle, nab, chouse, bilk, bite, pluck, swindle, victimize, outwit, overreach, palm upon, foist upon, fob off, balk, trump up.

Phr. To throw dust into the eyes ; to play a trick upon ; to cog the dice; to throw a tub to the whale ; to make one believe the moon is made of cream cheese.

Adj. Deceiving, cheating, &c.

Deceptive, deceitful, deceptious, illusive, illusory, delusory, elusive, insidious, *ad captandum.*

(546) UNTRUTH, falsehood, lie, falsity, fiction, fabrication, fib, story, fable, novel, romance, flam, bam, gammon, flim-flam, *guet-apens*, white lie.

Falsification, perjury, forgery, false swearing, misstatement, misrepresentation.

Pretence, pretext, subterfuge, irony, evasion, blind, disguise, plea, claptrap, shuffle, make believe, shift, mask, cloak, vizor, veil, masquerade, gloss, cobweb.

Phr. A tub to the whale ; a cock and bull story ; the grapes being sour.

127

(547) DUPE, gull, gudgeon, *gobe-mouche*, cully, victim, puppet, April-fool, done, *see* Credulity (486).
Phr. Qui vult decipi, decipiatur.

(548) DECEIVER, liar, hypocrite, tale-teller, shuffler, dissembler, serpent, cockatrice, Pharisee, Jesuit, Janus, Tartuffe.

Pretender, impostor, knave, cheat, rogue, trickster, swindler, sharper, jockey, blackleg, rook, shark, guinea-dropper, decoy-duck, gipsy.

Quack, chartalan, mountebank, empiric, quacksalver, salt in banco, medicaster, Rosicrucian, *soi-disant*.

Actor, player, mummer, tumbler, posture-master, jack-pudding.
Phr. A wolf in sheep's clothing.

(549) EXAGGERATION, hyperbole, stretch, strain, colouring, bounce, flourish, vagary, bombast, yarn, figure of speech, flight of fancy, *façon de parler*, extravagance, rhodomontade, Baron Munchausen, *see* Boasting (884).

V. To exaggerate, amplify, overcharge, overstate, overcolour, overlay, strain, stretch, bounce, flourish, *broder* ; to hyperbolize, aggravate.

Phr. To stretch a point ; spin a long yarn ; shoot with a long bow ; deal in the marvellous ; out-Herod Herod.

Adj. Exaggerated, &c., hyperbolical, turgid, extravagant, bombastic, *outré*.

Phr. All his geese are swans ; much cry and little wool ; to make a mountain of a mole-hill.

Section III. MEANS OF COMMUNICATING IDEAS.

1°. *Natural Means.*

(550) INDICATION, symbolization, notation, connotation, prefigurement, representation (554), exposition, notice (527), trace (551).

A sign, symbol, index, point or exponent, indice, indicator, mark, token, symptom, type, emblem, cypher, device, epigraph, motto, posy.

Lineament, feature, line, stroke, dash, trait, score, stripe, streak, scratch, tick, dot, point, notch, nick, asterisk, red letter, Italics, print, impress, imprint, sublineation, underlining, jotting.

For identification ; Badge, criterion, check, countercheck, countersign, label, ticket, billet, card, bill, witness, voucher, hall-mark, signature, handwriting, sign-manual, cypher, seal, sigil, signet, autograph, autography, superscription, endorsement, title, heading, docket, watchword, *mot du guet*.

Insignia ; Banner, banneret, flag, colours, streamer, standard, ensign, pennon, pennant, pendant, jack, ancient, oriflamb, gonfalon ; crest, arms, armorial bearings, shield, scutcheon, escutcheon, livery, cockade, epaulet, chevron.

Indication of locality ; Beacon, cairn, post, staff, flagstaff, hand, pointer, vane, guide-post, finger-post, directing post, land-mark, sea-mark, lighthouse, balize, polestar, loadstar, cynosure, guide, address, direction, rocket, blue-light, watch-fire.

Indication of an event ; Signal, nod, wind, beck, cue, gesture, gesticulation, dumb show, pantomime, touch, nudge, freemasonry, telegraph, semaphore.

Indication of danger ; Alarm, larum, alarm-bell, tocsin, beat of drum, fire-cross, sound of trumpet, war-cry, war-whoop.

V. To indicate, point out, be the sign, &c. of, denote, betoken, connote, connotate, represent, stand for, typify, shadow forth, argue, bear the impress of, witness, attest, testify.

To put an indication, mark, &c.; to note, mark, stamp, label, ticket, docket, endorse, sign, countersign; put, append, or affix a seal or signature; dot, jot down, book, score, dash, trace, chalk, underline, print, imprint, engrave, stereotype, make an impress of.

To make a sign, signal, &c., signalize; give or hang out a signal; give notice, beckon, beck, nod, wink, nudge, tip the wink, give the cue; wave, unfurl, hoist, or hang out a banner, flag, &c., show one's colours, give or sound an alarm, beat the drum, sound the trumpets, raise a cry, &c.

Adj. Indicating, &c., indicatory, indicative, denotative, typical, connotative, pathognomonic, symptomatic, exponential, emblematic, attesting, armorial.

Indicated, &c., typified, protypified, impressed, &c.

Capable of being denoted, denotable, indelible.

Phr. Ecce signum ; Ex pede Herculem ; Verbum satis.

---

(551) RECORD, trace, vestige, footstep, footmark, footprint, footfall, wake, trail, scent, *piste,* monument, relic, remains, trophy, hatchment, achievement, obelisk, pillar, column, testimonial, memorial.

Note, minute, register, registry, memorandum, document, voucher, protocol, inscription.

Paper, parchment, scroll, instrument, deed, indenture, debenture, roll, archive, schedule, tablet, cartulary, table, affidavit, certificate, attestation, entry, diploma, protest, round-robin, muster-roll, muster-book, note-book, commonplace-book, *adversaria,* portfolio.

Chronicle, annals, gazette, newspaper, gazetteer, almanac, calendar, ephemeris, diary, log, journal, *see* History (594).

Registration, tabulation, enrolment, entry, booking.

V. To record, note, register, chronicle, make an entry of, enter, book, take a note of, post, enrol, jot down, take down, mark, sign, &c. (550), tabulate, catalogue, file, calendar.

Adj. Registered, &c.

(552) Suppression of sign.

OBLITERATION, erasure, rasure, cancel, cancellation, circumduction, deletion, application of the sponge.

V. To efface, obliterate, erase, rase, expunge, cancel, blot out, take out, rub out, scratch out, strike out, wipe out, wash out, sponge, render illegible.

To be effaced, &c., to leave no trace.

Adj. Obliterated, effaced, &c., printless, leaving no trace.

Unrecorded, unattested, unregistered, intestate.

Adv. Dele.

---

(553) RECORDER, notary, clerk, registrar, registrary, prothonotary, secretary, scribe, remembrancer, historian, annalist, &c., bookkeeper.

(554) REPRESENTATION, delineation, representment.

Art, the fine arts, design, designing, illustration, imitation (19), copy (21).

An image, likeness, icon, effigies, effigy, fac-simile, imagery, stagery,

(555) MISREPRESENTATION, distortion (243), caricature, a bad likeness, daub, scratch, sign painting, anamorphosis; misprint, *erratum.*

129

figure, puppet, doll, manikin, mammet, marionette, *fantoccini* (599), wax-work.

Hieroglyphic, anaglyph, inscription, diagram, monogram, draught, outline, scheme, schedule.

Map, plan, chart, ground plan, projection, elevation, iconography, atlas.

V. To represent, delineate, design, figure, shadow out, copy, mould.

To imitate, impersonate, personate, personify, act, take off, hit off.

Adj. Representing, &c. ; artistic, imitative, figurative.

(556) PAINTING, depicting, &c., sciagraphy, photography, &c.
Drawing in pencil, crayons, chalk, water colours.
Painting in oils, in distemper, in fresco ; encaustic painting, enamel painting, scene painting.

A picture, drawing, painting, sketch, scratch, outline, *tableau*, cartoon, fresco ; pencil, &c. drawing ; oil, &c. painting ; daguerreotype, calotype, talbotype, photograph, catalistotype ; mosaic, tapestry, &c., picture gallery.
Portrait, portraiture, likeness, miniature, kitcat, shade, *silhouette*.
Landscape, seascape, view, still-life.

V. To paint, depict, pourtray, limn, draw, sketch, pencil, scratch, dash off, chalk out, shadow out, adumbrate ; daguerreotype, &c., to take a portrait, take a likeness.

Adj. Painted, &c. ; pictorial, graphic, picturesque ; like, &c. (17).

(557) SCULPTURE, insculpture, carving, modelling.
A statue, statuary, statuette, figure, *figurine*, model, bust, image, cast, marble, *intaglio*, anaglyph ; medallion, *cameo*.
V. To sculpture, carve, cut, chisel, model, mould, cast.
Adj. Sculptured, &c., anaglyptic.

(558) ENGRAVING, etching, xylography, &c.
A print, engraving, impression, plate, cut, wood-cut, vignette, gay.
An etching, mezzotint, aquatint, stippling, lithograph, lithotint, anastatic, glyphograph.
V. To engrave, etch, lithograph, print, &c.

(559) ARTIST, painter, limner, draughtsman, drawer, sketcher, designer, engraver, copyist.
Academician ; historical, landscape, portrait, miniature, scene, sign, &c. painter ; engraver ; an Apelles.
A sculptor, carver, modeller, *figuriste* ; a Phidias, a Praxiteles.
Implements of art ; pen, pencil, brush, crayon ; stump, graver, style, *burin*, canvass, easel ; studio.

2°. *Conventional Means.*

1. *Language generally.*

(560) LANGUAGE, tongue, lingo, vernacular, mother tongue, native tongue, the genius of a language.
Dialect, provincialism, brogue, *patois*, slang, broken English, *lingua franca.*

Pasigraphy, dactylonomy, pantomime, glossology, glottology.

Literature, letters, polite literature, the *belles lettres*, the muses, humanities, the republic of letters.

Scholarship (490), scholar (492).

Adj. Literary, linguistic, dialectic, polyglot, pantomimic.

(561) LETTER, alphabet, A B C, abecedary, Christ-cross-row ; character, hieroglyphic.

Syllable, monosyllable, polysyllable ; anagram, *majusculæ.*

(562) WORD, term, vocable, monogram, cypher, terminology, etymon.

Word similarly pronounced, homonym.

A dictionary, vocabulary, lexicon, index, polyglot, glossary, thesaurus, *gradus* ; lexicography ; a lexicographer.

Derivation, etymology.

Adj. Verbal, literal, titular.

Similarly derived, conjugate, paronymous.

Adv. Nominally, &c., *verbatim,* word for word, literally, *sic, totidem verbis, ipsissimis verbis, literatim,* chapter and verse.

(563) NEOLOGY, neologism, slang, cant, byeword, hard word, dog-latin, monkish latin.

A pun, play upon words, paragram, *jeu de mots,* palindrome, conundrum, acrostic, archaism.

———

(564) NOMENCLATURE, nuncupation.

A name, appellation, designation, appellative, denomination, term, cognomination, compellation, expression, noun, byeword, bye name, epithet, style, title, prenomen, cognomen, agnomen, patronymic, surname.

Synonym, namesake.

Quotation, citation, chapter and verse.

V. To name, call, term, denominate, designate, style, yclep, entitle, dub, christen, baptize, characterize, specify, define.

To be called, &c., to take the name of, quote, cite.

Phr. To call a spade a spade ; to rejoice in the name of.

Adj. Named, called, &c., hight, 'yclept, known as ; nuncupatory, nuncupative, cognominal, titular, nominal.

Literal, verbal, discriminative.

(565) MISNOMER, missaying, antiphrasis, nickname, *sobriquet,* assumed name or title, *alias, nom de guerre,* euphemism.

Phr. Lucus à non lucendo.

A neologist ; a Mrs. Malaprop.

V. To misname, missay, miscall, misterm, nickname.

To assume a name ; to coin words.

Adj. Misnamed, &c., *soi-disant,* self-called, self-styled, new-fangled expressions.

Nameless, anonymous, without a name, having no name, innominate, unnamed.

———

(566) PHRASE, expression, phraseology, paraphrase, periphrase, circumlocution, set phrase, round terms ; mode, or turn of expression ; idiom, wording, *façon de parler,* plain terms, plain English.

Sentence, paragraph, motto.

Figure, trope, metaphor (521), antiphrasis.

V. To express, phrase, couch, clothe in words.

Adj. Expressed, &c., couched in, periphrastic, circumlocutory.

131

(567) GRAMMAR, accidence, syntax, *praxis*, punctuation, philology.
V. To parse, punctuate.

(568) SOLECISM, bad or false grammar, slip of the pen or tongue, bull, *lapsus linguæ.*
V. To use bad or faulty grammar, to solecize, or commit a solecism.

Phr. To murder the king's English; to break Priscian's head.
Adj. Ungrammatical, incorrect, faulty, inaccurate.

(569) STYLE, diction, phraseology, turn of expression, idiom, manner, strain, composition, authorship, *la morgue littéraire.*

Various Qualities of Style.

(570) PERSPICUITY, lucidity, lucidness, clearness, perspicacity, plain speaking, intelligibility (518).
Adj. Perspicuous, clear, lucid, intelligible, plain, transparent.

(571) OBSCURITY, imperspicuity, ambiguity, &c., *see* Unintelligibility (519), involution, vagueness.
Adj. Obscure, confused, ambiguous, vague, unintelligible, &c., involved.

(572) CONCISENESS, brevity, terseness, compression, condensation, concision, closeness, laconism, pithiness, succinctness, quaintness, stiffness, ellipsis.
V. To be concise, &c., to condense, compress, abridge, abbreviate, cut short, curtail, abstract.
Adj. Concise, brief, short, terse, laconic, pithy, nervous, succinct, *guindé,* stiff, close, cramped, elliptical, quaint.
Adv. In short, briefly, in a word, to the point.
Phr. The short and the long; *multum in parvo.*

(573) DIFFUSENESS, prolixity, verbosity, pleonasm, tautology, battology, copiousness, exuberance, laxity, looseness, *verbiage,* flow, *flux de mots,* pleonasm, digression, circumlocution, ambages, periphrasis, redundance, macrology, perissology, episode, expletive, *see* Length (200).
V. To be diffuse, &c., to expatiate, enlarge, launch out, dilate, expand, spin out, swell out, inflate, dwell, harp on, descant, digress, ramble, rant.
Phr. To beat about the bush.
Adj. Diffuse, wordy, verbose, prolix, copious, exuberant, flowing, bombastic, lengthy, long-winded, longsome, spun out, long-spun, loose, lax, washy, slipslop, frothy, flatulent, digressive, discursive, excursive, tripping, rambling, ambagious, pleonastic, periphrastic, episodic.
Minute, detailed, particular, circumstantial.
Adv. In detail, *in extenso,* about it and about it.

(574) VIGOUR, power, force, spirit, point, raciness, liveliness, glow, piquancy, boldness, gravity, warmth, sententiousness, elevation, loftiness, sublimity, eloquence.
Adj. Vigorous, powerful, forcible, nervous, spirited, lively, glowing, racy, bold, slashing, piquant, pointed, antithetical, petulant, sententious, lofty, elevated, sublime, eloquent, full of point, poetic, &c.

(575) FEEBLENESS, baldness, tameness, meagreness, coldness, poverty, puerility, childishness, dulness.
Adj. Feeble, bald, tame, meagre, jejune, vapid, cold, poor, dull, languid, prosing, prosaic.

(576) PLAINNESS, simplicity, homeliness, chasteness, neatness, dryness, monotony, severity.

Adj. Simple, unornamented, plain, unadorned, dry, unvaried, monotonous, severe, &c.

(577) ORNAMENT, floridness, richness, flourish, flower of speech; big, high-sounding words; altiloquence, turgidity, pomposity, inflation, pretension, fustian, affectation, inversion, figurativeness, *sesquipedalia verba,* bombast, frothiness, well rounded periods.

V. To ornament, overcharge, overlay with ornament, to round a period.

Adj. Ornamented, &c., florid, rich, pedantic, affected, pompous, fustian, high-sounding, sententious, mouthy, inflated, bombastic, high-flowing, frothy, flowery, turgid, swelling, grandiose, grandiloquent, magniloquent, sesquipedalian.

Adv. Ore rotundo.

(578) ELEGANCE, grace, ease, nature, purity, concinnity, readiness, euphony, numerosity.

Phr. A ready pen.

Adj. Elegant, graceful, easy, natural, unlaboured, chaste, pure, flowing, mellifluous, euphonious, numerose.

(579) INELEGANCE, stiffness, uncouthness, barbarism, rudeness, abruptness, artificialness, cacophony.

Phr. Words that dislocate the jaw; — that break the teeth.

V. To be inelegant, &c.

Phr. To smell of the lamp.

Adj. Inelegant, stiff, forced, cramped, rude, uncouth, barbarous, artificial, graceless, abrupt.

2. *Spoken Language.*

(580) VOICE, vocality, vocalization, utterance, accent, cry, strain, articulate sound, prolation, articulation, enunciation, delivery, pronunciation, orthoepy.

Cadence, accent, accentuation, emphasis, stress, intonation, exclamation, ejaculation, vociferation, ventriloquism, polyphonism.

A ventriloquist, polyphonist.

Science of voice; Phonetics, Phonology.

V. To utter, breathe, cry, exclaim, shout, ejaculate, vociferate; raise, lift, or strain the voice or lungs; to vocalize, prolate, articulate, enunciate, pronounce, aspirate, deliver, mouth, rap out.

Adj. Vocal, oral, articulate.

Silvery, mellow, soft, *see* Melodious (413).

(581) APHONY, obmutescence, absence or want of voice, dumbness, muteness, speechlessness, hoarseness, vacuity, a dummy.

V. To render mute, to muzzle, to gag.

Phr. To stick in the throat; *Vox faucibus hæsit.*

Adj. Aphonous, dumb, speechless, mute, tongueless, muzzled, tongue-tied, inarticulate, inaudible, unspoken, mum, lips closed or sealed, wordless, deaf-mute, raucous, hoarse.

Phr. Mute as a fish; hoarse as a raven; with bated breath; *sotto voce;— Vox et præterea nihil.*

(582) SPEECH, locution, talk, parlance, verbal intercourse, prolation, oral communication, word of mouth, palaver, prattle, effusion, oration,

(583) Imperfect speech, inarticulateness.

STAMMERING, stuttering, impediment in one's speech, titubancy,

133

recitation, delivery, say, harangue, formal speech, speechifying.

Oratory, elocution, rhetoric, declamation, facundity, eloquence, gift of the gab, grandiloquence, magniloquence, *usus loquendi.*

A speaker, spokesman, prolocutor, mouth-piece, orator, soliloquy, *see* (589).

V. To speak, break silence, say, tell, open one's lips, give tongue, hold forth, make or deliver a speech, speechify, harangue, talk, discourse, declaim, flourish, spout, rant, recite, whisper in the ear, expatiate, run out on, quoth he, to lecture, sermonize, to soliloquize (589).

Phr. To have a tongue in one's head;—To have on the end of one's tongue;—To have on one's lips;—To pass one's lips.

Adj. Speaking, &c., oral, spoken, unwritten, outspoken.

Adv. Vivâ voce; ore rotundo.

(584) LOQUACITY, loquaciousness, talkativeness, garrulity, flow of words, *flux de bouche,* prate, gab, gift of the gab, gabble, jabber, chatter, prattle, cackle, clack, twattle, rattle, *caquet, caqueterie,* twaddle, bibble-babble, gibble-gabble.

Fluency, flippancy, volubility, *cacoëthes loquendi,* polylogy, perissology.

Phr. A thrice-told tale; a long yarn.

A chatterer, chatterbox, babbler, rattle, ranter, sermonizer, proser, driveller.

Magpie, jay, parrot, poll, Babel.

V. To be loquacious, &c., to prate, chatter, prattle, jabber, rattle, twaddle, twattle, babble, gabble, out-talk, descant, dilate, dwell on, expatiate, prose, launch out, palaver.

Phr. To din in the ears; to drum into the ear; *battre la campagne;* to spin a long yarn; to talk at random, to talk oneself out of breath.

Adj. Loquacious, talkative, garrulous, open-mouthed, chatty, cosy, chattering, &c.

Fluent, voluble, glib, flippant, hoarse with talking, long-winded, the tongue running fast.

Adv. Trippingly on the tongue.

faltering, hesitation, lisp, drawl, jabber, splutter, sputter, mumbling, mincing, muttering, mouthing, traulism, twang, a broken or cracked voice, broken accents or sentences, tardiloquence, *falsetto,* a whisper.

V. To stammer, stutter, hesitate, falter, hammer, balbutiate, bulbucinate, haw, hum and haw, mumble, lisp, jabber, mutter, sputter, splutter, muffle, mump, drawl, lisp, croak, speak through the nose, snuffle, clip one's words, mispronounce, missay.

Phr. To clip the king's English; *parler à tort et à travers;* not to be able to put two words together.

To speak aside, *sotto voce,* whisper.

Adj. Stammering, &c., inarticulate, guttural, nasal, unspeakable.

(585) TACITURNITY, closeness, reserve, muteness, silence, costiveness, pauciloquy.

V. To be silent, &c. (403), to hold one's tongue, keep silence, hold one's peace, say nothing, hold one's jaw, close one's mouth or lips.

To render silent, silence, put to silence, seal one's lips, smother, suppress, stop one's mouth, gag, muffle, muzzle.

Adj. Taciturn, close, reserved, mute, sparing of words, costive, buttoned up, breathless, close-tongued, uncommunicative.

Phr. Not a word escaping one; not having a word to say.

Int. Tush! silence! mum! hush! chut! hist! tut!

(586) ALLOCUTION, address, apostrophe, interpellation, appeal, invocation, salutation.

Feigned dialogue, dialogism, inquiry, *see* (461).

Phr. A word in the ear.

V. To speak to, address, accost, apostrophize, appeal to, invoke, hail, make up to, call to, halloo, salute.

Adj. Accosting, &c.

(587) RESPONSE, answer, reply, &c., *see* (462).

V. To answer, respond, reply, &c.

Adj. Answering, responding, &c.

(588) INTERLOCUTION, collocution, colloquy, conversation, converse, confabulation, talk, discourse, verbal intercourse, dialogue, trialogue, logomachy, communication, commerce.

Chat, chit-chat, small talk, table-talk, tattle, gossip, tittle-tattle, babblement, clack, prittle-prattle, *can-can*, idle talk, town-talk, *on dit*, the talk of the town.

Conference, parley, interview, audience, palaver.

A talker, interlocutor, gossip, tattler, chatterer, babbler, *dramatis personæ.*

Phr. " The feast of reason and the flow of soul ;" *Mollia tempora fandi.*

V. To talk together, converse, discourse with, engage in conversation ; hold, or carry on a conversation ; chat, gossip, put in a word, tattle, babble, prate, clack, prattle.

To confer with, hold conference, &c., to parley, palaver, commerce, hold intercourse with, be closeted with, commune with.

Adj. Conversing, &c., interlocutory, verbal, colloquial, cosy, chatty, gossiping, &c., conversible.

(589) SOLILOQUY, monologue, apostrophe.

V. To soliloquize ; to say or talk to oneself; to say aside, to think aloud, to apostrophize.

Adj. Soliloquizing, &c.

---

3. *Written Language.*

(590) WRITING, chirography, pencraft, penmanship, caligraphy.

Scribble, scrawl, scratch, cacography, scribbling, &c., *griffonage, barbouillage,* jotting, interlineation.

Transcription, inscription, superscription, minute.

Short-hand, stenography, brachygraphy, tachygraphy, steganography.

Secret writing, writing in cypher, cryptography, polygraphy, stelography.

Composition, authorship, *cacoëthes scribendi.*

Manuscript, copy, transcript, rough copy, fair copy, handwriting, autograph, signature, sign-manual.

A scribe, amanuensis, scrivener, secretary, clerk, penman, copyist, transcriber, penny-a-liner.

(591) PRINTING, print, letter-press, text, context, note, page, &c.

Typography, stereotypography, aprotype, &c., type, character, black letter, font, pie, &c.

V. To print, put to press, publish, edit, get out a work, &c.

Adj. Printed, &c.

Writer, author, scribbler, pamphleteer, essayist, editor: Grub street.

Pen, quill, pencil, paper, parchment, vellum, tablet, slate, marble, pillar, table, &c.

V. To write, pen, write out, copy, engross, write out fair, transcribe, scribble, scrawl, scratch, interline; to sign, undersign, countersign, endorse, set one's hand to.

To compose, indite, draw up, minute, jot down, make or take a minute of, put or set down in writing; to indite, to dictate.

Phr. To take up the pen; to spill ink; set or put pen to paper; put on paper.

Adj. Writing, &c., written, in writing, penned, &c.

Phr. Under one's hand; in black and white; off-hand; *currente calamo.*

(592) CORRESPONDENCE, letter, epistle, note, billet, missive, circular, favour, *billet-doux*, dispatch, bulletin, presents, rescript, rescription.

Letter-bag, mail, post.

V. To correspond, write to, send a letter to.

Phr. To keep up a correspondence.

(593) BOOK, writing, work, volume, tome, library, opuscule, tract, manual, pamphlet, enchiridion, circular, publication, part, number, journal, album.

Paper, bill, sheet, leaf, fly-leaf, page.

Chapter, section, paragraph, head article, passage, clause.

(594) DESCRIPTION, account, statement, report, return, delineation, sketch, representation, narration, narrative, relation, recital, rehearsal, annals, chronicle, *adversaria*, journal (551), itinerary, log-book.

Story, history, memoir, tale, tradition, legend, anecdote, ana, *analecta*, fable, novel, romance, apologue, parable; historic muse, Clio.

Biography, necrology, obituary, life, personal narrative, adventures, autobiography.

A historian, historiographer, narrator, annalist, biographer, fabulist, novelist.

V. To describe, state, set forth, sketch, delineate, represent, pourtray, depict, paint, shadow forth, adumbrate.

To relate, recite, recount, sum up, run over, recapitulate, narrate, rehearse, tell, give, or render an account of, report, draw up a statement, &c., unfold a tale.

To take up or handle a subject; to enter into particulars, detail, &c., to detail, retail; to descend to particulars; to come to the point.

Phr. To plunge *in medias res.*

Adj. Descriptive, graphic, historic, traditional, traditionary, legendary, anecdotic, described, &c.

(595) DISSERTATION, treatise, tract, tractate, essay, discourse, memoir, prolusion, disquisition, tractation, exposition, compilation, *bibliotheca*, sermon, homily, pandect.

V. To dissert, descant, treat of, discuss, write, compile, touch upon, handle a subject, do justice to a subject.

Adj. Discursive.

(596) COMPENDIUM, compend, summary, abstract, *précis*, epitome, *apperçu*, digest, sum and substance, *compte rendu*, draft, *exposé*, brief, re-

capitulation, *résumé*, abridgment, abbreviation, minute, note, synopsis, syllabus, *prodromus, spicilegium,* contents, heads, prospectus.

Scrap-book, album, note-book, commonplace-book, extracts, text-book, *excerpta,* flowers, anthology, *collectanea.*

V. To abridge, abstract, abbreviate, recapitulate, run over, make or prepare an abstract, &c., *see* (201).

Adj. Compendious, &c., synoptic, abridged, &c.

(597) POETRY, poetics, poesy, the Muse, Calliope.

Verse, metre, measure, foot, numbers, strain, rhyme, blank verse, versification, doggrel rhyme, prosody.

Poem, epic, *epopœa,* epic poem, ode, idyl, lyrics, eclogue, pastoral, bucolic, macaronic, dithramb, anacreontic, sonnet, lay, roundelay, *rondo,* madrigal, canzonet, opera, posy, anthology, distich, stanza, strophe, couplet, quartain, *cento.*

A poet, bard, scald, poetess, rhymer, rhymist, versifier, rhymester, sonneteer, poetaster.

Phr. Genus irritabile vatum ; disjecti membra poetæ.

V. To rhyme, versify, sing, make verses.

Adj. Poetical, poetic, lyric, metrical, epic, &c., catalectic, dithrambic.

(598) PROSE.

V. To prose.

Adj. Prosaic, prosing, rhymeless, unpoetical.

(599) THE DRAMA, stage, theatre, the histrionic art, acting, &c., stagery, the buskin, sock, Melpomene and Thalia.

Play, stage-play, piece, tragedy, comedy, melodrame, interlude, afterpiece, exode, opera, farce, *comédie iarmoyante, divertissement, extravaganza,* burletta, pantomine, dumb-show, *vaudeville.*

Puppet-show, *fantoccini, marionettes,* Punch and Judy, *pulcinello, polichinelle.*

Theatre, playhouse, stage, scene, the boards, green-room.

An actor, a player, stager, stage-player, performer, mime, *artiste,* comedian, tragedian, Thespian, clown, harlequin, *buffo,* buffoon, star, *prima donna, figurant,* &c.

Mummer, guiser, masque.

Dramatic writer, Mimographer.

V. To act, play, perform, personate (554), play a part, rehearse, spout, rant, to star it.

Phr. To strut one's hour on the stage.

Adj. Dramatic, theatric, theatrical, scenic, histrionic, comic, tragic, buskined, farcical, tragicomic.

CLASS V.

WORDS RELATING TO THE VOLUNTARY POWERS.

DIVISION I. INDIVIDUAL VOLITION.

Section I. VOLITION IN GENERAL.

1°. *Acts of Volition.*

(600) WILL, volition, velleity, free-will, spontaneity, spontaneousness.

Pleasure, wish, mind, *animus*, breast, mood, bosom, *petto*, heart, discretion, accord.

Determination, *see* (604), intention, *see* (620).

V. To will, list, think fit, think proper, determine, &c. (604), settle (609), to take upon oneself, to have one's will; to do as one likes, wishes, or chooses; to use or exercise one's own discretion, *see* Freedom (748), to volunteer, lend oneself to.

Phr. To have a will of one's own; *sic volo, sic jubeo; stet pro ratione voluntas;* to know one's own mind; to know what one is about; to see one's way.

Adj. Voluntary, volitional, willing, content, minded, spontaneous, free, left to oneself, unconstrained, unfettered, unbidden, unasked, uncompelled, of one's own accord, gratuitous, of one's own head, prepense, advised, express, designed, intended, calculated, premeditated, preconcerted, predetermined.

Adv. At will, at pleasure, *à volonté, ad libitum,* spontaneously, freely, of one's own accord, voluntarily, advisedly, designedly, intentionally, expressly, knowingly, determinately,

(601) NECESSITY, instinct, blind impulse, necessitation, fate, destiny, doom (152), foredoom, destination, election, predestination, preordination, compulsion (744), subjection (749).

The fates, the stars, astral influence.

Phr. Hobson's choice; A blind bargain; A *pis aller.*

V. To lie under a necessity, to be fated, doomed, destined, &c. (152), to need be, not to help, to leave to itself.

To necessitate, destine, doom, foredoom, predestine, preordain.

To compel, force, constrain, &c., cast a spell, &c. (992).

Phr. To make a virtue of necessity.

Adj. Necessitated, fated, destined, doomed, elect, spell-bound.

Compelled, forced, &c., unavoidable.

Compulsory, involuntary, unintentional, undesigned, unintended, instinctive, automatic, blind, mechanical, impulsive, unwitting, unaware.

Adv. Necessarily, needs, of necessity, perforce, forcibly, compulsorily; on or by compulsion or force, involuntarily, &c., impulsively (612), unwittingly (491).

Phr. It must be; it needs must

138

deliberately, pointedly, in earnest, in good earnest, studiously, purposely, *proprio motu, suo motu, ex mero motu.*

Phr. With one's eyes open; in cool blood.

(602) WILLINGNESS, voluntariness, disposition, inclination, leaning, *penchant*, humour, mood, vain, bent, bias, propensity, proclivity, aptitude, predisposition, predilection, proneness, propensedness, docility, assent (488).

V. To be willing, &c., to incline to, lean to, mind, *see* Desire (865), to have lief, to propend.

Phr. To find in one's heart; to set one's heart upon; to make no bones of.

Adj. Willing, fain, disposed, inclined, minded, bent upon, set upon, forward, predisposed, hearty, cordial, prepense, docile.

Free, spontaneous, unforced, unasked, unbiassed, unsolicited, undriven.

Adv. Willingly, freely, lief, heartily, with a good grace, without reluctance, &c., of one's own accord (600), certainly, be it so (488).

Phr. With all one's heart; *con amore;* with heart and soul; heart in hand; with a good grace; *à la bonne heure;* by all means; by all manner of means.

be; it cannot be helped; there is no help for it; there is no helping it; necessity has no law.

(603) UNWILLINGNESS, nolleity, nolition, involuntariness, indisposition, indisposedness, backwardness, disinclination, averseness, aversation, reluctance, repugnance, demur, renitence, remissness, slackness, indifference, *nonchalance.*

Hesitation, shrinking, recoil, suspense.

A recusant, *pococurante.*

V. To be unwilling, &c., to nill.

To demur, stick at, hesitate (605), waver, hang in suspense, scruple, stickle, boggle, falter, to hang back, hang fire.

Phr. To stick in the throat.

Decline, reject, refuse (764), refrain, keep from, abstain, recoil, shrink.

Adj. Unwilling, unconsenting, disinclined, indisposed, averse, reluctant, not content, laggard, backward, remiss, slack, indifferent, frigid, scrupulous, repugnant, disliking (867).

Demurring, wavering, &c., refusing (764).

Adv. Unwillingly, &c., perforce.

Phr. Against the grain; *invitâ Minervâ; à contre cœur; malgré soi;* nil he, will he; *bon gré, mal gré; nolens volens;* with a bad grace; not for the world.

Dislike (867), scrupulousness, scrupulosity, delicacy, demur, scruple, qualm.

(604) RESOLUTION, determination, decision, resolvedness, fixedness, steadiness, constancy, unchangeableness, inflexibility, firmness, doggedness, tenacity of purpose, perseverance, constancy, solidity.

Energy, manliness, vigour, spirit, spiritedness, pluck, bottom, game; self-reliance; mastery over one's self; self-control.

A devotee, zealot.

V. To be resolved, &c., to have

139

(605) IRRESOLUTION, indecision, indetermination, undetermination, demur, hesitation, suspense, hesitancy, vacillation, unsteadiness, inconstancy, wavering, fluctuation, flickering, changeableness, mutability, fickleness, levity, *légèreté*, trimming, softness, weakness.

A weathercock, a shuttlecock, a butterfly, a harlequin.

V. To be irresolute, &c., to hesitate, hang in suspense, demur, waver,

resolution, &c., to resolve, determine, conclude, make up one's mind ; to stand, keep or remain firm, &c., to come to a determination ; to form a resolution ; to take one's stand; to stand by, hold by, hold fast, stick to, abide by, adhere to, keep one's ground, persevere, keep one's course, hold on, not to fail.

To insist upon ; to make a point of.

Phr. To pass the Rubicon ; take a decisive step ; to nail one's colours to the mast ; to screw one's courage to the sticking place.

Adj. Resolved, resolute, firm, steady, steadfast, stanch, constant.

Decided, determinate, definitive, determined, fixed, unmoved, unshaken, unbending, unyielding, unflinching, inflexible, unwavering, unfaltering, unshrinking, undiverted, immoveable, not to be moved, unhesitating.

Peremptory, inexorable, indomitable, strenuous, persevering, irrevocable, irreversible, reverseless.

Strenuous, bent upon, set upon, intent upon, proof against, master of oneself, steeled, staid, serious, stiff, stiff-necked ; *see* Obstinate (606).

Phr. Firm as a rock ; steady as time; true to oneself.

Adv. Resolutely, &c., without fail.

Phr. Through thick and thin ; through fire and water ; *per fas aut nefas.*

vacillate, quaver, fluctuate, shuffle, boggle, flicker, falter, palter, debate, hang fire, dally with, swerve, &c.

Phr. To hang fire ; to hum and haw ; not to know one's own mind; to leave " *ad referendum.*"

Adj. Irresolute, undecided, unresolved, undetermined, vacillating, wavering, hesitating, faltering, shuffling, &c.

Unsteady, unsteadfast, fickle, changing, changeable, versatile, variable, inconstant, mutable, fluctuating, unsettled, unfixed, shilly-shally, infirm of purpose.

Weak, feeble-minded, frail, soft, pliant, giddy, volatile, fitful, frothy, freakish, lightsome, light-minded.

In suspense, in doubt, *see* (485).

Revocable, reversible.

---

(606) OBSTINACY, obstinateness, wilfulness, self-will, pertinacity, pertinacy, pertinaciousness, pervicacy, pervicacity, pervicaciousness, tenacity, tenaciousness, inflexibility, doggedness, stubbornness, headiness, *see* Resolution (604), restiveness, contumacy, obduracy, obduration, obdurateness, unruliness.

Intolerance, dogmatism, bigotry, opiniativeness, opiniatry, zealotry, infatuation, monomania, indocility, intractableness.

An opinionist, opinionatist, *opiniâtre,* opiniator, opinator, stickler, zealot, dogmatist, fanatic,—mule.

A fixed idea, rooted prejudice, blind side, &c. (481).

V. To be obstinate, &c., to persist, stickle, opiniate.

(607) Change of mind, intention, purpose, &c.

TERGIVERSATION, retractation, recantation, revocation, revokement, reversal, palinody, renunciation, abjuration, abjurement, relinquishment (624), repentance (950), vacillation, &c. (605).

Going over, ratting, apostacy.

A turn-coat, rat, Janus, renegade, apostate, trimmer, timeserver, Vicar of Bray, deserter, weathercock, &c. (605).

V. To change one's mind, &c., to retract, recant, revoke, abjure, renounce, apostatize, relinquish, trim, veer round, change sides, rat ; go over, pass, change, or skip from one side to another ; back out of, swerve, flinch, balance.

Adj. Obstinate, opinionative, opiniative, opinative, opinionate, opinionated, opinioned, wedded to an opinion, self-opinioned, prejudiced (481), wilful, self-willed, positive, tenacious.

Stiff, stubborn, starch, rigid, stiff-necked, dogged, pertinacious, restive (or restiff), pervicacious, dogmatic, unpersuadable, mulish, unmoved, uninfluenced, hard-mouthed, unyielding, pig-headed, wayward, intractable, haggard, headstrong, refractory, unruly, infatuated, heady, *entêté*, stiff-hearted, cross-grained, obdurate, contumacious, fanatical.

Phr. Obstinate as a mule.

Adv. Obstinately, &c., headlong, headforemost, heels over head; at any rate, risk, price, cost, or sacrifice.

Phr. Coûte qui coûte; quand même; through thick and thin; *per fas et nefas; à tort et à travers.*

Phr. To eat one's words; turn over a new leaf; think better of it; play fast and loose; blow hot and cold; *nager entre deux eaux.*

Adv. Changeful, changeable, mobile, unsteady (605), trimming, double-faced, ambidexter, fast and loose, timeserving.

Fugacious, fugitive, revocatory.

Phr. A change coming over the spirit of one's dream.

(608) CAPRICE, fancy, humor, whim, crotchet, *capriccio*, quirk, freak, maggot, vagary, whimsy, whim-wham, prank, fit, flim-flam, *escapade, boutade,* wild goose chase, freakishness, skittishness, volatility, fancifulness, whimsicality, giddiness, inconsistency; a mad cap.

V. To be capricious, &c.

Phr. To strain at a gnat and swallow a camel.

Adj. Capricious, inconsistent, fanciful, fantastic, whimsical, full of whims, &c., erratic, crotchetty, perverse, humorsome, wayward, captious, contrary, contrarious, skittish, fitful, sleeveless.

Phr. The head being turned; the deuce being in him; *Nil fuit unquam sic impar sibi.*

---

(609) CHOICE, option, election, arbitrament, adoption, selection, excerption, co-optation, gleaning, eclecticism, lief, preference, predilection, preoption.

Decision, determination, award, adjudication, vote, suffrage, verdict, voice, plumper.

Alternative, dilemma, ballot.

Persuasion, seduction, bringing over, *see* (615).

Thing chosen; *élite* (650).

V. To choose, decide, determine, elect, list, think fit, use one's discretion, fancy, shape one's course, prefer, have rather, have as lief, take one's choice, adopt, select, fix upon, pitch upon, pick out, single out, pick up, take up, catch at, jump at, cull, glean, pick, winnow.

Phr. To winnow the chaff from the wheat; to pick one's way; to indulge one's fancy; to make no bones; to make or have no scruple; to take a decided step; to pass the Rubicon.

(610) Absence of Choice, *see* Necessity (601).

REJECTION, refusal, *see* (764); declining, repudiation, exclusion.

Indifference, indecision (605).

V. To reject, refuse, &c., decline, give up, repudiate, exclude, lay aside, to refrain, spare.

Adj. Rejecting, &c., rejected, &c., rejectaneous, rejectitious, not chosen, &c.

Having no choice, indifferent, undecided (605).

Adv. Neither; neither the one nor the other.

To be persuaded, &c. ; to swallow the bait ; to gorge the hook ; to yield to temptation.

To persuade, overcome, seduce, entice, *see* (615).

Adj. Optional, discretional, eclectic, chasing, &c., chosen, &c., decided, &c.

Adv. Discretionally, at pleasure, *al piacere, à discrétion*, at will, *ad libitum*.

Decidedly, &c., rather, once for all, either the one or the other.

(611) PREDETERMINATION, premeditation, predeliberation, having no alternative, compulsory choice ; Hobson's choice.

V. To predetermine, premeditate, preresolve.

Adj. Prepense, premeditated, predetermined, advised.

(612) IMPULSE, sudden thought, inspiration, flash, spurt.

V. To flash on the mind.

Adj. Extemporaneous, impulsive, unmeditated, unpremeditated, *improvisé*, unprompted, spontaneous, natural, unguarded.

Adv. Extempore, off-hand, *impromptu, à l'improviste*, improviso.

Phr. On the spur of the moment, or of the occasion.

(613) HABIT, habitude, assuetude, wont, rule, routine, assuefaction.

Custom, use, usage, practice, run, way, prevalence, observance, fashion (852), etiquette, vogue.

Seasoning, training, hardening, &c. (673).

A second nature, *cacoëthes*, taking root, radication.

V. To be habitual, &c., to be in the habit of, be wont, be accustomed to, &c.

To follow, observe, conform to, obey, bend to, comply with, accommodate oneself to, adapt oneself to, fall into a habit, custom, or usage, to addict oneself to.

Phr. To follow the multitude ; *hurler avec les loups ;* go with the current, stream, &c.

(614) DESUETUDE, disuse, want of habit or of practice, inusitation, newness to.

Non-observance, infraction, violation, infringement.

V. To be unaccustomed, &c., to be new to, to leave off, wean oneself of, break off, break through, infringe, violate, &c., a habit, usage, &c., to disuse, to wear off.

Adj. Unaccustomed, unused, unusual, unwonted, uncustomary, unfashionable, non-observant, disused, weaned.

Unseasoned, uninured, unhabituated, untrained, unhackneyed.

To become a habit, to take root, to gain upon one, to run in the blood.

To habituate, inure, harden, season, form, train, accustom, naturalize, acclimatize.

To acquire a habit, to get into the way of, to learn, &c.

Adj. Habitual, accustomed, accustomary, habituated, &c.; in the habit, &c. of; used to, addicted to, attuned to, wedded to, usual, wonted, customary, hackneyed, fixed, rooted, permanent, inveterate, ingrained, running in the blood, hereditary, congenital, congenite, innate, inborn, natural, instinctive, &c. (5).

Fashionable, in fashion, in vogue, according to use, routine, &c.

Phr. Naturam expellas furca, tamen usque recurret.

Adv. As the world goes.

2°. *Causes of Volition.*

(615) MOTIVE, reason, ground, principle, mainspring, *primum mobile*, account, score, sake, the why and the wherefore, consideration, calculation, the *pro* and *con.*

Inducement, recommendation, encouragement, attraction, allectation, temptation, enticement, bait, allurement, allective, witchery, bewitchery.

Persuasibility, persuasibleness, softness.

Influence, prompting, dictate, instance, impulse, impulsion, incitement, incitation, press, instigation, excitement, provocation, invitation, solicitation, suasion, persuasion, hortation, exhortation, seduction, cajolery, tantalization, *agacerie*, seducement, bewitchment, inspiration.

Incentive, stimulus, spur, fillip, goad, vowel, provocative, *piquant*, dram, *prestige.*

Bribe, sap, lure, decoy, charm, spell, loadstone, the golden apple, the voice of the tempter, the song of the sirens.

Prompter, tempter, seducer, seductor, Siren, Circe, instigator.

V. To induce, move, lead, draw, draw over, carry, bring ; to influence, to weigh with ; bias ; to operate, work upon, engage, incline, dispose, predispose, prompt, whisper, call, call upon, recommend, encourage, entice, invite, solicit, press, enjoin, entreat (765), court, plead, advocate,

(616) Absence of motive, *see* Caprice (608).

Phr. Without rhyme or reason.

DISSUASION, dehortation, discouragement.

Cohibition, check, restraint, curb, bridle, rein, stay, damper, remonstrance, expostulation.

Scruple, qualm, demur (867), contraindication.

V. To dissuade, dehort, discourage, disincline, indispose, dispirit, damp, dishearten, disenchant, contraindicate, deter, keep back, render averse, &c.

To withhold, restrain, hold, check, bridle, curb, rein in, keep in, cohibit, inhibit, repel (751).

To cool, blunt, calm, quiet, quench, shake, stagger, remonstrate, expostulate, warn.

To scruple, refrain, abstain, &c. (603).

Phr. To throw cold water on ; to turn a deaf ear to.

Adj. Dissuading, &c., dissuasive, dehortatory.

Dissuaded, discouraged, &c., uninduced, unmoved, unactuated, uninfluenced, unbiassed, unincited, unimpelled, unswayed, unprovoked, uninspired, untempted, unattracted.

Repugnant, averse, scrupulous, &c. (867), unpersuadable.

———

exhort, enforce, dictate, tantalize, bait the hook, seduce, decoy, charm, conciliate, wheedle, coax, cajole, pat on the back or shoulder, talk over, inveigle, persuade, prevail upon, get to do, bring over, procure, lead by the nose, sway, turn the head, enlist.

To act upon, to impel, excite, suscitate, stimulate, exsuscitate, incite, animate, instigate, provoke, set on, urge, *pique*, spirit, inspirit, inspire, awaken, give a fillip, light up, kindle, enkindle, rekindle, quicken, goad, spur, prick, egg on, hurry on, stir up, work up, fan, fire, inflame, set on fire, fan the flame, blow the coals, stir the embers, put on one's mettle, set on, force, rouse, arouse.

Phr. To follow the bent of ; to follow the dictates of ; to make no scruple ; to make no bones.

Adj. Impulsive, motive, persuasive, hortatory, seductive, protreptical, suasory, suasive, honey-tongued, tempting, alluring, exciting, tantalizing, &c.

Persuadable, persuasible, suasible, soft, yielding, facile, easily persuaded, &c.

Induced, moved, disposed, led, persuaded, &c., spell-bound, instinct with or by.

Adv. Because, for, since, on account of, out of, from.

As, forasmuch as, therefore, hence, why, wherefore.

Phr. Hinc illæ lacrymæ.

(617) Ostensible motive, or reason assigned.

PLEA, allegation, pretext, pretence, excuse, cue, colour, gloss, *salvo,* loop-hole, handle, shift, quirk, guise, stalking-horse, starting-hole, make-shift, special pleading, a tub to the whale, *cheval de bataille,* clap-trap, advocation, soft sawder, a Canterbury tale, moonshine.

V. To make a pretext, &c. of; to use as a plea, &c.; to plead, allege, pretend, excuse, make a handle, &c. of.

Adj. Ostensible, colourable, pretended, alleged, &c.

Phr. Ad captandum; on the spur of the occasion; the grapes being sour.

3°. *Objects of Volition.*

(618) GOOD, benefit, advantage, service, interest, weal, boot, gain, profit, good-turn, blessing, *tanti;* behoof, behalf.

Luck, piece of luck, windfall, godsend, bonus; *bonanza,* prize.

Cause of good, *see* Utility (644), Goodness (648), and Remedy (662).

Adv. Aright, well.

In behalf of, in favour of.

(619) EVIL, harm, injury, wrong, scath, curse, detriment, hurt, damage, disservice, ill-turn, bale, grievance, prejudice, loss, mischief, disadvantage, drawback, trouble, annoyance, nuisance, molestation, oppression, persecution, plague, corruption (659).

Blow, bruise, scratch, wound, mutilation, outrage, spoliation, plunder, pillage, rapine, destruction, dilapidation, havoc, ravage, devastation, inroad, sweep, sack, foray (716), desolation, *razzia,* dragonade.

Misfortune, mishap, woe, disaster, calamity, catastrophe, downfall, ruin, prostration, curse, wrack, blight, blast; Pandora's box.

Cause of evil, *see* Bane (663).

Production of evil (649).

Adv. Amiss, wrong, evil.

Section II. PROSPECTIVE VOLITION.*

1°. *Conceptional Volition.*

(620) INTENTION, intent, intentionality, purpose, design, purport, mind, meaning, *animus,* view, set

(621) Absence of purpose in the succession of events.

CHANCE †, fortune, accident, ha-

---

* That is, volition having reference to a future object.

† See Note on (156).

purpose, point, bent, turn, proposal, study, scope.

Final cause, object, aim, end, drift, destination, mark, point, butt, goal, target, prey, quarry, game, quintain, the philosopher's stone.

Decision, determination, resolve, resolution (604), predetermination (611).

A hobby, ambition, wish ; *see* Desire (865).

Study of final causes, Teleology.

V. To intend, purpose, design, destinate, mean, aim at, propose to oneself, have in view, have *in petto*, have in one's eye, have an eye to.

To be at, drive at, be after, point at, level at, take aim, aspire at or after, endeavour after, destine.

To meditate, think of, dream of, premeditate (611), contemplate, compass.

To propose, project, devise, take into one's head, take upon oneself, to have to do ; to see one's way.

Adj. Intended, &c., intentional, minded, express, prepense, set upon, bent upon, intent upon, in view, in *petto*, in prospect, teleological.

Phr. In the wind ; *on the tapis.*

Adv. Intentionally, &c., expressly, designedly, purposely, on purpose, for, with a view to, for the purpose of, with the view of, in order to, to the end that, on account of, in pursuance of, pursuant to, with the intent, &c.

(622) Purpose in action.

Pursuit, undertaking, enterprize, emprise, adventure, game, endeavour.

Prosecution, search, angling, chase, hunt, race, scramble, course, direction, wild-goose-chase, steeple-chase.

V. To pursue, undertake, engage in, take in hand, carry on, prosecute, endeavour.

To court, seek, angle, chase, give chase, course, dog, hunt, follow, run after, hound, bid for, aim at, take aim, make a leap at, rush upon, jump at.

145

zard, hap, haphazard (156), lot, chance-medley, hit, casualty, contingency, fate, adventure, random shot.

A godsend, luck, a run of luck, a windfall, &c. (618).

Drawing lots, sortilegy, sortition.

Wager, bet, betting.

Phr. A blind bargain ; a pig in a poke.

V. To chance, hap, turn up ; to stand a chance.

To take one's chance, try one's luck, shuffle the cards, put into a lottery, bet, wager, lay a wager, gamble, raffle, toss up, cast lots, draw lots.

To risk, venture, hazard, stake, incur, or run the risk ; stand the hazard.

Phr. To buy a pig in a poke ; *alea jacta est ;* the die being cast.

Adj. Casual, fortuitous, accidental, contingent, random, adventitious, incidental.

Unintentional, aimless, driftless, designless, undesigned, undirected ; purposeless, causeless, without purpose, &c., unmeditated, unpurposed, indiscriminate, promiscuous.

On the cards, or dice ; possible (470), at stake.

Adv. Casually, &c., by chance, by accident, accidentally, &c., at haphazard ; heads or tails.

(623) Absence of pursuit.

Avoidance, forbearance, abstinence.

Flight, &c., evasion, elusion, contraindication.

V. To avoid, refrain, not to attempt ; to spare, hold, shun, fly, flee, eschew, run away from, get out of the way, steer clear of, shrink, hold back, draw back, *see* (286), recoil from, flinch, blench, shy, elude, evade, shirk, parry, dodge.

Phr. To give the slip, or go-by, to lead one a dance, to beat about the bush.

Take or hold a course ; tread a path ; shape one's course ; direct or bend one's steps or course ; run a race, rush headlong, rush headforemost, make a plunge, snatch at, &c., start game.

Phr. To run or ride full tilt at.

Adj. Pursuing, &c.

Adv. In order to, for the purpose of, with a view to, &c. (620).

Adj. Avoiding, &c., elusive, evasive, flying, unattempted, fugitive, &c., unsought.

Adv. Lest.

(624) RELINQUISHMENT, dereliction, abandonment, renunciation, desertion, see (607).

Dispensation, riddance.

V. To relinquish, give up ; lay, set, or put aside ; drop, abandon, renounce, desist from, desert, leave, leave off, back out of, quit, give over, forsake, forswear, swerve from, put away, discontinue (681).

Phr. To drop all idea of ; to think better of it ; to wash one's hands of ; to turn over a new leaf ; to throw up the game or the cards ; to have other fish to fry.

Adj. Relinquishing, &c., relinquished, &c., unpursued.

Int. Hands off ! keep off ! forbear !

(625) BUSINESS, affair, concern, task, work, job, errand, *agenda*, commission, office, charge, part, duty, *rôle*.

Province, department, beat, mission, function, vocation, calling, avocation, profession, cloth, faculty, trade, craft, mystery, walk, race, career, walk of life.

Place, post, orb, sphere, capacity, employment, engagement, exercise, occupation ; situation, undertaking (676).

V. To carry on a business, trade, &c.

To have to do with ; have on one's hands ; betake oneself to ; occupy or concern oneself with ; have on one's shoulders, make it one's business, go to do, act a part, perform the office of or functions of, to enter a profession, drive a trade, spend time upon.

Adj. Business-like, official, functional, professional, in hand.

Adv. On hand, on foot, afoot, afloat, going.

(626) PLAN, scheme, device, design, project, proposal, proposition.

Line of conduct, game, card, course, tactics, strategy, policy, polity (692), craft, practice, campaign.

Intrigue, cabal, plot, conspiracy, complot.

Measure, step, precaution, proceeding, procedure, process, system, economy, organization, expedient, contrivance, artifice, shift, stop-gap, manœuvre, stratagem, fetch, trick, machination, intrigue, stroke, stroke of policy, master-stroke, great gun, trump card.

Alternative, loophole, counterplot, counterproject, side-wind, *dernier ressort, pis aller.*

Sketch, outline, *programme*, draught (or draft), *ébauche*, rough draught, skeleton, forecast, prospectus, *carte du pays.*

Aftercourse, aftergame, *arrière pensée*, underplot.

A projector, designer, schemer, contriver, artist, schematist.

V. To plan, scheme, devise, imagine, design, frame, contrive, project, plot, invent, forecast, strike out, chalk out, sketch, lay out, lay down, cut out, cast, recast, countermine, hit upon, fall upon, arrange, mature, organize, concoct, digest, pack, prepare, hatch.

Phr. To have many irons in the fire ; to dig a mine ; to spring a project ; to take or adopt a course.

Adj. Planned, &c., strategic ; planning, scheming, &c.

Well-laid, deep-laid, cunning, well-devised, &c., maturely considered, well-weighed, prepared, organized, &c.

Adv. In course of preparation, on the anvil, on the stocks, on the *tapis.*

(627) METHOD, way, manner, wise, form, path, road, route, channel, walk, access, course, pass, ford, ferry, passage, line of way, trajectory, orbit, track, avenue, approach, beaten track, pathway, highway, roadway, causeway, footpath, turnpike-road, high road, railway, tram-way, the King's highway, thoroughfare, gateway, street, lane, alley, gangway, hatchway, by-path, by-way, by-walk, cross-road, cross-way, by-road, cut, short cut, royal road, cross cut, *carrefour.*

Bridge, stepping-stone, stair, corridor, staircase, flight of stairs, ladder, scaffold, scaffolding.

Inlet, gate, door, gateway, portal, porch, doorway.

Adv. How, in what way, in what manner, by what mode.

By the way, *en passant,* by-the-bye, *in transitu, chemin faisant.*

One way or another, any how.

Phr. Tout chemin va à Rome.

(628) MID-COURSE, middle course, mean, *juste milieu, mezzo termine, see* Middle (68) and Mean (29).

Direct, straight, straightforward course, path, &c.

V. To keep in a middle course, &c.

Adj. Undeviating, direct, straight, straightforward.

Phr. In medio tutissimus ibis.

(629) CIRCUIT, deviation, round-about way, *détour,* zigzag, circuition, circumbendibus, *see* (311), wandering, deviation (279).

V. To perform a circuit, &c., to deviate, wander, go round about, meander, &c. (279).

Adj. Circuitous, indirect, round about, zigzag, &c.

Adv. By a side wind, by an in direct course, &c.

(630) REQUIREMENT, requisition, need, lack, wants, necessities, *desidera tum,* exigency, pinch, *sine quâ non,* the very thing.

Needfulness, essentiality, necessity, indispensability, urgency, call for.

V. To require, need, want, have occasion for, stand in need of, lack, desire, be at a loss for, desiderate ; not to be able to do without or dispense with ; to prerequire ; to want but little.

To render necessary, to necessitate, to create a necessity for, to call for.

Adj. Requisite, required, &c., needful, necessary, exigent, essential, indispensable, prerequisite, that cannot be spared or dispensed with, urgent.

2°. *Subservience to 'Ends.*

1. *Actual Subservience.*

(631) INSTRUMENTALITY, medium, intermedium, intervention, dint, *see* Agency (170).

Key, master-key, passport, *passe partout,* "open sesame," a go-between, a cat's paw, mainstay, trump card.

Phr. Two strings to one's bow ; *cheval de bataille.*

Adj. Instrumental, intervening, intermediate, subservient.

Adv. Through, by, with, by means of, along with, thereby, through the medium, &c. of, wherewith.

(632) MEANS, resources, appliances, ways and means, expedients, step, measure (626), aid (707).

Machinery, mechanism, mechanics, engineering, mechanical powers.

Phr. Wheels within wheels.

Adj. Instrumental, subservient, mechanical, machinal.

Adv. How, by what means, by all means, by all manner of means, by the aid of, by dint of.

Phr. By hook or by crook.

(633) INSTRUMENT, tool, implement, apparatus, utensil, craft, machine, engine, lathe.

Weapon, arms, armory, battery.

Equipment, gear, tackle, tackling, rigging, harness, paraphernalia, equipage.

A wheel, jack, mill, clock-work, wheel-work, spring, screw, wedge, fly-wheel, lever, pinion, crank, wench, crane, capstan, windlass, monkey, hammer, mallet, mattock, mall, bat, sledge-hammer, mace, club, truncheon, pole, staff, bill, crow, crowbar, poleaxe, handspike, crutch, boom, bar.

Organ, limb, arm, hand, finger, claw, paw, talons, tentacle, wing, oar, paddle.

Handle, hilt, haft, heft, trigger, tiller, helm, treadle, pummel.

Edge tool, *see* (253), axis, *see* (312).

(634) SUBSTITUTE, shift, makeshift, *succedaneum,* jury-mast, *pis aller, see* Substitution (147) and Deputy (759).

(635) MATERIALS, stuff, *pabulum,* fuel, grist, provender, provisions, food, aliment, fodder, forage, prog, pasture, pasturage.

Supplies, munition, ammunition, reinforcement, relay.

Baggage, luggage, bag and baggage, effects, goods, chattels, household stuff, equipage, paraphernalia, stock in trade, pelf, cargo, lading.

Phr. A shot in the locker ; a hand at cards.

(636) STORE, stock, fund, supply, reserve, relay, budget, quiver, *corps de réserve,* reserved fund, mine, quarry, vein, lode, fountain, milch cow.

Collection, accumulation, heap (72), hoard, magazine, pile, rick, savings, bank (802), treasury, reservoir, repository, repertory, *repertorium,* depository, *dépôt,* treasure, thesaurus, museum, storehouse, promptuary, reservatory, conservatory, menagery, receptacle, warehouse, *entrepôt,* dock, larder, spence, garner, granary, storeroom, hanaper, cistern, well, tank, mill-pond, armory, arsenal, coffer, &c. (191).

V. To store, stock, treasure up, lay in, lay by, lay up, fund, garner, save, husband, hoard, deposit, accumulate (72).

To reserve, keep back, hold back.

Phr. To husband one's resources ; to have two strings to one's bow ; φειδεω των κτεανων.

Adj. Stored, &c., in store, in reserve.

(637) PROVISION, supply, providing, supplying, &c., purveyance, purveying, reinforcement, husbanding, commissariat, victualling.

Forage, pasture, food, &c. (299).

A purveyor, commissary, quartermaster, jackal.

(638) WASTE, consumption, expenditure, exhaustion, drain, leakage, wear and tear, dispersion (73), ebb.

V. To waste, spend, expend, use, consume, spill, leak, run out, run to waste, disperse (73), ebb, dry up,

V. To provide, supply, furnish, purvey, suppeditate, replenish, fill up, feed, stock with, recruit, cater, find, keep, lay in, lay in store, store, forage, husband.

Phr. To bring grist to the mill.

(639) SUFFICIENCY, adequacy, competence ; enough, satiety.

Fulness, plenitude, plenty, abundance, copiousness, amplitude, richness, fertility, luxuriance, uberty, the horn of plenty, cornucopia.

Impletion, repletion, saturation.

Riches (803), mine, store, fund (636); a bumper, a bellyful, a cartload, a plumper.

A flood, draught, shower, rain (347), stream, tide, spring tide, flush.

Moderation, *see* Mediocrity (651).

V. To be sufficient, &c., to suffice, to do, satisfy, saturate, make up.

To abound, teem, stream, flow, rain, shower down, pour, swarm.

To render sufficient, &c., to make up, to fill, replenish, pour in.

Adj. Sufficient, enough, adequate, commensurate, *quantum sufficit*, what will just do.

Moderate, measured.

Full, ample, plenty, copious, plentiful, plenteous, plenary, wantless, abundant, abounding, uberous, replete, laden, charged, fraught ; well stocked or provided, liberal, lavish, unstinted, to spare, unsparing, unmeasured.

Brimful, to the brim, chokefull, saturated, crammed, up to the ears, topful, rich, luxuriant.

Unexhausted, unwasted, exhaustless, inexhaustible.

Phr. Having two strings to one's bow ; enough and to spare ; cut and come again ; full as an egg ; full as a vetch ; ready to burst ; plenty as blackberries ; flowing with milk and honey ; enough in all conscience.

impoverish, drain, empty, exhaust; to fritter away.

Phr. To cast pearls before swine ; to employ a steam-engine to crack nuts ; to break a butterfly on a wheel.

Adj. Wasted, spent, &c., at a low ebb.

(640) INSUFFICIENCY, inadequacy, inadequateness, incompetence.

Deficiency, scantiness, scant, defect, defectiveness, defalcation, default, deficit, short-coming, falling short (304), what will not do, scantiness, slenderness.

Scarcity, dearth, want, need, lack, exigency, inanition, indigence, poverty, penury (804), destitution, dole, pittance, short allowance, short commons, a banyan day, a mouthful, starvation, famine, drought, emptiness, vacancy, flaccidity.

Phr. A beggarly account of empty boxes.

V. To be insufficient, &c., not to suffice, &c., to come short of, to fall short of, fail, stop short, to want, lack, need, require (630), caret.

To render insufficient, &c., to stint, grudge, hold back, withhold, starve, pinch, famish.

To empty, drain, &c., *see* (638).

Adj. Insufficient, inadequate, incompetent, not enough, &c., scant, scanty, deficient, defective, in default, scarce, empty, devoid, short of, wanting, &c.

Destitute, dry, drained, unprovided, unsupplied, unfurnished, unreplenished, unfed, unstored, untreasured, bare, meagre, poor, thin, spare, stinted, starved, famished, pinched, starveling, jejune, without resources.

Phr. Out at elbows ; not having a leg to stand upon.

---

(641) REDUNDANCE, superabundance, superfluity, superfluence, exuberance, profuseness, profusion, plethora, engorgement, congestion, glut, surfeit, load, turgidity, turgescence, dropsy.

149

Excess, an overdose, oversupply, overplus, surplusage, overflow, inundation, deluge, extravagance, prodigality (818), exorbitance, lavishment.

A drug; an expletive.

V. To overabound, run over, overflow, flow over.

To overstock, overdose, overlay, gorge, glut, load, overload, surcharge, overrun, drench, inundate, whelm, deluge.

Phr. To put butter upon bacon; it never rains but it pours.

Adj. Redundant, superfluous, exuberant, superabundant, excessive, in excess, overmuch, too much, *de trop*, needless, over and above (40), more than enough, *satis superque*, running to waste, overflowing, running over, over head and ears.

Turgid, gorged, plethoric, dropsical, profuse, lavish, prodigal, supervacaneous, *extra*, supernumerary, expletive, surcharged, overcharged, overloaded, overladen, overburdened, overrun.

Adv. Over, over and above, too much, overmuch, over and enough, too far, without measure, without stint.

2. *Degree of Subservience.*

(642) IMPORTANCE, consequence, moment, weight, gravity, seriousness, consideration, significance, import, influence (175), pressure, urgency, stress, emphasis, preponderance, prominence (250), greatness (31).

The substance, essence, quintessence, gist, pith, marrow, soul, *gravamen.*

The principal, prominent, or essential part.

Phr. A *sine quâ non.*

V. To be important, or of importance, &c., to signify, import, matter, boot, weigh, to be prominent, &c., to take the lead.

Phr. To be somebody, or something.

To attach, or ascribe importance to; to value, care for, &c. (897).

To over-estimate, &c. (482), to exaggerate (549).

Phr. To make much of; to make a stir, a fuss, a piece of work, or much ado about.

To mark, underline, score.

Adj. Important, of importance, &c., grave, serious, material, weighty, influential, significant, emphatic, momentous, earnest, pressing, critical, preponderating, pregnant, urgent, paramount, essential, vital, life and death.

(643) UNIMPORTANCE, indifference, insignificance, triflingness, paltriness, emptiness, nothingness, inanity, lightness, levity, frivolity, vanity, frivolousness, puerility, child's play.

Poverty, meagreness, meanness, shabbiness, &c.

A trifle, small matter, *minutiæ, bagatelle,* cipher, moonshine, molehill, joke, jest, snap of the fingers, fleabite, pinch of snuff, old song, *nugæ canoræ,* fiddlestick, fiddlestick end, paper pellet, bubble, bullrush.

A straw, pin, fig, button, rush, feather, farthing, brass farthing, doit, peppercorn, pebble, small fry.

Trumpery, trash, stuff, *fatras,* frippery, chaff, drug, froth, smoke, cobweb.

Toy, plaything, knick-knack, gimcrack, gewgaw, jiggumbob, bawble (or bauble), kickshaw.

Refuse, lumber, litter, orts, tares, weeds, sweepings, scourings, offscourings; rubble, *débris,* dross, *scoriæ,* dregs, scum, flue, dust, *see* Dirt (653).

Phr. "Leather or prunello;" *peu de chose;* much ado about nothing; much cry and little wool; *magno conatu, magnas nugas.*

V. To be unimportant, to be of little or no importance, &c.; not to signify, not to deserve, merit, or be

Great, considerable, &c., see (31), capital, leading, principal, superior, chief, main, prime, primary, cardinal, prominent, salient.

Signal, notable, memorable, remarkable, &c., grand, solemn, eventful, stirring ; not to be despised, or overlooked, &c., worth while.

Phr. Being no joke ; not to be sneezed at.

worthy of notice, regard, consideration, &c.

Phr. To catch at straws ; to make much ado about nothing ; *le jeu ne vaut pas la chandelle.*

Adj. Unimportant, secondary, inferior, immaterial, insignificant, unessential, non-essential, beneath notice, indifferent ; of little or no account, importance, consequence, moment, interest, &c.

Trifling, trivial, slight, slender, flimsy, trumpery, foolish, idle, puerile, childish, infantile, frothy, trashy, fribble, catch-penny, commonplace, contemptible.

Vain, empty, inane, poor, sorry, mean, meagre, shabby, scrannel, vile, miserable, scrubby, weedy, niggling, beggarly, piddling, peddling, pitiful, pitiable, despicable, priceless, ridiculous, farcical, finical, finikin, fiddle-faddle, fingle-fangle, gimcrack.

Phr. Not worth a straw.

Int. No matter! pshaw! pugh! pho-pho! fudge! fiddle-de-dee! nonsense! stuff! *n'importe!*

Adv. Meagrely, pitifully, vainly, &c.

(644) UTILITY, service, use, function, office, sphere, capacity, part, *rôle*, task, work.

Usefulness, worth, stead, avail, advantageousness, profitableness, serviceableness, merit, *cui bono*, applicability, adequacy, subservience, subserviency, efficacy, efficiency, help, money's worth.

V. To be useful, &c.

To avail, serve, subserve, help (707), conduce, serve one's turn, stand in stead, profit, advantage, accrue.

To render useful, to use (677), to turn to account, to utilize.

To serve an office, act a part, perform a function, serve a purpose, serve a turn.

Adj. Useful, beneficial, advantageous, serviceable, helping, gainful, profitable, proficuous.

Subservient, conducive, applicable, adequate, efficient, efficacious, effective, effectual.

Worth while, *tanti.*

Phr. Valeat quantum valere potest.
Adv. Usefully, &c.

(645) INUTILITY, uselessness, unsubservience, inefficacy, inefficiency, ineptness, inadequacy, inaptitude, fruitlessness, inanity, worthlessness, unproductiveness, barrenness, sterility, vanity, futility, triviality, paltriness, unprofitableness, unfruitfulness, rustiness, obsoleteness, discommodity, supererogation.

Litter, rubbish, lumber, trash, orts, weeds (643).

A waste, desert, wild, wilderness.

V. To be useless, &c., to be of no avail, use, &c. (644).

Phr. To use vain efforts ; to beat the air ; to fish in the air.

Adj. Useless, inutile, inservient, inefficient, inefficacious, unavailing, inoperative, bootless, supervacaneous, unprofitable, unproductive, sterile, barren.

Worthless, valueless, at a discount, gainless, fruitless, profitless, unserviceable, rusty, effete, washy, wasted, nugatory, futile, inept, withered, good for nothing, wasteful, ill-spent, not worth having, leading to no end.

Unneeded, unnecessary, uncalled for, incommodious, discommodious.

Phr. De lanâ caprinâ.
Adv. Uselessly, &c.

(646) Specific subservience.

EXPEDIENCE, expediency, fitness, suitableness, aptness, aptitude, appropriateness, pertinence, seasonableness (644), adaptation, congruity, consonance (23), convenience, eligibility, applicability, seemliness.

V. To be expedient, &c.

To suit, fit, square with, adapt itself to, agree with, consort with, tally with.

Adj. Expedient, fit, fitting, suitable, applicable, eligible, apt, appropriate, adapted, proper, advisable, desirable, pertinent, congruous, seemly, consonant, becoming, meet, due, consentaneous, congenial, well-timed, pat, seasonable, opportune, *à propos*, befitting, happy, felicitous, auspicious, acceptable, &c., convenient, commodious.

Phr. Being just the thing.

(648) Capability of producing good.

GOODNESS, excellence, value, worth, price, preciousness, estimation, rareness, exquisiteness.

Superexcellence, superiority, supereminence, transcendence, perfection (650).

Mediocrity, innocuousness, *see* (651).

V. To be good, &c.; to be superior, &c., to excel, transcend, top, vie, emulate, &c.

To be middling, &c. (651); to pass.

Phr. To challenge comparison; *probatum est;* to pass muster.

To produce good, benefit, &c., to benefit, to be beneficial, &c., to confer a benefit, &c., to improve (658).

Adj. Harmless, innocuous, hurtless, unobnoxious.

Good, beneficial, valuable, estimable, serviceable, advantageous, precious, favourable, palmary.

Sound, sterling, standard, true, genuine, household, fresh, unfaded, unspoiled, unimpaired, uninjured, un-

(647) INEXPEDIENCE, inexpediency, disadvantageousness, unsubservience, unserviceableness, disservice, unfitness, inaptitude, ineligibility, inappropriateness, impropriety, unseemliness, incongruity, impertinence, inopportuneness, unseasonableness.

Inconvenience, incommodiousness, incommodity, discommodity.

Inefficacy, inefficiency, inadequacy.

V. To be inexpedient, &c., to embarrass, cumber, lumber, &c.

Adj. Inexpedient, disadvantageous, unprofitable, unfit, unfitting, unsuitable, amiss, improper, unapt, inept, unadvisable, ineligible, objectionable, inadmissible, unseemly, inopportune, unseasonable; inefficient, inefficacious, inadequate.

Inconvenient, incommodious, in the way, cumbrous, cumbersome, lumbering, unwieldy, unmanageable, awkward, clumsy.

(649) Capability of producing evil.

BADNESS, hurtfulness, disserviceableness, injuriousness, banefulness, mischievousness, noxiousness, malignancy, venemousness, virulence, destructiveness, scathe, curse, bane (663).

Vileness, foulness, rankness, depravement, depravedness, pestilence; Deterioration, *see* (659).

V. To be bad, &c.

To cause, produce, or inflict evil; to harm, hurt, injure, mar, damage, damnify, endamage, scathe, prejudice, shend, inquinate.

To wrong, molest, annoy, grieve, aggrieve, trouble, oppress, persecute, weigh down, run down, overlay.

To maltreat, abuse, ill-use, ill-treat, bruise, scratch, maul, strike, smite, scourge (972), wound, lame, maim, scotch, cripple, mutilate, hamstring, hough, stab, pierce, &c., crush, crumble.

To corrupt, corrode, pollute, &c. (659).

To spoil, despoil, sweep, ravage, lay waste, devastate, dismantle, de-

demolished, undamaged, undecayed, natural, unsophisticated, unadulterated, unpolluted, unvitiated.

Choice, nice, fine, rare, felicitous, unexceptionable, excellent, admirable, first-rate, prime, crack, cardinal, superlative, superfine, superexcellent, exquisite, high wrought, inestimable, invaluable, incomparable, transcendent, matchless, none such, peerless, inimitable, unrivalled, *nulli secundus*, *facile princeps*, spotless, immaculate, perfect (650).

Moderately good (651).

Phr. Of the first water, precious as the apple of the eye, worth a Jew's eye; *ne plus ultra;* sound as a roach; worth its weight in gold.

---

molish, level, raze, consume, overrun, sac, plunder, destroy (162).

Phr. To play the deuce with; to break the back of; crush to pieces; crumble to dust; to grind to powder; to ravage with fire and sword.

Adj. Bad, evil, wrong, prejudicial, disserviceable, disadvantageous, unprofitable, unlucky, sinister, obnoxious, untoward, unadvisable, inauspicious.

Hurtful, injurious, grievous, detrimental, noxious, pernicious, mischievous, baneful, baleful.

Morbific, rank, peccant, malignant, tabid, corroding, corrosive, virulent, cankering, mephitic, narcotic.

Deleterious, deletory, poisonous, venemous, envenomed, pestilent, pestiferous, destructive, deadly, fatal, mortal, lethal, lethiferous.

Vile, sad, wretched, sorry, shabby, scurvy, scrubby, shocking, horrid.

Hateful, abominable, detestable, execrable, cursed, accursed, confounded, damnable, diabolic, devilish, demoniacal, infernal, hellish, Satanic.

Adv. Wrong, wrongly, badly, &c.

---

(650) PERFECTION, perfectness, bestness, indefectibility, impeccability, *beau idéal* (210).

Master-piece, *chef d'œuvre*, model, pattern, mirror, phœnix, *rara avis*, paragon, prime, flower, cream, none such, *non-pareil, élite.*

Gem, *bijou*, jewel, pearl, diamond, ruby, brilliant.

Phr. The philosopher's stone; the flower of the flock; the cock of the roost; the pink or acme of perfection; *le cygne noir; Natura lo fece, e poi rumpe la stampa;* the *ne plus ultra.*

V. To be perfect, &c., to excel, transcend, overtop, &c.

V. To carry everything before it; to play first fiddle.

To bring to perfection, to perfect, to ripen, mature, &c. (52, 729).

Adj. Perfect, best, faultless, finished, indeficient, indefective, indefectible, immaculate, spotless, transcendent, matchless, peerless, unparagoned, &c., *see* (648), inimit-
153

(651) IMPERFECTION, imperfectness, unsoundness, faultiness, deficiency, drawback, inadequacy, inadequateness.

Fault, defect, flaw, crack, twist, taint, peccancy.

Mediocrity, mean (29), indifference, inferiority.

V. To be imperfect, middling, &c., to fail, lie under a disadvantage.

Phr. To play second fiddle; barely to pass muster.

Adj. Imperfect, deficient, defective, faulty, inadequate, unsound, unremedied, cracked, warped, frail, gimcrack, gingerbread, tottering, decrepit, rickety, battered, worn out, threadbare, seedy, worm-eaten, used up, decayed, mutilated.

Indifferent, middling, *médiocre*, so so, *couci-couci*, secondary, second rate, second best, second-hand, second fiddle.

Tolerable, passable, pretty well, well enough, rather good, admissible, not bad, not amiss.

able, superlative, superhuman, divine.

(652) CLEANNESS, cleanliness, purity, neatness, tidiness, spotlessness, immaculateness.

Cleaning, purification, mundification, lustration, detersion, abstersion, epuration, depuration, expurgation, purgation, castration.

Washing, ablution, lavation, elutriation, lixiviation, clarification, defecation, despumation, edulcoration, colature, filtration.

Fumigation, ventilation, disinfection.

Scavenger; brush, broom, besom, sieve, riddle, screen, filter.

V. To be clean, &c.

To render clean, &c., to clean, to mundify, cleanse, wipe, mop, sponge, scour, swab, scrub, brush, sweep, brush up.

To wash, lave, buck, absterge, deterge, clear, purify, depurate, defecate, elutriate, lixiviate, edulcorate, clarify, rack, filter, filtrate.

To disinfect, fumigate, ventilate, purge, emasculate, castrate.

To sift, winnow, pick, weed.

Adj. Clean, pure, spotless, unspotted, immaculate, unstained, stainless, unsoiled, unsullied, taintless, untainted.

Spruce, tidy, washed, swept, &c., cleaned, purified, &c.

Phr. Clean as a whistle;—Clean as a new penny.

Phr. Having a screw loose; no great catch; milk and water; no great shakes; only better than nothing.

(653) UNCLEANNESS, immundicity, uncleanliness, soilure, soiliness, foulness, impurity, pollution, nastiness, offensiveness, beastliness, defilement, contamination, abomination, taint, tainture.

Slovenliness, slovenry, untidiness, sluttishness, coarseness, grossness.

Dirt, filth, soil, slop, dust, cobweb, smoke, soot, smudge, smut, raff, *sordes.*

Dregs, grounds, sediment, lees, settlement, dross, drossiness, precipitate, *scoriæ*, slag, scum, sweepings, off-scourings, *caput mortuum*, draff, fur, scurf, scurfiness, furfur, dandriff, riffraff, vermin.

Mud, mire, quagmire, slough, alluvium, silt, slime, spawn, offal, recrement, feces, excrement, ordure, dung, guano, manure, compost, dunghill, midden, bog, laystall, sink, cess, cesspool, sump, sough, *cloaca*, sewer, shore; hogwash, bilge-water.

Stye, pig-stye, lair, den.

Rottenness, corruption, decay, putrefaction, putrescence, putridity, purulence, feculence, rankness, rancidity, moulding, mustiness, mucidness, mould, mother, must, mildew, dry-rot, fœtor (401).

Phr. A sink of corruption.

V. To be unclean, dirty, &c. to rot, putrefy, mould, moulder, fester, &c.

To render unclean, &c., to dirt, dirty, soil, begrime, smear, besmear, bemire, spatter, bespatter, splash, bedaggle, bedraggle, daub, bedaub, slabber, beslabber, beslime, to cover with dust, &c.

To foul, befoul, pollute, defile, debase, contaminate, taint, corrupt, deflower, rot, &c.

Adj. Unclean, dirty, soiled, &c., dusty, dirtied, &c., sooty, smoky, reechy, thick, turbid, dreggy.

Slovenly, untidy, sluttish, dowdy, unkempt, unscoured, unswept, unwiped, unwashed, unstrained, unpurified.

Nasty, foul, impure, offensive, abominable, beastly.

Mouldy, musty, mildewed, rusty, mouldering, effete, reasty, rotten, rotting, tainted, high, fly-blown, maggoty, putrescent, putrid, pu-

154

trefied, festering, purulent, feculent, fecal, stercoraceous, excrementitious.

Phr. Wallowing in the mire ; rotten as a pear ; rotten as cheese.

(654) HEALTH, sanity, soundness, heartiness, haleness, vigour, freshness, bloom, healthfulness, incorruption, incorruptibility.

V. To be in health, &c., to flourish.

To return to health, to recover, to get the better of.

To restore to health, to cure, recall to life.

Phr. To keep on one's legs;— To take a new or fresh lease of life; — *Non est vivere sed valere vita.*

Adj. Healthy, in health, well, sound, healthful, hearty, hale, fresh, whole, florid, staunch, flush, hardy, vigorous, weather-proof.

Unscathed, uninjured, unmaimed, unmarred, untainted.

Phr. Having a clean bill of health ; being on one's legs ; sound as a roach ; fresh as a rose ; hearty as a buck.

(655) DISEASE, illness, sickness, ailment, ailing, indisposition, complaint, disorder, malady, distemper.

Sickliness, sicklishness, infirmity, diseasedness, discrasy, invalidation, cachexy, witheredness, atrophy, *marasmus*, incurableness, incurability.

Taint, pollution, infection, septicity, epidemic, endemic, murrain, plague, pestilence, virus, pox.

A sore, ulcer, abscess, fester, rot, canker, cancer, *caries*, gangrene, *sphacelus*, leprosy.

A valetudinarian, an invalid, a patient, a cripple.

Science of disease ; Pathology, Ætiology, Nosology.

V. To be ill, &c., to ail, suffer, be affected with, &c., to complain of, to lay up, droop, flag, languish, halt, gasp.

Adj. Diseased, ill, taken ill, seized, indisposed, unwell, sick, ailing, suffering, affected with illness, laid up, confined, bed-ridden, invalided.

Unsound, sickly, poorly, weakly, cranky, healthless, infirm, unbraced, drooping, flagging, withered, decayed, decrepit, lame, crippled, battered, halting, worn out, used up, moth-eaten, worm-eaten.

Morbid, tainted, vitiated, peccant, contaminated, tabid, mangy, poisoned, immedicable, recureless, gasping, moribund (360).

Phr. Out of sorts; out of joint; out of heart; good for nothing ; on the sick list; in a bad way; *hors de combat;* worn to the stump ; on one's last legs; at the last gasp.

(656) SALUBRITY, healthiness, wholesomeness, innoxiousness.

V. To be salubrious, &c., to agree with.

Adj. Salubrious, wholesome, healthy, salutary, salutiferous, healthful, agreeing with.

Innoxious, innocuous, harmless, uninjurious, innocent, uninfectious.

Remedial, restorative, sanatory, &c., *see* (662).

(657) INSALUBRITY, unhealthiness, unwholesomeness, deadliness, fatality, malaria, &c. (663).

Adj. Insalubrious, unhealthy, ungenial, uncongenial, unwholesome, morbific, septic, deleterious, pestilent, pestiferous, pestilential, virulent, poisonous, contagious, infectious, epidemic, zymotic, deadly, mortiferous.

Phr. "There is death in the pot."

(658) IMPROVEMENT, melioration, amelioration, betterment, mend, emendation, advance, advancement,

(659) DETERIORATION, wane, ebb, debasement, degeneracy, degeneration, degradation, degenerateness.

progress, elevation, preferment, convalescence, recovery, curableness.

Repair, reparation, cicatrization, correction, reform, reformation, epuration, purification, &c. (652), refinement, relief, redress, *limæ labor.*

New edition ; *réchauffé, rifacimento.*

V. To be, become, or get better, &c., to improve, mend, advance, progress (282), to get on, make progress, gain ground, make way, go ahead, pick up, rally, recover, get the better of, get well.

Phr. To be oneself again.

To render better, improve, mend, amend, better, meliorate, ameliorate, advance, push on, forward, enhance.

To relieve, refresh, restore, renew, redintegrate, heal, &c., *see* (660) ; to palliate, mitigate.

To repair, refit, retouch, botch, vamp, tinker, cobble, patch up, touch up, cicatrize, heelpiece, darn, finedraw, rub ub, furbish, polish, bolster up, calk, careen, to stop a gap, to stanch.

To purify, depurate (652), defecate, strain, filter, rack, refine, disinfect.

To correct, rectify, redress, reform, restore (660), mellow, cook, warm up.

Adj. Improving, &c., improved, &c., progressive, corrective, reparatory, emendatory.

Curable, corrigible.

———

Impairment, inquination, injury, vitiation, debasement, perversion, corruption, prostitution, pollution, alloy.

Decline, declension, declination, going down-hill, recession, retrogression, retrogradation (283), caducity, decrepitude, decadency, falling off.

Decay, disorganization, wear and tear, mouldiness, rottenness, moth and rust, dry-rot, blight, marasmus, falling to pieces, *délâbrement.*

Incurableness, remedilessness, *see* Hopelessness (859).

V. To be, or become deteriorated, to deteriorate, wane, ebb, degenerate, fall off, decline, go down-hill, sink, go down, lapse, droop, be the worse for, recede, retrograde, fall into decay, fade, break, break down, fall to pieces, wither, moulder, rot, rust, crumble, totter, shake, tumble, fall, topple, perish, die (360).

Phr. To go to rack and ruin ; to fall into the sear and yellow leaf ; to go to the dogs ; to go to pot ; to go on from bad to worse.

To render less good ; to deteriorate, impair, vitiate, inquinate, debase, alloy.

To spoil, embase, defile, taint, infect, contaminate, sophisticate, poison, canker, corrupt, pollute, deprave, leaven, envenom, debauch, prostitute, defile, adulterate, stain, spatter, bespatter, soil, tarnish.

To corrode, erode, wear away, wear out, gnaw, gnaw at the root of, sap, mine, undermine, shake, break up, disorganize, dismantle, dismast, lay waste, do for, ruin.

To embitter, acerbate, aggravate.

To injure, harm, hurt, damage, endamage, damnify, &c. (649).

Phr. To play the deuce with.

Adj. Deteriorated, become worse, impaired, &c., degenerate, on the decline, deciduous, unimproved, unrecovered, unrestored.

Remediless, hopeless, past cure, past mending, irreparable, irremediable, cureless, incurable, irremedicable, irrecoverable, irretrievable, irreclaimable, irreversible.

Decayed, &c., moth-eaten, worm-eaten, mildewed, rusty, timeworn, moss-grown, effete, wasted, worn, crumbling.

Phr. Out of the frying-pan into the fire ; the worse for wear ; worn to a thread ; worn to a shadow.

(660) RESTORATION, reinstatement, replacement, restoral, instauration, re-establishment, rectification, redintegration, refection, refocillation, cure, sanation, refitting, recruiting, redress, retrieval, &c.

Renovation, reanimation, recovery, recure, resuscitation, reviviscence, revival, rejuvenescence, reviction, regeneration, regeneracy, regenerateness, redemption ; a Phœnix.

V. To return to the original state, to right itself.

To restore, replace, re-establish, reinstate, re-estate, reconstitute, redintegrate, set right, set to rights, rectify, redress, reclaim, redeem, recover, recure, retrieve.

To refit, recruit, refresh, refocillate, rehabilitate, reconvert, reconstitute, renovate, revive, regenerate, resuscitate, reanimate, recal to life, set on one's legs, reseat.

To cure, heal, cicatrize, remedy, doctor, physic, medicate.

Adj. Restoring, &c., restored, &c., placed *in statu quo*, rising from its ashes, Phœnix-like.

Restorable, sanable, remediable, retrievable.

Adv. In statu quo ; as you were.

(661) RELAPSE, lapse, falling back, retrogression, retrogradation, &c. (659).

Return to, or recurrence of a bad state.

V. To relapse, lapse, fall back, return, retrograde, &c.

---

(662) REMEDY, help, redress, cure, antidote, counter-poison, prophylactic, corrective, restorative, sedative.

Physic, medicine, Galenicals, drug, medicament, *nostrum*, recipe, prescription, catholicon.

Panacea, elixir, balm, balsam, cordial, theriac, ptisan.

Salve, plaster, epithem, embrocation, cataplasm, poultice, vulnerary, cosmetic, &c.; sanativeness.

Pharmacy, Pharmacology, Acology, Materia Medica, Therapeutics, Dietetics, Dietary, Regimen, Chirurgery, Surgery.

An hospital, infirmary, pesthouse, lazaretto, *maison de santé, ambulance.*

Adj. Remedial, medical, medicinal, therapeutic, chirurgical, sanatory, sanative, salutary, salutiferous, healing, paregoric, restorative, tonic, corroborant, analeptic, balsamic, anodyne, sedative, lenitive, demulcent, emollient, depuratory, detersive, detergent, abstersive, disinfectant, corrective.

Dietetic, alexipharmic, alexiteric.

(663) BANE, rod, scourge, curse, scathe, sting.

Poison, leaven, virus, venom, miasm, *mephitis*, malaria, pest, rust, canker, cancer, cankerworm.

Hemlock, hellebore, nightshade, henbane, aconite.

A viper, adder, serpent, cobra, rattlesnake, cockatrice, scorpion, wireworm, torpedo, hornet, vulture, vampire, &c.; Demon, &c. (980); Fury, Attila, see (913).

Science of poisons, Toxicology.

---

3. *Contingent Subservience.*

(664) SAFETY, security, surety, impregnability, invulnerability, invulnerableness.

(665) DANGER, peril, insecurity, jeopardy, risk, hazard, venture, precariousness, slipperiness.

Safeguard, guard, guardianship, protection, tutelage, wardship, wardenship, safe-conduct, escort, convoy, garrison.

Watch, watch and ward, sentinel, scout, watchman, patrol, vedetta, picket, bivouac, watch-dog, ban-dog, Cerberus.

Protector, guardian, guard, defender, warden, warder, preserver, *chaperon*, tutelary saint, guardian angel; *see* Defence (717).

Custody, safe-keeping (751).

Precaution, quarantine.

V. To be safe, &c.

Phr. To save one's bacon.

To render safe, &c., to protect, guard, mount guard, shield, shelter, flank, cover, screen, shroud, ensconce, ward, secure, fence, hedge in, entrench, house, nestle.

To defend, forfend, escort, convoy, garrison.

Adj. Safe, in safety, in security, secure, sure, protected, guarded, &c., snug, scathless.

Invulnerable, unassailable, unattackable, impregnable, inexpugnable, imperdible.

Protecting, &c., guardian, tutelary.

Unthreatened, unmolested, unharmed, harmless, unhazarded.

Phr. Under lock and key; on sure ground; under cover; under the shadow of one's wing; the coast being clear; the danger being past; out of the wood.

(666) Means of safety.

REFUGE, asylum, sanctuary, fastness, retreat, ark, hiding-place.

Roadstead, anchorage, breakwater, mole, port, haven, harbour, harbour of refuge, pier.

Fort, citadel, fortification, &c., shield, &c., *see* Defence (717).

Screen, covert, wing, fence, rail, railing, wall, dike, ditch, &c. (232).

Anchor, kedger, grapnel, sheet-anchor, prop, stay, main-stay, jury-

Phr. The ground sliding from under one.

Liability, exposure (177), vulnerability, vulnerable point, the heel of Achilles.

Hopelessness (859), forlorn hope, alarm, *see* Fear (860), defencelessness.

V. To be in danger, &c., to be exposed to, to incur or encounter danger, run the danger of, run a risk.

To place or put in danger, &c., to endanger, expose to danger, imperil, jeopardize, compromise, adventure, risk, hazard, venture, stake.

Phr. To engage in a forlorn hope.

To ensnare, entrap, entangle, illaqueate.

Adj. In danger, peril, jeopardy, &c., unsafe, insecure, unguarded, unscreened, unsheltered, unprotected, guardless, helpless, guideless, exposed, defenceless, at bay, on a lee-shore, on the rocks, water-logged, *aux abois*, between two fires.

Unwarned, unadmonished, unadvised.

Dangerous, perilous, hazardous, parlous, fraught with danger, adventurous, precarious, breakneck, slippery, unsteady, shaky, tottering, top-heavy, harbourless.

Threatening, alarming, minatory, minaceous (909).

Phr. Not out of the wood; neck or nothing; out of the frying-pan into the fire; *latet anguis in herba; ne réveillez pas le chat qui dort; cane pejus et angue;* between Scylla and Charybdis.

(667) Source of danger.

PITFALL, rocks, reefs, sunken rocks, snags, sands, quicksands, breakers, shoals, shallows.

Trap, snare, gin, springe, toils, noose, net, spring-net, spring-gun, masked battery, mine.

Phr. The sword of Damocles; a snake in the grass; trusting to a broken reed.

mast, life-boat, plank, stepping-stone, umbrella, parachute, lightning-conductor.

(668) WARNING, caution, *caveat*, notice, premonition, premonishment, lesson, dehortation.

Beacon, lighthouse, pharos, watch-tower, signal-post, &c. *see* (550).

Sentinel, sentry, watch, watchman, patrol, vedette, &c. (664).

Phr. The writing on the wall.

V. To warn, caution, forewarn, prewarn, premonish, give notice, give warning, admonish, dehort.

Phr. To put on one's guard; to sound the alarm.

To take warning, to beware, to be on one's guard (864).

Adj. Warning, &c., premonitory, dehortatory.

Warned, &c., careful, on one's guard (459).

Int. Beware!

(669) Indication of danger.

ALARM, alarum, larum, alarm-bell, tocsin, signal of distress, blue-lights, &c., warning voice, Cassandra.

False alarm, cry of wolf, bugbear.

V. To give, raise, or sound an alarm, to alarm, warn, ring the tocsin, *battre la générale*, to cry wolf.

Adj. Alarming, &c.

(670) PRESERVATION, conservation, maintenance, support, sustentation, deliverance, salvation, rescue, redemption.

Means of preservation, prophylaxis, preservative, preserver, Hygiastics, Hygyantics.

V. To preserve, maintain, support, save, rescue.

To embalm, dry, cure, salt, pickle, season, kyanize, bottle, pot.

Adj. Preserving, conservative, prophylactic, preservatory, hygeianic.

Preserved, unimpaired, uninjured, unhurt, unsinged, unmarred.

(671) ESCAPE, scape, evasion, avolation, retreat, reprieve, reprieval, deliverance, redemption, rescue.

Narrow escape, hair's-breadth scape, *échappée belle*.

Means of escape; bridge, drawbridge, loophole, ladder, plank, stepping-stone, &c. (666).

V. To escape, scape, elude, evade, make or effect one's escape, make off, march off, pack off, slip away, steal away, slink away, flit, decamp, run away, abscond, fly, flee, bolt, elope, whip off, break loose, play truant.

Phr. To take oneself off; to beat a retreat; to slip the collar; to slip through the fingers; to make oneself scarce; to hop the twig; to take to one's heels; to cut and run; to run for one's life.

Int. Sauve qui peut! the devil take the hindmost!

Adj. Escaping, &c., escaped, &c., fugitive, runaway.

Phr. The bird having flown.

(672) DELIVERANCE, extrication, rescue, redemption, salvation, riddance, redeemableness.

V. To deliver, extricate, rescue, save, redeem, bring off, *tirer d'affaire*, to get rid of, to rid.

Phr. To save one's bacon; *se tirer d'affaire;* to find a hole to creep out of.

Adj. Delivered, saved, &c., scot free, scathless.

Extricable, redeemable, rescueable.

3°. *Precursory Measures.*

(673) PREPARATION, making ready, providing, provision, providence, anticipation, preconcertation, precaution, laying foundations, ploughing, sowing, semination, brewing, digestion, gestation, hatching, incubation, concoction, maturation, elaboration, predisposition.

Preparation of men; Training, drill, drilling, discipline, exercise, exercitation, *gymnasium, palæstra,* prenticeship, apprenticeship, qualification, inurement, education, noviciate, *see* Teaching (537).

Putting or setting in order, putting to rights, clearance, arrangement, disposal, organization, adjustment, adaptation, disposition, accommodation, putting in tune, tuning, putting in trim, dressing, putting in harness, outfit, equipment, accoutrement, &c., putting the horses to.

Phr. A stitch in time; clearing decks; a note of preparation.

Groundwork, basis, foundation, pedestal, &c., *see* (215), first stone, scaffold, scaffolding, *échaffaudage.*

State of being prepared, preparedness, ripeness, maturity, readiness, mellowness.

Preparer, pioneer, *avant courier, avant coureur,* warming-pan.

V. To prepare, get ready, make ready, get up, anticipate, forecast, pre-establish, preconcert, settle preliminaries, to found.

To arrange, set or put in order, set or put to rights, organize, dispose, cast the parts, adjust, adapt, accommodate, trim, betrim, fit, predispose, inure, elaborate, mature, ripen, nurture, hatch, cook, brew, tune, put in tune, attune, set, temper, anneal.

Phr. To prepare the ground; lay or fix the foundations, the basis, groundwork, &c.; to clear the ground, clear the way, clear decks, clear for action, close one's ranks, plough the ground, dress the ground, till the soil, sow the seed, open the way, pave the way, lay a train, dig a mine, prepare a charge.

To provide, provide against, make provision, keep on foot, take precautions, make sure.

To equip, arm, man, fit out, fit up, furnish, rigg, dress, dress up,

(674) NON-PREPARATION, want or absence of preparation, inculture, inconcoction, improvidence.

Immaturity, crudeness, crudity, greenness, rawness, disqualification.

Absence of art, nature.

An embryo, skeleton, rough copy, germ, &c., rudiment (153).

V. To be unprepared, &c., to want, or lack preparation.

Phr. S'embarquer sans biscuits.

To render unprepared, &c., to dismantle, dismount, dismast, disqualify, disable, unrig, undress (226).

Phr. To put *hors de combat.*

Adj. Unprepared, rudimental, immature, unripe, raw, green, crude, rough, rough-cast, rough-hewn, unhewn, unformed, unhatched, unfledged, unnurtured, uneducated, unlicked, untilled, natural, in a state of nature, unwrought, unconcocted, undigested, indigested, unmellowed, unblown, unfashioned, unlaboured, unleavened, fallow, uncultivated, untrained, undrilled, unexercised, unseasoned, disqualified.

Unbegun, unready, unarranged, unorganized, unsown, unfurnished, unprovided, unequipped, undressed, in *dishabille,* dismantled, untrimmed.

Shiftless, improvident, thoughtless, unthrifty.

Unpremeditated, off-hand (612), from hand to mouth, extempore.

---

furbish up, accoutre, array, fettle, vamp up, put in harness, sharpen one's tools, whet the knife, wind up, prime and load, put the horses to.

To prepare oneself, lay oneself out for, get into harness, gird up one's loins, buckle on one's armour.

To set on foot, lay the first stone, break ground.

To train, drill, discipline, break in, cradle, inure, habituate, harden, case-harden, season, acclimatize, qualify, educate, teach, &c.

Phr. To erect the scaffold ; to cut one's coat according to one's cloth ; to keep one's powder dry ; to beat up for recruits ; *venienti occurrite morbo ; principiis obsta ;* to sound the note of preparation.

Adj. Preparing, &c., in preparation, in course of preparation, in agitation, brewing, hatching, forthcoming, in embryo, afoot, afloat, on the anvil, on the carpet, on the stocks, on the *tapis,* provisional.

Prepared, trained, drilled, &c., forearmed, ready, in readiness, ripe, mature, mellow, fledged, ready to one's hand, cut and dried, annealed, concocted.

Phr. Armed to the teeth ; armed cap-à-pie ; the coast being clear.

Adv. In preparation, in anticipation of, &c., against.

(675) ESSAY, trial, experiment (463), probation, venture, adventure, *coup d'essai,* random shot.

V. To try, essay, make trial of, experiment, make an experiment, grope, feel one's way, *tâtonner,* pick one's way ; to venture, adventure.

Phr. To put out or throw out a feeler ; to send up a pilot balloon.

Adj. Essaying, &c., experimental, tentative, empirical, on trial, probative, probatory, probationary.

Adv. Experimentally, &c., *à tâtons,* at a venture.

(676) UNDERTAKING, enterprise, emprise, endeavour, attempt, move, first move, the initiative, first step, *see* Beginning (66), *début,* embarkation.

V. To undertake, take in hand, set about, go about, set to, fall to, set to work, engage in, launch into, embark in, plunge into, volunteer.

To endeavour, strive, use one's endeavours ; to attempt, make an attempt, tempt.

To begin, set on foot, set agoing, take the first step, take the initiative ; to break ground, break the ice, break cover.

Phr. To break the neck of the business ; to pass the Rubicon ; to take upon oneself ; to take on one's shoulders ; *ce n'est que le premier pas qui coute ; dimidium facti qui cœpit habet.*

To take the bull by the horns ; to rush *in medias res ;* to have too many irons in the fire ; to attempt impossibilities ; *prendre la lune avec les dents.*

Adv. Undertaking, attempting, &c.

(677) USE, employment, employ, application, appliance, adhibition, disposal, exercise.

Recourse, resort, avail, service, conversion to use, utilization.

Agency (170).

V. To use, make use of, employ, apply, adhibit, dispose of, work, wield, put to use ; turn or convert to use ; avail oneself of, resort to, recur to, take up with.

(678) DISUSE, forbearance, absti-nence, dispensation, desuetude, dispensableness.

V. To disuse, not to use, to do without, to dispense with, to let alone, to spare, wave.

To lay by ; set, put, or lay aside ; to discard, dismiss, cast off, throw off, turn off, turn out, turn away, throw away, shelve, do away with ; to keep back.

Phr. To take advantage of ; to turn to account ; to make the most of ; to make the best of ; to bring to bear upon ; to fall back upon ; to press or enlist into the service ; to make shift with.

To render useful, serviceable, available, &c. ; to utilize, draw, call forth, tax, task, try, exert, exercise, work up, consume, absorb, expend.

To practise, put in action, set to work, set in motion, ply, put in practice.

Phr. To pull the strings or wires ; to make a cat's-paw of.

To be useful, to serve one's turn, &c., *see* (644).

Adj. Used, employed, &c., applied, exercised, tried, &c.

To dismantle, dismast.

Phr. To lay on the shelf ; to lay up in ordinary ; to lay up in a napkin ; to cast, heave, or throw overboard ; to cast to the winds ; to turn out neck and heels.

Adj. Disused, &c., not used, unemployed, unapplied, unspent, unexercised, kept back.

Unessayed, untouched, ungathered, unculled, untrodden.

(679) MISUSE, misemployment, misapplication, misappropriation, abuse, profanation, prostitution, desecration.

Waste, wasting, spilling, exhaustion (638).

V. To misuse, misemploy, misapply, misappropriate, desecrate, abuse, profane, prostitute.

To waste, spill, fritter away, exhaust.

Adj. Misused, &c.

Section III.   VOLUNTARY ACTION.

1°. *Simple Voluntary Action.*

(680) ACTION, performance, work, operation, proceeding, procedure, process, handiwork, handicraft, workmanship, manœuvre, transaction, bout, job, doings.

Deed, act, overt act, stitch, touch, move, stroke, blow, *coup*, feat, exploit, passage, stroke of policy, *coup de main, coup d'état.*

V. To act, do, work, operate, do business, practise, perpetrate, perform, officiate, exercise, commit, inflict, strike a blow.

To labour, drudge, toil, ply, droil, set to work, pull the oar, serve, officiate, go about, turn one's hand to, dabble ; to have in hand.

Phr. To have a finger in the pie ; to take or play a part ; to discharge an office ; to go the whole hog.

Adj. Acting, &c., in action, in operation, &c., operative, in harness

Int. Here goes !

(681) INACTION, abstinence from action, *see* Inactivity (683).

V. Not to do, to let be, abstain from doing ; let or leave alone, refrain, desist, keep oneself from doing ; let pass, lie by, wait.

Phr. To bide one's time ; to cool one's heels ; to stay one's hand ; to wash one's hands of ; to leave in the lurch ; to have other fish to fry.

To undo, take down, take or pull to pieces.

Adj. Not doing, not done, let alone, undone, &c.

(682) ACTIVITY, briskness, quickness, promptness, readiness, alertness, smartness, sharpness, nimbleness, agility.

Spirit, vivacity, eagerness, alacrity, zeal, energy (171), vigour, intentness.

Movement, bustle, stir, fuss, ado, fidget, restlessness, fidgettiness.

Wakefulness, *pervigilium*, *insomnium*, sleeplessness.

Industry, assiduity, assiduousness, sedulity, sedulousness, diligence; perseverance, persistence, plodding, painstaking, drudgery, indefatigation, indefatigability, indefatigableness, patience, habits of business.

Dabbling, meddling, interference, interposition, intermeddling, tampering with, intrigue, *tripotage*, supererogation, superfluence.

A housewife, busy body, blade.

Phr. The thick of the action ; *in medias res;* too many cooks ; new brooms.

V. To be active, busy, stirring, &c., to busy oneself in, stir, bestir oneself, bustle, fuss, make a fuss, speed, hasten, push, make a push.

To plod, drudge, keep on, hold on, persist, stick to, buckle to, stick to work, take pains ; to take or spend time in ; to make progress, peddle, potter, pudder.

Phr. To look sharp ; to lay about one ; to have one's hands full ; to kick up a dust ; to stir one's stumps ; to exert one's energies ; to put one's best leg foremost ; to do one's best ; to do all one can ; to leave no stone unturned ; to have all one's eyes about one ; make the best of one's time ; to make short work of ; to seize the opportunity ; *battre le fer sur l'enclume;* to take time by the forelock ; to make hay while the sun shines ; to strike the iron while it is hot ; to take advantage of ; to kill two birds with one stone ; to move heaven and earth ; to go through fire and water ; to do wonders ; to go all lengths ; to stick at nothing ; to go the whole hog, *see* (684)

163

(683) INACTIVITY, inaction, idleness, sloth, laziness, indolence, indiligence, inertness, lumpishness, supineness, supinity, sluggishness, languor, torpor, lentor, listlessness, remissness.

Dilatoriness, cunctation, procrastination (133), relaxation, dronishness, truantship, lagging, dawdling, rust, rustiness, want of occupation.

Somnolence, drowsiness, doziness, nodding, oscitation, lethargicalness, sleepiness, sleepfulness, hypnology.

Sleep, nap, doze, slumber, snooze, *siesta*, dream, trance, snore, a wink of sleep, lethargy, *exstasis*, hybernation.

Phr. The Castle of Indolence ; *dolce far niente ;* the Fabian policy ; the thief of time.

An idler, laggard, lubbard, truant, do-little, lubber, sluggard, slumberer, *fainéant*, drone, dormouse, slowback, lourger, slug, marmot.

Cause of inactivity, *see* (174) ; torpedo.

V. To be inactive, &c., do nothing, to let alone, lie by, lie idle, lay to, keep quiet, hang fire, relax, slouch, loll, drawl, slug, dally, lag, dawdle, lounge, loiter, play truant ; to waste, lose, idle away, kill, trifle away, fritter away or fool away time ; faddle, dabble, fribble, piddle, fiddle-faddle.

Phr. To fold one's arms ; to rest upon one's oars ; to burn daylight ; *Ne battre que d'une aile.*

To sleep, slumber, nod, close the eyes, close the eyelids, doze, fall asleep, take a nap, go off to sleep, hybernate, yawn.

Phr. To sleep like a top ; to sleep as sound as a top ; to sleep like a log ; to sleep like a dormouse ; to eat the bread of idleness ; to loll in the lap of indolence.

To render idle, &c., to sluggardize.

Adj. Inactive, unoccupied, unemployed, unbusied, doing nothing (685).

Indolent, lazy, slothful, idle, lusk,

To meddle, moil, intermeddle, interfere, interpose, tamper with, agitate, intrigue, overact, overdo, overlay, outdo.

Phr. To have a hand in; to thrust one's nose in; to put in one's oar; to put one's foot in it; to mix oneself up with.

Adj. Active, brisk, quick, prompt, alert, on the alert, stirring, spry, sharp, smart, quick, nimble, agile, light-footed, featly, tripping, ready, awake, broad awake, wide awake, alive, at call, lively, vivacious, frisky, forward, eager, strenuous, zealous, enterprising, spirited, in earnest, up in arms.

Working, on duty, at work, hard at work, intent, industrious, assiduous, diligent, sedulous, notable, pains-taking, business-like, in harness, operose, plodding, toiling, hardworking, fagging, busy, bustling, restless, fussy, fidgetty, pottering, dabbling.

Persevering, indefatigable, untiring, unflagging, unremitting, unwearied, never-tiring, undrooping, unintermitting, unflinching.

Meddling, meddlesome, peddling, pushing, intermeddling, tampering, &c., officious, overofficious, intriguing, *intrigant.*

Phr. Up and stirring; busy as a bee; brisk as a bee; nimble as a squirrel; the fingers itching; *Nulla dies sine linea;* a rolling stone gathers no moss; the used key is always bright.

Adv. Actively, &c., *see* (684).

Int. Be alive!

(684) HASTE, dispatch, precipitancy, precipitation, precipitousness, impetuosity, post-haste, acceleration.

Hurry, flurry, bustle, fuss, splutter, scramble, *brusquerie,* fidget, fidgettiness (682).

V. To haste, hasten, urge, press on, push on, bustle, hurry, precipitate, accelerate, bustle, scramble, plunge, dash on, press on.

Phr. To make the most of one's time; to lose not a moment; *Festina lente; nec mora nec requies; Veni, vidi, vici.*

Adj. Hasty, hurried, precipitate, scrambling, &c., headlong, boisterous, impetuous, *brusque,* slapdash, cursory.

Adv. Hastily, &c., headlong, in haste, slapdash, amain, hurry-skurry, helter-skelter, head and shoulders, head over heels, by fits and starts, by spurts.

(686) EXERTION, labour, work, toil, heft, exercise, travail, exercitation, duty, trouble, pains, ado,

slack, inert, torpid, sluggish, languid, supine, heavy, dull, lumpish, exanimate, soulless, listless.

Dilatory, laggard, lagging, drawling, creeping, dawdling, faddling, rusty, lackadaisical, fiddle-faddle, shilly-shally.

Phr. With folded arms; *les bras croisés;* with the hands in the pockets.

Sleepy, dosy, drowsy, somnolent, dormant, asleep, lethargic, napping, sleepful, stubbering, somniferous, soporific, soporous, somnific, hypnotic, unawakened, unwakened.

Phr. The eyes beginning to draw straws.

———

(685) LEISURE, spare time, spare hours, breathing time, holiday, vacation, recess, red-letter day, repose.

Phr. Otium cum dignitate.

V. To have leisure, take one's leisure, repose (687), pause.

Adj. Leisurely, undisturbed, quiet, deliberate, calm, reposing, &c.

Adv. Leisurely, &c., at leisure.

———

(687) REPOSE, rest, halt, pause, relaxation, breathing time, respite, *see* Leisure (685).

drudgery, fagging, slavery, operoseness.

Effort, strain, tug, stress, throw, stretch, struggle, spell, &c., a stitch of work.

V. To labour, work, exert oneself, toil, strive, use exertion, fag, strain, drudge, take pains, take trouble, trouble oneself, slave, pull, tug, ply the oar, rough it, sweat, bestir oneself, fall to work, buckle to, stick to.

Phr. To set one's shoulder to the wheel; to strain every nerve; to do as much as in one lies; to work day and night; to do double duty; to work double tides; to put forth one's strength, &c.; to work like a galley slave, *see* (682).

Adj. Labouring, &c., laborious, toilsome, troublesome, operose, herculean, gymnastic, palestric.

Hardworking, pains-taking, strenuous (682).

Adv. Laboriously, &c.

Phr. By the sweat of the brow; with all one's might; *totis viribus;* with might and main; *vi et armis;* with tooth and nail; *unguibus et rostro;* hammer and tongs; through thick and thin.

V. To repose, rest, relax, take rest, breathe, take breath, take one's ease, gather breath, recover one's breath, respire, pause, halt, stay one's hand, lay to, lie by, lie fallow, recline, lie down, go to rest, go to bed, go to sleep, &c., unbend.

Phr. To rest upon one's oars; to take a holiday.

Adj. Reposing, resting, &c., unstrained.

----

(688) FATIGUE, lassitude, weariness, tiredness, fatigation, exhaustion, sweat, collapse, prostration, swoon, faintness, fainting, *deliquium, syncope,* yawning, pandiculation, oscitation, anhelation.

V. To be fatigued, &c., to droop, sink, flag, lose breath, lose wind, gasp, pant, puff, blow, yawn, drop, swoon, faint, succumb.

To fatigue, tire, weary, fag, jade, harass, exhaust, knock up, wear out, strain, overtask, overwork, overburden, overtax, overstrain.

Adj. Fatigued, tired, unrefreshed, weary, wearied, jaded, wayworn.

Breathless, out of breath, windless, out of wind, blown, anhelose, brokenwinded.

Drooping, flagging, faint, fainting, done up, knocked up, exhausted, sinking, prostrate, spent, overspent.

Worn out, battered, shattered, seedy, weatherbeaten, *hors de combat.*

Phr. Ready to drop; dog-weary; on one's last legs; off one's legs.

Fatiguing, &c., tiresome, irksome, wearisome.

(689) REFRESHMENT, recovery of strength, recruiting, repair, refection, refocillation, relief, bracing, regalement, restoration, revival.

Phr. A giant refreshed.

V. To refresh, recruit, repair, refocillate, give tone, restore, recover.

To recover, regain, renew, &c. one's strength.

Adj. Refreshing, &c., refreshed, &c., untired, unwearied, &c.

----

(690) AGENT, doer, performer, operator, hand, executor, maker, effector, stager.

Artist, workman, worker, artisan, artificer, architect, handicraftsman, mechanic, machinist, manufacturer, practitioner, operative, journeyman, labourer, smith, wright, day labourer, co-worker.

Bee, ant, working bee, drudge, fag, servant of all work.

(691) WORKSHOP, laboratory, manufactory, mill, factory, mint, forge, loom, cabinet, *studio, bureau, atelier*, hive, hive of industry, workhouse, nursery, hot-house, hot-bed, kitchen, dock, slip, yard.

Crucible, alembic, caldron, matrix.

2°. *Complex Voluntary Action.*

(692) CONDUCT, course of action, practice, procedure, transaction, dealing, ways, tactics, policy, polity, generalship, statesmanship, economy, strategy, husbandry, seamanship, housekeeping, housewifery (or huswifery).

Execution, manipulation, treatment, process, course, campaign, career.

Behaviour, deportment, comportment, carriage, *maintien*, demeanour, bearing, manner, observance.

V. To conduct, carry on, transact, execute, carry out, work out, get through, carry through, go through, dispatch, treat, deal with, proceed with, officiate, discharge, do duty, play a part or game, run a race.

To behave, comport, acquit onself, demean oneself.

Phr. To turn over a new leaf; to lead the way.

Adj. Conducting, &c.

(693) DIRECTION, management, government, bureaucracy, statesmanship, conduct (692), regulation, charge, agency, senatorship, ministry, ministration, managery, guidance, steerage, pilotage, superintendence, stewardship, supervision, *surveillance*, proctorship.

Committee, subcommittee.

V. To direct, manage, govern, guide, conduct, regulate, steer, pilot, have or take the direction, take the helm, have the charge of, superintend, overlook, supervise, control.

To head, lead, show the way, &c.

Adj. Directing, &c.

(694) DIRECTOR, manager, master (745), head minister, premier, governor, comptroller, superintendant, supervisor, supercargo, inspector, visitor, monitor, overseer, overlooker, taskmaster, Reis Effendi, official, red-tapist, officer (726).

Conductor, steersman, pilot, steersmate, guide, *cicerone*, guard, driver, charioteer, coachman, postilion, *vetturino*.

Steward, factor, factotum, bailiff, middleman, foreman, whipper-in, proctor, procurator, housekeeper, major domo.

(695) ADVICE, counsel, suggestion, recommendation, hortation, dehortation, instruction, charge, monition, admonition, submonition, caution, warning, expostulation, obtestation, injunction, persuasion.

Guidance, helm, cynosure, rudder, lode-star, guide, hand-book, manual, itinerary, reference, referment.

An adviser, senator, counsellor, counsel, monitor, mentor, guide, teacher (540), physician, leech.

Referee, arbiter, arbitrator, referendary.

V. To advise, counsel, give advice, admonish, submonish, caution, warn, forewarn.

To persuade, dehort, exhort, enjoin, expostulate, charge, instruct.

To deliberate, consult together, hold a council, &c., confer, call in, refer to, take advice, be closeted with.

Phr. To lay one's heads together.

Adj. Monitory, monitive, admonitory, recommendatory, dehortatory, warning, &c.

Int. Go to!

(696) COUNCIL, conclave, court, chamber, cockpit, house, committee, sub-committee, board, meeting, sitting.

Senate, *senatus*, parliament, synod, convocation, congress, consistory, diet, cortes, divan, Areopagus, sanhedrim, directory, &c.

A meeting, assembly, sitting, session.

(697) PRECEPT, direction, instruction, prescript, prescription.

Rule, canon, code, formula, formulary, maxim, apothegm, &c. (496).

(698) SKILL, skilfulness, clever-ness, ability, talent, ingenuity, capacity, calibre, shrewdness, sagacity, parts, genius, faculty, gift, forte, turn, invention, headpiece.

Address, dexterity, adroitness, felicity, knack, expertness, quickness, sharpness, readiness, excellence, habilitation, ambidexterity, ambidextrousness.

Qualification, proficiency, panurgy, accomplishment, acquirement, craft, mastership, seamanship, rope-dancing.

Tact, knowledge of the world, *savoir faire*, discretion, *finesse, usage du monde.*

Phr. A jack of all trades; a tactitian, a master-hand.

Prudence, discretion, *see* Caution (864).

Art, management, tactics, manœuvering, sleight, policy, strategy, jobbery, temporization, technology.

A master-stroke, *chef d'œuvre,* a master-piece, *tour de force,* a bold stroke.

V. To be skilful, skilled, &c., to excel in, be master of, to temporize.

Phr. To play one's cards well; to stoop to conquer; *reculer pour mieux sauter;* to cut one's coat according to one's cloth; *scire quid valeant humeri, quid ferre recusant.*

Adj. Skilled, skilful, &c., clever, able, accomplished, talented, ingeni-

(699) UNSKILFULNESS, inability, incompetence, incompetency, infelicity, inexpertness, indexterity, unaptness, lefthandedness, awkwardness, maladroitness, clumsiness, rawness, slovenliness, greenness, inexperience, disqualification, unproficiency.

Bungling, blundering, fumbling, floundering, stumbling, unteachableness, dulness.

Indiscretion, imprudence (863), thoughtlessness, giddiness, wildness, mismanagement, misconduct, maladministration, misrule, misgovernment, misapplication.

Absence of rule; the rule of thumb.

V. To be unskilled, unskilful, &c.

To mismanage, bungle, blunder, botch, bitch, boggle, fumble, mistake, misapply, missend.

Phr. To make a mess or hash of; to make sad work of; to put one's foot in it; to lose or miss one's way; to stand in one's own light; to quarrel with one's bread and butter; to have too many irons in the fire; to have too many eggs in one basket; to kill the goose which lays golden eggs.

Adj. Unskilled, &c., unskilful, bungling, &c., awkward, clumsy, unhandy, lubberly, *gauche, maladroit,* lefthanded, hobbling, slovenly, slatternly, giddy, gawky, dull.

Unapt, unqualified, inhabile, in-

ous, inventive, gifted, hard-headed, sagacious.

Expert, dextrous, adroit, apt, sharp, handy, deft, ready, quick, smart, spry, yare, nimble, ambidextrous, fine-fingered.

Conversant, versed, proficient, competent, qualified, good at, up to, master of, cut out for, at home in, knowing.

Experienced, practised, hackneyed, trained, initiated, prepared, primed, finished, thoroughbred.

Technical, artistic, workmanlike, dædalian, masterly, statesmanlike.

Discreet, politic, sure-footed, felicitous.

competent, disqualified, untalented, ill-qualified.

Unaccustomed, unused, unhackneyed, unexercised, untrained, unpractised, undisciplined, uneducated, undrilled, uninitiated, unschooled, unconversant, unversed, inexperienced, unstatesmanlike.

Unadvised, misadvised, ill-judged, ill-advised, unguided, misguided, foolish, wild.

Phr. Ne sutor ultra crepidam; Il se noyerait dans une goutte d'eau.

Phr. A nice hand; a clean hand; a dead shot; sharp as a needle; a jack of all trades.

Adv. Skilfully, &c., aright.

Phr. Suo marte; to the best of one's abilities.

(700) PROFICIENT, adept, genius, dab, master, masterhead, tactitian, politician, marksman, jobber, sharp blade, rope-dancer, funambulist, old stager, veteran, top-sawyer, picked man, cunning man, conjuror, wizard, &c. (994).

(701) BUNGLER, marplot, greenhorn, lubber, fumbler, novice, sloven, slattern, no conjuror, flat, the awkward squad.

(702) CUNNING, cunningness, craft, artfulness, subtlety, shrewdness, archness, insidiousness, shyness, artificialness, artificiality.

Artifice, strategem, wile, *finesse, ruse,* diplomacy, politics, *ruse de guerre.*

Duplicity, guile, circumvention, chicane, chicanery, sharp practice, Machiavelism, legerdemain, trickery, &c. (545).

Net, toils, trap, &c. (667).

A slyboots, Ulysses.

V. To be cunning, &c., to contrive, design, manœuvre, intrigue, temporize, circumvent.

(703) ARTLESSNESS, nature, naturalness, simplicity, ingenuousness, *bonhomie,* frankness, *naïveté,* openness, *abandon,* candour, sincerity, straightforwardness.

V. To be artless, &c.

Adj. Artless, natural, native, plain, simple-minded, ingenuous, candid, naive, sincere, frank, open, frankhearted, open-hearted, above-board, downright, guileless, inartificial, undesigning.

Phr. To stoop to conquer; *reculer pour mieux sauter;* to know on which side one's bread is buttered.

Adj. Cunning, crafty, artful, wily, sly, subtle, arch, designing, intriguing, contriving, insidious, canny, subdolous, deceitful (545), artificial, deep, profound, diplomatic, vulpine, Machiavelian, timeserving.

Phr. Cunning as a fox.

Section IV. ANTAGONISM.

1°. *Conditional Antagonism.*

(704) DIFFICULTY, delicacy, hardness, troublesomeness, laboriousness.

Impracticability, infeasableness, intractability, toughness, perverseness, *see* Impossibility (471).

Embarrassment, awkwardness, perplexity, intricacy, intrication, intricatenesss, inextricableness, entanglement, knot, Gordian knot, labyrinth, net, meshes, maze, &c. (248).

Dilemma, nice point, delicate point, knotty point, poser, puzzle, nonplus, quandary, strait, pass, critical situation, crisis, trial, emergency, exigency.

Scrape, hobble, lurch, *contretems*, slough, quagmire, hot water, stew, mess, ado, false position, set fast, stand, dead lock, encumbrance.

Phr. A ticklish card to play; a sea of troubles; a peck of troubles; a kettle of fish; "Ay, there's the rub."

V. To be difficult, &c.

To meet with, experience, labour under, get into, plunge into, be surrounded by, be encompassed with, be entangled by, to struggle, contend against or grapple with difficulties.

To come to a stand, to stick fast, to be set fast, to boggle, flounder.

Phr. To get into hot water, to get into a mess; to fish in troubled waters; to buffet the waves; to be put to one's shifts; not to know whether one stands on one's head or one's heels; *perdre son Latin.*

To render difficult, &c., to embarrass, perplex, put one out, bother, pose, puzzle, nonplus, ravel, entangle, gravel, run hard.

Phr. To lead a pretty dance; to put to one's shifts; to put a spoke in one's wheel.

Adj. Difficult, not easy, hard, troublesome, laborious, onerous, operose, awkward, unwieldy, beset with or full of difficulties.

Unmanageable, tough, stubborn, hard to deal with, ill conditioned, refractory, perverse, crabbed, intractable.

169

(705) FACILITY, practicability, feasibility, practicableness, *see* Possibility (470).

Ease, easiness, child's play, smoothness, tractableness, ductility, flexibility, malleability, tractility, capability, disencumbrance, disentanglement.

Plain sailing, smooth water, smooth sailing, fair wind, freedom, full play or swing, a clear coast, advantage, vantage-ground.

V. To be easy, &c., to flow, swim, or drift with the tide or stream.

To render easy, &c., to facilitate, smooth, ease, lighten, free, clear, disencumber, deobstruct, disembarrass, clear the way, smooth the way, disentangle, unclog, disengage, extricate, unravel, disburden, exonerate, emancipate, free from, deoppilate.

Phr. To leave a hole to creep out of.

Adj. Easy, facile, attainable, practicable, feasible, achievable, performable, possible (470), superable, surmountable, accessible.

Phr. The coast being clear; as easy as lying.

Easily managed or accomplished, &c., tractable, manageable, smooth, glib, pliant, yielding, malleable, ductile, tractible, flexible, submissive.

At ease, free, light, easy, unburdened, unencumbered, unloaded, disburdened, disencumbered, disembarrassed, exonerated, unrestrained, unobstructed, at home.

Phr. Being quite at home; being in one's element.

Adv. Easily, &c.

Embarrassing, perplexing, delicate, ticklish, intricate, thorny, knotty, invious, pathless, trackless, labyrinthic, labyrinthine.

Impracticable, not possible, impossible (471), not practicable, not feasible, infeasible, unachievable, uncomeatible, inextricable, impassable, innavigable, desperate, insuperable, insurmountable.

In difficulty, perplexed, &c., beset, waterlogged, put to it, hard put to it, run hard, hard pressed, thrown out, adrift, at fault, abroad.

Stranded, aground, stuck fast, at bay.

Phr. At a stand still; surrounded with shoals and breakers; thrown on one's beam ends; in the suds; out of one's depth; *au bout de son Latin;* put to one's shifts; in a cleft stick; on a wrong scent; driven from post to pillar; things being come to a pretty pass.

Adv. With difficulty, hardly, &c., against the stream, against the grain, uphill.

2°. *Active Antagonism.*

(706) HINDRANCE, prevention, preclusion, impedition, retardment, retardation.

Obstruction, stoppage, interruption, interclusion, oppilation, coarctation, restraint, inhibition, embargo, embarrassment.

Interference, interposition, obtrusion, discouragement, discountenance.

An impediment, hindrance, obstacle, obstruction, let, stumbling block, check, hitch, bar, barrier, barricade, turnpike, wall, dead wall, bulkhead, portcullis, &c. (717), dam, wier, boom.

Drawback, objection.

An encumbrance, clog, drag, weight, dead weight, lumber, pack, millstone, incubus, nightmare, Ephialtes; trammel, &c. (752).

Phr. A spoke in the wheel; a wet blanket; the old man of the sea.

A hinderer, a marplot; a killjoy, an interloper; an opponent (710).

V. To hinder, impede, impedite, prevent, preclude, retard, slacken, obviate, forefend, avert, turn aside, ward off, draw off, cut off, counteract, countercheck, antevert, undermine.

To obstruct, stop, stay, let, bar, debar, inhibit, cramp, restrain, check, discourage, discountenance, foreclose; to lay under restraint.

(707) AID, assistance, help, succour, support, relief, advance, furtherance, promotion.

Coadjuvancy, patronage, championship, countenance, favour.

Sustentation, alimentation, nutrition, nourishment; ministration, ministry, subministration, accommodation.

Supplies, reinforcements, succours, recruits; physical support, *see* (215).

V. To aid, assist, help, succour, support, promote, further, abet, advance, foster; to give, bring, furnish, afford or supply support, &c., to reinforce, nourish, nurture, suckle.

To favour, countenance, befriend, smile upon, encourage, patronize, make interest for.

To second, stand by, back, take part with, side with, to come or pass over to; to join, to rally round.

Phr. To take the part of; to take up the cause of; to espouse the cause of; to enlist under the banners of; to join hand in hand; to lend or bear a hand; to hold out a helping hand; to give one a lift; to give one a turn; to take in tow; to beat up for recruits.

To serve, do service, minister to, oblige, accommodate, work for, administer to, pander to; to tend, attend, take care of, wait on, nurse, dry nurse, entertain.

To thwart, traverse, contravene, interrupt, intercept, interclude, frustrate, defeat, disconcert, undo, intercept; to balk, cushion, spoil, mar.

To interpose, interfere, intermeddle, obtrude (682).

Phr. To stand in the way of; to break in upon; to run or fall foul of.

To hamper, clog, cumber, encumber, saddle with, load with, overload, overlay, lumber, block up, incommode, hustle; to curb, shackle, fetter.

To speed, expedite, forward, quicken, hasten, set forward.

Adj. Aiding, helping, assisting, &c., auxiliary, adjuvant, coadjuvant, coadjutant, ancillary, accessory, subsidiary.

Friendly, amicable, favourable, propitious.

Adv. On or in behalf of; in the service of; hand in hand.

Int. Help! save us!

Phr. To put a spoke in the wheel, to throw cold water on.

Adj. Hindering, &c., in the way of, impedient, inimical, unfavourable, onerous, burdensome.

Hindered, &c., wind-bound, water-logged.

Phr. Prevention being better than cure.

(708) OPPOSITION, antagonism, counteraction (179), contravention, control, clashing, collision, competition, rivalry, emulation.

Absence of aid, &c., counterplot (719).

V. To oppose, antagonize, cross, counteract, control, contravene, countervail, counterwork, stultify, thwart, overthwart, countermine, run counter, go against, clash, rival, emulate, pit against, militate against, beat against, stem, breast, encounter, compete with, withstand.

Phr. To set one's face against; to make a stand against; to fly in the face of; to fall foul of; to be or to play at cross purposes; to kick against the pricks; to buffet the waves.

Adj. Opposing, &c., adverse, antagonistic, opposed, contrary, unfavourable, cross; up in arms.

Unaided, unassisted, unhelped, unsustained, unseconded, &c., unsupported, unbefriended.

(709) CO-OPERATION, coadjuvancy, concert, collusion, co-efficiency, *see* Concurrence (178).

Alliance, colleagueship, joint-stock, co-partnership, coalition, federation, confederation (712).

V. To co-operate, concur, conspire, concert; draw or pull together, to join with, collude, unite one's efforts, club together, fraternize, be in league, &c. with, be a party to.

Phr. To understand one another; to be in the same boat; to play into the hands of.

Adj. Co-operating, &c., in co-operation, &c., in concert, allied, &c.

Phr. Wind and weather permitting.

Unopposed, unobstructed.

Adv. Against, counter to, against the stream, tide, wind, &c., in the way of, in spite of, in despite of, in the teeth of, in the face of, *per contra.*

Across, athwart, overthwart.

Though, although (179), even, *quand même.*

Phr. In spite of one's teeth.

(710) OPPONENT, antagonist, adversary, adverse party, rival, com-

(711) AUXILIARY, assistant, adjuvant, adjunct, adjutant, help, helper,

171

petitor, backfriend, enemy, foe, assailant.

_____

helpmate, colleague, partner, coadjutor, co-operator, ally, aide-de-camp, accomplice, complice, accessory.

Friend, confidant, champion, partisan, right-hand, sectarian, sectary; adherent, confederate, bottle-holder, candle-holder, servant, *see* (746).

(712) PARTY, partnership, fraternity, sodality, company, society, firm, house, body, corporation, corporate body, guild.

Fellowship, brotherhood, sisterhood, communion, clan, clanship, club, *clique*, junto, *coterie*, faction, *camarilla*, cabal, league, confederacy, confederation, federation : side, *esprit de corps ;* alliance.

Band, staff, crew, set, posse, phalanx.

V. To unite, join, club together, join forces, co-operate, befriend, aid, &c. (707), cement, form a party, league, &c.

Adj. In partnership, alliance, &c., bonded, bandied, linked, cemented, &c. together.

(713) DISCORD, variance, difference, dissent, misunderstanding, dissention, jar, jarring, clashing, odds.

Disunion, schism, breach, falling out, rupture, disruption, open rupture, *brouillerie*, feud, contentiousness.

Dispute, controversy, polemics, quarrel, tiff, *tracasserie*, altercation, bickering, snip-snap, chicanery, squabble, row, brawl.

Litigation, words, war of words, logomachy, wrangling, jangle, brabble, rixation, declaration of war, *see* Warfare (722).

Subject of dispute; ground of quarrel, disputed point, a bone to pick ; the bone of contention ; the apple of discord ; *casus belli.*

(714) CONCORD, accord, agreement (23), unison, unity, union, good understanding, quiet, peace, unanimity (488), harmony, amity, *entente cordiale*, alliance.

Phr. The bonds of harmony ; the happy family.

V. To agree, accord, be in unison, &c., to harmonize with.

Phr. To understand one another ; to remain at peace ; to keep the peace.

Adj. Concordant, agreeing, &c., united, in unison, &c., harmonious, allied, cemented, friendly, amicable, at peace, peaceful, pacific, tranquil.

Phr. In still water.

_____

V. To be discordant, &c., to differ, dissent, disagree, clash, jar, to misunderstand one another.

To fall out, dispute, controvert, litigate ; to quarrel, wrangle, squabble, bicker, spar, jangle, brangle, brawl ; to break with ; to declare war.

Phr. To be at odds with ; to have words with ; to have a bone to pick with ; to be at variance with ; to join issue ; to pick a quarrel with ; to break squares with ; to live like cat and dog.

To embroil, entangle, disunite, set against, pit against ; to sow dissention, disunion, discord, &c. among.

Phr. To set together by the ears.

Adj. Discordant, disagreeing, differing, disunited, clashing, jarring, dissentient, sectarian, at variance.

Quarrelsome, disputatious, litigious, litigant, factious, petty-fogging, polemic, schismatic ; unpacified, unreconciled.

Phr. At odds ; in hot water ; at daggers drawn ; up in arms ; at sixes and sevens ; at loggerheads.

(715) DEFIANCE, challenge, cartel, daring, war-whoop.

V. To defy, challenge, dare, beard, bluster, look big.

Phr. To set at naught ; snap the fingers at ; to bid defiance to ; to set at defiance ; to hurl defiance at ; to double the fist ; to stand akimbo ; to show a bold front ; to show fight ; to throw down the gauntlet (or gantlet) or glove.

Adj. Defying, &c.

Adv. In defiance of ; with arms akimbo.

Int. Come on !

(716) ATTACK, aggression, offence, assault, charge, onset, onslaught, brunt, thrust, pass, passado, cut, *estrapade*, impugnation, sally, inroad, invasion, irruption, *sortie, camisade*, storm, storming, boarding, *escalade*, foray, raid, *Jacquerie, razzia*, dragonade, *see* (619), siege, investment.

Fire, volley, cannonade, broadside, bombardment, raking fire, platoon-fire.

Kick, yerk, *ruade, coup de bec*, a run at, a dead set at.

An assailant, aggressor.

V. To attack, assault, assail, impugn, fall upon, close with, charge, bear down upon, set on, have at, strike at, run at, make a run at, butt, tilt at, poke at, make a pass at, thrust at, cut and thrust, pitch into, kick, yerk, buffet, beat, *see* (972), lay about one, lift a hand against, come on, have a fling at, slap on the face, pelt, throw stones, &c.

To shoot at, fire at, fire upon, pop at, let off a gun, shoot, let fly at, open fire, pepper, bombard, pour a broadside into, fire a volley.

To beset, besiege, lay siege to, invest, beleaguer, open the trenches, invade, storm, board, scale the walls.

To press one hard, be hard upon, drive one hard.

Phr. To take the bull by the horns ; to run a muck.

Adj. Attacking, &c., aggressive, offensive.

(717) DEFENCE, self-defence, self-preservation, protection, propugnation, ward, guard, guardianship, shielding, &c., *see* Resistance (718), and Safety (664).

Fence, wall, parapet, dyke, &c. (232), boom, picket, mound, mole, outwork, intrenchment, fortification, embankment, bulwark, barbacan, battlement, stockade, abattis, muniment, vallum, circumvallation, contravallation, sunk fence, haha, buttress, abutment, breastwork, hornwork, portcullis, glacis, bastion, redoubt, rampart.

Hold, stronghold, keep, donjon, palladium, fort, fortress, sconce, citadel, tower, castle, capitol, fastness, barracoon, asylum (666).

Shield, buckler, ægis, breastplate, coat of mail, cuirass, hawberk, habergeon, *chevaux de frise*, screen, &c. (666).

Defender, protector, guardian, *see* (664), champion, propugner, knight-errant.

V. To defend, shield, fend, fence, guard (644), keep off, keep at bay, ward off, beat off, parry, repel, propugn, bear the brunt of, put to flight.

To fall back upon, to act on the defensive, to maintain one's ground, to stand in the gap.

Adj. Defending, &c., defensive, defended, &c., armed, armed cap-à-pie, armed to the teeth.

Adv. Defensively, on the defence, on the defensive, at bay.

Phr. Pro aris et focis.

(718) RETALIATION, reprisal, retort, counter-stroke, reciprocation, *tu quoque*, retribution, counterplot, counter-project, *lex talionis, see* Revenge (919) and Compensation (30).

Phr. Tit for tat; a Roland for an Oliver; diamond cut diamond; the biter bit; catching a Tartar; *suo sibi gladio jugulo.*

V. To retaliate, retort, be even with one, pay off.

Phr. To turn the tables; return the compliment; to throw a stone in one's garden; to pay in one's own coin; to give a *quid pro quo;* to give a Roland for an Oliver.

Adj. Retaliating, retaliatory, retaliative.

Adv. In retaliation, *en revanche, tu quoque.*

---

(719) RESISTANCE, stand, oppugnation, reluctation, front, repulse, rebuff, kicking, &c., *see* Disobedience (742), recalcitration.

Strike, meeting, tumult, riot, *pronunciamento.*

Revolt, rising, insurrection, rebellion, *levée en masse, Jacquerie.*

V. To resist, not to submit, &c., to withstand, stand against, stand firm, make a stand, repugn, confront.

Phr. To present a front; to show a bold front; to make head against; to stand one's ground; to stand the brunt of; to keep at bay; to stem the torrent; to champ the bit; to sell one's life dearly.

To kick, kick against, recalcitrate, lift the hand against, *see* Attack (716), repel, repulse, to rise, revolt, mutiny.

Phr. To fly in the face of; to kick against the pricks; *Prendre le mors aux dents.*

Adj. Resisting, &c., resistive, refractory, mutinous, repulsive, recalcitrant, up in arms, *see* Disobedient (742).

Unyielding, unconquered, indomitable.

Int. Hands off! keep off.

---

(720) CONTENTION, contest, struggle, contestation, debate, logomachy, high words, rivalry, corrivalry, corrivalship, agonism, competition, *concours*, race, heat, steeplechase, bickering, bickerment.

Wrestling, pugilism, boxing, fisticuffs, spar, prize-fighting, set to, round, spree, *fracas*, row, rumpus, outbreak, clash, collision, shock, breach of the peace, brabble, brigue.

(721) PEACE, amity, truce, harmony, *see* Concord (714), tranquillity.

Phr. Piping time of peace.

V. To be at peace, &c., to keep, the peace, &c. (714).

Adj. Pacific, peaceable, peaceful, tranquil, untroubled.

Conflict, skirmish, rencounter, scuffle, encounter, *rencontre*, velitation, luctation, digladiation, colluctation, tussle, broil, fray, affray, *mêlée*, affair, brush, bout, fight, battle, combat, action, engagement, battle-royal, running fight, joust, tournament, tournay, pitched battle, death-struggle.

Naval engagement, *naumachia.*

Duel, satisfaction, monomachy, *passage d'armes.*

V. To contend, contest, struggle, vie with, outvie, battle with, cope with, compete, join issue, bandy, try conclusions with, close with, square, buckle with, wrestle, enter the lists, take up arms, take the field, encounter, struggle with, grapple with, reluct, engage with, fall to, encounter, join battle, fall foul of, have a brush with, break the peace, take up the cudgels, unsheath the sword, couch one's lance.

(722) WARFARE, war, hostilities, fighting, &c., open war, *ultima ratio*, war to the knife, internecine war, *guerre à mort, guerre à outrance.*

Battle array, campaign, crusade.

The art of war, tactics, strategy, military evolutions, arms, service, &c.

War-cry, fire-cross, trumpet, clarion, bugle, pibroch, war-whoop, beat of drum, *rappel,* to arms.

Phr. To your tents, O Israel!

V. To fight, set to, spar, justle, tussle, tilt, box, stickle, skirmish, fight hand to hand, stave, fence, measure swords, engage, combat, give battle, go to battle, join battle, engage in battle, wage war, go to war, come to blows, break a lance with, couch the lance, appeal to arms, appeal to the sword, give satisfaction, take the field, keep the field, fight it out, spill blood, carry on war, carry on hostilities, to fight one's way, to serve, to see service.

Adj. Contending, &c., unpeaceful, contentious, belligerent, bellicose, martial, warlike, military, militant, gladiatorial, chivalrous, in arms, armigerous.

Phr. Together by the ears.

Adv. Pendente lite, the battle raging, *flagrante bello.*

Int. Væ victis!

(723) PACIFICATION, reconciliation, accommodation, arrangement, adjustment.

Peace-offering, olive-branch, calumet of peace, preliminaries of peace.

Truce, armistice, suspension of arms, of hostilities, &c., convention.

Phr. Hollow truce, *pax in bello.*

Flag of truce, cartel.

V. To make peace, pacify, make it up, settle, arrange, accommodate matters, tranquillize, compose, hush up, settle differences, restore harmony, heal the breach.

Phr. To put up the sword; to sheath the sword; *tantas componere lites;* to bury the hatchet.

Adj. Pacified, &c.

---

(724) MEDIATION, intervention, interposition, interference, intermeddling, intercession, parley, negotiation, arbitration, mediatorship, good offices, diplomacy, peace offering.

A mediator, intercessor, peacemaker, make-peace, negotiator.

V. To mediate, intercede, interpose, interfere, negotiate, arbitrate.

Phr. Magnas componere lites.

(725) SUBMISSION, surrender, non-resistance, yielding, capitulation, cession.

V. To surrender, succumb, submit, yield, give in, bend, truckle to, knuckle to, knock under, capitulate, lay down or deliver up one's arms, retreat, give way, beat a retreat, strike one's flag or colours, surrender at discretion.

Adj. Surrendering, &c., non-resisting, submissive.

Undefended, untenable, indefensible.

(726) COMBATANT, armigerent, champion, disputant, litigant, competitor, rival, corrival, assailant, bully, fighter, duellist, fighting-man, pugilist, boxer, the fancy, prizefighter, fighting-cock, gladiator, fire-eater; swordsman, wrestler, Amazon.

Warrior, soldier, man-at-arms, red-coat, trooper, dragoon, huzzar, *voltigeur,* light horseman (or hussar), grenadier, fusileer, guardsman, life-guard, lancer, cuirassier, spearman, musketeer, carabineer, rifleman, sharpshooter; ensign, standard-bearer, halbardier; private, subaltern.

Artilleryman, gunner, cannonier, bombardier.

Marine, jolly.

Guerilla, Cossack, sepoy, spahee (or spahi), janissary.

Armed force, the army, the military, soldiery, infantry, fencibles, cavalry, horse artillery.

Militia, trainband, legion, phalanx, battalia, myrmidons, squadron, troop, cohort, regiment, corps, platoon, battalion, company (72), column, detachment, brigade, garrison, battle array.

Man-of-war, war-ship, privateer, &c. (273).

(727) ARMS, armament, armour, armoury, quiver, arsenal.

Mail, lorication; ammunition, powder, gunpowder, cartridge (635).

Artillery, park, ordnance-piece, gun, cannon, swivel, howitzer, carronade, culverin, field-piece, *bouche de feu,* basilisk, mortar, grenade, peterero (or pederera), petronel, petard.

Fire-arms, side-arms, stand of arms, musketry, musket, *fusil,* musketoon, caliver, firelock, matchlock, fowling-piece, rifle, revolver, carbine, blunderbuss, pistol.

Bow, harquebus, crossbow, balister, *arquebuse,* sling, catapult, catamaran.

Missile, projectile, shot, ball, grape, grape-shot, chain-shot, bullet, stone, shell, bomb, rocket, congreve, shrapnel.

Pike, lance, spear, spontoon, javelin, dart, arrow, reed, shaft, bolt, boomerang, harpoon.

Bayonet, sword, sabre, broadsword, cutlass, falchion, scimitar, rapier, skeen, toledo, tuck, claymore, cress, dagger, dirk, hanger, poniard, stiletto, stylet, dudgeon, axe, bill, poleaxe, battleaxe, halberd, tomahawk, bowie-knife, ataghah (or attaghan), assagais (or asseguay).

Club, mace, truncheon, staff, bludgeon, cudgel, life-preserver, shillelah, bat.

Catapult, battering-ram.

(728) ARENA, field, walk, battle-field, field of battle, lists, palæstra, course, stage, boards, race-course, *corso,* circus, cock-pit, bear-garden, scene of action, theatre of war, the enemy's camp, amphitheatre, hippodrome, coliseum.

Section V.   RESULTS OF VOLUNTARY ACTION.

(729) COMPLETION, accomplishment, performance, fulfilment, execution, achievement, dispatch, work done, superstructure, finish, termination, *dénouement,* consummation, *fait accompli,* winding up, the last stroke, finishing stroke, *coup de grâce,* last finish, final touch, crowning touch, *see* End (67), Arrival (293), and Completeness (52).

V. To complete, effect, perform, do, execute, go through, accomplish, fulfil, discharge, achieve, compass, dispatch, knock off, close, terminate, conclude, finish, end (67), consum-

(730) NON-COMPLETION, inexecution, short-coming (304), non-performance, neglect; incompleteness (53), a drawn battle, a drawn game.

V. Not to complete, perform, &c., to fall short of, leave unfinished, &c., neglect, leave undone, &c.

Adj. Not completed, &c., uncompleted, incomplete, unfinished, left undone (53), short, unaccomplished, unperformed, unexecuted.

Adv. Re infectâ.

mate, bring about, bring to bear, bring to pass, go through, carry through, bring through, work out, make good, carry out, wind up, bring to a close, termination, conclusion, &c.

To perfect, bring to perfection, stamp, give the last finish, put the seal to, crown.

To reach, arrive (293), touch, reach, attain the goal; to run one's race.

Phr. To give the last finish, or finishing touch; to put the last, or finishing hand to; to get in the harvest.

Adj. Completing, final, concluding, conclusive, crowning, &c., done, completed, wrought, highwrought, &c.

Phr. The race being run; *Finis coronat opus.*

(731) Success, successfulness, speed, thrift, advance, luck, good fortune (734), godsend, prize, trump card, hit, stroke; lucky or fortunate hit; bold stroke, master stroke, *coup de maitre*, check-mate, *see* Skill (698), time well spent.

Continued success, run of luck, tide, flood, high tide.

Advantage over, the upper hand, the whip-hand, ascendancy, mastery, conquest, subdual, victory, subjugation, triumph, exultation, &c. (884).

A conqueror, victor.

V. To succeed, to be successful, to come off successful, to be crowned with success, to come off well; to thrive, speed, prosper, bloom, blossom, flourish, go on well, be well off.

To gain, attain, carry, secure, or win a point or object; to triumph, be triumphant, &c.; to surmount, overcome, conquer, master, or get over a difficulty or obstacle.

To advance (282), get on, gain ground, make one's way, make progress, progress; to strive to some purpose; to gain an advantage.

To bring to bear, to bring about, to effect, accomplish, complete (729), make sure; to reap, gather, &c. the benefit of.

To master, get the better of, to get the upper hand, conquer, subdue, subjugate, reduce, overthrow, overpower, vanquish; get or gain the ascendancy, obtain a victory; to worst, beat, lick, floor, put down, trip up, beat hollow, check-mate, nonsuit, trip up the heels of,

(732) Failure, successlessness, non-success, disappointment, blow, frustration, abortion, miscarriage, lost trouble; vain, ineffectual, or abortive attempt or effort.

A mistake, error, fault, miss, oversight, blot, slip, trip, stumble, claudication, footfall, false step, wrong step, *faux pas*, titubation, scrape, *balourdise, bévue, faute*, botch, mess, lurch, stale-mate, botchery, sad work, bad job.

Mischance, mishap, misfortune, misadventure, disaster.

Repulse, rebuff, defeat, fall, downfall, rout, discomfiture, wreck, perdition, shipwreck, ruin, subjugation, overthrow, death-blow, destruction, &c.

A victim, bankrupt, insolvent (808).

Phr. A flash in the pan; *une affaire flambée;* a wild goose chase; a mare's nest; a sleeveless errand; the mountain bringing forth a mouse; *parturiunt montes.*

V. To fail, to be unsuccessful, &c., to come off ill, go on ill, go amiss, go wrong, go cross, turn out ill, work ill, lose ground, recede (283).

To miss, miss one's aim; to labour, toil, &c. in vain; to lose one's labour, flounder, limp, miss one's footing, miscarry, abort; to make vain, ineffectual, or abortive efforts; to make a slip; to make or commit a mistake, commit a fault, make a mess of; to botch, make a botch of, to bitch it.

To be defeated, overthrown, foiled,

capsize, shipwreck, victimize, put to flight, drown, &c.; to roll in the dust.

To baffle, disconcert, frustrate, foil, outgeneral, outmanœuvre, outwit, overreach, balk, outvote, circumvent.

To answer, succeed, work well, turn out well.

Phr. To sail before the wind; to swim with the tide; to stem the torrent; to turn a corner; to weather a point; to fall on one's legs or feet; *se tirer d'affaire;* to take a favourable turn; to turn up trumps; to have the ball at one's feet; to come off with flying colours; to win or gain the day; to win the palm; to get the upper hand; to get the whip hand of; to have on the hip; to get the start of; to have a run of luck; to make a hit; to reap or gather the harvest; to carry all before one.

Adj. Succeeding, &c., successful, prosperous, felicitous, blooming, &c., set up, triumphant.

Unfoiled, unbeaten, unsubdued, &c.

Phr. Flushed with success; the spoilt child of fortune.

Adv. Successfully, &c., triumphantly, with flying colours, in triumph, *à merveille,* to good purpose.

Phr. Veni, vidi, vici.

---

worsted, &c.; to break down, sink, drown, founder, go to ruin, &c., fall, slip, tumble, stumble, falter, be capsized, &c., run aground.

Phr. To come to nothing; to end in smoke; to slip through one's fingers; to take an ugly turn; to hang fire; to miss fire; to miss stays; to flash in the pan; to split upon a rock; to be thrown on one's back; to bite the dust; to be thrown on one's beam ends; to go to the wall; to go to the dogs; to go to pot; to break one's back; to be all up with; to be in the wrong box; to stand in one's own light; to catch a Tartar; to get hold of the wrong sow by the ear; to burn one's fingers; to shoot at a pigeon and kill a crow; to beat the air; *battre l'eau avec un bâton; donner un coup d'épée dans l'eau;* to skin a flint; to wash a blackamoor white; *se battre contre des moulins;* to roll the stone of Sisyphus; *vouloir rompre l'anguille au genou.*

Adj. Unsuccessful, failing, &c., unfortunate, in a bad way, unlucky, luckless, out of luck, ill-fated, illstarred, disastrous.

Unavailing, abortive, addle, stillborn, fruitless, bootless, ineffectual, unattained, lame, hobbling, *décousu.*

Aground, grounded, swamped, stranded, cast away, wrecked, foundered, capsized, shipwrecked, &c. (731).

Defeated, overcome, overthrown, overpowered, mastered, worsted, vanquished, conquered, &c., *see* (731), subjugated, routed, silenced, distanced, foiled, unhorsed, baffled, *flambé,* dished, tossed about, unhinged, stultified, undone, ruined, circumvented, planet-struck, being all up with.

Phr. Allant à tort et à travers; not having a leg to stand upon; ruined root and branch; the sport of fortune; the mountain bringing forth a mouse; hoisted by one's own petard.

Adv. Unsuccessfully, &c., in vain, to no purpose, all up with.

Phr. Out of the frying-pan into the fire; *tant va la cruche à l'eau qu'à la fin elle se casse.*

(733) TROPHY, laurel, palm, crown, bays, wreath, chaplet, civic crown, medal, prize, triumphal arch, ovation, triumph (883), flourish of trumpets, flying colours.

(734) PROSPERITY, *see* Success (731), thrift, good fortune, welfare, well-being, luck, good luck, a run of luck, fair weather, sunshine, fair wind, palmy days, the smiles of fortune, halcyon days, *Saturnia regna*, Saturnian age.

An upstart, *parvenu*, skipjack, mushroom, a made man.

V. To prosper, thrive, flourish, be well off; to flower, blow, blossom, bloom, fructify; to bask in the sunshine; to rise in the world; to make one's way; to have a run.

Phr. To feather one's nest.

Adj. Prosperous, fortunate, lucky, well off, well to do, thriving, set up, prospering, &c., blooming, palmy, halcyon.

Auspicious, propitious, in a fair way.

Phr. Born with a silver spoon in one's mouth.

(735) ADVERSITY, bad, ill, evil, adverse, &c. fortune, hap, or luck, reverse, broken fortunes, falling or going down in the world, hard times, the pressure of the times.

Fall, ruin, ruination, ruinousness, undoing, disaster, calamity, catastrophe, a hard life, evil star, evil genius.

Phr. The frowns of fortune; the ups and downs of life; the time being out of joint.

V. To be ill off; to decay, sink, fall, decline, go down in the world; to go hard with.

Adj. Unfortunate, unlucky, luckless, untoward, ill off, badly off, decayed, ill-fated, ill-starred, improsperous, unprosperous, adverse, untoward.

Disastrous, calamitous, ruinous, dire, deplorable, &c.

Phr. Behindhand in the world; having seen better days; born with a wooden ladle in one's mouth.

(736) MEDIOCRITY, the, golden mean, *aurea mediocritas*, moderate circumstances.

Division II.　INTERSOCIAL VOLITION.*

Section I.　General Intersocial Volition.

(737) AUTHORITY, influence, credit, power, prerogative, control, authoritativeness, absoluteness, despotism.

Command, empire, sway, rule, dominion, domination, supremacy, suzerainty, lordship, seigniory, mastery, mastership, government, gubernation, empire, body politic, accession.

Hold, grasp, gripe, grip, reach, fang, clutches, talons, helm, reins.

Reign, *régime*, directorship, proconsulship, prefecture, caliphate, senes-

(738) Absence of authority.

LAXITY, laxness, licence, licentiousness, relaxation, looseness, loosening, slackness, toleration, remission.

Misrule, anarchy, interregnum.

Deprivation of power, dethronement.

V. To be lax, &c., to hold a loose rein, tolerate, to relax, to misrule.

To dethrone.

Adj. Lax, loose, slack, remiss, relaxed, licensed, reinless, unbridled, anarchical.

* Implying the action of the will of one mind over the will of another.

chalship, magistrature, magistracy, presidency, presidentship.

Empire, monarchy, dynasty, kinghood, kingship, royalty, regality, kingcraft, aristocracy, oligarchy, democracy, demagogy, ochlocracy, mobocracy, military, stratocracy, *imperium in imperio*, dictatorship, protectorate, protectorship.

Vicarious authority, *see* (755) and (759).

V. To have, hold, possess, or exercise authority, &c.

To be master, &c.; to have the control, &c.; to over-rule, overawe.

To rule, govern, sway, command, control, direct, administer, lead, preside over; to dictate, reign, hold the reins; to possess or be seated on the throne; to ascend or mount the throne; to sway or wield the sceptre.

Phr. To have the upper hand; to have the whip hand; to have one's own way; to rule the roast; have under the thumb; to keep under; to lead by the nose; to wear the breeches; to have the ball at one's feet; to play first fiddle.

Adj. Ruling, &c., dominant, authoritative, executive, official, *ex officio*.

Imperial, regal, sovereign, royal, monarchical, imperatorial, princely, feudal.

Imperative, peremptory, overruling.

Adv. In the name of, by the authority of, in virtue of, *De par le Roi*.

Unauthorized (925).

Phr. An order being a dead letter.

---

(739) SEVERITY, strictness, rigour, rigidness, sternness, stringency, austerity, harshness, stiffness, rigorousness, inexorableness.

Arbitrary power, absolutism, despotism, dictatorship, autocracy, domineering, tyranny, iron rule.

Assumption, usurpation, arrogance, *see* (885).

A tyrant, disciplinarian, martinet, bashaw; a strong hand, a tight hand.

V. To be severe, &c.; to assume, usurp, arrogate, take liberties; to hold or keep a tight hand; to bear or lay a heavy hand on; to dictate; to domineer, tyrannize, inflict, wreak.

Phr. To lord it over; to carry matters with a high hand; to ride rough-shod over; to rule with a rod of iron.

Adj. Severe, strict, rigid, stern, stiff, strait-laced, rigorous, stringent, peremptory, absolute, positive, uncompromising, harsh, austere, haughty, arrogant, dictatorial, imperious, domineering, tyrannical, inflexible, inexorable, inclement.

Adv. Severely, &c.; with a high hand; with a strong, tight, or heavy hand.

(740) LENITY, mildness, lenience, gentleness, indulgence, clemency.

V. To be lenient, &c., to tolerate, indulge, to allow to have one's own way.

Adj. Lenient, mild, gentle, soft, indulgent, tolerant, clement.

---

(741) COMMAND, order, *fiat*, bidding, *dictum*, hest, behest, call, beck, nod, message, direction, injunction, charge, demand, exaction, imposition, requisition, requirement, claim.

Dictation, dictate, mandate, *caveat*, decree, enactment, precept, prescript, writ, rescript, law, ordinance, ordination, bull, regulation, prescription, brevet, *placit*, ukase, firman, warrant, passport, mittimus, mandamus, summons, subpœna, interpellation.

V. To command, to issue a command, order, give order, bid, require, enjoin, charge, claim, call for, demand, exact, insist on, make a point of, impose, set, tax, prescribe, direct, dictate, ordain, decree, enact; to issue a decree, &c.

To cite, summon, call for, send for, subpœna; to set or prescribe a task; to set to work; to give the word of command; to call to order.

Phr. The decree is gone forth.

Adj. Commanding, &c., authoritative, peremptory, &c., see (737).

(742) DISOBEDIENCE, non-compliance, insubordination, defection, infringement, infraction, violation.

See Defiance (715), Resistance (718), and Non-observance (773).

Rising, insurrection, revolt, rebellion, turn out, strike, riot, riotousness, mutinousness, mutiny, tumult, sedition, treason.

An insurgent, mutineer, rebel, rioter, traitor; *carbonaro*, radical, *frondeur*.

V. To disobey, resist (718), defy (715), turn restive, shirk, kick, strike, mutiny, rise, rebel, lift the hand against, turn out.

Phr. To champ the bit; to raise the fire-cross.

Adj. Disobedient, resisting, unruly, unsubmissive, uncomplying, uncompliant, restive, insubordinate, mutinous, riotous, seditious, refractory.

Unbidden, unobeyed, a dead letter.

Phr. The gray mare being the better horse.

(743) OBEDIENCE, submission, non-resistance, passiveness, resignation, cession, compliance, surrender (725), subordination, deference, allegiance, obeisance, homage, fealty, prostration, kneeling, genuflexion, curtsy, *kotou*, submissness, submissiveness, obsequiousness, see (886), servitorship, tendence, subjection (749).

V. To be obedient, &c.; to obey, submit, succumb, give in, knock under, cringe, yield (725), comply, surrender, follow, give up, give way, resign, bend to, bear obedience to.

To kneel, fall on one's knees, bend the knee, curtsy, *kotou*, bow, pay homage to.

Phr. To kiss the rod; to lick the dust; to eat humble pie; to play second fiddle.

To attend upon, tend; to be under the orders of, to serve.

Phr. To dance attendance on.

Adj. Obedient, submissive, resigned, passive, complying, compliant, yielding, unresisting, henpecked; restrainable, unresisted.

(744) COMPULSION, coercion, coaction, force, constraint, coarctation, enforcement, press, conscription.

V. To compel, force, coerce, constrain, enforce, put in force, oblige, force upon, press, extort, put down, bind, pin down, bind over.

Phr. To cram down the throat; to say it must be done.

Adj. Compelling, &c., compulsory, conpulsatory, forcible, coercive, coactive, peremptory, rigorous, stringent, inexorable, &c., see (739), being fain to do.

Adv. By force, perforce, by compulsion, &c., *vi et armis*, by main force, by brute force, in spite of one's teeth, *bon gré mal gré;* will he, nil he; *nolens volens.*

(745) MASTER, lord, chief, leader, captain, head, chieftain, com-

(746) SERVANT, servitor, *employé*, *attaché*, subaltern, retainer, vassal,

mander, commandant, director (694), ruler, potentate, dictator, liege, sovereign, monarch, autocrat, despot, tyrant, bashaw, demagogue, ringleader.

Emperor, king, majesty, tetrarch, *imperator*, protector, president, stadtholder, gubernator ; Empress, queen.

Cæsar, czar, sultan, soldan, caliph, Sophi, khan, cazique, shah, pascha, bashaw, dey, cham, judge, aga, vaivode (or waywode), hospodar, exarch.

Prince, seignior, highness, archduke, duke, margrave, landgrave, elector, doge, satrap, rajah, emir, bey, effendi, nizam, newaub, mandarin, beglerbeg, sirdar, ameer, sachem.

Princess, duchess, infanta, margravine, &c., maharajah, subahdar.

Nobility, *see* (875).

Military authorities, marshal, field-marshal, *maréchal*, generalissimo, commodore, commander-in-chief, admiral, general, colonel, lieutenant-colonel, officer, captain, major, lieutenant, adjutant, aide-de-camp, ensign, cornet, cadet, subaltern, non-commissioned officers, serjeant, corporal, centurion, seraskier.

Civil authorities, mayor, prefect, chancellor, provost, magistrate, palatine, syndic, alcade (or alcaid), burgomaster, *corregidor*, sheik, seneschal, burgrave, alderman, warden, constable, beadle, alguazil, cavass.

Statesman, politician, statist, statemonger.

President, chairman, speaker, moderator, vice-president, comptroller, director (694).

(747) Ensign, or badge of authority.

SCEPTRE, regalia, regality, crown, coronet, rod of empire, mace, *fasces*, wand, *bâton*, truncheon, staff.

Helm, bit, curb, reins, leading-strings.

A throne, chair, musnud, divan, woolsack.

Diadem, tiara, ermine, signet, seals, talisman, cap of maintenance, robes of state.

protégé, dependant, pensioner, hanger-on, emissary.

Retinue, *cortége*, staff, court.

An attendant, squire, henchman, led captain, chamberlain, follower, usher, page, donzel, train-bearer, domestic, butler, footman, lackey, flunkey, valet, waiter, equerry, groom, jockey, tiger, livery servant, cad, hireling, underling, menial, understrapper, journeyman, whipper-in, bailiff, castellan, seneschal, *major-domo*.

Serf, slave, helot, bondsman, *âme damnée*.

A maid, handmaid, *soubrette, confidente*, abigail, *femme de chambre, fille de chambre*, waiting maid, nurse, *bonne*, scullion, &c.

Badge of slavery, bonds, chains, &c., *see* (752).

V. To serve, attend upon, dance attendance, wait upon, squire.

Phr. To hang on the sleeve of; to pin oneself upon.

---

(748) FREEDOM, independence, liberty, scope, range, latitude, play, swing, free-play, full play, elbow-room, margin.

Franchise, immunity, exemption, emancipation (750).

Free land, allodium, *see* (780).

A freeman, denizen.

V. To be free, to have scope, &c.

Phr. To have the run of; to have one's own way; to stand on one's

(749) SUBJECTION, dependence, thrall, thraldom, subjugation, bondage, serfdom, servitude, slavery, vassalage, villanage, service, clientship, liability (177), enslavement.

Yoke, harness, collar (751).

V. To be subject, dependent, &c., to fall under, obey, serve (743).

Phr. To drag a chain; to be led by the nose; to be or lie at the mercy of.

legs; to stand on one's rights; to have a will of one's own.

To take a liberty; to make free with; *Prendre le mors aux dents.*

To render free, &c., to free, to emancipate, &c. (750).

Adj. Free, independent, loose, unconstrained, unrestrained, unchecked, unobstructed, unconfined, unsubject, unbound, uncontrolled, unchained, unshackled, unfettered, uncurbed, unbridled, unrestricted, unmuzzled, unenthralled, unbuttoned, unforced, uncompelled, unhindered, uncaught, unenslaved, unclaimed, ungoverned.

Free and easy, at ease, wanton, rampant, irrepressible, unprevented, unvanquished, exempt, enfranchised, emancipated, released, disengaged, &c., *see* (750).

Phr. A cat may look at a king.

(750) LIBERATION, disengagement, release, enlargement, emancipation, mancipation, affranchisement, enfranchisement, manumission, discharge, dismissal.

Escape (671), deliverance (672), redemption, extrication, acquittance, absolution (970), denization.

Licence, toleration.

V. To gain, obtain, acquire, &c. one's liberty, freedom, &c., to deliver oneself from, to cast off trammels.

To break loose, escape, slip away, make one's escape, cut and run, slip the collar, bolt, &c. (671), shake off the yoke, tear asunder one's bonds, break prison.

To liberate, free, set free, set at liberty, release, loose, let loose, loosen, relax, unloose, untie, unbind, unhand, unchain, unshackle, unfetter, unclog, disengage, unharness, &c., *see* (44).

To enlarge, set clear, let go, let out, disincarcerate, unbar, unbolt, uncage, unclose, uncork, discharge, disenthral, dismiss, deliver, extricate, let slip, enfranchise, affranchise, manumit, denizen, emancipate, assoil.

To clear, acquit, redeem, ransom.

Phr. To give one one's head; to let one paddle one's own canoe; to send to the right about.

To subject, enthral, enslave, keep under, control, &c. (751), to reduce to slavery, to bethrall.

Phr. To have one on the hip.

Adj. Subject, dependent, subjected, in subjection to, feudatory, feudal, a slave to, at the mercy of, stipendiary, in leading-strings, enthralled, controlled, constrained, &c., *see* (751), the puppet, sport, plaything of, &c.

Phr. Under the thumb of; on the hip.

(751) RESTRAINT, constraint, coertion, cohibition, discipline.

Confinement, durance, duress, imprisonment, incarceration, prisonment, coarctation, entombment, "durance vile," limbo, captivity.

Arrest, arrestation, custody, keep, care, charge, ward, restringency.

Curb, &c., *see* (753).

V. To be under restraint, to be coerced, &c.

To restrain, constrain, coerce, curb, cramp, keep under, enthral, put under restraint, debar; to chain, enchain, fasten, tie up (43), picket, fetter, shackle, trammel, bridle, muzzle, gag, pinion, pin down, tether.

To confine, shut up, shut in, clap up, lock up, cage, encage, impound, pen, coop, hem in, jam in, enclose, mew, wall in, rail in, cloister, bolt in, close the door upon, imprison, incarcerate, immure, entomb.

Phr. To put in irons; to put in a strait-waistcoat.

To take charge of, lead captive, send or commit to prison, give in charge, or in custody, arrest, commit.

Adj. Restrained, coerced, &c., buttoned up, pent up.

Coactive, stiff, restringent, strait-laced.

Phr. In limbo; in Lob's pound; laid by the heels.

(752) Means of restraint.

PRISON, jail, gaol, prison-house, cage, coop, den, cell, stronghold, fortress, keep, dungeon, bastille, *oubliette*, bridewell, toll-booth, panopticon, penitentiary, guardroom, hold, roundhouse, blackhole, station, enclosure, pen, fold, pound, paddock, stocks.

Fetter, shackle, trammel, bond, chain, iron, collar, pinion, gyve, fetlock, manacle, handcuff, strait-waistcoat; muzzle, gag, bridle, curb, bit, snaffle, rein, martingale, leadingstring, tether, picket, band, brake.

Bolt, bar, lock, padlock, rail, wall, paling, palisade (232), fence, barricade.

(753) KEEPER, custodian, *custos*, jailor, castellan, guard, watch, watch-man, watch and ward, sentry, sentinel, escort.

(755) Vicarious authority.

COMMISSION, delegation, consignment, assignment, procuration, deputation, legation, mission, agency, clerkship, agentship; errand, charge, *brevet*, diploma.

Appointment, nomination, ordination, installation, inauguration.

Vicegerency, regency, regentship.

V. To commission, delegate, depute, send out, consign, charge.

To appoint, name, nominate, ordain, install, induct, inaugurate.

(754) PRISONER, captive, *détenu*, in custody, in charge.

(756) ABROGATION, annulment, cancel, revocation, repeal, rescission, rescinding, deposal, defeasance, dismissal, *congé*.

Abolition, abolishment, counter-order, countermand, repudiation, nullification, recantation, retraction, *see* (607).

V. To abrogate, annul, cancel, revoke, repeal, rescind, over-rule, abolish, disannul, dissolve, quash, repudiate, nullify, retract, recant, recall, countermand, counter-order, break off, disclaim, declare null and void, set aside.

To dismiss, send off, send away, discard, turn off, turn away, cashier, oust, unseat, unthrone, dethrone, depose, unsaddle, uncrown, send back, send about one's business.

Adj. Abrogated, &c.; *functus officio*.

Int. Get along with you! begone! go about your business.

(757) RESIGNATION, retirement, abdication, renunciation, abjuration.

V. To resign, give up, throw up, retire, abdicate, lay down, abjure, renounce, forego, disclaim, retract, &c., *see* (756); to tender one's resignation.

Phr. "Othello's occupation's gone."

(758) CONSIGNEE, delegate, commissary, commissioner, vicegerent, legate, representative, secondary, nominee, surrogate, functionary, plenipotentiary, emissary, nuncio, internuncio.

Agent, factor, attorney, broker, factotum, bailiff, man of business, go-between, middleman, *employé*, *attaché*, curator, clerk, placeman.

(759) DEPUTY, substitute, vice, proxy, *locum tenens*, delegate.

Regent, viceroy, vicegerent, satrap, exarch, vizier, minister, premier, commissioner, chancellor, prefect, warden, lieutenant, archon, consul, Reis Effendi, legate, surrogate.

V. To be deputy, &c. for; to appear for.

Phr. To stand in the shoes of.

Section II. Special Intersocial Volition.

(760) Permission, leave, allowance, sufferance, tolerance, toleration, liberty, law, licence, concession, grant, vouchsafement, authorization, accordance, admission, favour, dispensation, exemption, connivance.

A permit, warrant, *brevet*, precept, authority, firman, pass, passport, furlough, licence, *carte blanche*.

V. To permit; give leave or permission; to let, allow, admit, suffer, tolerate, concede, accord, vouchsafe, humour, indulge, to leave it to one; to leave alone; to grant, empower, authorize, warrant, licentiate; to give licence; to give a loose to.

Phr. To give *carte blanche;* to give one rope; to give a horse his head; to stretch a point; leave the door open.

To let off, absolve, dispense with, favour, wink, connive at.

To take a liberty; to use a freedom.

Adj. Permitting, &c., permissive, conceding, &c.

Unforbid, unforbidden.

(761) Prohibition, inhibition, *veto*, disallowance, interdiction, hindrance (706), restriction, restraints (751), embargo, an interdict, ban, taboo, proscription.

V. To prohibit, forbid, inhibit, disallow, bar, debar, interdict, keep in, hinder, restrain (751), cohibit, restrict, withhold, limit, circumscribe, keep within bounds.

To exclude, shut out, proscribe.

Phr. To clip the wings of.

Adj. Prohibitive, restrictive, exclusive, prohibitory, forbidding, &c.

Not permitted, prohibited, &c., unlicensed, &c.

Int. Hands off! keep off!

---

(762) Consent, compliance, acquiescence, assent (488), agreement, yieldance, yieldingness, acknowledgment, settlement, ratification, confirmation.

V. To consent, give consent, assent, comply with, acquiesce, agree to, accede, accept.

To concede, yield, satisfy, grant, settle, acknowledge, confirm, ratify, deign, vouchsafe.

Adj. Consenting, &c., unconditional, *see* Assent (488).

(763) Offer, proffer, tender, present, overture, proposition, motion, proposal, invitation, presentation, offering, oblation, bid, bribe, sacrifice, immolation.

V. To offer, proffer, tender, present, invite, volunteer, propose, move, make a motion, start, press, bid, hold out, hawk about.

Adj. Offering, &c.

(764) Refusal, rejection, declining, non-compliance, incompliance, declension, dissent, denial, repulse, rebuff, discountenance; *see* (489).

Disclaimer, recusancy, abnegation, protest.

Revocation, violation, abrogation (756), flat refusal, peremptory denial.

V. To refuse, reject, deny, decline, nill, disclaim, protest, resist, repel, refuse or withhold one's assent, to negative, grudge, begrudge.

To discard, set aside, rescind, revoke, discountenance, forswear.

Phr. To turn a deaf ear to; to shake the head; to send to the right about; to hang fire; to wash one's hands of.

Adj. Refusing, &c., recusant, uncomplying, unconsenting.

Phr. Your humble servant; *bien obligé.*

(765) REQUEST, asking, petition, demand, suit, solicitation, craving, entreaty, begging, postulation, solicitation, canvass, prayer, supplication, impetration, imploration, instance, obsecration, obtestation, importunity, application, address, appeal, motion, overture, invocation, interpellation, apostrophe, orison, incantation, imprecation.

Mendicancy, begging letter, grace, *brigue*.

Claim, reclamation, revendication.

V. To request, ask, beg, crave, pray, petition, solicit, beg a boon, demand, prefer a request or petition, ply, apply to, make application, put to, make bold to ask, invite, beg leave, put up a prayer, pop the question.

To beg hard, entreat, beseech, supplicate, implore, conjure, adjure, invoke, evoke, kneel to, fall on one's knees, impetrate, imprecate, appeal to, apply to, put to, address, call for, press, urge, beset, importune, dun, tax, besiege, cry to, throw oneself at the feet of.

Prithee, do, please, be good enough, pray, be so good as, have the goodness, vouchsafe.

To bespeak, canvass, tout, make interest, court.

To claim, revendicate, reclaim, sue.

Adj. Requesting, asking, beseeching, &c., precatory, suppliant, supplicatory, importunate, bowing, &c., supplicant, postulant.

Phr. Cap in hand.

Adv. For heaven's sake, for goodness' sake, for God's sake.

(767) PETITIONER, solicitor, applicant, suppliant, supplicant, mendicant, beggar, suitor, candidate, postulant, canvasser.

(766) Negative request.

DEPRECATION, expostulation, intercession.

V. To deprecate, protest, expostulate; to enter a protest; to intercede for.

Adj. Deprecating, &c., deprecatory, expostulatory, deprecated, protested. Unsought, unbesought.

Adv. By no means; on no account; not for the world; cry you mercy.

Int. God forbid! forbid it heaven

Section III. CONDITIONAL INTERSOCIAL VOLITION.

(768) PROMISE, word, troth, plight, *parole*, word of honour, assurance, vow, oath.

Engagement, insurance, contract (769), obligation, affiance, betrothment.

V. To promise, give a promise, assure; to give, pass, pledge or plight one's word, honour, credit, &c.; to swear, vow, be sworn; take oath, make oath, kiss the book; to attest, adjure.

Phr. To call heaven to witness; swear by bell, book, and candle.

To engage; to enter on, make or form an engagement, take upon oneself; to bind, tie, or pledge oneself; to be in for it; to contract an obligation; to be bound; to undertake; to hold out an expectation.

To answer for, be answerable for, secure, give security (771).

(768 *a*) Release from engagement, *see* Liberation (750).

Adj. Absolute, unconditional.

Adj. Promising, &c., promised, pledged, sworn, &c. ; votive.
Phr. Under one's hand and seal ; as one's head shall answer for.
Int. So help me God !

(769) COMPACT, contract, agreement, bargain, pact, paction, stipulation, covenant, settlement, convention, *nudum pactum*, charter, treaty, indenture, *concordat, Zollverein,* Pragmatic sanction.

Negociation, transaction, bargaining, haggling, chaffering, bargain by inch of candle ; diplomacy.

Ratification, settlement, signature, seal, signet, bond.

A negociator, diplomatist, agent, attorney, broker, &c. (759).

V. To contract, covenant, bargain, agree for, strike a bargain, engage, &c., *see* Promise (768); to underwrite.

To treat, negociate, bargain, stipulate, haggle (or higgle), chaffer, stickle for, insist upon, make a point of, compound for.

To conclude, close, confirm, ratify, clench, come to an understanding, take one at one's word, come to terms.

To subscribe, sign, seal, indent, put the seal to.

(770) CONDITIONS, terms, articles, articles of agreement, clauses, *proviso,* provisions, *salvo,* covenant, stipulation, *ultimatum, sine quâ non.*

V. To make it a condition, &c., to stipulate, insist upon, &c.

Adj. Conditional, provisional, guarded, fenced, hedged in, &c.

Adv. Conditionally, with the understanding ; provided, unless, *see* (469).

Phr. Wind and weather permitting.

(771) SECURITY, surety, guaranty, guarantee, mortgage, warranty, bond, pledge, tie, plight, caution, sponsion, mainpernor, hostage, sponsor, bail.

Deed, instrument, deed-poll, indenture, warrant, charter, cartel, protocol, recognizance ; verification, acceptance, indorsement, signature, execution.

Stake, deposit, pool, earnest, handsel.

(772) OBSERVANCE, performance, fulfilment, satisfaction, discharge, compliance, acquittance, acquittal, adhesion, acknowledgment, fidelity (939).

V. To observe, perform, keep, fulfil, discharge, comply with, meet, satisfy, adhere . to, be faithful to, stand to one's engagement, acquit oneself.

Phr. To redeem one's pledge.

Adj. Observant, faithful, true, honourable, &c. (939), strict, rigid, punctilious.

Adv. Faithfully, &c.

(773) NONOBSERVANCE, failure, neglect, laches, laxity, infringement, infraction, violation, forfeiture, transgression.

Retraction, repudiation, nullification, protest.

Informality, lawlessness, disobedience, bad faith (742).

V. To break, violate, fail, neglect, omit, forfeit, infringe, transgress.

To retract, discard, protest, go from one's word, repudiate, nullify, ignore, wipe off, cancel, &c. (552), to fob off, palter, elude, evade.

Phr. To apply the sponge.

Adj. Violating, &c., elusive, evasive, transgressive, unfulfilled, &c. compensatory (30).

(774) COMPROMISE, composition, middle term, *mezzo termine;* bribe, hush-money.

V. To compromise, compound, take the mean, split the difference, come to terms.

Section IV. Possessive Relations.*

1°. *Property in general.*

(775) ACQUISITION, obtainment, gaining, earning, procuration, procuring, gathering, gleaning, picking, collecting.

Gain, profit, benefit, emolument, the main chance, pelf, lucre, loaves and fishes, produce, return, fruit.

Inheritance, bequest, legacy.

Fraudulent acquisition, subreption.

V. To acquire, get, gain, win, earn, realize, regain, receive (785), take (789), obtain, procure, derive, secure, collect, reap, come in for, step into, inherit, come by, scrape together, get hold of.

To profit, make profit, turn to profit, make money by, obtain a return, make a fortune, coin money.

Phr. To turn a penny; to bring grist to the mill; to feather one's nest; to reap or gain an advantage.

To be profitable, to pay, to answer.

To fall to, come to, accrue.

Adj. Acquiring, acquired, &c., profitable, remunerative, paying.

(776) Loss, perdition, deperdition, forfeiture.

Privation, bereavement, deprivation (789), dispossession, riddance.

V. To lose; incur, experience, or meet with a loss; to miss, mislay, throw away, forfeit, allow to slip through the fingers; to get rid of (782), to waste (638, 679).

Adj. Losing, &c., lost, &c.

Devoid of, not having, unobtained, unpossessed, unblest with.

Shorn of, deprived of, bereaved of, dispossessed.

Irrecoverable, irretrievable, irremediable, irreparable.

———

(777) POSSESSION, ownership, proprietorship, occupancy, hold, holding, preoccupancy.

Exclusive possession, impropriation, monopoly, inalienableness.

Future possession, heritage, inheritance.

V. To possess, have, hold, own, be master of, be in possession of, enjoy, occupy, be seised of, be worth, to have in hand or on hand; to inherit.

To engross, monopolize.

To be the property of, belong to, appertain to, pertain to, be in the hands of, be in the possession of.

Adj. Possessing, &c., possessed of, worth, endowed with, instinct with, fraught, laden with, charged with.

Possessed, &c., on hand, in hand, unsold, unshared; inalienable.

(778) Joint possession.

PARTICIPATION, joint stock, common stock, partnership, copartnership, communism, possession in common, communion, community of possessions or goods.

Snacks, co-portion.

A partner, copartner.

V. To participate, partake, share, go snacks, go halves, share and share alike; to have or possess, &c. in common; to come in for a share.

Adj. Partaking, &c.

Adv. Share and share alike.

(779) POSSESSOR, owner, holder, proprietor, proprietary, master, heritor, occupier, landlord, tenant; proprietress.

Future possessor, heir, inheritor.

* That is, relations which concern property.

(780) PROPERTY, possession, ownership, *meum et tuum*, occupancy.

Estate, effects, assets, stock, goods, chattels, fixtures, moveables, furniture, things, traps, trappings, paraphernalia, luggage, baggage, bag and baggage, cargo, lading : patrimony, heir-loom.

Real property, land, landed estate, manor, demesne, domain, tenement, hereditament, household, freehold, farm, fief, feoff, *appanage*, seigniority, allodium.

Ground, acres, field, close.

State, realm, empire, kingdom, principality.

Adj. Predial, manorial, freehold, &c.

(781) RETENTION, keep, holding, keeping, retaining, detention, custody, grasp, gripe, tenacity.

Fangs, teeth, clutches, claws, talons, nails.

Incommunicableness.

Phr. A bird in hand.

V. To retain, keep, keep in hand, detain, hold fast, grasp, clutch, clench, gripe, hug, withhold, keep back.

Adj. Retaining, &c., retentive, tenacious.

Unforfeited, undeprived, undisposed, uncommunicated, incommunicable.

(782) RELINQUISHMENT, cession, abandonment, renunciation, surrender, riddance (776), resignation (758).

V. To relinquish, give up, let go, lay aside, resign, forego, renounce, surrender, part with, get rid of, lay down, abandon, cede, yield, dispose of, divest oneself of, spare, give away, throw away, cast away, fling away, let slip, make away with, make way for.

Adj. Relinquished, &c., left, unculled.

2°. *Transfer of Property.*

(783) TRANSFER, interchange, exchange, transmission, barter (794), abalienation, demise.

V. To transfer, consign, make over, pass, transmit, interchange, exchange.

To change hands, change from one to another, alienate, devolve.

To dispossess, abalienate, disinherit.

(784) GIVING, bestowal, donation, accordance to, presentation, oblation, presentment, delivery, granting.

Cession, concession, consignment, dispensation, benefaction, charity, almsgiving.

Gift, donation, boon, present, fairing, benefaction, grant, offering, contribution, subscription, donative, meed, tribute, gratuity, *douceur*, *pour-boire*, bribe, free gift, favour, bounty, largess, subsidy, allowance, endowment, charity, alms, sportule, peace-offering, *see* Payment (807).

Bequest, legacy, demise, dotation.

V. To give, bestow, accord, confer, grant, concede, present, give away, deliver, deliver over, make over, consign, hand, tip, render,

(785) RECEIVING, reception, acceptance, suscipience, admission.

A recipient, sportulary, stipendiary, beggar.

V. To receive, take (789), accept, admit, catch, catch at, jump at, take in.

Adj. Receiving, &c., suscipient, recipient.

Not given, unbestowed.

———

impart, hand over, part with, yield, dispose of, put into the hands of, vest in, assign, put in possession, settle upon, endow.

To bequeath, leave, demise, devise.

To give out, dispense, deal, deal out, dole out, mete out.

To contribute, subscribe, pay (807), spend.

To furnish, supply, afford, spare, accommodate with, indulge with.

To bribe, suborn.

Adj. Giving, &c., given, &c., charitable, eleemosynary, sportulary, tributary.

(786) APPORTIONMENT, distribution, allotment, partition, division, deal.

Dividend, portion, contingent, share, allotment, lot, measure, dole, pittance, *quantum*, ration, *quota, modicum*, allowance, appropriation.

V. To apportion, divide, distribute, billet, allot, cast, share, mete, parcel out, deal, partition, appropriate.

Adj. Apportioning, &c.

(787) LENDING, loan, advance, mortgage, accommodation, feneration, pawn, pignoration, hypothecation, investment.

Lender, pawnbroker, uncle.

V. To lend, advance, mortgage, invest, pawn, impawn, hypothecate, impignorate, place or put out to interest, accommodate with.

Adj. Lending, &c., unborrowed.

Adv. In advance.

(788) BORROWING, pledging, replevin, borrowed plumes, plagiarism, plagiary.

V. To borrow, raise money, desume, raise the wind.

Adj. Borrowing, &c., borrowed, second-hand.

(789) TAKING, appropriation, prehension, prensation, capture, caption, abreption, seizure, deprehension, abduction, ablation, catching, seizing, &c.

Abstraction, subtraction, deduction, subduction.

Dispossession, deprivation, deprivement, bereavement, divestment, sequestration, confiscation.

Resumption, reprise, reprisal.

Clutch, swoop, wrench.

V. To take, lay one's hands on; lay, take, or get hold of; to help oneself to; to possess oneself of, take possession of, make sure of, make free with.

(790) RESTITUTION, return, reddition, rendition, restoration, rehabilitation, reinvestment, reparation, atonement.

Redemption, recovery, recuperation, release, replevin.

V. To return, restore, give back, bring back, render, refund, reimburse, rehabilitate, repair, reinvest.

To let go, unclutch, disgorge, regorge, regurgitate.

Adj. Restoring, &c.

To appropriate, impropriate, pocket, put into one's pocket, bag, sack; to ease one of.

To pick up, gather, collect, reap, glean, crop, get in the harvest, intercept.

To take away, carry away, carry off, bear off, hurry off with, abduct, kidnap, crimp.

To lay violent hands on, fasten upon, pounce upon, catch, seize, snatch, nip up, whip up, jump at, snap at, hook, claw, cam, grasp, gripe, grab, clutch, wring, wrest, wrench, pluck, tear away, catch, nab, capture, collar, throttle.

To take from, deduct, subduct (38), subtract, curtail, retrench, abridge of, dispossess, take away from, abstract, deprive of, bereave, divest, despoil, strip, fleece, levy, distrain, confiscate, sequester, sequestrate, oust, extort, usurp, suck, drain, gut, dry, exhaust.

Phr. To suck like a leech.

Adj. Taking, &c., prehensile, predatory, rapacious, raptorial, ravenous.

(791) STEALING, theft, thieving, thievery, appropriation, plagiarism, depredation, pilfering, rape, larceny, robbery, shoplifting, burglary.

Spoliation, plunder, pillage, sack, rapine, *brigandage*, foray, dragoonade, marauding.

Peculation, embezzlement, swindling (545), smuggling, thievishness; the den of Cacus.

Licence to plunder; letters of marque.

V. To steal, rob, abstract, appropriate, filch, pilfer, purloin, nab, nim, prig, grab.

To convey away, carry off, make off with, run off with, abduct, kidnap, crimp, seize, lay violent hands on, &c. (789).

To cabbage, crib, sponge, swindle, peculate, embezzle, poach, run, smuggle.

To plunder, pillage, rifle, sack, ransack, spoil, spoliate, despoil, strip, fleece, gut, forage, levy black-mail, pickeer.

Phr. To live by one's wits; to rob Peter to pay Paul; to set a thief to catch a thief.

Adj. Stealing, &c., thievish, light-fingered, stolen, furtive, &c.

(792) THIEF, robber, spoiler, pickpocket, cutpurse, depredator, footpad, highwayman, burglar, house-breaker, shop-lifter; swell mob; the light-fingered gentry.

Swindler, smuggler, sharper, blacklegs, shark, stork, trickster, harpy, *chevalier d'industrie*, peculator, plagiarist.

Brigand, freebooter, bandit, pirate, corsair, buccaneer, thug, picqueerer, picaroon, moss-trooper, raparee, marauder.

(793) BOOTY, spoil, plunder, prey, grab, forage, black-mail.

3°. *Interchange of Property.*

(794) BARTER, exchange, truck, interchange, commutation, scorse.

Traffic, trade, commerce, dealing, business, custom, negotiation, jobbing, *agiotage*, bargain, commercial enterprize, speculation, brokery.

Phr. A Roland for an Oliver; a *quid pro quo;* robbing Peter to pay Paul; a blind bargain; a pig in a poke; taking for better for worse.

V. To barter, exchange, truck, interchange, commute, scorse, traffic, trade, speculate, transact or do business with, deal with, have dealings with; open, or keep an account with; to carry on a trade.

To bargain; drive, make, or strike a bargain; negotiate, bid for, haggle (or higgle), chaffer, stickle, cheapen, compound for, beat down, outbid, come to terms.

Phr. To give a sprat to catch a herring.

Adj. Commercial, mercantile, interchangeable; wholesale, retail.

(795) PURCHASE, emption, buying, purchasing; pre-emption, bribery, coemption.

A buyer, purchaser, customer, *emptor*.

V. To buy, purchase, procure, hire, rent, farm, pay, fee, repurchase, keep in one's pay, bribe, suborn.

Adj. Purchased, &c.

Phr. Caveat emptor.

(796) SALE, vent, disposal, custom. Auction, roup, nundination.

Lease, mortgage.

Vendibility, vendibleness.

A vendor, seller, &c. (797).

To sell, vend, dispose of, retail, dispense, hawk, put up to sale or auction, bring to the hammer, undersell.

To let, lease, set, mortgage.

Adj. Unpurchased, unbought, on one's hands.

(797) MERCHANT, trader, dealer, tradesman, buyer and seller, vendor, monger, shopkeeper, shopman, salesman.

Retailer, chapman, hawker, huckster, regrater, higgler, pedlar, cadger, sutler, Autolycus, middleman, costerman, costermonger; auctioneer, broker, money-broker, jobber, factor, go-between, money-lender.

House, firm, concern, partnership, company, guild.

Buyer, customer, purchaser.

(798) MERCHANDISE, ware, mercery, commodity, effects, goods, article, stock, cargo, produce, freight.

(799) MART, market, change, exchange, market-place, fair, hall, staple, bazaar, guildhall, toll-booth, custom-house.

Office, shop, counting-house, *bureau*, counter, stall, chambers.

Warehouse, *dépôt*, store (636), interposit, *emporium*.

4°. *Monetary Relations.*

(800) MONEY, funds, treasure, capital, stock, proceeds, assets, cash, bullion, ingot.

Circulating medium, specie, coin, hard cash, pounds, shillings, and pence.

Ready, rhino, blunt, dust, mopus, tin.

Gold, silver, copper, *rouleau*, dollar, &c.

Currency, finance.

Pocket-money, change, small coin; doit, farthing, penny, shilling, &c.

Sum, amount, balance.

Paper-money, note, bank-note, note of hand, promissory note, I. O. U.

Bill, draught (or draft), check (or cheque), order, warrant, *coupon*, debenture, bill of exchange, exchequer bill, *assignat*.

A drawer; a drawee.

False money, base coin, flash note, slip, kite.

Science of coins, Numismatics.

Phr. The sinews of war.

V. To draw, draw upon, endorse.

Adj. Monetary, pecuniary, crumenal, fiscal, financial, sumptuary; numismatical.

Phr. To touch the pocket; *argumentum ad crumenam.*

(801) TREASURER, purse-bearer, purser, questor, bursar, banker, moneyer, paymaster, cashier, teller, cash-keeper, bursary.

Chancellor of the exchequer, financier.

(802) TREASURY, bank, exchequer, coffer, chest, stocks, money-box, money-bag, strong-box, stronghold, till, tiller, purse, purse-strings, pocket, breeches-pocket, fisc.

(803) WEALTH, fortune, riches, opulence, affluence, independence, solvency, competence, easy circumstances, command of money.
Phr. A well-lined purse ; the purse of Fortunatus ; a mint of money.
Means, provision, substance, revenue, income, alimony, livelihood, loaves and fishes, pelf, Mammon, lucre, dower, pension, annuity.
A rich man ; a capitalist ; a *millionnaire* ; a Nabob, Crœsus, Midas.
V. To be rich, &c., to afford.
Phr. To roll in riches ; to wallow in wealth ; to hold one's head above water.
To enrich, fill one's coffers, &c.
Adj. Wealthy, rich, affluent, opulent, flush.
Phr. Made of money ; rich as Crœsus ; rich as a Jew ; rolling in riches, &c.

(804) POVERTY, indigence, penury, pauperism, destitution, want, need, lack, necessity, privation, distress, an empty purse, bad circumstances, straits, insolvency, beggary, mendicancy, mendicity.
Phr. Res angusta domi.
A poor man, pauper, mendicant, beggar, starveling; *un pauvre diable ; qui n'a pas le sou.*
V. To be poor, &c., to want, lack, starve.
Phr. To live from hand to mouth; come upon the parish ; not to have a penny ; *tirer le diable par la queue ; zonam perdidit ; cantabit vacuus, &c.*
To render poor, &c., to reduce, to impoverish, reduce to poverty, ruin.
Phr. To bring to the parish.
Adj. Poor, indigent, penniless, unmonied, moneyless, short of money, out of money, out of cash, out of pocket, needy, destitute, necessitous, seedy, distressed, hard up, in need, in want, in distress, pinched, dowerless, fortuneless, reduced, insolvent, *see* (806), bereft, bereaved, fleeced, stripped.
Phr. Unable to make both ends meet ; out at elbows; under hatches ; not having a penny ; not worth a *sou ;* poor as a rat; poor as a church mouse; out at the heels.
Adv. In formâ pauperis.

(805) CREDIT, trust, tick, score. Letter of credit, duplicate.
A creditor, lessor, mortgagee ; a dun.
V. To keep an account with, to credit, accredit.
Adj. Crediting.
Adv. On credit, on tick, on account.

(806) DEBT, obligation, liability, debit, indebtment, arrears, deficit, default, insolvency.
Interest, usance, usury.
A debtor, debitor, lessee, mortgagor ; a defaulter (808).
V. To be in debt, to owe, to answer for, to incur a debt, *see* Borrow (788).
Phr. To run up a bill ; to go on tick.
Adj. In debt, indebted, owing, due, liable, answerable for, insolvent.
unpaid, in arrear, being minus, Unrepaid, unrequited, unrewarded.

(807) PAYMENT, defrayment, discharge, quittance, acquittance, settle-

(808) NONPAYMENT, default, defalcation, protest.

ment, clearance, liquidation, satisfaction, reckoning, arrangement, acknowledgment, release.

Repayment, reimbursement, retribution, reward, *see* (973).

Bill, cheque, cash, ready money, &c. (800).

V. To pay, defray, discharge; settle, quit, acquit oneself of; account or reckon with; clear, liquidate, release.

Phr. To fork out money; to pay on the nail; to honour a bill; to strike a balance; to settle, balance, or square accounts with; to be even with; to wipe off old scores; to satisfy all demands; to pay in full of all demands.

To repay, refund, retribute, reimburse.

Adj. Paying, &c.; paid, owing nothing, out of debt, unowed.

Insolvency, bankruptcy, repudiation, application of the sponge.

Waste paper, bonds, dishonoured bills, &c.

A defaulter, a bankrupt, an insolvent debtor.

V. Not to pay, to fail, to break to become insolvent or bankrupt.

To protest, dishonour, repudiate, nullify.

Phr. To apply the sponge; to pay over the left shoulder.

Adj. Not paying, in debt, insolvent, bankrupt.

Phr. Being *minus*, or worse than nothing; deep in debt; plunged, or over head and ears in debt.

(809) EXPENDITURE, money going out; outgoings, expenses, disbursement, outlay.

Money paid; pay, payment, fee, hire, wages, perquisites, vails, allowance, stipend, salary, appointments, subsidy; batta, shot, scot.

Remuneration, recompense, reward, *see* (973), drink-money, *pourboire*, largess, *honorarium*, modicum, bribe, *douceur*, hush-money.

Pay in advance; earnest, handsel.

Contribution, donation, subscription, deposit, contingent, dole, quota.

Investment, purchase, &c., *see* (795), alms, *see* (784).

V. To expend, spend, pay, disburse, lay out; lay, or pay down; to cash; to come down with; to fork out; bleed, make up a sum; to invest, sink money.

Phr. To unloose the purse strings; to pay the piper; to pay through the nose.

Adj. Expending, &c., expended, &c., sumptuary.

(810) RECEIPT, money coming in, incomings.

Income, revenue, rent, rental, rent-roll, rentage, return, proceeds, premium, bonus.

Pension, annuity, jointure, dower, dowry, alimony.

Emoluments, perquisites, recompense, &c., *see* (809), sinecure.

V. To receive, pocket, bag, sac, &c.; *see* Take (785 & 789), to draw from, derive from.

To bring in, yield, afford, pay, accrue.

Phr. To get what will make the pot boil.

Adj. Receiving, &c., received, &c.

Gainful, profitable, remunerative, lucrative, advantageous, &c.

(811) ACCOUNTS (or accompts), money matters, bills, score, balance-sheet, books, account books, ledger, debtor and creditor accounts.

Book-keeping, audit.

An accountant, auditor, actuary, bookkeeper.

V. To keep accounts, enter, post, credit, debit, carry over; balance, make up accounts, take stock, audit.

To falsify, garble, or cook accounts.

(812) PRICE, cost, expense, charge, demand, run upon, damage, fare.

Dues, duty, toll, tax, cess (or sess), levy, gabelle (or gavel), assessment, benevolence, custom, exactment, ransom, salvage, excise, tariff, brokerage.

Bill, account, score, reckoning.

Worth, rate, value, valuation, appraisement; money's worth, pennyworth.

V. To set or fix a price, appraise, assess, price, charge, demand, ask, require, exact.

Phr. To run up a bill.

To fetch, sell for, cost, bring in, yield, stand one in, afford.

Adj. Priced, charged, &c., to the tune of, *ad valorem.*

Phr. No penny, no paternoster ; *point d'argent, point de Suisse.*

(813) DISCOUNT, abatement, reduction, allowance, drawback, poundage, *agio,* per centage, rebate, set off, salvage.

V. To discount, bate, abate, rebate, reduce, take off, allow, give, discount, tax.

Adj. Discounting, &c.

Adv. At a discount.

---

(814) DEARNESS, costliness, high-price, expensiveness, rise in price, overcharge, extravagance, exorbitance.

V. To be dear, &c., to cost much, to overcharge.

To pay too much, to pay through the nose.

Adj. Dear, high, high-priced, expensive, costly, dear-bought, precious, unreasonable, extravagant, exorbitant.

Adv. Dear, at great cost, *à grands frais.*

(815) CHEAPNESS, low price, bargain, absence of charge, gratuity, &c., peppercorn rent.

V. To be cheap, &c., to cost little, to come down or fall in price.

Phr. To have one's money's worth.

Adj. Cheap, low, moderate, reasonable, inexpensive, unexpensive, low-priced, worth the money, half-price.

Gratuitous, gratis, free, for nothing, free of cost, without charge, not charged, untaxed, scot free, shot free, expenseless, free of expense, free of all demands.

Phr. Cheap as dirt ; dog cheap.

(816) LIBERALITY, generosity, bounty, munificence, bounteousness, bountifulness, charity, hospitality.

V. To be liberal, &c., spend freely.

Phr. To open one's purse strings ; to bleed freely.

Adj. Liberal, free, generous, charitable, hospitable, bountiful, bounteous, handsome, ungrudging, fullhanded, openhearted, freehearted, munificent, princely.

(817) ECONOMY, frugality, thrift, thriftiness, care, husbandry, good huswifery (or housewifery), savingness, retrenchment, savings, a aveall.

Phr. Cheese parings and candle ends.

V. To be economical, &c., to save, economise, meet one's expenses, retrench.

Phr. To cut one's coat according to one's cloth ; to make both ends meet.

Adj. Economical, frugal, thrifty, careful, saving, chary, spare, sparing.

(818) PRODIGALITY, unthriftiness, waste, profusion, profuseness, extravagance, prodigence, squandering, malversation.

(819) PARSIMONY, stint, stinginess, niggardliness, illiberality, closeness, penuriousness, avarice, tenacity, straithandedness, covetousness, gree-

A prodigal, spendthrift, squanderer, wastethrift.

V. To be prodigal, &c., to squander, lavish, waste, dissipate, exhaust, run out, spill, misspend, throw away money, drain.

Phr. To burn the candle at both ends; to make ducks and drakes of one's money.

To outrun the constable; to fool away, potter, muddle away, fritter away, &c. one's money; to pour water into a sieve.

Adj. Prodigal, profuse, thriftless, unthrifty, wasteful, extravagant, lavish, dissipated.

Phr. Penny wise and pound foolish.

diness, avidity, rapacity, venality, mercinariness, cupidity.

Phr. Auri sacra fames.

A miser, niggard, churl, screw, skinflint, crib, codger, muckworm, hunks, curmudgeon, harpy.—Harpagon.

V. To be parsimonious, &c., to grudge, stint, pinch, screw.

Phr. To skin a flint.

Adj. Parsimonious, stingy, miserly, mean, shabby, near, niggardly, close, close-fisted, close-handed, fast-handed, chary, illiberal, ungenerous, churlish, hide-bound, sordid, mercenary, venal, covetous, avaricious, greedy, griping, pinching, rapacious.

Phr. Having an itching palm.

CLASS VI.

WORDS RELATING TO THE SENTIENT AND MORAL POWERS.

~~~~~~~~~~~~~~~

SECTION I.   AFFECTIONS IN GENERAL.

(820) AFFECTIONS, character, qualities, disposition, nature, spirit, temper, temperament; cast, or frame of mind, or soul; turn, bent, bias, turn of mind, predisposition, proneness, proclivity, vein, humour, grain, mettle, *verve.*

Soul, heart, breast, bosom, the inner man, inmost heart, heart's core, heart-strings, heart's blood, heart of hearts, *penetralia mentis.*

Passion, pervading spirit, ruling passion, master passion; flow of soul, fulness of the heart, heyday in the blood, flesh and blood.

V. To have or possess affections, &c.; be of a character, &c.; to breathe.

Adj. Affected, characterized, formed, moulded, cast, tempered, attempered, framed, disposed, predisposed, prone, inclined, having a bias, &c., inbred, inborn, ingrained.

(821) FEELING, endurance, experience, suffering, tolerance, sufferance, patience, content (831).

Non-endurance, *see* (825).

Impression, sensation, affection, response, emotion, pathos, warmth, glow, fervour, fervency, heartiness, cordiality, ardour, zeal, eagerness, passion, enthusiasm.

Blush, suffusion, flush, hectic, tingling, thrill, turn, shock, agitation (315), heaving, flutter, flurry, fluster, twitter, tremor, throb, throbbing, panting, palpitation, trepidation, perturbation, ruffle, hurry of spirits, the heart swelling, throbbing, thumping, pulsating, melting, bursting, &c.

Transport, rapture, ecstasy, ravishment, *see* (827).

V. To feel, receive an impression, &c.; to be impressed with, affected with, moved with, touched with, &c.

To bear, suffer, endure, brook, tolerate, experience, taste, meet with, go through, prove; to harbour, cherish, support, abide, undergo, aby.

To blush, tingle, twitter, throb, heave, pant, palpitate, go pit-a-pat, agitate, thrill, tremble, shake, quiver, wince.

To swell, glow, warm, flush, catch the flame, catch the infection, respond.

To possess, pervade, penetrate, imbue, absorb, &c., the soul.

Phr. To come home to one's feelings, or bosom.

Adj. Feeling, suffering, enduring, &c.

Impressed, moved, touched, affected with, &c., penetrated, *pétri.*

Warm, quick, lively, smart, strong, sharp, keen, acute, cutting, piercing, pungent, racy, *piquant,* poignant.

Deep, profound, indelible, deep-felt, home-felt, heart-felt, warm-hearted, hearty, cordial, swelling, thrilling, soul-stirring, deep-mouthed, heart-expanding, electric.

Earnest, eager, glowing, fervent, fervid, ardent, burning, red-hot, fiery, flaming, boiling, boiling over, zealous, pervading, penetrating, absorbing, over head and ears, the heart being big, full, swelling, bursting.

Wrought up, excited, passionate, enthusiastic, *see* (825).

(822) SENSIBILITY, impressiveness, impressibility, sensibleness, sensitiveness, affectibility, susceptibleness, susceptibility, susceptivity, excitability, mobility, vivacity, vivaciousness, tenderness, softness, intolerance.

Physical sensibility, *see* (375).

V. To be sensible, &c., shrink, &c., to be without skin.

Phr. "To die of a rose in aromatic pain."

Adj. Sensible, sensitive, impressible, susceptive, susceptible, excitable, mobile, thin-skinned, tremblingly alive, lively, vivacious, mettlesome, tender, soft, sentimental, romantic, enthusiastic, *romanesque*.

Adv. Sensibly, &c., to the quick.

(823) INSENSIBILITY, inertness, insensibleness, impassibility, impassibleness, apathy, phlegm, dulness, habitude, coolness, coldness, supineness, stoicism, *insouciance, nonchalance,* indifference, lukewarmness, frigidity, cold blood, *sang froid,* dry eyes, cold heart, deadness, torpor, torpidity.

Lethargy, coma, trance, stupor, stupefaction, paralysis, palsy, hebetation, anæsthesia (381), stock and stone, neutrality.

Physical insensibility, *see* (376).

V. To disregard, be insensible, not to be affected by, not to mind, to vegetate, *laisser aller,* not to care.

To render insensible, numb, benumb, paralyze, deaden, render callous, sear, inure, harden, steel, case-harden, stun, stupefy, brutalize, hebetate.

Adj. Insensible, unconscious, impassive, unsusceptible, insusceptible, impassible, unimpressible, dead to, passionless, spiritless, unfeeling, apathetic, phlegmatic, callous, thick-skinned, pachydermatous, obtuse, proof against, case-hardened, inured, steeled against, stoical, dull, frigid, cold, cold-blooded, cold-heartened, flat, maudlin, obtuse, inert, supine, sluggish, torpid, languid, tame, numb, numbed, sleepy, yawning, stupefied, comatose, anæsthetic.

Indifferent, *insouciant,* lukewarm, careless, *pococurante, sans souci.*

Unfelt, unaffected, unruffled, unimpressed, unmoved, uninspired, untouched, &c.; with withers unrung, unshocked, unstruck, without being moved, &c.; with dry eyes, platonic, imperturbable, vegetative.

Adv. Insensibly &c., *æquo animo.*

Phr. No matter; *n'importe;* it matters not; it does not signify; it is of no consequence or importance (643); it cannot be helped; nothing coming amiss; being all the same to.

(824) EXCITATION of feeling, excitement, suscitation, galvanism, stimulation, provocation, calling forth, infection, animation, agitation, perturbation, subjugation, fascination, intoxication, enravishment, unction.

Repression of feeling, *see* (826).

V. To excite, affect, touch, move, stir, wake, awaken, raise, raise up, evoke, call up, summon up, rake up, rip up.

To impress, strike, quicken, impassion, mantle, swell, work upon.

To warm, kindle, stimulate, whet, animate, inspire, impassion, inspirit, provoke, irritate, sting, rouse, work up, hurry on.

To agitate, ruffle, flutter, fluster, flush, shake, thrill, penetrate, pierce, cut, work oneself up.

To soften, subdue, overcome, master, overpower, overwhelm.

To shock, stagger, stun, astound, electrify, galvanize, give one a shock, petrify.

To madden, intoxicate, fascinate, transport, ravish, enrapture, enravish, entrance.

Phr. To come home to one's feelings ; to prey on the mind ; to give one a turn ; to cut to the quick ; to go through one; to strike one all of a heap ; to make one's blood boil.

Adj. Excited, affected, &c., *see* (825), wrought up, worked up, *bouleversé,* lost, *éperdu,* wild, haggard, feverish, mantling.

Exciting, &c., impressive, warm, glowing, fervid, swelling.

Phr. Being all of a twitter; all in a pucker ; ready to sink.

(825) Excess of sensitiveness.

EXCITABILITY, intolerance, impatience, wincing, disquiet, disquietude, restlessness, fidgets, fidgettiness, fuss, hurry, agitation, flurry, fluster, flutter, irritability (901).

Phr. Noli me tangere.

Passion, excitement, vehemence, impetuosity, flush, heat, fever, fire, flame, fume, turbulence, boisterousness, tumult, effervescence, ebullition, boiling, boiling over, whiff, gust, storm, tempest, breaking out, burst, fit, paroxysm, the blood boiling.

Fierceness, rage, fury, *furor,* raving, delirium, phrenzy, intoxication, fascination, infection, infatuation, fanaticism, Quixotism, *la tête montée.*

V. To be intolerant, &c., not to bear, to bear ill, wince, chafe, fidget, fuss, not to be able to bear, stand, tolerate, &c.

To break out, fly out, burst out, explode, run riot, boil, boil over, fly off, flare up, fire, take fire, fume, rage, rave, run mad.

Phr. To fly off at a tangent.

Adj. Excitable, &c., excited, &c.

Intolerant, impatient, unquiet, restless, fidgetty, irritable, mettlesome, chafing, wincing, &c.

Vehement, boisterous, impetuous, fierce, fiery, flaming, boiling, overzealous, passionate, impassioned, enthusiastic, rampant, mercurial,

(826) Absence of excitability.

INEXCITABILITY, dispassion, inirritability, hebetude, tolerance, patience.

Coolness, composure, calmness, imperturbation, *sang froid,* collectedness, tranquilness, quiet, quietude, quietness, sedateness, soberness, graveness, staidness, gravity, stayedness, placidity, sobriety, philosophy, stoicism, demureness, meekness, gentleness, mildness.

Submission, resignation, sufferance, endurance, longanimity, longsufferance, forbearance, fortitude, equanimity.

Repression of feeling, composure, &c., hebetation.

V. To be composed, &c., to bear, to bear well, tolerate, put up with, take up with, bear with, stand, bide, abide, aby, abide with, take easily, rub on, make the best of, acquiesce, submit, yield, bow to, resign oneself, suffer, endure, support, go through, reconcile oneself to, bend under.

To brook, digest, eat, swallow, pocket, stomach, brave.

Phr. To pocket the affront ; to swallow the pill ; to swallow the leek ; to shrug the shoulders ; *avaler des couleuvres.*

To be borne, endured, &c., to go down.

To allay, compose, calm, still lull, allay, pacify, quiet, tranquillize,

199

high-wrought, overwrought, hot-headed, hurried, turbulent, furious, fuming, boiling, raging, raving, frantic, delirious, intoxicated, demoniacal.

Overpowering, overwhelming, uncontrolled, stanchless, irrepressible, ungovernable, uncontrollable.

Int. Pish! pshaw!

hush, smoothe, appease, assuage, mitigate, soothe, soften, temper, alleviate, moderate, sober down, mollify, lenify, tame, blunt, obtund, dull, deaden, slacken, damp, repress, restrain, check, curb, bridle, rein in, smother, quell, lay, *see* (174).

Phr. To set one's heart at rest or at ease.

Adj. Inexcitable, unexcited, calm, cool, temperate, composed, collected, placid, quiet, tranquil, unstirred, undisturbed, unruffled, serene, demure, sedate, staid, sober, dispassionate, unimpassioned, unpassionate, philosophic, stoical, imperturbable, cold-blooded.

Meek, tolerant, patient, submissive, unoffended, unresented, content, resigned, subdued, bearing with, longsuffering, gentle, mild, inirritable, unpassionate, unpathetic, sober-minded, coolheaded.

Phr. Gentle as a lamb; patient as Job; armed with patience.

Section II. PERSONAL AFFECTIONS.*

1°. Passive Affections.

(827) PLEASURE, gratification, enjoyment, fruition, oblectation, relish, zest, *gusto.*

Well-being, satisfaction, content (831), comfort, *sans souci,* bed of roses, bed of down, velvet.

Joy, gladness, delight, glee, cheer, sunshine, physical pleasure, *see* (377).

Treat, regale, feast, *délice,* luxury, voluptuousness, clover.

Happiness, felicity, bliss, beatitude, beatification, enchantment, transport, rapture, ravishment, ecstasy, heaven, *summum bonum,* paradise, elysium, empyrean, third heaven (981).

Honeymoon, palmy days, halcyon days, golden age, *Saturnia regna.*

V. To be pleased, &c., to feel, receive, or derive pleasure, &c.; to take pleasure or delight in; to delight in, rejoice in, relish, like, enjoy, take in good part.

(828) PAIN, suffering, physical pain, *see* (378).

Displeasure, dissatisfaction, discontent, discomfort, *malaise.*

Uneasiness, disquiet, inquietude, weariness, dejection, *see* (837).

Annoyance, irritation, plague, bore, bother, botheration.

Care, anxiety, mortification, vexation, chagrin, trouble, trial, solicitude, cark, dole, fret.

Grief, sorrow, distress, affliction, woe, bitterness, heartache, a heavy heart, a bleeding heart, a broken heart, heavy affliction, &c.

Unhappiness, infelicity, misery, wretchedness, desolation.

Dolour, sufferance, ache, aching, hurt, smart, cut, twitch, twinge, stitch, shoot, cramp, spasm, nightmare, *ephialtes,* convulsion, throe.

Pang, anguish, agony, torture, torment, rack, cruciation, crucifixion, martyrdom, purgatory, hell (982).

* Or those which concern one's own state of feeling.

To indulge in, treat oneself, solace oneself, revel, luxuriate in, to be on velvet, in clover, in heaven, &c. ; to enjoy oneself.

Phr. To slake the appetite ; *faire ses choux gras ;* to bask in the sunshine ; to tread on enchanted ground.

Adj. Pleased, enjoying, relishing, liking, gratified, glad, gladdened, rejoiced, delighted, charmed.

Cheered, enlivened, flattered, tickled, indulged, regaled, treated, &c.

Comfortable, at ease, satisfied, content (831), luxurious, on velvet, in clover, on a bed of roses, *sans souci,* unalloyed, without alloy.

Happy, blest, blessed, blissful, overjoyed, enchanted, captivated, fascinated, transported, raptured, enraptured, in raptures, in ecstasies, in a transport, beatified, in heaven, in paradise, &c.

Phr. With a joyful face ; with sparkling eyes ; happy as a king ; pleased as Punch ; in the lap of luxury ; happy as the day is long.

Adv. Happily, &c.

___

Phr. The cankerworm of care ; a peck of troubles ; a sea of troubles ; the ills that flesh is heir to ; the iron entering the soul.

A sufferer, victim, prey, martyr.

V. To feel, suffer, or experience pain, &c. ; to suffer, ache, smart, ache, ail, bleed, shoot, twinge, tingle, gripe, lancinate, wince, writhe.

To grieve, fret, pine, mourn, bleed, worry oneself, chafe, yearn, droop, sink, give way, despair (859).

Phr. To sit on thorns ; to be on pins and needles ; to take to heart ; to labour under afflictions ; to drain the cup of misery to the dregs ; *"hæret lateri lethalis arundo."*

Adj. In pain ; feeling, suffering, enduring, &c. pain ; in a state of pain, of suffering, &c., sore, aching, suffering, ailing, &c., pained, hurt, stung, &c., *see* (830).

Displeased, annoyed, dissatisfied, discontented, weary, &c. (832), uneasy, ungratified, uncomfortable, ill at ease.

Concerned, afflicted, in affliction, sorry, sorrowful, in sorrow, *au désespoir,* bathed in tears.

Unhappy, unfortunate, hapless, unblessed, luckless, unlucky, ill-fated, ill-starred, fretting, wretched, miserable, careworn, carking, disconsolate, inconsolable, woebegone, forlorn, a prey to grief, &c., despairing, in despair (859), heart-broken, broken-hearted, the heart bleeding, doomed, devoted, accursed, undone.

___

(829) Capability of giving pleasure.

PLEASURABLENESS, pleasantness, gratefulness, welcomeness, acceptableness, agreeableness, delectability, deliciousness, daintiness, sweetness, luxuriousness, lusciousness, voluptuousness.

Charm, attraction, attractiveness, attractability, fascination, *prestige,* loveliness, takingness, invitingness.

A treat, dainty, tit bit, *bon-bon, bonne bouche,* sweet, sweetmeat, sugar-plumb, nuts, *sauce piquante.*

V. To cause, produce, create, give, afford, procure, offer, present, yield, &c., pleasure, gratification, &c.

To please, take, gratify, satisfy,

(830) Capability of giving pain.

PAINFULNESS, disagreeableness, unpleasantness, irksomeness, displeasingness, unacceptableness, bitterness, vexatiousness, troublesomeness.

Trouble, care, cross, annoyance, burden, load, nuisance, plague.

Scourge, bitter pill, worm, canker, cancer, ulcer, curse, gall and wormwood, sting, scorpion, thorn, briar, bramble, hornet, whip, lash, rack, wheel.

Phr. A thorn in one's side.

A mishap, misadventure, mischance, pressure, infestation, grievance, trial, crosses, hardship, blow,

indulge, flatter, tickle, humour, regale.

To charm, rejoice, cheer, gladden, delight, enliven (836), to transport, captivate, fascinate, enchant, entrance, bewitch, ravish, enrapture, enravish, beatify.

Phr. To do one's heart good.

Adj. Causing or giving pleasure, &c., pleasing, agreeable, grateful, gratifying, pleasant, pleasurable, acceptable, welcome, glad, gladsome, comfortable.

Sweet, delectable, nice, palatable, dainty, delicate, delicious, dulcet, savoury, toothsome, luscious, luxurious, voluptuous, genial, cordial, refreshing.

Fair, lovely, favourite, attractive, engaging, winning, taking, prepossessing, inviting, captivating, bewitching, fascinating.

Charming, delightful, exquisite, enchanting, ravishing, rapturous, heart-felt, thrilling, heavenly, celestial, elysian, empyrean, seraphic.

Palmy, halcyon, Saturnian.

Phr. To one's heart's content; doing one's heart good.

———

stroke, affliction, misfortune, reverse, infliction, dispensation, visitation, disaster, undoing, tragedy, calamity, catastrophe, adversity (735).

Provocation, infestation, affront, indignity, outrage, *see* (900, 929).

V. To cause, produce, give, &c. pain, uneasiness, suffering, &c., to disquiet, &c.

To pain, hurt, wound, sting, pinch, grate upon, regrate, irk, gall, chafe, gnaw, prick, lancinate, lacerate, pierce, cut, cut up, stick, gravel, hurt one's feelings, shock, smite, twinge, gripe.

To wring, harrow, torment, torture, rack, scarify, cruciate, crucify, convulse, agonize.

To displease, annoy, incommode, discompose, trouble, disquiet, grieve, cross, tease, tire, vex, worry, plague, bother, pester, bore, pother, harass, importune.

To irritate, provoke, nettle, aggrieve, enchafe, enrage, gravel.

To maltreat, bite, assail, badger, harry, persecute.

To sicken, disgust, revolt, turn the stomach, mumble.

To horrify, prostrate.

Phr. To barb the dart; to set the teeth on edge; to stink in the nostrils; to tweak the nose; to break the heart; to add a nail to one's coffin; to plant a dagger in the breast; to put to the question; to break on the wheel, &c. (972).

Adj. Causing, occasioning, giving, producing, creating, inflicting, &c., pain, &c., hurting, &c.

Painful, dolorific, dolorous, unpleasant, unpleasing, displeasing, disagreeable, distasteful, uncomfortable, unwelcome, unsatisfactory, unpalatable, unacceptable, thankless, undesirable, untoward, unlucky, undesired, obnoxious.

Distressing, bitter, afflicting, afflictive, affective, cheerless, joyless, depressing, depressive, mournful, dreary, melancholy, grievous, pathetic, woeful, disastrous, calamitous, tragical, deplorable, dreadful.

Irritating, provoking, stinging, biting, vexatious, annoying, unaccommodating, troublesome, tiresome, irksome, plaguing, plaguy, teazing, pestering, bothering, harassing, worrying, tormenting, importunate, deuced.

Intolerable, insufferable, insupportable, unbearable, unendurable, shocking, frightful, terrific, grim, appalling, dire, heart-breaking, heart-rending, heart-wounding, heart-corroding, horrid, harrowing, horrifying, horrific, execrable, accursed.

Odious, hateful, unpopular, repulsive, offensive, nauseous, disgust-ing, sickening, nasty, revolting, shocking, vile, abominable.

Sharp, acute, sore, severe, grave, hard, harsh, bitter, cruel, biting, corroding, consuming, racking, excruciating, &c.

Phr. What flesh and blood cannot bear.

Adv. Painfully, &c.

(831) CONTENT, contentment, con-tentedness, satisfaction, entire satis-faction, serenity, sereneness, ease, heart-ease.

Comfort, snugness, well-being.

Moderation, patience, endurance, resignation, reconciliation.

Phr. " Patience sitting on a monu-ment ; " "patience, sovereign o'er transmuted ill."

V. To be content, &c.; to rest satisfied, to put up with ; to take up with ; to be reconciled to.

Phr. To make the best of ; to let well alone.

To render content, &c., to set at ease, to conciliate, reconcile, satisfy, indulge, slake, gratify, &c.

Phr. To set one's heart at ease, or at rest ; to speak peace.

Adj. Content, contented, satisfied, at ease, snug, comfortable.

Patient, resigned to, reconciled to, unrepining.

Unafflicted, unvexed, unmolested, unplagued, &c.

(834) RELIEF, easement, allevi-ation, mitigation, palliation, solace, consolation, comfort, encouragement, refreshment, lullaby.

Delivery from evil, &c.

Lenitive, balm, oil, restorative, cataplasm, &c. (662), cushion, pillow, bolster, bed, &c. (215).

V. To relieve, ease, alleviate, mi-tigate, palliate, soften, soothe, as-suage, allay, cheer, comfort, encourage, bear up, refresh, restore, re-medy, cure.

Phr. To dry the tears ; to wipe the tears ; to pour balm into ; to lay the flattering unction to one's soul.

Adj. Relieving, &c., consolatory ; balmy, balsamic, lenitive, ano-dyne, &c. (662), remedial, curative.

(836) CHEERFULNESS, gaiety (or gayety), cheer, spirits, high spirits, high glee, joyfulness, joyousness,

(832) DISCONTENT, discontentment, dissatisfaction, disappointment, mor-tification.

Repining, taking on, inquietude, heart-burning, heart-grief, *see* Regret (833).

V. To be discontented, &c., dis-satisfied ; to repine, regret (833), grumble (839).

To cause discontent, &c., to dis-appoint, dissatisfy, mortify.

Adj. Discontented, dissatisfied, un-satisfied, malcontent, mortified, dis-appointed, cut up.

Repining, glum, grumbling, exi-gent, exacting.

Phr. Out of sorts ; in the dumps ; down in the mouth.

Disappointing, unsatisfactory.

(833) REGRET, bitterness, repin-ing ; lamentation (839) ; *see* Peni-tence (950).

V. To regret, deplore, lament, rue, repent (950).

Adj. Regretting, &c., regretful.

Phr. 'Tis pity ; what a pity !

(835) AGGRAVATION, heightening, exacerbation, exasperation.

V. To aggravate, to render worse, heighten, embitter, sour, acerbate, envenom, exacerbate, exasperate.

Adj. Aggravating, &c., aggra-vated, &c., unrelieved ; aggravable.

---

(837) DEJECTION, depression, low spirits ; lowness or depression of spirits, dejectedness ; weight or op-

gaieté de cœur, hilarity, exhilaration, liveliness, sprightliness, briskness, vivacity, *allégresse*, jocundity, levity, sportiveness, sportfulness, jocularity, sprightfulness.

Phr. A flow of spirits.

Mirth, merriment, merry-making, laughter, *see* (838), amusement, *see* (840), Nepenthe.

Gratulation, rejoicing, exultation, jubilation, jubilee, triumph, pæan, *te deum*.

V. To be cheerful, &c.; to be of good cheer, to cheer up, brighten up, light up; take heart, bear up.

To rejoice, make merry, exult, congratulate oneself, triumph, clap the hands, crow, sing, carol, frisk.

Phr. To drive dull care away; to give a loose to mirth; to keep up one's spirits; *Ride si sapis.*

To cheer, enliven, elate, exhilarate, entrance, &c.

Adj. Cheerful, gay, blithe, cheery, cheerly, of good cheer, in spirits, in good or high spirits, *allegro*, light, lightsome, buoyant, debonnair, bright, light-hearted, hearty, free and easy, airy, canty, sprightly, lively, vivacious, sprightful, sunny.

Merry, joyous, joyful, jocund, bonny, buxom, playful, playsome, *folâtre*, frisky, frolicsome, sportive, sportful, gamesome, jocose, jocular, jolly.

Rejoicing, elated, exulting, jubilant, palmy, flushed, rollicking, cock-a-hoop.

Phr. In high feather; gay as a lark; playful as a kitten; merry as a grig; *ridentem dicere verum.*

Adv. Cheerfully, cheerily, &c.

Int. Tant mieux! hurrah! huzza! tol de roll loll!

pression on the spirits, damp on the spirits, sadness.

Heaviness, dulness, infestivity, joylessness, gloom, dolefulness, dolesomeness, weariness (841), heaviness of heart, failure of heart.

Melancholy, melancholiness, dismals, mumps, dumps, blue devils, megrims, spleen, hypochondriasis; *tædium vitæ*; the cave of Trophonius.

Despondency, despair, disconsolateness, prostration, prosternation; the cave of despair, *see* (859).

Demureness, seriousness, gravity, solemnity, solemnness, sullenness, &c.

A hypochondriac, a seek-sorrow, self-tormentor, *malade imaginaire.*

V. To be dejected, sad, &c.; to grieve, to take on, to take to heart, to give way, droop, sink, lower, look downcast, mope, pout, brood over, fret, pine, yearn, frown, *see* Despair (859).

Phr. To look blue; to hang down the head; to wear the willow; to laugh on the wrong side of the mouth.

To refrain from laughter; to keep one's countenance.

To depress, discourage, dishearten, dispirit, dull, deject, lower, sink, dash, unman, prostrate.

Phr. To prey on the mind or spirits.

Adj. Cheerless, uncheerful, unlively, joyless, dull, flat, dispirited, out of spirits, out of sorts, out of heart, in low spirits, spiritless, lowering, frowning, sulky.

Discouraged, disheartened, downcast, cast down, depressed, chapfallen, jaw-fallen, crest-fallen, dashed, drooping, sunk, soulsick, dumpish, mumpish, desponding.

Dismal, melancholy, sombre, tristful, pensive, *pensieroso*, mournful, doleful, moping, splenetic, gloomy, lugubrious, funereal, forlorn, heart-struck.

Melancholic, hipped, hypochondriacal, bilious, jaundiced, atrabilious, saturnine.

Disconsolate, despairing, in despair (859).

Grave, serious, sedate, staid, sober, solemn, demure, grim, grim-faced, grim-visaged, rueful, sullen.

Phr. Down in the mouth; sick at heart; in the suds; with a long face; a prey to melancholy; dull as a beetle; dull as ditch-water; as melancholy as a gib cat.

Depressing, preying upon the mind, &c.

(838) Expression of pleasure.

REJOICING, exultation, triumph, jubilation, jubilee, *see* (884).

Smile, simper, smirk, grin, broad grin.

Laughter, giggle, titter, crow, cheer, chuckle, shout, hearty laugh, horse laugh, a shout, burst, or peal of laughter.

Derision, risibility (856).

Momus, Democritus the Abderite.

V. To rejoice, exult, triumph (884).

To smile, simper, smirk, grin, mock; to laugh, giggle, titter, crow, cackle; to burst out, split, shout.

Phr. To laugh in one's sleeve; to shake one's sides; to hold both one's sides; to split one's sides; to die with laughter.

To cause, create, occasion, raise, excite, or produce laughter, &c.; to tickle.

Phr. To tickle one's fancy; to set the table in a roar; to convulse with laughter; to be the death of one.

Adj. Laughing, &c.; jubilant, triumphant.

Laughable, risible, ludicrous.

Phr. Ready to burst or split; *risum teneatis amici?*

(839) Expression of pain.

LAMENTATION, complaint, murmur, mutter, plaint, lament, wail, sigh, suspiration, heaving.

Cry, whine, whimper, sob, tear, moan, grumble, groan.

Outcry, scream, screech, howl, whoop, brawl, yell, roar.

Weeping, crying, &c.; lachrymation, complaining, frown, scowl, sardonic grin or laugh.

Dirge, elegy, monody, threnody, jeremiade.

Plaintiveness, querimoniousness, languishment, querulousness.

Mourning, weeds, willow, cypress.

A grumbler, croaker, brawler; Heraclitus, Niobe.

Phr. The melting mood; wringing of hands and gnashing of teeth; *Laudator temporis acti.*

V. To lament, complain, murmur, mutter, grumble, sigh; give, fetch, or heave a sigh.

To cry, weep, sob, greet, blubber; snivel, bibber, whimper; to shed tears; maunder, pule, take on.

To grumble, groan, grunt, croak, whine, moan, bemoan, wail, bewail, frown, scowl.

To cry out, growl, mew, mewl, squeak, squeal, sing out, scream, cry out lustily, screech, bawl, hollow, bellow, yell, roar.

Phr. To melt or burst into tears; *fondre en larmes;* to cry oneself blind; to cry one's eyes out; to beat one's breast; to wring one's hands; to gnash one's teeth; to tear one's hair; to roll on the ground; to roar like a bull; to bellow like an ox.

Adj. Lamenting, complaining, &c.; lachrymose, plaintive, plaintful, querulous, querimonious.

Phr. Being in the melting mood; with tears in one's eyes; bathed or dissolved in tears; the eyes suffused, swimming, brimful, or overflowing with tears; with moistened or watery eyes; the tears standing in the eyes, or starting from the eyes; *les larmes aux yeux.*

Int. Heigh ho! alas! alack! O dear! ah me! well-a-day! well-a-way! alas the day!

(840) AMUSEMENT, diversion, entertainment, sport, divertisement, recreation, holiday, relaxation, pastime, *passetems.*

Fun, frolic, pleasantry, drollery, jocoseness, laughter (838).

Play, game, gambol, romp, prank, quip, quirk, rig, lark, *escapade*, *échappée*, heyday.

Dance, ball, *ballet*, hop, real, cotillon, rigadoon, saraband, hornpipe, fandango, minuet, quadrille, waltz, &c.

Festivity, festival, jubilee, merry-making, rejoicing, *fête*, gala, ridotto, revelry, revels, carnival, saturnalia.

Feast, banquet, entertainment, carousal, jollification, regale, junket, wake, *fête champêtre, symposium,* wassail; jollity, joviality, jovialness.

Buffoonery, mummery, tomfoolery, raree-show, puppet-show, masquerade.

Bonfire, fireworks, *feu de joie.*

Toy, plaything, bauble, &c., see (643).

A master of ceremonies or revels.

Phr. Deus nobis hæc otia fecit; "Quips and cranks and wanton wiles; Nods and becks and wreathed smiles."

V. To amuse, divert, entertain, rejoice, cheer, recreate, enliven, solace; to beguile or while away the time; to drown care.

To play, sport, disport, make merry, take one's pleasure, make holiday, keep holiday; to game, gambol, revel, frisk, frolic, romp, dally; to dance, hop, foot it, jump, caper, cut capers, skip.

To treat, feast, regale, carouse, banquet.

Phr. To play the fool; to jump over the moon; *desipere in loco.*

Adj. Amusing, diverting, &c., amused, &c.

Sportive, jovial, festive, jocose, rompish, &c.

Phr. Playful as a kitten; "On the light fantastic toe."

(841) WEARINESS, tedium, *ennui*, lassitude, fatigue, dejection, *see* (837).

Disgust, nausea, loathing, sickness, disgust of life, *tædium vitæ.*

Wearisomeness, irksomeness, tiresomeness, monotony.

A bore, a button-holder, proser.

Phr. A twice-told tale; time hanging heavily on one's hands.

V. To tire, weary, fatigue, bore; set to sleep, send to sleep.

To sicken, disgust, nauseate.

Phr. To harp on the same string.

Adj. Wearying, &c., wearisome, tiresome, irksome, uninteresting, devoid of interest, monotonous, humdrum, mortal, flat, prosy, prosing, soporific, somniferous.

Disgusting, sickening, nauseating.

Weary, tired, &c.; unenjoyed, uninterested, flagging, used up, *blasé*, life-weary, weary of life; drowsy, somnolent, sleepy, &c.

Adv. Wearily, &c.

Phr. Usque ad nauseam.

(842) WIT, humor, fancy, fun, pleasantry, drollery, whim, jocularity, facetiousness, waggery, waggishness, wittiness, salt, atticism, attic wit, attic salt, *esprit*, smartness, banter, *badinage*, farce, *espiéglerie.*

Jest, joke, conceit, quip, quirk, crank, *concetto*, witticism, repartee, *bon-mot, plaisanterie,* flash of wit, sally, point, bob, dry joke, idle conceit, *turlupinade*, epigram, *quipro-*

(843) DULNESS, heaviness, stolidness, stupidity (499), flatness, infestivity, gravity (837), solemnity; prose, matter of fact.

V. To be dull, &c.

To render dull, &c., damp, depress.

Phr. To throw cold water on; to lay a wet blanket on; to catch napping.

Adj. Dull, prosaic, prosing, un-

quo, quibble, *jeu de mots,* pun, conundrum, *quodlibet.*

Phr. The cream of the jest.

V. To joke, jest, retort; to cut jokes, gleck, crack a joke, perpetrate a joke, or pun.

To laugh at, banter, jeer, to make fun of, make merry with.

Phr. To set the table in a roar.

Adj. Witty, facetious, humorous, quickwitted, nimblewitted, *spirituel,* smart, jocose, jocular, waggish, comic, comical, laughable, droll, ludicrous, drollish, funny, risible, farcical, roguish, sportive, pleasant.

entertaining, unlively, flat, pointless, stolid, stupid, plodding, humdrum; Bœotian.

Phr. Davus sum non Œdipus; Aliquando bonus dormitat Homerus.

---

(844) A HUMORIST, wag, wit, reparteeist, epigrammatist, *bel esprit,* witsnapper, jester, spark, Joe Miller, *gaillard.*

A buffoon, *farceur,* merryandrew, tumbler, mountebank, charlatan, posturemaster, harlequin, punch, *pulcinello,* scaramouch, clown, pickle-herring, pantaloon, gipsy, jack-pudding.

Phr. The life of the party.

2°. DISCRIMINATIVE AFFECTIONS.

(845) BEAUTY, handsomeness, beauteousness, beautifulness, pulchritude, το καλον.

Form, elegance, grace, symmetry, *belle tournure.*

Comeliness, seemliness, shapeliness, fairness, prettiness, neatness, spruceness, attractiveness, loveliness, quaintness, speciousness, polish, gloss.

Bloom, brilliancy, radiance, splendour, magnificence, sublimity, sublimification.

Concinnity, delicacy, refinement.

Venus, Hebe, the Graces, Peri, Houri, Cupid, Apollo, Hyperion, Adonis, Antinous, Narcissus.

Peacock, butterfly; the flower of, the pink of, &c.; a garden.

Phr. Je ne sais quoi; le beau idéal.

V. To render beautiful, &c., to beautify, embellish, adorn, deck, bedeck, decorate, set out, set off, ornament, *see* (847), dight, bedight, array, garnish, furbish, smarten, trick out, prank, prink, trim, embroider, emblazon.

To polish, burnish, gild, varnish, japan, lacker, &c.

(846) UGLINESS, deformity, inelegance, plainness, homeliness, uncomeliness, ungainliness, uncouthness, clumsiness, stiffness, disfigurement, distortion, contortion, malformation, monstrosity, misproportion, want of symmetry, roughness, repulsiveness, squalor, hideousness, unsightliness, odiousness.

Phr. A forbidding countenance, a hanging look; a wry face; "*spretæ injuria formæ.*"

An eyesore, an object, a figure, a sight, fright, spectre, scarecrow, hag, harridan, satyr, sibyl, toad, baboon, monster, Caliban.

Phr. "*Monstrum horrendum informe cui lumen ademptum.*"

V. To be ugly, &c.

To render ugly, &c., to deform, deface, distort, disfigure, misshape, blemish, spot, stain, distain, soil, tarnish, sully, blot, daub, bedaub, begrime, blur, smear, besmear, bespatter, maculate.

Phr. To make faces.

Adj. Ugly, plain, homely, beautiless, unsightly, sightless, ill-looking, ordinary, unseemly, ill-favoured,

Phr. " To snatch a grace beyond the rules of art."

Adj. Beautiful, handsome, fine, pretty, lovely, graceful, elegant, delicate, refined, fair, personable, comely, seemly, bonny, well-favoured, proper, shapely, well-made, well-formed, well-proportioned, symmetrical, becoming, goodly, neat, dapper, tight, spruce, sleek, quaint, janty, bright-eyed, attractive, tricksy, curious.

Blooming, brilliant, shining, beaming, splendid, resplendent, dazzling, gorgeous, superb, magnificent, sublime.

Picturesque, artistical.

Phr. Fait à peindre.

Passable, not amiss, undeformed, undefaced, spotless, unspotted.

----

disstained, sullied, blurred, splashed, smeared, begrimed, garnished.

hard-favoured, evil-favoured, hard-featured, hard-visaged, ungainly, uncouth, slouching, ungraceful, clumsy, graceless, rude, rough, rugged, homespun, gaunt, rawboned, haggard, scraggy.

Misshapen, shapeless, misproportioned, deformed, ill-made, ill-shaped, disfigured, distorted, unshapen, humpbacked, crooked, bandy-legged, stumpy, dumpy, squat, stubby, bald, ricketty.

Squalid, grim, grisly, grim-faced, grim-visaged, ghastly, ghost-like, death-like, cadaverous, repulsive, forbidding, grotesque.

Frightful, odious, hideous, horrid, shocking, monstrous.

Phr. Ugly as sin ; ugly as a toad ; ugly as a dead monkey ; ugly as a scarecrow.

Foul, soiled, tarnished, stained, blotted, spotted, maculated, spotty, spattered, bedaubed, besmeared ; un-

(847) ORNAMENT, adornment, decoration, embellishment, ornature, ornateness, gaud, pride.

Garnish, polish, varnish, gilding, japanning, lacquer, &c.

Jewel, gem, brilliant, &c. (650), spangle, trinket.

Embroidery, broidery, brocade, galloon, lace, fringe, trapping, trimming, hanging.

Wreath, festoon, garland, chaplet, tassel, knot, epaulette, frog, ermine.

Feather, plume, panache.

Nosegay, *bouquet,* posy.

Tracery, moulding, arabesque.

Frippery, finery, gewgaw, tinsel, spangle, *clinquant,* tawdriness, &c.

Trope, flourish, flowers of rhetoric (577).

Excess of ornament, *see* (851).

V. To ornament, embellish, decorate, adorn, beautify, garnish, polish, gild, &c., bespangle, dizen, bedizen ; embroider, &c., *see* (845).

Adj. Ornamented, &c., beautified, ornate, showy, gaudy, gairish (or garish), gorgeous.

Phr. Fine as a May-day queen ; fine as fivepence.

(848) BLEMISH, disfigurement, eyesore, defect, flaw.

Stain, blot, spot, speck, blur, *macula,* blotch, speckle, spottiness ; soil, tarnish, smudge, smut, dirt, soot, &c. (653).

Excrescence, pimple, &c., *see* (250).

V. To disfigure, deface, &c., *see* (846).

(849) SIMPLICITY, plainness, undress, chastity ; freedom from ornament or affectation, homeliness.

Phr. Simplex mundities.

V. To be simple, &c., to render simple, &c., to simplify.

Adj. Simple, plain, homely, chaste, homespun, unaffected.

Unadorned, unornamented, undecked, ungarnished, unarrayed, untrimmed.

----

(850) Good taste.

TASTE, delicacy, refinement, gust, *gusto*, nicety, finesse, grace, *virtu*, το πρεπον, polish, elegance.

Science of taste, Æsthetics.

A man of taste, *connoisseur*, judge, critic, *conoscente*, *virtuoso*, *amateur*, an Aristarchus.

V. To appreciate, judge, discriminate, criticize (465).

Adj. In good taste, tasty, unaffected, pure, chaste, classical, attic, refined, æsthetic, elegant.

Adv. Elegantly, &c.

Phr. To one's taste or mind; after one's fancy; *tiré à quatre épingles ; comme il faut.*

(852) FASHION, *ton*, style, *bon ton*, mode, vogue.

Manners, breeding, politeness, gentility, decorum, *bienséance*, punctilio, form, formality, *etiquette*, custom, demeanour, air, port, carriage, presence.

Show, equipage, turn out, &c., *see* (882).

The world, the fashionable world, the *beau monde*, high life, town, court, gentility, civilization, civilized life, *see* Nobility (875).

V. To be fashionable, &c.

Phr. To fall in with the prevailing taste.

Adj. Fashionable, in fashion, in vogue, *à la mode*, modish, stylish, courtly, *recherché*, genteel, *comme il faut*, well-bred, well-mannered, polished, gentlemanlike, ladylike, well-spoken, civil, presentable, refined, thoroughbred, *dégagé*, janty, unembarrassed.

Phr. Having a run.

Adv. Fashionably, in fashion, &c.

(851) Bad taste.

VULGARITY, vulgarism, barbarism, Vandalism, Gothicism.

Coarseness, grossness, indecorum, lowness, homeliness, low life, *mauvais ton*, clownishness, rusticity, boorishness, brutishness, brutality, awkwardness, want of tact.

A bad joke; *une mauvaise plaisanterie.*

A rough diamond, a hoiden, tomboy, slattern, sloven, dowdy, cub, clown, &c. (876).

Excess of ornament, false ornament, tawdriness, finery, frippery, trickery, tinsel, gewgaw, *clinquant.*

V. To be vulgar, &c.

Phr. To smell of the shop.

Adj. In bad taste, vulgar, coarse, unrefined, gross, heavy, rude, unpolished, homely, homespun, homebred, uncouth, awkward, ungraceful, slovenly, slatternly, dowdy, unlicked, ungenteel, impolite, ill-mannered, uncivil, underbred, ungentlemanlike, unladylike, unfeminine, unseemly, unpresentable, unkempt, uncombed.

Rustic, boorish, clownish, barbarous, barbaric, gothic, unclassical, heathenish, tramontane, outlandish, untamed (876).

Obsolete, out of fashion, unfashionable, antiquated, old-fashioned, gone by.

New-fangled, odd, fantastic, grotesque, *see* ridiculous (853), affected, meretricious, extravagant, monstrous, shocking, horrid, revolting.

Gaudy, tawdry, bedizened, tricked out.

Adv. Out of fashion, &c.

_____

(853) RIDICULOUSNESS, ludicrousness, risibility.

Oddness, oddity, whimsicality, comicality, grotesqueness, fancifulness, quaintness, frippery, gawkiness, preposterousness, extravagance, monstrosity.

Bombast, bathos, fustian, *amphigouri, extravaganza.*

Adj. Ridiculous, extravagant, *outré*, monstrous, preposterous.

Odd, whimsical, quaint, grotesque, fanciful, eccentric, *bizarre*, strange, out of the way, fantastic, *baroque.*

Laughable, risible, ludicrous, comic, ludibrious, comical, funny, derisive, farcical, burlesque, *pour rire*, quizzical, bombastic, inflated.

Awkward, gawky, lumpish, hulky, uncouth, &c.

Phr. As whimsical as a dancing bear.

(854) FOP, dandy, exquisite, coxcomb, beau, macaroni, blade, blood, jemmy, buck, spark, swell, popinjay, puppy, prig, *petit-maître*, jack-a-napes, jack-a-dandy.

(855) AFFECTATION, mannerism, pretension, airs, conceit, foppery, affectedness, charlatanism, quackery, foppishness, pedantry, teratology, acting a part.

Prudery, demureness, coquetry, *minauderie*, stiffness, formality, buckram.

Pedant, mannerist.

Phr. A lump of affectation.

V. To affect, to give oneself airs, to simper, mince, to act a part, overact.

Adj. Affected, conceited, pedantic, pragmatical, priggish, smug, puritanical, prim, starch, stiff, formal, demure.

Foppish, namby-pamby, slip-slop, coxcomical, slipshod, simpering, mincing.

Over-wrought, over-acted.

(856) RIDICULE, derision, mockery, quiz, banter, irony, *persiflage*, raillery, irrision.

Jeer, gibe, quip, taunt, satire, scurrility, scoffing.

A parody, burlesque, travesty, farce, comedy, tragicomedy, doggrel, blunder, bull, *lapsus linguæ*, slip of the tongue, anticlimax.

Buffoonery, vagary, antic, mummery, tom-foolery, grimace, *simagrée*, monkey trick, *escapade*, prank, tumbling, *gambade*.

V. To ridicule, deride, laugh at (929), scoff, mock, jeer, banter, quiz, rally, fleer, flout, gleek, roast, taunt, point at, grin at.

To parody, caricature, burlesque, travesty.

Phr. To raise a smile; to set the table in a roar; *risum teneatis.*

To turn into ridicule; to play upon; to make merry with; to make a fool of; to make fun of; to make game of; to make faces at; to make mouths at; to lead one a dance; to run a rig upon; to make an April fool of.

To laugh in one's sleeve.

Adj. Derisory, scurrilous, burlesque.

(857) Object and cause of ridicule.

LAUGHING-STOCK, jesting-stock, gazing-stock, butt, quiz, put, square-toes, queer fish; an original, oddity, monkey, buffoon, jester (844), mime, mimer, &c. (599), scaramouch, punch, *pulcinello,* mountebank.

3°. PROSPECTIVE AFFECTIONS.

(858) HOPE, trust, confidence, reliance, faith, assurance, credit, security, expectation, affiance, promise, assumption, presumption.

Hopefulness, bright prospect, millennium, optimism, enthusiasm, &c., utopia.

Phr. Castles in the air, *châteaux en Espagne; le pot au lait.*

Anchor, mainstay, sheet-anchor, staff &c., *see* Support (215).

(859) Absence, want or loss of hope.

HOPELESSNESS, despair, desperation, forlornness, a forlorn hope.

V. To despair, to give over; to lose, give up, abandon, relinquish, &c. all hope; to yield to despair.

To inspire or drive to despair; to dash, crush, or destroy one's hopes.

Phr. To trust to a broken reed; *jetter la manche après la cognée;*

Phr. A ray, gleam, or flash of hope.

V. To hope; to feel, entertain, harbour, cherish, feed, nourish, encourage, foster, &c. hope or confidence.

To trust, confide, rely on, feel or rest assured, confident, secure, &c.; to flatter oneself, expect, presume.

Phr. To see land; to look on the bright side of; *voir en couleur de rose;* to pin one's hope or faith upon; to apply the flattering unction to one's soul.

To give, or inspire hope; to augur well, encourage, assure, promise, flatter, buoy up, reassure, embolden, raise expectations, &c.

Adj. Hoping, &c., in hopes, &c., hopeful, confident, secure, buoyant, buoyed up, sanguine, enthusiastic, utopian.

Fearless, unsuspecting, unsuspicious; free or exempt from fear, suspicion, distrust, &c., undespairing.

Auspicious, promising, propitious, *de bon augure.*

Phr. Nil desperandum; never say die.

" Lasciate ogni speranza voi ch' entrate."

Adj. Hopeless, having lost or given up hope, losing, &c. hope, past hope, forlorn, desperate, incurable.

Inauspicious, unpropitious, unpromising, threatening, &c.

(860) Fear, timidity, diffidence, nervousness, restlessness, inquietude, disquietude, solicitude, anxiety, distrust, hesitation, misgiving, suspicion, qualm, want of confidence.

Apprehension, flutter, trepidation, tremor, shaking, trembling, palpitation, quivering, ague-fit, fearfulness, despondency.

Fright, affright, affrightment, alarm, dread, awe, terror, horror, dismay, panic, consternation, despair (859).

Intimidation, terrorism, reign of terror. An alarmist.

Object of fear; bugbear, bugaboo, scarecrow, goblin, &c. (980), *bête noire,* night-mare, Gorgon, mormo, ogre, raw head and bloody bones, Fee faw fum.

V. To fear, be afraid, &c.; to distrust, hesitate, have qualms, misgivings, suspicions, &c.

To apprehend, take alarm, start, wince, boggle, skulk, cower, crouch, tremble, shake, quake, shudder, quail, boggle, turn pale, blench, flutter, flinch.

Phr. To smell a rat; to shake all over; to shake like an aspen leaf; *ante tubam trepidat.*

To excite fear, raise apprehensions, to give, raise, or sound an alarm, to intimidate, put in fear, frighten, fright, affright, alarm, scare, haunt, strike terror, daunt, terrify, awe, horrify, dismay, petrify, appal.

To overawe, abash, cow, browbeat, bully.

Phr. To fright from one's propriety; to strike all of a heap.

Adj. Fearing, timid, fearful, nervous, diffident, apprehensive, restless, haunted with the fear, apprehension, dread, &c. of.

Frightened, pale, alarmed, scared, terrified, petrified, aghast, awe-struck, dismayed, horror-struck, horrified, appalled, panic-struck.

Inspiring fear, alarming, formidable, redoubtable, portentous, perilous (665), fearful, dreadful, dire, shocking, terrible, tremendous, horrid, horrible, horrific, ghastly, awful.

Phr. White as a sheet; the hair standing on end; not daring to say one's soul's one's own; more frightened than hurt; frightened out of one's senses or wits.

(861) Absence of fear.

Courage, bravery, valour, valiantness, boldness, spirit, spiritedness,

(862) Excess of fear.

Cowardice, pusillanimity, cowardliness, timidity, fearfulness, spirit-

daring, gallantry, intrepidity, contempt of danger, defiance of danger, fearlessness, audacity, dreadlessness.

Manhood, nerve, pluck, mettle, game, bottom, heart, spunk, face, virtue, hardihood, fortitude, firmness, resolution.

Prowess, heroism, chivalry.

A hero, Hector, Hotspur, Amazon, bully, fire-eater, &c. (863).

A lion, tiger, bull-dog, game-cock, fighting-cock.

V. To be courageous, &c., to face, front, affront, confront, despise, brave, defy, &c. danger ; to take courage, to summon up courage, to pluck up courage.

To venture, make bold, face, defy, brave, beard, hold out, bear up against.

Phr. To look in the face ; to come to the scratch ; to " screw one's courage to the sticking place."

To give, infuse, or inspire courage ; to encourage, embolden, inspirit.

Phr. To pat on the back ; to make a man of.

Adj. Courageous, brave, valiant, valorous, gallant, intrepid.

Spirited, high-spirited, high-mettled, mettlesome, spiritful, manly, manful, resolute, stout, stout-hearted, iron-hearted, heart of oak, firm, indomitable.

Bold, daring, audacious, fearless, dreadless, undaunted, aweless, unappalled, undismayed, unawed, unabashed, unalarmed, unflinching, unshrinking, unblenching, unblenched, unapprehensive.

Enterprising, venturous, adventurous, venturesome, dashing, chivalrous, heroic, fierce, savage.

Unfeared, undreaded, &c.

Phr. Up to the scratch ; brave as a lion ; bold as brass ; brave to the back-bone.

lessness, faint-heartedness, softness, effeminacy.

Poltroonery, baseness, dastardness, dastardy, Dutch courage, the white feather, a faint heart.

A coward, poltroon, dastard, recreant, shy-cock, dunghill-cock, milksop, white liver, nidget.

A runaway, fugitive.

V. To quail, &c. (860), to flinch, fight shy, shy, turn tail, run away, cut and run, fly for one's life.

Phr. To show the white feather.

Adj. Coward, cowardly, pusillanimous, shy, timid, skittish, timorous, poor-spirited, spiritless, weak-hearted, faint-hearted, chicken-hearted, lily-hearted, pigeon-hearted, white-livered, lily-livered, milk-livered, milksop, smock-faced.

Dastard, dastardly, base, craven, dunghill, recreant, unwarlike.

Phr. " In face a lion, but in heart a deer."

Sauve qui peut ; the devil take the hindmost.

———

(863) RASHNESS, temerity, audacity, presumption, precipitancy, precipitation, recklessness, fool-hardiness, desperation, Quixotism.

Impudence, indiscretion.

Phr. A blind bargain.

A desperado, rashling, bully, bravo, dare-devil, *enfant perdu,* Hotspur, Don Quixote, knight-errant.

V. To be rash, incautious, &c.

Phr. To buy a pig in a poke ; to go on a forlorn hope ; *donner tête baissée ;* to rush on destruction.

(864) CAUTION, cautiousness, discretion, prudence, wariness, cautel, heed, circumspection, calculation, deliberation, *see* (459).

Coolness, self-possession, presence of mind, *sang froid,* self-command, steadiness.

Phr. " The better part of valour."

V. To be cautious, &c., to take care, to have a care, take heed, to be on one's guard, to look about one.

Phr. To look before one leaps ;

Adj. Rash, temerarious, head-strong, foolhardy, reckless, desperate, hot-headed, hair-brained, headlong, hot-brained, precipitate, Quixotic.

Imprudent, indiscreet, uncalculating, incautious, improvident.

Phr. Without ballast; hand over head; *tête baissée;* post haste; neck or nothing; head foremost; *à corps perdu.*

(865) DESIRE, wish, mind.

Inclination, leaning, bent, fancy, fantasy, partiality, *penchant,* pre-dilection, liking, fondness, relish.

Want, need, exigency.

Longing, hankering, solicitude, anxiety, yearning, coveting, aspiration, ambition, over-anxiety.

Appetite, appetence, appetition, the edge of appetite, keenness, hunger, stomach, thirst, thirstiness, mouth-watering, itch, prurience, *cacoëthes,* cupidity, lust, concupiscence.

Avidity, greediness, covetousness, craving, voracity, canine appetite, rapacity.

Passion, rage, *furore,* mania, *manie,* inextinguishable desire, vaulting ambition, impetuosity.

A *gourmand,* glutton, cormorant, *see* (957).

An *amateur,* votary, devotee, aspirant, solicitant, candidate.

Object of desire; *Desideratum,* attraction, allurement, fancy, temptation, magnet, whim, whimsy, maggot, hobby, hobby-horse, *prestige.*

Phr. The height of one's ambition; *hoc erat in votis;* the wish being father to the thought; *sua cuique voluptas.*

V. To desire, wish, long for, fancy, have a mind to, be glad of, want, miss, need, feel the want of, would fain have, to care for.

To hunger, thirst, crave, lust after, hanker after.

To desiderate, sigh, cry, gape, gasp, pine, pant, languish, yearn for, aspire after, catch at, jump at.

To woo, court, solicit, &c.

Phr. To have at heart; to find in

to see which way the wind blows; to have one's wits about one.

Adj. Cautious, wary, careful, heedful, cautelous, chary, circumspect, prudent, discreet.

Unenterprising, unadventurous, cool, steady, self-possessed.

(866) INDIFFERENCE, coldness, coolness, unconcern, *insouciance,* inappetency, listlessness, lukewarmness, *see* Disdain (930).

V. To be indifferent, &c.; to have no desire, wish, taste or relish for; not to care for; to disdain, spurn (930).

Adj. Indifferent, undesirous, cool, cold, unconcerned, unsolicitous, unattracted, &c., lukewarm, listless, unambitious, unaspiring.

Unattractive, unalluring, undesired, undesirable, &c., uncared for, unwished, unvalued.

Vapid, tasteless, insipid, mawkish, flat, stale, vain.

(867) DISLIKE, distaste, disrelish, disinclination, reluctance, backwardness, demur.

Repugnance, disgust, queasiness, turn, nausea, loathing, averseness, aversion, abomination, antipathy, abhorrence, horror, hatred, detestation, *see* (898), hydrophobia.

V. To dislike, mislike, disrelish.

To shun, avoid, eschew, withdraw from, shrink from, shrug the shoulders at, recoil from, shudder at.

To loathe, nauseate, abominate, detest, abhor, *see* Hate (898).

Phr. Not to be able to bear or endure.

To cause or excite dislike; to disincline, repel, sicken, render sick, nauseate, wamble, disgust, shock.

Phr. To go against the grain; to turn one's stomach; to go against the stomach; to make one's blood run cold.

Adj. Disliking, disrelishing, &c., averse from, adverse, shy of, disinclined.

one's heart; to set one's heart upon; to cast a sheep's eye upon; to set one's cap at; to run mad after.

To cause, create, raise, excite, or provoke desire; to allure, attract, solicit, tempt, hold out temptation or allurement, to tantalize.

Phr. To whet the appetite; to make one's mouth water; *faire venir l'eau à la bouche.*

To gratify desire, slake, satiate (827).

Adj. Desirous, inclined, fain, wishful, wishing, optative, desiring, wanting, needing, hankering after, partial to.

Craving, hungry, sharp-set, peckish, thirsty, athirst, dry.

Greedy, voracious, open-mouthed, agog, covetous, ravenous, rapacious, unsated, unslacked, insatiable, insatiate.

Phr. Pinched with hunger; greedy as a dog; hungry as a horse; hungry as a hunter; having a sweet tooth; devoured by desire; nothing loth.

Eager, bent on, intent on, aspiring, ambitious, vaulting.

Desirable, desired, desiderated, &c., *see* Pleasing (829).

Int. O for!

Loathing, nauseating, sick of, dog-sick, queasy, sea-sick, abominating, abhorrent

Disliked, disagreeable, unpalatable, unpopular, offensive, loathsome, loathful, sickening, nauseous, nauseating, repulsive, disgusting, detestable, execrable, abhorred (830).

Adv. Disagreeably, &c.

Phr. Usque ad nauseam.

Int. Faugh! foh!

(868) FASTIDIOUSNESS, nicety, daintiness, squeamishness, niceness, difficulty in being pleased, *friandise*, epicurism.

Excess of delicacy, prudery.

V. To be fastidious, &c., to disdain.

Phr. To turn up one's nose at.

Adj. Fastidious, nice, difficult, dainty, squeamish, queasy, squeasy, difficult to please.

(869) SATIETY, repletion, glut, saturation, surfeit.

A spoiled child; *enfant gâté.*

V. To sate, satiate, satisfy, saturate, quench, slake, pall, glut, gorge, surfeit, tire, spoil.

Adj. Satiated, sated, *blasé*, used up.

Phr. Toujours perdrix.

Int. Enough! *Eheu jam satis!*

4°. CONTEMPLATIVE AFFECTIONS.

(870) WONDER, surprise, marvel, astonishment, amazement, wonderment, awe, bewilderment, stound, stupefaction, fascination, *prestige*, thaumaturgy (992), amazedness, &c.

V. To wonder, marvel, be surprised, &c.; to stare, gape, start.

Phr. To open one's mouth or eyes; *tomber des nues;* to stand agog; to stand aghast; not to believe one's eyes; not to account for; not to know whether one stands on one's head or one's heels.

To surprise, astonish, amaze, astound, dumfounder, strike, startle, take by surprise, take aback, strike with wonder, &c., electrify, petrify, confound, stagger belief, stupefy, bewilder, fascinate.

To be wonderful, &c.

(871) Absence of wonder.

EXPECTANCE, expectation (507).

V. To expect, not to be surprised, not to wonder, &c., *nil admirari.*

Phr. To make nothing of.

Adj. Expecting, &c., foreseen, unamazed, astonished at nothing, *blasé* (841).

Common, ordinary, *see* (82).

Phr. To beggar description.

Adj. Surprised, astonished, amazed, astounded, struck, startled, taken by surprise, taken aback, struck dumb, awe-struck, aghast, agape, dumfoundered, flabbergasted, thunderstruck, planet-struck, stupefied, open-mouthed, petrified.

Phr. Struck all of a heap; like a duck in thunder.

Wonderful, wondrous, surprising, astonishing, amazing, astounding, startling, unexpected, unforeseen, strange, uncommon, unheard of, unaccountable, incredible, inexplicable, indescribable, inexpressible, ineffable, unutterable, monstrous, prodigious, stupendous, beggaring description, miraculous, passing strange.

Adv. With wonder, &c., with gaping mouth, all agog.

Int. Lo! heyday! hallo! what! indeed! really! surely! humph! you don't say so! lack-a-daisy! my stars! my goodness! good gracious! gracious goodness! bless us! bless my heart! odzookens! O gemini! hem! dear me! only think! hoity-toity! strong! *Mirabile dictu!* who'd have thought it!

(872) PRODIGY, phenomenon, wonder, marvel, miracle, monster (83), unicorn, phœnix, gazing-stock, curiosity, *rara avis,* lion, sight, spectacle, wonderment, sign, portent (512).

Thunderclap, thunderbolt, bursting of a shell or bomb, volcanic eruption.

5°. Extrinsic Affections.*

(873) REPUTE.

Distinction, note, name, repute, reputation, figure, notoriety, *éclat,* celebrity, fame, famousness, popularity, renown, memory, immortality.

Glory, honor, credit, account, regard, respect, reputableness, respectability, respectableness, illustriousness, gloriousness.

Dignity, stateliness, solemnity, grandeur, splendour, nobleness, lordliness, majesty, sublimity.

Greatness, highness, eminence, supereminence.

Elevation, ascent (305), exaltation, superexaltation, dignification, aggrandizement.

Rank, standing, *pas,* station, place, *status,* order, degree, *locus standi.*

Dedication, consecration, enshrinement, glorification, posthumous fame.

Chief, leader, &c. (745), cock of the roost, *prima donna.*

A star, sun, constellation, galaxy, paragon (650), honor, ornament, mirror.

(874) DISREPUTE, discredit, ingloriousness, derogation, abasement, degradation, odium.

Dishonor, shame, disgrace, slur, scandal, obloquy, opprobrium, ignominy, baseness, turpitude, vileness, infamy.

Tarnish, taint, defilement, pollution.

Stain, blot, spot, blur, stigma, champain, brand, reproach, slur.

Phr. A burning shame; *scandalum magnatum;* a badge of infamy; a blot in one's escutcheon; a byeword of reproach.

V. To be conscious of shame, to feel shame, to blush, to be ashamed, humiliated, humbled, abashed, &c., *see* (879) and (881).

Phr. To feel disgrace; to take shame to oneself; to hide one's face; to look foolish; to hang one's head; to laugh on the wrong side of the mouth; to go away with a flea in one's ear; not to dare to show one's face; to hide its diminished head.

---

* Or personal affections derived from the opinions or feelings of others.

Phr. A halo of glory, a fair name, blushing honors, *aura popularis.*

V. To be conscious of glory, to glory in, to be proud of, *see* (878), to exult, &c. (884), to be vain of (880).

To be glorious, distinguished, &c., to shine, to figure, to make or cut a figure, dash, or splash.

To live, flourish, glitter, flaunt.

Phr. To acquire or gain honor, &c.; to bear the palm; to bear the bell; to win laurels; to make a noise in the world ; to have a run.

To confer or reflect honor, &c., on ; to honor; to do honor to; to redound to one's honor ; *fama volat.*

To pay or render honor, &c. to ; to honor, dignify, glorify, ennoble, nobilitate, exalt, enthrone, signalize, immortalize.

To consecrate, dedicate to, devote to, to enshrine.

Phr. To exalt one's horn ; to exalt to the skies.

Adj. Distinguished, noted, notable, respectable, reputable, notorious, celebrated, famous, famed, far-famed, honored, renowned, popular ; imperishable, immortal, *œre perennius.*

Illustrious, glorious, splendid, bright, brilliant, radiant, full-blown, heroic.

Eminent, prominent, high, preeminent, signalized, exalted, dedicated, consecrated, enshrined.

Great, dignified, proud, noble, worshipful, lordly, grand, stately, august, imposing, transcendant, majestic, sacred, sublime.

To be inglorious, abased, dishonored, &c., to incur disgrace, &c.

Phr. To lose caste.

To cause shame, &c.; to shame, disgrace, put to shame, dishonor, throw, cast, fling or reflect shame, &c. upon, to derogate from.

To tarnish, stain, blot, sully, taint, discredit, degrade, debase, defile.

To impute shame to, to brand, post, stigmatize, vilify, defame, slur.

Phr. To hold up to shame.

To abash, humiliate, humble, dishonor, discompose, disconcert, shame, ashame, put down, confuse, mortify; to obscure, eclipse, outshine.

Phr. To put to the blush; to put out of countenance ; to cast into the shade ; to take out the shine ; to tread or trample under foot.

Adj. Feeling shame, disgrace, &c., ashamed, abashed, &c., disgraced, &c., blown upon, branded, tarnished, &c.

Inglorious, mean, base, &c. (940), shabby, nameless, renownless, unnoticed, unnoted, unhonored.

Shameful, disgraceful, despicable, discreditable, unbecoming, unworthy, disreputable, derogatory, vile, ribald, dishonorable, scandalous, infamous.

Phr. Infra dignitatem ; shorn of its beams ; unknown to fame ; in bad odour ; loaded with shame, infamy, &c.

Int. Fie ! shame ! for shame ! *proh pudor !*

Phr. Redounding to one's honor ; one's name living for ever.

Int. Hail! all hail! *Ave!* Glory be to! honor be to!

(875) NOBILITY, *noblesse,* aristocracy, peerage, gentry, gentility, optimacy, quality, rank, blood, birth, donship, fashionable world, &c. (852), *le beau monde,* distinction, &c.

A personage, man of distinction, rank, &c.; a nobleman, noble, lord, peer, grandee, *magnifico, hidalgo,* don, gentleman, squire, patrician, lordling.

Gentlefolk, squirearchy, *magnates, primates, optimates.*

(876) COMMONALTY, the lower or humbler classes or orders, the vulgar herd, the crowd, the people, the multitude, οι πολλοι, the populace, the million, the mobility, the peasantry.

The mob, rabble, rabble-rout, *canaille;* the scum or dregs of the people, or of society; *fæx populi ; profanum vulgus ;* low company, vermin, nobody.

A commoner, one of the people, a proletary, *prolétaire, roturier ;* a

Prince, duke, marquis, earl, viscount, baron, thane, banneret, baronet, knight, count, armiger, esquire, &c.; nizam, begum, rajah, &c.

V. To be noble, &c.

Adj. Noble, exalted, of rank, titled, patrician, aristocratic, highborn, well-born, genteel, *comme il faut*, gentlemanlike, princely, &c., fashionable, &c. (852).

(877) TITLE, honour, knighthood, &c.

Highness, excellency, grace, lordship, worship, reverence, esquire, sir, master, &c.

Decoration, laurel, palm, wreath, medal, ribbon, cross, star, garter, feather, crest, epaulette, colours, cockade, livery; order, arms, shield, scutcheon.

(878) PRIDE, haughtiness, loftiness, *hauteur*, stateliness, vain-glory, superciliousness, assumption, lordliness, stiffness, primness, crest, arrogance.

A proud man, &c., a highflier.

V. To be proud, &c., to presume, assume, swagger, strut, bridle.

Phr. To look big, toss the head, give oneself airs, hold up one's head, perk oneself up; to take the wall.

To pride oneself on, glory in, pique oneself, plume oneself, to stand upon.

Phr. To put a good face upon.

Adj. Proud, haughty, lofty, high, mighty, high-flown, high-minded, puffed up, flushed, blown, supercilious, disdainful, overweening, consequential, on stilts, swollen, arrogant.

Stately, stiff, starch, prim, perked up, in buckram, strait-laced, vain-glorious, lordly, magisterial, purse-proud.

Unabashed, unblushing, &c.

217

peasant, boor, carle, churl, serf, kern, tyke (or tike), chuff, ryot.

A swain, clown, hind, clodhopper, bog-trotter, bumpkin, ploughman, ploughboy, gaffer, loon, looby, lout, underling, *gamin.*

An upstart, *parvenu*, skipjack, *novus homo*, snob, mushroom.

A beggar, pariah, muckworm, *sans culotte*, raff, tatterdemallion, tag-rag and bobtail, ragamuffin, riff-raff, caitiff.

Phr. A man of straw; nobody one knows.

A Goth, Vandal, Hottentot, savage, barbarian, Yahoo, an unlicked cub.

Barbariousness, barbarism.

V. To be ignoble, &c.

Adj. Ignoble, mean, low, plebeian, vulgar, untitled, homespun, subaltern, underling, homely.

Base, base-born, beggarly, earthborn, rustic, cockney, menial, sorry, scrubby, mushroom, dunghill, vile, uncivilized, loutish, boorish, churlish, rude, brutish, raffish, unlicked, barbarous, barbarian, barbaric.

(879) HUMILITY, humbleness, meekness, lowness, lowliness, affability, condescension, abasement, self-abasement, humiliation, submission, resignation; verecundity, *see* Modesty (881).

V. To be humble, &c.; to condescend, humble, or demean oneself; stoop, submit, knuckle to.

Phr. To lower one's flag; fall on one's knees, &c.; to knock under; to sing small; to eat humble pie; to eat dirt; to pocket an affront; to stoop to conquer.

To render humble; to humble, humiliate, set down, abash, abase, take down, snub.

Phr. To throw into the shade; to put out of countenance; to teach one's distance; to take down a peg lower; to send away with a flea in one's ear.

Adj. Humble, lowly, meek, sober-minded, submissive, resigned, unoffended.

Phr. High and mighty ; on one's high horses ; on one's tight ropes ; proud as a peacock ; proud as Lucifer.

(880) VANITY, conceit, conceitedness, self-conceit, self-confidence, self-sufficiency, self-esteem, self-approbation, self-praise, self-laudation, self-admiration, *amour propre.*

Pretensions, mannerism, egotism, coxcombery, gaudery, vain-glory (943).

A coxcomb, &c., *see* (858).

V. To be vain, &c.

Phr. To have a high or overweening opinion of oneself, one's talents, &c. ; to blind oneself as to one's own merit ; not to think small beer, or *vin ordinaire*, of oneself ; to put oneself forward ; to fish for compliments.

To render vain, &c., to puff up, to inspire with vanity, &c.

Adj. Vain, conceited, overweening, forward, vain-glorious, puffed up, high-flown, inflated, flushed.

Self-satisfied, self-confident, self-sufficient, self-flattering, self-admiring, self-applauding, self-opinioned.

Unabashed, unblushing, unconstrained, unceremonious, free and easy, *sans façon.*

Phr. Vain as a peacock.

Adv. Vainly, &c., ostentatiously, &c. (882), with beat of drum, &c.

Humbled, humiliated, &c.

Phr. Out of countenance ; shorn of one's glory; down on one's knees; humbled in the dust.

(881) MODESTY, humility (879), diffidence, timidity, bashfulness, shyness, coyness, sheepishness, *mauvaise honte*, shamefacedness, blushing, verecundity.

Reserve, constraint, demureness.

V. To be modest, humble, &c. ; to retire, keep in the background, keep private, reserve oneself.

Phr. To draw in one's horns.

Adj. Modest, diffident, humble (879), timid, bashful, timorous, shy, skittish, coy, sheepish, shamefaced, blushing.

Unpretending, unobtrusive, unassuming, unostentatious, unboastful, unaspiring.

Abashed, ashamed, dashed, out of countenance, down in the mouth, chop-fallen, crest-fallen, dumfoundered, flabbergasted.

Reserved, constrained, demure.

Adv. Humbly, &c., quietly, privately, unostentatiously.

Phr. Without beat of drum.

(882) OSTENTATION, display, show, flourish, parade, *étalage*, pomp, state, solemnity, pageantry, dash, splash, glitter, strut, magnificence, pomposity, showing off, *coup de théâtre.*

Flourish of trumpets, *fanfare*, salvo of artillery, salute, *feu de joie.*

Pageant, spectacle, procession, turn out, set out, *fête*, gala, regatta.

Ceremony, ceremonial, mummery ; formality, form, etiquette, punctilio, punctiliousness, *puncto*, frippery, court dress, &c.

V. To be ostentatious, &c. ; to display, *prôner*, exhibit, show off, come forward, put oneself forward, flaunt, emblazon, prink, glitter ; make or cut a figure, dash, or splash.

To observe or stand on ceremony, etiquette, &c.

Adj. Ostentatious, showy, gaudy, gairish (or garish), dashing, flaunting, janty, glittering, pompous, sumptuous, theatrical.

Pompous, solemn, stately, high-sounding, formal, stiff, ceremonious, punctilious.

Phr. Ad captandum vulgus.

Adv. With flourish of trumpets, with beat of drum.

(883) CELEBRATION, jubilee, commemoration, solemnization, ovation, pæan, triumph.

Triumphal arch, bonfire, salute, salvo, *feu de joie*, flourish of trumpets.

Inauguration, installation.

V. To celebrate, keep, signalize, do honour to, pledge, drink to, toast, commemorate, solemnize.

To inaugurate, install.

Adj. Celebrating, &c., in honour of, in commemoration of, &c.

Int. Hail! all hail!

(884) BOASTING, boast, vaunt, vaunting, brag, crake, puff, puffing, puffery, flourish, *fanfaronade*, gasconade, braggardism, bravado, jactitation, venditation, vapouring, rhodomontade, bombast, teratology, *see* Exaggeration (549).

Exultation, gloriation, triumph, flourish of trumpets, *fanfare*, jubilation.

A boaster, braggart, braggadocio, Gascon, *fanfaron*, puppy ; a pretender, *soi-disant*.

V. To boast, make a boast of, brag, vaunt, puff, flourish, crake, crack, strut, swagger.

To exult, croak, crow, neigh, chuckle, triumph.

Phr. To talk big ; *se faire valoir ; faire clacquer son fouet.*

Adj. Boasting, vaunting, &c., vainglorious, braggart.

Elate, elated, flushed, jubilant.

Phr. On stilts ; cock-a-hoop.

(885) Undue assumption of superiority.

INSOLENCE, haughtiness, arrogance, imperiousness, contumeliousness, superciliousness, swagger.

Impertinence, sauciness, pertness, flippancy, dicacity, petulance, malapertness.

Assumption, forwardness, impudence, assurance, front, face, brass, shamelessness, a hardened front, effrontery, audacity, procacity.

V. To be insolent, &c. ; to bluster, vapour, swagger, swell, roister, arrogate, assume.

To domineer, bully, beard, snub, huff, outface, outlook, outstare, outbrazen, bear down, beat down, trample on, tread under foot, outbrave, hector.

Phr. To give oneself airs; to lay down the law ; to put on big looks; to ride the high horse ; to lord it over ; *traiter, ou regarder du haut en bas ;* to ride roughshod over.

(886) SERVILITY, obsequiousness, suppleness, fawning, slavishness, abjectness, prostration, prosternation, genuflexion, &c. (990).

Fawning, mealymouthedness, sycophancy, *see* Flattery (833) and Humility (879).

A sycophant, parasite, toad-eater, toady, spaniel, lickspittle, hanger-on, tufthunter, timeserver, reptile (941).

V. To cringe, bow, stoop, kneel, fall on one's knees, &c.

To sneak, crawl, crouch, truckle to, grovel, fawn.

Phr. To pay court to ; to dance attendance on ; to pin oneself upon ; to hang on the sleeve of.

To go with the stream ; to worship the rising sun ;. to hold with the hare and run with the hounds.

Adj. Servile, obsequious, supple, mean, cringing, fawning, slavish, grovelling, snivelling, beggarly, sycophantic, parasitical, abject.

Adj. Insolent, &c.; haughty, arrogant, imperious, dictatorial, contumelious, supercilious, overbearing, intolerant.

Flippant, pert, cavalier, saucy, forward, impertinent, malapert.

Blustering, swaggering, vapouring, bluff, roistering, rollicking, high-flown, assuming, impudent, brazen, brazen-faced, shameless, unblushing, unabashed.

(887) BLUSTERER, bully, swaggerer, roister, prig, puppy, saucebox, malapert, jackanapes, jack-pudding, jack-in-office, drawcansir, Captain Bobadil, Sir Lucius O'Trigger.

SECTION III.   SYMPATHETIC AFFECTIONS.

1°. SOCIAL AFFECTIONS.

(888) FRIENDSHIP, amity, amicableness, friendliness, brotherhood, fraternity, sodality, confraternity, fraternization, harmony, good understanding, concord (714), *entente cordiale.*

Acquaintance, introduction, intimacy, familiarity, fellowship, welcomeness, favoritism.

V. To be friends, to be friendly, &c., to fraternize, sympathize with (897), to be well with, to befriend (707).

To become friendly, to make friends with.

Phr. To take in good part; to hold out the right hand of fellowship.

Adj. Friendly, amical, amicable, brotherly, fraternal, harmonious, cordial, neighbourly, on good terms, on a friendly, a familiar, or an intimate footing, or on friendly, &c. terms, well-affected, unhostile.

Acquainted, familiar, intimate, thick, hand and glove.

Firm, staunch, intimate, familiar, bosom, cordial, tried, devoted, lasting, fast, warm, ardent.

Adv. Friendly, amicably, &c.

(889) ENMITY, *see* Hate (898) and Discord (713).

Unfriendliness, alienation, estrangement.

Animosity, umbrage, pique, hostility.

V. To be inimical, &c., to estrange, to fall out, alienate.

Adj. Inimical, unfriendly, at variance, at daggers drawn, hostile.

_____

(890) FRIEND, well-wisher, *amicus curiæ, alter ego*, bosom friend, *fidus Achates*, favourer, fautor.

Neighbour, acquaintance, associate, compeer, comrade, companion, *camarade*, messmate, shopmate, crony, chum, boon companion, copesmate, pot-companion, schoolfellow, playfellow, playmate, bedfellow, bedmate.

Arcades ambo, Pylades and Orestes, Castor and Pollux.

Host, Amphitryon, guest, visitor.

(891) ENEMY, foe, opponent, *see* (710), back-friend.

_____

(892) SOCIALITY, sociability, sociableness, companionship, companionableness, consortship, intercommunity.

Conviviality, good fellowship, hospitality, heartiness, welcome, *savoir vivre*, festivity, merry-making.

Society, association, copartnership, fraternity, sodality, coterie, circle, *clique*, party, welcomeness.

Esprit de corps, nepotism (11).

An entertainment, party, levee, *soirée*, *conversazione*, rout, *ridotto*, at home, house-warming, festival (840), interview, assignation, appointment, visit, visiting, reception (588).

V. To be sociable, &c., to associate with, keep company with, to club together, sort with, consort; make, pick, or scrape acquaintance with.

To visit, pay a visit, interchange visits or cards, call upon, leave a card, make advances.

Phr. To beat up one's quarters; to make oneself at home.

To entertain, give a party, rout, &c.; to keep open house; to receive, to welcome.

Adj. Sociable, social, companionable, homiletical, neighbourly, gregarious, conversible, &c., on visiting terms, welcome, hospitable, convivial, festive.

Phr. Free and easy; hail fellow well met.

Adv. En famille; in the family circle.

(894) COURTESY, good manners, good breeding, mannerliness, *bienséance*, urbanity, civilization, politeness, civility, amenity, suavity, good temper, easy temper, gentleness, mansuetude, graciousness, affability, obligingness, *prévenance*, amiability, amability.

Compliment, fair words, soft words, sweet words, salutation, reception, presentation, introduction, *accueil*, greeting, welcome, *abord*, respect, *dévoir*.

(893) SECLUSION, privacy, retirement, recess, retiredness, rustication.

Solitude, singleness, estrangement from the world, loneliness, lonesomeness, isolation.

Wilderness, depopulation.

EXCLUSION, excommunication, banishment, exile, ostracism, cut, cut direct, dead cut, inhospitality, inhospitableness.

A recluse, hermit, cenobite, anchoret (or anchorite), Santom, *solitaire*, pilgarlic, ruralist, outcast.

V. To be secluded, &c., to retire, to live retired, secluded, &c.; to keep aloof; to keep snug; to shut oneself up, deny oneself.

Phr. Aller planter ses choux.

To cut, refuse to associate with or acknowledge; repel, blackball, excommunicate, exclude, banish, exile, ostracize.

Phr. To send to Coventry; to turn one's back upon; look cool upon.

To depopulate, dispeople.

Adj. Secluded, sequestered, retired, private, bye, snug, domestic.

Unsociable, unsocial, isolated, inhospitable, cynical, inconversible.

Solitary, lonesome, isolated, single, estranged, unfrequented.

Unvisited, cut, blackballed, uninvited, unwelcome, friendless, deserted, abandoned, lorn, forlorn.

(895) DISCOURTESY, ill-breeding; ill, bad, or ungainly manners; rusticity, inurbanity, impoliteness, uncourtliness, insuavity, rudeness, incivility, barbarism, misbehaviour, *grossièreté*, roughness, ruggedness, *brusquerie*.

Bad or ill temper, churlishness, crabbedness, tartness, crossness, peevishness, moroseness, sullenness, sulkiness, morosity, acrimony, sternness, austerity, moodishness, asperity, captiousness, sharpness, per-

Obeisance, reverence, bow, curtsey, scrape, salaam, *kotou*, capping, shaking hands, embrace, hug, squeeze, *accolade*, salute, kiss, buss, kissing hands, presenting arms, kneeling, genuflexion, prostration, obsequiousness.

Mark of recognition, nod, pledge, hob and nob.

Valediction, *see* (292).

V. To be courteous, civil, &c., to show courtesy, civility, &c.

To visit, wait upon, present oneself, pay one's respects, kiss hands.

To receive, do the honours, greet, welcome, bid welcome, bid God speed ; hold or stretch out the hand ; shake, press, or squeeze the hand.

To salute, kiss, smack, embrace, hug, drink to, pledge, hob and nob ; to move to, nod to, smile upon, bow, curtsey, scrape, uncover, cap, present arms, take off the hat, &c.

Phr. To make a leg ; to steal a kiss.

To pay homage or obeisance, kneel, bend the knee, prostrate oneself, &c.

To render polite, &c., to polish, civilize, humanize.

Adj. Courteous, civilized, polite, well-bred, well-mannered, mannerly, urbane, gentlemanlike, obliging.

Gracious, affable, familiar, well-spoken, fair-spoken, soft-spoken, fine-spoken, oily, bland, mild, obsequious.

Phr. With open or outstretched arms ; *suaviter in modo.*

Int. Hail !. welcome ! well met ! ave ! all hail !

versity, sauciness, procacity, irascibility, *see* (901).

Sulks, dudgeon, mumps, black looks.

A bear, brute, blackguard, beast.

V. To be rude, &c., frown, scowl, glower, pout ; to cut, insult, &c.

Phr. To turn one's back upon ; to turn on one's heel ; to look black upon ; turn a cold shoulder on.

To render rude, &c., to brutalize.

Adj. Discourteous, uncourteous, uncourtly, ill-bred, ill-mannered, ill-behaved, unmannerly, unmannered, impolite, unpolite, unpolished, ungenteel, ungentlemanlike, unladylike, uncivilized.

Uncivil, rude, ungracious, cool, repulsive, uncomplaisant, unaccommodating, ungainly, unceremonious, ungentle, rough, rugged, bluff, blunt, gruff, churlish, bearish, brutal, *brusque*, stern, harsh, austere,

Ill-tempered, out of temper or humour, cross, crusty, tart, sour, crabbed, sharp, short, snappish, testy, peevish, waspish, captious, grumpy, snarling, caustic, acrimonious, petulant, pert.

Perverse, cross-grained, ill-conditioned, wayward, humoursome, restiff, cantankerous, intractable, curst, froward, sulky, glum, grim, morose, scowling, glowering, surly, sullen, sinistrous, growling, spleenly, spleenish, moody, dogged.

Phr. Cross as a cat ; cross as two sticks ; cross as a dog ; cross as a crab ; surly as a bear ; like a cat in pattens.

Adv. With a bad grace.

(896) CONGRATULATION, felicitation, wishing joy.

V. To congratulate, felicitate, give or wish joy, tender or offer one's congratulations, &c.

Adj. Congratulatory, &c.

(897) LOVE, fondness, liking, inclination, regard, good graces, partiality, predilection, dilection.

Affection, sympathy, fellow-feeling, heart, affectionateness.

Attachment, yearning, amour, passion, tender passion, flame, devo-

(898) HATE, hatred, disaffection, disfavour, alienation, estrangement, odium, *see* Dislike (867) and Animosity (900).

Umbrage, pique, grudge, dudgeon, spleen, bitterness, acrimony, malice (907), implacability.

tion, enthusiasm, enchantment, infatuation, adoration, idolatry.

Cupid, Venus ; the myrtle.

Maternal love, *storge.*

Attractiveness, &c., popularity.

Abode of love ; agapemone.

A lover, suitor, follower, admirer, adorer, wooer, beau, sweetheart, flame, love, truelove, leman, paramour, *amoroso, cicisbeo, caro sposo;* turtledoves.

Inamorata, idol, doxy, Dulcinea, goddess.

Betrothed, affianced, *fiancée.*

V. To love, like, affect, abide, fancy, care for, regard, revere, cherish, admire, dote on, adore, idolize.

To bear love to ; to take to ; to be in love with ; to be taken, smitten, &c. with ; to have, entertain, harbour, cherish, &c. a liking, love, &c. for, *aimer éperdument.*

Phr. To take a fancy to ; to make much of ; to look sweet upon ; to fall in love with ; to set one's affections on ; to lose one's heart ; become enamoured, &c.

To excite love ; to win, gain, secure, &c. the love, affections, heart, &c. ; to take the fancy of ; to attract, attach, seduce, charm, fascinate, captivate, enamour, enrapture.

Disgust, repugnance, aversion, aversation, loathing, abomination, horror, detestation, antipathy, abhorrence.

Object of hatred ; an abomination, aversion, antipathy.

Phr. The phials of hate.

V. To hate, dislike, disrelish, &c. (867), loathe, nauseate, detest, abominate, shudder at, recoil at, abhor.

To excite hatred, estrange, alienate, set against, to be hateful, &c.

Phr. To make one's blood run cold.

Adj. Hating, &c., abhorrent, averse from, set against.

Unloved, disliked, unlamented, undeplored, unmourned, unbeloved, uncared for, unendeared, unvalued.

Crossed in love, forsaken, rejected, lovelorn.

Obnoxious, hateful, odious, repulsive, offensive, shocking, loathsome, sickening, nauseous, disgusting, abominable, horrid.

Invidious, spiteful, malicious.

Insulting, irritating, provoking.

Phr. (Mutual hate ;) there being no love lost between them ; being at daggers drawn.

To get into favour ; to ingratiate oneself, insinuate oneself, curry favour with, pay one's court to, *faire l'aimable.*

Adj. Loving, liking, &c., attached to, fond of, taken with, struck with, sympathetic, sympathizing with, charmed, captivated, fascinated, lovesick, lovelorn.

Affectionate, tender, sweet upon, loving, amorous, amatory, erotic, uxorious, ardent, passionate, devoted.

Phr. Over head and ears in love.

Loved, beloved, &c., dear, darling, favourite (899), pet, popular.

Phr. To one's mind, taste, or fancy ; in one's good graces ; dear as the apple of one's eye ; nearest to one's heart ; the idol of the people.

Lovely, sweet, dear, charming, engaging, amiable, winning, attractive, adorable, enchanting, captivating.

(899) FAVOURITE, pet, cosset, dear, darling, jewel, minion, spoiled child, *enfant gâté.*

Phr. The apple of one's eye.

(900) RESENTMENT, anger, wrath, indignation.

Soreness, dudgeon, moodiness, acerbity, bitterness, asperity, spleen, gall, heartburning, heartswelling, rankling, animosity.

Excitement, irritation, warmth, bile, choler, ire, fume, passion, fit, tantarem (or tantrum), burst, explosion, storm, rage, fury.

Phr. The blood being up; the blood rising; the blood boiling; a towering passion; the phials of wrath.

Temper, petulance, procacity, angry mood, taking, pique, huff, tiff, miff, pet, umbrage.

Cause of umbrage; affront, provocation, offence, indignity, insult (929), *casus belli.*

The Furies; the Eumenides.

V. To resent, take amiss, take offence, take umbrage, take huff, bridle up, bristle up, frown, scowl, lower, snarl, growl, gnarl, snap.

To chafe, mantle, fume, froth up; kindle, get, fall, or fly into a passion, rage, &c.; fly out, take fire, boil, boil over, rage, storm, foam.

Phr. To take in bad part; to take exception; to stick in one's gizzard; *ne pas entendre raillerie;* to stand on one's hind legs; to show one's teeth; to stamp the foot; to foam with rage; to breathe revenge; to cut up rough; to pour out the phials of one's wrath; *" Manet altâ mente repôstum."*

To cause or raise anger; to affront, offend, give offence or umbrage; discompose, fret, ruffle, nettle, irritate, provoke, chafe, wound, sting, incense, inflame, enrage, aggravate, embitter, exasperate.

Phr. To stir up one's bile; to raise one's dander or choler; to work up into a passion.

Adj. Angry, wrath, irate, warm, boiling, fuming, raging, &c., nettled, ruffled, chafed, &c.

Fierce, rageful, furious, infuriate, mad with rage, fiery, savage, rankling, bitter, *acharné*, set against.

Relentless, ruthless, implacable, unpitying, pitiless (919), inexorable, remorseless.

Phr. One's back being up; up in arms; in a stew; the gorge rising; on one's high ropes; *" Tantæne animis celestibus iræ?"*

(901) IRASCIBILITY, susceptibility, excitability, temper, procacity, petulance, irritability, fretfulness, testiness, frowardness, peevishness, snappishness, hastiness, tartness, huffiness, acerbity, protervity, pugnacity, *see* (895).

A shrew, vixen, termagant, virago; a brabbler, a tartar.

V. To be irascible, &c.; to take fire, fire up, flare up, &c., *see* (900).

Adj. Irascible, susceptible, excitable, irritable, fretful, on the fret, fidgetty, peevish, hasty, quick, warm, hot, touchy, testy, techy, pettish, waspish, snappish, petulant, peppery, fiery, passionate, choleric.

Ill-tempered, cross, churlish, sour, crabbed, out of sorts, exceptious, fractious, splenetic, froward, shrewish.

Quarrelsome, querulous, disputatious, cantankerous, sarcastic, resentful, resentive, vindictive, pugnacious.

Phr. Like touchwood or tinder.

(902) Expression of affection or love.

ENDEARMENT, caress, blandishment, blandiment, *épanchement*, fondling, billing and cooing, embrace, salute, kiss, buss, smack, osculation, deosculation.

Courtship, wooing, suit, addresses, flirtation, philandering, gallivanting, serenading.

Love-letter, billet-doux, valentine.

V. To caress, fondle, wheedle, dandle, dally, coddle, cockle, cosset, nestle, clasp, hug, embrace, kiss, salute.

To court, woo, flirt, philander, serenade.

Phr. To make much of; to smile upon; to pat on the cheek; to make love; pay one's court or one's addresses to.

To win the heart, affections, love, &c. of.

Adj. Caressing, &c., caressed, &c.

(903) MARRIAGE, matrimony, wedlock, union, match, intermarriage, coverture, *vinculum matrimonii.*

Wedding, nuptials, Hymen, spousals, espousals; leading to the altar; the torch of Hymen; nuptial benediction, *epithalamium,* the honeymoon.

A married man, a husband, spouse, bridegroom, benedict, neogamist, consort.

A married woman, a wife, bride, mate, helpmate, rib, better half, *feme covert.*

Monogamy, bigamy, digamy, deuterogamy, trigamy, polygamy; a Turk, a Bluebeard.

V. To marry, wed, espouse, wive, to take to oneself a wife.

Phr. To lead to the altar.

To marry, join, give away, handfast.

Phr. To tie the nuptial knot; to give in marriage.

Adj. Matrimonial, conjugal, connubial, nuptial, hymeneal, spousal, bridal, marital.

(904) Unlawful marriage; a left-handed marriage; *mésalliance.*

CELIBACY, singleness, misogamy, single blessedness.

An unmarried man, bachelor, agamist, misogamist.

An unmarried woman, a spinster, maid, maiden, virgin, *feme sole.*

V. To live single.

(905) DIVORCE, separation, widowhood.

A widow, widower, dowager, a *divorcée.*

V. To live separate.

2°. DIFFUSIVE SYMPATHETIC AFFECTIONS.

(906) BENEVOLENCE, good-will, good-nature, kindness, kindliness, benignity, beneficence, charity, humanity, fellow-feeling, sympathy, good-feeling, kindheartedness, amiability, loving-kindness.

Charitableness, bounty, bounteousness, bountifulness, almsgiving.

Acts of kindness, a good turn, kind offices, good treatment.

Phr. The milk of human kindness; the good Samaritan.

V. To be benevolent, &c., to do good to, to benefit, confer a benefit, be of use, aid, assist (707), render a service, treat well, to sympathize with.

Phr. To have one's heart in the right place.

Adj. Benevolent, well-meaning,

(907) MALEVOLENCE, ill-will, unkindness, diskindness, ill-nature, malignity, malice, maliciousness, spite, spitefulness, despite, despitefulness, the evil eye.

Uncharitableness, venom, incompassionateness, gall, rancour, rankling, bitterness, acerbity, harshness, mordacity.

Cruelty, hardness of heart, cruelness, brutality, brutishness, savageness, ferity, ferocity, barbarity, bloodthirstiness, immanity, truculence.

An ill turn, a bad turn.

Phr. A heart of stone.

V. To injure, hurt, harm, molest, disoblige, do harm to, ill-treat, maltreat, do an ill office to.

To worry, harass, oppress, grind,

kind, obliging, accommodating, kind-hearted, tender-hearted, charitable, beneficent, humane, clement, benignant.

Good-natured, well-natured, *bon enfant*, spleenless, sympathising, sympathetic, complacent, complaisant, amiable, gracious.

Kindly, well-meant, well-intentioned.

Adv. With a good intention, with the best intentions.

persecute, hunt down, dragoon, wreak one's malice on, *see* (830).

To bear or harbour malice against.

Phr. To dip or imbrue one's hands in blood.

Adj. Malevolent, evil-minded, ill-intentioned, unbenign, unbenevolent, maleficent, malign, malignant.

Ill-natured, disobliging, inofficious, unfriendly, unkind, uncandid, uncharitable, ungracious, unamiable, unfriendly.

Surly, grim, spiteful, despiteful, ill-conditioned, foul-mouthed, mordacious, *acariâtre*.

Cold, cold-blooded, cold-hearted, hard-hearted, flint-hearted, marble-hearted, stony-hearted.

Pitiless, unpitying, incompassionate, uncompassionate, bowelless, merciless, unmerciful, inexorable, relentless, unrelenting.

Cruel, brutal, savage, untamed, ferine, inhuman, barbarous, fell, ruthless, bloody, bloodstained, bloodthirsty, bloody-minded, truculent.

Fiendish, fiendlike, infernal, demoniacal, diabolical, hellish.

Phr. Betraying the cloven foot, having no bowels.

Adv. Malevolently, &c., with bad intent or intention, despitefully.

(908) MALEDICTION, curse, imprecation, denunciation, execration, anathema, ban, proscription, excommunication, commination (909), fulmination, cursing, scolding, railing, Billingsgate language.

V. To curse, accurse, imprecate, beshrew, scold, rail, execrate, fulminate.

To denounce, proscribe, excommunicate.

Phr. To devote to destruction ; to invoke or call down curses on one's head.

Adj. Cursing, &c., cursed, &c.

Int. Woe to ! beshrew ! *ruat cœlum !*

(909) THREAT, menace, defiance (715), abuse, minacity, intimidation.

V. To threaten, threat, menace, defy, snarl, growl, gnarl, mutter ; to intimidate (860).

Phr. To hurl defiance ; to throw down the gauntlet ; to show one's teeth ; to shake the fist at.

Adj. Threatening, menacing, minatory, minacious, abusive.

(910) PHILANTHROPY, humanity, public spirit.

Patriotism, civism, nationality, love of country, *amor patriæ*.

A philanthropist, utilitarian, cosmopolite, citizen of the world, patriot, *amicus humani generis*.

Adj. Philanthropic, utilitarian, patriotic, &c., public-spirited.

Phr. " *Nihil humanum à me alienum puto ;*" *Pro bono publico.*

(911) MISANTHROPY, egotism, incivism, moroseness, *see* Selfishness (943).

A misanthrope, egotist, cynic, man-hater, woman-hater, misogynist.

Adj. Misanthropic, selfish, egotistical, morose, unpatriotic.

(912) BENEFACTOR, saviour, good genius, tutelary saint, guardian angel, good Samaritan.

Phr. Deliciæ humani generis.

———

(913) Maleficent being.

EVIL DOER, evil worker, mischief-maker, marplot, firebrand, incendiary, evil genius.

Savage, brute, ruffian, barbarian, caitiff, desperado, jail-bird.

Fiend, tiger, hyæna, bloodhound, bloodsucker, hellhound, hellhag, beldam.

Monster, demon, imp, devil (980), anthropophagi, Attila.

Phr. A snake in the grass; a scourge of the human race.

3°. Special Sympathetic Affections.

(914) PITY, compassion, commiseration, sympathy, fellow-feeling, tenderness, yearning.

Forbearance, mercy, clemency, leniency, ruth, long-suffering, quarter, *coup de grâce.*

Phr. The melting mood; bowels of compassion; *Argumentum ad misericordiam.*

V. To pity, commiserate, compassionate, sympathize, feel for, yearn for, enter into the feelings of, have pity, &c.; show or have mercy; to forbear, relent, spare, relax, give quarter.

To excite pity, touch, soften, melt, propitiate.

To ask for pity, mercy, &c.; to supplicate, implore, deprecate, appeal to, cry for quarter, &c.; beg one's life, kneel, fall on one's knees, &c.

Adj. Pitying, commiserating, &c.

Pitiful, compassionate, tender, clement, merciful, lenient, relenting, exorable, &c.; soft-hearted, sympathetic, tender, weak, soft, melting, unhardened.

Phr. Tender as a chicken.

Int. For pity's sake! mercy! cry you mercy! God help you!

(915) CONDOLENCE, lamentation, lament, *see* (839), sympathy, consolation.

V. To condole with, console, sympathize; express, testify, &c. pity; to afford or supply consolation, lament with, weep with, &c. (839).

4°. Retrospective Sympathetic Affections.

(916) GRATITUDE, thankfulness, feeling of obligation.

Acknowledgment, recognition, thanksgiving, giving thanks, benediction.

Thanks, praise, pæan, *Te Deum* (990).

Requital, thank-offering.

V. To be grateful, &c.; to thank, to give, render, return, offer, tender thanks, acknowledgments, &c.; to acknowledge, requite.

To lie under an obligation, to be obliged, beholden, &c., *savoir gré.*

(917) INGRATITUDE, thanklessness, oblivion of benefits.

Phr. "Benefits forgot."

V. To be ungrateful, &c.; to forget benefits.

Phr. To look a gift-horse in the mouth.

Adj. Ungrateful, unmindful, unthankful, thankless.

Forgotten, unacknowledged, unthanked, unrequited, unrewarded.

Phr. Thank you for nothing.

———

Phr. To overflow with gratitude; to thank one's stars.

Adj. Grateful, thankful, obliged, beholden, indebted to, under obligation, &c.

Int. Thanks! many thanks! grammercy! much obliged! thank heaven! heaven be praised!

(918) FORGIVENESS, pardon, condonation, grace, remission, absolution, amnesty, oblivion, indulgence, reprieve.

Reconcilement, reconciliation, shaking of hands, pacification (723).

Excuse, exoneration, quittance, acquittal, propitiation, exculpation.

Longanimity, placability.

Phr. Amantium iræ; locus penitentiæ.

V. To forgive, pardon, excuse, pass over, overlook, forgive and forget, absolve, pass, let off, remit, reprieve, exculpate, exonerate.

To conciliate, propitiate, placate, make it up, reconcile.

To allow for; to make allowance for.

Phr. To heal the breach.

Adj. Forgiving, &c., placable.

Forgiven, &c., unresented.

(919) REVENGE, vengeance, revengement, avengement, avengence, retaliation.

Rancour, vindictiveness, implacability, Nemesis.

V. To revenge, take revenge, avenge.

Phr. To wreak one's vengeance; to visit the sins on; to breathe vengeance; to have a crow to pick with; to have accounts to settle; to have a rod in pickle.

Adj. Revengeful, vindictive, vengeful, rancorous, unforgiving, pitiless, unrelenting, implacable, rigorous.

Phr. "*Æternum servans sub pectore vulnus.*"

(920) JEALOUSY, jealousness.

Phr. A jaundiced eye; the green-eyed monster.

V. To be jealous, &c.; to view with jealousy.

Adj. Jealous, jaundiced, yellow-eyed, unrevenged, hornmad.

(921) ENVY, rivalry; a Zoilus.

V. To envy.

Adj. Envious, invidious.

Phr. Alieni appetens.

SECTION IV. MORAL AFFECTIONS.

1°. MORAL OBLIGATION.

(922) RIGHT, what ought to be, what should be, το πρεπον.

Justice, equity, equitableness, fitness, fairness, fair play, impartiality, reasonableness, propriety.

Astræa, Nemesis; the scales of justice.

Phr. Even-handed justice; *suum cuique;* a clear stage and no favour; a fair field and no favour; *lex*

(923) WRONG, what ought not to be, what should not be.

Injustice, unfairness, foul play, partiality, favour, favoritism, undueness (925), unreasonableness, unlawfulness (964), encroachment, imposition, &c.

V. To be wrong, unjust, &c.; to favour, lean towards, to encroach, impose upon, &c.

talionis ; " Fiat justitia, ruat cœlum."

Morality, morals, &c., *see* Duty (926).

V. To be right, just, &c.

Phr. To see justice done; to hold the scales even; to see fair play; to see one righted; to serve one right; to put the saddle on the right horse; to give the devil his due.

To deserve, merit; to be worthy of, to be entitled to, *see* (924).

Adj. Right, just, equitable, fair, equal, even-handed, legitimate, justifiable, fit, proper, becoming, decorous, &c., *see* Duty (926).

Deserved, merited, condign, entitled to (924).

Adv. Rightly, in justice, in equity, fairly, &c.

Phr. En règle ; selon les règles.

Adj. Wrong, unjust, unfair, undue, inequitable, unequal, partial, unreasonable, unfit, immoral, *see* (945).

Unjustified, unjustifiable, unwarranted, unallowed, unauthorized, unallowable.

Phr. In the wrong; in the wrong box.

Adv. Wrongly, &c.

----

(924) DUENESS, due.

Right, privilege, prerogative, title, claim, licitness, pretension, birthright, immunity, licence, liberty, franchise.

Sanction, authority, warranty, tenure, bond, security, lien, constitution, charter.

A claimant, appellant.

V. To be due, &c. to.

To have a right to, to be entitled to, to have a claim upon, a title to, &c.; to deserve, merit, be worthy of, to deserve richly.

To demand, claim, call upon, exact, insist on, challenge, make a point of, enforce, put in force, use a right.

To appertain to, belong to, &c. (777).

To lay claim to, assert, assume, arrogate, make good, vindicate a claim, &c.

To give or confer a right; to entitle, authorize, warrant, sanction, sanctify, privilege, licence, legalize, ordain, prescribe.

Adj. Having a right to, a claim to, &c.; entitled to, deserving, meriting.

Privileged, allowed, sanctioned, warranted, authorized, permitted, ordained, prescribed.

Prescriptive, presumptive, absolute, indefeasible, unalienable, inalienable, imprescriptible, inviolable.

Condign, merited, deserved.

(925) Absence of right.

UNDUENESS, unlawfulness, impropriety, unfitness.

Falseness, spuriousness, emptiness or invalidity of title, illegitimacy.

Loss of right, disfranchisement.

Usurpation, violation, breach, encroachment, stretch, relaxation.

V. Not to be due, &c. to; to be undue, &c.

To infringe, encroach, violate; to stretch or strain a point; to usurp.

To disfranchise, disentitle; to relax, to disqualify, invalidate.

To misbecome, misbehave (945).

Adj. Undue, unlawful, unmerited, undeserved, unearned.

Unauthorized, unwarranted, unsanctioned, unjustified, unprivileged, illegitimate, spurious, false, usurped, unchartered, unfulfilled.

Unentitled, disentitled, unqualified.

Improper, unmeet, unbecoming, unfit, misbecoming, unseemly.

Phr. Not being the thing.

Allowable, permissible, lawful, legitimate, legal, legalized (963), equitable, unexceptionable, reasonable.

Adv. Ex officio, by divine right, *Dei gratiâ, jure divino.*

(926) DUTY, what ought to be done; moral obligation, accountableness, liability, *onus*, responsibility, bounden duty; dueness.

Allegiance, fealty, tie, office, function, province, post, engagement.

Morality, morals, conscience, accountableness, conscientiousness.

Dueness, το πρεπον, propriety, fitness, seemliness.

The thing, the proper thing, a case of conscience.

Science of morals; Ethics, Deontology, Aretology; Moral or Ethical Philosophy, Casuistry.

Observance, fulfilment, discharge, performance, acquittal, satisfaction, redemption.

V. To be the duty of, to be due to; ought to be; to be incumbent on, to behove, befit, become, beseem, belong to, pertain to, devolve on, to lie on one's head, to owe to oneself.

To be, or stand, or lie under the obligation, to be beholden or indebted to, to have to answer for, to be accountable for.

To impose a duty or obligation; to require, exact, saddle with, prescribe, assign, call upon, look to, oblige; must be.

(927) Dereliction of duty, guilt, &c., *see* (947).

EXEMPTION, freedom, irresponsibility, immunity, liberty, licence, release, exoneration, excuse, dispensation, absolution, franchise, renunciation, discharge.

Non-observance, non-performance, neglect, infraction, violation, transgression, failure, evasion.

V. To be exempt, free, at liberty, released, excused, exonerated, absolved, &c.

To exempt, release, excuse, exonerate, absolve, acquit, free, set at liberty, discharge, set aside, let off, license, dispense with.

To violate, break through, break, infringe, set at naught, slight, neglect, trample on, evade, renounce, repudiate, escape, transgress, fail.

Adj. Exempt, free, released, at liberty, absolved, exonerated, excused, let off, discharged, licensed, acquitted, unincumbered, dispensed, scot free.

Irresponsible, unaccountable, unanswerable, unbound.

To do one's duty, to enter upon a duty; to perform, observe, fulfil, discharge, adhere to; acquit oneself of, satisfy a duty, &c., to redeem one's pledge.

Phr. To be at one's post.

Adj. Obligatory, binding, behoving, incumbent on, chargeable on, meet, due to.

Being under obligation, obliged by, beholden to, bound by, tied by, saddled with, indebted to.

Amenable, liable, accountable, responsible, answerable, lying on one's head.

Right, proper, fit, due, seemly, fitting, befitting, being quite the thing.

Moral, ethical, casuistical, conscientious.

Phr. In foro conscientiæ.

2°. MORAL SENTIMENTS.

(928) RESPECT, deference, reverence, honor, esteem, distance, decorum, veneration.

(929) DISRESPECT, irreverence, dishonor, disparagement, slight, neglect, disesteem, superciliousness,

Homage, fealty, obeisance, genu-flexion, kneeling, salaam, *kotou*, pre-senting arms, &c., *see* (896), pros-tration, *égards*, obsequiousness, de-votion, worship (990).

V. To respect, honor, reverence, defer to, pay respect, deference, &c. to, render honor to, look up to, es-teem, revere, to think much of, to think highly of, to venerate.

To pay homage to, kneel to, bend the knee to, present arms, fall down before, prostrate oneself.

Phr. To keep one's distance.

Adj. Respecting, &c., respectful, reverential, obsequious, ceremonious, bareheaded, cap in hand, &c.

Int. Hail! all hail! *Esto per-petua!*

vilipendency, contumely, indignity, insult.

Ridicule (856), derision, mockery, scoffing, sibilation.

A jeer, gibe, hiss, hoot, fling, flout, grin; *see* Contempt (940).

V. To treat with disrespect, &c., to disparage, dishonor, misprize, vilipend, slight, disregard, make light of, hold in no esteem, esteem of no account, set at naught, speak slightingly of, set down, pass by, overlook, look down upon, *see* (930).

To deride, scoff, sneer at, laugh at, ridicule (856), mock, jeer, taunt, hiss, hoot, make game of, point the finger at, make a fool of, turn into ridicule.

Adj. Disrespectful, slighting, dis-paraging, dishonoring, &c., scorn-ful (940), irreverent, supercilious, contumelious, deriding, derisive.

Unrespected, unregarded, disregarded, unsaluted.

Adv. Disrespectfully, cavalierly, &c.

(930) CONTEMPT, despisal, despiciency, vilipendency, disdain, scorn, contumely, slight, sneer, spurn; a byeword.

Scornfulness, disdainfulness, haughtiness, contemptuousness.

The state of being despised; despisedness.

Phr. "*Spretæ injuria formæ.*"

V. To despise, contemn, scorn, disdain, scout, spurn, look down upon, disregard, slight, make light of, hold cheap, hold in contempt, pooh-pooh, sneeze at, whistle at, hoot, flout, kick, trample upon.

Phr. Not to care a straw, fig, button, &c. for, *see* (643); to turn up one's nose at; to shrug one's shoulders; to snap one's fingers at; to turn a cold shoulder upon; to laugh to scorn; to take the shine out of; to tread or trample under foot; *traiter du haut en bas.*

Adj. Contemptuous, disdainful, scornful, derisive, supercilious.

Contemptible, despicable, poor, &c., *see* (643).

Phr. A fig for! pish! fudge! pooh-pooh! fiddlestick! fiddle-de-dee!

(931) APPROBATION, approval, approvement, esteem, estimation, good opinion, appreciation, regard, account, popularity.

Commendation, praise, laud, good word; meed or tribute of praise, encomium, eulogium, eulogy, *éloge*, panegyric.

Laudation, applause, plaudit, clap, clapping, clapping of hands, accla-mation; pæan, benediction, blessing, benison.

(932) DISAPPROBATION, disap-proval, blame, censure, odium, dis-placency, disesteem, disvalue, depre-ciation, detraction, condemnation, ostracism.

Reprobation, improbation, expro-bation, insinuation, animadversion, stricture, objection, exception, criti-cism, *critique*, correction, discom-mendation.

Satire, sneer, fling, wipe, gibe, skit, squib, quip, taunt, quib, sar-

Phr. A peal, shout, or chorus of applause.

V. To approve, think well of, think good or highly of, esteem, appreciate, value, admire, countenance.

To commend, speak well of, recommend, praise, laud, compliment, bepraise, clap, clap hands, applaud, panegyrize, eulogize, cry up, extol, glorify, magnify, exalt, swell, hosannah, bless, give a blessing to.

Phr. To sing the praises of; to extol to the skies; to ring with the praises of.

To deserve praise, &c., to be praised, &c.

Phr. To win golden opinions; *laudari à laudato viro.*

Adj. Approving, &c., commendatory, complimentary, benedictory, laudatory, panegyrical, eulogistic, encomiastic.

Approved, praised, uncensured, admired, &c., deserving or worthy of praise, &c., praiseworthy, commendable, plausible.

Phr. Probatum est.

Int. Well done! *bravo! bravissimo! viva! euge! macte!*

---

casm, lampoon, cavil, pasquinade, invective, castigation.

Remonstrance, reprehension, reproof, admonition, expostulation, reproach, rebuke, reprimand.

Evil speaking, hard words, foul language, sauce, Billingsgate language.

Upbraiding, abuse, vituperation, scolding, objurgation, railing, jobation, increpation, reviling, contumely.

A set down, trimming, slap, frown, scowl, black look.

A lecture, curtain lecture, blow up, *diatribe*, jeremiade, *tirade*, philippic; clamour, outcry, hue and cry, hiss, hissing, sibilation.

A scold, shrew, vixen.

Phr. A rap on the knuckles; *un coup de bec*; a slap on the face.

V. To disapprove, dispraise, find fault with, criticize, glance at, insinuate, cut up, carp at, cavil, point at, peck at, nibble at, object to, take exception to, *fronder*, animadvert upon, protest against, frown upon.

To disparage, depreciate, disvalue, speak ill of, avile, decry, vilify, vilipend, defame, detract, *see* (934), revile, satirize, smoke, sneer, gibe, lampoon, inveigh against.

To blame; lay or cast blame upon; to reflect upon; to censure; pass censure on; impugn, censure, brand, stigmatize, reprobate, exprobate.

To reprehend, admonish, remonstrate, expostulate, reprove, pull up, take up, set down, snub, twit, taunt, reprimand, reproach, load with reproaches, rebuke.

To chide, scold, rate, objurgate, upbraid, vituperate, abuse, call names, exclaim against, jaw, mob, trounce, trim, rail at, bark at, revile, blow up, roast, lecture; castigate, chastise, lash.

To cry out against, cry down, run down, clamour, hiss, hoot; to accuse, *see* (938).

Phr. To set one's face against; to view with dark or jaundiced eyes; to bend or knit the brows; to pick a hole in; to pluck a crow with; to have a fling at; to read a lecture; to take to task; to bring to book; to call over the coals; to give a rap on the knuckles; to pick to pieces; to cast in one's teeth; to abuse like a pickpocket; *laver la tête.*

To incur blame; to excite disapprobation; to scandalize, shock, revolt.

Phr. To forfeit the good opinion of.

To take blame; to stand corrected.

Adj. Disapproving, &c., condemnatory, damnatory, reproachful, abusive, objurgatory, clamorous, vituperative.

Censorious, critical, carping, satirical, sarcastic, cynical, hypercritical, captious, sharp ; severe, squeamish, fastidious, straitlaced, &c. (868).

Phr. *Omnia suspendens naso.*

Disapproved, &c., unapproved, blown upon, unblest, unlamented, unbewailed, &c.

Worthy of blame, uncommendable, exceptionable, *see* (649, 945).

Int. Out upon it ! *O tempora, O mores !*

(933) FLATTERY, adulation, sycophancy, blandishment, cajolery, fawning, wheedling, coaxing, flunkeyism, toadeating, blandiloquence.

Incense, honeyed words, flummery, soft sawder, blarney, *placebo.*

V. To flatter, wheedle, cajole, fawn upon, coax, humour, glose, glaver, butter, bespatter, beslaver, earwig, cog, collogue, pander (or pandar) to, court, pay court to.

Phr. To curry favour with ; to lay it on thick ; to lick the dust ; to lay the flattering unction to the soul.

Adj. Flattering, adulatory, mealy-mouthed, smooth, oily, unctuous, fair spoken, servile, sycophantic ; courtierly, courtier-like.

(935) FLATTERER, eulogist, encomiast, whitewasher, toady, sycophant, toadeater, *flaneur, proneur,* touter, *claqueur,* spaniel, clawback, flunkey, lickspittle, pick-thank, earwig, hanger-on, courtier, parasite, doer of dirty work, *âme damnée.*

(937) VINDICATION, reply, justification, exoneration, exculpation, acquittal, whitewashing.

Extenuation, palliation, softening.

Plea, excuse, apology, defence, gloss, varnish, salvo (617).

V. To vindicate, justify, exculpate, acquit, clear, set right, exonerate, disculpate, whitewash.

To extenuate, palliate, excuse, apologize, varnish, slur, gloss over.

To plead, advocate, defend, stand up for, speak for, make good, vindicate, say in defence, contend for, propugn.

(934) DETRACTION, obloquy, scurrility, defamation, aspersion, traducement, slander, calumny, backbiting.

Libel, lampoon, skit, sarcasm.

V. To detract, asperse, depreciate, blow upon, bespatter, blacken, defame, malign, backbite, libel, lampoon, traduce, slander, calumniate.

Phr. To speak ill of one behind one's back.

Adj. Detracting, &c., libellous, scurrilous, scurrile, foul-tongued, foul-mouthed, slanderous, defamatory, calumnious.

(936) DETRACTOR, disapprover, critic, censor, caviller, carper, *frondeur,* defamer, backbiter, slanderer traducer, libeller, calumniator.

(938) ACCUSATION, charge, imputation, inculpation, exprobation, crimination, accrimination, recrimination, invective, jeremiade, &c. (932).

Denunciation, denouncement, challenge, indictment, libel, delation, citation, arraignment, impeachment, appeachment, bill of indictment, *scandalum magnatum.*

Phr. The gravamen of a charge ; *argumentum ad hominem.*

V. To accuse, charge, tax, impute, twit, taunt with, slur, reproach, criminate, inculpate, &c., *see* (932).

To inform against ; to indict, de-

Phr. To put in a good word for; to put a good face upon; to help a lame dog over a style; to take the will for the deed.

Adj. Vindicatory, exculpatory; vindicating, &c.

Excusable, defensible, pardonable, venial, specious, plausible, justifiable.

nounce, arraign, impeach, appeach, challenge, show up, pull up, cite, summons.

Phr. To lay to one's door; to lay to one's charge; to throw in one's teeth; to call to account; to bring to book; to take to task; to pick a hole in one's coat; to catch tripping; to put in the black book; to trump up a charge; to keep a rod in pickle for.

Adj. Accusing, &c., accusatory, accusative, imputative, criminatory, accusable, imputable.

Indefensible, inexcusable, unpardonable, unjustifiable.

3°. MORAL CONDITIONS.

(939) PROBITY, integrity, uprightness, honesty, faith, good faith, fairness, honor, fair play, justice, principle, fidelity, incorruptibility.

Trustworthiness, trustiness, grace, uncorruptedness, impartiality, equity, candour, veracity (545), straightforwardness, truth, equitableness, singleness of heart.

Conscientiousness, punctiliousness, nicety, scrupulosity, punctuality.

Dignity, reputableness, *see* (873).

A man of honor, a gentleman, a man of his word, a truepenny, *preux chevalier.*

Phr. The court of honor; *Argumentum ad verecundiam.*

V. To be honorable, &c.; to keep one's word; to deal honorably, squarely, impartially, fairly, &c.

Phr. To give the devil his due.

Adj. Upright, honest, honorable, fair, right, just, equitable, impartial, evenhanded, square, loyal, *see* (944).

Trustworthy, trusty, uncorrupt, straightforward, ingenuous (703), frank, open-hearted.

Conscientious, tender-conscienced, high-principled, high-minded, scrupulous, nice, punctilious, punctual, inviolable, inviolate, unviolated, unbroken.

Chivalrous, gentlemanlike, unbought, unbribed, unstained, stainless, untarnished, unsullied, untainted, unperjured (946).

(940) IMPROBITY, bad faith, unfairness, infidelity, faithlessness, want of faith, dishonesty, disloyalty, onesidedness, disingenuousness, shabbiness, littleness, meanness, baseness, vileness, abjection, turpitude, mouth honor, insidiousness, knavery, knavishness, fraud, &c. (545).

Disgrace, ignominy, infamy, tarnish, blot, stain, spot, slur, pollution, derogation, degradation, &c., *see* Dishonor (874).

Perfidy, perfidiousness, treason, high treason, perjury, *punica fides,* apostacy, backsliding, breach of faith, defection, disloyalty, foul play, double dealing, disingenuousness.

V. To be of bad faith, dishonest, &c.; to play false, break one's word, faith, &c., betray, forswear, shuffle (545).

To disgrace oneself, stoop, demean oneself, lose cast.

Phr. To seal one's infamy.

Adj. Dishonest, unfair, fraudulent, knavish, false, faithless, unfaithful, foul, trothless, trustless, slippery, double, crooked, unscrupulous, insidious, treacherous, perfidious, falsehearted, perjured.

Base, vile, grovelling, dirty, scurvy, scabby, low, mean, paltry, pitiful, scrubby, beggarly, putid, indign, disgraceful, dishonorable, derogatory, low-thoughted, disreputable, unhandsome, unbecoming, unbefitting, un-

234

Phr. Jealous of honor ; as good as one's word ; *sans tache et sans reproche.*

Adv. Honorably, &c., *bonâ fide.*

gentlemanlike, base-minded, recreant, low-minded.

Phr. Double-tongued ; lost to shame ; dead to honor ; *Parthis mendacior.*

Adv. Dishonestly, &c., *malâ fide.*

(941) KNAVE, truant, trimmer, time-server, time-pleaser, turncoat, turn-tippet, Vicar of Bray.

Apostate, renegade, traitor, archtraitor, recreant, miscreant, cullion, mean wretch, *âme de boue,* slubberdegullion.

(942) DISINTERESTEDNESS, generosity, high-mindedness, nobleness, elevation, liberality, greatness, loftiness, exaltation, magnanimity, chivalry, chivalrous spirit, heroism, sublimity.

Self-denial, self-abnegation, self-sacrifice, devotion, stoicism.

Adj. Disinterested, generous, unselfish, handsome, liberal, noble, great, high, high-minded, elevated, lofty, exalted, spirited, stoical, self-devoted, magnanimous, chivalrous, heroic, sublime.

Unbought, unbribed, pure, uncorrupted, incorruptible.

(943) SELFISHNESS, egotism, self-love, self-indulgence, worldliness, earthly-mindedness.

Illiberality, meanness, baseness.

A time-server, tuft-hunter, fortune-hunter, jobber, worldling.

V. To be selfish, &c., narrow-minded.

Phr. To look after one's own interest ; to take care of number one.

Adj. Selfish, egotistical, egoistical, illiberal, mean, ungenerous, narrow-minded.

Worldly, earthly, mundane, time-serving, worldly-minded.

Phr. The dog in the manger ; *après nous le déluge.*

(944) VIRTUE, goodness, righteousness, morality, morals, rectitude, correctness, dutifulness, conscientiousness, integrity, probity (939), uprightness, nobleness.

Merit, worth, worthiness, desert, excellence, credit, self-control, self-conquest, self-government.

Well-doing, good actions, the discharge, fulfilment, or performance of duty ; a well-spent life.

V. To be virtuous, &c. ; to act well ; to do, fulfil, perform, or discharge one's duty, to acquit oneself, to practise virtue ; to command or master one's passions, *see* (926).

Phr. To have one's heart in the right place ; to keep in the right path.

Adj. Virtuous, good, meritorious, deserving, worthy, desertful, correct, dutiful, duteous, moral, righteous, &c., *see* (939), laudable, well-intentioned, praiseworthy, excellent, admirable, sterling, pure, noble.

(945) VICE, wickedness, sin, iniquity, unrighteousness, demerit, unworthiness, worthlessness.

Immorality, incorrectness, impropriety, indecorum, laxity, looseness of morals, want of principle, obliquity, backsliding, gracelessness, demoralization, depravity, obduracy, hardness of heart, brutality, corruption, pollution, dissoluteness, grossness, baseness, roguery, rascality, villany, profligacy, flagrancy, atrocity.

Criminality, &c., *see* Guilt (947).

Infirmity, weakness, feebleness, frailty, imperfection, error, weakside, blind-side, foible, failing, failure, defect, deficiency, indiscretion, peccability.

Phr. The cloven foot ; the lowest dregs of vice ; a sink of iniquity.

V. To be vicious, &c. ; to sin, commit sin, do amiss, misdo, err, transgress, go astray, misdemean or misconduct oneself, misbehave ; to fall, lapse, slip, trip, offend, trespass.

Exemplary, matchless, peerless, saintly, saint-like, heaven-born, angelic, seraphic, godlike.

Phr. Above or beyond all praise ; *mens sibi conscia recti.*

Adv. Virtuously, &c.

Phr. To deviate from the line of duty, or from the paths of virtue, rectitude, &c.; to hug a sin or fault ; to sow one's wild oats.

Adj.* Vicious, sinful, wicked, unprincipled, demoralized, unconscionable, worthless, unworthy, good for nothing, graceless, heartless, virtueless, immoral, unduteous.

Wrong, culpable, guilty, naughty, incorrect, criminal, dissolute, corrupt, profligate, depraved, abandoned, graceless, shameless, recreant, villanous, sunk, lost, obdurate, incorrigible, irreclaimable.

Weak, frail, lax, infirm, imperfect, indiscreet, erring, transgressing, sinning, &c., peccable.

Blamable, blameworthy, uncommendable, discreditable, disreputable, exceptionable.

Indecorous, unseemly, sinister, base, foul, vile, black, felonious, nefarious, scandalous, infamous, villanous, heinous, grave, flagrant, atrocious, satanic, diabolic, hellish, infernal, stygian, fiend-like, miscreated, misbegotten, hell-born, demoniacal.

Unpardonable, indefensible, inexcusable, irremissible, inexpiable.

Phr. Contra bonos mores ; of a deep dye.

Adv. Wrong, &c. ; without excuse.

(946) INNOCENCE, guiltlessness, inculpableness, harmlessness, innocuousness, incorruption, impeccability, blamelessness, sinlessness.

A lamb.

V. To be innocent, &c.

Phr. Nil conscire sibi, nullâ pallescere culpâ.

Adj. Innocent, guiltless, unguilty, faultless, sinless, clear, spotless, stainless, immaculate, unspotted, innocuous, unblemished, untarnished, unsullied, undefiled.

Inculpable, unculpable, unblamed, blameless, irreproachable, irreprovable, irreprehensible, unreproached, unimpeachable, unimpeached, unexceptionable, inerrable, unerring.

Harmless, inoffensive, dovelike, lamblike, pure, uncorrupted, undefiled, undepraved, undebauched, unhardened, unreproved.

Adv. Innocently, &c., with clean hands, with a clear conscience.

(947) GUILT, guiltiness, culpability, criminality, criminousness, sinfulness.

Misconduct, misbehaviour, misdoing, malpractice, malefaction, misprision, deviation from rectitude, dereliction.

Indiscretion, *peccadillo*, lapse, slip, trip, *faux pas*, fault, error, flaw, blot, omission.

Misdeed, offence, trespass, transgression, misdemeanour, delinquency, felony, sin, crime, enormity, atrocity.

(948) SAINT, lamb, worthy, example, pattern, mirror, model, paragon, phœnix, *rara avis*, hero, demigod, seraph, angel, see Perfection (650)..

(949) SINNER, evil-doer, culprit, delinquent, criminal, malefactor, wrong-doer, outlaw, felon, convict, outcast.

Knave, rogue, rascal, scoundrel, scamp, scapegrace, varlet, *vaurien,*

---

* Most of these adjectives are applicable both to the act and to the agent.

blackguard, loose fish, vagabond, *mauvais sujet*, sad dog, *drôle de corps*, jade, raff, rascallion, rapscallion, slubberdegullion, cullion, roister, reprobate, *roué*, recreant, *guet-a-pens*, villain, outlaw, outcast, ruffian, miscreant, caitiff, wretch, *âme damnée*, castaway, monster.

Cur, dog, hound, viper, serpent, cockatrice, basilisk, reptile, urchin, tiger, imp, demon, devil, devil incarnate, cannibal, Mephistophiles (978), Jezabel, hellhound, hangman, cut-throat, *particeps criminis*.

Int. Sirrah!

(950) PENITENCE, contrition, compunction, regret (833), repentance, remorse.

Self-reproach, self-reproof, qualms or prickings of conscience.

Confession, acknowledgment, shrift, apology, *peccavi, locus penitentiæ, meâ culpâ.*

Phr. The stool of repentance; the cutty stool.

V. To repent, regret, rue, repine, deplore.

Phr. To plead guilty; to sing *miserere;* to cry *peccavi;* to eat humble pie; to turn over a new leaf.

To confess, acknowledge, apologize, to shrive, humble oneself, to reclaim, to turn from sin.

Adj. Penitent, repentant, contrite, repenting, &c.

Not hardened, unhardened, reclaimed.

Adv. In sackcloth and ashes, &c.

(951) IMPENITENCE, obduracy, recusance, hardness of heart, a seared conscience, induration, irrepentance.

V. To be impenitent, &c.; to steel or harden the heart.

Adj. Impenitent, uncontrite, obdurate, hard, hardened, seared, recusant, relentless, unrepentant, graceless, shriftless, lost, incorrigible, irreclaimable, unatoned, unreclaimed, unreformed, unrepented.

(952) ATONEMENT, reparation, compromise, composition, compensation (30), quittance, quits; propitiation, expiation, redemption.

Amends, apology, *amende honorable*, satisfaction, peace-offering, sin-offering, scapegoat, sacrifice.

Penance, fasting, maceration, sackcloth and ashes, white sheet, lustration, purgation, purgatory.

V. To atone, expiate, propitiate, make amends, redeem, make good, absolve, do penance, apologize, purge.

Phr. To wipe off old scores.

Adj. Propitiatory, piacular, expiatory.

4°. MORAL PRACTICE.

(953) TEMPERANCE, moderation, forbearance, abnegation, self-denial, self-conquest, self-control, sobriety, frugality.

Abstinence, abstemiousness, system of Pythagoras.

V. To be temperate, &c.; to ab-

(954) INTEMPERANCE, epicurism sensuality, luxury, animalism, pleasure, effeminacy, silkiness; the lap of pleasure or luxury; indulgence, inabstinence, self-indulgence, voluptuousness.

Excess, dissipation, licentiousness,

stain, forbear, refrain, deny oneself, spare.

Adj. Temperate, moderate, sober, frugal, sparing, abstemious, abstinent, Pythagorean, vegetarian.

———

debauchery, dissoluteness, crapulence, brutishness, revels, debauch, orgies.

Phr. The Circean cup ; system of Epicurus ; the swine of Epicurus.

V. To be intemperate, sensual, &c.

To indulge, exceed, revel ; give a loose to indulgence, sensuality, &c. ; to wallow in voluptuousness, luxury, &c. ; to plunge into dissipation.

To pamper, pander (or pandar), slake.

Adj. Intemperate, sensual, pampered, self-indulgent, inabstinent, licentious, wild, dissolute, rakish, debauched, brutish, crapulous, Epicurean, Sybaritical, voluptuous, swinish.

Indulged, pampered, milksop.

A Sybarite, a debauchee, a man of pleasure, voluptuary, rake, *roué*, a votary of Epicurus, pig, hog, swine, *see* (962).

(955) Asceticism, austerity, mortification, maceration, sackcloth and ashes, flagellation, &c., martyrdom.

An ascetic, anchorite, anchoret, martyr ; a recluse, hermit, &c. (893).

Adj. Ascetic, puritanical.

(956) Fasting, fast, spare diet, Lent, *jour maigre*, a lenten entertainment, famishment, starvation, banyan-day, Ramadan (or Ramazan), a Barmecide feast.

V. To fast, starve.

Phr. To dine with Duke Humphrey.

Adj. Fasting, &c., unfed.

(957) Gluttony, epicurism, greediness, good cheer, high living, edacity, voracity, gulosity, crapulence.

A glutton, epicure, *bon vivant*, cormorant, *gourmand*, hog, bellygod, Apicius.

V. To gormandize, gorge, stuff, guttle, pamper.

Adj. Gluttonous, greedy, gormandizing, edacious, crapulent, swinish, pampered.

(958) Sobriety, teetotalism, hydropathy.

A water-drinker, teetotaler (or teetotalist), hydropathist.

V. To take the pledge.

Adj. Sober.

Phr. Sober as a judge.

———

(959) Drunkenness, insobriety, ebriety, inebriety, inebriation, intoxication, ebriosity, temulency, bibacity, drinking, toping, tippling, sottishness, bacchanals, compotation.

A drunkard, sot, toper, tippler, bibber, wine-bibber, soaker, tun, toss-pot, reveller, carouser, Bacchanal, Bacchanalian, Bacchal, Bacchante, a devotee to Bacchus.

V. To drink, tipple, tope, booze (or bouse) ; to guzzle, swill, carouse, get drunk, &c ; to take to drinking, &c.

To inebriate, intoxicate, fuddle, fuzzle.

Phr. To get into the head.

Adj. Drunk, drunken, tipsy, intoxicated, in liquor, inebriated, temulent, temulentive, fuddled, mellow, cut, boosy, fou, fresh, flush, flushed, flustered, groggy, topheavy, potvaliant, potulent, overcome, overtaken, whittled, screwed, corned, sewed up, lushy, nappy, muddled, muzzy, maudlin, dead drunk, disguised.

Bibacious, sottish, bacchanal, bacchanalian.

Phr. In one's cups ; the worse for liquor ; half seas over ; under the table ; drunk as a piper ; drunk as a fiddler ; drunk as a lord ; drunk as Chloe ; drunk as an owl.

(960) PURITY, modesty, decency, decorum, delicacy, continence, chastity.

A vestal, a virgin, a Joseph.

Adj. Pure, modest, delicate, decent, decorous.

Chaste, continent, Platonic, honest.

---

(961) IMPURITY, immodesty, grossness, coarseness, indelicacy, impudicity, indecency, obscenity, ribaldry, smut, obsceneness, smuttiness, bawdiness, bawdry, *double entendre, équivoque.*

Concupiscence, lust, carnality, flesh, salacity, lewdness, pruriency, lechery, lasciviousness, lasciviency, voluptuousness, lubricity.

Incontinence, intrigue, gallantry, debauchery, libertinism, *libertinage,* fornication, *liaison,* wenching.

Seduction, defloration, violation, rape, adultery, incest, harlotry, stupration.

A seraglio, harem, brothel, bagnio, stew, bawdy-house.

V. To intrigue, &c.

Adj. Impure, immodest, indecorous, indelicate, indecent, loose, coarse, gross, broad, equivocal, nasty, smutty, fulsome, ribald, obscene, bawdy.

Concupiscent, prurient, lickerish, rampant, carnal, lustful, lascivious, lecherous, libidinous, erotic, ruttish, salacious.

Unchaste, light, wanton, debauched, dissolute, carnal-minded, riggish, incontinent, meretricious, rakish, gallant, dissipated, adulterous, incestuous.

Phr. On the town, on the *pavé ;* who is no better than she should be.

(962) A LIBERTINE, voluptuary, man of pleasure, rake, debauchee, *intrigant,* gallant, seducer, fornicator, lecher, satyr, whoremonger, cuckold, *palliard,* adulterer.

A courtesan, strumpet, harlot, whore, punk, *fille de joie,* woman of the town, street-walker, piece, the frail sisterhood, loose fish, demirep, wench, trollop, trull, baggage, hussey, drab, rig, quean, mopsy, minx, harridan, Jezabel, Messalina.

Concubine, mistress, doxy, *chère amie.*

Pimp, pander (or pandar), bawd, *conciliatrix,* procuress.

5°. INSTITUTIONS.

(963) LEGALITY, legitimateness, legitimacy.

Law, code, constitution, pandect, enactment, edict, statute, rule, order, ordinance, injunction, precept, regulation, decree, firman, bull, ukase.

Legal process, form, formula, formality, rite.

---

(964) Absence or violation of law.

ILLEGALITY, arbitrariness, antinomy, violence, brute force, despotism, despoticalness.

Mob law, lynch law, club law.

Phr. La loi du plus fort ; argumentum bacculinum.

Science of law ; Jurisprudence, Legislation, Codification.

Equity, common law, *lex non scripta*, *lex scripta*, law of nations, international law, *jus gentium*.

V. To enact, ordain, enjoin, prescribe, order ; to pass a law, issue an edict or decree ; to legislate, codify.

Adj. Legal, according to law, legitimate, constitutional.

Legislative, statutable, statutory.

Adv. Legally, &c.

Phr. In the eye of the law.

Informality, unlawfulness, illegitimacy.

Smuggling, poaching.

V. To smuggle, run, poach.

Phr. To take the law into one's own hands ; to set the law at defiance.

Adj. Illegal, unlawful, illicit, illegitimate, unauthorized, unconstitutional, informal, contraband.

Arbitrary, extrajudicial, despotic, irresponsible, unanswerable, unaccountable.

Phr. The law being a dead letter.

(965) JURISDICTION, judicature, soc, administration of justice.

The executive ; municipality, magistracy, police, police force.

Sheriff, constable, bailiff, tipstaff, bum-bailiff, catchpoll, beadle.

Sbirri, alguazil, *gendarme*, lictor, macebearer.

Adj. Juridical, judicial, forensic, municipal, executive, administrative, inquisitorial, causidical.

(966) TRIBUNAL, court, guild, board, bench, judicatory, court of law, court of justice, justice-seat, judgment-seat, mercy-seat, star-chamber, durbar, bar, dock, forum, hustings, drum-head, woolsack, jury-box, witness-box.

Assize, sessions, eyre, court-martial, wardmote, bailiwick.

(967) JUDGE, justice, chancellor, magistrate, arbiter, arbitrator, umpire, referee.

Mollah, ulema, cadi or (kadi).

Prosecutor, plaintiff, accuser, appellant.

Defendant, panel, prisoner, the accused.

(968) LAWYER, the bar, advocate, counsellor, counsel, pleader, special pleader, conveyancer, bencher, proctor, civilian, barrister, jurist, equity draughtsman, attorney, solicitor, marshal.

Phr. The gentlemen of the long robe ; the learned in the law ; a limb of the law.

(969) LAWSUIT, suit, action, cause, trial.

Denunciation, citation, arraignment, prosecution, indictment, impeachment, apprehension, arrest, committal, imprisonment, *see* (751).

Pleadings, writ, summons, subpœna, plea, bill, affidavit, &c.

Verdict, sentence, judgment, finding, decree, arbitrament, adjudication, award, *plébiscite*.

V. To go to law ; to take the law of ; to appeal to the law ; to join issue ; file a bill, file a claim.

To denounce, cite, apprehend, sue, prosecute, bring to trial, indict, attach, distrain, to commit, give in charge or custody ; throw into prison.

To try, hear a cause, sit in judgment.

To pronounce, find, judge, sentence, give judgment ; bring in a verdict ; doom, to arbitrate, adjudicate, award, report.

Phr. Adhuc sub judice lis est.

(970) ACQUITTAL, acquitment, absolution, *quietus, see* Pardon (918), clearance, discharge, release, reprieve, respite.

Exemption from punishment ; impunity.

V. To acquit, absolve, whitewash, clear, assoil, discharge, release, reprieve, respite.

Adj. Acquitted, &c.

Uncondemned, unpunished, unchastised.

(971) CONDEMNATION, conviction, proscription, damnation.

Attainder, attainture, attaintment.

V. To condemn, convict, cast, find guilty, proscribe, attaint, damn.

Adj. Condemnatory, &c.

(972) PUNISHMENT, punition, chastisement, castigation, correction, chastening, discipline, infliction.

Retribution, requital, reward (973), Nemesis.

A blow, slap, hit, knock, rap, thump, bang, stroke, cuff, kick, thwart, douse, box, punch, pummel.

Beating, lash, flagellation, flogging, &c., dressing, lacing, fustigation, *bastinado, estrappade, strappado,* pillory, gantlet, picketting.

Execution, hanging, beheading, decollation, guillotine, *garotto, auto-da-fé,* crucifixion, impalement, &c., martyrdom.

V. To punish, chastise, castigate, chasten, correct, inflict punishment, pay, do for, serve out, visit upon, lynch.

Phr. To make an example of; to serve one right.

To strike, hit, smite, knock, slap, flap, rap, bang, thwack, thump, kick, punch, pelt, beat, buffet, thresh (or thrash), baste, pummel, drub, trounce, baste, belabour, lace, strap, comb, lash, lick, whip, flog, scourge, wallop, leather, flagellate, horsewhip, bastinado.

Phr. To give a dressing ; to lace one's jacket; to tweak or pull the nose; to box the ears; to beat to a mummy, or jelly; to tar and feather.

To execute, hang, behead, decapitate, decollate, guillotine, shoot, gibbet, picket, hang, draw and quarter ; break on the wheel; crucify, empale, torture, &c.

To be hanged, &c.

Phr. To come to the gallows; to die in one's shoes.

Adj. Punishing, &c., punitory, punitive, inflictive, castigatory.

Punished, &c.

(973) REWARD, recompence, remuneration, meed, guerdon, reguerdon, premium, indemnity, indemnification, compensation, reparation, requital, retribution, quittance, acknowledgment, amends, sop, atonement, redress, consideration, return, tribute.

Crown, laurel, bays, cross, medal, ribbon, decoration, &c.

V. To reward, recompense, requite, remunerate, compensate, make amends, atone, satisfy, acknowledge, acquit oneself.

(974) PENALTY, pain, penance.

Fine, mulct, amercement, forfeit, forfeiture, escheat, damages, deodand, sequestration, confiscation.

V. To fine, mulct, amerce, sconce, confiscate, sequestrate.

(975) Instrument of punishment.

SCOURGE, rod, cane, stick, ratan, cane, switch, ferule, birch, cudgel.

Whip, lash, strap, thong, knout, cat, cat-o'-nine-tails.

Pillory, stocks, whipping-post, ducking-stool.

Rack, wheel, stake, tree, block, scaffold, gallows, gibbet, axe, maiden, guillotine, halter, bowstring.

Section V. RELIGIOUS AFFECTIONS.

1°. Superhuman Beings and Objects.

(976) Deity, Divinity, Godhead, Omnipotence, Providence. Quality of being divine; divineness, divinity.

God, Lord, Jehovah, The Almighty; The Supreme Being; The First Cause, *Ens Entium;* The Author, &c. of all things, The Infinite, The Eternal, The All-powerful, The All-wise, The All-merciful, The All-holy.

Attributes and Perfections; Infinite Power, Wisdom, Goodness, Justice, Mercy, Omnipotence, Omniscience, Omnipresence, Unity, Immutability, Holiness, Glory, Majesty, Sovereignty, Infinity, Eternity.

The Trinity, The Holy Trinity, The Trinity in Unity, The Triune God. God the Father, The Maker, The Creator.

(Functions) Creation, Preservation, Divine Government, Theocracy, Thearchy, Providence, the ways, the dispensations, the visitations of Providence.

God the Son, Christ, Jesus, The Messiah, The Saviour, The Redeemer, The Mediator, The Intercessor, The Advocate, The Judge, The Anointed, The Son of Man, The Lamb of God, The Word, λογος.

The Incarnation, The Hypostatic Union.

(Functions) Salvation, Redemption, Atonement, Propitiation, Mediation, Intercession, Judgment.

God the Holy Ghost, The Holy Spirit, Paraclete, The Comforter, The Spirit of Truth, The Dove.

(Functions) Inspiration, Unction, Regeneration, Sanctification.

V. To create, uphold, preserve, govern, &c.

To atone, redeem, save, propitiate, mediate, &c.

To predestinate, elect, call, ordain, bless, justify, sanctify, glorify, &c.

Adj. Almighty, &c., holy, hallowed, sacred, divine, heavenly, celestial.

Superhuman, ghostly, spiritual, supernatural, theocratic.

(977) Beneficent spirits.

Angel, archangel.

The heavenly host; the host of heaven, the sons of God.

Seraphim, cherubim, ministering spirits, morning stars.

Adj. Angelic, seraphic.

(978) Maleficent spirits.

Satan, the devil, Lucifer, Beelzebub, the Prince of the Devils.*

The tempter, the evil one, the wicked one, the old Serpent, the Prince of darkness, the Prince of this world, the Prince of the power of the air; the foul fiend, the archfiend, the common enemy; Mephistophiles.

Diabolism, devilism, devilship; Manicheism.

Fallen Angels, unclean spirits; devils; the Rulers or Powers of darkness; inhabitants of Pandemonium.

Adj. Satanic, diabolic, devilish.

* I have not inserted in the text the slang synonyms Old Nick, Old Scratch, Old Horny, Old Harry, the Deuce, the Old Gentleman, &c.

Mythological and other fabulous Deities and Powers.

(979) JUPITER, Jove, &c., &c., Brahma, Vishnu, Siva, Krishna, Buddha, Moloch, Baal, Asteroth, &c.

Good genius, Demiurge, familiar; fairy, fay, sylph, Ariel, Peri, Banshee (or Benshi), Ormuzd; Puck, Oberon, Mab, Robin Goodfellow, Hamadryad, Mermaid, *Ondine*, pigwidgeon, &c., &c.

Adj. Fairy-like, sylph-like, sylphid.

(980) DEMON, evil genius, fiend, Belial, cacodemon, succubus and succuba.

Ariman; fury, harpy, Siren, satyr, &c.

Vampire, ghoule, affreet (or effreet), ogre, gnome, imp, gin, lamiæ, bogie, bogle, nis, kobold, brownie, pixy, elf, dwarf, urchin, troll, dwerger, sprite, oufe, &c.

Ghost, spectre, apparition, shade, vision, goblin, hobgoblin, wraith, spook.

Adj. Supernatural, ghostly, elfish; unearthly, spectral, ghost-like, fiendish, fiend-like, impish; demoniacal.

(981) HEAVEN, the kingdom of heaven; the kingdom of God, the heavenly kingdom; the throne of God, the presence of God.

Phr. The inheritance of the Saints in Light.

Paradise, Eden, the abode of the blessed; celestial bliss, glory, &c.

Mythological heaven, Olympus. Mythological paradise, Elysium.

Translation, apotheosis.

Adj. Heavenly, celestial, supernal, unearthly, from on high, paradisaical.

(982) HELL, bottomless pit, place of torment; the habitation of fallen angels, Pandemonium.

Hell fire, everlasting fire, the lake of fire and brimstone.

Phr. The fire that is never quenched; the worm that never dies.

Purgatory, limbo, gehenna, abyss.

Mythological hell; Tartarus, Hades, Pluto, Avernus, the Stygian creek, the pit of Acheron, Erebus, Cocytus, Tophet.

Phr. The infernal regions, the shades below, the realms of Pluto.

Adj. Hellish, infernal, stygian.

2°. RELIGIOUS DOCTRINES.

(983) Religious knowledge.

THEOLOGY (natural and revealed), divinity, religion, monotheism.

Creed, belief, faith, persuasion, tenet, dogma, articles of faith, declaration, profession or confession of faith.

ORTHODOXY, true faith, Christianity, Christianism, Catholicism.

Phr. "The faith once delivered to the Saints."

A theologian, a divine.

A Christian, a true believer.

The Church, the Catholic or Universal Church; the Church of

(984) HETERODOXY, heresy, schism, schismaticalness, dissent, latitudinarianism, sectarism, sectarianism, recusancy, apostacy, back-sliding.

Antichrist.

Idolatry, superstition, bigotry, credulity, fanaticism.

Paganism, heathenism, ethnicism, mythology, polytheism, tritheism, pantheism; Judaism, Gentilism, Mahometanism, Turcism, Buddhism (or Boodhism), &c.

A heretic, pagan, heathen, painim (or paynim), pantheist, idolater, sacrilegist, non-conformist, separatist,

Christ, the body of Christ, the Bride, the members of Christ, the disciples or followers of Christ, the Christian community, the collective body of Christians, the temple of the Holy Ghost.

Adj. Theological, divine, religious.

Orthodox, sound, faithful, true, scriptural, Christian, Catholic, schismless.

(985) REVELATION, Word, Word of God, inspiration, Scripture, the Scriptures, Holy Writ, the Bible.

Old Testament; Septuagint, Vulgate, Pentateuch, Hagiographa, the Law, the Prophet, the Apocrypha, &c.

New Testament; the Gospel, the Evangelists, the Epistles, the Apocalypse.

Talmud, Mishna, Massora.

A Prophet, Evangelist, Apostle, Disciple, Saint.

Phr. The Holy Men of old.

Adj. Scriptural, biblical, sacred, evangelical, apostolic, apostolical.

schismatic, sectarian, sectarist, sectary, recusant, bigot, fanatic.

Jew, Mahometan, Mussulman, Moslem, Brahmin (or Brahman), Parsee, Sofi, Magi, Gymnosophist, Fireworshipper, &c.

Adj. Heterodox, heretical, unorthodox, unscriptural, schismatic, sectarian, non-conformist, recusant.

Credulous, bigoted, fanatical.

Pagan, heathen, ethnic, gentile, painim, pantheistic; Brahminical, Mahometan, &c.

(986) PSEUDO-REVELATION.

The Koran (or Alcoran), Ly-king, Shaster, Veda, Zendavesta, Vendidad, Purana, &c.

False prophets and religious founders; Buddha, Zoroaster (or Zerdhusht), Confucius, Mahomet, &c.

Idols; Golden calf, Baal, Moloch, Dagon, &c.

Adj. Antiscriptural, antichristian, profane, idolatrous, heathen, heathenish.

3°. RELIGIOUS SENTIMENTS.

(987) PIETY, religion, theism, faith, religiousness, godliness, reverence, humility, veneration, devoutness, devotion, theopathy, grace, unction, edification; holiness, sanctity, sanctitude, sacredness, consecration.

Phr. The odour of sanctity; the beauty of holiness.

Theopathy, beatification, adoption, regeneration, conversion, justification, salvation, inspiration.

A believer, theist, Christian, saint, one of the elect, a devotee.

V. To be pious, &c., to believe, have faith; to convert, edify, sanctify, beatify, regenerate, inspire; to consecrate, to enshrine.

Phr. To work out one's salvation.

Adj. Pious, religious, devout,

(988) IRRELIGION, atheism, indevotion, devoutlessness, ungodliness, unholiness, gracelessness.

Scepticism, doubt, unbelief, disbelief, incredulity, incredulousness, faithlessness, want of faith or belief (485, 487).

Deism, infidelity, freethinking, unchristianness, antichristianity.

An atheist, sceptic, unbeliever, deist, freethinker, infidel, alien.

V. To be irreligious, disbelieve, lack faith, doubt, question, &c.

Adj. Irreligious, indevout, undevout, devoutless, godless, atheistic, ungodly, unholy, unsanctified, graceless, without God.

Sceptical, unbelieving, freethinking, incredulous, unconverted, faithless, lacking faith, unhallowed.

reverent, godly, heavenly-minded, pure, holy, spiritual, saintly, saint-like.

Believing, faithful, Christian, Catholic, &c.

Sanctified, regenerated, justified, adopted, elected, inspired, consecrated, converted, unearthly, sacred, solemn, not of the earth.

Deistical, antichristian, unchristian, worldly-minded, mundane, carnal, earthly-minded.

Adv. Irreligiously, &c.

(989) IMPIETY, irreverence, profaneness, profanity, blasphemy, desecration, sacrilegiousness; scoffing, reviling.

Assumed piety; hypocrisy, pietism, lip-devotion, lip-service, lip-reverence, formalism, sanctimony, sanctimoniousness, precisianism, sabbatism.

Hardening, backsliding, declension, reprobation.

A scoffer, hypocrite, pietist, religionist, precisian, formalist; sons of men, sons of Belial, blasphemer.

A bigot, enthusiast, fanatic, sabbatarian.

V. To be impious, &c.

To profane, desecrate, blaspheme, revile, scoff.

Adj. Impious, profane, irreverent, sacrilegious, desecrating, blasphemous, unhallowed, unsanctified, hardened, reprobate.

Bigoted, priest-ridden, fanatical, enthusiastic.

Hypocritical, pietistical, sanctimonious, over-righteous, righteous overmuch.

4°. ACTS OF RELIGION.

(990) WORSHIP, adoration, devotion, latria, homage, service, humiliation, kneeling, genuflexion, prostration.

Prayer, invocation, supplication, rogation, petition, orison, holy breathing, asking, suffrage, &c. (765), litany, the Lord's prayer, paternoster, collect.

Thanksgiving, giving, or returning thanks, praise, glorification, benediction, doxology, hosanna, hallelujah, *Te Deum*.

Psalmody, psalm, hymn, plainsong, chaunt, antiphon, response, anthem. Oblation, sacrifice, incense, libation, burnt-offering.

Discipline, self-discipline, self-examination, self-denial, fasting.

V. To worship, adore, do service, pay homage, humble oneself, kneel, bend the knee, prostrate oneself.

To pray, invoke, supplicate, petition, put up prayers or petitions; to ask, implore, beseech, &c. (765).

To return or give thanks; to bless, praise, laud, glorify, magnify, sing praises, give benediction, lead the choir.

To propitiate, offer sacrifice, fast, deny oneself; vow, offer vows, give alms.

Phr. To work out one's salvation.

Adj. Worshipping, &c., devout, solemn, reverent, pure, fervid, heartfelt, &c.

(991) IDOLATRY, idol-worship, idolism, demonism, fire-worship, devil-worship, fetichism.

Deification, apotheosis, canonization.

Sacrifices, hecatomb, holocaust; human sacrifices, immolation, infanticide, self-immolation, *suttee*.

Idol, fetich.

V. To worship idols, pictures, relics, &c.; to deify, to canonize.
Adj. Idolatrous.

(992) SORCERY, magic, the black art, necromancy, theurgy, thaumaturgy, *diablerie*, demonship, demonomy, witchcraft, witchery, glamour, fetichism, sortilege, conjuration, fascination, mesmerism, clairvoyance, second-sight, divination, enchantment, hocus-pocus (545), ordeal.

V. To practise sorcery, &c.; to conjure, exorcise, charm, enchant, bewitch, entrance, mesmerize, fascinate; to taboo, wave a wand, cast a spell, call up spirits.

Adj. Magic, magical, cabalistic, talismanic, phylacteric, incantatory, charmed, exorcised, &c.

(993) SPELL, charm, incantation, exorcism, weird, cabala, exsufflation, abracadabra, open sesame, taboo, counter-charm.

Talisman, amulet, periapt, telesm, phylactery.

Caduceus, rod, divining rod.

(994) SORCERER, magician, conjurer, necromancer, seer, wizard, witch, weird, warlock, charmer, exorcist, mage, soothsayer (513), cunning-man, figure-flinger.

5°. RELIGIOUS INSTITUTIONS.

(995) CHURCHDOM, ministry, apostleship, priesthood, prelacy, hierarchy, church government, church:—(in a bad sense) priestcraft.

Monachism, monasticism, monachy.

Ecclesiastical offices and dignities; Primacy, archbishopric, bishopric, bishopdom, episcopate, episcopacy, see, diocese; deanery, stall, canonry, canonicate, prebend, prebendaryship; benefice, incumbency, living, cure, rectorship, vicarship, vicariate, deaconry, deaconship, curacy, chaplaincy, chaplainship.

Holy orders, ordination, institution, consecration, induction, preferment, translation.

Council, conclave, *sanhedrim*, synod, consistory, chapter, vestry (696).

V. To call, ordain, induct, prefer, translate.

Adj. Ecclesiastical, clerical, sacerdotal, priestly, prelatical, pastoral, ministerial.

Pontifical, episcopal, canonical; monastic, monachal, monkish.

(996) CLERGY, ministers, priesthood.

A clergyman, divine, ecclesiastic, churchman, priest, hierophant, pastor, father, shepherd, minister, father in Christ.

Dignitaries of the church; Primate, archbishop, bishop, prelate, diocesan, suffragan; dean, subdean, arch-deacon, prebendary, canon, residentiary, beneficiary; Rector, vicar, incumbent, parson, chaplain, curate, deacon, preacher; capitular.

Churchwarden, sidesman; clerk, precentor, choir, almoner, verger, beadle, sexton (or sacristan), acolyth (or acolothyst).

(997) LAITY, flock, fold, congregation, assembly, brethren, people.

Temporality, secularization.

A layman, parishioner.

V. To secularize.

Adj. Secular, lay, laical, civil, temporal, profane.

Roman Catholic priesthood; Pope, pontiff, high priest, cardinal, (ancient) flamen.

Cenobite, conventual, abbot, prior, monk, friar; mendicant; Franciscan (or Grey Friars, Friars minor, Observant, Capuchin), Dominican (or Black Friars), Carmelite, Augustin (or Austin Friars), Crossed or Crutched Friars, Bonhomme, &c.

Abbess, prioress, canoness, *religieuse*, nun, novice.

(Under the Jewish dispensation). Prophet, priest, high priest, Levite, Rabbi (or Rabbin), scribe.

Mahomedan, &c., mollah, ulema, imaum, sheik, sofi (or sophi), mufti, dervish, fakir (or faquier), brahmin, druid, bonze, santon, abdal.

(998) RITE, ceremony, ordinance, observance, formulary, ceremonial, solemnity, sacrament.

Baptism, christening, chrism, baptismal regeneration.

Confirmation, imposition or laying on of hands.

The Eucharist, the Lord's Supper, the communion, the sacrament, consubstantiation.

Matrimony (903), burial (363), visitation of the sick, &c., offertory, &c.

Roman Catholic rites and ceremonies; Mass, high mass, low mass, dry mass; matins, vespers; the seven sacraments, transubstantiation, impanation, extreme unction, viaticum, invocation of saints, canonization, transfiguration, auricular confession, maceration, flagellation, sackcloth and ashes, telling of beads, &c.

Relics, rosary, beads, reliquary, pix (or pyx), host, crucifix, *Agnus Dei*, &c.

Liturgy, ritual, euchology, book of common prayer, litany, &c.; rubric, breviary, missal, processional, &c.

Service, duty, ministration, psalmody, &c., *see* (990); preaching, predication; sermon, homily, lecture.

V. To perform service, do duty, minister, officiate; to baptize, dip, sprinkle, &c.; to confirm, lay hands on, &c.; to give or administer the sacrament; to take or receive the sacrament; to communicate.

To preach, sermonize, predicate, lecture.

Adj. Ritual, ceremonial, baptismal, &c.

(999) CANONICALS; robe, gown, pallium, surplice, cassock, scapulary, tonsure, cowl, hood, calote, bands, &c.

Mitre, tiara, triple crown, crosier.

(1000) Place of worship, house of God.

TEMPLE, cathedral, minster, church, kirk, chapel, chaplet, meeting-house, tabernacle, conventicle, basilic, fane, holy place.

Synagogue, mosque, pantheon, pagoda, joss-house, &c.

Parsonage, rectory, vicarage, manse, deanery, bishop's palace.

Altar, shrine, sanctuary, *sanctum sanctorum*, sacristy, communion table, baptistry, font, holy table, table of the Lord.

Chancel, choir, nave, aisle, transept, vestry, crypt, stall, pew, pulpit, ambo, reading-desk, confessional.

Monastery, priory, abbey, convent, nunnery, cloister.

INDEX.

N.B. The numbers refer to the headings under which the words occur. When the same word may be used in various senses, the several headings under which it will be found, according to those meanings, are indicated by the words printed in Italics. These words in Italics are not intended to explain the meanings of the word to which they are annexed, but only to assist in the required reference.

Words borrowed from another language have an asterisk prefixed to them.

Aback, 235.
Abacus, 85.
Abaft, 235.
Abalienate, 783.
Abandon *a purpose*, 624.
  property, 782.
*Abandon, 703.
Abandoned, *forsaken*, 893.
  vicious, 945.
Abase, *depress*, 308.
  degrade, 879.
Abasement, 886.
Abash, *daunt*, 860.
  humiliate, 879.
  shame, 874.
Abashed, 881.
Abate, *lessen*, 36.
  a price, 813.
Abattis, 717.
*Abattoir, 361.
Abbess, 996.
Abbey, 1000.
Abbot, 996.
Abbreviate, *shorten*, 201.
  style, 572.
Abdal, 996.
Abderite, 838.
Abdicate, 757.
Abduction, 288, 789.
Abecedarian, 541.
Abecedary, 561.
Aberrant, *divergent*, 290.
  erroneous, 495.
  exceptional, 83.
Aberration, *deviation*, 279.
  mental, 503.
Abet, 707.
Abeyance, *expectation*, 507.
  extinction, 2.
249

Abhor, *hate*, 898.
  dislike, 867.
Abide, *continue*, 142, 143.
  endure, 821.
  dwell, 186.
Abide by, 604.
Abigail, 746.
Ability, *power*, 157.
  skill, 698.
Abject, *servile*, 886.
  vile, 940.
Abjure, *renounce*, 607.
  resign, 757.
  deny, 536.
Ablation, *subduction*, 38.
  taking, 789.
Able, *skilful*, 698.
Ablebodied, 159.
Ablegate, 185.
Ablepsy, 442.
Ablude, 18.
Ablution, 652.
Abnegation, *denial*, 536.
  self-denial, 942.
  forbearance, 953.
Abnormity, 83.
Aboard, *ship*, 273.
  present, 186.
Abode, 189.
Abodement, 511.
Abolish, *destroy*, 162.
  abrogate, 756.
Abominable, *hateful*, 898.
  bad, 649.
  painful, 830.
Abominate, *hate*, 898.
  dislike, 867.
Abomination, *foulness*, 653.
*Abord, 894.

Aboriginal, 66.
Aborigines, 188.
Abortion, 732.
Abound, 639.
About, *relative to*, 9.
  near, 32.
  around, 227.
Above, 206.
Above-board, *visible*, 446.
  plain, 518.
  artless, 703.
  true, 543.
Above ground, *alive*, 359.
Above par, 31.
Abracadabra, 993.
Abrasion, 330, 331.
Abreast, *lateral*, 236.
  parallel, 216.
Abreption, 789.
Abridge, *shorten*, 201.
  lessen, 36.
  deprive, 789.
  in writing, 596.
Abroach, 73.
Abroad, *distant*, 196.
  ignorant, 491.
  perplexed, 704.
Abrogation, 756.
Abrupt, *sudden*, 132.
  violent, 173.
  transient, 111.
  steep, 217.
  style, 579.
Abscess, 655.
Abscission, *retrenchment*, 38.
  division, 44.
Abscond, *escape*, 671.
  fly from, 286.

Absence, *nonpresence*, 187.
  inattention, 458.
  thoughtlessness, 452.
Absentee, 187.
Absolute, *not relative*, 1.
  certain, 474.
  true, 494.
  unconditional, 768.
  authoritative, 737.
  severe, 739.
Absolve, *forgive*, 918.
  exempt, 927.
  liberate, 750.
  permit, 760.
Absonant, *unreasonable*, 495.
Absonous, *unmusical*, 414.
Absorb, *take in*, 297.
  think, 451.
  attend to, 457.
  feel, 821.
  consume, 677.
Abstain, *refrain*, 603.
  temperance, 953.
Abstemious, 953.
Absterge, 652.
Abstersive, 662.
Abstinent, 953.
Abstract, *separate*, 44.
  idea, 451.
  to abridge, 596.
  to take, 789.
  to steal, 791.
Abstruse, *recondite*, 519.
  hidden, 528.
Absurd, 497.
Abundant, *copious*, 639.
  great, 31.
Abuse, *misuse*, 679.
  ill-treat, 649.
  upbraid, 932.
  deceive, 545.
  of language, 523.
Abut, *rest on*, 215.
  touch, 199.
Aby, *remain*, 142.
  endure, 821.
Abyss, *depth*, 208.
  space, 180.
  hell, 982.
Academic, 537.
Academy, 542.
Accede, 762.
Accelerate, *velocity*, 274.
  earliness, 132.
Accension, 384.
Accent, *tone of voice*, 580.
  sound, 402.
Accept, *receive*, 785.
  consent, 762.
250

Acceptable, *agreeable*, 829.
  expedient, 646.
Acceptance, *security*, 771.
Acceptation, *meaning*, 516.
Access, 627.
Accessible, 705.
Accession, *increase*, 35.
  addition, 37.
  to power, 737.
Accessory, *adjunct*, 39.
  auxiliary, 711.
  aiding, 707.
Accidence, 567.
Accident, *chance*, 156, 621.
  event, 151.
Accidental, 6.
Acclamation, 931.
Acclimatize, *enure*, 613.
  train, 673.
Acclivity, 217.
*Accolade, 894.
Accommodate, *suit*, 23.
  reconcile, 723.
  lend, 787.
  prepare, 673.
  aid, 707.
  give, 784.
Accommodating, *kind*, 906.
Accompaniment, *musical*, 415.
Accompany, *coexist*, 88.
  add, 37.
Accomplice, 711.
Accomplish, *execute*, 161.
  finish, 729.
Accomplishment, *talent*, 698.
  learning, 490.
Accord, *agree*, 23.
  assent, 488.
  concord, 714.
  give, 784.
  grant, 760.
  spontaneous, 600.
Accordingly, 476.
According to, *conformably*, 15.
  evidence, 467.
Accordion, 417.
Accost, 586.
Account, *money*, 811.
  bill, 812.
  computation, 85.
  list, 86.
  description, 594.
  value, 644.
  estimation, 484.
  judgment, 480.
  approbation, 931.
  fame, 873.

Account, *sake*, 615.
Account for, 155.
Accountable, 926.
Accountant, 811.
Accoutre, *dress*, 225.
  equip, 673.
Accredit, *money*, 805.
  honor, 873.
Accretion, 46.
Accrue, *result*, 154.
  add, 37.
  acquire, 775.
  receive, 810.
  benefit, 644.
Accubation, 213.
*Accueil, 894.
Accumbent, 213.
Accumulate, *collect*, 72.
  store, 636.
Accurate, *exact*, 494.
  likeness, 17.
Accurse, 908.
Accursed, *undone*, 828.
  painful, 830.
  disastrous, 649.
Accuse, *charge*, 938.
  disapprove, 932.
Accuser, 967.
Accustom, *habituate*, 613.
  usual, 82.
Ace, *unit*, 87.
  small in quantity, 32.
  small in size, 193.
Aceldama, 361.
Acerbate, *embitter*, 659.
  aggravate, 835.
Acervate, 72.
Acetose, 397.
Acetous, 397.
*Acharné, 900.
Ache, *physical pain*, 378.
  moral pain, 828.
Acheron, 982.
Achieve, *accomplish*, 729.
  end, 67.
Achievable, *possible*, 470.
  easy, 705.
Achievement, *sign*, 551.
Achromatism, 429.
Acicular, 253.
Acid, 397.
Acknowledge, *avow*, 535.
  disclose, 529.
  assent, 488.
  consent, 762.
  reward, 973.
  repent, 950.
  answer, 462.
  observe, 772.
  receive, 82.

Acme, *summit*, 210.
  highest degree, 33.
  perfection, 650.
Acology, 662.
Acolyth, 996.
Aconite, 663.
Acoustics, 402.
Acquaint, 527.
Acquaintance, *knowledge*, 490.
  friendship, 888.
  friend, 890.
Acquiesce, *assent*, 488.
  consent, 762.
Acquire, 775.
Acquirement, *knowledge*, 490.
  learning, 539.
  talent, 698.
Acquisition, *gain*, 775.
  knowledge, 490.
Acquit, *absolve*, 970.
  exempt, 927.
  vindicate, 937.
  liberate, 750.
Acquit oneself *of a duty*, 926.
  of an agreement, 772.
Acquittance, *payment*, 807.
Acres, 780.
Acrid, 395.
Acrimony, *physical*, 171.
  taste, 395.
  hatred, 898.
  discourtesy, 895.
Acroatic, 490.
Across, *transverse*, 219.
  opposition, 708.
Acrostic, 563.
Act, *physical*, 170.
  voluntary, 680.
  to feign, 544.
  to personate, 599.
  to imitate, 19.
Action, *physical*, 170.
  voluntary, 680.
  battle, 720.
  at law, 969.
Activity, *physical*, 171.
  voluntary, 682.
Actor, *impostor*, 548.
  player, 599.
Actual, *existing*, 1.
  real, 494.
  present, 118.
Actually, *truly*, 31.
Actuary, 811.
Actuate, 615.
Acuity, 253.
Aculeated, 253.

251

Acumen, 498.
Acuminated, 253.
Acupuncture, 260.
Acute, *pointed*, 253.
  violent, physically, 173.
  sensible, } 375.
  physically,
  painful, morally, 830.
  strong feeling, 820.
  musical tone, 410.
  perspicacious, 498.
Acutely, *much*, 31.
Adage, 496.
Adagio, 275.
Adamant, *hard*, 323.
  strong, 159.
Adapt, *fit*, 646.
  adjust, 673.
  agree, 23.
Add, *join*, 37.
  increase, 35.
  numerically, 85.
*Addendum, 39.
Adder, *viper*, 663.
  maleficent being, 913.
Addict, *habit*, 613.
Additament, 39.
Addition, *adjunction*, 37.
  thing added, 39.
  arithmetical, 85.
Addle, *barren*, 169.
  incomplete, 730.
Addle-headed, 499.
Address, *speak to*, 586.
  skill, 698.
  request, 765.
  residence, 189.
  direction, 550.
Addresses, *courtship*, 902.
Adduce, *bring to*, 289.
  evidence, 467.
Adept, 700.
Adequate, *sufficient*, 639.
  power, 157.
  strength, 159.
  for a purpose, 644.
Adhere, *stick*, 46.
  fidelity, 772.
Adherent, *follower*, 711.
Adhesive, 46.
Adhibit, 677.
*Ad hominem, 79.
*Adieu, 292.
*Ad interim, 106.
Adipose, 355.
Adit, *conduit*, 350.
  orifice, 260.
Adjacent, 197.
Adjection, 37.
Adjective, 39.

Adjoin, 197.
Adjourn, 133.
Adjudge, 969.
Adjudicate, 969.
Adjunct, *thing added*, 39.
  aid, 707.
Adjure, *request*, 765.
  promise, 768.
Adjust, *fit*, 27.
  prepare, 673.
  settle, 723.
Adjutage (*or* ajutage),
  pipe, 350.
  opening, 260.
Adjutant, *auxiliary*, 711.
  military, 745.
Adjuvant, *helper*, 707.
Admeasurement, 466.
Administer, *give*, 784.
  exercise authority, 737.
Administration, *of justice*, 965.
Admirable, *excellent*, 648.
  virtuous, 944.
Admiral, 745.
Admire, *approve*, 931.
  love, 897.
  wonder, 870.
Admissible, *tolerable*, 651.
Admission, *ingress*, 295, 297.
Admit, *let in*, 297.
  accept, 785.
  include, 76.
  composition, 54.
  concede in argument, 467.
  allow, 760.
Admit of, 470.
Admixture, 41.
Admonish, *advise*, 695.
  warn, 668.
  reprove, 932.
  predict, 511.
Ado, *exertion*, 686.
  activity, 682.
  difficulty, 704.
Adolescence, 131.
Adonis, 845.
Adopt, 609.
Adore, *love*, 897.
  worship, 990.
Adorn, 845.
Adown, 207.
Adrift, *unrelated*, 10.
  dispersed, 73.
  at fault, 704.
Adroit, 698.
Adscititious, *intrinsic*, 6.
  added, 37.
  supplementary, 52.

Adulation, 933.
Adult, 131.
Adulterate, *mix*, 41.
  deteriorate, 659.
  falsify, 495.
Adulterer, 962.
Adultery, 961.
Adumbrate, *sketch*, 594.
  painting, 556.
  faint likeness, 21.
  imitate, 19.
Aduncity, 244.
Adustion, 384.
Advance, *progress*, 282.
  to promote, 658.
  forward, 707.
  increase, 35.
  lend, 787.
  assert, 535.
Advances (to make), 892.
Advanced guard, 234.
Advantage, *good*, 618.
  utility, 644.
  goodness, 648.
  superiority, 33.
  inequality, 28.
  success, 731.
Advene, 37.
Advent, *arrival*, 293.
  event, 151.
  futurity, 121.
Adventitious, *extrinsic*, 6.
  casual, 156, 621.
Adventure, *event*, 151.
  chance, 156, 621.
  pursuit, 622.
  trial, 675.
Adventurous, *courageous*,
  861.
  dangerous, 665.
*Adversaria, *register*, 551.
  chronicle, 594.
Adversary, 710.
Adverse, *opposed*, 708.
  disliking, 867.
  unprosperous, 735.
Adversity, 735.
Advert, 457.
Advertise, 531.
Advice, *counsel*, 695.
  notice, 527.
Advisable, 646.
Advise, *inform*, 527.
  counsel, 695.
  predict, 511.
Advised, *voluntary*, 600.
Adviser, *counsellor*, 695.
  teacher, 540.
Advocate, *counsellor*, 968.
  to prompt, 615.
252

Advocate, *to vindicate*, 937.
  Saviour, 976.
*Adytum, *secret place*, 528.
  room, 191.
  prediction, 511.
Ægis, 717.
Aerial, *aëriform*, 338.
  elevated, 206.
Aeriform, 334.
Aerie, 189.
Aerology, 338.
Aeromancy, 511.
Aeronautics, 267.
Aerostatics, 334, 267.
Aerostation, 267.
Æsthetic, *taste*, 850.
  sensibility, 375.
Ætiology, 655.
Afar, 196.
Affable, *courteous*, 874.
  humble, 879.
Affair, *business*, 625.
  event, 151.
  topic, 454.
  battle, 720.
Affect, *desire*, 865.
  love, 897.
  lend to, 176.
  touch, 824.
Affectability, 822.
Affectation, *pretension*, 855.
  in style, 577.
Affection, *state of soul*, 820.
  love, 897.
Affiance, *trust*, 858.
  promise, 768.
*Affiche, 531.
Affidavit, *evidence*, 467.
  record, 551.
Affiliation, *relation*, 9.
  kindred, 11.
Affinity, 9.
Affirm, *assert*, 535.
  confirm, 488.
Affirmatively, 488.
Affix, *to join*, 43.
  sequel, 39.
Afflation, 349.
Afflict, 830.
Affliction, 828.
Afflictive, 830.
Affluence, 803.
Afflux, 287.
Afford, *supply*, 784.
  wealth, 803.
  accrue, 810.
Affranchise, 750.
Affreet, 980.
Affriction, 331.
Affright, 860.

Affront, *insult*, 900.
  courage, 861.
  molest, 830.
Affuse, 337.
Afire, 382.
Afloat, *at sea*,
  on shipboard, } 273.
  unstable, 149.
Afoot, 625.
  in preparation, 673.
Afore, 116.
Aforesaid, 104.
Afraid, 860.
Afresh, *new*, 123.
  repeated, 104.
  frequent, 136.
Aft, 235.
After, *in order*, 63.
  in time, 117.
Afterage, 124.
Afterall, 469.
Afterclap, 509.
Aftercourse, 626.
Aftergame, 626.
Afterlife, 121.
Afternoon, 126.
Afterpart, 65.
Afterpiece, 599.
Aftertaste, 390.
Afterthought, 607.
Aftertime, 121.
Afterwards, 117.
Aga, 745.
*Agacerie, 615.
Again, *repeated*, 104.
  frequent, 136.
Against, *physical opposi-*
  tion, 179.
  voluntary opposition,
  708.
  anteposition, 237.
  provision, 673
Agape, *wonder*, 870.
  curiosity, 455.
Age, *period*, 108.
  advanced life, 128.
Agency, *physical*, 170.
  instrumentality, 631.
  direction, 693.
*Agenda, 625.
Agent, *physical*, 153.
  voluntary, 690.
  consignee, 758.
Agentship, 755.
Agglomerate, 72.
Agglutinate, 46.
Aggrandize, *in degree*, 35.
  in bulk, 194.
  honor, 873.
Aggravate, *increase*, 35.

Aggravate, *vehemence*, 173.
   distress, 835.
   render worse, 659.
   exasperate, 900.
   exaggerate, 549.
Aggregate, *whole*, 50.
   collection, 72.
Aggregation, 46.
Aggression, 716.
Aggrieve, *distress*, 830.
   injure, 649.
Aghast, *with wonder*, 870.
   with fear, 860.
   disappointed, 509.
Agile, *swift*, 274.
   active, 682.
Agio, 813.
Agiotage, 794.
Agitate, *motion*, 315.
   activity, 682.
   to affect the mind, 821.
   to excite, 824.
Agnate, 9.
Agnation, 11.
*Agnomen, 564.
*Agnus Dei, 999.
Ago, 122.
Agog, *curiosity*, 455.
   wonder, 870.
   desire, 865.
Agonize, 830.
Agony, *physical*, 378.
   mental, 828.
Agrarian, 371.
Agree, *accord*, 23.
   concur, 178.
   assent, 488.
   consent, 762.
   concord, 714.
Agreeable, 829.
Agreeably, *conformably*, 82.
Agreement, *bargain*, 769.
Agriculture, 371.
Aground, *stranded*, 265.
   failure, 732.
Ague-fit, 860.
Agueish, 383.
Ahead, *in front*, 234.
Ahead (go), *activity*, 282.
   to improve, 658.
Aid, *to help*, 707.
   charity, 906.
Aide-de-camp, *auxiliary*, 711.
   officer, 745.
Ail, *sick*, 655.
   in pain, 828.
Ailment, 655.
Aim, *direction*, 278.
   purpose, 620.
   253

Aimless, 621.
Air, *gas*, 334.
   atmospheric, 338.
   wind, 349.
   tune, 415.
   appearance, 448.
   unsubstantial, 4.
   fashion, 852.
   affectation, 855.
Air-balloon, 273.
Air-built, 515.
Airiness, 320.
Airing, 266.
Air-pipe, 351.
Airy, *atmospheric*, 338.
   gay, 836.
Aisle, *passage*, 260.
   in a church, 1000.
Ajutage (*or* adjutage),
   pipe, 350.
   opening, 260.
Akimbo (to stand), 715.
   angular, 244.
Akin, 11.
Alabaster colour, 430.
Alack! 839.
Alacrity, *activity*, 682.
   cheerfulness, 836.
Alarm, *fear*, 860.
   notice of danger, 669.
   signal, 550.
   threatening, 665.
Alarum, 668.
Alas! 839.
Albeit, 179.
Albification, 430.
Albino, 443.
Album, *book*, 593.
   compendium, 596.
Albuminous, 352.
Alcade (*or* alcaid), 745.
Alcoran, 986.
Alcove, *cave*, 252.
   dwelling, 189.
Alderman, 745.
Alectryomancy, 511.
Alembic, *vessel*, 191.
   laboratory, 691.
Alert, *active*, 682.
   watchful, 459.
Aleuromancy, 511.
Alexandrine, 200.
Alexipharmic, 662.
Alexiteric, 662.
Algebra, 85.
Algid, 383.
Algorithm, 85.
Alguazil, 965.
*Alias, 565.
*Alibi, 187.

Alien, *irrelevant*, 10.
   foreign, 57.
   irreligious, 988.
Alienate, *transfer*, 783.
   estrange, 889.
   set against, 898.
Alienation (mental), 503.
Alight, *descend*, 306.
   stop, 265.
   arrive, 293.
Alike, 17.
Aliment, *food*, 299.
   materials, 635.
Alimentation, 707.
Alimony, *dowry*, 810.
   provision, 803.
Aliquot, 51.
Alive, *living*, 359.
   active, 682.
All, *whole*, 50.
   complete, 52.
Allay, *moderate*, 174.
   repress excitement, 826.
Allective, 615.
Allege, *evidence*, 467.
   assert, 535.
   plea, 617.
Allegiance, 926.
Allegory, 464.
*Allegresse, } 836.
*Allegro, }
Allemande, 840.
Alleviate, *moderate*, 174.
   allay, 826.
   relieve, 834.
Alley, *passage*, 260.
   way, 627.
   court, 189.
Alliance, *relation*, 9.
   kindred, 11.
   physical co-operation, 178.
   voluntary co-operation, 709.
   union, 714.
Alligation, 43.
Alliteration, 17.
Allocation, 60.
Allocution, 586.
Allodium, 780.
Allot, *arrange*, 60.
   distribute, 786.
Allow, *permit*, 760.
   assent, 488.
   concede, 467.
   give, 784.
   discount, 813.
   allot, 786.
   pay, 809.

Allowance, *qualification*, 469.
  forgiveness, 918.
Alloy, *mixture*, 41.
  debase, 659.
Allude, *mean*, 516.
  refer to, 521.
Allure, 615.
Allurement, *desire*, 865.
Allusion, *meaning*, 516.
  reference, 521.
Allusive, 9.
Alluvial, 344.
*Alluvium, *deposit*, 40.
  soil, 653.
Ally, 711.
Alma mater, 542.
Almanac, 114, 551.
Almighty (the), 976.
Almoner, 996.
Almost, 32.
Alms, 784.
Aloft, 206.
Alomancy, 511.
Alone, 87.
Along, 200.
Along with, *together*, 88.
  by means of, 631.
Alongside, 216.
Aloof, *distant*, 196.
  high, 206.
  secluded, 893.
Aloud, 404.
*Alpha, 66.
Alphabet, 561.
Alps, 206.
Already, *antecedently*, 116.
  even now, 118.
  past time, 122.
Also, 37.
Altar, *marriage*, 903.
  church, 1000.
Alter, *vary*, 20.
  change, 140.
Alterable, 149.
Altercation, 713.
Alternate, *reciprocal*, 12.
  periodic, 138.
  discontinuous, 70.
Alternative, *plan*, 626.
  choice, 609.
Although, *counteraction*, 179.
  opposition, 708.
  counterevidence, 468.
Altiloquence, 577.
Altimetry, 466.
Altitude, 206.
Altogether, *collectively*, 50.
  entirely, 31.
2 £ 4

Alveolus, 252.
Always, 112.
Amalgam, *mixture*, 41.
  compound, 48.
Amalgamate, 48.
Amanuensis, 590.
Amaritude, 395.
*Amateur, 865, 850.
Amatory, 897.
Amass, *whole*, 50.
  to collect, 72.
Amaze, 870.
Amazingly, 31.
Amazon, *warrior*, 726.
  courage, 861.
*Ambages, 279.
Ambagious, 573.
Ambassador, 534.
Amber colour, 436.
Ambidexter, *clever*, 698.
  fickle, 607.
  right and left, 238.
Ambient, 227.
Ambiguous, *uncertain*, 475.
  obscure, 571.
  unintelligible, 519.
Ambit, 229.
Ambition, *desire*, 865.
  intention, 620.
Amble, *pace*, 266.
  fleet, 274.
Ambo, *school*, 542.
  pulpit, 1000.
Ambrosial, 394.
*Ambulance, 662.
Ambulation, 266.
Ambuscade, 530.
Ambush, 530.
Ambustion, 384.
Ameer, 745.
Ameliorate, 658.
Amen, 488.
Amenable, 926.
Amend, 658.
Amends, *compensation*, 30.
  reward, 973.
  atonement, 952.
Amenity, 894.
Amerce, 974.
Amethyst, 437.
Amiable, 906.
Amicable, *friendly*, 888.
  assisting, 707.
Amidst, 228.
Amiss, 647.
Amity, *friendship*, 888.
  concord, 714.
  peace, 721.
Ammunition, *materials*, 635.

Ammunition, *warlike*, 727.
Amnesty, 918.
Among, 228.
Amorous, 897.
Amorphous, *formless*, 241.
  irregular, 83.
Amotion, 185.
Amount, *quantity*, 25.
  whole, 50.
  sum of money, 800.
Amour, 897.
Amphibious, 83.
Amphibology, 520.
Amphictryon, 890.
*Amphigouri, 497, 853.
Amphilogy, 520.
Amphitheatre, *arena*, 728.
  prospect, 441.
  school, 542.
Ample, *much*, 31.
  copious, 639.
  large, 192.
  broad, 202.
  spacious, 181.
Amplify, *enlarge*, 35.
  dilate, 194.
  exaggerate, 549.
Amplitude, *degree*, 26.
  size, 192.
  breadth, 202.
Amputate, 38.
Amulet, 993.
Amuse, 840.
Amylaceous, 352.
An (*if*), 514.
Ana, 594.
Anachronism, 115.
Anacreontic, 597.
Anæsthesia, 823.
Anaglyph, 557.
Anagogics, 528.
Anagram, 561.
*Analecta, 594.
Analeptic, 662.
Analogy, *relation*, 9.
  similarity, 17.
Analysis, *decomposition*, 49.
  arrangement, 60.
  algebra, 85.
  inquiry, 461.
Anamorphosis, *optical*, 443.
  misrepresentation, 555.
Anarchy, *disorder*, 59.
  social, 738.
Anastatic printing, 558.
Anastomosis, *junction*, 43.
  crossing, 219.
Anastrophe, 218.
Anathema, 908.
Anatomy, *dissection*, 44.

Anatomy, *skeleton*, 329.
  inquiry, 461.
Ancestor, } 166.
Ancestry, }
Anchor, *safeguard*, 666.
  hope, 858.
Anchorage, *roadstead*, 189.
Anchorite, 955.
Anchylosis, 150.
Ancient, 124.
Ancillary, 707.
Androgynous, 83.
Anecdote, 594.
Anent, 9.
Anew, 123.
Anfractuosity, *angle*, 244.
  convolution, 248.
Angel, *supernatural being*,
  977.
  object of love, 948.
Angelic, 944.
Anger, 900.
Angle, 244.
Angle (*to*), 622.
Anguilliform, *narrow*, 203.
  serpentine, 248.
Anguish, *physical*, 378.
  moral, 828.
Angularity, 244.
Angustation, 203.
Anhelation, 688.
Anhydrous, 340.
Anility, 128.
Animadvert,*reprehend*, 932
  consider, 451.
Animal, 366.
Animal cries, 412.
Animalcule, *minute*, 193.
Animalism, *sensuality*, 954.
Animality, 364.
Animate, *excite*, 824.
  stimulate, 615.
Animation, *life*, 359.
  animality, 364.
  excitation, 824.
Animosity, *enmity*, 889.
  hatred, 898.
  anger, 900.
*Animus, *will*, 600.
  intention, 620.
Annals, *record*, 551.
  history, 114.
  account, 551.
Annalist, 553.
Anneal, 763.
Annex, *add*, 37.
  join, 43.
Annihilate, *extinguish*, 2.
  destroy, 162.
Anniversary, 138.

Annotation, *note*, 550.
  glossary, 522.
Announce, *inform*, 527.
  publish, 531.
  predict, 511.
  assert, 535.
Annoy, 830.
Annoyance, *pain*, 828.
  evil, 619.
  badness, 649.
Annual, *year*, 108.
  periodic, 138.
Annuity, 803.
Annul, 756.
Annular, 247.
Annulet, 247.
Annunciate, *inform*, 527.
  publish, 531.
Anodyne, 656.
Anoint, *coat*, 222.
  oil, 355.
Anointed, 976.
Anomaly, *irregularity*, 83.
  disorder, 59.
Anomalastic, 83.
Anon, *ere long*, 132.
  shortly, 111.
Anonymous, 565.
Another, 15.
Answer, *to an inquiry*,
  462.
  reply, 587.
  to suceeed, 731.
Answer for, 768.
Answer to, *correspond*, 9.
Answerable, 926.
Ant, 690.
Antagonism, *difference*, 14.
  voluntary, 708.
  physical, 179.
Antagonist, 710.
Antecedence, *in order*, 62.
  in time, 116.
Antecedent, 64.
Antechamber, 191.
Antedate, 115.
Antediluvian, 124.
Antelope, 274.
Anteposition, 237.
Anterior, *in order*, 62.
  in time, 116.
  in place, 234.
Anteroom, 191.
Anthem, 990.
Anthology, *poem*, 597.
  collection, 596.
Anthropology, 372.
Anthropophagi, 913.
Antic, 856.
Antichristian, 988.

Antichronism, *false time*,
  115.
Anticipate, *early*, 132.
  future, 121.
  anachronism, 115.
  expect, 507.
  foresee, 510.
  prepare, 673.
Anticlimax, *depth*, 208.
  bathos, 856.
Antidote, 662.
Antilogarithm, 84.
Antinomy, 964.
Antinous, 845.
Antiparallel, 217.
Antiphon, *music*, 415.
  answer, 462.
  rites, 998.
Antiphrasis, 565.
Antipodes, *distance*, 196.
  anteposition, 237.
  difference, 14.
  depth, 208.
Antique, 124.
Antiquated, 851.
Antithesis, *contrast*, 14.
  style, 574.
Antitype, 22.
Anvil, *support*, 215.
  (*on the*) *plan*, 626.
  preparing, 673.
Anxiety, *pain*, 828.
  fear, 860.
  desire, 865.
Aorist, *indefinite time*, 119.
Apace, *swift*, 274.
  short time, 111.
  early, 132.
Apart, *distance*, 196.
  singleness, 87.
Apartment, 191.
Apathy, *physical*, 376.
  moral, 823.
Ape, 19.
Apelles, 559.
*Aperçu, 596.
Apertness, } 260.
Aperture, }
Apex, 210.
Aphelion, 196.
Aphony, 581.
Aphorism, 496.
Aplanatic, 429.
Apicius, 957.
Apocalypse, 985.
Apocryphal, 475.
Apodetical, 478.
Apograph, 21.
Apollo, *music*, 415.
  beauty, 845.

Apologue, 594.
Apology, *penitence*, 950.
   vindication, 937.
   atonement, 952.
Apophysis, 250.
Apoplexy, 160.
Apostacy, *palinody*, 607.
   dishonor, 940.
   heterodoxy, 984.
Apostate, 941.
Apostle, 540.
Apostolic, 985.
Apostrophe, *appeal*, 765.
   address, 586, 589.
Apothegm, 496.
Apotheosis, 991.
Apozem, 335.
Appal, 860.
Appalling, 830.
Appanage, 780.
Apparatus, 633.
Apparel, 225.
Apparent, 446.
Apparition, *ghost*, 980.
   appearance, 448.
Appeach, 938.
Appeal, *request*, 765.
   address, 586.
Appear for, 759.
Appearance, *sight*, 448.
   probability, 472.
Appease, *physically*, 174.
   morally, 826.
Appellant, 924.
Appellation, 564.
Append, 37.
Appendage, 39.
Appendix, 65.
Appertain, *belong*, 777.
   related to, 9.
   right, 922.
Appetite, 865.
Applaud, 931.
Apple green, 435.
Apple of discord, 713.
Appliances, 632.
Applicable, *to use*, 644.
   expedient, 646.
   relative, 23.
Application, *use*, 677.
   request, 765.
   study, 457.
Appoint, 755.
Appointment, *salary*, 809.
   interview, 892.
Apportion, *allot*, 786.
   arrange, 60.
   portion, 51.
Apposite, *agreeing*, 23.
   relative, 9.
256

Apposition, *closeness*, 199.
Appraise, *value*, 812.
   estimate, 466.
Appreciate, *measure*, 466.
   taste, 850.
   judge, 480.
   approve, 931.
Apprehend, *know*, 490.
   believe, 484.
   fear, 860.
   seize, 965.
Apprentice, 541.
Apprenticeship, *learning*, 539.
   training, 673.
Apprize, 527.
Approach, *move*, 287.
   nearness, 197.
   path, 627.
   of time, 121.
Approbation, 931.
Appropinquation, 287.
Approve, *commend*, 931.
   corroborate, 467.
Approximate, *approach*, 287.
   nearness, 197.
   in mathematics, 85.
   resemble, 17.
   related to, 9.
Appulse, *convergence*, 291.
   collision, 276.
Appurtenance, *part*, 51.
   component, 56.
Apricot, *colour*, 439.
April-fool, 501.
Apron, 666.
*Apropos, 9, 646.
Aprotype, 591.
Apt, *consonant*, 23.
   clever, 698.
   docile, 539.
   willing, 602.
   expedient, 646.
   tendency, 176.
Aquatic, 337.
Aquatint, 558.
Aqueduct, 350.
Aqueous, 337.
Aquiline, 244.
Arabesque, 847.
Arable, 371.
Arbiter, *judge*, 967.
   adviser, 695.
Arbitrament, *sentence*, 969.
   judgment, 480.
   choice, 609.
Arbitrary, *without law*, 964.
   irregular, 83.
   without relation, 10.

Arbitrate, *mediate*, 724.
   judge, 480.
Arbor, 215.
Arborescent, 256.
*Arboretum, 367.
Arboriculture, 371.
Arbour, 189.
Arc, 245.
*Arcanum, 533.
Arch, *curve*, 245.
   great, 31.
   cunning, 702.
   clever, 498.
Archaism, 563.
Archæology, 122.
Archæus, 359.
Archangel, 977.
Archbishop, 996.
Archdeacon, 996.
Archduke, 745.
Archfiend, 978.
Architect, *constructer*, 164.
   agent, 690.
Architecture, *construction*, 161.
   fabric, 329.
Archive, 551.
Archness, *cunning*, 702.
   cleverness, 498.
   intelligence, 450.
Archtraitor, 941.
Arcuation, 245.
Ardent, *fiery*, 382.
   feeling, 821.
Arduous, 704.
Area, 181.
Arefaction, 340.
Arena, *field*, 728.
   workshop, 691.
Arenaceous, 330.
Areopagus, 696.
Areolar, 219.
Areometer, *density*, 321.
   measure, 466.
Aretology, 926.
Argent, 430.
Argillaceous, 324.
Argosy, 273.
Argue, *reason*, 476.
   evidence, 467.
   indicate, 550.
Argument, *evidence*, 467.
   topic, 454.
   meaning, 516.
Argus-eyed, *sight*, 441.
   vigilant, 459.
Argute, 498.
Aria, 415.
Arid, 340.
Ariel, *messenger*, 534.

Assess, *judge*, 480.
Assets, *property*, 780.
  money, 800.
Asseverate, 535.
Assiduous, 682.
Assign, *attribute*, 155.
  give, 784.
*Assignat, 800.
Assignation, 892.
Assimilate, *resemble*, 17.
  imitate, 19.
  agree, 23.
Assist, *aid*, 707.
  benefit, 906.
Assistant, 711.
Assize, *measure*, 466.
  tribunal, 966.
Associate, *accompany*, 88.
  unite, 43.
  collect, 72.
  friend, 890.
  society, 892.
Association, *relation*, 9.
  (*See* Associate.)
Assoil, *free*, 750.
  acquit, 970.
Assort, 60.
Assortment, *class*, 75.
  collection, 72.
Assuage, *physically*, 174.
  morally, 826.
  relieve, 834.
Assuetude, 613.
Assume, *suppose*, 514.
  evidence, 467.
  hope, 858.
  right, 924.
  insolence, 885.
  pride, 878.
  falsehood, 544.
Assumption (*See* Assume).
  qualification, 469.
  severity, 739.
Assurance, *assertion*, 535.
  promise, 768.
  certainty, 474.
  belief, 484.
  hope, 858.
  insolence, 885.
Assymptote, 291.
Asterisk, 550.
Astern, 235.
Asteroid, 318.
Asteroth, 979.
Asthenia, 160.
Astonish, 870.
Astonishing, *great*, 31.
Astound, *surprise*, 870.
  excite, 824.
Astræa, 922.
258

Astral, 318.
Astray, 279.
Astriction, 43.
Astride, 215.
Astringent, 195.
Astrology, 511.
Astronomy, 318.
Astute, 498.
Asunder, *separate*, 44.
  distant, 196.
Asylum, *retreat*, 666.
  defence, 717.
Ataghan, 727.
*Atelier, 691.
Athanor, 386.
Atheism, 988.
Athirst, 865.
Athletic, 159.
Athwart, *oblique*, 217.
  crossing, 219.
  opposing, 708.
Atlas, *support*, 215.
  maps, 554.
Atmosphere, *air*, 338.
  circumambience, 227.
Atom, *small in degree*, 32.
  in size, 193.
Atone, 952.
Atonement, *religious*, 976.
Atony, 160.
Atrabilious, 837.
Atramentous, 431.
Atrocious, 945, 947.
Atrophy, *shrinking*, 195.
  disease, 655.
Attach, *join*, 43.
  love, 897.
  legal, 969.
*Attaché, 746, 758.
Attack, 716.
Attain, *arrive*, 293.
  succeed, 730.
Attainable, *possible*, 470.
  easy, 705.
Attainder, 971.
Attainment, *learning*, 539.
Attemper, *mix*, 41.
  moderate, 174.
Attempt, 676.
Attend, *accompany*, 88.
  follow, 281.
  apply the mind, 457.
  be present, 186.
Attendant, 746.
Attention, 457.
Attenuate, *lessen*, 36.
  contract, 195.
  narrow, 203.
Attest, *bear testimony*, 467.
  adjure, 768.

Attic, *garret*, 191.
  high, 206.
  wit, 842.
  taste, 850.
Atticism, 842.
Attila, 663, 913.
Attire, 225.
Attitude, *posture*, 240.
  circumstance, 8.
Attorney, *consignee*, 758.
  in law, 968.
Attract,*bring towards*, 289.
  please, 829.
Attractive, *beautiful*, 845.
  desirable, 865.
  lovely, 897.
Attrahent, 289.
Attribute, 157.
Attribution, 155.
Attrition, 331.
*Attroupement, 72.
Attune, *music*, 415.
  prepare, 673.
Auburn, 433.
Auction, 796.
Audacity, *courage*, 861.
  insolence, 885.
Audible, 402.
Audience, *hearing*, 418.
  conversation, 588.
Audit, *accounts*, 811.
  numeration, 85.
Audition, 418.
Auditor, 418.
Auditory, 418.
Auger, 262.
Aught, 51.
Augment, *to increase*, 35.
  thing added, 39.
Augur (to), 511.
  soothsayer, 513.
Augury, 511.
August, 873.
Augustine, 996.
*Aura, 380.
Aurate, 436.
Auricular, 418.
Aurora, *light*, 420.
  dawn, 125.
Auscultation, 418.
Auspicious, *hopeful*, 858.
  prosperous, 734.
  expedient, 646.
  opportune, 134.
Austere, *harsh taste*, 395.
  severe, 739.
  discourteous, 895.
  ascetic, 955.
Austromancy, 511.
Authentic, 494.

Bald, *bare*, 226.
  ugly, 846.
  in style, 575.
Balderdash, 497.
Baldric, *girdle*, 247.
  belt, 229.
Bale, *bundle*, 72.
  evil, 619.
Bale out, 296.
Baleful, 649.
Balister, *arms*, 727.
Balize, 550.
Balk, *hinder*, 706.
  fail, 731.
  disappoint, 509.
  deceive, 545.
Ball, *globe*, 249.
  missile, 284.
  (cannon), 727.
  dance, 840.
Ballad, *song*, 415.
  poem, 597.
Ballast, *weight*, 319.
  wisdom, 498.
*Ballet, 840.
Balloon, 273.
Ballot, 609.
Balm, *fragrance*, 400.
  relief, 834.
  remedy, 662.
*Balourdise, 732.
Balsam. *See* Balm.
Balsamic, *salubrious*, 656.
Balustrade, 232.
Bam, 546.
Bamboozle, 545.
Ban, *prohibition*, 761.
  denunciation, 908.
Band, *ligature*, 45.
  assemblage, 72.
  party, 712.
  of music, 416.
  shackle, 752.
Bandage, *ligature*, 45.
  to tie, 43.
Bandbox, 191.
Bandit, 792.
Bandog, 668.
Bands, 999.
Bandy, *agitate*, 315.
  contest, 720.
  exchange, 148.
Bandy-legged, 846.
Bane, 663.
Baneful, 649.
Bang, *sound*, 406.
  to impel, 276.
  to beat, 972.
Banian, *fast*, 950.
  scanty, 640.
260

Banish, *exclude*, 55.
  seclude, 893.
Bank, *side of lake*, 343.
  acclivity, 217.
  store, 636.
  money, 802.
Banker, 801.
Bankruptcy, *failure*, 732.
  non-payment, 808.
Banner, 550.
Banneret, 875.
Banquet, *meal*, 299.
  feast, 840.
Banshee, 979.
Banter, *wit*, 842.
  ridicule, 856.
Bantling, *child*, 129.
  offspring, 167.
Baptism, 998.
Baptize, *name*, 564.
Baptistry, 1000.
Bar, *hindrance*, 706.
  line, 200.
  to exclude, 55.
  inclosure, 232.
  prison, 752.
  prohibition, 761.
  tribunal, 966.
  legal profession, 968.
*Baragouin, 497.
Barb, *spike*, 253.
  nag, 271.
Barbacan, 717.
Barbarian, 913.
Barbarism, 895.
Barbarous, *maleficent*, 907.
  vulgar, 851.
  rude, 876.
  style, 579.
*Barbouillage, 590.
Bard, 597.
Bare, *mere*, 32.
  nude, 226.
  scanty, 640.
  exposed to view, 446.
Barebone, 203.
Barefaced, 446.
Bareheaded, 928.
Barely, 32.
Bargain, *compact*, 769.
  barter, 794.
  promise, 768.
  cheap, 813.
Barge, 273.
Bark, *rind*, 223.
  ship, 273.
  to yelp, 412.
  to censure, 932.
Barn, 189.
Barnacles, 445.

Barometer, 466.
Baron, 875.
Baronet, 875.
*Baroque, 853.
Barrack, 189.
Barracoon, 717.
Barred, *crossed*, 219.
  striped, 440.
Barrel, *vessel*, 191.
  cylinder, 249.
Barren, *sterile*, 169.
  useless, 645.
Barricade, *fence*, 232.
  prison, 752.
  obstacle, 706.
Barrier, *fence*, 232.
  obstacle, 706.
Barring, *except*, 83.
  save, 38.
Barrister, 968.
Barrow, *vehicle*, 272.
  grave, 363.
Barter, 794.
Base, *lowest part*, 211.
  support, 215.
  music, 413.
  grave note, 408.
  bad, 649.
  dishonorable, 940.
  shameful, 874.
  vicious, 945.
  cowardly, 862.
  plebeian, 876.
Baseless, *unreal*, 2.
  erroneous, 495.
Basement, 211.
Baseminded, 940.
Bashaw, *ruler*, 745.
  tyrant, 739.
Bashful, 881.
Basilic, 1000.
Basilisk, *serpent*, 949.
  cannon, 727.
Basin, *hollow*, 252.
  vessel, 191.
  plain, 344.
  dock, 189.
Basis, *preparation*, 673.
Bask, *warmth*, 382.
  physical enjoyment, 377.
  moral enjoyment, 827.
  prosperity, 734.
Basket, 191.
Bass, *in music*, 408.
Bass-viol, 417.
Bassoon, 417.
Bastard, *spurious*, 544.
  erroneous, 495.
Baste, *beat*, 276.
  punish, 972.

Bastile, 752.
Bastinado, 972.
Bastion, 717.
Bat, *club*, 727.
 mall, 633.
Batch, 72.
Bate, *diminish*, 36.
 reduce price, 813.
Bath, 301.
Bathe, 301.
Bathos, *depth*, 208.
 anticlimax, 497.
 ridiculous, 853.
*Bâton, 747.
Battalion, *troop*, 726.
 assemblage, 72.
Batten, 297.
Batter, *beat*, 276.
 destroy, 162.
Battered, 651.
Battering-ram, 727.
Battery, 633.
Battle, 720.
Battle array, 722.
Battle-axe, 727.
Battle-field, 728.
Battlement, *bulwark*, 666.
 defence, 717.
 inclosure, 232.
 embrasure, 257.
Battology, *repetition*, 104.
 diffuseness, 573.
*Bavardage, 497.
Bawble, *trifle*, 643.
 toy, 840.
Bawd, 962.
Bawdy, 961.
Bawl, 411.
Bay, *gulf*, 343.
 brown, 433.
 to howl, 412.
Bay (at), 717.
Bayard, 271.
Bayonet, 727.
Bays, *trophy*, 733.
 reward, 973.
Bazaar, 799.
Be (to), 1.
Be off, 292.
Beach, 342.
Beacon, *sign*, 550.
 warning, 668.
Beadle, *janitor*, 263.
 officer, 745.
 law officer, 965.
 church, 996.
Beads, 998.
Beak, 250.
Beam, *support*, 215.
 of a balance, 466.
261

Beam, *of light*, 420.
 beauty, 845.
Beamless, 421.
Bear, *sustain*, 215.
 produce, 161.
 carry, 270.
 suffer, 821.
 admit, 470.
Bear, *brute*, 895.
Bear down upon, 716.
Bear off, 789.
Bear out, *confirm*, 467.
 vindicate, 937.
Bear up, 836.
Bear upon, *influence*, 175.
 evidence, 467.
 to relate to, 9.
Beard, *sharp*, 253.
 rough, 256.
 to defy, 715.
 courage, 861.
 insolence, 885.
Beardless, 127.
Bearer, 271.
Bear-garden, 728.
Bearing, *support*, 215.
 direction, 278.
 meaning, 516.
 demeanour, 692.
Bearish, 895.
Bear-leader, 540.
Beast, 366.
Beastly, 653.
Beat, *strike*, 972.
 be superior, 33.
 periodic, 138.
 oscillation, 314.
 agitation, 315.
 crush, 330.
 sound, 407.
 succeed, 731.
 line of pursuit, 625.
Beat about, 461.
Beat down, *chaffer*, 794.
 insolence, 885.
Beat off, 717.
Beat time, 114.
Beatify, *enrapture*, 829.
 sanctify, 987.
Beatitude, 827.
Beau, *fop*, 854.
 admirer, 897.
*Beau-idéal, 845.
*Beau monde, *fashion*, 852.
 nobility, 875.
Beautiless, 846.
Beauty, 845.
Beaver, *hat*, 225.
Bec, 550.
Becalm, 265.

Because, *attribution*, 155.
 reasoning, 476.
 motive, 615.
Bechance, 151.
Beck, *rill*, 348.
 mandate, 741.
Beckon, 550.
Becloud, 421.
Become, *change to*, 144.
 behove, 926.
Becoming, *proper*, 646.
 beautiful, 845.
Bed, *layer*, 204.
 support, 215.
 lodgment, 191.
Bedarken, 421.
Bedaub, *cover*, 222.
 dirt, 653.
 deface, 846.
Bedazzle, 420.
Bedeck, 845.
Bedew, 339.
Bedfellow, 890.
Bedight, 845.
Bedim, 421.
Bedizen, *beautify*, 845.
 ornament, 851.
Bedlam, 503.
Bedlamite, 504.
Bedridden, 655.
Bee, *agent*, 690.
 active, 682.
Beef-witted, 499.
Beelzebub, 678.
Beetle, *high*, 206.
 projecting, 250.
Beetle-head, 501.
Beetle-headed, 499.
Befall, 151.
Beg, 765.
Beget, 161.
Beggar, 767.
Beggarly, *mean*, 643.
 vulgar, 876.
 servile, 886.
 vile, 940.
Begilt, 847.
Begin, 66.
Beginner, 541.
Begird, 231.
Begirt, 227.
Beglerbeg, 745.
Begone, *depart*, 292.
 disappear, 449.
 repel, 288.
Begrime, *soil*, 653.
 deface, 846.
Begrudge, 764.
Beguile, *deceive*, 545.
 amuse, 840.

Begum, 875.
Behalf, *advantage*, 618.
  aid, 707.
Behave, 692.
Behead, 975.
Behest, 741.
Behind, 63.
Behindhand, *late*, 133.
  adversity, 735.
Behold, 441.
Beholden, *grateful*, 916.
  obligatory, 926.
Behoof, 618.
Behoove, 926.
Being, *abstract*, 1.
  concrete, 3.
Belabour, *thump*, 972.
  buffet, 276.
Belated, 491.
Belay, 43.
Belch, 296.
Beldam, 913.
Beldame, 173.
Beleaguer, 716.
Belial, 980.
Belie, *falsify*, 544.
  misinterpret, 523.
  deny, 536.
Belief, *credence*, 484.
  religious creed, 987.
Belike, 472.
Bell, *sound*, 417.
  funereal, 363.
  alarm, 669.
Bell-shaped, *globose* 4 9.
  concave, 252.
Belle, 374.
*Belles lettres, 560.
Bellicose, 720.
Belligerent, 720.
Bellow, *cry*, 412.
  complain, 839.
Bellows, 349.
Bellyful, 639.
Belly-god, 957.
Belly-timber, 299.
Belomancy, 511.
Belong to, *related*, 9.
  property, 777.
  attribute, 157.
  duty, 926.
Beloved, 899.
Below, 207.
Belt, *girdle*, 247.
  outline, 229.
Belvedere, 441.
Bemingle, 41.
Bemoan, 839.
Bench, *support*, 215.
  council, 696.

Bench, *tribunal*, 966.
Bencher, 968.
Bend, *curve*, 245.
  angularity, 244.
  circle, 247.
  circuit, 311.
  obliquity, 217.
  descent, 306.
  deviation, 279.
  stoop, 879.
Bend to, *tend*, 176.
Bending, *pliant*, 324.
Beneath, *under*, 207.
  unbecoming, 940.
Benedict, 903.
Benediction, *approval*, 931.
  gratitude, 916.
  worship, 990.
Benefaction, 784.
Benefactor, 912.
Benefice, 995.
Beneficent, 906.
Beneficial, *useful*, 644.
  good, 648.
Beneficiary, 996.
Benefit, *advantage*, 618.
  acquisition, 775.
  benevolence, 906.
Benevolence, *kindness*, 906.
  tax, 812.
Benighted, 491.
Benignant, 906.
Benison, 931.
Bent, *direction*, 278.
  inclination, 602.
  desire, 865.
  intention, 629.
  affections, 820.
Bent on, *willing*, 602.
  resolved, 604.
  desirous, 865.
Benumb, *cold*, 383.
  general insensibility,
    376.
  tactual insensibility, 381
Bepraise, 931.
Bequeath, 784.
Bequest, *gift*, 784.
  acquisition, 775.
Bereave, *take away*, 789.
Bereavement, *loss*, 776.
Bereft, *poor*, 804.
Berlin, 272.
Berry, *brown*, 433.
Berth, *lodging*, 189.
  bed, 191.
  repose, 215.
Beseech, *request*, 765.
  pray, 990.
Beseem, 926.

Beset, *surround*, 227.
  difficulty, 704.
  entreaty, 765.
  beshrew, 908.
  by the side of, 216.
Beside, *except*, 83.
Beside oneself, 503.
Besides, *moreover*, 37.
Besiege, *attack*, 716.
  solicit, 765.
Beslabber, 653.
Beslaver, 933.
Beslime, 653.
Besmear, *soil*, 653.
  deface, 846.
Besom, 652.
Besotted, *prejudiced*, 481.
  foolish, 499.
Bespangle, 847.
Bespatter, *soil*, 653.
  spoil, 659.
  deface, 846.
  revile, 932.
  flatter, 933.
Bespeak, *indicate*, 516.
  hire, 755.
Bespeckle, 440.
Bespotted, 440.
Besprinkle, *mix*, 41.
  spirt, 296.
Best, 650.
Bestial, 961.
Bestir, 682.
Bestow, 784.
Bestride, 206.
Bet, 621.
Betake, 625.
Bethink, 505.
Bethrall, 749.
Betide, 151.
Betimes, 132.
Betoken, *indicate*, 550.
  predict, 511.
Betray, *disclose*, 529.
  deceive, 545.
  dishonor, 940.
Betroth, 768.
Better (to), 658.
Between, 228.
Betwixt, 228.
Bevel, 217.
Bever, 299.
*Bévue, 732.
Bevy, 72.
Bewail, 839.
Beware, *warn*, 668.
  afraid, 862.
Bewilder, *confuse*, 458.
  mislead, 538.
  perplex, 528.

Bewilder, *astonish*, 870.
Bewildered, *ignorant*, 491.
Bewitch, *please*, 829.
   exorcise, 992.
Bey, 745.
Beyond, 196.
Bias, *slope*, 217.
   prepossession, 481.
   (*mental*), 602.
   motive, 615.
   disposition, 820.
Bibacious, 959.
Bibber, *toper*, 959.
   to weep, 839.
Bible, 985.
Bibliomancy, 511.
Bibliomania, *curiosity*, 455.
   erudition, 490.
Bibliotheca, 595.
Bibulous, 322.
Bicker, *flutter*, 315.
   discord, 713.
   quarrel, 720.
Bid, *order*, 741.
   offer, 763.
Bid for, *bargain*, 794.
Bide, 133, 142.
Bidet, 271.
*Bienséance, *polish*, 852.
   manners, 894.
Bier, 363.
Bifarious, 91.
Bifold, 90.
Biform, 90, 91.
Bifurcation, *fork*, 244.
Big, *in degree*, 31.
   in size, 192.
Bigamy, 903.
Bight, 343.
Bigot, 989.
Bigoted, 499.
Bigotry, *prejudice*, 481.
   obstinacy, 606.
   heterodoxy, 984.
Big-wig, *sage*, 500.
   (*ironically*), 493.
*Bijou, 650.
Bilander, 273.
Bilbo, 727.
Bilboes, 752.
Bile, 900.
Bilge-water, 653.
Bilious, 837.
Bilk, 545.
Bill, *money account*, 811.
   charge, 812.
   money order, 800.
   in law, 969.
   ticket, 550.
   hatchet, 633.
263

Bill, *weapon*, 727.
Bill of fare, 632.
Billet, *epistle*, 592.
   ticket, 500.
   to locate, 184.
Billingsgate, *scolding*, 932.
   imprecatory, 908.
Billion, 98.
Bin, 191.
Binary, 90.
Bind, *connect*, 43.
   compel, 744.
   obligation, 926.
   condition, 770.
Binomial, 90.
Biography, 594.
Biology, 357.
Bipartition, 91.
Biplicity, 90.
Biquadratic, 95.
Birch, 975.
Bird, 366.
Bird's-eye view, 448.
Bird-lime, 45.
Birth, *beginning*, 66.
   nobility, 875.
Birth-place, 153.
Birth-right, 924.
*Bise, 349.
Bisection, 91.
Bishop, 996.
Bishopric, 995.
Bisulcate, 258.
Bit, *part*, 51.
   small quantity, 32.
   curb, 747, 752.
Bit by bit, 51.
Bite, *pain*, 378.
   painful, 830.
   cheat, 545.
Biting, *cold*, 383.
   pungent, 392.
   painful, 830.
Bitter, *taste*, 395.
   cold, 383.
   animosity, 898.
   wrath, 900.
   regret, 833.
   painful, 830.
*Bivouac, *repose*, 265.
   to encamp, 186.
   camp, 189.
   watch, 664.
*Bizarre, 853.
Blab, 529.
Black, *colour*, 431.
   crime, 945.
Blackamoor, 431.
Blackball, *exclude*, 55.
   seclude, 893.

Blacken, 932.
Blackguard, *rude*, 895.
   vagabond, 949.
Blackhole, 752.
Blackleg, *sharper*, 548.
   thief, 792.
Black letter, 591.
Black looks, 895.
Blackmail, *theft*, 791.
   booty, 793.
Bladder, 191.
Blade, 372, 854.
Blain, 250.
Blamable, 945.
Blame, 932.
Blameless, 946.
Blameworthy, 945.
Blanch, 430.
Bland, *courteous*, 894.
   mild, 174.
Blandiloquence, 933.
Blandishment, 933.
Blank, 4.
Blarney, 933.
*Blasé, 841.
Blasphemy, 989.
Blast, *wind*, 349.
   sound, 404.
   evil, 619.
   explosion, 173.
Blatant, *cry*, 412.
   silly, 499.
Blaze, *light*, 420.
   heat, 382.
Blaze about, 531.
Blazon, 531.
Bleach, 429.
Bleak, 383.
Blear-eyed, 443.
Bleat, 412.
Bleb, *swelling*, 250.
   bubble, 353.
Bleed, *physical pain*, 378.
   moral pain, 828.
Blemish, *ugly*, 846.
   defect, 848.
Blench, *avoid*, 623.
   fear, 860.
Blend, *mix*, 41.
   combine, 48.
Bless, 931.
Blessing, 618.
Blight, *evil*, 619.
   deterioration, 689.
Blind, *cecity*, 442.
   ignorant, 491.
   screen, 424.
   falsehood, 546.
   deception, 545.
   concealment, 528.

Blind, *necessity*, 601.
   pretext, 617.
   imperforate, 261.
Blind alley, 261.
Blindfold, *sightless*, 442.
   ignorant, 491.
Blind side, *obstinacy*, 606.
   prejudice, 481.
Blink, *wink*, 442.
   neglect, 460.
   overlook, 458.
Bliss, 827.
Blister, 250.
Blithe, 836.
Bloated, 192.
Block, *mass*, 192.
   dense, 321.
   fool, 501.
   execution, 975.
Block-up, *plug*, 261.
   impede, 706.
Blockade, 261.
Blockhead, 501.
Blockish, 499.
Blonde, 430.
Blood, *killing*, 361.
   affections, 820.
   nobility, 875.
   fop, 854.
Bloodhound, 913.
Blood-red, 434.
Bloodshed, 361.
Bloodstained, *murderous*,
   361.
   maleficent, 907.
Bloodsucker, 913.
Bloodthirsty, 907.
Bloody, 907.
Bloom, *youth*, 127.
   prosperity, 734.
   success, 731.
   blueness, 438.
Blooming, 845.
Blossom, 731, 734.
Blot, *obliterate*, 552.
   darken, 431.
   disappear, 449.
   decoloration, 429.
   forget, 506.
   ugly, 846.
   blemish, 848.
   disgrace, 874.
   dishonor, 940.
   guilt, 947.
Blotch, *blackness*, 431.
   blemish, 848.
*Blouse, 225.
Blow, *wind*, 349.
   knock, 276.
   action, 680.
264

Blow, *evil*, 619.
   pain, 828.
   disappointment, 732.
   to prosper, 734.
Blow down, 162.
Blow-hole, 351.
Blow out, 385.
Blow over, 122.
Blow up, *fan*, 615.
   wind, 349.
   inflate, 194.
   eruption, 173.
   objurgation, 932.
Blow upon, *censure*, 934.
Blown, *fatigued*, 688.
   consequential, 878.
Blowsy, 434.
Blubber, *cry*, 839.
   fat, 356.
Bludgeon, *club*, 276.
   weapon, 727.
Blue, *colour*, 438.
   learned, 490.
Blue devils, 837.
Blue lights, 423.
Blue stocking, 492.
Bluff, *high*, 206.
   blunt, 254.
   insolent, 885.
   discourteous, 895.
Blunder, *error*, 495.
   folly, 499.
   awkwardness, 699.
   ridiculous, 856.
Blunderbuss, 727.
Blunderheaded, 499.
Blunt, *inert*, 172.
   obtuse, 254.
   insensible, 376.
   inexcitable, 826.
   stupid, 499.
   cash, 800.
   discourteous, 895.
   frank, 543.
   to moderate, 174.
   to damp, 616.
Blunt-witted, 499.
Blur, *deformity*, 846.
   blemish, 848.
Blurred, 447.
Blurt out, 529.
Blush, *redden*, 434.
   feel, 821.
   be ashamed, 874.
   appearance, 448.
Bluster, *violence*, 173.
   insolence, 885.
   defiance, 715.
Blusterer, 887.
Board, *layer*, 204.

Board, *support*, 215.
   food, 299.
   to attack, 716.
   council, 696.
   tribunal, 966.
   theatre, 599.
Boast, 884.
Boat, 273.
Bob, *rise*, 305.
   stoop, 306.
   oscillate, 314.
   agitate, 315.
Bobadil, 887.
Boddice, 225.
Bode, 511.
Bodily, 3.
Bodkin, *perforator*, 262.
   go-between, 228.
Body, *substance*, 3.
   matter, 316.
   whole, 50.
   person, 373.
   assemblage, 72.
   party, 712.
   political, 737.
Bœotian, *dull*, 843.
   foolish, 499.
Bog, *swamp*, 343.
   dunghill, 653.
Boggle, *demur*, 603.
   hesitate, 605.
   difficulty, 704.
   awkward, 699.
Bogie, 980.
Bogle, 980.
Boil, *heat*, 382.
   to heat, 384.
   bubble, 353.
   effervesce, 315.
   be excited, 825.
   be irate, 900.
Boiler, 386.
Boisterous, *violent*, 173.
   hasty, 684.
   excitable, 825.
Bold, *brave*, 861.
   prominent, 250.
Bolster, *support*, 215.
   aid, 707.
   repair, 658.
   relief, 834.
Bolt, *fastening*, 45.
   to fasten, 43.
   to propel, 284.
   swallow, 297.
   move rapidly, 274.
   escape, 671, 750.
   shackle, 752.
   upright, 212.
Bolthead, 191.

Bolus, *mouthful*, 299.
Bomb, 727.
Bombard, 716.
Bombardier, 726.
Bombast, *absurd*, 497.
  ridiculous, 853.
  boasting, 884.
Bombastic style, 577.
*Bonâ fide, 543.
*Bonbon, 396, 829.
Bond, *tie*, 45.
  compact, 769.
  security, 771.
  right, 924.
  fetters, 752.
Bondage, 749.
Bondsman, 746.
Bones, *corpse*, 362.
Bone of contention, 713.
Bonfire, 838.
*Bonhommie,*credulity*,486.
  veracity, 543.
  candour, 703.
*Bonmot, 842.
*Bonne, 746.
*Bonnebouche, 67, 829.
Bonnet, 225.
Bonny, *pretty*, 845.
  cheerful, 836.
*Bon-ton, 852.
Bonus, *advantage*, 618.
  money, 810.
*Bonvivant, 957.
Bonze, 996.
Booby, *fool*, 501.
  ignoramus, 493.
Boodhism, 984.
Book, *volume*, 593.
  to enter accounts, 811.
  to record, 551.
  to register, 86.
Book-keeper, 553.
Book-keeping, 811.
Bookish, *erudite*, 490.
  scholar, 492.
Bookworm, 492.
Boom, *bar*, 633.
  defence, 717.
  obstacle, 706.
  to sail, 267.
  rush, 274.
  sound, 404.
Boomerang, *arms*, 727.
  recoil, 277.
Booming, 276.
Boon, 784.
Boor, *clown*, 876.
  ridiculous, 851.
Boot (to), *addition*, 37.
  dress, 225.
2E5

Boot, *advantage*, 618.
  punishment, 975.
Booth, 189.
Bootless, *useless*, 645.
  failing, 732.
Booty, 793.
Bopeep, 441.
Border, *edge*, 230.
  to be near, 197.
Bore, *hole*, 260.
  diameter, 202.
  to trouble, 828.
  to plague, 830.
  to weary, 841.
Boreal, 383.
Boreas, 349.
Borer, 262.
*Borné, 499.
Borough, 189.
Borrow, 788.
Bosom, *breast*, 221.
  mind, 450.
  will, 600.
  affections, 820.
Bosom friend, 890.
Boss, 250.
Botanic, 367.
Botanomancy, 511.
Botany, 369.
Botch, *to mend*, 658.
  to fail, 732.
  unskilful, 699.
Both, 89.
Bother, *trouble*, 828.
  to trouble, 830.
Bottle, 191.
Bottle-green, 432.
Bottle up, *inclose*, 231.
  preserve, 670.
  remember, 505.
Bottom, *lowest part*, 211.
  ship, 273.
  pluck, 604.
  courage, 861.
Bottomless, 208.
*Boudoir, 191.
Bough, *part*, 51.
  curve, 245.
Bought, *flexure*, 245.
*Bouleversé, 824.
Bounce, *violence*, 173.
  motion, 274.
  exaggeration, 549.
Bounce upon, 293.
  surprise, 508.
Bouncing, *large*, 192.
Bound, *limit*, 233.
  circumscribe, 231.
  spring, 274.
  ascend, 305.

Bound, *leap*, 309.
Boundary, 233.
Bounden duty, 926.
Boundless, *great*, 31.
  infinite, 105.
  space, 180.
Bounteous, 906.
Bountiful, 816.
Bounty, *gift*, 784.
  liberality, 816.
  benevolence, 906.
*Bouquet, 400.
Bourn, 233.
Bournouse, 225.
Bouse, 959.
Bout, *job*, 680.
  fight, 720.
*Boutade, 497.
Bow, *curve*, 245.
  fore part, 234.
  propeller, 284.
  arms, 727.
  to stoop, 306.
  reverence, 894.
  obeisance, 743.
  servility, 886.
  respect, 928.
  prominence, 250.
Bowels, *interior*, 221.
  of compassion, 914.
Bowelless, 907.
Bower, *alcove*, 189.
  chamber, 191.
Bowie knife, 727.
Bow-kneed, 245.
Bowl, *vessel*, 191.
  hollow, 252.
  to propel, 284.
Bowling-green, 213.
Bow-shot, 197.
Bowstring, 975.
Box, *chest*, 191.
  house, 189.
  to strike, 972.
  to fight, 720.
Boxer, 726.
Boxing, 720.
Boy, 129.
Brabble, *discord*, 713.
  contest, 720.
Brabbler, 901.
Brace, *to tie*, 43.
  fastening, 45.
  two, 89.
  to refresh, 689.
  to strengthen, 159.
Bracelet, 247.
Brachygraphy, 590.
Bracing, 159.
Bracket, *tie*, 43.

Bracket, *support*, 215.
  couple, 89.
Brackish, 392.
Brad, 45.
Brag, 884.
Braggadocio, 884.
Braggart, 884.
Brahma, 979.
Brahmin, 996.
Braid, *to tie*, 43.
  ligature, 45.
  intersection, 219.
Brain, *intellect*, 450.
  skill, 498.
Brainless, 499.
Brainsick, *giddy*, 460.
Brake, *copse*, 367.
  curb, 752.
Bramble, *thorn*, 253.
  painful, 830.
Bran, 330.
Brancard, 272.
Branch, *member*, 51.
  duality, 91.
  posterity, 167.
Branch off, 290.
Branch out, *style*, 573.
Brand, *to burn*, 384.
  fuel, 388.
  to stigmatize, 932.
  to accuse, 938.
  reproach, 874.
Brandish, *oscillate*, 314.
  flourish, 315.
Brangle, 713.
Brasier, 386.
Brass, 885.
Brass, *colour*, 439.
Brat, 129.
Bravado, 884.
Brave, 861.
*Bravo, *assassin*, 361.
  applause, 931.
*Bravura, 415.
Brawl, *cry*, 411.
  weeping, 839.
  discord, 713.
Brawny, *strong*, 159.
  stout, 192.
Bray, *cry*, 412.
  to grind, 330.
Brazenfaced, 885.
Breach, *crack*, 44.
  quarrel, 713.
  violation, 925.
  exception, 83.
Bread, 299.
Bread-stuffs, 299.
Breadth, 202.
Break, *fracture*, 44.
266

Break, *shatter*, 162.
  interval, 70.
  violation, 773.
  bankruptcy, 808.
  to infringe, 927.
  to disclose, 529.
  to tame, 749.
  to decline, 659.
Break down, *fail*, 732.
Break ground, 676.
Break in, *teach*, 537.
  train, 673.
Break loose, *escape*, 671.
  liberate, 750.
Break off a habit, 614.
  leave off, 141.
  abrogate, 756.
Break out, *fly out*, 825.
Break up, *destroy*, 162.
  decompose, 49.
Break with, 713.
Breaker, *wave*, 346, 348.
  danger, 667.
Breakfast, 299.
Breakneck, *perilous*, 665.
  precipitous, 217.
Breakwater, 666.
Breast, *interior*, 221.
  mind, 450.
  will, 600.
  soul, 820.
  to oppose, 708.
Breast-plate, 717.
Breast-work, 717.
Breath, *air*, 349.
  sound, 405.
  life, 359.
Breathe, *exist*, 1.
  live, 359.
  blow, 349.
  mean, 516.
  utter, 580.
  repose, 687.
Breathless, *speechless*, 585.
  out of breath, 688.
Breech, 235.
Breeches, 225.
Breed, *kind*, 75.
  to multiply, 161.
  progeny, 167.
Breeding, 852.
Breeze, 349.
Brevet, *warrant*, 741.
  commission, 755.
Brevity, 201.
Brew, *mix*, 41.
  prepare, 673.
  impend, 121.
Briar, *sharp*, 253.
  painful, 830.

Bribe, *buy*, 795.
  offer, 763.
  gift, 784.
  tempt, 615.
Brick, 635.
Brickbat, 284.
Bride, 903.
Bridegroom, 903.
Bridewell, 752.
Bridge, *intermedium*, 45.
  way, 627.
  escape, 671.
Bridge over, 43.
Bridle, *curb*, 752.
  to restrain, 751.
  to moderate, 174.
  to swagger, 878.
Bridle up, 900.
Brief, *time*, 111.
  space, 201.
  style, 572.
  compendium, 596.
Briefly, 111.
Brig, 273.
Brigade, 726.
Brigand, 792.
Brigantine, 273.
Bright, *shining*, 420.
  colour, 428.
  cheerful, 836.
  glorious, 873.
Brilliant, *shining*, 420.
  beautiful, 845.
  glorious, 873.
  perfect, 650.
  gem, 847.
Brim, 230.
Brimful, 639.
Brinded, 433.
Brindled, 440.
Brine, *salt*, 392.
  sea, 341.
Bring, *transfer*, 270.
  induce, 615.
Bring about, *cause*, 153.
  achieve, 729.
  succeed, 731.
Bring forth, 161.
Bring forward, 525.
Bring in, 812.
Bring off, 672.
Bring out, 525.
Bring over, *persuade*, 484.
Bring up, *educate*, 537.
Brink, 230.
Brisk, *quick*, 274.
  active, 682.
  prompt, 111.
Bristle, 253.
Bristle up, 900.

Brittle, 328.
Broach, 535.
Broad, *space*, 202.
   indelicate, 961.
Broadcast, *scattered*, 73.
   shed, 290.
Broadside, *side*, 236.
   cannonade, 716.
Broadsword, 727.
Brobdignagian, 192.
Brocade, 847.
*Broder, 549.
Brogue, 560.
Broidery, 847.
Broil, *heat*, 382.
   to fry, 384.
   fray, 720.
Broken, 160.
Broken-winded, 688.
Broker, *agent*, 758.
   merchant, 797.
Brokerage, *pay*, 812.
Brood, 167.
Brood over, *think*, 451.
   mope, 837.
Brook, *stream*, 348.
   to bear, 821.
Broom, 652.
Brougham, 272.
Broth, 299.
Brothel, 961.
Brother, *kin*, 11.
   similar, 17.
   friend, 888.
*Brouillerie, 713.
*Brouillon, *rough copy*, 21.
Brow, *summit*, 210.
   edge, 230.
Browbeat, *intimidate*, 860.
   swagger, 885.
Brown, 433.
Brownie, 980.
Brown-study, *reverie*, 458.
Browse, 297.
Bruise, *hurt*, 619.
   to injure, 649.
*Bruit, 531, 532.
Brumal, 383.
Brunette, 433.
Brunt, *impulse*, 276.
   attack, 716.
Brush, *rapid motion*, 274.
   to clean, 652.
   painting, 559.
   fight, 720.
Brushwood, 367.
*Brusquerie, *haste*, 684.
   discourtesy, 895.
Brustle, 406.
Brutal, *vicious*, 945.
267

Brutal, *savage*, 907.
Brutalize, 823, 895.
Brute, *animal*, 366.
   rude, 895.
   maleficent, 913.
Brute force, 964.
Brute matter, *materiality*,
   316.
   inanimate matter, 358.
Brutish, *vulgar*, 876.
   intemperate, 954.
Bubble, *air*, 353.
   light, 320.
   trifle, 643.
   error, 495.
   vision, 515.
   deceit, 545.
Buccaneer, 792.
Buck, *to wash*, 652.
   fop, 854.
Bucket, 191.
Buckle, *to tie*, 43.
   fastening, 45.
Buckle to,*apply oneself*,682.
Buckle with, *grapple*, 720.
Buckler, *defence*, 666, 717.
Buckram, 323, 855.
Bucolic, *pastoral*, 371.
   poem, 597.
Bud, *beginning*, 60.
   to expand, 194.
   effect, 154.
   graft, 301.
Buddha, 979, 986.
Buddhism, 984.
Budge, 264.
Budget, *heap*, 72.
   store, 636.
   news, 532.
   finance, 811.
Buff colour, 436.
Buffet, *cupboard*, 191.
   beat, 276, 972.
   attack, 716.
Buffoon, *humorist*, 844.
   butt, 857.
   actor, 599.
Buffoonery,*amusement*,840.
   ridiculous, 856.
Bugaboo, 860.
Bugbear, *fear*, 860.
   alarm, 669.
   imaginary, 515.
Bugle, *instrument*, 417.
   war-cry, 722.
Buggy, 272.
Build, *construct*, 161.
   compose, 54.
Builder, 164.
Building, 189.

Bulb, *knob*, 249.
   projection, 250.
Bulge, 250.
Bulk, *whole*, 50.
   size, 192.
Bulkhead, 706.
Bulky, 192.
Bull, *absurdity*, 497.
   error, 495.
   solecism, 568.
   law, 963.
   ordinance, 741.
Bull-calf, 501.
Bulldog, 861.
Bullet, *ball*, 249.
   missile, 284.
   arms, 727.
Bulletin, 592.
Bullhead, 501.
Bullion, 800.
Bullrush, 643.
Bully, *to bluster*, 885.
   blusterer, 887.
   fighter, 726.
   courage, 861.
   rashness, 863.
   to frighten, 860.
Bulwark, *defence*, 717.
   refuge, 666.
Bum-bailiff, 965.
Bumboat, 273.
Bump, *projection*, 250.
   thump, 276.
Bumper, 639.
Bumpkin, 876.
Bunch, *protuberance*, 250.
   collection, 72.
Bundle, *packet*, 72.
   to move, 275.
Bung, 263.
Bungalow, 189.
Bungle, 699.
Bungler, 701.
Buoy, *float*, 320.
   to raise, 307.
   to hope, 858.
Buoyant, *floating*, 305.
   levity, 320.
   elastic, 325.
   hopeful, 858.
   cheerful, 836.
Bur, *rough*, 256.
   clinging, 46.
Burden, *weight*, 319.
   clog, 706.
   chorus, 104.
   frequency, 136.
   lading, 190.
   oppression, 828.
*Bureau, *cabinet*, 691.

*Bureau, *office,* 799.
Bureaucracy, 693.
Burgess, *citizen,* 188, 373.
Burglar, 792.
Burglary, 791.
Burgomaster, 745.
Burgrave, 745.
Burial, 362.
Buried, 208.
*Burin, 599.
Burke, *kill,* 361.
   destroy, 162.
Burlesque, *imitation,* 19.
   travestie, 21.
   ridicule, 856.
   ridiculous, 853.
Burletta, 599.
Burly, 192.
Burn, *heat,* 382.
   consume, 384.
   passions, 821.
   rivulet, 348.
Burnish, *polish,* 255.
   beautify, 845.
   shine, 420.
Burnoose, 225.
Burrow, *excavate,* 252.
   lodge, 186.
Bursar, 801.
Bursary, 802.
Burst, *explosion,* 173.
   sound, 406.
   of anger, 900.
   paroxysm, 825.
Burst forth, *appear,* 446.
Bury, *inter,* 363.
   conceal, 528.
Buskin, 225.
Bush, *branch,* 51.
   shrub, 367.
Bushel, 191.
Bushy, 256.
Business, *occupation,* 625.
   event, 151.
   topic, 454.
   barter, 794.
Business-like, 682.
Buskin, *dress,* 225.
   drama, 599.
Buss, *carriage,* 272.
   kiss, 902.
Bustle, *activity,* 682.
   haste, 684.
   energy, 171.
   earliness, 132.
Busy, 682.
Busy-body, 682.
But, *exception,* 83.
   counter-evidence, 468.
Butcher, 913.
268

Butchery, 361.
Butler, 746.
Butt, *aim,* 620.
   laughing-stock, 857.
   to push, 276.
   to attack, 716.
Butt-end, 67.
Butter, *softness,* 324.
   oiliness, 356.
Butterfly, *beauty,* 845.
   fickleness, 605.
Button, *knob,* 250.
   to fasten, 44.
   fastening, 45.
   hanging, 214.
   trifle, 643.
Buttoned up, *reserved,* 528.
   taciturn, 585.
Button-holder, 841.
Buttress, 717.
Buxom, 836.
Buy, 795.
Buyer, 797.
Buzz, *sound,* 409.
   to publish, 531.
   news, 532.
Buzzard, 501.
Bye, *departure,* 292.
   sequestered, 893.
By the bye, 134.
Bygone, *former,* 122.
   forgotten, 506.
By-path, *by-road,* 627.
*Byssus, 256.
By-stander, *spectator,* 444.
   near, 197.
By-way, 627.
By-word, *maxim,* 496.
   cant term, 563.

C.

Cabal, *confederacy,* 712.
   plan, 626.
Cabala, 993.
Cabalistic, *mysterious,* 526.
Cabbage, *purloin,* 791.
Cabin, *room,* 189.
   receptacle, 191.
Cabinet, *receptacle,* 191.
   workshop, 691.
   council, 696.
Cable, 45.
Cabriolet, 272.
Cachexy, 655.
Cachinnation, 838.
Cackle, *of geese,* 412.
   talk, 588.
   laughter, 838.
Cacodemon, 980.

*Cacoëthes, *habit,* 613.
   itch, 865.
   writing, 590.
Cacography, 590.
Cacophony, *stridor,* 410.
   discord, 414.
   style, 579.
Cacus, 791.
Cad, 746.
Cadaverous, *pale,* 429.
   hideous, 846.
Cadence, *accent,* 580.
   music, 415.
Cadenza, 413.
Cadet, *junior,* 129.
   officer, 745.
Cadger, 797.
Cadi, 967.
Caduceus, 993.
Caducity, 111.
Cæsar, 745.
*Cæsura, *break,* 70.
Caftan, 225.
Cage, *prison,* 752.
   to immure, 751.
*Cahotage, 315.
Caique, 273.
Cairn, *grave,* 363.
   sign, 550.
Caisson, 191.
Caitiff, *ruffian,* 913.
   villain, 949.
   churl, 876.
Cajole, *persuade,* 615.
   flatter, 933.
Cake, *aggregate,* 46.
   density, 321.
Calabash, 191.
Calamity, *evil,* 619.
   adversity, 735.
   suffering, 830.
Calash, *vehicle,* 272.
   cap, 225.
Calcine, 384.
Calcitrate, 276.
Calculate, *reckon,* 85.
   expect, 507.
   believe, 484.
   investigate, 461.
Calculated, *tending to,* 176.
   premeditated, 600.
Calculating, *prudent,* 498.
Calculation, *consideration,*
   615.
   caution, 864.
Calculus, 85.
Caldron, *vessel,* 191.
   heating, 386.
   laboratory, 691.
Calefaction, 384.

Calendar, *of time*, 114.
  list, 86.
  record, 551.
  to glaze, 255.
Calf, 501.
Caliban, 846.
Calibre, *size*, 192.
  breadth, 202.
  opening, 260.
  intellectual capacity, 698.
Calidity, 382.
Caligenous, 421.
Caligraphy (or calligraphy), 590.
Caliph, 745.
Caliphate, 737.
Calk, 658.
Call, *to name*, 564.
  motive, 615.
  inspiration, 985.
Call down, 908.
Call for, *order*, 741.
  ask, 765.
  require, 630.
Call forth, *resort to*, 677.
Call on, 892.
Call over, 85.
Call up, 505.
Call upon, *behove*, 926.
  visit, 892.
  claim, 924.
Calligraphy, 590.
Calling, 625.
Callipers, 466.
Callosity, 323.
Callous, *obtuse*, 376.
  insensible, 823.
Callow, *infant*, 129.
  young, 127.
Calm, *physical*, 174.
  moral, 826.
  quiet, 265.
Calorific, 382.
Calorimeter, 389.
Calote, 999.
Calumet, 723.
Calumny, 934.
Calumniator, 936.
Cam, 789.
*Camarade, 890.
Camel, 271.
Cameo, 557.
Camera lucida, 445.
Camera obscura, 445.
Camilla, 274.
*Camisade, 716.
Camp, *to locate*, 184.
  abode, 186.
Campaign, *warfare*, 722.
269

Campaign, *plan*, 626.
  conduct, 692.
Campaniliform, *bell-shaped*, 249.
  cupped, 252.
Campestrian, 344.
Can, *power*, 157.
  mug, 191.
*Canaille, 876.
Canal, 260.
Canaliculated, 259.
*Cancan, 588.
Cancel, *obliterate*, 552.
  abrogate, 756.
Cancellated, 219.
Cancer, *disease*, 655.
  foulness, 653.
  painful, 830.
Candelabra, 423.
Candid, *sincere*, 543.
  ingenuous, 703.
  honorable, 939.
Candidate, 865.
Candle, 423.
Candleholder, 711.
Candlestick, 423.
Candour, *veracity*, 543.
  artlessness, 703.
  honor, 939.
Candy, 396.
Cane, *scourge*, 975.
  to beat, 276.
  punish, 972.
Canicular, 382.
Canister, 191.
Canker, *disease*, 655.
  bane, 663.
  deterioration, 659.
  pain, 830.
Cankering, 649.
Cannibal, 949.
Cannon, *arms*, 727.
  collision, 276.
Cannonade, 716.
Cannonier, 726.
Canny, 702.
Canoe, 273.
Canon, *rule*, 80.
  precept, 697.
  priest, 996.
Canonicals, 999.
Canonize, *rites*, 998.
  to deify, 991.
Canopy, *height*, 206.
  roof, 210.
  covering, 222.
Cant, *neology*, 563.
  oblique, 217.
  hypocrisy, 544.
Cantankerous, 895.

*Cantata, 415.
*Cantatrice, 416.
Canted, 217.
Canteen, 191.
Canter, *move*, 266.
  gallop, 274.
Canticle, 415.
Cantle, 51.
Canto, 415.
Canton, 181.
Cantonment, *location*, 184.
  abode, 189.
Canty, 836.
Canvass, *investigate*, 461.
  solicit, 765.
  sail, 267.
Canzonet, *song*, 415.
  poem, 597.
Caoutchouc, 325.
Cap, *hat*, 225.
  height, 206.
  to be superior, 33.
  to salute, 894.
Capability, *power*, 157.
  strength, 159.
  facility, 705.
  endowment, 5.
Capacity, *space*, 180.
  size, 192.
  endowment, 5.
  intellect, 450.
  talent, 698.
  wisdom, 498.
  utility, 644.
  office, 625.
*Cap-a-pie, 673.
Caparison, 225.
Cape, *land*, 342.
  projection, 250.
  height, 206.
Caper, *rise*, 305.
  leap, 309.
  dance, 840.
Capillary, 203.
Capillament, *fibre*, 205.
Capital, *excellent*, 648.
  important, 642.
  summit, 210.
  money, 800.
  wealth, 803.
Capitalist, 803.
Capitation, 85.
Capitol, 717.
Capitular, 996.
Capitulate, 725.
Capnomancy, 511.
Capote, 225.
Caprice, 608.
Capricious, *irregular*, 139.
Capriole, 309.

Capsize, *inversion*, 218.
   wreck, 731.
Capsized, 732.
Capstan, 633.
Capsule, *vessel*, 191.
   tunicle, 222.
Captain, 745.
Caption, 544.
Captious, *capricious*, 608.
   censorious, 932.
   discourteous, 895.
Captive, 754.
Captivating, *pleasing*, 829.
   lovely, 897.
Captivity, 751.
Capuchin, 997.
*Caput mortuum, 40.
*Caquet, 584.
Car, 272.
Carabineer, 726.
*Caracole, *rise*, 305.
   leap, 309.
*Carambole, 276.
Caravan, 272.
Caravansary, 189.
Carbine, 727.
Carboy, 191.
Carcass, 362.
Card, *ticket*, 550.
   plan, 626.
   to unravel, 60.
Cardinal, *important*, 642.
   excellent, 648.
   dress, 225.
   priest, 996.
Care, *attention*, 459.
   pain, 828, 830.
   custody, 751.
Care for, *desire*, 865.
   love, 897.
Careen, 658.
Career, *business*, 625.
   conduct, 692.
Careful, 864.
Careless, *inattentive*, 458.
   neglectful, 460.
   insensible, 826.
Caress, 902.
*Caret, *incomplete*, 53.
   to want, 640.
Careworn, 828.
Cargo, *goods*, 798.
   contents, 190.
   property, 780.
   materials, 635.
   large quantity, 31.
Caricature, *likeness*, 19.
   misrepresentation, 555.
   ridicule, 856.
Cariole, 272.

Carking, 828.
Carle, 876.
Carmelite, 996.
Carmine, 434.
Carnage, 361.
Carnal, *impure*, 961.
   irreligious, 988.
Carnation, 434.
Carnival, 840.
Carol, *music*, 415.
   cheerful, 836.
Carouse, *feast*, 297.
   festivity, 840.
   drink, 959.
Carp, 932.
Carper, 936.
Carpet (on the), 673.
Carriage, *transference*, 270.
   vehicle, 272.
   gait, 264.
   aspect, 448.
   fashion, 852.
Carrier, 271.
Carrion, *carcass*, 362.
   foulness, 653.
Carronade, 727.
Carrotty, 434.
Carry, *support*, 215.
   transfer, 270.
   tend, 176.
   induce, 615.
Carry on, *conduct*, 692.
   continue, 143.
   pursue, 622.
Carry off, *take*, 789.
   steal, 791.
Carry out, *complete*, 729.
   conduct, 692.
Carry through, 729, 692.
Cart, 272.
Cartage, 270.
*Carte blanche, 760.
*Cartel, *defiance*, 715.
   truce, 723.
   security, 771.
Cartload, *quantity*, 31.
   abundance, 639.
Cartoon, 556.
Cartridge, 727.
Cartulary, 551.
Caruncle, 250.
Carve, *sculpture*, 857.
   to form, 240.
   to produce, 161.
Carver, 559.
Caryatides, 215.
Cascade, 348.
Case, *state*, 7.
   sheath, 222.
   stout, 192.

Caseharden, *harden*, 823.
   strengthen, 159.
   train, 673.
Casemate, 717.
Cash, 800.
Cashier, *to dismiss*, 756.
   treasurer, 801.
Cask, 191.
Casket, 191.
Cassock, *dress*, 225.
   canonicals, 999.
Cast, *to throw*, 284.
   state, 7.
   mould, 21.
   form, 240.
   to throw down, 308.
   small quantity, 32.
   tinge, 428.
   aspect, 448.
   to peel, 226.
   to condemn, 971.
   to allot, 786.
Cast of the eye, 443.
Cast about, 461.
Cast anchor, *stop*, 265.
   arrive, 293.
Cast away, *lost*, 732.
   to relinquish, 782.
   reprobate, 949.
Cast down, 837.
Cast forth, 73.
Cast out, 296.
Cast up, *add*, 85.
   happen, 151.
   eject, 296.
Castanet, 417.
Castaway, 949.
Caste, 75.
Castellan, *keeper*, 753.
   servant, 746.
Caster, 191.
Castigate, *punish*, 972.
   reprove, 932.
Casting, 270.
Castle, *defence*, 717.
   edifice, 189.
Castle-building, 515.
Castor, 225.
Castor and Pollux, 890.
Castrametation, 189.
Castrated, *weakened*, 160.
   purified, 652.
Casual, *by chance*, 621.
   uncertain, 475.
Casualty, *event*, 151.
   chance, 156, 621.
Casuistry, *sophistry*, 477.
   scruple, 485.
   ethics, 926.
Cat, 975.

Cat's cradle, 219.
Cat's paw, 631.
Catachresis, *metaphor*, 521.
   misinterpretation, 523.
Cataclysm, *deluge*, 348.
   redundance, 641.
Catacomb, 363.
Catafalque, 363.
Catalectic, 597.
Catalepsy, 265.
Catalogue, 86.
Catamaran, *vessel*, 273.
   armament, 727.
Cataplasm, 662.
Catapult, *projection*, 284.
   arms, 727.
Cataract, 348.
Catastrophe, *end*, 67.
   disaster, 619.
   adversity, 735.
   calamity, 830.
Catch, *take*, 789.
   receive, 785.
   learn, 539.
   gather meaning, 518.
   cheat, 545.
Catch at, 785.
Catch the eye, 446.
Catchpenny, *trumpery*, 643.
   false, 544.
Catchpoll, 965.
Catechize, 461.
Catechretical, 461.
Catechumen, 541.
Categorical, *true*, 494.
   positive, 474.
   demonstrative, 478.
   affirmative, 535.
Category, *class*, 75.
   state, 7.
Catenation, 69.
Cater, 637.
Caterwalling, 412.
Cates, 299.
Cathedral, 1000.
Catholic, *universal*, 78.
   religion, 987.
Catholicism, 983.
Catholicon, 662.
Cat-o'-nine-tails, 975.
Catoptromancy, 511.
Caucus, 72.
Caudal, 67.
Cauldron. *See* Caldron.
Caudate, 214.
Causality, 157.
Cause, *source*, 153.
   final, 620.
   lawsuit, 969.
Causeless, *casual*, 156.

271

Causeless, *aimless*, 621.
Causeway, 627.
Causidical, 965.
Caustic, *energetic*, 171.
   gruff, 895.
Cautel, 459.
Cautelous, 864.
Cautery, 384.
Caution, *care*, 459.
   warning, 668.
   prudence, 864.
   advice, 695.
   security, 771.
Cavalcade, 69.
Cavalier, *horseman*, 268.
   insolent, 885.
Cavalierly, 458.
Cavalry, 726.
Cavass, 745.
Cave, *cavity*, 252.
   cell, 191.
   dwelling, 189.
*Caveat, 668.
Cavern, *hollow*, 252.
   cave, 191.
   dwelling, 189.
Cavernous, *hollow*, 252.
   rarity, 322.
Caviar, *pungent*, 392.
   energetic, 171.
Cavil, *censure*, 932.
Caviller, 936.
Cavity, 252.
Caw, 412.
Cayenne, *condiment*, 393.
   pungent, 171.
Cazique, 745.
Cease, 141.
Ceaseless, 112.
Cecity, 442.
Cede, 782.
Ceiling, 206, 210.
Celebration, 883.
Celebrity, 873.
Celerity, 274.
Celestial, *physical*, 318.
   moral, 829.
   religious, 976.
Celibacy, 904.
Cell, *cavity*, 252.
   receptacle, 191.
   abode, 189.
   prison, 752.
Cellar, 191.
Cellaret, 191.
Cellule, 191.
Cement, *uniting medium*, 45.
   to unite, 46.
   concord, 714.
Cemetery, 363.

Cenobite, *recluse*, 893.
   anchorite, 996.
Cenotaph, 363.
Censer, 1000.
Censor, 936.
Censorious, 932.
Censure, 932.
Census, 85.
Centaur, 83.
Centenary, 98.
Centennial, 98.
Centesimal, 99.
*Cento, 597.
Central, 223.
Centralize, 48.
Centre, *in order*, 68.
   in space, 223.
Centre in, 291.
Centrifugal, 290.
Centripetal, 291.
Centurion, 745.
Century, 108.
Cerberus, *janitor*, 263
   custodian, 664.
Cerebrum, 450.
Cerement, 363.
Ceremony, *parade*, 882.
   religious, 998.
Ceremonious, 928.
Certain, *sure*, 474.
   special, 79.
   indefinite number, 100.
Certainly, 488.
Certificate, *voucher*, 551.
   evidence, 467.
Certify, *evince*, 467.
   inform, 527.
Certitude, 474.
Cerulean, 438.
Cess, *tax*, 812.
   sewer, 653.
Cessation, 141.
Cession, *surrender*, 725.
   gift, 784.
Cesspool, 653.
Cestus, *girdle*, 225.
   ligature, 45.
   ring, 247.
Chafe, *warm*, 384.
   pain, 378.
   irritate, 825, 828.
   vex, 830.
   incense, 900.
Chafing-dish, 386.
Chaff, *trash*, 643.
   vulgar, 876.
Chaffer, *bargain*, 769.
   sale, 794.
Chagrin, 828.
Chain, *series*, 69.

Chain, *to fasten*, 43.
 vinculum, 45.
 to imprison, 752.
Chain-shot, 727.
Chair, *support*, 215.
 vehicle, 272.
 professorship, 540.
 school, 542.
 throne, 747.
Chairman, 745.
Chalice, *cup*, 191.
 hollow, 252.
Chaise, 272.
Chalk, *mark*, 550.
 drawing, 556.
Chalk out, 626.
Challenge, *defy*, 715.
 accuse, 938.
 claim, 924.
Cham, 745.
Chamber, *room*, 191.
 council, 696.
 mart, 799.
Chamberlain, 746.
Chameleon, 440.
Chamfer, 259.
Champ, 297.
Champaign, 344.
Champion, *auxiliary*, 711.
 defence, 717.
 combatant, 726.
Championship, 707.
Chance, *absence of cause*, 156.
 absence of aim, 621.
Chancel, 1000.
Chance-medley, 156.
Chancellor, *president*, 745.
 judge, 967.
Chandelier, 423.
Change, *alteration*, 140.
 mart, 799.
 small coin, 800.
Changeable, *mutable*, 149.
 irresolute, 605.
Changeful, *mutable*, 149.
 volition, 607.
Changeling, *changed*, 147.
 fool, 501.
Channel, *opening*, 260.
 conduit, 350.
 way, 627.
 furrow, 259.
Chant(*or* chaunt),*sing*,415.
 worship, 990.
 rites, 998.
Chaos, *disorder*, 59.
 secret, 533.
Chaomancy, 511.
Chap, 373.
272

Chapel, 1000.
*Chaperon, 664.
Chapfallen, 837.
Chaplin, 996.
Chaplet, *circle*, 247.
 dress, 225.
 ornament, 847.
 trophy, 733.
Chapman, 797.
Chaps, 66.
Chapter, *part*, 51.
 topic, 454.
 book, 593.
 church, 995.
Char, 384.
Character, *nature*, 5.
 disposition, 820.
 state, 7.
 letter, 561.
 type, 591.
Characteristic, *special*, 79.
 intrinsic, 5.
Characterize, 564.
Charade, 533.
Charcoal, *fuel*, 388.
 black, 431.
Charge, *business*, 625.
 direction, 693.
 advice, 695.
 commission, 755.
 load, 639.
 order, 741.
 accusation, 938.
 attack, 716.
 price, 812.
 custody, 751.
Charger, 271.
Chariot, 272.
Charioteer, 694.
Charitable, *giving*, 784.
 liberal, 816.
 benevolent, 906.
Charity, *giving*, 784.
 benevolence, 906.
*Charivari, 404.
*Charlatan, *impostor*, 548.
 mountebank, 844.
Charlatanism, 855.
Charm, *to please*, 829.
 love, 897.
 motive, 615.
 to conjure, 992.
 spell, 993.
Charnel-house, 363.
Chart, 554.
Charter, *privilege*, 924.
 compact, 769.
 security, 771.
 commission, 755.
Chary, *economical*, 817.

Chary, *cautious*, 864.
Chase, *pursue*, 622.
 follow, 281.
 wood, 367.
Chasm, *discontinuity*, 70.
 interval, 198.
Chaste, *simple*, 849.
 good taste, 850.
 pure, 960.
Chasten, 972.
Chastise, 972.
Chat, 588.
*Chateau, 189.
*Chatoyant, 440.
Chattels, *goods*, 635.
 property, 780.
Chatter, *talk*, 584.
 cold, 383.
Chatterbox, 584.
Chaunt, *sing*, 415.
 worship, 990.
 rites, 998.
Chaunter, 416.
Cheap, *low price*, 815.
 worthless, 643.
Cheapen, 794.
Cheat, *deceiver*, 548.
 to deceive, 545.
Check, *restrain*, 174.
 pacify, 826.
 slacken, 275.
 counteract, 179.
 hinder, 706.
 dissuade, 616.
 evidence, 467.
 ticket, 550.
 money order, 800.
 numerical, 85.
Checked, 440.
Checker, 440.
Checkered, 440.
Checkmate, 731.
Cheek, 236.
Cheer, *mirth*, 836.
 rejoicing, 838.
 amusement, 840.
 pleasure, 827.
 to give pleasure, 830.
 relief, 834.
 cry, 411.
 repast, 290.
Cheered, 827.
Cheerful, 836.
Cheerless, 837.
Cheeseparings, 40.
*Chef-d'œuvre, *master-piece*, 650.
 master-stroke, 698.
*Chemise, 225.
Chemistry, 144.

Close in upon, 291.
Close with, *arrive*, 293.
   combat, 720.
   assent, 488.
   compact, 769.
Close-fisted, 819.
Closeness, 43.
Close quarters, 197.
Closet, 191.
Closure, 261.
Clot, *concrete*, 46.
   density, 321.
   earth, 342.
Clothes, 225.
Clotpoll, 501.
Cloud, *dimness*, 422.
   shade, 424.
   opacity, 426.
   concealment, 528.
   crowd, 72.
   smoke, 334.
Cloud-capt,   cloud-topt,
   cloud-touching, 206.
Clouded, *variegated*, 440.
Cloudless, 420.
Cloudy, *opaque*, 426.
   dark, 421.
Cloven, 91.
Cloven-foot, 907.
Clover, *luxury*, 377.
   comfort, 827.
Clown, *rustic*, 876.
   buffoon, 844.
   pantomimic, 599.
Clownish, *vulgar*, 851.
Cloy, 869.
Club, *bludgeon*, 276.
   instrument, 633.
   weapon, 727.
   party, 712.
   to co-operate, 709.
   social meeting, 892.
Club-law, 964.
Cluck, 412.
Clump, *projecting mass*,
   250.
   assemblage, 72.
   trees, 367.
Clumsy, 699.
Cluster, 72.
Clutch, *seize*, 789.
   retain, 781.
Clutches, 737.
Clutter, 407.
Coacervation, 72.
Coach, *carriage*, 272.
   to teach, 537.
   tutor, 540.
Coachman, 694.
Coaction, 744.

Coadjutant, 707.
Coadjutor, 711.
Coadjuvant, 707.
Coagency, 709.
Coagmentation, 72.
Coagulate, 321.
Coagulum, 321.
Coal, 388.
Coal-black, 431.
Coalesce, *identity*, 13.
   combine, 48.
Coalition, 709.
Coaptation, 23.
Coarctation, *narrow*, 203.
   decrease, 36.
   impede, 706.
   coercion, 744.
Coarse, *texture*, 329.
   vulgar, 851.
   dirty, 653.
   impure, 961.
Coast, *land*, 342.
   to navigate, 267.
Coat, *layer*, 204.
   exterior, 220.
   habit, 225.
   to paint, 222.
   lining, 224.
Coating, 222.
Coax, *persuade*, 615.
   flatter, 933.
Cob, 271.
Cobble, *to mend*, 658.
   ship, 273.
Cobra, 663.
Cobweb, *light*, 320.
   flimsy, 643.
   dirt, 653.
   untruth, 546.
Cock and bull, 497.
Cock up, *stick up*, 212.
   project, 250.
Cockade, *badge*, 550.
   title, 877.
Cock-a-hoop, *exulting*, 884.
   gay, 836.
Cockatrice, *bane*, 663.
   miscreant, 949.
Cock-boat, 273.
Cock-crow, 125.
Cocker, *fold*, 258.
   caress, 902.
Cockle up, 258.
Cockney, 876.
Cock-pit, *arena*, 728.
   of a ship, 191.
   council, 696.
Coction, 384.
Cocytus, 982.
Coddle, 902.

Code, *law*, 963.
   precept, 697.
Codger, 819.
Codicil, 39.
Codify, 963.
Codlin, 129.
Coefficient,   *co-operating*,
   709.
   accompanying, 88.
   factor, 84.
Coemption, 795.
Cœnobite, 893.
Coequal, 27.
Coerce, *restrain*, 751.
   compel, 744.
   dissuade, 616.
Coetaneous, 120.
Coeternal, 112.
Coeval, 120.
Coexist, *synchronism*, 120.
   accompany, 88.
   contiguity, 199.
Coextension, *equality*, 27.
   parallelism, 216.
Coffer, *chest*, 191.
   money-chest, 802.
   store, 636.
Coffin, 363.
Cog, *tooth*, 253.
   ship, 273.
   deceive, 545.
   flatter, 933.
Cogent, *powerful*, 157.
   argument, 476.
Cogitate, 451.
Cognate, 80.
Cognation, 9.
Cognition, 490.
Cognizance, 490.
Cognomen, 564.
Cognoscence, 490.
Cognoscible, 490.
Cohabitation, 184.
Cohere, *unite*, 46.
   dense, 321.
Cohesive, 46.
Cohibit, *restrain*, 751.
   prohibit, 761.
   counteract, 179.
Cohort, 726.
*Cohue, 72.
Coif, 225.
Coil, *convolution*, 248.
   circuition, 311.
   disorder, 59.
Coin, *money*, 800.
   to fabricate, 161.
   to imagine, 515.
Coinage of the brain, 515.
Coincidence, *identity*, 13.

Coincidence, *in time*, 120.
  in place, 199.
  in opinion, 488.
Coke, 388.
Colander, 260.
Colature, 652.
Cold, *frigidity*, 383.
  style, 575.
  insensible, 823.
  indifferent, 866.
Cold-blooded, *malevolent*, 907.
  dispassionate, 826.
Coliseum, 728.
Collapse, *contraction*, 195.
  prostration, 160.
Collar, *dress*, 225.
  shackle, 752.
  seize, 789.
Collate, 464.
Collateral, *relation*, 11.
  lateral, 236.
Collation, 299.
Colleague, *auxiliary*, 711.
  co-operating, 709.
Collect, *assemble*, 72.
  take, 789.
  acquire, 775.
  learn, 539.
  opine, 480.
  understand, 518.
  prayer, 990.
Collected, *calm*, 826.
Collection, *store*, 636.
  assemblage, 72.
Collectiveness, 50.
College, 542.
Collide, *throw*, 276.
Collier, 273.
Colligate, 72.
Collimation, 278.
Colliquate, 333.
Colliquefaction, 335.
Collision, *approach*, 287.
  percussion, 276.
  clashing, 179.
  opposition, 708.
  encounter, 720.
Collocate, *arrange*, 60.
  assemble, 72.
Collocution, 588.
Collogue, *wheedle*, 933.
Collop, 51.
Colloquy, 588.
Colluctation, 720.
Collusion, *deceit*, 545.
  conspiring, 709.
Colon, 141.
Colonel, 745.
Colonize, 184.
276

Colonnade, 69.
Colony, 188.
*Colophon, 67.
Coloration, 428.
Colossal, *size*, 192.
  height, 206.
Colossus, 192.
Colour, *hue*, 428.
  plea, 617.
  disguise, 545.
Colourable, *deceptive*, 545.
  ostensible, 472.
Colouring, *meaning*, 516.
  exaggeration, 549.
Colourless, 429.
Colours, *standard*, 550.
  decoration, 877.
Colt, *fool*, 501.
  horse, 271.
Column, *series*, 69.
  height, 206.
  monument, 551.
  cylinder, 249.
  troop, 726.
Coma, 823.
Comb, 972.
Combat, 720.
Combatant, 726.
Combine, 48.
Combinations, *arithmetical*, 84.
Combustible, *heating*, 384.
  fuel, 388.
Come, *arrive*, 293.
  approach, 287.
  happen, 151.
Come about, 151.
Come after, 63.
Come away, 286.
Come before, 62.
Come by, 775.
Come down, *descend*, 306.
  cheapness, 815.
  pay, 809.
Come from, 154.
Come near, 287.
Come on, *follow*, 63.
  defy, 715.
Come out, 294.
Come up to, *equal*, 27.
Come up with, 292.
Come upon, 293.
Comedian, 599.
Comedy, *drama*, 599.
  ridicule, 856.
Comely, 845.
Comestible, 299.
Comet, *wanderer*, 268.
Comfit, 396.
Comfort, *pleasure*, 827.

Comfort, *content*, 831.
  relief, 834.
Comfortable, *pleased*, 827.
  pleasing, 829.
Comforter, 976.
Comic, *witty*, 842.
  ridiculous, 853.
*Comitium, 72, 696.
Comma, 141.
Command. *order*, 741.
  authority, 737.
Commander, 745.
Commemorate, 883.
Commence, 66.
Commend, 931.
Commensurate, *accordant*, 23.
  adequate, 639.
Comment, *reason*, 476.
  interpret, 522.
Commerce, 794.
Commination, 909.
Commingle, 41.
Comminute, 330.
Commiserate, 917.
Commissariat, 637.
Commissary, *consignee*, 758.
  deputy, 759.
Commission, 755.
Commissioner, 758.
Commissure, 43.
Commit, *act*, 680.
  delegate, 755.
  imprison, 751.
  arrest, 969.
Committee, *directors*, 693.
  council, 696.
Commix, 41.
Commode, 191.
Commodious, 646.
Commodity, 798.
Commodore, 745.
Common, *ordinary*, 82.
  general, 78.
  plain, 344.
Commoner, 876.
Commonalty, 876.
Common-place, 643.
Common-sense, 450.
Commons, 299.
Commonwealth, 373.
Commorant, 188.
Commotion, 315.
Commune, 451.
Communicate, *tell*,.
  join, 43.
Communion, *society*, 712.
  participation, 778.
Communism, 778.

Community, 373.
Commute, *barter*, 794.
  substitution, 147.
Commutual, 12.
Compact, *close*, 43.
  dense, 321.
  compendious, 201.
  bargain, 769.
*Compages, *whole*, 50.
  texture, 329.
Compagination, 43.
Companion, 890.
Companionable, 892.
Companionship, *accompaniment*, 88.
  sociality, 892.
Company, *assembly*, 72.
  accompaniment, 88.
  partnership, 797.
Comparable, 9.
Comparative, *degree*, 26.
  magnitude, 31.
Compare, 464.
Compartment, *cell*, 191.
  region, 181.
  place, 182.
Compass, *degree*, 26.
  space, 180.
  azimuth, 278.
  measure, 466.
  enclose, 231.
  to achieve, 729.
  intend, 620.
Compassion, 917.
Compatible, *consentaneous*, 23.
  possible, 470.
Compeer, *equal*, 27.
  friend, 890.
Compel, 744.
Compellation, 564.
Compendious, 596.
Compendium, *short*, 201.
  writing, 596.
Compensate, *make up for*, 30.
  requite, 973.
Compete, *oppose*, 708.
  contend, 720.
Competence, *power*, 157.
  sufficiency, 639.
  wealth, 803.
  skill, 698.
Competition, 708.
Competitor, *opponent*, 710.
  combatant, 726.
Compilation, 595.
Complacent, *content*, 831.
  kind, 906.
Complaint, *murmur*, 839.
277

Complaint, *illness*, 655.
Complaisant, 906.
Complement, *adjunct*, 39.
  remainder, 40.
  part, 52.
  arithmetical, 84.
Complete, *entire*, 52.
  great, 31.
  end, 67.
  to finish, 729.
Complex, 59.
Complexion, *state*, 7.
  appearance, 448.
Compliance, *observance*, 772.
  obedience, 743.
Complicated, 59.
Complice, 711.
Compliment, *courtesy*, 894.
  praise, 931.
Comply, *consent*, 762.
  obey, 743.
Component, 56.
Comport, 692.
Comport with, *agree*, 23.
*Compos, 502.
Compose, *make up*, 54.
  produce, 161.
  moderate, 174.
  pacify, 723.
  assuage, 826.
  music, 415.
  write, 590.
Composed, *self-possessed*, 826.
Composite, 41.
Composition, *constitution*, 54.
  music, 415.
  style, 569.
  compromise, 774.
  atonement, 952.
Compost, 653.
Composure, 826.
Compotation, 959.
Compound, *mix*, 41.
  combination, 48.
  compromise, 774.
Compound for, *compact*, 769.
  barter, 794.
Comprehend, *include*, 76.
  compose, 54.
  understand, 518.
  know, 490.
Compress, *condense*, 321.
  narrow, 203.
  curtail, 201.
  contract, 195.
Comprise, 76.

Comprobation, *evidence*, 467.
  demonstration, 478.
Compromise, *compound*, 774.
  atone, 952.
  to endanger, 665.
*Compte rendu, 596.
Comptroller, *director*, 694.
  master, 745.
Compulsion, 744.
Compunction, 950.
Compurgation, 970.
Compute, 85.
Comrade, 890.
Con, 451, 505.
Concatenation, 69.
Concave, 252.
Conceal, *hide*, 528.
  invisible, 447.
Concede, *consent*, 762.
  admit, 467.
  give, 784.
  assent, 488.
  permit, 760.
Conceit, *idea*, 453.
  belief, 484.
  supposition, 514.
  imagination, 515.
  affectation, 855.
  vanity, 880.
  wit, 842.
Conceited, 499.
Conceive, *believe*, 484.
  imagine, 515.
Concentrate, *assemble*, 72.
  converge, 291.
Concentric, 223.
Concentual, 413.
Conception, *intellect*, 450.
  idea, 453.
  belief, 484.
  knowledge, 490.
  imaginaton, 515.
Concern, *relation*, 9.
  grief, 828.
  business, 625.
  firm, 797.
Concerning, 9.
Concert, *music*, 415.
  co-operation, 709.
Concertina, 417.
Concession, *grant*, 784.
  permit, 760.
*Concetto, 842.
Conchoid, 245.
Conciliate, *talk over*, 615.
  satisfy, 831.
Concinnity, *style*, 578.
  beauty, 845.
Concise, 572.

Conclave, *assembly*, 72.
   council, 696.
   church, 995.
Conclude, *end*, 67.
   infer, 476.
   opine, 480.
   complete, 729.
   determine, 604.
Conclusions (to try), 720.
Conclusive, 478.
Concoct, *prepare*, 673.
   plan, 626.
Concomitant, *synchronous*, 120.
   accompanying, 88.
Concord, *agreement*, 23.
   in music, 413.
   assent, 488.
   harmony, 714.
   amity, 888.
Concordance. *See* Concord.
*Concordat, 769.
*Concours, 720.
Concourse, *assemblage*, 72.
   convergence, 291.
Concrete, *mass*, 46.
   density, 321.
Concubine, 962.
Concupiscence, *desire*, 865.
   impurity, 961.
Concur, *co-operate*, 178.
   in concert, 709.
   converge, 291.
   assent, 488.
Concussion, 276.
Condemn, *censure*, 932.
   convict, 971.
Condense, 195, 321.
Condescend, 879.
Condign, 924.
Condiment, 393.
Condisciple, 541.
Condition, *state*, 7.
   term, 770.
   modification, 469.
Conditionally, 8.
Condole, 915.
Condonation, 918.
Conduce, *tend*, 176.
   concur, 178.
   avail, 644.
   contribute, 153.
Conduct, *lead*, 693.
   transfer, 270.
   procedure, 692.
Conductor, *guard*, 666.
   director, 694.
   conveyer, 271.
Conduit, 350.
Condyle, 250.

Cone, *round*, 249.
   pointed, 253.
Confabulation, 588.
Confection, 396.
Confederacy, *party*, 712.
   co-operation, 709.
Confederate, 711.
Confer, *give*, 784.
   converse, 588.
   advise, 695.
Confess, *avow*, 529.
   assert, 488.
   penitence, 950.
   rite, 998.
Confessional, 1000.
Confidant, 711.
Confide, *trust*, 484.
   hope, 858.
Confidential, 528.
Configuration, 240.
Confine, *limit*, 233.
   imprison, 751.
   circumscribe, 231.
   frontier, 199.
Confined, 655.
Confirm, *corroborate*, 467.
   consent, 762.
   rites, 998.
Confiscate, *condemn*, 971.
   take, 789.
Conflagration, 384.
Conflict, 720.
Confluence, 291.
Conflux, 72.
Conform, *assent*, 488.
   accustom, 613.
Conformation, *form*, 240.
   frame, 7.
Conformity, *to rule*, 82.
Confound, *disorder*, 61.
   injure, 649.
   perplex, 475.
   confuse, 519.
   astonish, 870.
Confounded, 31.
Confraternity, 888.
Confront, *face*, 234.
   compare, 467.
   resist, 719.
Confucius, 986.
Confuse, *derange*, 61.
   obscure, 519.
   perplex, 458.
   abash, 874.
   style, 571.
Confusion, *disorder*, 59.
   shame, 874.
Confutation, 479.
*Congé, 756.
Congeal, *cold*, 385.

Congealed, *dense*, 321.
Congener, *similar*, 17.
   included, 76.
Congenial, *agreeing*, 23.
   expedient, 646.
Congenital, 5.
Congeries, 72.
Congestion, *collection*, 72.
   redundance, 641.
Conglaciation, 385.
Conglobation, 72.
Conglomerate, 72.
Conglutinate, 46.
Congratulate, 896.
Congregate, 72.
Congregation, 997.
Congress, *assemblage*, 72.
   council, 696.
Congreve, 727.
Congruous, *agreeing*, 23.
   expedient, 646.
Conjecture, 514.
Conjoin, 43.
Conjugal, 903.
Conjugate words, 562.
Conjugation, *junction*, 43.
   pair, 89.
   phase, 144.
Conjunct, 43.
Conjuncture, *contingency*, 8.
   occasion, 134.
Conjuration, *deception*, 545.
   sorcery, 992.
Conjure, *entreat*, 765.
   exorcise, 992.
Conjurer, *sorcerer*, 994.
   adept, 700.
Connate, 153.
Connatural, *uniform*, 16.
   similar, 17.
Connect, *relate*, 9.
   link, 43.
Connection, *kindred*, 11.
Connective, 45.
Connive, *overlook*, 460.
   allow, 760.
*Connoisseur, 850.
Connotation, 550.
Connubial, 903.
*Conoscente, 850.
Conquer, 731.
Conquered, 732.
Conqueror, 731.
Conquest, 731.
Consanguinity, 11.
Conscience, *moral sense*, 926.
   knowledge, 490.

Conscientious, *virtuous*, 944.
  scrupulous, 939.
  true, 494.
Consciousness, *intuition*, 450.
  knowledge, 490.
Conscription, 744.
Consecrate, *dedicate*, 873.
  sanctify, 987.
Consectary, 467.
Consecution, 63.
Consecutive, *following*, 63.
  continuous, 69.
Consent, *grant*, 762.
  assent, 488.
Consentaneous, *agreeing*, 23.
  expedient, 646.
Consequence, *effect*, 154.
  event, 151.
Consequent, 63.
Consequential, *arrogant*, 878.
  deducible, 467.
Consequently, 476.
Conservation, 670.
Conservative, 142.
Conservatory, *store*, 636.
  hot-house, 386.
Conserve, 396.
Consider, *think*, 451.
  attend to, 457.
  inquire, 461.
Considerable, *in degree*, 31.
  in size, 192.
  important, 642.
Considerate, *judicious*, 498.
Consideration, *motive*, 615.
  qualification, 469.
  importance, 642.
  requital, 973.
Considering, 476.
Consign, *transfer*, 783.
  commission, 755.
  give, 784.
Consignee, 758.
Consignment, 755.
Consist of, 54.
Consistent, 23.
Consistence, *density*, 321.
Consistency, *uniformity*, 16.
Consistory, *council*, 696.
  church, 995.
Consociation, 892.
Console, *relieve*, 834.
  pity, 914.
  table, 215.
Consolidate, *unite*, 46.
  condense, 321.
279

Consonant, *agreeing*, 23.
  expedient, 646.
  musical, 413.
Consort, *accompany*, 88.
  associate, 892.
  spouse, 903.
Consortship, 892.
Conspicuous, 446.
Conspiracy, 626.
Conspire, 178.
Constable, *governor*, 745.
  officer, 965.
Constant, *immutable*, 150.
  regular, 80, 82.
  resolute, 604.
  faithful, 939.
Constellation, *stars*, 318.
  glory, 873.
Consternation, 800.
Constipate, 321.
Constituent, 56.
Constitute, *compose*, 54.
  produce, 161.
Constitution, *nature*, 5.
  state, 7.
  charter, 924.
Constrain, *power*, 157.
  restrain, 751.
  compel, 744.
  abash, 881.
Constrict, 203.
Constringe, 203.
Construct, 161.
Construction, *meaning*, 522.
Construe, 522.
Consubstantiation, 998.
Consul, 759.
Consult, 695.
Consume, *destroy*, 162.
  waste, 638.
  use, 677.
  ravage, 649.
Consuming, 830.
Consummate, *great*, 31.
  complete, 729.
Consummation, *end*, 67.
Consumption, *shrinking*, 195.
  waste, 638.
  use, 677.
Contact, 199.
Contagious, 657.
Contain, *include*, 76.
  be composed of, 54.
Contaminate, *spoil*, 659.
  soil, 653.
Contemn, 930.
Contemper, 174.
Contemplate, *view*, 441.
  think, 451.

Contemplate, *purpose*, 620.
  expect, 507.
Contemporary, 120.
Contempt, 930.
Contemptible, 643.
Contend, *fight*, 720.
  assert, 535.
Content, *satisfied*, 831.
  calm, 826.
  patience, 821.
  will, 600.
Contention, *discord*, 713.
  struggle, 720.
Contents, *ingredients*, 56.
  components, 190.
  list, 86.
  compendium, 596.
  conterminate, end, 67.
  limit, 233.
Conterminous, *adjoining*, 199.
Contest, 720.
Context, 591.
Contexture, *state*, 7.
  texture, 329.
Contiguous, 199.
Continence, 960.
Continent, *land*, 342.
Contingent, *conditional*, 8.
  eventual, 151.
  liable, 177.
  possible, 470.
  uncertain, 475.
  casual, 621.
  allotment, 786.
Continually, 136.
Continuation, *sequence*, 63.
  sequel, 65.
Continue, *persist*, 143.
  endure, 106.
Continuity, 69.
Contortion, *distortion*, 243.
  convolution, 246.
  deformity, 846.
Contour, 229.
Contra, 708.
Contraband, *illicit*, 964.
  false, 544.
Contract, *decrease*, 36.
  shrivel, 195.
  curtail, 201.
  narrow, 203.
  promise, 768.
  bargain, 769.
Contractility, *corrugation*, 195.
  elasticity, 325.
Contradict, *evidence*, 468.
  deny, 536.
  dissent, 489.

Contradiction, 14.
Contradistinction, 15.
Contraindicate, 616.
Contraposition, *reversion*, 237.
  inversion, 218.
Contrary, *opposite*, 14.
  opposing, 708.
Contrarious, 608.
Contrast, *contrariety*, 14.
  comparison, 464.
Contravallation, 717.
Contravene, *counteract*, 179.
  oppose, 708.
  hinder, 706.
  counterevidence, 468.
  deny, 536.
*Contretems, 704.
Contribute, *tend*, 176.
  concur, 178.
  give, 784.
  cause, 153.
Contrition, *abrasion*, 331.
  penitence, 950.
Contrive, *plan*, 626.
Contriving, *artful*, 702.
Control, *power*, 157.
  authority, 737.
  to regulate, 693.
  to check, 179, 708.
Controversy, *discussion*, 476.
  dispute, 713.
Controvertible, *dubious*, 475.
Contumacy, 606.
Contumely, *disrespect*, 929.
  arrogance, 885.
  rudeness, 895.
  reproach, 932.
Contund, 330.
Contuse, 330.
Conundrum, *secret*, 533.
  pun, 563.
  wit, 842.
  problem, 461.
Convalescence, 658.
Convection, 270.
Convene, 72.
Convenient, 646.
Convent, 1000.
Conventicle, *church*, 1000.
  assembly, 72.
Convention, *compact*, 769.
  treaty of peace, 723.
Conventual, 996.
Converge, 291.
Conversant, *knowing*, 490.
280

Conversant, *skilful*, 698.
Conversation, 588.
Converse, *reverse*, 14.
  talk, 588.
Conversible, 892.
Conversion, 144.
Convert, *opinion*, 484.
  learner, 541.
  to change to, 144.
  to use, 677.
Convertible, *identical*, 13.
Convex, 250.
Convey, 270.
Conveyance, 272.
Conveyancer, 968.
Convict, *condemn*, 971.
  to convince, 537.
  condemned, 949.
Conviction, 484.
Convince, 537.
Convincement, 484.
Convivial, 892.
Convocate, 72.
Convoke, 72.
Convolution, *coil*, 248.
  rotation, 312.
Convoy, *transfer*, 270.
  guard, 664.
Convulse, *violent*, 173.
  agitate, 315.
Coo, 412.
Cook, *heat*, 384.
  prepare, 673.
  falsify, 544.
  accounts, 811.
Cool, *cold*, 383.
  to refrigerate, 385.
  to moderate, 174.
  to allay, 826.
  indifferent, 866.
  torpid, 826.
Cooler, 387.
Coolheaded, *torpid*, 826.
  judicious, 498.
Cooli, 271.
Coop, *confine*, 752.
  restrain, 751.
Co-operate, *physically*, 178.
  voluntarily, 709.
Co-operator, 711.
Co-ordinate, 27.
Coot, 189.
Copartner, *participator*, 778.
  associate, 892.
  accompanying, 88.
Cope, *contend*, 720.
  equal, 27.
Copious, *abundant*, 639.
  style, 573.

Copist, 590.
Coportion, 778.
Copper, *money*, 800.
Copper-coloured, 439.
Coppice (or copse), 367.
Copula, 45.
Copy, *imitation*, 21.
  prototype, 22.
  to write, 590.
  represent, 554.
Copying, *imitating*, 19.
Coquetry, 855.
Coracle, 273.
*Corbeille, 191.
Cord, *tie*, 45.
  filament, 205.
Cordage, 45.
Cordial, *grateful*, 829.
  warm, 821.
  willing, 602.
  friendly, 888.
  remedy, 662.
*Cordon, 229.
Core, 223.
Coriaceous, 327.
Co-rival. *See* Corrival.
Cork, *lightness*, 320.
  plug, 263.
Cork up, 261.
Corkscrew, 262.
  spiral, 248.
Cormorant, 957.
Corn, *projection*, 250.
Corned, 959.
Corner, *place*, 182.
  receptacle, 191.
Cornet, *music*, 417.
  officer, 745.
Cornice, 210.
Cornucopia, 639.
Cornute, 253.
Corollary, *deduction*, 480.
  addition, 37.
Corona, 247.
Coronet, 747.
Corporate, 43.
Corporation, *association*, 712.
  bulk, 192.
Corporeal, 316.
Corps, *assemblage*, 72.
  troops, 726.
Corpse, 362.
Corpulent, 192.
Corpuscle, *atom*, 193.
  jot, 32.
Corradiation, 74.
Correct, *true*, 494.
  virtuous, 944.
  to improve, 658.

Covenant, 769.
Cover, *dress*, 225.
   superpose, 222.
   conceal, 528.
   retreat, 530.
   safety, 664.
   to compensate, 30.
   stopper, 263.
Covercle, 222.
Covert, 447.
Coverture, 903.
Covert-way, 260.
Covetous, *miserly*, 819.
   desirous, 865.
Covey, 72.
Cow, *intimidate*, 860.
Coward, 862.
Cower, *fear*, 860.
   stoop, 306.
Cowl, *dress*, 225.
   sacerdotal, 999.
Coxcomb, 854.
Coxcomical, *vain*, 880.
   affected, 855.
Coy, 881.
Cozen, 545.
Crab, 397.
Crabbed, *sour*, 397.
   difficult, 704.
   uncivil, 895.
   testy, 901.
Crack, *split*, 44.
   fissure, 198.
   furrow, 259.
   to destroy, 162.
   sound, 406.
   to boast, 884.
   excellent, 648.
Crackbrained, 499.
Cracked, *mad*, 504.
   faulty, 651.
Cracker, 406.
Crackle, 406.
Cradle, *bed*, 215.
   origin, 153.
   infancy, 127.
   to place, 184.
   to train, 673.
Craft, *cunning*, 702.
   skill, 698.
   plan, 626.
   apparatus, 633.
   business, 623.
   shipping, 273.
Crag, 253.
Cragged, *rough*, 256.
Craig, 206.
Crake, 884.
Cram, *stuff*, 194.
   fill, 639.
282

Cram, *gorge*, 297.
   teach, 537.
   choke, 261.
Cramp, *hinder*, 706.
   restrain, 751.
   narrow, 203.
   fasten, 45.
   paralyze, 158.
   weaken, 160.
   spasm, 378.
Cramped, *style*, 572, 579.
Crane, 633.
Crane-neck, 245.
Cranium, 450.
Crank, *instrument*, 633.
   wit, 842.
Cranny, 198.
Crapulence, 954.
Crash, *sound*, 406.
   destruction, 162.
Crasis, *nature*, 5.
   coherence, 46.
Crass, 32.
Crassitude, *breadth*, 202.
   thickness, 352.
Crate, 272.
Crater, *hollow*, 252.
   depth, 208.
Craunch, *bruise*, 44.
   masticate, 297.
Cravat, 225.
Crave, *ask*, 765.
   desire, 865.
Craven, 862.
Craw, 191.
Crawl, *move*, 275.
   servility, 886.
Crayon, *painting*, 556.
   pencil, 559.
Crazy, *weak*, 160.
   mad, 503.
Creak, 410.
Cream, *emulsion*, 354.
   oil, 355.
   perfection, 650.
Cream-coloured, 430.
Creamy, 352.
Crease, 258.
Create, *produce*, 161.
   cause, 153.
   imagine, 515.
Creator, 976.
Creature, *animal*, 366.
   thing, 3.
   effect, 154.
Creature comforts, 299.
Credence, 484.
Credential, 467.
Credible, 472.
Credit, *belief*, 484.

Credit, *authority*, 737.
   pecuniary, 805.
   account, 811.
   influence, 737.
   hope, 858.
   repute, 873.
   desert, 944.
Creditor, 805.
Credulity, 486.
   superstition, 984.
Creed, *belief*, 484.
   tenet, 983.
Creek, 343.
Creep, *crawl*, 275.
Creeping, *sensation*, 380.
Creeper, 367.
Cremation, *burning*, 384.
   of corpses, 363.
Cremona, 417.
Crenated, 257.
Crepitate, 406.
Crepuscule, *dawn*, 125.
   dimness, 422.
Crescendo, 35.
Crescent, *curve*, 245.
   street, 189.
Crest, *summit*, 210.
   tuft, 256.
   armorial, 550.
Crest-fallen, *dejected*, 837.
   humiliated, 881.
Crevice, 198.
Crew, *assemblage*, 72.
   party, 712.
   inhabitants, 188.
Crib, *bed*, 215.
   to steal, 791.
Cribble, 260.
Crick, *pain*, 378.
Crier, 534.
Crime, *guilt*, 947.
Criminal, *culprit*, 949.
   vicious, 945.
Criminality, 947.
Criminate, 938.
Crimp, *brittle*, 328.
   to steal, 791.
Crimson, 434.
Cringe, *submit*, 743.
   servility, 886.
Crinkle, *fold*, 258.
   angle, 244.
Cripple, *weaken*, 160.
   disable, 158.
   injure, 649.
   disease, 655.
Cris-cross-row, 562.
Crisis, *conjuncture*, 8.
   event, 151.
   difficulty, 704.

Crisis, *opportunity*, 134.
Crisp, *brittle*, 328.
  rough, 256.
  rumpled, 248.
Criterion, *trial*, 463.
  evidence, 467.
Crithomancy, 511.
Critic, *taste*, 850.
  detractor, 936.
Critical, *opportune*, 134.
  important, 642.
Criticism, 932.
Criticize, *taste*, 850.
Croak, *cry*, 412.
  stammer, 583.
  complain, 839.
  boast, 884.
  predict, 511.
Crocodile tears, 544.
Crœsus, 803.
Croft, 189.
Cromlech, 363.
Crone, *veteran*, 130.
  fool, 501.
Crony, 890.
Crooked, *angular*, 244.
  distorted, 243.
  sloping, 217.
  dishonorable, 940.
Crop, *stomach*, 191.
  to shorten, 201.
  to gather, 775.
  to take, 789.
  to eat, 297.
  harvest, 154.
Crosier, 999.
Cross, *intersection*, 219.
  opposition, 708.
  vexation, 828.
  vexatiousness, 830.
  ill-tempered, 895.
  fretful, 901.
  failure, 732.
  decoration, 877.
  reward, 973.
  rites, 998.
Cross-bow, 727.
Cross-cut, 627.
Cross-examine, 461.
Cross-grained, *obstinate*, 606.
  ill-tempered, 895.
Cross-purposes, 495, 523.
Cross-question, 461.
Cross-reading, 523.
Cross-road, 627.
Crossing, 219.
Crotch, 244.
Crotchet, *music*, 413.
  caprice, 608.
283

Crotchetty, 499.
Crouch, *stoop*, 306.
  lower, 207.
  servility, 886.
  fear, 860.
Croup, 235.
Crow, *cry*, 412.
  laugh, 838.
  boast, 884.
  exult, 836.
  lever, 633.
Crow-bar, 633.
Crowd, *assemblage*, 72.
  multitude, 102.
  closeness, 197.
  the vulgar, 876.
Crown, *top*, 210.
  end, 67.
  circle, 247.
  trophy, 733.
  sceptre, 747.
  reward, 973.
  to complete, 729.
Crucial, 219.
Cruciate, *pain physically*, 378.
  mentally, 828, 830.
Crucible, 191.
  laboratory, 691.
Crucifix, 998, 999.
Cruciform, 219.
Crucify, *torture (physical)*, 378.
  agony, mental, 828.
  torturing, 830.
  execution, 972.
Crude, 674.
Cruel, *painful*, 830.
  inhuman, 907.
Cruet, 191.
Cruise, *vessel*, 191.
  navigation, 267.
Crum, *small part*, 51.
  grain, 193.
  powder, 330.
  bit, 32.
Crumble, *pulverize*, 330.
  destroy, 162.
  spoil, 659.
  brittleness, 328.
Crumenal, 800.
Crump, 245.
Crumple, *ruffle*, 256.
  crease, 258.
Crusade, 722.
Crush, *pulverize*, 330.
  destroy, 162.
  injure, 649.
Crust, 222.
Crusty, 895.

Crutch, *support*, 215.
  angle, 244.
  instrument, 633.
Cry, *animal*, 422.
  human, 421.
  loudness, 404.
  voice, 580.
  publish, 531.
  weep, 839.
Cry down, 932.
Cry for, *desire*, 865.
Cry to, *beseech*, 765.
Cry up, *praise*, 931.
Crypt, *cell*, 191.
  grave, 363.
  ambush, 530.
  altar, 1000.
Cryptography, 590.
Crystalline, *dense*, 321.
  transparent, 425.
Cub, *young*, 129.
  clown, 876.
Cube, 92.
Cuckold, 962.
Cuckoo, *repetition*, 104.
  imitation, 19.
  sound, 407.
  cry, 412.
Cuddle, 902.
Cudgel, *beat*, 975.
  bludgeon, 276, 727.
Cue, *hint*, 527.
  watchword, 550.
  plea, 617.
Cuff, *beat*, 276, 972.
*Cui-bono ? 644.
Cuirass, 717.
Cuirassier, 726.
*Cuisine, 299.
*Culbute, 218.
*Cul-de-sac, 252.
Culinary, 299.
Cull, 609.
Cullender, 260.
Cullibility, 486.
  dupe, 547.
Cullion, *wretch*, 941, 949.
Cully, *to deceive*, 545.
  dupe, 547.
Culminate, *maximum*, 33.
  height, 206, 210.
Culpability, 947.
Culpable, 945.
Culprit, 949.
Cultivate, *improve*, 658.
  till, 371.
Culverin, 727.
Culvert, 350.
Cumber, *load*, 319.
  to incommode, 647.

Cumber, *to obstruct*, 706.
Cumulation, 72.
Cumulus, 353.
Cunctation, *delay*, 133.
   inactivity, 683.
Cuneiform, 244.
Cunning, *art*, 702.
   sagacity, 698.
Cup, *hollow*, 252.
   vessel, 191.
Cupboard, 191.
Cupid, 845, 897.
Cupidity, *avarice*, 819.
   desire, 865.
Cupola, *dome*, 250.
   height, 206.
Cur, 949.
Curable, 658.
Curacy, 995.
Curate, 996.
Curator, 758.
Curb, *restrain*, 751.
   hinder, 706.
   shackle, 752.
   moderate, 174.
   check, 826.
   dissuade, 616.
   counteract, 179.
   slacken, 275.
Curd, *mass*, 46.
   density, 321.
   pulp, 354.
Curdle, *condense*, 321.
   coagulate, 46.
Cure, *remedy*, 662.
   reinstate, 660.
   preserve, 670.
   improve, 656.
Cureless, 659.
Curfew, 126.
Curiosity, 455.
   phenomenon, 872.
Curious, *true*, 494.
   exceptional, 83.
   beautiful, 845.
Curl, *bend*, 245.
   cockle up, 258.
Curmudgeon, 819.
Currency, *publicity*, 531.
   money, 800.
Current, *existing*, 1.
   present, 118.
   stream, 347.
   river, 348.
   opinion, 484.
   prevailing, 82.
Curricle, 272.
*Curriculum, 537.
Curry, 393.
Curry favour, 933.
284

Curse, *malediction*, 908.
   bane, 663.
   evil, 619.
   badness, 649.
   painfulness, 830.
Cursory, *transient*, 111.
   inattentive, 458.
   neglecting, 460.
Curst, 895.
Curt, 201.
Curtail, *shorten*, 201.
   retrench, 38.
   decrease, 36.
   deprive, 789.
Curtain, 530.
Curtsey, *obeisance*, 743, 894.
   stoop, 306.
Curve, 245.
Curvet, *rise*, 305.
   leap, 309.
   oscillate, 314.
   agitate, 315.
Cushion, *pillow*, 215.
   softness, 324.
   to frustrate, 706.
   relief, 834.
Cusp, *point*, 253.
   angle, 244.
Custodian, 753.
Custody, *captivity*, 751.
   captive, 754.
Custom, *rule*, 80.
   habit, 613.
   fashion, 852.
   sale, 796.
   barter, 794.
   tax, 812.
Custom-house, 799.
Customer, *purchaser*, 795.
   dealer, 797.
Cut, *divide*, 44.
   bit, 51.
   sculpture, 557.
   curtail, 201.
   layer, 204.
   notch, 257.
   form, 240.
   road, 627.
   print, 558.
   pain, 828.
   to give pain, 830.
   affect, 824.
   decline acquaintance, 893, 895.
   state, 7.
   tipsy, 959.
   cold, 385.
Cut across, 302.
Cut along, 274.

Cut and run, *escape*, 671.
Cut capers, *leap*, 309.
   dance, 840.
Cut down, *diminish*, 36.
   destroy, 162.
   shorten, 201.
   lower, 308.
   kill, 361.
Cut off, *kill*, 361.
   subduct, 38.
   impede, 706.
Cut out, *surpass*, 33.
   retrench, 38.
   plan, 626.
Cut short, *shorten*, 201.
   decrease, 36.
   contract, 195.
Cut up, *divide*, 44.
   destroy, 162.
   censure, 932.
Cutaneous, 222.
Cuticle, 222.
Cutlass, 727.
Cut-purse, 792.
Cutter, 273.
Cutting, *cold*, 383.
   affecting, 821.
Cut-throat, 361, 949.
Cycle, *period*, 138.
   circle, 247.
Cycloid, 247.
Cyclopædia, 490.
Cyclops, 872.
Cylinder, 249.
Cymbal, 417.
Cynical, *censorious*, 932.
   detracting, 483.
   cross, 895.
Cynosure, 550.
Cypher, *zero*, 101.
   number, 84.
   to compute, 85.
   mark, 550.
   monogram, 562.
   writing, 590.
Cypress, 839.
Cyst, 191.
Czar, 745.

D.

Dab, *clever*, 700.
   to paint, 222.
   to slap, 276.
Dabble, *meddle*, 680.
   fribble, 683.
*Da-capo, 104.
Dactyliomancy, 511.
Dactylonomy, 560.

Dad, 166.
Dædalian, 698.
Daft, 503.
Dagger, 727.
Daggers drawn, *discord*, 713.
  enmity, 889.
Daggle, 214.
Daguerreotype, 556.
Dainty, *savoury*, 394.
  pleasing, 829.
  fastidious, 868.
Dais, 215.
Dale, 252.
Dally, *irresolute*, 605.
  delay, 133.
  inactive, 683.
  amuse, 840.
  fondle, 902.
Dam, *parent*, 166.
  lock, 350.
  close, 261.
  obstruct, 706.
Damage, *evil*, 619.
  to injure, 649.
  to spoil, 659.
  payment, 812.
Damages, 974.
Damask, 434.
Dame, 374.
Damn, 971.
Damnify, *damage*, 649.
  spoil, 659.
Damocles, 667.
Damp, *moist*, 339.
  cold, 386.
  to moderate, 174.
  to dissuade, 616.
  depress, 837.
  calm, 826.
Damsel, *youth*, 129.
  lady, 374.
Dance, *oscillate*, 314.
  agitate, 315.
  rise, 305.
  jump, 309.
  sport, 840.
Dander, 900.
Dandle, 902.
Dandriff, 653.
Dandy, 854.
Danger, 665.
Dangle, *hang*, 214.
  swing, 314.
Dank, 339.
Darn, 658.
Dapper, *thin*, 203.
  elegant, 845.
Dapple, 433.
Dappled, 440.
285

Dare-devil, 863.
Daring, 861.
Dark, *obscure*, 421.
  dim, 422.
  invisible, 447.
  unintelligible, 519.
  ignorant, 491.
  blind, 442.
  latent, 526.
Darling, *favourite*, 899.
  beloved, 897.
Darn, 658.
Dart, *missile*, 727.
  to propel, 284.
  swift, 274.
Dash, *sprinkling*, 32, 193.
  to mix, 41.
  throw down, 308.
  display, 882.
  depress, 837.
  shine, 873.
  mark, 550.
Dash off, *sketch*, 556.
Dash out, *rush*, 274.
  haste, 684.
Dashing, *brave*, 861.
Dastard, 862.
Data, *evidence*, 467.
  reasoning, 476.
Date, 114.
Daub, *cover*, 222.
  dirt, 653.
  bad painting, 555.
  to deform, 846.
Daughter, 167.
Daunt, 860.
Dauntless, 861.
Dawdle, *slow*, 275.
  tardy, 133.
  inactive, 683.
Dawn, *morning*, 125.
  precursor, 116.
  dim, 422.
  glimpse, 490.
Day, *period*, 108.
  light, 420.
Day-break, 125.
Day-dream, 515.
Day-labourer, 690.
Day-light, 420.
Dazzle, 420.
  confuse, 442.
Deacon, 996.
Dead, *lifeless*, 360.
  insensible, 823.
  colourless, 429.
Deaden, *weaken*, 158.
  moderate, 174, 826.
  benumb, 823.
Dead drunk, 959.

Dead-lock, *stoppage*, 265.
  hindrance, 706.
Deadly, *mortal*, 361, 657.
  pernicious, 649.
Deadness, *numbness*, 381.
  inertness, 172.
Dead shot, 700.
Dead weight, 706.
Deaf, 419.
Deafen, 404.
Deal, *quantity*, 31.
  mingle, 41.
  give, 784.
  allot, 786.
  barter, 794.
  conduct, 692.
Deal out, 73.
Dealer, 797.
Dean, 996.
Deanery, *office*, 995.
  house, 1000.
Dear, *loved*, 897.
  high-priced, 814.
Dear-bought, 644.
Dearth, 640.
Death, 360.
Deathless, 112.
Death-like, *hideous*, 846.
  silence, 403.
*Débâcle, 348.
Debar, *prohibit*, 761.
  hinder, 751.
Debark, 293.
Debase, *depress*, 308.
  deteriorate, 659.
  foul, 653.
Debased, *lowered*, 207.
Debate, *reason*, 476.
  dispute, 720.
  hesitate, 605.
Debateable, 475.
Debauch, *spoil*, 659.
  intemperance, 954.
  impurity, 961.
Debenture, 880.
  certificate, 551.
Debility, 160.
Debit, *debt*, 806.
  accounts, 811.
Debitor, 806.
*Debonnair, 836.
*Débris, 51, 643.
Debt, 806.
Debtor, 806.
*Début, 676.
Decade, 98.
Decadency, 659.
Decamp, 286, 671.
Decant, 270.
Decanter, 191.

Decapitate, 972.
Decay, *spoil*, 659.
  disease, 655.
  shrivel, 195.
Decayed, *imperfect*, 651.
  old, 124.
  adversity, 735.
Decease, 360.
Deceit, 545.
Deceiver, 548.
Decent, 960.
Deception, 545.
  sophistry, 477.
Decide, *judge*, 480.
  choose, 609.
Decided, *resolved*, 604.
  great, 31.
Deciduous, *transitory*, 111.
  spoiled, 659.
Decimal, 84, 98.
Decimate, *subduct*, 38, 99.
Decipher (*or* decypher),
  462, 522.
Decision, *intention*, 620.
  conclusion, 480.
Deck, *floor*, 211.
  to beautify, 845.
Declaim, 582.
Declare, *assert*, 535.
  inform, 527.
Declensions, 5.
Declension, *descent*, 306.
  deterioration, 659.
Decline, *decrease*, 36.
  weaken, 160.
  disease, 655.
  become worse, 659.
  reject, 610.
  refuse, 764.
  be unwilling, 603.
Declivity, 217.
Decoction, 384.
Decollate, 972.
Decoloration, 429.
Decompose, 49.
Decorate, *embellish*, 845.
Decoration, 873, 877.
Decorticate, 226.
Decorum, *politeness*, 852.
  respect, 928.
  purity, 960.
*Décousu, 70, 732.
Decoy, *entice*, 615.
  deceive, 545.
  deceiver, 548.
Decrease, *in degree*, 36.
  in size, 195.
Decrepit, *old*, 124, 128.
  weak, 160.
  frail, 651.
286

Decrepitate, 406.
Decrepitude, *age*, 128.
  feebleness, 160.
Decry, *depreciate*, 483.
  censure, 932.
Decumbent, 213.
Decuple, 98.
Decurtation, 201.
Decussation, 219.
Decypher, *interpret*, 522.
  solve, 462.
Dedicate, 873.
Deduce, *infer*, 480.
  retrench, 38.
Deducible, 467.
Deduct, *retrench*, 38.
  deprive, 789.
Deed, *act*, 680.
  record, 551.
  security, 771.
Deem, 484.
Deep, *profound*, 208.
  the sea, 341.
  cunning, 702.
  feeling, 821.
  sound, 404.
Deeply, 31.
Deep-mouthed, 404.
Deep-seated, *interior*, 221.
  deep, 208.
Deep-toned, 408.
Deface, *render ugly*, 846.
  destroy form, 241.
Defalcation, *short-coming*,
  304.
  contraction, 195.
  incompleteness, 53.
  insufficiency, 640.
  non-payment, 808.
Defame, *detract*, 934.
  shame, 874.
  censure, 932.
Defamer, 936.
Default, *insufficiency*, 640.
  non-payment, 808.
Defaulter, 806.
Defeat, 732.
Defecate, *clean*, 652.
  improve, 658.
Defect, *incomplete*, 53.
  imperfect, 651.
  failing, 945.
Defection, 940.
Defective, *incomplete*, 53.
  imperfect, 651.
  insufficient, 640.
Defence, *resistance*, 717.
  vindication, 937.
  safety, 664.
Defenceless, *weak*, 160.

Defenceless, *exposed*, 665.
Defendant, 967.
Defer, 133.
Defer to, *respect*, 928.
  assent, 488.
Deference, 928.
Defiance, *daring*, 715.
  threat, 909.
Deficient, *incomplete*, 53.
  imperfect, 651.
  insufficient, 640.
Deficit, *debt*, 806.
Defigure, 846.
Defile, *ravine*, 203.
  march, 266.
  dirt, 652.
  spoil, 659.
  shame, 874.
Define, *name*, 564.
  explain, 522.
Definite, *exact*, 494.
  special, 79.
  visible, 446.
  limited, 233.
  intelligible, 518.
Definitive, *decided*, 604.
  final, 67.
Deflagration, 384.
Deflect, 245.
Defloration, 961.
  soil, 653.
Defluxion, 348.
Deformity, 846.
Defraud, *cheat*, 545.
  non-payment, 808.
Defray, 807.
Deft, *clever*, 698.
  suitable, 23.
Defunct, 360.
Defy, *dare*, 715.
  disobey, 742.
  threaten, 909.
Degenerate, 659.
Deglutition, 297.
Degradation, *shame*, 874.
  dishonor, 940.
  deterioration, 659.
Degree, 26.
  term, 71.
  honor, 873.
Degustation, 390.
Dehortation, *dissuasion*, 616
  advice, 695.
  warning, 668.
Deification, 991.
Deign, *condescend*, 879.
  consent, 762.
Deism, 988.
Deity, 976.
  fabulous, 979.

Deject, 837.
*Déjeûné, 299.
*Délâbrement, 659.
Delation, 938.
Delay, 133.
*Dele, 552.
Delectable, *savoury*, 394.
  agreeable, 829.
Delegate, 758.
  to commission, 755.
Deleterious,*pernicious*,649.
  unwholesome, 657.
Deletion, 552.
Deliberate, *think*, 451.
  cautious, 864.
  advised, 695.
Deliberately, 600.
Delicacy, *of texture*, 329.
  slenderness, 203.
  weak, 160.
  tender, 655.
  savoury, 394.
  dainty, 299.
  of taste, 850.
  fastidiousness, 868.
  exactness, 494.
  pleasing, 829.
  beauty, 845.
  honor, 939.
  purity, 960.
  difficulty, 704.
  scruple, 616.
*Délice, 827.
Delicious, *taste*, 394.
  pleasing, 829.
Delight, *pleasure*, 827.
Delightful, 829.
Delineate, *describe*, 594.
  represent, 554.
Delinquency, 947.
Delinquent, 949.
Deliquation, 333.
Deliquescent, 333.
Deliquium, 160.
Delirium, *raving*, 503.
  passion, 825.
Delitescence, 526.
Deliver, *transfer*, 270.
  give, 784.
  liberate, 750.
  relieve, 834.
  utter, 582.
  rescue, 672.
  escape, 671.
Dell, 252.
Delude, 545.
Deluge, 348.
  redundance, 641.
Delusion, *error*, 495.
  deceit, 545.
287

Delusion (self), 486.
Delve, *dig*, 252.
  depth, 208.
Demagogue, 745.
Demagogy, 737.
Demand, *claim*, 924.
  ask, 765.
  inquire, 461.
  order, 741.
  price, 812.
Demarcation, 233.
Demean, *humble*, 879.
  dishonor, 940.
Demeanour, *conduct*, 692.
  air, 448.
  fashion, 852.
Demency, 503.
Dementation, 503.
Demerit, *vice*, 945.
  inutility, 645.
Demesne, 780.
Demi, 91.
Demigod, 948.
Demigration, 266.
Demirep, 962.
Demise, *death*, 360.
  to transfer, 783.
  to give, 784.
Demiurge, 979.
Democracy, 737.
Demolish, *destroy*, 162.
  damage, 649.
Demon, *devil*, 980.
  wretch, 913.
  bane, 663.
  violent, 173.
Demoniacal, *wicked*, 945.
  furious, 825.
  diabolic, 649.
Demonism, 991.
Demonomy, 992.
Demonship, 992.
Demonstrate, *prove*, 478.
  manifest, 525.
Demoralize, 945.
Demulcent, *mild*, 174.
  soothing, 662.
Demur, *unwillingness*, 603.
  hesitation, 605.
  to disbelieve, 485.
  dislike, 867.
Demure, *grave*, 826.
  sad, 837.
  modest, 881.
  affected, 855.
Den, *cell*, 189.
  prison, 752.
  stye, 653.
Denary, 98.
Denaturalized, 83.

Dendriform, 256.
Denial, 536.
Denigrate, 431.
Denization, 750.
Denizen, *inhabitant*, 188.
  man, 373.
Denominate, 564.
Denomination, 75.
Denominator, 84.
Denote, 550.
*Dénouement, *result*, 154.
  end, 67.
  elucidation, 522.
Denounce, *accuse*, 908.
  cite, 965.
Dense, *close*, 321.
  crowded, 72.
Dent, *notch*, 257.
  hollow, 252.
Denticulated, 253.
Denude, 226.
Denunciation, 969.
Deny, *negative*, 536.
  dissent, 489.
  refuse, 764.
Deobstruct, 705.
Deodand, 974.
Deontology, 926.
Deoppilation, 705.
Depart, *set out*, 292.
  die, 360.
Department, *class*, 75.
  region, 181.
  business, 625.
Depend, *hang*, 214.
  be contingent, 475.
Depend upon, *trust*, 484.
  be the effect of, 154.
  affirm, 535.
Dependent, *liable*, 177.
  servant, 746.
Dependence,*subjection*,749.
Deperdition, 776.
Dephlegmation, 340.
Depict, *paint*, 556.
  describe, 594.
Depletion, 640.
Deplorable, *bad*, 649.
  painful, 830.
Deplore, *regret*, 833.
  complain, 839.
  remorse, 950.
Deploy, 194.
Deponent, 467.
Depopulate, *displace*, 185.
  desert, 893.
Deportation, *displace*, 185.
  transfer, 270.
  emigration, 296.
Deportment, 692.

Depose, *evidence*, 467.
tell, 527.
record, 551.
dethrone, 756.
declare, 535.
Deposit, *place*, 184.
secure, 771.
store, 636.
Depository, 636.
*Dépôt, 636.
Deprave, *spoil*, 659.
Depraved, *bad*, 649.
vicious, 945.
Deprecate, 766.
pity, 914.
Depreciate, *detract*, 483.
censure, 932.
Depredation, 791.
Depredator, 792.
Deprehension, 789.
Depression, *lowering*, 308.
lowness, 207.
depth, 208.
concavity, 252.
dejection, 837.
Deprive, *take*, 789.
subduct, 38.
lose, 776.
Depth, *physical*, 208.
mental, 450.
Depurate, *clean*, 652.
improve, 658.
remedy, 662.
Depute, 755.
Deputy, 757, 759.
Dequantitate, 36.
Derange, 61.
Derangement, *mental*, 503.
Dereliction, *relinquishment*,
624.
guilt, 947.
Deride, *ridicule*, 856.
disrespect, 929.
trifle with, 643.
Derisive, 853.
Derivation, *origin*, 153.
verbal, 562.
Derive, *attribute*, 155.
receive, 785.
acquire, 775.
income, 810.
Dermal, 222.
Derogate, *disparage*, 483.
demean, 940.
shame, 874.
Dervish, 996.
Descant, *dissert*, 595.
dwell upon, 584.
diffuseness, 573.
Descendant, 167.
288

Descendent, 306.
Descent, 306.
Describe, 594.
Description, *kind*, 75.
Descry, 441.
Desecrate, *misuse*, 679.
profane, 989.
Desert, *solitude*, 101, 893.
waste, 645.
empty, 4.
Desert, *merit*, 944.
to relinquish, 624.
to escape, 671.
Deserter, 607.
Desertful, 944.
Desertless, 945.
Deserve, *merit*, 944.
right, 922, 924.
Desiccate, 340.
Desiderate, 865.
Desideratum, 865.
Design, *intention*, 620.
cunning, 702.
plan, 626.
delineation, 554.
prototype, 22.
Designate, 564.
Designation, *kind*, 75.
Designed, *intended*, 600.
Designer, *artist*, 559.
Designing, *false*, 544.
artful, 702.
Designless, 621.
Desinence, *end*, 67.
discontinuance, 141.
Desirable, 646.
Desire, 865.
Desist, *discontinue*, 141.
relinquish, 624.
inaction, 681.
Desk, *support*, 215.
receptacle, 191.
*Désobligeant, 272.
Desolate, *alone*, 87.
secluded, 893.
afflicted, 828.
to ravage, 162.
Desolation, *evil*, 619.
Despair, *hopelessness*, 859.
grief, 828.
Despatch, 532.
Desperado, 863.
Desperate, *great*, 31.
violent, 173.
rash, 863.
difficult, 704.
impossible, 471.
Desperation, 859.
Despicable, *shameful*, 874.
contemptible, 930.

Despicable, *trifling*, 643.
Despise, *contemn*, 930.
deride, 483.
Despite, *notwithstanding*,
179, 708.
malevolence, 907.
Despoil, *take*, 789.
rob, 791.
hurt, 649.
Despond, 859.
Despot, 745.
Despotism, *arbitrariness*,
964.
authority, 737.
severity, 739.
Despumation, 652.
Desquamation, 226.
Dessert, 299.
Destine, 620.
Destination, *fate*, 152.
arrival, 293.
intention, 620.
Destiny, *fate*, 601.
chance, 152.
Destitute, *insufficient*, 640.
poor, 804.
Destroy, *demolish*, 162.
injure, 649.
deface, 241.
Destroyed, 2.
Destruction, *demolition* 162
evil, 619.
Destructive, 649.
Desuetude, 614.
disuse, 678.
Desultory, *discontinuous*, 70.
irregular in time, 139.
disordered, 59.
multiform, 81.
deviating. 279.
agitated, 315.
Detach, *separate*, 44.
Detached, *irrelated*, 10.
Detachment, *part*, 51.
army, 726.
Detail, *to describe*, 594.
special portions, 79.
Detain, 781.
Detect, 480.
Detention, 781.
*Détenu, 754.
Deter, 616.
Deterge, 652.
Detergent, *remedy*, 662.
remedial, 656.
Deteriorate, 659.
Determinate, *special*, 79.
exact, 474.
resolute, 604.
Determination, 604.

Determine, *judge*, 480.
  intend, 620.
  direction, 278.
Detersion, 652.
Detest, 898.
Detestable, *bad*, 649, 867.
Dethrone, 756.
Dethronement, *anarchy*, 738.
Detonate, *sound*, 406.
  explode, 173.
Detortion, 243.
*Détour, 629.
Detract, *subduct*, 38.
  depreciate, 483.
  censure, 932.
  slander, 934.
Detractor, 936.
Detriment, 619.
Detrimental, 649.
*Detritus, 51, 330.
Detrude, *cast out*, 296.
  cast down, 308.
Detruncation, 38.
Deuce, *duality*, 89.
  demon, 980.
Deuced, 31.
Deuterogamy, 903.
Devastate, *destroy*, 162.
  injure, 649.
  havoc, 619.
Develope, *cause*, 153.
  produce, 161.
  increase, 35.
  expand, 194.
  evolve, 313.
Devexity, *bending*, 217.
  curvature, 245.
Deviate, *differ*, 15.
  vary, 20.
  turn, 279.
  circuit, 629.
Device, *expedient*, 626.
  motto, 550.
Devil, *Satan*, 978.
  maleficent being, 913.
  culprit, 949.
  seasoned food, 392.
Devilish, 31.
  bad, 649.
Devious, *deviating*, 279.
  different, 15.
Devise, *plan*, 626.
  imagine, 515.
  bequeathe, 784.
Devoid, *empty*, 640.
  absent, 187.
  not having, 776.
*Devoir, 894.
Devolve, 783.

289

Devolve on, 926.
Devote, *give up*, 457.
  curse, 908.
  employ, 677.
  consecrate, 873.
Devotee, *piety*, 987.
  resolute, 604.
Devoted, *loving*, 897.
  friendly, 888.
  doomed, 152, 828.
Devotion, *piety*, 987.
  worship, 990.
  respect, 928.
  love, 897.
  disinterestedness, 942.
Devour, *eat*, 297.
  destroy, 162.
Devout, 987.
Devoutless, 988.
Dew, 339.
Dextrality, 238.
Dextrous, 698.
Dey, 745.
*Diablerie, 992.
Diabolic, *malevolent*, 907.
  wicked, 945.
  bad, 649.
Diadem, 747.
Diagnostic, 5.
Diagonal, 217.
Diagram, 554.
Dial, 114.
Dialect, 560.
Dialectic, *argumentation*, 476.
  language, 560.
Dialogue, 588.
Diameter, 202.
Diamond, *lozenge*, 244.
  gem, 650.
Diapason, 413.
Diaphanous, 425.
Diaphragm, *partition*, 228.
  middle, 68.
Diary, *record*, 551.
  journal, 114.
Diastole, 194.
Diathermancy, 384.
*Diathesis, 7.
Diatonic, 413.
*Diatribe, 932.
Dibble, 262.
Dicacity, 885.
Dice, 156.
Dichotomy, 91.
Dichroism, 440.
Dictate, *command*, 741.
  authority, 737.
Dictate, *enjoin*, 615.
  write, 590.

Dictator, 745.
Dictatorial, 885.
Dictatorship, 737.
Diction, 569.
Dictionary, 562.
*Dictum, *maxim*, 496.
  affirmation, 535.
Didactic, 537.
Didder, *shiver*, 383.
Diddle, 545.
Diduction, 44.
Die, *chance*, 156.
  to expire, 360.
  cease, 142.
Die for, *desire*, 865.
Diet, *food*, 299.
  council, 696.
Dietetics, 662.
Difference, 15.
  discord, 713.
  numerical, 84.
Differential, 84.
Differentiation, 85.
Difficult, *fastidious*, 868.
Difficulty, 704.
Diffident, *modest*, 881.
  fearful, 860.
Diffuse, *style*, 573.
  disperse, 73.
  publish, 531.
  permeate, 186.
Dig, *excavate*, 252.
  deepen, 208.
Digamy, 903.
Digest, *arrange*, 60.
  think, 451.
  plan, 626.
  compendium, 596.
Dight, 225.
Digit, 84.
Digitated, 253.
Digladiation, 720.
Dignify, 873.
Dignitary, 997.
Dignity, *glory*, 873.
  honor, 939.
Digress, *deviate*, 279.
  style, 573.
Dijudication, 480.
Dike, *ditch*, 198.
  defence, 717, 666.
Dilaceration, 44.
Dilapidated, 160.
Dilate, *increase*, 35.
  swell, 194.
  lengthen, 202.
  rarefy, 322.
  style, 573.
  discourse, 584.
Dilatory, *slow*, 275.

Dilatory, *inactive*, 683.
Dilection, 897.
Dilemma, *difficulty*, 704.
    logic, 476.
    doubt, 485.
*Dilettante, 492, 850.
Diligence, *coach*, 272.
    activity, 682.
Dilution, 337.
Diluvian, 124.
Dim, *dark*, 421.
    obscure, 422.
    invisible, 447.
Dimension, 192.
Dimidiate, 91.
Diminish, *lessen*, 36.
    con'ract, 195.
Diminutive, *in degree*, 32.
    in size, 193.
Dimness, 422.
Dimple, *concavity*, 252.
    notch, 257.
Dimsighted, 443.
    foolish, 499.
Din, *noise*, 404.
    repetition, 104.
    loquacity, 584.
Dine, 297.
Ding, *repeat*, 104.
    noise, 407.
Dingle, 252.
Dingy, *dark*, 421.
    dim, 422.
    colourless, 429.
    boat, 273.
Dinner, 299.
Dint, *power*, 157.
    instrumentality, 631.
Diocesan, 996.
Diocese, 995.
Diorama, *view*, 448.
    painting, 556.
Dip, *plunge*, 310.
    leap, 309.
    stoop, 308.
    dive, 208.
    insert, 301.
    immerse, 337.
Diploma, *commission*, 755.
    document, 551.
Diplomacy, *mediation*, 724.
    artfulness, 702.
    negociation, 769.
Diplomatic, 544.
Dire, *fearful*, 860.
    grievous, 830.
    calamitous, 649.
Direct, *straight*, 246.
    to order, 737.
    to command, 741.

Direct, *to teach*, 537.
    artless, 703.
Directly, *soon*, 111.
    towards, 278.
Direction, *tendency*, 278.
    management, 693.
    precept, 697.
Director, *manager*, 694.
    master, 745.
    teacher, 540.
Directorship, 737.
Directory, 696.
Dirge, *song*, 415.
    lament, 839.
    funeral, 363.
Dirk, 727.
Dirt, *uncleanness*, 653.
    trifle, 643.
    ugly, 846.
    blemish, 848.
Dirty, *dishonorable*, 940.
Disability, 158.
Disabuse, 529.
Disadvantage, *evil*, 619.
    inexpedience, 647.
    badness, 649.
Disaffection, 898.
Disagreeable, *unpleasing*,
830.
    disliked, 867.
Disagreement, *incongruity*,
24.
    difference, 15.
    discord, 713.
    dissent, 489.
Disallow, 761.
Disannul, 756.
Disapparel, 226.
Disappear, 449.
    vanish, 2.
Disappoint, *discontent*, 832.
    fail, 732.
    balk, 509.
Disapprobation, 932.
Disarm, *incapacitate*, 158.
    weaken, 160.
Disarrange, 61.
Disarray, *disorder*, 59.
    undress, 226.
Disaster, *evil*, 619.
    failure, 732.
    adversity, 735.
    calamity, 830.
Disavow, 536.
Disband, *disperse*, 73.
    separate, 44.
Disbelief, 485.
    (*religious*), 988.
Disbranch, 44.
Disburden, *facilitate*, 705.

Disburden, *disclose*, 529.
Disburse, 809.
Disc, 220.
Discard, *dismiss*, 756.
    disuse, 678.
    refuse, 764.
    thought, 452.
    repudiate, 773.
Discern, 441.
Discernible, 446.
Discerning, 498.
Discernment, 498.
Discerption, 44.
Discharge, *emit*, 296.
    sound, 406.
    violence, 173.
    propel, 284.
    excrete, 298.
    flow, 348.
    duty, 926.
    acquit oneself, 692.
    observe, 772.
    pay, 807.
    exempt, 927.
    liberate, 750.
    forget, 506.
    acquit, 970.
Discind, 44.
Disciple, 541.
Disciplinarian,   *master*,
546.
    martinet, 739.
Discipline, *order*, 58.
    teaching, 537.
    training, 673.
    restraint, 751.
    religious, 990.
Disclaim, *deny*, 536.
    refuse, 764.
    repudiate, 756.
    abjure, 757.
Disclose, 529.
Discolour, 429.
Discomfit, 731.
Discomfiture, 732.
Discomfort, 828.
Discommendation, 932.
Discommodious, 645.
Discommodity, 647.
Discompose, *derange*, 61.
    hinder, 706.
    put out, 458.
    to vex, 830.
    disconcert, 874.
    provoke, 900.
Disconcert, *hinder*, 706.
    frustrate, 731.
    confuse, 874.
Disconcerted, 458.
Disconformity, 24.

Discongruity, 24.
Disconnect, 44.
Disconsolate, *sad*, 837.
  grief, 828.
Discontent, 832.
Discontented, 828.
Discontinuance, 141.
Discontinuity, 70.
Discord, *disagreement*, 24.
  dissention, 713
  musical, 414.
Discordance, *incongruity*, 24.
  sound, 410.
  dissent, 489.
Discount, 813.
Discountenance, *refuse*, 764.
  disfavour, 706.
  rudeness, 895.
Discourage, *dissuade*, 616.
  sadden, 837.
  disfavour, 706.
Discourse, *talk*, 588.
  speech, 582.
  dissert, 595.
Discourtesy, 895.
Discover, *perceive*, 441.
  find, 480.
  solve, 462.
Discredit, *disbelief*, 485.
  dishonor, 874.
Discreditable, 945.
Discreet, *careful*, 459.
  cautious, 864.
  clever, 698.
Discrepancy, 24.
Discrete, *separate*, 44.
  single, 87.
Discretion, *wisdom*, 498.
  skill, 698.
  will, 600.
Discretional, 609.
Discrimination, *distinction*, 465.
  difference, 15.
  taste, 850.
  wisdom, 498.
Disculpate, 937.
Discursion, 266.
Discursive, *moving*, 264.
  migratory, 266.
  wandering, 279.
  style, 573.
Discuss, *reason*, 476.
  inquire, 461.
  reflect, 451.
Disdain, *contempt*, 930.
  indifference, 866.
  fastidiousness, 868.
291

Disdainful, *proud*, 878.
Disease, 655.
Disembark, 293.
Disembarrass, 705.
Disembody, 317.
Disembogue, *flow out*, 348.
  emit, 294.
Disembroil, 60.
Disenable, 158.
Disenchant, *dissuade*, 616.
  displease, 830.
Disencumber, 705.
Disengage, *detach*, 44.
  facilitate, 705.
  liberate, 750.
Disentangle, *separate*, 44.
  arrange, 60.
  facilitate, 705.
  decipher, 522.
Disentitled, 925.
Disesteem, *disrespect*, 929.
  censure, 932.
Disfavour, *hate*, 898.
  to oppose, 708.
Disfigure, *deface*, 241.
  deform, 846.
  blemish, 848.
Disfranchise, 925.
Disgorge, *emit*, 296.
  restore, 790.
  flow out, 348.
Disgrace, *shame*, 874.
  dishonor, 940.
Disguise, *conceal*, 528.
  falsify, 544.
  deceive, 545.
  mask, 530.
  untruth, 546.
Disguised, *in liquor*, 959.
Disgust, *dislike*, 867.
  hatred, 898.
  offensive, 830.
  weary, 841.
  taste, 395.
Dish, *plate*, 191.
  food, 299.
Dishabille, *undress*, 225.
  unprepared, 674.
Dishearten, *dissuade*, 616.
  deject, 837.
Dished, 732.
Dishevel, *loose*, 47.
  disordered, 61.
  intermixed, 219.
Dishonest, *false*, 544.
Dishonor, *baseness*, 940.
  to repudiate a bill, 808.
  disrespect, 929.
Dishonorable, 874.
Disincline, *dissuade*, 616.

Disincline, *dislike*, 867.
Disinclined, 603.
Disinfect, *purify*, 652.
  improve, 658.
Disinfectant, 662.
Disinherit, 783.
Disingenuous, *false*, 544.
  dishonorable, 940.
Disintegrate, *separate*, 44.
  pulverize, 330.
Disinter, *exhume*, 363.
  discover, 525.
Disinterested, 942.
Disinthral, 750.
Disjoin, 44.
Disjointed, 44.
  in disorder, 59.
Disk, *face*, 234.
  exterior, 220.
Dislike, 867, 898.
  reluctance, 603.
Dislocate, 44.
Dislodge, 185.
Disloyal, 940.
Dismal, 837.
Dismantle, *destroy*, 162.
  disuse, 678.
  despoil, 649.
  injure, 659.
Dismast, *disuse*, 678.
  dismantle, 659.
Dismay, 860.
Dismember, 44.
Dismiss, *discard*, 678.
  liberate, 750.
Dismount, *descend*, 306.
Disobey, 742.
Disobliging, 907.
Disorder, *confusion*, 59.
  to derange, 61.
  disease, 655.
Disorganize, *derange*, 61.
  destroy, 162.
  spoil, 659.
Disown, 536.
Dispair, 44.
Disparage, *depreciate*, 483.
  disrespect, 929.
  censure, 932.
Disparate, *different*, 15.
  dissimilar, 18.
  single, 87.
  disagreeing, 24.
  unequal, 28.
Dispart, 44.
Dispassion, 826.
Dispatch, *speed*, 274.
  haste, 684.
  earliness, 132.
  to conduct, 692.

Dispatch, *complete*, 729.
  kill, 361.
  epistle, 592.
Dispel, *destroy*, 162.
  scatter, 73.
Dispensable, 678.
Dispensation, *licence*, 760.
  calamity, 830.
Dispense, *exempt*, 927.
  permit, 760.
  disuse, 678.
  relinquish, 624.
  give, 784.
  disperse, 73.
  retail, 796.
Dispeople, 893.
Disperse, *scatter*, 73.
  separate, 44.
  diverge, 290.
Dispirit, *sadden*, 837.
  discourage, 616.
Displace, *remove*, 185.
  transfer, 270.
  derange, 61.
Displacency, *dislike*, 867.
  disapprobation, 932.
Display, *show*, 525.
  appear, 448.
  parade, 882.
Displease, 830.
Displeased, 828.
Displeasure, 828.
  anger, 900.
Displosion, 173.
Disport, 840.
Dispose, *arrange*, 60.
  prepare, 673.
  tend, 176.
  induce, 615.
Dispose of, *sell*, 796.
  give, 784.
  relinquish, 782.
  use, 677.
Disposition, *order*, 58.
  arrangement, 60.
  inclination, 602.
  mind, 820.
Dispossess, *take away*, 789.
  transfer, 783.
Dispraise, 932.
Disprize, 483.
Disproof, 479.
Disproportion, *irrelation*, 10.
  disagreement, 24.
Disprove, *confute*, 479.
Disputant, 726.
Disputatious, *irritable*, 901.
Dispute, *discord*, 713.
  denial, 536.
292

Dispute, *discussion*, 476.
Disqualify, *incapacitate*, 158
  weaken, 160.
  disentitle, 925.
  unprepared, 674.
  unskilful, 699.
Disquiet, *excitement*, 825.
  uneasiness, 828.
  to give pain, 830.
Disquietude, *apprehension*,
  860.
Disquisition, 595.
Disregard, *overlook*, 458.
  neglect, 460.
  slight, 483.
Disrelish, *dislike*, 867.
  hate, 898.
Disreputable, *vicious*, 945.
Disrepute, 874.
Disrespect, 929.
Disrobe, 226.
Disruption, 44.
Dissatisfaction, *discontent*,
  832.
  sorrow, 828.
Dissect, *anatomize*, 44.
  investigate, 461.
Dissemble, 544.
Dissembler, 548.
Disseminate, *scatter*, 73.
  diverge, 290.
  publish, 531
  pervade, 186.
Dissent, *disagree*, 489.
  refuse, 764.
  heterodoxy, 984.
  discord, 713.
Dissertation, 595.
Disservice, *disadvantage*,
  619.
  inexpedience, 647.
Disserviceable, 649.
Dissever, 44.
Dissidence, 24.
Dissilience, 173.
Dissimilar, 18.
Dissimilitude, 18.
Dissimulate, 544.
Dissipate, *scatter*, 73.
  waste, 638.
  prodigality, 818.
  dissolute, 961.
  licentiousness, 954.
Dissociation, *irrelation*, 10.
  separation, 44.
Dissolute, *intemperate*, 954.
  profligate, 945.
  debauched, 961.
Dissolution, *decomposition*,
  49.

Dissolution,   *liquefaction*,
  335.
  death, 360.
Dissolve, *vanish*, 2.
  disappear, 449.
  abrogate, 756.
  liquefy, 335.
  debauched, 961.
Dissonance,   *disagreement*,
  24.
  discord, 414.
Dissuade, 616.
Distain, 846.
Distance, 196.
  to overtake, 282.
  to leave behind, 732.
  respect, 928.
  of time, 110.
Distaste, *dislike*, 867.
Distasteful,   *disagreeable*,
  830.
Distemper, *disease*, 655.
  painting, 556.
Distend, 194.
Distended, 192.
Distich, 597.
Distil, *evaporate*, 336.
  flow, 348.
  drop, 294.
Distinct, *visible*, 446.
  intelligible, 518.
Distinction, *difference*, 15.
  discrimination, 465.
  fame, 873.
Distinguish, *perceive*, 441.
Distortion, *obliquity*, 217.
  twist, 243.
  of vision, 443.
  perversion, 523.
  ugliness, 846.
Distracted, *insane*, 503.
  foolish, 499.
  confused, 491.
Distrain, *seize*, 789.
*Distrait, 452, 458.
Distress, *affliction*, 828.
  cause of pain, 830.
  poor, 804.
Distribute, *disperse*, 73.
  arrange, 60.
  allot, 786.
  diverge, 290.
District, 181.
Distrust, *disbelief*, 485.
  fear, 860.
Disturb, *derange*, 61.
  agitate, 315.
Disunion, *separation*, 44.
  discord, 713.
Disuse, *unemploy*, 678.

Disuse, *desuetude*, 614.
Disvalue, 932.
Ditch, *conduit*, 350.
  hollow, 252.
  trench, 259.
Ditto, 104.
Ditty, 415.
Diurnal, 108.
Diuturnal, 110.
Divan, *sofa*, 215.
  council, 696.
Divarication, *divergence*, 290.
  deviation, 279.
  difference, 15.
Dive, *plunge*, 310.
  inquire, 461.
Divergence, *variation*, 20.
  difference, 15.
  separation, 290.
  deviation, 279.
Divers, *many*, 102.
  different, 15.
  multiform, 81.
Diversion, 840.
Diversity, *difference*, 15.
  dissimilarity, 18.
  multiform, 81.
Divert, *amuse*, 840.
  abstract, 452.
Divest, *denude*, 226.
  take, 789.
Divest oneself of, 782.
Divide, *separate*, 44.
  part, 51.
  apportion, 786.
Dividend, *part*, 51.
  number, 84.
  portion, 786.
Divination, *prediction*, 511.
  sorcery, 992.
Divine, *Deity*, 976.
  clergyman, 996.
  to guess, 514.
  perfect, 650.
Divining rod, 993.
Divinity, *Deity*, 976.
  theology, 983.
Division, *separation*, 44.
  class, 75.
  arithmetical, 85.
  discord, 713.
Divisor, 84.
Divorce, *matrimonial*, 905.
  separation, 44.
Divulge, 529.
Divulsion, 44.
Dizen, *beautify*, 845.
  ornament, 847.
Dizzard, 501.
293

Dizzy, *confused*, 458.
  vertigo, 503.
Do, *act*, 680.
  produce, 161.
  complete, 729.
  cheat, 545.
Do away with, *remove*, 185.
  destroy, 162.
Do for, *injure*, 659.
  punish, 972.
Do into, 522.
Do over, 220.
Docile, 539.
Dock, *cut off*, 38.
  diminish, 36.
  shorten, 201.
  port, 189.
  yard, 691.
  tribunal, 966.
Docked, 53.
Docket, 550.
Doctor, *sage*, 492.
  to restore, 660.
  remedy, 658.
Doctrinal, 537.
Doctrine, *tenet*, 484.
  knowledge, 490.
Document, 551.
Dodge, *oscillate*, 314.
  pursue, 461.
  deceive, 545.
  avoid, 623.
  shift, 264.
Doer, *agent*, 690.
  originator, 164.
Doff, 226.
Dog, *to pursue*, 622.
Dog-cheap, 815.
Dog's-ear, 258.
Dog days, 382.
Doge, 745.
Dogged, *obstinate*, 606.
  discourteous, 895.
Dogger, 273.
Doggrel, *verse*, 597.
  ridiculous, 853.
Dog-hole, 189.
Dogma, *tenet*, 484.
  theological, 983.
Dogmatic, *obstinate*, 606.
  assertion, 535.
Dog-trot, 275.
Doings, *actions*, 680.
  events, 151.
Doit, *trifle*, 643.
  coin, 800.
Dole, *small quantity*, 32.
  to give, 784.
  to allot, 786.
  grief, 828.

Doleful, 837.
Do-little, 683.
Doll, *image*, 554.
  small, 193.
Dollar, 800.
Dolorific, 830.
Dolour, *physical*, 378.
  moral, 828.
Dolt, 501.
Doltish, 499.
Domain, *region*, 181.
  property, 780.
Dome, 250.
Domestic, *interior*, 221.
  servant, 746.
  secluded, 893.
Domicile, 189.
Dominance, 175.
Dominant, *prevailing*, 737.
  note in music, 413.
Domination, 737.
Domineer, *tyrannize*, 739.
  insolence, 885.
Dominican, 996.
Domino, *dress*, 225.
  mask, 530.
Don, *to put on*, 225.
  noble, 875.
Donation, 784.
Done, *finished*, 729.
  cheated, 547.
Donjon, 717.
Donkey, *ass*, 271.
  fool, 501.
*Donna, 374.
Donzel, 746.
Doodle, 501.
Doom, *fate*, 152.
  necessity, 601.
  destruction, 162.
  to sentence, 969.
Doomed, *undone*, 828.
Doomsday, 121.
Door, *opening*, 260.
  passage, 627.
  brink, 230.
  entrance, 66.
  barrier, 232.
Door-keeper, 263.
Door-way, 260.
Dormant, *latent*, 526.
  inert, 172.
Dormitory, 191.
Dormouse, 683.
Dorsal, 235.
Dose, 51.
Dot, *speck*, 32, 193.
  mark, 550.
Dotage, 499.
Dotard, 501.

Dotation, 784.
Dote, *drivel*, 503.
  love, 897.
Dotted, 440.
Double, *duplex*, 90.
  turn, 283.
  fold, 258.
  false, 544.
Double-dealing, 544.
  dishonor, 940.
Double-edged, 171.
*Double entendre, 520, 961.
Double-faced,*deceitful*,544
  trimming, 607.
Double-meaning, 520.
Double-tongued, 544.
Doublet, 225.
Doubt, *disbelief*, 485.
  scepticism, 988.
Doubtful, *uncertain*, 475.
  incredulous, 485.
Doubtless, 474.
Douceur, 809.
*Douche, 337.
Dough, *pulp*, 354.
  inelastic, 324.
Doughty, 861.
Douse, *immerse*, 310.
  splash, 337.
  blow, 972.
Dove, 976.
Dove-like, 946.
Dove-tail, *intervene*, 228.
  intersect, 219.
  insert, 301.
  angular, 244.
  join, 43.
  agree, 23.
Dowager, *widow*, 905.
  lady, 374.
Dowdy, *vulgar*, 851.
  dirty, 653.
  ugly, 846.
Dower, 803.
Dowerless, 804.
Down, *levity*, 320.
  smoothness, 255.
  plumose, 256.
  bed of, 377.
  below, 207.
Downcast, 837.
Downfall, *ruin*, 732.
  calamity, 619.
Downhill, 217.
Downright, *absolute*, 31.
  sincere, 703.
Downs, *plains*, 344.
  uplands, 206.
Downwards, 207.
294

Downy, 324.
Dowry, 803.
Dowse, *strike*, 276.
Doxology, 990.
Doxy, 899.
Doze, 683.
Dozen, 98.
Drab, *colour*, 432.
  hussey, 962.
Draff, 653.
Draft, *copy*, 21.
  transfer, 270.
  sketch, 554.
  abstract, 596.
  depth, 208.
  plan, 626.
  cheque, 800.
Drag, *traction*, 285.
  attract, 289.
  crawl, 275.
Drag up, 307.
Draggle, *hang*, 214.
Drag-net, 78.
Dragoman, 524.
Dragon, *violence*, 173.
Dragonnade, 619.
Dragoon, 726.
  to persecute, 907.
Drain, *conduit*, 350.
  to dry, 340.
  exhaust, 789.
  waste, 638.
  dissipate, 818.
  flow out, 294.
  empty itself, 348.
  drink up, 297.
Dram, *stimulus*, 615.
Drama, 599.
Drapery, 225.
Drastic, 171.
Draught, *drink*, 297.
  traction, 285.
  stream of air, 349.
  abundance, 639.
  cheque, 800.
Draughtsman, 559.
Draw, *pull*, 285.
  attract, 289.
  extract, 300.
  induce, 615.
  delineate, 556.
  money order, 800.
Draw back, *regress*, 283.
  avoid, 623.
Draw in, *contract*, 195.
Draw near, *approach*, 287.
  time, 121.
Draw on, *event*, 151.
Draw out, *extract*, 300.
  prolong, 200.

Draw out, *protract*, 110.
  exhibit, 525.
Draw up, 590.
Draw together, 72.
Drawback, *hindrance*, 706.
  imperfection, 651.
  discount, 813.
  evil, 619.
Drawbridge, *escape*, 671.
Drawcansir, 887.
Drawee, 800.
Drawer, *receptacle*, 191.
  money, 800.
Drawers, *dress*, 225.
Drawing, *sketch*, 556.
Drawing-room, 191.
Drawl, *creep*, 275.
  prolong, 200.
  in speech, 583.
  sluggish, 683.
Dray, 272.
Dread, 860.
Dreadful, *great*, 31.
  fearful, 860.
  calamitous, 830.
Dreadless, 861.
Dream, *vision*, 515.
  unsubstantial, 4.
  error, 495.
  inactivity, 683.
Dream of, *think*, 451.
  intend, 620.
Dreamy, *inattentive*, 458.
Dreary, *solitary*, 87.
  melancholy, 830.
Dredge, *raise*, 307.
  extract, 300.
  collect, 72.
Dregs, *refuse*, 643.
  dirt, 653.
  remainder, 40.
Drench, *drink*, 297.
  affusion, 337.
  redundance, 641.
Dress, *cloathe*, 225.
  prepare, 673.
Dressing, *punishment*, 972.
Dresser, 215.
Dribble, *flow out*, 294.
  drop, 348.
Dribblet, *part*, 51.
  scanty, 193.
Drift, *direction*, 278.
  meaning, 516.
  intention, 620.
  approach, 287.
  to float, 267.
  to accumulate, 72.
Driftless, 621.
Drill, *auger*, 262.

Drill, *to train*, 673.
  teach, 537.
  pierce, 260.
Drink, *to swallow*, 297.
  liquor, 299.
  to tipple, 959.
Drink in, *learn*, 539.
  imbibe, 297.
Drip, *ooze*, 294.
  flow, 348.
Drive, *impel*, 276.
  propel, 284.
  repel, 288.
  urge, 615.
  airing, 266.
Drive at, *intend*, 620.
  mean, 516.
Drive in, *insert*, 301.
  ingress, 295.
Drive out, 296.
Drivel, *folly*, 499.
  fatuity, 503.
Driveller, *fool*, 501.
  loquacious, 584.
Driver, 694.
Drizzle, 348.
Droil, 680.
Droll, 842.
Drollery, 840.
Dromedary, 271.
Drone, *inactive*, 683.
  slow, 275.
  sound, 412.
Droop, *sink*, 306.
  flag, 688.
  weakness, 160.
  disease, 655.
  sorrow, 828.
  dejection, 837.
  decline, 659.
Drop, *fall*, 306.
  discontinue, 141.
  expire, 360.
  relinquish, 624.
  faint, 160.
  fatigue, 688.
  flow out, 348.
  spherule, 249.
  small quantity, 193.
Drop astern, 283.
Drop in, *immerse*, 301.
  arrive, 293.
Drop off, *die*, 360.
Dropsical, *swollen*, 192.
  redundant, 641.
*Droschke, 272.
Dross, *dirt*, 653.
  trash, 643.
Drought, 640.
Drove, 72.
295

Drown, *kill*, 361.
  immerse, 301.
  affusion, 337.
  ruin, 731.
Drowsy, *slow*, 275.
  inactive, 683.
  weary, 841.
Drub, *beat*, 276.
  punish, 972.
Drudge, *agent*, 690.
  to work, 680.
  to plod, 682.
Drug, *remedy*, 662.
  superfluity, 641.
  trash, 643.
Druid, 996.
Drum, *cylinder*, 249.
  music, 417.
  sound, 407.
  to repeat, 104.
Drum-head, 966.
Drunk, 959.
Dry, *arid*, 340.
  style, 575.
  thirsty, 865.
  scanty, 640.
Dry up, 638.
Dry-nurse, *aid*, 707.
  teach, 537.
  teacher, 540.
Dry-rot, 659.
Duality, 89.
Dub, 564.
Dubious, 475.
Dubitation, 485.
Duchy, 181.
Duck, *immerse*, 301.
  plunge, 310.
  affuse, 337.
  stoop, 308.
Ducking-stool, 975.
Duct, 350.
Ductile, *flexible*, 324.
  easy, 705.
Dudgeon, *anger*, 900.
  discourteous, 895.
  club, 727.
Due, *proper*, 924.
  expedient, 646.
Duel, 720.
Duellist, 726.
Dueness, 924.
Duenna, 540.
Duergar, 980.
Dues, 812.
Duet, 415.
Duke, *noble*, 875.
  ruler, 745.
Dulcet, *sound*, 405.
  melodious, 413.

Dulcet, *agreeable*, 829.
Dulcify, 396.
Dulcimer, 417.
Dulcinea, 899.
Dulcorate, 396.
Dull, *inert*, 172.
  insensible, 376.
  callous, 823.
  blunt, 254.
  weak, 160.
  moderate, 174.
  colourless, 429.
  dejected, 837.
  inexcitable, 826.
  stolid, 499.
  prosing, 843.
  unapt, 699.
Dullard, 501.
Dull-brained, 499.
Dull-head, 501.
Dull-witted, 499.
Dumb, 581.
Dumb-show, 599.
Dumfounder, *astonish*, 870.
  abash, 881.
  disappoint, 509.
Dummy, 581.
Dumps, *sadness*, 837.
  mortification, 832.
Dumpy, *big*, 192.
  broad, 202.
  ugly, 846.
Dun, *colour*, 432.
  to importune, 765.
  a creditor, 805.
Dunce, *ignoramus*, 493.
  fool, 501.
Dunderhead, 501.
Dung, 653.
Dungeon, 752.
Dunghill, *vulgar*, 876.
  cowardly, 862.
Duodecimal, 99.
Duodenary, 98.
Dupe, *to deceive*, 545.
  deceived, 547.
  credulous, 486.
Duplex, 90.
Duplicate, *double*, 90.
  copy, 21.
  pledge, 805.
Duplication, *imitation*, 19.
Duplicature, *fold*, 258.
Duplicity, 544.
Durable, 110.
Durance, 751.
Duration, 106.
Durbar, 966.
Duress, 751.
During, 106.

Durity, 323.
Dusk, *evening*, 126.
  obscurity, 422.
Dusky, 421.
Dust, *powder*, 330.
  levity, 320.
  dirt, 653.
  trash, 643.
  money, 800.
Duteous, 944.
Dutiful, 944.
Duty, *obligation*, 926.
  business, 625.
  work, 686.
  tax, 812.
  rite, 998.
Dwarf, *small*, 193.
  to lessen, 36.
Dwell, *tarry*, 265.
  reside, 186.
Dweller, 188.
Dwelling, *abode*, 189.
  residence, 184.
Dwindle, *diminish*, 195.
  lessen, 36.
Dyadic, 89.
Dye, 428.
Dying, 360.
Dynamics, 276.
Dynasty, 737.
Dythrambic, 597.

E.

Each, 79.
Eager, *ardent*, 821.
  desirous, 865.
  active, 682.
Eagle, *swift*, 274.
  sight, 441.
Ear, 418.
Ear-deafening, 404.
Earl, 875.
Earless, 419.
Early, 132.
Earn, 775.
Earnest, *intention*, 620.
  strenuous, 682.
  emphatic, 642.
  pledge, 771.
  pay in advance, 809.
  eager, 821.
Ear-piercing, 404.
Ear-shot, 197.
Earth, *land*, 342.
  ground, 211.
  world, 318.
Earth-born, 876.
Earthlyminded, *selfish*, 943.
296

Earthlyminded, *worldly*, 988.
Earthquake, 173.
Earwig, *to flatter*, 933.
  flatterer, 935.
Ear-witness, 467.
Ease, *facility*, 705.
  relief, 834.
  content, 831.
  in style, 578.
Easel, *frame*, 215.
  painter's, 559.
Easy, *gentle*, 275.
Eat, 297.
Eatable, 299.
Eaves, 250.
Eaves-dropping, 418.
*Ebauche, 626.
Ebb, *regress*, 283.
  decrease, 36.
  contract, 195.
  waste, 638.
  spoil, 659.
Ebb of life, 360.
Ebony, 431.
Ebriety, 959.
Ebullition, *heat*, 384.
  energy, 171.
  violence, 173.
  excitation, 825.
Eccentric, *irregular*, 83.
  exterior, 220.
  wrong-headed, 499.
Ecclesiastic, 996.
*Ecervelé, 501.
*Echaffaudage, 673.
Echo, *repeat*, 104.
  imitate, 19.
  loudness, 404.
  resonance, 408.
  answer, 462.
*Eclaircissement, 522.
*Eclat, 873.
Eclectic, 609.
Eclipse, *hide*, 528.
  darkness, 421, 422.
  outshine, 874.
Eclogue, 597.
Economy, *order*, 58.
  plan, 626.
  conduct, 692.
  frugality, 817.
Economy (animal), 359.
Ecstasy, 827.
Ectype, 21.
Ecumenical, 78.
Edacity, 957.
Eddy, *current*, 348.
  whirlpool, 312.
Eden, 981.

Edge, *brink*, 230.
  energy, 171.
Edge-tool, 253.
Edible, 299.
Edict, 963.
Edifice, 189.
Edify, *build*, 161.
  teach, 537.
  piety, 987.
Edit, 531.
Educate, *teach*, 537.
  train, 673.
Education, *learning*, 490.
Educe, 525.
Educt, 40.
Edulcorate, *sweeten*, 396.
  clean, 652.
Eel, 248.
Efface, *obliterate*, 552.
  oblivion, 506.
  disappear, 449.
Effect, *consequence*, 154.
  to produce, 161.
  to complete, 729.
Effects, *property*, 780.
  goods, 798.
  materials, 637.
Effective, } *capable*, 157.
Effectual, } *useful*, 644.
Effeminate, *weak*, 160.
  sensual, 954.
  timorous, 862.
Effendi, 745.
Effervesce, *bubble up*, 353.
  agitate, 315.
  energy, 171.
  violence, 173.
  excited, 825.
Effete, *old*, 124.
  weak, 160.
  useless, 645.
  foul, 653.
  spoiled, 659.
Efficacy, } *power*, 157.
Efficiency, } *utility*, 644.
Effigy, *representation*, 554.
  copy, 21.
*Effleurer, *skim*, 267.
  slur over, 458.
Efflorescence, 330.
Effluence, } *egress*, 294.
Efflux, } *flow*, 348.
Effluvium, *odour*, 398.
  vapour, 334.
Effort, 686.
Effreet, 980.
Effrontery, 885.
Effulgence, 420.
Effuse, *pour out*, 294.
  excrete, 298.

Effusion, *speech*, 582.
Eft, *soon*, 111.
   early, 132.
*Egards, 928.
Egestion, 296.
Egg on, *urge*, 615.
Egg-shaped, 247, 249.
Egotism, *selfishness*, 943.
   vanity, 880.
Egregiously, 32.
Egress, 294.
Either, 609.
Ejaculate, *propel*, 284.
   utter, 580.
Eject, *displace*, 185.
   emit, 296.
Eke, *also*, 37.
   to complete, 52.
   spin out, 110.
Elaborate, 673.
Elaine, 356.
Elapse, *pass*, 122.
   flow, 109.
Elastic, *resilient*, 325.
   strong, 159.
Elate, *to cheer*, 836.
   boast, 884.
Elbow, *angle*, 244.
   projection, 250.
   to push, 276.
Elbow-room, 748.
Elder, 124, 128, 130.
Elect, 609.
Election, *necessity*, 601.
   numerical, 84.
Elector, 745.
Electricity, 274.
Electric, 821.
Electrify, *excite*, 824.
   astonish, 870.
Eleemosynary, 784.
Elegance, *beauty*, 845.
   in style, 578.
Elegy, *dirge*, 415.
   plaint, 839.
Element, *component*, 56.
   matter, 316.
   cause, 153.
   rudimental knowledge,
     490.
Elementary, *simple*, 42.
Elench, 477.
Elephant, *large*, 192.
   carrier, 271.
Elevation, *height*, 206.
   raising, 307.
   plan, 554.
   improvement, 658.
   of mind, 942.
   glory, 873.
   2J7

*Elève, 541.
Elf, *infant*, 129.
   little, 193.
   demon, 980.
Elicit, *manifest*, 525.
   discover, 480.
   draw out, 300.
Eligible, 646.
Eliminate, *exclude*, 55.
   extract, 300.
   weed, 103.
Elision, *separation*, 44.
   shortening, 201.
*Elite, 650.
Elixation, 384.
Elixir, 662.
Ellipse, 247.
Ellipsis, *curtailment*, 201.
   style, 572.
Ellipsoid, 247, 249.
Elocation, 270.
Elocution, 582.
*Eloge, 931.
Elongation, *lengthening*, 200
   distance, 196.
Elope, 671.
Eloquence, *of style*, 574.
   speech, 582.
Else, 37.
Elsewhere, 187.
Elucidate, 522.
Elude, *avoid*, 623.
   escape, 671.
   palter, 773.
   sophistry, 477.
   succeed, 731.
Elusory, 544.
Elutriation, 652.
Elysium, *paradise*, 981.
   bliss, 827.
Emaciation, *contraction*, 193
   smallness, 195.
   slenderness, 203.
Emaculate. *See* Immaculate.
Emanate, *go out of*, 294.
   excrete, 298.
   proceed from, 154.
Emanation, *odour*, 398.
Emancipate, *free*, 750.
   facilitate, 705.
Emasculate, 160.
Embalm, *preserve*, 670.
   memory, 505.
   to perfume, 400.
Embankment, 666.
Embargo, *prohibition*, 761.
   stoppage, 265.
Embark, *depart*, 292.
   engage in, 676.

Embarrass, *render difficult*,
   704.
   hinder, 706.
   hesitation, 485.
Embase, 659.
Embed, 184.
Embellish, *beautify*, 845.
   ornament, 847.
Embers, 388.
Embezzle, 791.
Embitter, *aggravate*, 835.
   deteriorate, 659.
   acerbate, 900.
Emblazon, *colour*, 428.
   beautify, 845.
   display, 882.
Emblem, 550.
Embody, *combine*, 48.
   compose, 54.
   join, 43.
   form a whole, 50.
Embolden, *encourage*, 861.
   hope, 858.
*Embonpoint, 192.
Embosomed, *middle*, 68.
   lodged, 184.
   begirt, 227.
Embossed, 250.
*Embouchure, 260.
Embrace, *include*, 76.
   compose, 54.
   enclose, 227.
   courtesy, 894.
   endearment, 902.
Embrasure, 257.
Embrocation, 662.
Embroider, 845, 847.
Embroil, *discord*, 713.
   derange, 61.
Embryo, *cause*, 153.
   preparation, 673.
   beginning, 66.
Emendation, 658.
Emerald colour, 435.
Emerge, 294.
Emergency, *difficulty*, 704.
   conjuncture, 8.
   event, 151.
Emersion, 294.
Emication, 420.
Emigrant, 268.
Emigrate, *remove*, 266.
   egress, 294.
Eminence, *height*, 206.
   fame, 873.
Eminently, 33.
Emir, 745.
Emissary, *messenger*, 534.
   consignee, 758.
Emission, 296.

Emmet, 193.
Emollient, 662.
Emolument, 775.
   receipt, 810.
Emotion, 821.
Empale, *transfix*, 260.
   pass through, 302.
   execute, 972.
Emperor, 745.
Emphasis, *accent*, 580.
Emphatic, *positive asser-*
   tion, 535.
   important, 642.
Empierce, *perforate*, 260.
   insert, 301.
Empire, *dominion*, 737.
   domain, 780.
Empirical, *tentative*, 675.
Empiricism,*experiment,*463
   quackery, 545.
Employ, *use*, 677.
   commission, 755.
   business, 625.
*Employé, *servant*, 746.
   agent, 758.
*Emporium, 799.
Empower, *power*, 157.
   commission, 755.
   permit, 760.
Emprise, 676.
Emption, 795.
*Emptor, 795.
Empty, *vacant*, 187.
   transfer, 270.
Empty-headed, 491.
Empyrean, *sky*, 318.
   blissful, 827, 829.
Empyreumatic, 401.
Emulate, *rival*, 708.
   imitate, 19.
   glory, 873.
Emulsion, *milk*, 352.
   oil, 354.
Emunctory, 350.
Enable, 157.
Enact, *order*, 741.
   a law, 963.
Enamel, *painting*, 556.
Enamour, 897.
Encage, 231.
Encamp, *locate*, 184.
   inhabit, 186.
Encase, 231.
Encaustic, *painting*, 556.
*Enceinte, *region*, 181.
Enchain, 43.
Enchant, *please*, 829.
   love, 897.
   conjure, 992.
   spell, 993.
298

Enchase, 43.
Enchiridion, 593.
Encircle, 227.
Enclose, 231.
Enclosure, *fence*, 752.
   space, 181.
Encomiast, 935.
Encomium, 931.
Encompass, 227.
*Encore, 104.
Encounter, *meet*, 293.
   clash, 276.
   contest, 720.
   withstand, 708.
Encourage, *animate*, 615.
   aid, 707.
   embolden, 861.
   hope, 858.
   comfort, 834.
Encroach, *transgress*, 303.
   infringe, 925.
Encrust, 222.
Encumber, 706.
Encyclical, 531.
Encyclopædia, 490.
End, *termination*, 67.
   object, 620.
Endammage, *injure*, 659.
   harm, 649.
Endanger, 665.
Endeavour, *attempt*, 676.
   pursue, 622.
   intend, 620.
Endemic, *special*, 79.
   disease, 655.
Endless, *infinite*, 105.
   multitudinous, 102.
Endorsement,   *evidence*,
   467.
   sign, 550.
Endosmose, 302.
Endow, *confer power*, 157.
Endowment, *give*, 784.
   capacity, 5.
   power, 157.
   talent, 698.
Endue, *empower*, 157.
Endure, *time*, 106.
   to continue, 142.
   to last, 110.
   event, 151.
   to bear, 821.
   to submit, 826.
Enemy, 891.
Energy, *physical*, 171.
   strength, 159.
   activity, 682.
Enervate, 160.
Enfeeble, 160.
Enfilade, *pierce*, 260.

Enfilade,*pass through*, 302.
Enforce, *urge*, 615.
   compel, 744.
   require, 924.
Enfranchise, 750.
Engage, *induce*, 615.
   the attention, 457.
   in a pursuit, 622.
Engagement, *business*, 625.
   contest, 720.
   duty, 926.
Engaging, *pleasing*, 829.
   amiable, 897.
Engender, 161.
Engine, 633.
Engineering, 632.
Engird, 227.
Engorge, 297.
Engorgement, 641.
Engraft, 43.
Engrave, *mark*, 550.
   on the memory, 505.
Engraver, 559.
Engraving, 558.
Engross, *possess*, 777.
   write, 590.
   the thoughts, 451.
   the attention, 457.
Engulph, *destroy*, 162.
   plunge, 310.
   swallow up, 297.
Enhance, *increase*, 35.
   improve, 658.
Enharmonic, 413.
Enigma, *secret*, 533.
   question, 461.
Enigmatic, *concealed*, 528.
   obscure, 519.
   uncertain, 475.
Enjoin, *command*, 741.
   induce, 615.
   enact, 963.
Enjoy, *physically*, 377.
   morally, 827.
   possess, 777.
Enkindle, 615.
Enlarge, *increase*, 35.
   swell, 194.
   liberate, 750.
   in writing, 573.
Enlist, *commission*, 755.
   engage, 615.
Enliven, *amuse*, 840.
   cheer, 836.
   delight, 829.
Enmity, *hate*, 889.
   discord, 713.
Ennoble, 873.
*Ennui, 841.
Enormity, *crime*, 947.

Enormous, *in degree*, 31.
  in size, 192.
Enough, *much*, 31.
  sufficient, 639.
  satiety, 869.
Enrage, *incense*, 900.
  provoke, 830.
Enrapture, *excite*, 824.
  beatify, 829.
  love, 897.
Enravish, *beatify*, 829.
Enrich, 803.
Enrobe, 225.
Enrol, *commission*, 755.
  record, 551.
Enrolment, *list*, 86.
Ens, *essence*, 1.
Ensample, 22.
Ensconce, *safety*, 664.
  conceal, 528.
*Ensemble, 50.
Enshrine, *memory*, 505.
  sanctify, 987.
Ensiform, 253.
Ensign, *standard*, 550.
  officer, 726.
  master, 745.
Enslave, 749.
Ensue, *follow*, 63.
  happen, 151.
Ensure, 474.
Entablature, 210.
Entail, 153.
Entangle, *derange*, 61.
  disorder, 59.
  perplex, 528.
*Entente cordiale, 888.
Enter, *go in*, 295.
  note, 551.
  accounts, 811.
Enter in, *converge*, 291.
Enter upon, 66.
Enterprise, *pursuit*, 622.
  attempt, 676.
Enterprising, *active*, 682.
  courageous, 861.
Entertain, *amuse*, 840.
  support, 707.
  sociality, 892.
Entertainment, *repast*, 299.
*Entêté, *obstinate*, 606.
  prejudiced, 481.
Enthral, 749.
Enthrone, 873.
Enthusiasm, *feeling*, 821.
  imagination, 515.
  love, 897.
  hope, 850.
Enthusiast, 989.
Enthusiastic, 822, 825.

Enthymeme, 476.
Entice, 615.
Enticing, 829.
Entire, *whole*, 50.
  complete, 52.
Entitle, *name*, 564.
  give a right, 924.
Entity, 1.
Entomb, *inter*, 363.
  immerse, 231.
  imprison, 751.
Entrails, 221.
Entrance, *beginning*, 66.
  ingress, 295.
  to enrapture, 824, 829.
  to conjure, 992.
Entrap, *deceive*, 545.
  ensnare, 665.
Entreat, 765.
*Entremet, 299.
*Entrepôt, 636.
Entry, *ingress*, 295.
  beginning, 66.
  record, 551.
  evidence, 467.
Entwine, *join*, 43.
  intersect, 219.
  convolve, 248.
Enumerate, 85.
Enunciate, *publish*, 531.
  inform, 527.
  voice, 580.
Envelope, *covering*, 222.
  inclosure, 232.
Envenom, *poison*, 649.
  deprave, 659.
  exasperate, 835.
Environ, 227.
*Environs, 197.
Envoy, 534.
Envy, 921.
Enwrap, 225.
Eolus, 349.
*Epanchement, 902.
Epaulette, *badge*, 550.
  decoration, 877.
  ornament, 847.
*Eperdu, 824.
Ephemeral, *transient*, 111.
  changeable, 149.
Ephemeris, *calendar*, 114.
  record, 551.
*Ephialtes, 378, 828.
Epic, 597.
Epicedium, 363.
Epicene, *exceptional*, 83.
  multiform, 81.
Epicure, *sensual*, 954.
  glutton, 957.
  fastidious, 868.

Epicycle, 247.
Epicycloid, 247.
Epidemic, *disease*, 655.
*Epidermis, 222.
Epigram, 842.
Epigrammatist, 844.
Epigraph, 550.
Epilepsy, 315.
Epilogue, 65.
Episcopal, 995.
Episodic, *unrelated*, 10.
  style, 573.
Epistle, 593.
Epitaph, 363.
*Epithalamium, 903.
Epithem, 662.
Epithet, 564.
Epitome, *compendium*, 596.
  miniature, 193.
Epoch, *time*, 113.
  period, 114.
Epopœa, 597.
Epuration, *detersion*, 652.
  purification, 658.
Equable, 922.
Equal, 27.
  equitable, 922.
Equate, 27.
Equator, 68.
Equerry, 746.
Equestrian, 268.
Equidistant, 68.
Equilibrium, 27.
Equip, *dress*, 225.
  prepare, 673.
Equipage, *vehicle*, 272.
  instrument, 633.
  materials, 635.
Equipoise, 27.
Equipollent, *equal*, 27.
  identical, 13.
Equiponderant, 27.
Equitable, *just*, 922.
  fair, 939.
Equitation, 266.
Equity, *justice*, 922.
  honor, 939.
Equivalence, 27.
Equivalent, 13.
Equivocal, *dubious*, 475.
  double meaning, 520.
*Equivoque, 520, 961.
Era, 106.
Eradicate, 162.
Erase, *efface*, 552.
Erato, 415.
Ere, 116.
Erebus, *dark*, 421.
  hell, 982.
Erect, *raise*, 307.

Erect, *build*, 161.
  vertical, 212.
Erection, *house*, 189.
Erelong, 132.
Erewhile, 122.
*Ergo, 476.
Eriometer, 445.
Ermine, *ornament*, 847.
  badge of authority, 747.
Erode, *destroy*, 162.
  injure, 659.
Erotic, *amorous*, 897.
  impure, 961.
Err, *in opinion*, 495.
  morally, 945.
Errand, *commission*, 755.
  business, 625.
  message, 532.
Erratic, *capricious*, 608.
  wandering, 264.
*Erratum, *error*, 495.
  misprint, 555.
Erring, 945.
Error, *false opinion*, 495.
  failure, 732.
  vice, 945.
  guilt, 947.
Erst, 122.
Erubescence, 434.
Eructate, 296.
Erudition, 490.
Eruption, *egress*, 294.
  violence, 173.
*Escalade, *attack*, 716.
  mounting, 305.
*Escamoter, 545.
*Escapade, *freak*, 608.
  prank, 840.
  vagary, 856.
Escape, *flight*, 671.
  liberate, 750.
  evade, 927.
Escarpment, 217.
Escharotic, *pungent*, 392.
  acrid, 171.
Escheat, 974.
Eschew, *avoid*, 623.
  dislike, 867.
Escort, *to accompany*, 88.
  safeguard, 664.
  keeper, 753.
Esculent, 299.
Escutcheon, 550.
Esoteric, *private*, 79.
  concealed, 528.
Especial, 79.
Espial, 441.
*Espièglerie, 842.
*Espionage, 461.
Esplanade, *flat*, 213.
300

Esplanade, *plain*, 344.
Espousal, 903.
*Esprit, *shrewdness*, 498.
  wit, 842.
*Esprit de corps, 712.
Espy, 441.
Esquire, 877.
Essay, *try*, 463.
  endeavour, 675.
  dissertation, 593.
Essayist, 590.
Essence, *nature*, 5.
  odour, 398.
  pith, 642.
Essential, *great*, 31.
Establish, *fix*, 184.
  demonstrate, 478.
  create, 161.
Established, *received*, 82.
*Estafette, 534.
Estate, *condition*, 7.
  property, 780.
Esteem, *judge*, 480.
  believe, 484.
  approve, 931.
Estimable, 648.
Estimate, *measure*, 466.
  judge, 480.
Estimation, *opinion*, 484.
  good, 648.
Estrade, 213.
Estrange, *alienate*, 889.
  hate, 898.
  seclude, 893.
*Estrapade, 972.
Estuary, 343.
Estuation, 384.
*Et cætera, 37.
*Etalage, 882.
Etch, 558.
Eternal, 112.
Ether, *vapour*, 334.
  levity, 320.
Ethics, 926.
Ethiopic, 431.
Ethnic, 984.
Ethnology, 372.
Etiolate, *bleach*, 429.
  whiten, 430.
Etiology, *knowledge*, 490.
  causes, 155.
Etiquette, *fashion*, 852.
  custom, 613.
  ceremony, 882.
*Etourderie, 460.
Etymology, 562.
Etymon, *origin*, 153.
  verbal, 562.
Eucharist, 998.
Euchology, 998.

Eulogy, 931.
Euphemism, 565.
Euphonic, *musical*, 413.
  style, 578.
Euphony, 413.
Euripus, 343.
Euterpe, 415.
*Euthanasia, 360.
Evacuate, *emit*, 296.
  excrete, 298.
Evade, *avoid*, 623.
  escape, 671.
  sophistry, 477.
  exempt, 927.
Evanescent, *transient*, 111.
  minute, 32, 193.
  disappearing, 449.
Evangelist, 985.
Evaporate, 336.
Evasion, *escape*, 671.
  falsehood, 544.
  untruth, 546.
Eve, 126.
Even, *equal*, 27.
  level, 213.
  smooth, 255.
  straight, 246.
  although, 179.
Even so, 488.
Evenhanded, *equitable*, 922.
  honorable, 939.
Evening, 126.
Event, 151.
Eventful, *stirring*, 151.
  remarkable, 642.
Eventide, 126.
Eventual, 121.
Ever, *always*, 112.
  seldom, 137.
Everchanging, 149.
Evergreen, 123.
Everlasting, 112.
Evermore, 112.
Ever-recurring, 104.
Eversion, 218.
Every, 78.
Every-day, 82, 112.
Every where, 180.
Evidence, 467.
Evident, *visible*, 446.
  demonstrable, 478.
Evil, *harm*, 619.
  producing evil, 649.
Evil doer, *maleficent*, 913.
  culprit, 949.
Evil-eye, 907.
Evil-minded, *malevolent*, 907.
  vicious, 945.
Evil-speaking, 934.

Evince, *show*, 467.
  prove, 478.
Evoke, *call upon*, 765.
  excite, 824.
Evolution, *numerical*, 85.
  turning out, 313.
  circuition, 311.
Evulsion, 300.
Ewer, 191.
Exacerbate, *increase*, 35.
  aggravate, 835.
  exasperate, 173.
Exact, *true*, 494.
  similar, 17.
  require, 741.
  claim, 924.
  tax, 812.
Exactly, *just so*, 488.
Exaggerate, *increase*, 35.
  over-estimate, 482.
  misrepresent, 549.
Exalt, *increase*, 35.
  elevate, 307.
  extol, 931.
  boast, 884.
Exalted, *heroic*, 942.
Examine, 461.
Example, *instance*, 82.
  pattern, 22.
  model, 948.
Exanimate, 360.
Exarch, *ruler*, 745.
  deputy, 759.
Exasperate, *increase*, 35.
  exacerbate, 173.
  aggravate, 835.
  inflame, 900.
Excavate, 252.
Exececation, 442.
Exceed, *surpass*, 33.
  expand, 194.
  transgress, 303.
Exceeding, *remaining*, 40.
Exceedingly, 31.
Excel, 648.
Excellent, *good*, 648.
  virtuous, 944.
Excellency, *skill*, 698.
  title, 877.
Excentric, 220.
Except, *subduct*, 38.
  exclude, 55.
Exception, *to a rule*, 83.
  qualification, 469.
  censure, 932.
Exceptionable, *vicious*, 945.
Exceptional, *special*, 79.
Exceptious, 901.
Excern, 298.
*Excerpta, 51.
301

Excess, *remainder*, 40.
  redundance, 641.
  intemperance, 954.
Excessive, 31.
Exchange, *mutual change*,
  148.
  transfer, 783.
  barter, 794.
  mart, 799.
Exchequer, 802.
Excise, 812.
Excision, 38.
Excitability, *excitement*, 825
  irascibility, 901.
Excitation, 824.
Excite, *violent*, 173.
  morally, 824.
  anger, 900.
Exclaim, 580.
Exclude, *leave out*, 55.
  prohibit, 761.
Exclusive, *omitting*, 55.
  special, 79.
  irregular, 83.
Excogitation, *thought*, 451.
  imagination, 515.
Excommunicate, *exclude*, 55
  hate, 898.
  curse, 908.
Excoriate, 226.
Excrement, 653.
Excrescence, *projection*, 250
  blemish, 848.
Excretion, 298.
Excruciating, 830.
Exculpate, *forgive*, 918.
  vindicate, 937.
Excursion, *tour*, 266.
  circuit, 311.
Excursive, *style*, 573.
Excuse, *plea*, 617.
  exempt, 927.
  forgive, 918.
  vindicate, 937.
Execrable, *bad*, 649.
  offensive, 830.
  nauseous, 867.
Execrate, 908.
Execute, *conduct*, 692.
  perform, 729.
  in law, 771.
  music, 415.
Executioner, 361.
Executive, 965.
Executor, 690.
*Exegesis, 522.
*Exemplar, 22.
Exemplary, 944.
Exemplify, *quote*, 82.
  illustrate, 522.

Exempt, *absolve*, 927.
  free, 748.
  permit, 760.
Exemption, *exception*, 83.
Exequies, 363.
Exercise, *employ*, 677.
  act, 680.
  exert, 686.
  teach, 537.
  train, 673.
  task, 625.
Exert, 686.
Exertion, *physical*, 171.
Exfoliation, 226.
Exhalation, *vapour*, 336.
  odour, 398.
  excretion, 298.
Exhaust, *drain*, 638.
  fatigue, 688.
  weaken, 160.
  misemploy, 679.
  squander, 818.
Exhaustless, *infinite*, 105.
  plentiful, 639.
Exhibit, *show*, 525.
  display, 882.
Exhilarate, 836.
Exhort, *advise*, 695.
  induce, 615.
Exhume, 363.
Exigency, *crisis*, 8.
  difficulty, 704.
  requirement, 630.
  need, 865.
  dearth, 640.
Exiguous, 193.
Exile, *displace*, 185.
  send out, 296.
  seclude, 893.
Exility, 203.
Existence, *being*, 1.
  thing, 3.
  in time, 118.
  in space, 186.
Exit, *departure*, 292.
  egress, 294.
Exode, 599.
Exonerate, *exempt*, 927.
  vindicate, 937.
  forgive, 918.
  disburden, 705.
  release, 756.
Exorable, 914.
Exorbitant, *enormous*, 31.
  redundant, 641.
  dear, 814.
Exorcise, 992.
Exorcism, 993.
Exorcist, 994.
*Exordium, 66.

Exosmose, 302.
Exostosis, 250.
Exoteric, *disclosed*, 531.
  public, 529.
Exotic, *alien*, 10.
  exceptional, 83.
Expand, *swell*, 194.
  increase, 35.
  in breadth, 202.
  rarefy, 322.
  in writing, 573.
Expanse, *space*, 180.
  size, 192.
Exparte, 467.
Expatiate, *in writing*, 573.
  in discourse, 584.
Expatriate, *deport*, 294.
  exclude, 55.
Expect, *look for*, 507.
  not wonder, 871.
Expedience, *utility*, 646.
Expedient, *means*, 632.
  plan, 626.
Expedite, *accelerate*, 274.
  earliness, 132.
  aid, 707.
Expedition, *speed*, 274.
  march, 266.
Expel, *displace*, 185.
  drive from, 296.
Expend, *use*, 677.
  waste, 638.
  pay, 809.
Expense, *price*, 812.
Expenseless, 815.
Expensive, 814.
Experience, *knowledge*, 490.
  undergo, 821.
  event, 151.
Experienced, *skilled*, 698.
Experiment, *trial*, 463.
  endeavour, 675.
Expert, 698.
Expiate, 952.
Expire, 360.
Explain, *expound*, 522.
  inform, 527.
  teach, 537.
  answer, 462.
Explain away, 523.
Expletive, 641.
Explication, 522.
Explicit, 518.
Explode, *burst*, 173.
  sound, 406.
  passion, 825.
  anger, 900.
Exploit, 680.
Explore, *investigate*, 461.
  experiment, 463.
302

Explosion. *See* Explode.
Exponent, *index*, 550.
  numerical, 84.
Export, 294.
*Exposé, *account*, 596.
  disclosure, 529.
Expose, *show*, 525.
  interpret, 522.
  confute, 479.
  denude, 226.
  endanger, 665.
Exposition, *answer*, 462.
  disclosure, 529.
Expositor, *interpreter*, 524.
  teacher, 540.
Expository, 527.
Expostulate, *deprecate*, 766
  reprehend, 932.
  advise, 695.
Exposure to, 177.
Expound, *interpret*, 522.
  teach, 537.
  answer, 462.
Express, *voluntary*, 600.
  intentional, 620.
  declare, 525.
  mean, 516.
  inform, 527.
  intelligible, 518.
  name, 564.
  squeeze out, 300.
  rapid, 274.
Expression, *aspect*, 448.
Exprobate, 932.
Expulsion. *See* Expel.
Expunge, *efface*, 552.
  destroy, 162.
  disappear, 449.
Expurgation, 652.
Exquisite, *excellent*, 648.
  pleasurable, 829.
  savoury, 394.
  fop, 854.
Exquisitely, 31.
Exsiccate, 340.
Exsufflation, 992.
Exsuscitate, *rouse*, 615.
Extant, 1.
Extasy. *See* Ecstasy.
Extempore, *instantly*, 113.
  early, 132.
  off-hand, 612.
  unprepared, 674.
Extend, *prolong*, 200.
  expand, 194.
  reach, 196.
  increase, 35.
Extensile, 324.
Extensive, *spacious*, 180.
  considerable, 31.

Extent, *degree*, 26.
  space, 180.
Extenuate, *decrease*, 36.
  diminish, 192.
  excuse, 937.
Exterior, 220.
Exterminate, 162.
Exterminator, 165.
External, 220.
Extinction, *destruction*, 162.
  of life, 360.
Extinguish, *destroy*, 162.
  darken, 421.
  blow out, 385.
Extinguisher, 165.
Extirpate, 162.
Extispicious, 511.
Extol, *praise*, 931.
  over-estimate, 482.
Extort, *despoil*, 789.
  compel, 744.
*Extra, *additional*, 37.
  supernumerary, 641.
Extract, *take out*, 300.
  quotation, 596.
Extradition, *deportation*
270.
  expulsion, 296.
Extrajudicial, 964.
Extramundane, 317.
Extraneous, *extrinsic*, 6.
  not related, 10.
  foreign, 57.
Extraordinary, 83.
Extraregarding, 220.
Extravagant, *exaggerated*,
549.
  absurd, 497.
  ridiculous, 853.
  foolish, 499.
  high-priced, 814.
  prodigal, 818.
  vulgar, 851.
  inordinate, 31.
*Extravaganza, *fanciful*,
515.
  burlesque, 853.
Extravagation, 303.
Extravasate, 298.
Extreme, 31.
Extremity, *end*, 67.
  exterior, 220.
Extricate, *take out*, 300.
  liberate, 750.
  deliver, 672.
  facilitate, 705.
Extrinsic, 6.
Extrude, 296.
Exuberant, *redundant*, 641.
  style, 573.

Exude, 298.
Exult, *crow*, 836.
   rejoice, 838.
   boast, 884.
*Exuviæ, 40.
Eye, *organ of sight*, 441.
   opening, 260.
   circle, 247.
Eye-glass, 445.
Eyeless, 442.
Eyelet, 260.
Eyesight, 441.
Eyesore, 846.
Eye-witness, 467.
Eyre, 965.
Eyry, 189.

F.

Fabian policy, *inactivity*,
   683.
   delay, 133.
Fable, *fiction*, 546.
   error, 495.
   description, 594.
Fabric, *texture*, 329.
   house, 189.
   effect, 154.
   state, 7.
Fabricate, *make*, 161.
   invent, 515.
   forge, 544.
   falsify, 546.
Fabulous, 515.
*Façade, 234.
Face, *exterior*, 220.
   front, 234.
   confront, 861.
   aspect, 448.
Face about, 279.
Face to face, 525.
Facet, 220.
Facetious, 842.
Facile, *irresolute*, 605.
Facility, 707.
Facing, 224.
Facinorous, 945.
Fac-simile, *copy*, 21.
   representation, 554.
Fact, *event*, 151.
   truth, 494.
   existence, 1.
Faction, *party*, 712.
Factious, 713.
Factor, *numerical*, 84.
   director, 694.
   consignee, 758.
   merchant, 797.
Factory, 691.
303

Factotum, *manager*, 694.
   employé, 758.
Faculty, *power*, 157.
   skill, 698.
   profession, 625.
Facundity, 582.
Faddle, 683.
Fade, *vanish*, 2.
   disappear, 449.
   lose colour, 429.
   spoil, 659.
   droop, 160.
   become old, 124.
*Fade, *insipid*, 391.
Fadge, 23.
Fæces, *excretion*, 298.
   foulness, 653.
Fag, *labour*, 686.
   activity, 682.
   fatigue, 688.
   drudge, 690.
Fag-end, *remainder*, 40.
   end, 67.
Fagot, *bundle*, 72.
   fuel, 388.
Fail, *incomplete*, 53.
   short-coming, 304.
   non-observance, 732.
   non-payment, 808.
   droop, 160.
   vice, 945.
Fain, *wish*, 865.
   willing, 602.
   compulsive, 744.
*Fainéant, 683.
Faint, *weak*, 160.
   sound, 405.
   colour, 429.
   small in degree, 32.
   swoon, 688.
Faint-hearted, 862.
Fair, *in degree*, 31.
   white, 430.
   just, 922.
   honorable, 939.
   true, 543.
   pleasing, 829.
   beautiful, 845.
   mart, 799.
Fair sex, 374.
Fairly, 31.
Fairing, 784.
Fair-play, *justice*, 922.
   honor, 939.
Fair-spoken, 894.
Fairy, 979.
Faith, *belief*, 484.
   hope, 858.
   honor, 939.
   creed, 983.

Faith, *piety*, 987.
Faithful, *likeness*, 17.
Faithless, *false*, 544.
   dishonorable, 940.
   sceptical, 988.
Fakir, 997.
Falcated, *curved*, 245.
   sharp, 244.
Falchion, 727.
Falciform, 244, 245.
Fall, *descend*, 306.
   slope, 217.
   fail, 732.
   die, 360.
   adversity, 735.
   decline, 659.
   happen, 151.
   vice, 945.
Fall away, *decrease*, 36.
   shrink, 195.
Fall back, *recede*, 283.
   relapse, 661.
Fall down, 306.
   worship, 990.
Fall in, *marshal*, 60.
   happen, 151.
Fall in with, *find*, 480.
   agree, 23.
Fall off, 659.
Fall out, *happen*, 151.
   quarrel, 713.
   drop, 296.
Fall short, *short-coming*,
   304.
   insufficiency, 640.
Fall to, *work*, 686.
   fight, 722.
Fall under, 76.
Fall upon, *attack*, 716.
   discover, 480.
   devise, 626.
Fallacy, *error*, 495.
   uncertainty, 475.
   sophistry, 477.
Fallible, 475.
Fallow, *yellow*, 436.
   unready, 674.
False, *untrue*, 544.
   error, 495.
   sophistry, 477.
   spurious, 925.
   dishonorable, 940.
False-hearted, 940.
Falsehood, *lie*, 546.
*Falsetto, 413.
Falsify, *misinterpret*, 523.
   accounts, 811.
Falter, *stammer*, 583.
   hesitate, 605.
   demur, 603.

Falter, *slowness*, 275.
Fame, *renown*, 873.
   rumour, 531.
   news, 532.
Familiar, *common*, 80.
   known, 490.
   friendly, 888.
   affable, 894.
   spirit, 979.
Family, *class*, 75.
   consanguinity, 11.
Famine, 640.
Famishment, 956.
Famous, 873.
Fan, *blow*, 349.
   excite, 615.
Fan the flame, 384.
Fanaticism, *folly*, 499.
   obstinacy, 606.
   religious, 984.
Fanatic, 515.
Fanciful, *capricious*, 608.
   imaginative, 515.
   mistaken, 495.
   sanguine, 858.
Fancy, *think*, 451.
   believe, 484.
   idea, 453.
   suppose, 514.
   imagine, 515.
   caprice, 608.
   choice, 609.
   desire, 865.
   pugilism, 726.
Fandango, 840.
*Fane, 1000.
*Fanfare, 404.
Fanfaronade, 884.
Fang, 737.
*Fantasia, *music*, 415.
   madness, 503.
   error, 495.
Fantastic, *odd*, 83.
   capricious, 608.
   ridiculous, 853.
Fantasy, *desire*, 865.
*Fantoccini, 554, 599.
Faquier, 997.
Far, 196.
Farce, *drama*, 599.
   ridiculous, 856.
*Farceur, 844.
Farcical, *ridiculous*, 856.
   witty, 842.
   trifling, 643.
Fardel, 72.
Fare, *circumstance*, 8.
   event, 151.
   to eat, 297.
   food, 299.
304

Fare, *price*, 812.
Farewell, 292.
Far-fetched, *irrelevant*, 24.
   obscure, 519.
Farm, *house*, 189.
   property, 780.
   to rent, 795.
Farrago, *mixture*, 41.
   confusion, 59.
Farthing, *coin*, 800.
   worthless, 643.
*Fasces, 747.
*Fascia, *band*, 205.
   circle, 247.
*Fasciculus, 72.
Fascinate, *please*, 829.
   excite, 824, 825.
   astonish, 870.
   love, 897.
   conjure, 992.
Fascination, *spell*, 993.
Fashion, *form*, 240.
   custom, 613.
   mode, 852.
   nobility, 875.
Fast, *rapid*, 274.
   stuck, 265.
   joined, 43.
   not to eat, 956.
Fast and loose, *false*, 544.
   tergiversation, 607.
Fasten, 43.
Fastening, 45.
Fast-handed, 817.
Fastidious, 868.
Fasting, *abstinence*, 956.
   atonement, 952.
Fastness, *asylum*, 666.
   defence, 717.
Fat, *oleaginous*, 356.
   unctuous, 355.
   corpulent, 192.
Fatal, *lethal*, 361.
   pernicious, 649.
Fatalism, 152.
Fate, *necessity*, 601.
   chance, 152, 621.
Father, *paternity*, 166.
   priest, 996.
Father upon, 155.
Fatherless, 160.
Fathom, *measure*, 466.
   investigate, 461.
Fathomless, 208.
Fatidical, 511.
Fatigation, 688.
Fatigue, *lassitude*, 688.
   weariness, 841.
*Fatras, 643.
Fatten on, 297.

Fatuity, 499.
Fatuous, 499.
Fat-witted, 499.
*Faubourg, 227.
Faugh! 867.
Fault, *imperfection*, 651.
   vice, 945.
   guilt, 947.
   error, 495.
   failure, 732.
   ignorance, 491.
Faultless, *perfect*, 650.
   innocent, 946.
*Fauna, 367.
*Faute, 732.
*Fauteuil, 215.
*Fautor, 890.
*Faux pas, *failure*, 732.
   vice, 945.
Favour, *aid*, 707.
   permit, 760.
   partiality, 923.
   gift, 784.
   letter, 592.
Favourable, 648.
Favourite, *pleasing*, 829.
   beloved, 897, 899.
Favouritism, 923.
Fawn, *colour*, 433.
   cringe, 886.
   flatter, 933.
Fay, 979.
Fealty, *duty*, 926.
   respect, 928.
Fear, 860.
Fearful, *great*, 31.
Fearless, *hopeful*, 858.
   courageous, 861.
Feasible, *possible*, 470.
   easy, 705.
Feast, *repast*, 299.
   to devour, 297.
   revel, 840.
   enjoyment, 827.
Feat, 680.
Feather, *tuft*, 256.
   lightness, 320.
   trifle, 643.
   ornament, 847.
   decoration, 877.
Feather-bed, 324.
Feathery, 256.
Featly, 682.
Feature, *character*, 5.
   form, 240.
   appearance, 448.
   lineament, 550.
Feculence, 653.
Fecund, 168.
Federation, 709, 712.

Fee, 809.
Feeble, *weak*, 160.
  scanty, 32.
  writing, 575.
Feeble-minded, *foolish*, 499.
  irresolute, 605.
Feed, *eat*, 297.
  supply, 637.
  meal, 299.
Feel, *touch*, 379.
  sensibility, 375.
  moral, 821.
Feel for, *seek*, 461.
Feet, 266.
Feign, 544.
Feint, 545.
Feld-marshal, 745.
Felicitate, 896.
Felicitous, *expedient*, 646.
  favourable, 648.
  skilful, 699.
  successful, 731.
  happy, 827.
Felicity, *happiness*, 827.
  skill, 698.
Fell, *mountain*, 206.
  to cut down, 308.
  dire, 162.
  wicked, 907.
Fellow, *similar*, 17.
  companion, 88.
  dual, 89.
Fellow-creature, 373.
Fellow-feeling, 897.
Fellowship, *sociality*, 892.
  partnership, 712.
  friendship, 888.
Felo-de-se, 361.
Felon, 949.
Felonious, 945.
Felony, 947.
Felt, 219.
Felucca, 273.
Female, 374.
Feminality, *feebleness*, 160.
Feminine, 374.
Fen, 345.
Fence, *circumscribe*, 231.
  enclose, 232.
  defence, 717.
  safety, 664.
  refuge, 666.
  prison, 752.
  to evade, 544.
Fencible, 726.
Fend, 717.
Feneration, 787.
Feoff, 780.
Ferine, 907.
305

Ferity, 907.
Ferment, *disorder*, 59.
  energy, 171.
  violence, 173.
  agitation, 315.
  effervesce, 353.
Ferocity, *brutality*, 907.
  violence, 173.
Ferret out, 480.
Ferry, *transference*, 270.
  way, 627.
Fertile, *productive*, 168.
  abundant, 639.
Ferule, 975.
Fervour, *heat*, 382.
  animation, 821.
Fester, *disease*, 655.
  corruption, 653.
Festival, 840.
Festive, 840, 892.
Festivity, 892.
Festoon, 847.
Fetch, *bring*, 270.
  arrive, 293.
  stratagem, 626.
  evasion, 545.
  price, 812.
*Fête, 840, 882.
  convivial, 892.
Fetichism, 991, 992.
Fetid, 401.
Fetlock, *chain*, 45.
  shackle, 752.
Fetter, *hinder*, 706.
  restrain, 751.
  shackle, 752.
Fettle, 673.
Feud, 713.
Feudal, 737.
Feudatory, 749.
*Feu-de-joie, 840.
Fever, *heat*, 382.
  excitement, 825.
Few, 103.
Fez, 225.
*Fiat, 741.
Fib, 544, 546.
Fibre, *link*, 45.
  filament, 205.
Fibrous, 203.
Fickle, 605.
Fictile, 240.
Fiction, *untruth*, 546.
  fancy, 515.
Fictitious, 544.
Fiddle, *to play*, 415.
  violin, 417.
Fiddle - de - dee, *trifling*, 643.
  contemptible, 930.

Fiddle-faddle, *trifle*, 643.
  dawdle, 683.
Fiddler, 416.
Fiddlestick, *contemptible*, 930.
  absurd, 497.
  trifling, 643.
Fidelity, *honor*, 939.
  observance, 772.
Fidget, *excitability*, 825.
  irascibility, 901.
Fiducial, 484.
Fie! 874.
Fieff, 780.
Field, *plain*, 344.
  arena, 728.
  scope, 180.
  property, 780.
Field of view, *vista*, 441.
  idea, 453.
Field-piece, 727.
Fiend, *demon*, 980.
  ruffian, 913.
Fiendish, *malevolent*, 907.
  wicked, 945.
Fierce, *violent*, 173.
  passion, 825.
  daring, 861.
  angry, 900.
Fiery, *violent*, 173.
  excitable, 825.
Fife, 417.
Fig, 643.
Fight, 720.
Fighter, 726.
Figment, 515.
*Figurante, 599.
Figurate number, 84.
Figurative, *metaphorical*, 521.
  style, 577.
  comparison, 464.
Figure, *state*, 7.
  number, 84.
  form, 240.
  metaphor, 521.
  imagine, 515.
  represent, 550.
  reputation, 873.
  ugliness, 846.
*Figurine, 557.
*Figuriste, 559.
Filament, *slender*, 205.
  ligature, 45.
Filamentous, 203.
Filch, 791.
File, *to smooth*, 255.
  to pulverize, 330.
  to string together, 60.
  row, 69.

File, *list*, 86.
File off, *march*, 266.
  diverge, 290.
Filiation, *consanguinity*, 11.
  posterity, 167.
Filigree, 219.
Filings, 330.
Fill, 186.
Fill up, *complete*, 52.
  close, 261.
  compensate, 30.
Fillet, *band*, 45.
  circle, 247.
Fillip, *stimulus*, 615.
  impulse, 276.
Filly, 271.
Film, *layer*, 204.
  dimness, 421.
Filter, *clean*, 652.
  percolate, 294.
  amend, 658.
Filth, 653.
Fimbriated, 256.
Fin, 633.
Final, 67.
Finance, 800.
Financier, 801.
Find, *discover*, 480.
  provide, 637.
  sentence, 969.
Fine, *rare*, 322.
  good, 648.
  beautiful, 845.
  mulct, 974.
Finedraw, 658.
Finery, 847.
Finespoken, 894.
Finespun, 203.
*Finesse, *cunning*, 702.
  manœuvre, 545.
  tact, 698.
  taste, 850.
Finger, *touch*, 379.
  instrument, 633.
Finger-post, 550.
Fingle-fangle, 643.
Finical, 643.
Finikin, 643.
*Finis, 67.
Finish, *complete*, 52.
  achieve, 729.
  end, 67.
  symmetry, 242.
Finished, *perfect*, 650.
  accomplished, 698.
Finite, 32.
Fire, *heat*, 382.
  to excite, 825.
  to urge, 615.
  to attack, 716.
306

Fire off, 284.
Fire up, 900.
Firebrand, *brand*, 388.
  incendiary, 913.
Fire-cross, 722.
Fire-drake, 420.
Fire-eater, 726.
Fire-fly, 423.
Firelock, 727.
Fireplace, 386.
Fire-ship, 273.
Fire-side, 189.
Fire-work, *fire*, 382.
  light, 420.
Fire-worshipper, 984.
Firing, *fuel*, 388.
  explosion, 406.
Firkin, 191.
Firm, *hard*, 323.
  junction, 43.
  resolute, 604.
  brave, 861.
  party, 712.
  partnership. 797.
  friendship, 888.
Firmament, 318.
*Firman, *order*, 741.
  permit, 760.
  decree, 963.
First, 66.
First-born, 124.
First-rate, *ship*, 273.
  excellent, 648.
Firth, 343.
Fisc, 802.
Fiscal, 800.
Fish, 366.
Fish out, 480.
Fish up, 307.
Fisk, 266.
Fissible, 328.
Fissure, *chink*, 198.
Fistulous, 260.
Fit, *state*, 7.
  paroxysm, 173.
  caprice, 608.
  to prepare, 673.
  excitement, 825.
  anger, 900.
  duty, 926.
  expedient, 646.
  right, 922.
Fit out, 673.
Fit up, 673.
Fitful, *capricious*, 608.
  irresolute, 605.
  irregular, 139.
Fitness, 23.
Fitting, *expedient*, 646.
  right, 922, 926.

Five, 98.
Fix, *place*, 184.
  solidify, 321.
Fix together, 43.
Fix upon, *choose*, 609.
Fixed, *determined*, 604.
  permanent, 142.
  quiescent, 265.
Fixture, 780.
Fizgig, 423.
Fizz, 409.
Fizzle, *shine*, 420.
  hiss, 409.
Flabbergasted, 881.
Flabby, 324.
Flaccid, *shrivelled*, 193.
  empty, 640.
Flag, *streamer*, 550.
  flat stone, 204.
  weakness, 160.
  floor, 211.
  droop, 688.
  infirm, 655.
  slowness, 275.
Flagellation, *flogging*, 972.
  asceticism, 955.
Flageolet, 417.
Flagitious, 945.
Flagrant, *notorious*, 531.
  atrocious, 945.
Flagration, 382.
Flag-ship, 273.
Flag-staff, *sign*, 550.
  high, 206.
Flail, 276.
Flake, 204
*Flam, 546.
Flambé, 732.
Flambeau, 423.
Flame, *light*, 420.
  luminary, 423.
  love, 897.
  favourite, 899.
Flame-colour, 439.
Flamen, 996.
Flaming, *feeling*, 821.
  excited, 825.
*Flaneur, 935.
Flange, 215.
Flank, *side*, 236.
  safety, 664.
Flap, *appendix*, 39.
  hanging, 214.
  move about, 315.
  beat, 972.
Flapper, 505.
Flapping, *loose*, 47.
Flare, *glare*, 420.
  violence, 173.
Flare up, *kindle*, 825.

Flare up, *anger*, 900.
Flaring, *colour*, 428.
Flash, *instant*, 113.
  light, 420.
  thought, 451.
  sudden act, 612.
  violence, 173.
Flash note, 800.
Flashy, *gaudy colour*, 428.
  ornamented, 847.
Flask, 191.
Flasket, 191.
Flat, *level*, 251.
  horizontal, 213.
  low, 207.
  vapid, 391.
  inert, 172, 823.
  dull, 843.
  dejected, 837.
  sound, 408.
  indifferent, 866.
Flatter, *please*, 829.
  encourage, 858.
  adulation, 933.
Flatterer, 935.
Flatulent, *windy*, 338.
  style, 573.
Flatus, 349.
Flaunt, *display*, 882.
  gaudy, 428.
  ornament, 847.
Flavour, *taste*, 390.
Flavous, *yellow*, 436.
Flaw, *crack*, 198.
  imperfection, 651.
  blemish, 848.
  fault, 947.
Flay, 226.
Fleabite, 643.
Fleckered, 440.
Fledged, 673.
Flee, *escape*, 671.
  avoid, 623.
Fleece, *tegument*, 222.
  to rob, 791.
  to strip, 789.
  impoverish, 804.
Fleer, 856.
Fleet, *swift*, 274.
  ships, 273.
Fleeting, 111.
Flesh, *mankind*, 372.
  carnality, 961.
Flesh-colour, 434.
Flesh-pots, 299.
Fleshy, *corpulent*, 192.
Flexible, *curve*, 245.
  pliant, 324.
  easy, 735.
Flexion, *bending*, 245.
307

Flexion, *fold*, 258.
Flexuous, 248.
Flexure, *bending*, 245.
  fold, 258.
Flicker, *flutter*, 315.
  waver, 605.
Flight, *departure*, 290.
  volitation, 267.
  swiftness, 274.
Flight of fancy, *imagina-*
  tion, 515.
  idea, 453.
Flighty, 503.
Flim-flam, *lie*, 546.
  caprice, 608.
Flimsy, *texture*, 329.
  soft, 324.
  trifling, 643.
Flinch, *fear*, 860.
  avoid, 623.
  swerve, 607.
Fling, *propel*, 284.
  censure, 932.
  attack, 716.
  jeer, 929.
Fling away, 782.
Flint, 323.
Flint-hearted, 907.
Flippant, *pert*, 885.
  fluent, 584.
Flirt, *propel*, 284.
  coquette, 902.
Flit, *move*, 264, 266.
  depart, 292.
  escape, 671.
  swift, 274.
  thought, 451.
Flitter, *scrap*, 51.
  flutter, 315.
Flitting, *evanescent*, 111.
Float, *navigate*, 267.
  buoy up, 305.
  lightness, 320.
  sound, 405.
Flocculent, *soft*, 324.
  pulverulent, 330.
Flock, *herd*, 366.
  assemblage, 72.
  laity, 997.
Flog, 972.
Flood, *water*, 378.
  abundance, 639.
  increase, 35.
  of light, 420.
Floodgate, 350.
Floor, *base*, 211.
  level, 204.
  horizontal, 213.
  support, 215.
  to overthrow, 731.

Flop, *flutter*, 315.
Florid, *colour*, 428.
  red, 434.
  health, 654.
  style, 577.
Flotilla, 273.
Flounce, *quick motion*, 274.
  agitation, 315.
  trimming, 230.
Flounder, *toss*, 315.
  mistake, 495.
  to blunder, 499.
  bungle, 699.
Flourish, *brandish*, 314.
  succeed, 731, 734.
  display, 882.
  boast, 884.
  of speech, 577.
Flout, *mock*, 856.
  sneer, 929.
Flow, *stream*, 347.
  motion, 264.
  result from, 154.
Flow out, 294.
Flow over, *run over*, 348.
  abound, 641.
Flower, *ornament*, 845.
  perfection, 650.
  prosper, 734.
  of life, 127.
  of speech, 577.
  honor, 873.
Flowing, *style*, 573.
  sound, 405.
  abundant, 639.
Fluctuate, *oscillate*, 314.
  wavering, 605.
Flue, *air-pipe*, 351.
  egress, 294.
  opening, 260.
  down, 320.
  trifle, 643.
Fluent, *speech*, 584.
  flowing, 348.
Flugleman, 22.
Fluid, 333.
Fluke, 244.
Flummery, *vain*, 643.
  flattery, 933.
  absurd, 497.
Flunkey, *lacquey*, 746.
  flatterer, 935.
Flurry, *hurry*, 684.
  agitation, 825.
Flush, *flat*, 251.
  flood, 348.
  heat, 382.
  light, 420.
  redness, 434.
  abundance, 639.

Flush, *feeling*, 821.
  passion, 825.
  in liquor, 959.
Fluster, *excitement*, 824.
  tipsy, 959.
Flute, 417.
Fluted, 259.
Flutter, *move*, 315.
  fear, 860.
  excitement, 824.
Fluviatile, 348.
Flux, *flow*, 348.
  motion, 264.
  changes, 140.
Fluxion, 85.
Fly, *depart*, 292.
  take wing, 267.
  escape, 671.
  recede, 286.
  shun, 623.
  run away, 862.
  lose colour, 429.
  minute, 193.
  time, 111.
  burst, 173.
Fly at, 716.
Fly-boat, 273.
Fly back, *recoil*, 277.
  elastic, 325.
Fly-blown, 653.
Fly-leaf, 228.
  book, 593.
Fly out, *burst*, 173.
  passion, 825.
  anger, 900.
Fly-wheel, 633.
Flying, *swiftness*, 274.
  volitation, 267.
Foam, *spray*, 353.
  passion, 900.
Fob, *pocket*, 191.
  to cheat, 545.
  evade, 773.
Focus, *reunion*, 74.
  centre, 223.
  furnace, 386.
Fodder, 635.
Foe, *antagonist*, 710.
  enemy, 891.
Fœtid, 401.
Fœtus, 129.
Fog, 422.
Foggy, *obscure*, 447.
  shaded, 426.
Foh! 867.
Foible, 945.
Foil, 731.
Foiled, 732.
Foist, 301.
Foist in, 228.

308

Foist upon, 545.
*Folâtre, 836.
Fold, *plait*, 258.
  pen, 752.
  congregation, 996.
  bisect, 91.
Foliaceous, 204.
Foliage, 367.
Foliated, 204.
Folk, 373.
Follicle, *hollow*, 252.
  opening, 260.
  cyst, 191.
Follow, *in order*, 63.
  in time, 117.
  in motion, 281.
  to imitate, 19.
  pursue, 622.
  result from, 154.
  obey, 743.
Follow up, 461.
Follower, 281.
  partizan, 746.
Folly, *irrationality*, 499.
  nonsense, 497.
  building, 189.
Foment, *promote*, 707.
  excite, 173.
Fond, 897.
Fondle, 902.
Fondling, 899.
Fondness, *love*, 897.
  desire, 865.
Font, *types*, 591.
  origin, 153.
  altar, 1000.
Food, *eatable*, 299.
  materials, 635.
Fool, 501.
Foolhardy, 863.
Foolish, *unwise*, 499.
  trifling, 643.
Foot, *stand*, 211.
  metre, 597.
Foot it, *walk*, 266.
  dance, 840.
Footfall, *motion*, 264.
  trace, 551.
  stumble, 732.
Footing, *situation*, 8.
  foundation, 211.
  place, 58.
  rank, 71.
  influence, 175.
Footman, 746.
Footmark, 551.
Footpad, 792.
Foot-path, 627.
Footprint, 551.
Footstep, 551.

Footstool, 215.
Fop, 854.
Foppery, 855.
Foppish, 855.
For, *reason*, 476.
  motive, 615.
Forage, *provision*, 637.
  materials, 635.
  booty, 793.
  to steal, 791.
Foraminous, 260.
Forasmuch as, 476.
Foray, *attack*, 716.
  robbery, 791.
  havoc, 619.
Forbear, *avoid*, 623.
  spare, 678.
  pity, 914.
  abstain, 953.
  sufferance, 826.
Forbid, 761.
Forbidding, *repulsive*, 846.
Force, *power*, 157.
  strength, 159.
  agency, 170.
  to compel, 744.
  to induce, 615.
  of style, 574.
Forced, *out of place*, 24.
Ford, 627.
Fore, 234.
Forearmed, 673.
Forebode, 511.
Forecast, *foresee*, 510.
  plan, 626.
  prepare, 673.
Foreclose, 706.
Foredoom, 601.
Forefather, *old*, 130.
  ancestor, 166.
Forefend, *guard*, 717.
  hinder, 706.
Forego, *relinquish*, 782.
  renounce, 757.
Foregoing, *past*, 122.
  preceding, 62.
Foreground, 234.
Forehead, 234.
Foreign, *alien*, 10.
  extraneous, 57.
Forejudge, 481.
Foreknow, 510.
Foreland, *high*, 206.
  projection, 250.
Foreman, 694.
Foremost, *front*, 234.
  beginning, 66.
Forenoon, 125.
Forensic, 965.
Forerank, 234.

Forerun, 116.
Forerunner, *in order*, 64.
  in time, 116.
  omen, 512.
Foresee, *foreknow*, 510.
  expect, 507.
Foreshadow, 511.
Foreshorten, 201.
Foresight, 510.
Forest, 367.
Forestall, *early*, 132.
  expect, 507.
Foretaste, 510.
Foretell, 511.
Forethought, 459.
Foretoken, 511.
Forewarn, *warn*, 668.
  advise, 695.
  predict, 511.
Forfeit, *lose*, 776.
  fail, 773.
  penalty, 974.
Forge, *produce*, 161.
  workshop, 691.
  trump up, 544.
Forgery, 546.
Forget, 506.
Forgive, 918.
Forgotten, *unremembered*, 506.
  ingratitude, 917.
Fork, 244.
Forlorn, *abandoned*, 893.
  dejected, 837.
  wobegone, 828.
Forlorn hope, *hopeless*, 859.
  danger, 665.
Form, *shape*, 240.
  state, 7.
  arrange, 60.
  rule, 80.
  to make up, 54.
  produce, 161.
  educate, 537.
  habituate, 613.
  bench, 215.
  fashion, 852.
  etiquette, 882.
  law, 963.
  manner, 627.
  beauty, 845.
  likeness, 21.
  pupils, 541.
Formal, *regular*, 82.
  affected, 855.
Formality, *ceremony*, 852.
  parade, 882.
  law, 963.
Formation, *production*, 161.
  shape, 240.
309

Formed of, 54.
Former, *in order*, 62.
  in time, 122.
Formication, 380.
Formidable, 860.
Formless, 241.
Formula, *rule*, 80.
  precept, 697.
  law, 963.
Fornication, 961.
Fornicator, 962.
Forsake, 624.
Forsooth, 494.
Forswear, *renounce*, 624.
  refuse, 764.
  perjure, 544, 940.
Fort, *defence*, 717.
  refuge, 666.
  excellence, 698.
Forth, 282.
Forthcoming, 121.
Forthwith, 111.
Fortification, *defence*, 717.
  refuge, 666.
Fortify, 159.
Fortitude, *courage*, 861.
  endurance, 826.
Fortress, *defence*, 716.
  prison, 752.
Fortuitous, 621.
Fortunate, 734.
Fortune, *chance*, 156.
  accident, 621.
  wealth, 803.
Fortuneless, 804.
Fortune-teller, 513.
Fortune-telling, 511.
Forum, *tribunal*, 966.
  school, 542.
Forward, *early*, 132.
  to advance, 282.
  to help, 707.
  active, 682.
  willing, 602.
  vain, 880.
  impertinent, 885.
Foss, 259.
Fosse, 232.
Fossil, 358.
Foster, 707.
Fou, 959.
Foul, *bad*, 649.
  corrupt, 653.
  odour, 401.
  ugly, 846.
  vicious, 945.
Foulmouthed, 907.
Foultongued, 932.
Found, *cause*, 153.
  prepare, 673.

Foundation, *base*, 211.
  support, 215.
Founder, *originator*, 164.
  sink, 732.
Fountain, *cause*, 153.
  river, 348.
  store, 636.
Four, 95.
Fourfold, 96.
Fourscore, 98.
Fourth, 97.
Fowl, 366.
Fowling piece, 727.
Fox, 702.
*Fracas, 720.
Fraction, *part*, 51.
  numerical, 84.
Fractious, 901.
Fracture, 44.
Fragile, 328.
Fragment, 51.
Fragrant, 400.
Frail, *brittle*, 328.
  irresolute, 605.
  imperfect, 651.
  failing, 945.
Frame, *condition*, 7.
  support, 215.
  texture, 329.
  form, 240.
  substance, 316.
  to construct, 161.
  border, 230.
Frame-work, 215.
Franchise, *right*, 924.
  freedom, 748.
  exemption, 927.
Franciscan, 996.
Frank, *artless*, 703.
  open, 525.
  sincere, 543.
  honorable, 939.
Frankincense, 400.
Frantic, *delirious*, 503.
  violent, 173.
  excited, 825.
Fraternal, *brotherly*, 11.
  friendly, 888.
Fraud, *deception*, 545.
  dishonor, 940.
Fraught, *having*, 777.
  full of, 639.
Fray, 720.
Freak, 608.
Freakish, 605.
Freckle, 848.
Freckled, 440.
Free, *detached*, 44.
  at liberty, 748.
  spontaneous, 602.

Free, *exempt*, 927.
  unobstructed, 705.
  liberal, 816.
  gratuitous, 815.
Freebooter, 792.
Freeborn, 748.
Free-gift, 784.
Freehold, 780.
Freemasonry, *secrecy*, 528.
  sign, 550.
Free-play, 748.
Free-spoken, 543.
Freethinking, 988.
Freewill, 600.
Freeze, 385.
Freezing mixture, 387.
Freight, *contents*, 190.
  cargo, 798.
  transfer, 270.
Frenzy, 503.
Frequent, *in time*, 136.
  in number, 102.
  in space, 186.
Fresco, *cold*, 383.
  painting, 556.
Fresh, *new*, 123.
  cold, 383.
  colour, 428.
  flood, 348.
  healthy, 654.
  good, 648.
  tipsy, 959.
Freshman, 541.
Freshwater sailor, 674.
Fret, *suffer*, 378.
  grieve, 828.
  to gall, 830.
  sadness, 837.
  to irritate, 900.
Fretful, 901.
Fretwork, 219.
Friable, 330.
*Friandise, 868.
Friar, 996.
Fribble, *trifle*, 643.
  dawdle, 683.
Frication, 331.
Friction, *rubbing*, 331.
  obstacle, 179.
Friend, *well-wisher*, 890.
  auxiliary, 711.
Friendless, 893.
Friendly, *amical*, 888.
  helping, 707.
Friendship, 888.
Frieze, 210.
Frigate, 273.
Fright, *alarm*, 860.
  ugliness, 846.
Frightful, *great*, 31.
310

Frightful, *hideous*, 846.
  dreadful, 830.
Frigefaction, 385.
Frigid, *cold*, 383.
  callous, 823.
  reluctant, 603.
Frill, *border*, 230.
Fringe, *lace*, 256.
  ornament, 847.
Frippery, *dress*, 225.
  trifle, 643.
  ornament, 847.
  ostentation, 882.
  ridiculous, 853.
Frisk, *brisk*, 682.
  gay, 836.
  amuse, 840.
Frisky, *nimble*, 274.
  in spirits, 836.
Frith, *strait*, 343.
  chasm, 198.
Fritter, *small part*, 51.
  waste, 638.
  misuse, 679.
Frivolous, 643.
Frizzled, 248.
Frock, 225.
Frog, 847.
Frolic, 840.
Frolicsome, 836.
*Frondeur, 742, 936.
Front, *fore part*, 234.
  beginning, 66.
  exterior, 220.
  resistance, 719.
Frontal, *beginning*, 66.
  exterior, 220.
Frontier, *limit*, 233.
  vicinity, 199.
Fronting, 237.
Frontispiece, *prefix*, 64.
  front, 234.
Frost, 383.
Froth, *bubble*, 353.
  trifle, 643.
  style, 577.
Frounce, 258.
Frousy, 401.
Froward, *irascible*, 901.
  discourteous, 895.
Frown, *disapprove*, 932.
  anger, 900.
  scowl, 839.
  lower, 837.
Fructify, 168, 734.
Frugal, *temperate*, 953.
  economical, 817.
Fruit, *result*, 154.
  acquisition, 775.
Fruitful, 168.

Fruition, 827.
Fruitless, *useless*, 645.
  abortive, 732.
Frump, 900.
Frustrate, *defeat*, 731.
  prevent, 706.
Frustration, 732.
Frustum, 51.
Fry, *child*, 129.
  heat, 384.
Frying-pan, 386.
Fuddled, 959.
Fudge, *nonsense*, 497.
  trivial, 643.
Fuel, *combustible*, 388.
  materials, 635.
Fugacious, *transitory*, 111.
Fugitive, *escape*, 671.
Fugue, 415.
Fulciment, 215.
Fulcrum, 215.
Fulfil, *observe*, 772.
  duty, 926.
  complete, 729.
Fulgent, 420.
Fulguration, 420.
Fuliginous, *black*, 431.
  opaque, 426.
Full, *much*, 31.
  complete, 52.
  sound, 404.
  abundant, 639.
Full blown, 194.
Full grown, 194.
Fullhanded, 816.
Fully, 31.
Fulminate, *loud*, 404.
  violent, 173.
  malediction, 908.
Fulsome, *nauseous*, 395.
  fetid, 401.
  impure, 961.
Fulvous, 436.
Fumble, *derange*, 61.
  handle, 379.
  awkward, 699.
Fumbler, 701.
Fume, *exhalation*, 334.
  odour, 398.
  violence, 173.
  excitement, 825.
  anger, 900.
Fumigate, 652.
Fun, 840.
Funambulist, 700.
Function, *business*, 625.
  duty, 926.
  utility, 644.
Functionary, 758.
Fund, *capital*, 800.

Fund, *store*, 636.
Fundamental, *basis*, 211, 215.
    in music, 413.
Funds, 800.
Funebrial, 363.
Funeral, 363.
Fungus, 250.
Funnel, 260.
Funnel-shaped, 252.
Funny, *witty*, 842.
    ridiculous, 853.
    boat, 273.
Fur, *hair*, 256.
    dirt, 653.
Furbish, *improve*, 658.
    prepare, 673.
    beautify, 845.
    ornament, 847.
Furfur, 653.
Furfuraceous, 330.
Furious, *great*, 31.
    violent, 173.
    passion, 825.
    enraged, 900.
Furl, 312.
Furlough, 760.
Furnace, 386.
Furnish, *provide*, 637.
    prepare, 673.
    give, 784.
Furniture, *materials*, 635.
    goods, 780.
Furrow, 259.
Further, 707.
Furthermore, 37.
Furtive, *clandestine*, 528.
    false, 544.
    stealing, 791.
Furuncle, 250.
Fury, *violence*, 173.
    excitation, 825.
    anger, 900.
    demon, 980.
    bane, 663.
Fuscous, 433.
Fuse, *melt*, 335.
    heat, 382.
    combine, 48.
Fusiform, *pointed*, 253.
    angular, 244.
Fusileer, 726.
Fusillade, 361.
Fusion, *heat*, 384.
    union, 48.
Fuss, *haste*, 684.
    activity, 682.
    hurry, 825.
Fustian, *nonsense*, 497.
    ridiculous, 853.

311

Fustian, *style*, 577.
Fusty, 401.
Futile, *useless*, 645.
Future, 121.
Fuzzle, 959.
Fy! 874.

G.

Gab, 582.
Gabble, 584.
Gabelle, 812.
Gaberdine, 225.
Gad about, 266.
Gaffer, *man*, 373.
    clown, 876.
Gag, *speechless*, 585.
    muzzle, 751.
Gage, *measure*, 466.
    security, 771.
Gaiety, 836.   *See* Gay.
*Gaillard, 844.
Gain, *acquisition*, 775.
    advantage, 618.
    to learn, 539.
Gain ground, 658.
Gain upon, *approach*, 287.
    become a habit, 613.
Gainful, 644.
Gainless, 645.
Gainsay, 536.
Gairish (or garish), *colour*, 428.
    light, 420.
    ornament, 847.
    display, 882.
Gait, *walk*, 264.
    speed, 274.
Gaiter, 225.
Gala, *festival*, 840.
    display, 882.
Galaxy, *stars*, 318.
    luminary, 423.
    glory, 873.
Gale, 349.
Galenicals, 662.
*Galimathias, 497.
Galiot, 273.
Galipot, 191.
Gall, *bitterness*, 395.
    pain, 378.
    to pain, 830.
    malevolence, 907.
    anger, 900.
Gallant, *brave*, 861.
    licentious, 961.
Galleon, 273.
Gallery, *room*, 191.
    passage, 260.
Galley, 273.

Gallimaufry, 41.
Galliot, 273.
Gallipot, 191.
Gallop, *ride*, 266.
    scamper, 274.
Galloway, 271.
Gallows, 975.
Galoche, 225.
Galvanism, 824.
*Gamach, 225.
*Gambade, *leap*, 309.
    prank, 856.
Gambado, 225.
Gamble, 156, 621.
Gambol, 840.
Game, *chance*, 156.
    pursuit, 622.
    plan, 626.
    intent, 620.
    amusement, 840.
    resolute, 604.
    brave, 861.
Gamecock, 861.
Gamesome, 836.
*Gamin, 876.
Gammon, 546.
Gamut, 413.
Gang, *party*, 712.
    knot, 72.
Gangrene, 655.
Gangway, 627.
Gantlet. *See* Gauntlet.
Gap, *discontinuity*, 70.
    chasm, 198.
Gape, *open*, 260.
    wonder, 870.
    curiosity, 455.
    desire, 865.
Gar, 161.
Garb, 225.
Garbage, 653.
Garble, *retrench*, 38.
    exclude, 55.
    misinterpret, 523.
    falsify, 544.
Garbled, *incomplete*, 53.
Garden, 845.
Gardening, 371.
Garish. *See* Gairish.
Garland, 847.
Garment, 225.
Garner, *collect*, 72.
    store, 636.
Garnish, *adorn*, 845.
    ornament, 847.
    addition, 39.
Garret, *room*, 191.
    high, 206.
Garrison, 726.
Garrulity, 584.

Gas, 322, 334.
Gasconade, 884.
Gash, 44.
Gasp, *pant*, 688.
   desire, 865.
   droop, 655.
Gate, *beginning*, 66.
   way, 627.
   mouth, 260.
   barrier, 232.
Gather, *collect*, 72.
   acquire, 775.
   learn, 539.
   conclude, 480.
   fold, 258.
   unite in a focus, 74.
*Gauche, 699.
Gaud, 847.
Gaudery, 880.
Gaudy, *colouring*, 428.
   ornamented, 847.
   flaunting, 882.
Gauge, 466.
Gaunt, *hulky*, 192.
   spare, 203.
Gauntlet, *defiance*, 715.
   punishment, 972.
   anger, 909.
Gauze, 424.
Gavel, 812.
Gawky, *awkward*, 699.
   ridiculous, 853.
Gay, *cheerful*, 836.
   colour, 428.
Gaze, 441.
Gazebo, 441.
Gazelle, 274.
Gazette, *publication*, 531.
   record, 551.
Gazing-stock, 872.
Gear, *clothes*, 225.
   harness, 633.
Gehenna, 982.
Gelatin, 354.
Gelatinous, 352.
Gelding, 271.
Gelid, 383.
Geloscopy, 511.
Gem, *ornament*, 847.
   jewel, 650.
Gemination, 90.
*Gendarme, 965.
Gender, 75.
Genealogy, 69.
General, *generic*, 78.
   officer, 745.
Generalissimo, 745.
Generality, 78.
Generalship, 692.
Generate, 161.
312

Generation, *mankind*, 372.
Gew-gaw, 847.
Ghost, 980.
Gift, *given*, 784.
   power, 157.
   talent, 698.
Gig, 272, 273.
Gigantic, *large*, 192.
   tall, 206.
Giggle, 838.
Gild, *adorn*, 845.
   ornament, 847.
   coat, 222.
Gilding, 222.
Gilt, 348.
Gimcrack, *brittle*, 328.
   valueless, 645.
   imperfect, 651.
   ornament, 847.
   whim, 865.
Gimlet, 262.
Gin, *trap*, 667.
   demon, 980.
Gingerbread, *imperfect*, 651.
   ornament, 847.
Gingerly, *carefully*, 459.
   slowly, 275.
Gingle, 408.
Gipsy, 548.
Girandole, 423.
Gird, *bind*, 43.
   surround, 227.
   enclose, 231.
   strengthen, 159.
Girder, *bond*, 45.
   beam, 215.
Girdle, 247.
Girl, *young*, 129.
   female, 374.
Girth, *band*, 45.
   outline, 229.
Gist, *essence*, 5.
   important, 642.
   meaning, 516.
Gittern, 417.
Give, 784.
Give back, 790.
Give in, *submit*, 725.
   obey, 743.
Give notice, *inform*, 527.
   warn, 668.
Give out, *emit*, 296.
   bestow, 784.
   publish, 531.
   teach, 537.
Give over, *relinquish*, 624.
   cease, 141.
   lose hope, 859.
Give up, *relinquish*, 624.

Give up, *resign*, 757.
   reject, 610.
   property, 782.
Give way, *yield*, 725.
   obey, 743.
   despond, 837.
Gizzard, 191.
Glabrous, 255.
Glacial, 383.
Glaciate, 385.
Glacier, 383.
Glacis, 717.
Glad, 827.
Gladden, 829.
Glade, *opening*, 260.
   hollow, 252.
   thicket, 367.
Gladiator, 726.
Gladiatorial, 722.
Gladsome, 829.
Glairy, 352.
Glamour, 992.
Glance, *look*, 441.
   rapid motion, 274.
   attend to, 457.
   hint, 527.
Glare, *light*, 420.
   visible, 446.
   colour, 428.
   obvious, 518.
Glass, *vessel*, 191.
   brittle, 328.
   spectacles, 445.
Glassy, *dim*, 422.
   transparent, 425.
   colourless, 429.
Glaucous, 435.
Glaver, 933.
Glazed, 255.
Gleam, *ray*, 420.
Glean, *choose*, 609.
   take, 789.
   acquire, 775.
   learn, 539.
Glebe, 342.
Glee, *satisfaction*, 827.
   merriment, 836.
Glen, 252.
Glib, *voluble*, 584.
   facile, 705.
Glide, *move*, 266.
   slowly, 275.
Glimmer, *light*, 420.
   dimness, 422.
Glimmering, *slight knowledge*, 490, 491.
Glimpse, *sight*, 441.
   knowledge, 490.
Glisten, 420.
Glitter, *shine*, 420.

Glitter, *display*, 882.
Gloat, *look*, 441.
  revel, 827.
Globe, *sphere*, 249.
  world, 318.
Globule, *spherule*, 249.
  minute, 193.
Glomeration, 72.
Gloom, *darkness*, 421.
  sadness, 837.
Gloriation, 884.
Glorify, *approve*, 931.
  worship, 990.
Glory, *honor*, 873.
  light, 420.
  pride, 878.
Glose, 933.
Gloss, *light*, 420.
  smoothness, 255.
  beauty, 845.
  plea, 617.
  falsehood, 546.
  interpretation, 522.
Gloss over, *neglect*, 460.
  inattention, 458.
  sophistry, 477.
  vindication, 937.
  falsehood, 544.
Glossary, *interpretation*,
  522.
  verbal, 562.
Glossy, 255.
Glove, *cartel*, 715.
Glow, *shine*, 420.
  colour, 428.
  warmth, 382.
  passion, 821.
  style, 574.
Glow-worm, 423.
Glue, *cement*, 45.
  to cement, 46.
Glum, *discontented*, 832.
  sulky, 895.
Glut, *redundance*, 641.
  satiety, 869.
Glutinous, 46, 352.
Gluttony, *excess*, 957.
  desire, 865.
Glyphography, 558.
Gnarl, } *malevolence*, 907.
Gnash, } *anger*, 900.
Gnat, 193.
Gnaw, *eat*, 297.
  corrode, 659.
  pain, 378.
  give pain, 830.
Gnome, 980.
Go, *move*, 264.
  depart, 292.
Go across, 302.

Go ahead, *advance*, 282.
  improve, 658.
Go beyond, 303.
Go-by, 303.
  evade, 623.
Go down, *sink*, 306.
  decline, 659.
Go forth, *depart*, 292.
  publish, 531.
Go near, 287.
Go off, *cease*, 142.
  die, 360.
Go on, 143.
Go over, 607.
Go round, 311.
Go through, *pass*, 302.
  complete, 729.
  endure, 821.
Go to, *direction*, 278.
  remonstrance, 695.
Go up, 305.
Go with, *assent*, 488.
Goad, 615.
Goal, *object*, 620.
  reach, 293.
Go-between, *agent*, 758.
  intermedium, 631.
Gobble, *devour*, 297.
  cry, 412.
*Gobemouche, *credulous*,
  486.
  fool, 501.
  dupe, 547.
Goblin, *ghost*, 980.
  bugbear, 860.
Go-by, *deceive*, 545.
God, 976.
Goddess, 899.
Godless, 988.
Godlike, 944.
Godliness, 987.
Godsend, *luck*, 621.
  advantage, 618.
  success, 731.
Goer, *horse*, 271.
Goggle, 445.
Goggle-eyed, 443.
Going, *futurity*, 121.
Gold, 800.
Gold-coloured, 436.
Golden, 436.
Golden-age, 827.
Goloshes, 225.
Gondola, 273.
Gone, *non-extant*, 2.
  absent, 187.
Gone by, *past*, 123.
Gonfalon, 550.
Gong, 417.
Good, *advantage*, 618.

Good, *advantageous*, 648.
  virtuous, 944.
Good-bye, 292.
Goodfellowship, 892.
Goodly, *large*, 192.
  beautiful, 845.
Good manners, 894.
Good nature, 906.
Good will, 906.
Goods, *effects*, 780.
  merchandise, 798.
  materials, 635.
Goody, 374.
Goose, 501.
Goose-cap, 501.
Goose-skin, 383.
Gordian knot, *problem*,461.
  difficulty, 704.
Gore, 260.
Gorge, *ravine*, 198.
  narrowness, 203.
  to devour, 297.
  full, 641.
  gluttony, 957.
  satiety, 869.
Gorgeous, *colour*, 428.
  splendid, 845.
  ornamented, 847.
Gorgon, 860.
Gormandize, 957.
Gospel, *scripture*, 985.
  truth, 494.
  certainty, 474.
Gossamer, *texture*, 329.
  slender, 205.
  light, 320.
Gossip, *conversation*, 588.
  news, 532.
Goth, 876.
Gothic, 851.
*Gourmand, 957.
Govern, *direct*, 693.
  authority, 737.
Governor, *director*, 694.
  tutor, 540.
Gown, 225.
Grab, *snatch*, 789.
  steal, 791.
  booty, 793.
Grabble, *fumble*, 379.
Grace, *elegance*, 845.
  polish, 850.
  forgiveness, 918.
  honor, 939.
  title, 877.
  piety, 987.
  worship, 990.
  beseech, 765.
  style, 578.
Graceless, *ungraceful*, 846.

Graceless, *vicious*, 945.
  impenitent, 951.
Gracious, *courteous*, 894.
  good-natured, 906.
Gradation, *degree*, 26.
  order, 58.
  arrangement, 60.
  continuity, 69.
Grade, *degree*, 26.
  term, 71.
Gradient, 217.
Gradual, *degree*, 26.
  continuity, 69.
Graduate, *to arrange*, 60.
  to adapt, 23.
  to measure, 466.
  scholar, 492.
*Gradus, 562.
Graft, *join*, 43.
  insert, 301.
  locate, 184.
  teach, 537.
Grain, *essence*, 5.
  minute, 32.
  particle, 193.
  texture, 329.
  soul, 820.
Grammar, 567.
Grammercy, 916.
Granary, 636.
Grand, *important*, 642.
  glorious, 873.
Grandam, 130.
Grandee, 875.
Grandeur, 873.
Grandiloquence, *eloquence*, 582.
  style, 577.
Grandiose, *style*, 577.
Grandsire, *old*, 130.
  ancestor, 166.
Grange, 189.
Granite, 323.
Grant, *give*, 784.
  allow, 760.
  consent, 762.
  assent, 488.
Granulate, 330.
Granule, 193.
Grape-shot, 727.
Graphic, *painting*, 556.
  description, 594.
  intelligible, 518.
Grapnel, *anchor*, 666.
Grapple, 720.
Grappling-iron, *fastening*, 45.
  safety, 666.
Grasp, *seize*, 789.
  retain, 781.
314

Grasp, *comprehend*, 518.
  power, 737.
Grass, 367.
Grass-green, 435.
Grate, *rub*, 330.
  friction, 331.
  furnace, 386.
  pain physical, 378.
  moral, 830.
Grateful, *thankful*, 916.
  agreeable, 829.
Gratification, *animal*, 377.
  moral, 827.
Gratify, 829.
Grating, *noise*, 410.
  lattice, 219.
Gratis, 815.
Gratitude, 916.
Gratuitous, *spontaneous*, 600.
  payless, 815.
Gratuity, 784.
Gratulation, 836.
Gravamen, 642.
Grave, *sad*, 837.
  serious, 642.
  distressing, 830.
  heinous, 945.
  to engrave, 559.
  impress, 505.
  tomb, 363.
  sound, 408.
Gravel, *offend*, 830.
  puzzle, 704.
Graveolent, 398.
Graver, 559.
Graveyard, 363.
Gravity, *weight*, 319.
  dulness, 843.
  seriousness, 837.
  importance, 642.
Gravy, 333.
Gray, *colour*, 432.
  age, 128.
Graze, *browse*, 297.
  touch, 199.
Grease, 355, 356.
Great, *much*, 31.
  big, 192.
  important, 642.
  glorious, 873.
  magnanimous, 942.
Great-coat, 225.
Greater, 33.
Greatest, 33.
Greaves, 225.
Greedy, *voracious*, 957.
  desirous, 865.
  avaricious, 819.
Green, *colour*, 435.

Green, *unskilled*, 699.
  unprepared, 674.
  a novice, 491.
Green-eyed, 920.
Greenhorn, *fool*, 501.
  novice, 491.
  bungler, 701.
Green-room, 599.
Greet, *hail*, 894.
  weep, 839.
Gregarious, 892.
Grenade, 727.
Grenadier, *soldier*, 726.
  tall, 206.
Grey. See Gray.
Greybeard, 130.
Greyhound, *swift*, 274.
Gride, 44.
Gridelin, 437.
Gridiron, 219.
Grief, 837.
Grievance, *injury*, 619.
  pain, 830.
Grieve, *complain*, 839.
  afflict, 830.
  injure, 649.
Griffin, 83.
*Griffonage, 590.
Grig, 836.
Grill, 384.
Grim, *ugly*, 846.
  discourteous, 846.
  ferocious, 907.
Grimace, 856.
Grime, 653.
Grim-visaged, 837.
Grin, *laugh*, 838.
  ridicule, 856.
  scorn, 929.
Grind, *pulverize*, 330.
  an organ, 415.
  oppress, 907.
  learn, 539.
Grinder, 540.
Grip, *power*, 737.
Gripe, *seize*, 789.
  retain, 781.
  pain, 378, 828.
  to give pain, 830.
  power, 737.
Griping, *avaricious*, 819.
*Grisette, 374.
Grisly, 846.
Grist, *provision*, 637.
  materials, 635.
Grit, 330.
Gritty, *hard*, 323.
Grizzled, 440.
Grizzly, *gray*, 432.
Groan, *cry*, 411.

Groan, *lament*, 839.
Groggy, 959.
Groin, 244.
Groom, 746.
Groove, 259.
Grope, *feel*, 379.
   experiment, 463.
   inquire, 461.
   try, 676.
Gross, *whole*, 51.
   vulgar, 851.
   vicious, 945.
   impure, 961.
Gross-head, 501.
*Grossièreté, 895.
Grot. *See* Grotto.
Grotesque, 853.
Grotto, *alcove*, 189.
   hollow, 252.
Ground, *land*, 342.
   support, 215.
   base, 211.
   region, 181.
   cause, 153.
   motive, 615.
   plea, 617.
   property, 780.
   teach, 537.
Grounded, *knowing*, 490.
   wrecked, 732.
Groundling, 876.
Groundless, *erroneous*,
495.
   sophistical, 477.
Ground-swell, *surge*, 348.
   agitation, 315.
Ground-work, *basis*, 211.
   support, 215.
   cause, 153.
   precursor, 64.
   preparation, 673.
Grounds, *lees*, 653.
Group, *cluster*, 72.
   to marshal, 58.
Grout, 45.
Grove, *wood*, 367.
   house, 189.
Grovel, *move slowly*, 275.
   be low, 207.
   cringe, 886.
   base, 940.
Grow, *increase*, 35.
   expand, 194.
Grow from, 154.
Growl, *cry*, 412.
   complain, 839.
   threaten, 909.
   anger, 900.
Growth, *in degree*, 35.
   in size, 194.
315

Grub, 192.
Grub up, *extract*, 300.
   destroy, 162.
   discover, 480.
Grudge, *hate*, 898.
   stingy, 819.
Gruff, *morose*, 895.
   sound, 410.
Grumble, *sound*, 411.
   complain, 839.
Grumous, *dense*, 321.
   semiliquid, 352.
Grumpy, 895.
Grunt, *cry*, 412.
   complain, 839.
Guano, 693.
Guant, 846.
Guarantee, 771.
Guard, *defend*, 717.
   safety, 664.
Guarded, *circumspect*, 459.
Guardian, 664.
Guardless, 665.
Guard-room, 752.
Guardsman, 726.
Gubernation, 737.
Gubernator, 745.
Gudgeon, 547.
Guerdon, 973.
Guerilla, 726.
Guess, 514.
Guest, 890.
*Guet-à-pens, 546, 949.
Guggle, *bubble*, 353.
   gush, 348.
   resound, 408.
   cry, 412.
Guidance, 693.
Guide, *direct*, 693.
   director, 694.
   advice, 695.
   teach, 537.
   teacher, 540.
   road-book, 266.
Guideless, 665.
Guide-post, *indicator*, 550.
   warning, 668.
Guild, *corporation*, 712.
   tribunal, 966.
   partnership, 797.
Guildhall, 799.
Guile, *cunning*, 702.
   deceit, 545.
Guileless, *artless*, 703.
   sincere, 543.
Guillotine, *engine*, 975.
   to decapitate, 972.
Guilt, *crime*, 947.
   vice, 945.
Guiltless, 946.

*Guindé, 572.
Guise, *state*, 7.
   appearance, 448.
   plea, 617.
Guiser, 599.
Guitar, 417.
Gules, 434.
Gulf (or gulph), 208, 343.
Gull, *dupe*, 547.
   credulous, 486.
Gullet, *throat*, 260.
   rivulet, 348.
Gullible, 486.
Gully, *conduit*, 350.
   opening, 260.
   hollow, 252.
Gulosity, 957.
Gulp, *swallow*, 297.
   believe, 484.
Gulph, *sea*, 343.
   depth, 208.
Gum, 45, 46.
Gumption, *capacity*, 498.
Gun, 727.
Gunner, 726.
Gurge, *eddy*, 312.
   torrent, 348.
Gurgle, *sound*, 405.
   bubble, 353.
Gush, *flow*, 294.
   flood, 348.
Gust, *wind*, 349.
   physical taste, 390.
   enjoyment, 826.
   moral taste, 850.
Gustable, 390.
Gustation, 390.
Gustful, 394.
Gustless, 391.
*Gusto, *relish*, 827.
   taste, 850.
Gut, *opening*, 260.
   to sack, 789.
   vitals, 221.
Gutter, *conduit*, 350.
   groove, 259.
Guttle, *devour*, 297.
   gorge, 957.
Guttural, 583.
Guzzle, *drink*, 297.
   tipple, 959.
Gybe, 932.
Gymbals, 312.
*Gymnasium, *school*, 542.
   training, 673.
Gymnastic, 686.
Gymnosophist, 984.
Gyration, 312.
Gyre, 312.
Gyromancy, 511.

Gyve, *chain*, 45.
  shackle, 752.

H.

Habergeon, 717.
Habiliment, 225.
Habilitation, 698.
Habit, *custom*, 613.
  coat, 225.
Habitation, *abode*, 189.
  location, 184.
Habitual, *regular*, 82.
Habituate, *accustom*, 613.
  train, 673.
Habitude, *relation*, 9.
  habit, 613.
Hack, *cut*, 44.
  shorten, 201.
  horse, 271.
Hackle, *cut*, 44.
Hacknied, *regular*, 82.
  habitual, 613.
  experienced, 698.
Hades, 982.
Haft, 633.
Hag, *ugly*, 846.
  wretch, 913.
Haggard, *ugly*, 846.
  wild, 824.
  insane, 503.
  intractable, 606.
Haggle, *cut*, 44.
  bargain, 769.
  chaffer, 794.
Haha, *ditch*, 198.
  defence, 717.
Haic, 225.
Hail, *call*, 586.
  salute, 928.
  ice, 383.
Hair, *thread*, 45.
  filament, 205.
  roughness, 256.
Hair-brained, 863.
Hair-breadth, 203.
Hake, 225.
Halberd, 727.
Halberdier, 726.
Halcyon, *prosperous*, 734.
  joyful, 827.
  calm, 174.
Hale, 654.
Half, 91.
Half and half, 41.
Half-blood, 83.
Half-moon, 245.
Half seas over, 959.
Half way, 68.
316

Half wit, 501.
Half-witted, 499.
Hall, *chamber*, 189.
  receptacle, 191.
  mart, 799.
Hallelujah, 990.
Hallo! *call*, 586.
  wonder, 870.
Halloo, 411.
Hallowed, 976.
Hallucination, *error*, 495.
  delusion, 503.
Halo, *light*, 420.
  glory, 873.
Halt, *stop*, 265.
  rest, 687.
  limp, 275.
Halter, *rope*, 45.
  punishment, 975.
Halting, *lame*, 160.
Hamadryad, 979.
Hamlet, 189.
Hammer, *to knock*, 276.
  instrument, 633.
  auction, 796.
  stammer, 583.
  think, 451.
Hammock, 215.
Hamper, *basket*, 191.
  obstruct, 706.
Hamstring, *injure*, 649.
  weaken, 160.
  incapacitate, 158.
Hanaper, 636.
Hand, *instrument*, 633.
  indicator, 550.
  agent, 690.
  side, 236.
  writing, 590.
  to give, 784.
  agency, 170.
Hand in hand, 88.
Hand (in), *possession*, 777.
  business, 625.
Hands off! *resist*, 719.
  prohibit, 761.
Hand-barrow, 272.
Handbook, 695.
Handcuff, *tie together*, 43.
  manacle, 752.
Handful, 25.
Handgallop, 274.
Handicraft, 680.
Handicraftsman, 690.
Handiwork, 680.
Handkerchief, 225.
Handle, *instrument*, 633.
  plea, 617.
  feel (touch), 379.
  describe, 594.

Handle, *dissert*, 595.
Handmaid, 746.
Handsel, *security*, 771.
  pay, 809.
Handsome, *beautiful*, 845.
  liberal, 816.
  disinterested, 942.
Handspike, 633.
Hand-writing, *omen*, 512.
  signature, 550.
  autograph, 590.
Handy, 698.
Hang, *pendency*, 214.
  kill, 361.
  execute, 972.
Hang fire, *reluctance*, 603.
  vacillation, 605.
  refuse, 764.
  slowness, 275.
Hang over, *futurity*, 121.
  destiny, 152.
  height, 206.
Hanger, 727.
Hanger on, *servant*, 746.
  accompany, 88.
  flatterer, 935.
Hangings, *ornaments*, 847.
Hangman, *ruffian*, 913.
  miscreant, 949.
Hanker, 865.
Hap, 156, 621.
Hap-hazard, 156, 621.
Hapless, *hopeless*, 859.
  miserable, 828.
Haply, 156.
Happen, 151.
Happy, *glad*, 827.
  expedient, 646.
Harangue, 582.
Harass, *worry*, 907.
  fatigue, 688.
  vex, 830.
Harbinger, 512.
Harbour, *refuge*, 666.
  haven, 293.
Harbourless, *exposed*, 665.
Hard, *dense*, 323.
  difficult, 704.
  grievous, 830.
  sour, 397.
Harden, *accustom*, 613.
  train, 673.
  render callous, 823.
  impious, 989.
  impenitent, 951.
Hard-favoured, 846.
Hard-headed, 698.
Hard-hearted, 907.
Hardihood, 861.
Hardly, *scarcely*, 32.

Hardly, *infrequency*, 137.
Hard-mouthed, 606.
Hardness of heart, 945.
Hardship, 830.
Hard-working, 686.
Hardy, *strong*, 159.
   healthy, 654.
Hare, 274.
Hare-brained, 460.
Harem, 961.
Hark, 418.
Harlequin, *motley*, 440.
   pantomimic, 599.
   nimble, 274.
   humorist, 844.
Harlot, 962.
Harlotry, 961.
Harm, *evil*, 619.
   badness, 649.
   malevolence, 907.
Harmattan, 349.
Harmless, *safe*, 664.
   innocent, 946.
   innocuous, 648.
Harmonic, 413.
Harmonica, 417.
Harmony, *agreement*, 23.
   melody, 413.
   concord, 714.
   peace, 721.
   friendship, 888.
Harness, *fasten*, 43.
   fastening, 45.
   accoutrement, 225.
   instrument, 633.
   subjection, 749.
Harp, *musical instrument*, 417.
   to repeat, 114.
   to weary, 841.
Harper, 416.
Harpoon, 727.
Harpsichord, 417.
Harpy, *demon*, 980.
   thief, 792.
   miser, 819.
Harquebus, 727.
Harridan, *hag*, 846.
   trollop, 962.
Harrow, 830.
Harry, 830.
Harsh, *severe*, 739.
   morose, 895.
   disagreeable, 830.
   malevolent, 907.
   acrid, 171.
   sound, 410.
Harum-scarum, 59.
Haruspicy, 511.
Harvest, 775.

Hash, *mixture*, 41.
   to cut, 44.
Hasp, *lock*, 45.
   to lock, 43.
Hassock, 215.
Haste, *in time*, 132.
   in motion, 274.
   in action, 684.
   activity, 682.
Hasten, *to promote*, 707.
Hasty, *transient*, 111.
   irritable, 901.
Hat, 225.
Hatch, *produce*, 161.
   plan, 626.
   prepare, 673.
Hatchet, 633.
Hatchment, 551.
Hatchway, 627.
Hate, 898.
Hateful, *noxious*, 649.
   painful, 830.
Hauberk, 717.
Haughty, 878.
Haul, 285.
Haunch, 236.
Haunt, *presence*, 186.
   alarm, 860.
   abode, 189.
   trouble, 830.
Hautboy, 417.
Haut-goût, 392.
Have, 777.
Have it, 484.
Haven, 666.
Haversac, 191.
Havoc, 619.
Haw, 583.
Hawk, *sell*, 796.
   publish, 531.
Hawk-eyed, 441.
Hawker, 797.
Hawser, 45.
Hazard, *chance*, 156, 621.
   danger, 665.
Haze, *mist*, 353.
   dimness, 422.
   opacity, 426.
Hazle, 433.
Hazy, 447.
Head, *beginning*, 66.
   class, 75.
   summit, 210.
   froth, 353.
   intellect, 450.
   wisdom, 498.
   master, 745.
   direction, 693.
   director, 694.
   topic, 454.

Headache, 378.
Head-foremost, *rash*, 863.
   obstinate, 606.
Head-gear, 225.
Headiness, 606.
Heading, *title*, 550.
   beginning, 66.
Headland, *projection*, 250.
   cape, 342.
   height, 206.
Headlong, *rashly*, 863.
   hastily, 684.
   swiftly, 274.
Head-piece, *intellect*, 450.
   skill, 698.
   wisdom, 498.
Head-quarters, 74.
Heads, *compendium*, 596.
Headstrong, *rash*, 863.
   obstinate, 606.
Headway, 180.
Headwork, 451.
Heady, 606.
Heal, *repair*, 658.
   forgive, 918.
Health, 654.
Healthless, 655.
Healthy, 656.
Heap, *collection*, 72.
   store, 636.
   much, 31.
Hear, *audition*, 418.
   learn, 539.
Hearer, 418.
Hearing, 418.
Hearsay, 532.
Hearse, 363.
Heart, *interior*, 221.
   centre, 223.
   mind, 450.
   will, 600.
   affections, 820.
   courage, 861.
   love, 897.
Heart-ache, 828.
Heart-breaking, 830.
Heart-broken, 828.
Heart-burning, 900.
Heart-ease, 831.
Heart-felt, 821.
Heart-grief, 832.
Hearth, 189.
Heartiness, *feeling*, 821.
   sociality, 892.
Heartless, 945.
Heart-rending, 830.
Heart-sinking, 860.
Heart-strings, 820.
Heart-swelling, 900.
Hearty, *healthy*, 654.

Hearty, *willing*, 602.
   feeling, 821.
   cheerful, 831.
Heat, *warmth*, 382.
   calefaction, 384.
   contest, 720.
   violence, 173.
   excitement, 825.
Heath, 344.
Heathen, *pagan*, 984.
   irreligious, 988.
Heathenish, *vulgar*, 851.
Heather, 344.
Heave, *raise*, 307.
   pant, 821.
Heave in sight, 446.
Heaven, *paradise*, 981.
   bliss, 827.
Heaven-born, 944.
Heaven-directed, 498.
Heavenly, *divine*, 976.
   rapturous, 829.
   celestial, 318.
Heavens, 318.
Heaviness, *inertia*, 172.
   dejection, 837.
Heavy, *weighty*, 319.
   inert, 172.
   slow, 275.
   stupid, 499.
   rude, 851.
   large, 31.
Hebdomadal, 108.
Hebe, 845.
Hebetate, 823.
Hebetude, 499.
Hectic, *fever*, 382.
   flush, 821.
Hector, *courage*, 861.
   bully, 885.
Hedge, 666.
Hedge in, *inclose*, 231.
   safe, 664.
Hedgehog, 253.
Heed, *attend*, 457.
   care, 459.
   caution, 864.
Heedful, 459.
Heedless, *inattentive*, 458.
   neglectful, 460.
Heel, 311.
Heel-piece, 658.
Heel-tap, 40.
Heels, 235.
Heels over head, 460.
Heft, *handle*, 633.
   exertion, 686.
Heigh ho! 839.
Height, *altitude*, 206.
   degree, 26.
318

Heighten, *increase*, 35.
   aggravate, 835.
Heinous, 945.
Heir, *possessor*, 779.
   futurity, 121.
Heir-loom, 780.
Helix, 248.
Hell, *gehenna*, 982.
   abyss, 208.
Hell-born, 945.
Hellebore, 663.
Hell-hound, *miscreant*, 949.
   ruffian, 913.
Hellish, *bad*, 649.
   malevolent, 907.
   vicious, 945.
Helm, *handle*, 633.
   authority, 737.
   sceptre, 747.
Helmet, 225.
Helot, 746.
Help, *aid*, 707.
   auxiliary, 711.
   utility, 644.
   remedy, 662.
   (not to) 601.
Helpless, *weak*, 160.
   incapable, 158.
   exposed, 665.
Helpmate, *auxiliary*, 711.
   wife, 903.
Helter-skelter, *disorder*, 59.
   haste, 684.
Hem, *edge*, 230.
Hem! 870.
Hem in, *inclose*, 231.
   restrain, 751.
*Hemi, 91.
Hemlock, 663.
Henbane, 663.
Hence, *arising from*, 155.
   deduction, 476.
Henceforth, 121.
Henceforwards, 121.
Henchman, 746.
Henpecked, 743.
Herald, *messenger*, 534.
   omen, 512.
   to predict, 511.
   to proclaim, 531.
Herb, 367.
Herculean, 159.
Herd, *animal*, 366.
   flock, 72.
Here, 186.
Hereabouts, 197.
Hereafter, 121.
Hereditament, 780.
Hereditary, *derivative*, 154.
   habit, 613.

Heresy, *error*, 495.
   religious, 984.
Heretofore, 122.
Herewith, 88.
   possession, 777.
Heritage, *futurity*, 121.
Heritor, 779.
Hermaphrodite, 83.
Hermetically, 261.
Hermit, 893.
Hermitage, 189.
Hero, *brave*, 861.
   saint, 948.
Heroic, *brave*, 861.
   glorious, 873.
   magnanimous, 942.
Herring, *pungent*, 392.
Hesitate, *reluctant*, 603.
   irresolute, 605.
   fearful, 860.
   sceptical, 485.
   to stammer, 583.
Hest, 741.
Heteroclite, 83.
Heterodox, 984.
Heterogeneous, *mixed*, 41.
   multiform, 81.
   exceptional, 83.
Hew, *cut*, 44.
   shorten, 201.
   fashion, 240.
Heyday, *wonder*, 870.
   festivity, 840.
   exultation, 836.
*Hiatus, *interval*, 198.
   opening, 260.
   discontinuity, 70.
Hibernal, 383.
Hibernicism, 497.
Hid, *invisible*, 447.
   concealed, 528.
Hidalgo, 875.
Hide, *conceal*, 528.
   skin, 222.
Hideous, 846.
Hiding-place, *refuge*, 666.
   ambush, 530.
Hie, 274.
Hierarchy, 995.
Hieroglyphic, *letter*, 561.
   representation, 554.
Hierogram, 985.
Hierographa, 985.
Hieromancy, 511.
Hierophant, 996.
Hieroscopy, 511.
Higgle, *chaffer*, 794.
   bargain, 769.
Higgledy-piggledy, 59.
Higgler, 797.

High, *lofty*, 206.
   proud, 878.
   magnanimous, 942.
Highborn, 875.
Higher, 33.
Highflier, 515.
Highflown, *proud*, 878.
   vain, 880.
   insolent, 885.
   dashing, 882.
Highland, 342.
High-life, 852.
Highly, 31.
Highminded, *proud*, 878.
   generous, 942.
   honorable, 940.
Highness, *title*, 877.
   prince, 745.
High-priced, 814.
High-seasoned, 392.
High-spirited, 861.
Hight, 564.
Highway, 627.
Highwayman, 792.
Highwrought, *perfect*, 650.
   finished, 729.
   excited, 825.
Hilarity, 836.
Hill, 206.
Hillock, 206.
Hilt, 633.
Hind, *back*, 235.
   clown, 876.
Hinder, *back*, 235.
   end, 67.
   to impede, 179.
   obstruct, 706.
   prohibit, 761.
Hindrance, 706.
Hinge, *depend upon*, 154.
   cause, 153.
   rotate, 312.
Hinny, 271.
Hint, *suggest*, 505.
   inform, 527.
   suppose, 514.
Hip, 236.
Hipped, 837.
Hippocentaur, 83.
Hippogriff, 83.
Hire, *commission*, 755.
   purchase, 795.
Hireling, *servant*, 746.
Hirsute, 256.
Hispid, 256.
Hiss, *sound*, 409.
   disapprobation, 932.
   disrespect, 929.
Histology, 329.
Historian, 553.

Historic, 550.
History, *record*, 551.
   narrative, 594.
Histrionic, 599.
Hit, *strike*, 276.
   punish, 972.
   succeed, 731.
   chance, 156, 621.
   reach, 293.
Hit off, 19.
Hit upon, *find*, 480.
Hitch, *difficulty*, 704.
   hang, 214.
Hither, 293.
Hitherto, 122.
Hive, *workshop*, 691.
   dwelling, 186.
Hoar, *white*, 430.
   aged, 128.
Hoar-frost, 363.
Hoard, 636.
Hoarse, *sound*, 405.
   voice, 581.
Hoary, *white*, 430.
   aged, 128.
Hoax, 545.
Hob, 215.
Hobbardy-hoy, 129.
Hobble, *limp*, 275.
   difficulty, 704.
   lame, 732.
   awkward, 699.
Hobby, *pursuit*, 622.
   desire, 865.
Hobgoblin, 980.
Hob-nob, 894.
Hobson's choice, 601.
Hocus, 545.
Hocus-pocus, *cheat*, 545.
   conjuration, 992.
Hod, *receptacle*, 191.
   vehicle, 272.
Hoddy-doddy, 501.
Hodge-podge, *mixture*, 41.
   confusion, 59.
Hog, *sensuality*, 954.
   gluttony, 957.
Hogwash, 653.
Hoiden, 851.
Hoist, 307.
Hoity-toity! 870.
Hold, *possess*, 777.
   believe, 484.
   retain, 781.
   cohere, 46.
   stop, 265.
   discontinue, 141.
   continue, 142, 143.
   refrain, 623.
   contain, 54.

Hold, *influence*, 175.
   prison, 752.
   in a ship, 207.
Holdfast, 45.
Hold forth, *declaim*, 582.
   teach, 537.
Hold good, 494.
Hold in, 174.
Hold on, *move*, 264.
   continue, 142, 143.
   determination, 604.
Hold out, *resist*, 718.
   offer, 763.
Hold together, 43.
Hold the tongue, 403, 585.
Hold up, *sustain*, 707.
   continue, 143.
Holder, 779.
Hole, *opening*, 260.
   place, 182.
   receptacle, 191.
   ambush, 530.
   hovel, 189.
Holiday, *amusement*, 840.
   repose, 687.
   leisure, 685.
   time, 134.
Holiness, 976.
Hollow, *concavity*, 252.
   depth, 208.
   incomplete, 53.
   false, 544.
   unsubstantial, 4.
   sound, 408.
   cry, 839.
Holm, 346.
Holocaust, 991.
Holt, 367.
Holy, 976, 987.
HOLY GHOST, 976.
Holy Writ, 985.
Homage, *reverence*, 928.
   approbation, 931.
   worship, 990.
Home, *habitation*, 189.
   interior, 221.
   near, 197.
   arrival, 293.
Homebred, 851.
Homefelt, 821.
Homely,   } *simple*, 849.
Homespun, }
   ugly, 846.
   vulgar, 851.
   low, 876.
   style, 575.
Homestall, 189.
Homestead, 189.
Homicide, 361.
Homiletical, 892.

Homily, *advice*, 595.
    sermon, 998.
Homœopathic, 193.
Homogeneity, *relation*, 9.
    uniformity, 16.
    simplicity, 42.
Homology, *relation*, 9.
    simplicity, 16.
Homonym, *word*, 562.
    equivocal, 520.
Honest, *pure*, 960.
    true, 543.
    honor, 939.
Honey, 396.
Honeycomb, 252.
Honeymoon, *wedding*, 903.
    happiness, 827.
Honor, 939.
    glory, 873.
    title, 877.
    respect, 928.
    to pay, 807.
*Honorarium, 809.
Honorary, 815.
Hood, *cowl*, 999.
    cap, 225.
Hoodwink, *blind*, 442.
    conceal, 528.
    ignore, 491.
Hook, *to fasten*, 43.
    fastening, 45.
    hang, 214.
    angle, 244.
    take, 780.
Hoop, *circle*, 247.
    cry, 412.
    loud, 404.
Hoot, *cry*, 411.
    deride, 929.
    scout, 932.
Hop, *leap*, 305, 309.
    dance, 840.
Hop the twig, *move off*, 286.
    die, 360.
Hope, 858.
Hopeful, *probable*, 472.
Hopeless, *desperate*, 859.
    impossible, 471.
    irreparable, 659.
Horde, 72.
Horizon, *distance*, 196.
    view, 441.
    futurity, 121.
Horn, *sharpness*, 253.
    (French), 417.
Horn-book, 542.
Horn-mad, 920.
Horn of plenty, 639.
Hornet, 6: 3.
Hornpipe, 840.
3.0

Hornwork, 717.
Horology, 114.
Horoscope, 511.
Horrible, *great*, 31.
    fearful, 860.
Horrid, *noxious*, 649.
    ugly, 846.
    dire, 830.
    vulgar, 851.
    fearful, 860.
    hateful, 898.
Horripilation, 383.
Horror, *dislike*, 867.
    hate, 898.
Horse, *animal*, 271.
    cavalry, 726.
    stand, 215.
Horse-laugh, 838.
Horseman, 268.
Horseshoe, 245.
Horsewhip, 972.
Hortation, 695.
Horticulture, 371.
Hortus siccus, 367.
Hosanna, 990.
Hospice, 189.
Hospitable, *social*, 892.
    liberal, 816.
Hospital, 662.
Hospodar, 745.
Host, *multitude*, 100.
    collection, 72.
    friend, 890.
    religious, 999.
Hostage, 771.
Hostilities, 722.
Hostility, 889.
Hot, *warm*, 382.
    pungent, 392.
    irascible, 901.
Hot-bed, *workshop*, 691.
    cause, 153.
    school, 542.
Hotch-potch, *mixture*, 41.
    confusion, 59.
Hotel, 189.
Hot-brained, } *rash*, 863.
Hot-headed, } *excited*, 825.
Hothouse, *conservatory*, 386
    workshop, 691.
Hotspur, *rashness*, 863.
    courage, 861.
Hottentot, 876.
Hot-water, 704.
Hough, 649.
Hound, *follow*, 281.
    pursue, 622.
    wretch, 949.
Hour, 108.
Hour-glass, *time*, 114.

Hour-glass, *form*, 203.
Houri, 845.
House, *abode*, 189.
    to locate, 184.
    safety, 664.
    party, 712.
    senate, 696.
    partnership, 797.
Housebreaker, 792.
Householder, *abode*, 189.
    genuine, 648.
    property, 780.
Housekeeper, 694.
Housekeeping, 692.
Houseless, 185.
Housewarming, 892.
Housewife, 682.
Housewifery, *conduct*, 692.
    economy, 817.
Housing, *lodging*, 189.
Hovel, 189.
Hover, *soar*, 267.
    rise, 305.
    high, 206.
How, *in what way*, 627.
    by what means, 632.
Howbeit, 179.
However, *except*, 83.
    notwithstanding, 179.
    degree, 23.
Howitzer, 727.
Howl, 411, 412.
Howsoever, 26.
Hoy, 273.
Hubbub, *noise*, 402.
    discord, 713.
Huckster, 797.
Huddle, *mix*, 41.
    disorder, 59.
    derange, 61.
    collect, 72.
    don, 225.
    nearness, 197.
Hue, 428.
Hue and cry, *noise*, 404.
    proclaim, 531.
Hueless, 429.
Huff, *anger*, 900.
    insolence, 885.
Huffiness, 901.
Hug, *cohere*, 46.
    retain, 781.
    endearment, 902.
    courtesy, 894.
Huge, *in degree*, 31.
    in size, 192.
Huke, 225.
Hulk, 50.
    ship, 273.
Hulky, *big*, 192.

Hulky, *awkward*, 853.
Hullabaloo, *noise*, 404.
   cry, 411.
Hum, *faint sound*, 405.
   continued sound, 407.
   to sing, 415.
   deceive, 545.
Hum and haw, *hesitate*,583.
   demur, 605.
Humane, *benevolent*, 906.
   philanthropic, 910.
Humanities, *letters*, 560.
Humanity, *human nature*,
   372.
Humanize, 894.
Humble, *meek*, 879.
   modest, 881.
   to abash, 874.
   pious, 987.
Humbug, *deception*, 545.
   falsehood, 544.
Humectate, *moisten*, 339.
Humid, 339.
Humiliate, *humble*, 879.
   shame, 874.
   worship, 990.
Humility, *piety*, 987.
Humming-top, 417.
Hummock, 206.
Humorist, 844.
Humour, *essence*, 5.
   liquid, 333.
   disposition, 602.
   caprice, 608.
   indulge, 760.
   affections, 820.
   to please, 829.
Humoursome, *capricious*,
   608.
   discourteous, 895.
Hump, 250.
Humpback, 846.
Humph! 870.
Hunch, 250.
Hundred, 99.
Hunger, 865.
Hunks, 819.
Hunt, *follow*, 281.
   pursue, 622.
   inquire, 461.
Hunter, 271.
Hurdle, 272.
Hurdy-gurdy, 417.
Hurl, 284.
Hurly-burly, *confusion*, 59.
   turmoil, 315.
Hurrah! 836.
Hurricane, *tempest*, 349.
   violence, 173.
Hurried, 825.

Hurry, *haste*, 684.
   swiftness, 274.
   earliness, 132.
   to urge, 615.
   to excite, 824.
Hurst, 367.
Hurt, *evil*, 619.
   physical pain, 378.
   moral pain, 828.
   to injure, 649.
   to molest, 830.
Hurtful, 649.
Hurtless, 648.
Husband, *spouse*, 903.
   to store, 636.
Husbandman, 371.
Husbandry,*agriculture*,371
   conduct, 692.
   economy, 817.
Hush, *silence*, 403.
   moderate, 174.
   assuage, 826.
   pacify, 723.
Hush up, *conceal*, 528.
Hush-money, 809.
Husk, 222.
Husky, *dry*, 340.
   faint sound, 405.
Hussar, 726.
Hussey, 962.
Hustings, *tribunal*, 966.
   school, 542.
Hustle, *push*, 276.
   agitate, 315.
Huswifery, *economy*, 817.
   conduct, 692.
Hut, 189.
Huzza! 836.
Huzzar (*or* hussar), 726.
Hyaline, 425.
Hydra, 83.
Hyæna (*or* hyena), 913.
Hybernation, 683.
Hybrid, 83.
Hydraulicostatics, 348.
Hydraulics, 348.
Hydrology, 333.
Hydromancy, 511.
Hydromel, 396.
Hydrometer, 321.
Hydropathy, 958.
Hydrophobia, 867.
Hydrostatics, 333.
Hyemal, 383.
Hyena, 913.
Hygiastics, 670.
Hymen, 903.
Hymn, 990.
Hyperbole, 549.
Hyperboreal, 383.

Hypercritical, 932.
Hyperion, 845.
Hypertrophy, 192.
Hyphen, 45.
Hypnology, 683.
Hypochondriac, 837.
Hypocrisy, *deception*, 545.
   religious, 989.
Hypocrite, 548.
Hypocritical, 544.
Hypostasis,*substantiality*,3.
Hypostatic, 976.
Hypothecation, 787.
Hypothesis, 514.
Hysteric, 173.

I.

Icarus, 305.
Ice, 383.
Ice-house, 387.
Ichnography, 554.
Ichor, 333.
Ichthyomancy, 511.
Icicle, 383.
Icon, 554.
Idea, *notion*, 453.
   belief, 484.
   knowledge, 490.
   small degree, 32.
   small quantity, 192.
   inexistence, 2.
Ideal, *erroneous*, 495.
   unreal, 2.
Ideality, *intellect*, 450.
   imagination, 515.
Identify, 464.
Identity, 13.
Idiocrasy, 5.
Idiocy, 499.
Idiology, 450.
Idiosyncrasy, *essence*, 5.
   speciality, 79.
Idiom, *phrase*, 566.
   style, 569.
Idiot, *imbecile*, 501.
   foolish, 499.
Idle, *slothful*, 683.
   trivial, 643.
Idolatry, *superstition*, 984.
   impious worship, 991.
   love, 897.
Idolism, 991.
Idolize, *love*, 897.
   impiety, 989.
Idyl, 597.
Ieromancy, 511.
If, *supposition*, 514.
   qualification, 469.

Igneous, 382.
*Ignis fatuus, *light*, 420.
   phantom, 515.
Ignite, 384.
Ignition, 382.
Ignoble, 876.
Ignominy, *dishonor*, 940.
   shame, 874.
Ignoramus, 493.
Ignorance, 491.
Ignore, *repudiate*, 773.
   dissent, 489.
Ilk, 13.
Ill, *sick*, 655.
   evil, 619.
Ill-advised, 499, 699.
Illaqueate, *entrap*, 665.
Illation, 480.
Ill-bred, 895.
Ill-conditioned, *difficult*, 704.
   discourteous, 895.
   malevolent, 907.
Ill-devised, 499.
Illegal, 964.
Illegible, 519.
Illegitimate, *undue*, 925.
   illegal, 964.
   erroneous, 495.
Ill-favoured, 846.
Ill-flavoured, 395.
Illiberal, *selfish*, 943.
   stingy, 819.
Illicit, 964.
Illimited, *infinite*, 105.
   great, 31.
Illiterate, 491.
Ill-looking, 846.
Ill-natured, 907.
Illness, 655.
Ill-judged, *foolish*, 492, 499.
   ill-advised, 699.
Ill-off, 735.
Illogical, *sophistical*, 477.
   erroneous, 495.
Ill-starred, 735.
Ill-temper, *discourtesy*, 895.
   irascibility, 901.
Ill-timed, 24.
Ill-treat, 649.
Ill-turn, 619.
Illuminate, *enlighten*, 420.
   colour, 428.
*Illuminati, 492.
Illusion, *error*, 495.
   deceit, 545.
Illusive, } *erroneous*, 495.
Illusory, } *sophistical*, 477.
   deceitful, 544.

Illustrate, *interpret*, 522.
Illustrious, 873.
Ill-will, 907.
Image, *representation*, 554.
   idea, 453.
   statue, 557.
   likeness, 17.
Imagery, *metaphor*, 521.
   fancy, 515.
Imaginary, *non-existing*, 2.
   erroneous, 495.
   quantity, 84.
Imagine, 515.
Imaum, 996.
Imbecile, *foolish*, 499.
   weak, 160.
   incapable, 158.
Imbibe, *receive*, 297.
   learn, 539.
Imbricated, 222.
Imbrue, *moisten*, 339.
   impregnate, 301.
Imbue, *mix*, 41.
   tinge, 428.
   impregnate, 301.
   moisten, 339.
   feel, 821.
Imitate, *to copy*, 19.
   to represent, 554.
Imitation, *copy*, 21.
Immaculate, *excellent*, 648.
   spotless, 652.
   faultless, 650.
   innocent, 946.
Immanent, *inherent*, 5.
Immanity, 907.
Immaterial, *spiritual*, 317.
   trifling, 643.
Immature, *new*, 123.
   unprepared, 674.
Immeasurable, *infinite*, 105.
   great, 31.
Immediate, 111.
Immedicable, 659.
Immemorial, 124.
Immense, *in degree*, 31.
   in size, 192.
Immensurable, 105.
Immerge, } *introduce*, 301.
Immerse, } *dip*, 337.
Immethodical, 59.
Immigration, *migration*, 266.
   entrance, 295.
Imminent, 121.
Immission, 297.
Immitigable, *ire*, 900.
   ruin, 659.
Immix, 41.

Immobility, *immutability*, 150.
   quiescence, 265.
   resolution, 604.
Immoderately, 31.
Immodest, 961.
Immolate, *destroy*, 162.
   kill, 361.
   offer, 763.
Immoral, *vicious*, 945.
   wrong, 923.
Immortal, *perpetual*, 112.
   glorious, 873.
   celebrated, 883.
Immovable, 150, 604.
Immundicity, 653.
Immunity, *exemption*, 927.
   right, 924.
   freedom, 748.
Immure, *enclose*, 231.
   imprison, 751.
Immutable, 150.
Imp, *demon*, 980.
   ruffian, 913.
   wretch, 943.
Impact, *contact*, 43.
   insertion, 301.
Impair, 659.
Impale. *See* Empale.
Impalpable, *small*, 193.
   powder, 330.
   intangible, 381.
Impanation, 998.
Imparity, 28.
Impart, *give*, 784.
   inform, 527.
Impartial, *just*, 922.
   honorable, 939.
Impassable, *closed*, 261.
Impassion, *excite*, 824.
Impassive, 823.
Impatient, 825.
Impawn, 787.
Impeach, 938.
Impeccability, 650.
Impede, 706.
Impedite, 706.
Impel, *push*, 276.
   induce, 615.
Impend, *future*, 121.
   height, 206.
   destiny, 152.
Impenetrable, *latent*, 526.
   hidden, 528.
Impenitence, 951.
Imperative, 737.
Imperceptible, *invisible*, 447.
   minute, 193.
Impercipient, 376.

Imperfect, *incomplete*, 53.
  failing, 651.
  vicious, 945.
  small, 32.
Imperforate, 261.
Imperial, 737.
Imperil, 605.
Imperious, *stern*, 739.
  insolent, 885.
Imperishable, *eternal*, 112.
  glorious, 873.
Impermeable, *closed*, 261.
  dense, 321.
Impersonal, 78.
Impersonate, 554.
Impertinent, *inexpedient*, 647.
  irrelevant, 10.
  disagreeing, 24.
  insolent, 885.
Imperturbable, 826.
Impervious, 261.
Impetrate, *beseech*, 765.
  refuse, 764.
Impetuous, *boisterous*, 173.
  hot, 825.
  hasty, 684.
  eager, 865.
Impetus, 276.
Impiety, 989.
Impignorate, 787.
Impinge, 276.
Implacable, *hatred*, 898.
  wrath, 900.
  unforgiving, 919.
Implanted, *adventitious*, 6.
Implant, *insert*, 301.
  teach, 537.
Implement, 633.
Impletion, 639.
Implex, 41.
Implicate, *accuse*, 938.
  involve, 54.
Implication, *metaphor*, 521.
Implicit, *understood*, 516.
  metaphorical, 521.
  trust, 484.
Implore, *beseech*, 765.
  pray, 990.
  pity, 914.
Imply, *mean*, 516.
  latent, 526.
  evidence, 467.
  metaphor, 521.
Impolite, *rude*, 895.
  vulgar, 851.
Impolitic, 499.
Imponderable, 320.
Imponderous, 320.
Imporous, *closed*, 261.

323

Imporous, *dense*, 321.
Import, *ingress*, 295.
  insert, 301.
  mean, 516.
  be of consequence, 642.
Important, 642.
Importation, 297.
Importunate, 830.
Importune, *ask*, 765.
  pester, 830.
Impose, *order*, 741.
  cheat, 545.
  be unjust, 923.
  palm upon, 486.
Imposing, *glorious*, 873.
Impossible, 471.
Impost, 812.
Impostor, 548.
Imposture, 545.
Impotence, 158.
Impound, *enclose*, 231.
  imprison, 751.
Impoverish, *drain*, 638.
  render poor, 804.
Impracticable, *difficult*, 704.
  impossible, 471.
Imprecate, 765.
Imprecation, *request*, 765.
  malediction, 908.
Impregnable, 664.
Impregnate, *insert*, 301.
  mix, 41.
  teach, 537.
Imprescriptible, 924.
Impress, *mark*, 550.
  memory, 505.
  excite, 824.
Impressible, 822.
Impression, *belief*, 484.
  idea, 453.
  feeling, 821.
  engraving, 558.
*Imprimis, 66.
Imprint, 505.
Imprison, *shut up*, 751.
  circumscribe, 231.
Improbable, 473.
Improbate, 932.
Improbity, 940.
*Impromptu, 612.
Improper, *wrong*, 923.
  inexpedient, 647.
  incongruous, 24.
Impropriate, *take*, 789.
  possess, 777.
Improsperous, 735.
Improve, 658.
Improvident, *careless*, 460.
  not preparing, 674.

*Improvisé, 612.
Imprudent, *rash*, 863.
  unwise, 699.
  neglectful, 460.
Impudent, 885.
Impudicity, 961.
Impugn, *blame*, 932.
  attack, 716.
  deny, 536.
Impuissance, 158.
Impulse, *push*, 276.
  unpremeditation, 612.
  necessity, 601.
Impunity, 970.
Impure, *foul*, 653.
  licentious, 961.
Impute, *ascribe*, 155.
  accuse, 938.
Inability, *want of power*, 158.
  want of skill, 699.
Inaccessible, 196.
Inaccurate, 495.
Inaction, 681.
Inactivity, 683.
Inadequate, *insufficient*, 640.
  imperfect, 651.
  weak, 160.
Inadmissible, *inexpedient*, 647.
  incongruous, 24.
  excluded, 55.
Inadvertence, 458.
Inalienable, *right*, 924.
  possession, 777.
*Inamorata, 897.
Inane, *trivial*, 643.
  void, 4.
Inanimate, *dead*, 360.
  inorganic, 358.
Inanition, 640.
Inanity, *inutility*, 645.
  insignificance, 643.
Inappetency, 866.
Inapplicable, 24.
Inapposite, 24.
Inappreciable, *in size*, 193.
  in degree, 32.
Inappropriate, 24.
Inapt, *inexpedient*, 647.
  incongruous, 24.
Inarticulate, 583.
Inartificial, 703.
Inattention, 458.
Inaudible, *silent*, 403.
  mute, 581.
Inaugurate, *begin*, 66.
  celebrate, 883.
Inauspicious, *hopeless*, 859.

Inauspicious, *untimely*, 135.
   untoward, 649.
Inbeing, 5.
Inborn, 5.
Inbred, 5.
Incage, 751.
Incalculable, *infinite*, 105.
   much, 31.
Incalescence, 382.
Incandescence, 382.
Incantation,   *invocation*,
   765.
   spell, 993.
Incapable, *weak*, 160.
   unable, 158.
Incapacious, 203.
Incapacity, *impotence*, 158.
   weakness, 160.
   stupidity, 499.
   indocility, 538.
Incarcerate,   *imprison*,
   751.
   surround, 231.
Incarnadine, 434.
Incarnation, 5.
Incautious, 460, 863.
Incendiary, 913.
Incense, *fragrance*, 400.
   to provoke, 900.
   hatred, 898.
   flattery, 933.
   worship, 990.
Incentive, 615.
Inception, 66.
Inceptor, 541.
Incertitude, 475.
Incessant, 112.
Incest, 961.
Inch, 193.
Inchoation, 66.
Incide, 44.
Incidence, 278.
Incident, 151.
Incidental, *extrinsic*, 6.
   liable, 177.
   casual, 621.
   irrelative, 10.
Incinerate, 384.
Incipience, 66.
Incircumspect, 460.
Incision, *cut*, 44.
   open, 260.
Incite, *urge*, 615.
   exasperate, 173.
Incivility, 895.
Incivism, 911.
Inclement, *cold*, 383.
   severe, 739.
Incline, *slope*, 217.
   direction, 278.

Incline, *tendency*, 176.
   willing, 602.
   desire, 862.
   love, 897.
   induce, 615.
Inclose, 232.
Inclusive, *in a compound*,
   54.
   in a class, 76.
Incogitable, 452.
Incogitancy, 452.
*Incognito, 528.
Incoherence, *physical*, 47.
   mental, 503.
Incombustible, 383.
Income, *receipt*, 810.
   wealth, 803.
Incommensurable, *quantity*,
   84.
   irrelation, 10.
   disagreeing, 24.
Incommode,   *to hinder*,
   706.
Incommodious,   *inconve-*
   nient, 647.
Incommunicable, 781.
Incomparable, 648.
Incompassionate, 907.
Incompatible, 24.
Incompetence,   *inability*,
   158.
   incapacity, 499.
Incomplete, *defective*, 53.
   not completed, 730.
Incomprehensible, 519.
Incompressible, 321.
Inconceivable, 519.
Inconcinnity, 24.
Inconclusive, 477.
Inconcoction, 674.
Incongruous, 24.
Inconnexion, 44.
Inconsiderable, *in size*, 193.
   in degree, 32.
Inconsiderate, *thoughtless*,
   452.
   heedless, 460.
   foolish, 699.
Inconsistent, *contrary*, 14.
   disagreeing, 24.
   absurd, 497.
Inconsolable, 828.
Inconstant, 605.
Incontestible, 474.
Incontiguous, 196.
Incontinent, 961.
Incontinently, 111.
Incontrovertible, 474.
Inconvenient, 647.
Inconversible, 893.

Inconvertible, 150.
Inconvincible, 487.
Incorporal, 317.
Incorporate, 48.
Incorporeity, 317.
Incorrect, *erroneous*, 495.
   sophistical, 477.
Incorrigible, *vicious*, 945.
   impenitent, 951.
   irremediable, 649.
Incorruptible,   *honorable*,
   939.
   pure, 942.
Incorruption, *health*, 654.
   innocence, 946.
Incrassate, *thickness*, 202.
   density, 321.
Increase, *in degree*, 35.
   in size, 194.
Incredible, *impossible*, 471.
   improbable, 473.
   much, 31.
   wonderful, 870.
Incredulity, *unbelief*, 487.
   religious, 988.
Increment, *in degree*, 35.
   in size, 194.
   addition, 39.
Increpation, 932.
Incrust, *line*, 224.
   coat, 222.
Incubation, 673.
*Incubus, 706.
Inculcate, 537.
Inculpate, 938.
Inculture, 674.
Incumbent, *height*, 206.
   weight, 319.
   duty, 926.
   clergyman, 996.
Incur, 177.
Incurable, 655.
Incuriosity, 456.
Incursion, 295.
Incurvation, 245.
Indagation, 461.
Indebted, *owing*, 806.
   duty, 926.
   gratitude, 916.
Indecent, 961.
Indecision, 605.
Indecisive, 475.
Indeclinable, 150.
Indecorum, *vice*, 945.
   impurity, 961.
   vulgarity, 851.
Indeed, *very*, 31.
   wonder, 870.
   truth, 494.
   assertion, 535.

Infantile, *puerile*, 643.
  foolish, 499.
Infantry, 726.
Infarction, 261.
Infatuation, *folly*, 499.
  obstinacy, 606.
  credulity, 486.
  insanity, 503.
  passion, 825.
  love, 897.
Infeasible, 471, 704.
Infection, *disease*, 655.
  contamination, 659.
  excitation, 824.
Infectious, 657.
Infecund, 169.
Infelicity, *unhappiness*, 828.
  inexpertness, 699.
Infer, 480.
Inference, 480, 522.
Inferiority, 34.
Infernal, *bad*, 649.
  wicked, 945.
  malevolent, 907.
Infertility, 169.
Infest, 830.
Infestivity, *dulness*, 843.
  sadness, 837.
Infidelity, *dishonor*, 940.
  irreligion, 988.
Infiltrate, *intervene*, 228.
  imbue, 339.
  teach, 537.
Infinite, *in quantity*, 105.
  in degree, 31.
Infinitesimal, *in degree*, 32.
  in quantity, 193.
Infirm, *weak*, 160.
  irresolute, 605.
  vicious, 945.
Infirmary, 662.
Infirmity, *weakness*, 160.
  disease, 655.
  failing, 945.
Infix, 537.
Inflame, *burn*, 384.
  incite, 615.
Inflate, *expand*, 194.
  rarefy, 322.
  blow, 349.
  style, 573, 577.
  ridiculous, 853.
  vanity, 880.
Inflect, 245.
Inflexible, *hard*, 323.
  resolved, 604.
  stern, 739.
Inflexion, 245.
Inflict, *condemn*, 971.
  act upon, 680.
326

Inflict, *give pain*, 830.
Influence, *physical*, 175.
  authority, 737.
  inducement, 615.
  importance, 642.
Influential, 642.
Influx, 295.
Infold, 231.
Inform, 527.
Inform against, 938.
Informal, *irregular*, 83.
  lawless, 964.
Information, *knowledge*, 490.
  communication, 527.
Infraction, *non-observance*,
  773.
  exemption, 927.
  disobedience, 742.
  violation, 614.
Infrequency, 137.
Infrigidation, 385.
Infringe, *transgress*, 303.
  violate, 773, 925, 927.
  disobey, 742.
  break through, 614.
Infundibuliform, 252.
Infuriate, *wrathful*, 900.
  violent, 173.
Infuscate, 431.
Infuse, *mix*, 41.
  insert, 301.
  teach, 537.
Ingannation, 90.
Ingenious, 698.
*Ingénu, 543.
Ingenuous, *artless*, 703.
  sincere, 543.
  guileless, 939.
Ingest, 297.
Ingle, 388.
Inglorious, 874.
Ingot, 800.
Ingraft, *insert*, 301.
  join, 43.
  add, 37.
  teach, 537.
  implant, 6.
Ingrained, *imbued*, 5.
  combined, 48.
Ingratiate, 897.
Ingratitude, 917.
Ingredient, 56.
Ingress, 295.
Ingulf, 297.
Ingurgitate, 297.
Inhabile, 699.
Inhabit, 186.
Inhabitant, 188.
Inhale, 297.
Inharmonious, 414.

Inherence, 5.
Inherit, *acquire*, 775.
  possess, 777.
Inhesion, 5.
Inhibit, *prohibit*, 761.
  hinder, 706.
Inhospitable, 893.
Inhuman, 907.
Inhume, 363.
Inimical, 889.
Inimitable, *perfect*, 650.
  good, 648.
Iniquity, *wrong*, 923.
  vice, 945.
Inirritability, 826.
Initiate, *begin*, 66.
  teach, 537.
Initiated, *skilful*, 698.
Inject, 301.
Injudicious, 499.
Injunction, *command*, 741.
  advice, 695.
  decree, 963.
Injure, *to damage*, 659.
  malevolence, 907.
Injury, *harm*, 649.
Injustice, 923.
Ink, 431.
Inkling, *information*, 527.
  knowledge, 490.
Inlaid, 440.
Inland, 221.
Inlay, 440.
Inlet, *opening*, 260.
  way, 627.
  beginning, 66.
  of the sea, 343.
Inly, 221.
Inmate, 188.
Inmost, 221.
Inn, 189.
Innate, 5.
Innavigable, 704.
Inner, 221.
Innocence, 946.
Innocuous, 648.
Innominate, 565.
Innovation, *newness*, 123.
  change, 140.
Innoxious, *innocent*, 946.
  salubrious, 656.
Innuendo, 527.
Innumerable, 105.
Inoculate, *insert*, 301.
  teach, 537.
Inodorous, 399.
Inoffensive, 946.
Inofficious, 907.
Inoperative, *unproductive*,
  169.

Inoperative, *useless*, 645.
Inopportune, *untimely*, 135.
 inexpedient, 647.
Inordinate, *size*, 192.
 excessive, 31.
Inorganic, 358.
Inosculate, *intersect*, 219.
 convoluted, 248.
 joined, 43.
Inquest, 461.
Inquietude, *uneasiness*, 828.
 apprehension, 860.
 discontent, 832.
 restlessness, 264.
 disorder, 59.
Inquinate, *deteriorate*, 659.
 badness, 649.
Inquiry, *search*, 461.
 curiosity, 455.
Inquisition, 965.
Inroad, *ingress*, 295.
 invasion, 716.
 devastation, 619.
Insalubrity, 657.
Insane, 504.
Insanity, 503.
Insatiable, 865.
Inscribe, *write*, 590.
 label, 551.
 represent, 554.
Inscrutable, 519.
Insculpture, 557.
Insect, *animal*, 366.
 minute, 193.
Insecure, 665.
Insensate, *foolish*, 499.
 mad, 503.
Insensibility, *physical*, 376.
 moral, 823.
Inseparable, *cohering*, 46.
 attached, 43.
Insert, *put in*, 301.
 locate, 184.
 interpose, 228.
 enter, 295.
Inservient, 645.
Inside, 221.
Insidious, *false*, 544.
 cunning, 702.
 dishonorable, 940.
Insight, 490.
Insignia, 550.
Insignificant, 643.
Insincere, 544.
Insinuate, *intervene*, 228.
 ingress, 295.
 mean, 516.
 suppose, 514.
 hint, 527.
 blame, 932.

Insipid, *tasteless*, 391.
 indifferent, 866.
Insist, 741.
Insnare, *cheat*, 545.
 endanger, 665.
Insobriety, 959.
Insolation, 382.
Insolence, 885.
Insolvable, 519.
Insolvent, 808.
Insomuch, 31.
*Insouciance, *thoughtless-
 ness*, 458.
 supineness, 823.
 indifference, 866.
Inspect, *look*, 441.
 attend to, 457.
Inspector, *spectator*, 444.
 director, 694.
Inspiration, *impulse*, 612.
 imagination, 515.
 wisdom, 498.
 piety, 987.
 revelation, 985.
Inspire, *prompt*, 615.
 animate, 824.
Inspirit, *urge*, 615.
 animate, 824.
 courage, 861.
Inspissation, 352.
Instability, 149.
Install, *locate*, 184.
 commission, 755.
 celebrate, 883.
Instalment, *portion*, 51.
Instance, *example*, 82.
 solicitation, 765.
 motive, 615.
Instant, *moment*, 113.
 present, 118.
 future, 121.
*Instanter, 132.
Instauration, 660.
Instead, 147.
Instigate, 615.
Instil, *insert*, 301.
 mix, 41.
Instinct, *intellect*, 450.
 intuition, 477.
 impulse, 601.
 innate, 5.
Institute, 542.
Institutor, 540.
Instruct, *teach*, 537.
 advise, 695.
 precept, 697.
Instructor, 540.
Instrument, *implement*, 633.
 record, 551.
 security, 771.

Instrumentality, 631.
Insuavity, 895.
Insubordinate, 742.
Insubstantiality, 4.
Insufferable, 830.
Insufficient, 640.
Insufflation, 349.
Insular, *island*, 346.
 detached, 44.
 single, 87.
Insulse, 499.
Insult, *rudeness*, 895.
 offence, 900.
Insuperable, 704.
Insupportable, 830.
Insuppressible, 173.
Insurance, 768.
Insurgent, 742.
Insurmountable, 704.
Insurrection, *disobedience*,
 742.
 resistance, 719.
Insusceptible, 823.
Intact, 142.
Intaglio, 252.
Intangible, 381.
Integer, 50.
Integral calculus, 84.
Integrant part, 56.
Integrate, *consolidate*, 50.
 complete, 52.
Integration, 84.
Integrity, *whole*, 50.
 virtue, 944.
 probity, 939.
Integument, 222.
Intellect, 450.
Intelligence, *mind*, 450.
 news, 532.
Intelligent, 498.
Intelligible, 518.
Intemperate, 954.
Intempestivity, 135.
Intended, 600.
Intensity, *degree*, 26.
 greatness, 31.
 energy, 171.
Intention, *design*, 620.
Intentional, 600.
Intentness, *attention*, 457.
 thought, 451.
Inter, *bury*, 363.
 insert, 301.
Intercalate, *insert*, 301.
 intervene, 228.
Intercede, *mediate*, 724.
 deprecate, 766.
Intercept, *hinder*, 706.
 take, 789.
Intercession, 766.

Interchange, 148.
  barter, 794.
  transfer, 783.
Interclude, 706.
Intercommunity, *sociality*, 892.
Intercourse, 588.
Intercurrence, 302.
Interdict, 761.
Interdigitate,*intervene*,228.
  intersect, 219.
Interest, *advantage*, 618.
  concern, 9.
  debt, 806.
Interfere, *intervene*, 228.
  meddle, 680.
  disagree, 24.
  counteract, 179.
  thwart, 706.
  mediate, 724.
  activity, 682.
Interim, 106.
Interior, 221.
Interjacence, *coming between*, 228.
  middle, 68.
Interject, *insert*, 301.
  interpose, 228.
Interlace, *twine*, 219.
  join, 43.
Interlard, *interpose*, 228.
  mix, 41.
  insert, 301.
Interleave, 228.
Interline, *insert*, 228.
  write, 590.
Interlink, 43.
Interlocation, 228.
Interlocution, 588.
Interloper, *intervene*, 228.
  obstruct, 706.
  extraneous, 57.
Interlude, *dramatic*, 599.
  time, 106.
Intermarriage, 903.
Intermeddle, *hinder*, 706.
  interfere, 682.
Intermediate, *mean*, 29.
  middle, 68.
  intervening, 228.
Intermedium, *link*, 45.
  instrument, 631.
  intervention, 228.
Interment, 363.
Interminable, *infinite*, 105.
  eternal, 112.
  long, 200.
Intermingle, 41.
Intermission, *discontinuance*, 141.
328

Intermit, *interrupt*, 70.
  discontinue, 141.
  recur, 138.
  suspend, 265.
  in time, 106.
Intermix, 41.
Internal, *interior*, 221.
  intrinsic, 5.
International,*reciprocal*,12
  law, 963.
Internecine, *slaughter*, 361.
  war, 722.
Internuncio,*messenger*,534
  consignee, 758.
Interpel, 141.
Interpellation,*inquiry*, 461.
  address, 586.
  appeal, 765.
  summons, 741.
Interpenetration, *passage*, 302.
  ingress, 295.
Interpolate, *intervene*, 228.
  mix, 41.
  analytical, 85.
Interpose, *intervene*, 228.
  mediate, 724.
  act, 682.
  hinder, 706.
Interposit, 799.
Interpret, *explain*, 522.
  answer, 462.
Interpreter, 524.
Interregnum, *laxity*, 738.
  intermission, 106.
  cessation, 141.
  discontinuity, 70.
Interrogate, 461.
Interrupt,*discontinuity*, 70.
  hindrance, 706.
  cessation, 141.
  pause, 265.
Intersect, 219.
Interspace, *interval*, 198.
  interior, 221.
Intersperse, *diffuse*, 73.
  mix, 41.
  intervene, 228.
Interstitial,*interjacent*,228.
  internal, 221.
Intertexture, *tissue*, 329.
  intersection, 219.
Intertwine, *cross*, 219.
Intertwist, *unite*, 43.
Interval, *of space*, 198.
  of order, 70.
  of time, 106.
Intervene, *in space*, 228.
  in time, 106.
  in order, 68.

Intervention, *mediation*, 724.
  instrumentality, 631.
Interview, *conference*, 588.
  society, 892.
Intervolved, 43.
Interweave, 219.
Intestate, 552.
Intestine, 221.
Inthrall, 751.
Intimate, *to tell*, 527.
  friendly, 888.
  close, 197.
Intimidate, *frighten*, 860.
  insolence, 885.
  threat, 909.
Intolerable, 830.
Intolerant, *impatient*, 825.
  insolent, 885.
  prejudice, 481.
Intomb, 363.
Intonation, *sound*, 402.
  voice, 580.
Intoxicate, *excite*, 824, 825.
  inebriate, 959.
Intractable, *difficult*, 704.
  obstinate, 606.
  discourteous, 895.
Intransient, 110.
Intransitive, 110.
Intransmutable, 110.
Intraregarding, 221.
Intrench, 717.
Intrepid, 861.
Intricate, *difficult*, 704.
  confused, 59.
  perplexed, 519.
Intrigue, *plot*, 626.
  cunning, 702.
  activity, 682.
  licentiousness, 961.
Intrinsic, 5.
Introduction, *ingress*, 295.
  insertion, 301.
  precursor, 64.
  acquaintance, 888.
  presentation, 894.
Introductory,*preceding*,62
  precursory, 116.
  beginning, 66.
Introgression, 295.
Intromit, *receive*, 297.
  discontinue, 141.
Introspection,*look into*,441.
  attend to, 457.
Introvert, *invert*, 218.
  evolve, 313.
Intrude, *intervene*, 228.
  enter, 295.
  inopportune, 135.

Intrude, *interfere*, 24.
Intruder, 57.
Intuition, *mind*, 450.
 knowledge, 490.
Intuitive, 477.
Intumescence, 250.
Intwine, 43.
Inunction, 222.
Inundate, *effusion*, 337.
 flow, 348.
 redundance, 641.
Inunderstanding, 452.
Inurbanity, 895.
Inure, *habituate*, 613.
 train, 673.
 harden, 823.
Inusitation, 614.
Inutility, 645.
Invade, *ingress*, 295.
 attack, 716.
Invalid, 655.
Invalidate, *disable*, 158.
 disentitle, 925.
 confute, 479.
 rebut, 468.
Invalidity, 479.
Invaluable, 648.
Invariable, 150.
Invasion, *ingress*, 295.
 attack, 716.
Invective, 938.
Inveigh, *blame*, 932.
Inveigle, *deceive*, 546.
 seduce, 615.
Invent, *imagine*, 515.
 devise, 626.
 falsehood, 544.
Inventive, *skilful*, 698.
Inventory, 86.
Inversion, *reversion*, 145.
 of position, 218, 237.
 of relation, 14.
 of order, 59, 61.
Invest, *give*, 784.
 lend, 787.
 empower, 157.
 ascribe, 155.
 clothe, 225.
 besiege, 716.
Investigate, 461.
Investiture. *See* Invest.
Investment. *See* Invest.
Inveterate, *habit*, 613.
 old, 124.
Invidious, *envy*, 921.
 hatred, 898.
Invigoration, 159.
Invincible, 159.
Inviolable, *right*, 924.
 honor, 939.
320

Inviolable, *secret*, 528.
Invious, *close*, 261.
 pathless, 704.
Invisible, *not to be seen*, 447.
 small, 193.
 concealed, 526.
Invite, *ask*, 765.
 offer, 763.
 induce, 615.
Inviting, *pleasing*, 829.
Invoke, *implore*, 765.
 pray, 990.
 curse, 908.
Invoice, 86.
Involution, *disorder*, 59.
 convolution, 248.
 numerical, 85.
 style, 571.
Involve, *derange*, 61.
 include, 54.
 wrap, 225.
 evidence, 467.
 meaning, 516.
Involved, 59.
Invulnerable, 664.
Inward, 221.
Inweave, 219.
Iota, *particle*, 32.
 minute, 193.
Irascible, 901.
Irate, 900.
Ire, 900.
Iridescent, 440.
Iris, 440.
Irishism, 497.
Irk, 830.
Irksome, *tiresome*, 688.
 tedious, 841.
 oppressive, 830.
Iron, *strength*, 159.
 hardness, 323.
 to smooth, 255.
Ironhearted, 861.
Irony, *ridicule*, 856.
 untruth, 544, 546.
Irradiate, 420.
Irrational, *number*, 84.
 silly, 477.
Irreducible, *out of order*, 59.
 discordant, 24.
Irreclaimable, *degenerate*, 659.
 impenitent, 951.
Irreconcileable, *discordant*, 24.
 unrelated, 10.
Irrecoverable, *lost*, 776.
 hopeless, 659.
Irrefragable, *certain*, 475.
 proved, 478.

Irrefutable, *certain*, 475.
 proved, 478.
Irregular, *out of order*, 59.
 against rule, 83.
 in time, 139.
 multiform, 81.
Irrelation, 10.
Irrelevant, *unrelated*, 10.
 unaccordant, 24.
 sophistical, 477.
Irreligion, 988.
Irremediable, *lost*, 776.
 spoiled, 659.
 bad, 649.
Irremissible, 945.
Irremovable, 150, 265.
Irreparable, *loss*, 776.
 bad, 649.
 incurable, 659.
Irrepentance, 951.
Irreprehensible, 946.
Irrepressible, *violent*, 173.
 excitement, 825.
Irreproachable, 946.
Irreprovable, 946.
Irresistible, 159.
Irresolute, 605.
Irrespective, 10.
Irresponsible, *exempt*, 927.
 arbitrary, 964.
Irretrievable, 776.
Irreverence, *disrespect*, 929.
 impiety, 989.
Irreversible, *past*, 122.
 immutable, 150.
Irrevocable, 150.
Irrigate, 337.
Irrision, 836.
Irritable, *excitable*, 825.
 irascible, 901.
Irritate, *provoke*, 898.
 incense, 900.
 fret, 828.
 excite, 171.
Irruption, *ingress*, 295.
 invasion, 716.
Island, 346.
Isochronous, 120.
Isolation, *singleness*, 87.
 seclusion, 893.
 detachment, 44.
 irrelation, 10.
Isomorphism, 240.
Issue, *effect*, 154.
 event, 151.
 posterity, 167.
 depart, 292.
 stream, 347.
 distribute, 73.
 (*to join*), 476.

Issueless, 169.
Isthmus, *narrowness*, 203.
   connexion, 45.
Italics, 550.
Itch, *desire*, 865.
   titillation, 380.
Item, *addition*, 37.
   speciality, 79.
Iteration, 104.
Itinerant, *moving*, 266.
   traveller, 268.
Itinerary, *description*, 594.
   guide, 695.
Ivory, 430.

J.

Jabber, *chatter*, 584.
   stammer, 583.
Jacent, 213.
Jack, *instrument*, 633.
   ensign, 550.
Jack in office, 887.
Jack-a-dandy, 854.
Jackal, 637.
Jackanapes, *fop*, 854.
   bully, 887.
Jackass, 271.
Jacket, 225.
Jack-o'-lantern, *vision*, 515.
   light, 420.
Jack-pudding, *blusterer*, 887
   boaster, 884.
*Jacquerie, *tumult*, 719.
   attack, 716.
Jactitation, *tossing*, 315.
   boasting, 884.
Jaculate, 276.
Jade, *to fatigue*, 688.
   scamp, 949.
   horse, 271.
Jagged, *angular*, 244.
   notched, 257.
Jail, 752.
Jailor, 753.
Jam, *to squeeze*, 43.
   confection, 396.
Jangle, *sound*, 410.
   discord, 713.
Janissary, 726.
Janitor, 263.
Janty, *showy*, 882.
   pretty, 845.
Janus, 548.
Japan, *varnish*, 222.
   beautify, 845.
   ornament, 847.
Jar, *vessel*, 191.
   stridor, 410.
330

Jar, *discord*, 713.
   agitation, 315.
   clash, 24.
Jargon, *unmeaning*, 519.
   absurdity, 497.
Jasper-coloured, 435.
Jaundiced, *prejudiced*, 481.
   jealous, 920.
   dejected, 837.
Jaunt, 266.
Jaunty, *fashionable*, 852.
   showy, 882.
Javelin, 727.
Jaw, *mouth*, 230.
   to scold, 932.
Jaws of death, 360.
Jawfallen, 837.
Jay, 584.
Jealousy, 920.
Jeer, *banter*, 856.
   flout, 929.
   joke, 842.
Jehovah, 976.
Jejune, *scanty*, 640.
   style, 575.
Jelly, 354.
Jemmy, 854.
Jeopardy, 665.
Jeremiade, *accusation*, 938.
   invective, 932.
   lamentation, 839.
Jerk, *throw*, 284.
   draw, 285.
   agitate, 315.
Jesabel, *wicked*, 913.
   wretch, 949.
   courtezan, 962.
Jest, *wit*, 842.
   trifle, 643.
Jester, *humorist*, 844.
   buffoon, 857.
Jesuit, 548.
Jesuitry, *deception*, 544
   sophistry, 477.
JESUS, 976.
Jet, *water*, 347.
   stream, 348.
   blackness, 431.
Jetty, 250.
Jew, 984.
Jew's-harp, 417.
Jewel, *gem*, 650.
   ornament, 847.
   favorite, 899.
Jiffy, 113.
Jig, 415.
Jiggumbob, 643.
Jilt, 545.
Jingle, 408.
Job, *business*, 625.

Job, *action*, 680.
   unfairness, 940.
Jobation, 932.
Jobber, *merchant*, 797.
   trickster, 943.
   tactician, 700.
Jobbernowl, 501.
Jobbing, *skill*, 698.
Jockey, *horseman*, 268.
   servant, 746.
   to deceive, 545.
   deceiver, 548.
Jocose, *witty*, 842.
Jocular, *gay*, 836.
   amusing, 840.
Jocund, 836.
Joe Miller, 844.
Jog, *push*, 276.
   shake, 315.
Jog on, *advance*, 282.
   slowness, 275.
   trudge, 266.
Joggle, 315.
Join, 43.
Joint, *part*, 51.
   junction, 43.
   accompanying, 88.
Joint-stock, 778.
Jointure, 810.
Joist, 215.
Joke, *wit*, 842.
   trifle, 643.
Jole, 236.
Jollity, 840.
Jolly, *gay*, 836.
   plump, 192.
Jolly-boat, 273.
Jolt, 315.
Jolthead, 501.
Jorum, 191.
Joss-house, 1000.
Jostle, *clash*, 24.
   push, 276.
Jot, *small quantity*, 32.
   particle, 193.
   to record, 551.
Jounce, 315.
Journal, *annals*, 114.
   record, 551.
   description, 594.
   book, 593.
Journey, 266.
Journeyman, *agent*, 690.
   servant, 746.
Joust, 720.
Jove, 979.
Jovial, *gay*, 836.
   amusement, 840.
Joy, 827.
Joyful, 836.

Joyless, 837.
Joyous, 836.
Jubilant, *joyous*, 836.
   boastful, 884.
Jubilee, *rejoicing*, 836, 838.
   festival, 840.
   celebration, 883.
Jucundity, 836.
Judaism, 984.
Judge, *arbitrator*, 967.
   master, 745.
   taste, 850.
Judgment, *decision*, 480.
   intellect, 450.
   belief, 484.
   wisdom, 498.
   sentence, 969.
Judgment-seat, 966.
Judicature, 965.
Judicious, 498.
Jug, 191.
Juggle, 545.
Juice, 333.
Juicy, 339.
Julep, 396.
Jumble, *confusion*, 59.
   derangement, 61.
   mixture, 41.
Jument, 271.
Jump, *rise*, 305.
   leap, 309.
   dance, 840.
Jump at, *seize*, 789.
   pursue, 622.
   desire, 865.
Jump over, 460.
Junction, 43.
Juncture, *period*, 134.
   circumstance, 8.
   junction, 43.
Jungle, 367.
Junior, 127.
Junk, 273.
Junket, *merry-making*, 840.
   dish, 299.
Junto, 712.
Jupiter, 979.
Jurisdiction, 965.
Jurisprudence, 963.
Jurist, 968.
Jury, 967.
Jury-mast, *substitute*, 634.
   resource, 666.
Just, *accurate*, 494.
   equitable, 939.
Just so, 488.
Justle, 276.
Justice, *right*, 922.
   magistrate, 967.
Justification, *religious*, 987.
331

Justification, *vindication*, 937.
Justify, 976.
Justle, 315.
Jutt out, 250.
Jutty, 250.
Juvenile, 127.
Juxta-position, 199.

K.

Kadi, 967.
Kaleidoscope, 445.
Kalendar, 114.
Keck, 296.
Kedge, *anchor*, 666.
   ship, 273.
Keel, 211.
Keen, *energetic*, 171.
   poignant, 821.
Keenwitted, 498.
Keep, *retain*, 781.
   custody, 751.
   prison, 752.
   to observe, 772.
   to celebrate, 883.
   to persist, 142.
   to continue, 143.
   food, 299.
   provision, 637.
Keep back, *conceal*, 528.
   disuse, 678.
   dissuade, 616.
Keep from, *refrain*, 603.
Keep on, 143.
Keep under, *restrain*, 751.
Keep up, 143.
Keeper, 753.
Keeping, *congruity*, 24.
Keepsake, 505.
Keg, 191.
Ken, 490.
Kennel, *ditch*, 259.
   conduit, 350.
   hovel, 189.
Kerbstone, 233.
Kerchief, 225.
Kern, 876.
Kernel, 223.
Ketch, *ship*, 273.
   horse, 271.
Kettle, *vessel*, 191.
   caldron, 386.
Kettle-drum, 417.
Key, *interpretation*, 522.
   answer, 462.
   music, 413.
   cause, 153.
   instrument, 631.

Key-hole, 260.
Key-note, *music*, 413.
   model, 22.
Key-stone, 215.
Khan, 745.
Kibitka, 272.
Kick, *strike*, 276.
   attack, 716.
   disobey, 742.
   resist, 719.
   punish, 972.
Kickshaw, 643.
Kidnap, 791.
Kidney, 75.
Kilderkin, 191.
Kill, 361.
Kiln, 386.
Kilt, 225.
Kimbo, 244.
Kin, 75.
Kind, *class*, 75.
   benevolent, 906.
Kindle, *set fire to*, 384.
   cause, 153.
   quicken, 171.
   incite, 615.
   excite, 824.
   incense, 900.
Kindred, 11.
King, 745.
Kingcraft, 737.
Kingdom, 780.
Kingship, 737.
Kinsfolk, 11.
Kinsman, 11.
Kirk, 1000.
Kirtle, 225.
Kiss, *endearment*, 902.
   courtesy, 894.
Kit, *bottle*, 191.
   fiddle, 417.
   class, 75.
Kitcat, 556.
Kitchen, *workshop*, 691.
   room, 191.
Kite, *flying*, 273.
   bill, 800.
Kith and kin, 11.
Knack, *skill*, 698.
   toy, 840.
Knap, *ridge*, 206.
Knapsac, 191.
Knave, *deceiver*, 548.
   rogue, 941.
   dishonor, 949.
Knavish, 940.
Knead, *mix*, 41.
   soften, 324.
Knee, 244.
Kneel, *beg*, 765.

Kneel, *respect*, 928.
   pray, 990.
   servility, 886.
Knell, 363.
Knick-knack, 643.
Knife, 253.
Knight, *noble*, 875.
Knight-errant, 717.
Knighthood, 877.
Knit, 43.
Knob, *protuberance*, 250.
   ball, 249.
Knock, *blow*, 276.
   sound, 406.
   beat, 972.
Knock down, 162.
Knock off, *finish*, 729.
Knock-under, *yield*, 725.
   obey, 743.
Knock-up, 688.
Knock-kneed, 245.
Knoll, 206.
Knot, *ligature*, 45.
   entanglement, 59.
   group, 72.
   intersection, 219.
   difficulty, 704.
   ornament, 847.
Knotted, 219.
Knotty, *difficult*, 704.
   dense, 321.
Knowing, 698.
Knowledge, 490.
Knuckle, 244.
Knuckle to, *submit*, 725.
   humble, 879.
Koran, 986.
*Kotou, *bow*, 894.
   respect, 928.
   obedience, 743.
Kraal, 189.
Kraken, 83.
Kyanize, 670.

L.

Label, 550.
Laboratory, 691.
Labour, *exertion*, 686.
   work, 680.
Labourer, 690.
Labyrinth, *secret*, 533.
   difficulty, 704.
   convolution, 248.
Lace, *tie*, 43.
   net, 219.
   to beat, 972.
Lacerate, 44.
Laches, *neglect*, 460.
332

Laches, *omission*, 773.
Lachrymation, 839.
Lack, *insufficiency*, 640.
   destitution, 804.
   requisition, 630.
   number, 98.
Lacker, *varnish*, 222.
   adorn, 845.
Lackey, 746.
Lackbrain, 501.
Lacklustre, *dim*, 423.
   discoloured, 429.
Laconic, 572.
Lacquer, 222.
*Lacuna, *orifice*, 260.
   pit, 252.
Lacustrine, 343.
Lad, 129.
Ladder, 627.
Lade, *transfer*, 270.
Laden, *charged*, 639.
Lading, *cargo*, 635.
   baggage, 780.
Ladle, *spoon*, 272.
   vessel, 191.
Lady, 374.
Lady-like, 852.
Lag, *linger*, 275.
   follow, 281.
   dawdle, 683.
Laggard, *slack*, 603.
Lagoon, 343.
Laical, 997.
Lair, *den*, 189.
   stye, 653.
Laity, 997.
Lake, 343.
Lamb, *innocent*, 946.
   Saviour, 976.
   saint, 948.
Lambent flame, 420.
Lamblike, 946.
Lame, *weak*, 160.
   bad, 649.
   failing, 732.
   laxity, 738.
Lamella, 204.
Lament, *complain*, 839.
   regret, 833.
   pity, 914.
Lamiæ, 980.
Lamina, *layer*, 204.
   part, 51.
Lamp, 423.
Lampoon, 932.
Lance, *throw*, 284.
   javelin, 727.
Lancer, 726.
Lancet, 262.
Lancinate, *pain*, 378, 828.

Lancinate, *painful*, 830.
Land, *ground*, 342.
   to arrive, 293.
   to stop, 265.
   estate, 780.
Landau, 272.
Landgrave, 745.
Landing-place, 215.
Land-locked, 227.
Landlord, 779.
Landmark, 550.
Landscape, *view*, 448.
   delineation, 556.
Lane, *street*, 189.
   way, 627.
Language, 560.
Languid, *weak*, 160.
   slow, 275.
   torpid, 823.
   style, 575.
Languish, *desire*, 865.
   illness, 655.
Languor, *weakness*, 160.
   inactivity, 683.
Lank, 193.
Lantern, 423.
Lap, *seat*, 189.
   interior, 221.
   to wrap, 222.
   encompass, 227.
   drink, 297.
Lapidescence, 321.
Lapidification, 321.
Lappet, 39.
Lapse *of time*, 109.
   past time, 122.
   fall, 306.
   degeneracy, 659.
   guilt, 947.
*Lapsus linguæ, 568.
Larboard, 239.
Larceny, 791.
Lard, 355, 356.
Larder, *store*, 636.
   food, 299.
Large, *in quantity*, 31.
   in size, 192.
Largess, 784.
*Largo, 275.
Lark, *mount*, 305.
   frolic, 840.
Larum, *alarm*, 669.
   signal, 550.
   loudness, 404.
Larva, 127.
Lascivious, 961.
Lash, *tie together*, 43.
   punish, 972.
   scourge, 975, 830.
   censure, 932.

Lash, *violence*, 173.
Lass, 129.
Lassitude, *fatigue*, 688.
   weariness, 841.
Lasso, 45.
Last, *in order*, 67.
   endure, 106.
   continue, 142.
   durable, 110.
   model, 22.
Latch, 45.
Latchet, 45.
Late, *tardy*, 133.
   past, 122.
Latent, *concealed*, 526.
   inert, 172.
Later, 117.
Lateral, 236.
Lath, 205.
Lathe, 633.
Lather, 353.
Latitant, 526.
Latitude, *scope*, 180.
   place, 182.
   breadth, 202.
   freedom, 748.
Latitudinarian, 984.
Latration, 412.
Latria, 990.
Latter, *sequent*, 63.
   past, 122.
Lattice, 219.
Laud, *praise*, 931.
   worship, 990.
Laudable, 944.
Laudation, 931.
Laugh, 838.
Laugh at, *ridicule*, 856.
   sneer, 929.
   joke, 842.
Laughable, *ridiculous*, 853.
Laughing-stock, 857.
Laughter, 838.
Launch, *propel*, 284.
   begin, 66.
   adventure, 876.
Launch out, *expatiate*, 584.
   style, 573.
Laurel, *trophy*, 733.
   reward, 973.
   glory, 873.
   decoration, 877.
Lave, 652.
Lavender colour, 437.
Lavish, *prodigal*, 818.
   profuse, 641.
Law, *rule*, 80.
   ordination, 963.
   command, 741.
   permission, 760.

Lawful, 924.
Lawless, *arbitrary*, 964.
   irregular, 83.
Lawn, 344.
Lawsuit, 969.
Lawyer, 968.
Lax, *incoherent*, 47.
   soft, 324.
   diffuse, 573.
   remiss, 738.
   licentious, 945.
Lay, *place*, 184.
   assuage physically,174.
   morally, 826.
   bet, 151.
   poetry, 597.
   music, 415.
   secular, 997.
Lay aside, *relinquish*, 624.
   give up, 782.
   reject, 610.
Lay by, *store*, 636.
   economize, 817.
Lay down, *assert*, 535.
   renounce, 757.
Lay in, *store*, 636.
Lay open, *disclose*, 529.
   show, 525.
   divest, 226.
Lay to, *stop*, 265.
   be inactive, 683.
   repose, 687.
Lay up, *illness*, 655.
   store, 636.
Lay waste, *ravage*, 649.
   disorganize, 659.
Layer, 204.
Layman, 997.
Laystall, 653.
Lazaretto, 662.
Lazy, *inactive*, 683.
   slow, 275.
Lea, 343.
Lead, *to precede in order*,62.
   precede in motion, 280.
   to tend, 176.
   to direct, 693.
   to induce, 615.
   authority, 737.
   heaviness, 319.
Lead off, 66.
Leader, 745.
Leading, *important*, 642.
Leading-strings, *reins*, 747.
   subjection, 749.
Leaf, *part*, 51.
   of a book, 593.
Leaflet, 51.
League, 712.
Leak, *dribble*, 294.

Leak, *waste*, 638.
Lean, *thin*, 193.
   narrow, 203.
   oblique, 217.
   recline, 215.
Leaning, *direction*, 278.
   willingness, 602.
Leap, 305, 309.
Leap to, *change*, 140.
Learned, 490.
Learner, 541.
Learning, *acquiring*, 539.
   erudition, 490.
Lease, 796.
Leash, *tie*, 43.
   couple, 92.
Least, 34.
Leather, *trifle*, 643.
   to beat, 972.
Leave, *quit*, 292.
   relinquish, 624.
   permission, 760.
   bequeath, 784.
Leave off, 141.
Leave out, 55.
Leaven, *cause*, 153.
   bane, 663.
   dirt, 153.
   to spoil, 659.
Leavings, 40.
Leaward, 236.
Lecher, 962.
Lechery, 961.
Lecture, *teach*, 537.
   censure, 932.
   discourse, 582.
Lecturer, 541.
Ledge, 215.
Ledger, *accounts*, 811.
   list, 86.
Lee, 236.
Leech, *suck*, 789.
   physician, 695.
Lee-shore, 667.
Lee-way, 304.
Leer, 441.
Lees, 652.
Left, *remaining*, 40.
   sinistral, 239.
Left-handed, 699.
Legacy, *gift*, 784.
   acquisition, 775.
Legal, *legitimate*, 924.
   relating to law, 963.
Legate, *consignee*, 750.
   messenger, 534.
   deputy, 759.
Legation, 755.
Legend, *narrative*, 594.
   record, 551.

Legerdemain, *trick*, 545.
   cunning, 702.
*Legèreté, 605.
Legging, 225.
Legible, 518.
Legion, *army*, 726.
   multitude, 102.
   assemblage, 72.
Legislate, 963.
Legislature, 963.
Legitimate, *true*, 494.
   due, 924.
   legal, 963.
Legs, 266.
Leisure, *unoccupied*, 685.
   opportunity, 134.
Leisurely, 133.
Leman, 899.
Lemma, 467.
Lemon colour, 436.
Lend, 787.
Length, 200.
Lengthy, *diffuse*, 573.
Lenient,   *compassionate*,
  914.
   moderate, 174.
   mild, 740.
Lenify, 174.
Lenitive, *remedy*, 662.
   relief, 834.
Lenity, 740.
Lens, 445.
Lent, 956.
Lenticular, 245.
Lentor, *slowness*, 275.
   inertness, 172.
   inactivity, 683.
Lentous, *viscid*, 352.
Leopard, 440.
Leprosy, 655.
Less, *inferior*, 34.
   subduction, 38.
Lessee, 806.
Lessen, *in quantity or de-*
  gree, 36.
   in size, 195.
Lesson, *teaching*, 537.
   warning, 668.
Lessor, 805.
Lest, 623.
Let, *hindrance*, 706.
   sell, 796.
   permit, 760.
Let down, 308.
Let fall, 308.
Let fly, 284.
Let go, *liberate*, 750.
   relinquish, 782.
   unclutch, 790.
Let in, *admit*, 297.
334

Let in, *insert*, 301.
Let off, *exempt*, 927.
   forgive, 918.
   explode, 173.
Let out, *eject*, 296.
   release, 750.
Lethal, *deadly*, 361.
   pernicious, 649.
Lethargy, *insensibility*, 823.
   inactivity, 683.
Lethe, 506.
Letter, *character*, 561.
   epistle, 592.
Lettered, 490.
Letter-press, 591.
Letters, 560.
Levee, 892.
Level, *horizontal*, 213.
   flat, 251.
   smooth, 255.
   to equalize, 27.
   to direct, 278.
   to lower, 308.
   to raze, 649.
Level at, 620.
Lever, 633.
Leverage, 175.
Leviathan, 192.
Levigate, 330.
Levite, 996.
Levity, *lightness*, 320.
   trifle, 643.
   irresolution, 605.
   jocularity, 836.
Levy, *demand*, 812.
   distrain, 789.
Lewd, 961.
Lexicography, 562.
Lexicon, 562.
Liable, *subject to*, 177.
   debt, 806.
   duty, 926.
*Liaison, 961.
Liar, 548.
Libation, *potation*, 297.
   worship, 990.
Libel, *detraction*, 934.
   censure, 932.
Liberal, *generous*, 816.
   disinterested, 942.
   ample, 639.
Liberate, *release*, 750.
   disjoin, 44.
Libertine, 962.
Libertinism, 961.
Liberty, *freedom*, 748.
   right, 924.
   exemption, 927.
   permission, 760.
Libidinous, 961.

Library, 593.
Librate, 314.
Licence, *permission*, 760.
   laxity, 738.
   right, 924.
   exemption, 927.
   toleration, 750.
Licentious, *dissolute*, 954.
   debauched, 961.
Licitness, 924.
Lick, *beat*, 972.
Lickerish, *fastidious*, 868.
   licentious, 961.
Lickspittle, *flatterer*, 935.
   servile, 886.
Lictor, 965.
Lid, *cover*, 263.
   integument, 222.
Lie, *place*, 186.
   exist, 1.
   recline, 213, 215.
   descend, 306.
   to deceive, 545.
   untruth, 546.
   contradict, 489.
Lie over, *postpone*, 133.
   future, 121.
Lie to, 265.
Lief, 602.
Liege, 745.
Lien, 924.
Lieu, 182.
Lieutenant, *officer*, 745.
   deputy, 759.
Life, *vitality*, 359.
   events, 151.
Life and death, *important*,
  642.
Life-blood, 359.
Life-boat, *boat*, 273.
   safety, 666.
Lifeless, *dead*, 360.
   inert, 172.
Lifeweary, 841.
Lift, *raise*, 307.
   aid, 707.
Ligament, 45.
Ligature, 45.
Light, *luminosity*, 420.
   levity, 320.
   to kindle, 384.
   luminary, 423.
   small, 32.
   trifling, 643.
   gay, 836.
   idea, 453.
   knowledge, 490.
   to arrive, 293.
   loose, 961.
Light up, *illuminate*, 420.

Light up, *cheer*, 836.
  awaken, 615.
Light upon, *find*, 480.
  arrive, 293.
Lighten, *render easy*, 705.
Lighter, *ship*, 273.
Light-footed, *swift*, 274.
  active, 682.
Light-headed, *delirious*, 503
  foolish, 499.
Light-hearted, 836.
Light-house, *beacon*, 668.
  luminary, 423.
Light-legged, 274.
Lightless, 421.
Light-minded, 605.
Lightness. *See* Light.
Lightning, *velocity*, 274.
  luminousness, 420.
Lightsome, *cheerful*, 836.
  fickle, 605.
Likelihood, 472.
Likely, 472.
Likeness, *similitude*, 17.
  copy, 21.
  representation, 554.
  portrait, 556.
Likewise, 37.
Liking, *love*, 897.
  desire, 865.
Lilac, 437.
Lilliputian, 193.
Lily, 430.
Lily-hearted, 862.
Lily-livered, 862.
Limature, 330, 331.
Limb, *member*, 51.
  component, 56.
  instrument, 633.
Limber, 324.
Limbo, *incarceration*, 751.
  purgatory, 982.
Lime, 545.
Limit, *boundary*, 233.
  to circumscribe, 231.
  qualify, 469.
  prohibit, 761.
Limitless, *infinity*, 105.
  space, 180.
Limn, 556.
Limner, 559.
Limp, *halt*, 275.
  fail, 732.
Limpid, 425.
Line, *length*, 200.
  filament, 205.
  band, 45.
  contour, 229.
  continuity, 69.
  direction, 278.
335

Line, *feature*, 550.
  appearance, 448.
  posterity, 167.
Lineage, *posterity*, 167.
  series, 69.
  kindred, 11.
Lineament, *appearance*, 448
  mark, 550.
Linear, 200.
Linger, *loiter*, 275.
  delay, 133.
  protract, 110.
Lingo, 560.
Linguist, 492.
Liniment, 355.
Lining, 224.
Link, *connecting*, 45.
  to connect, 43.
  part, 51.
  flambeau, 423.
Linsey woolsey, *mixed*, 41.
Lion, *courage*, 861.
  prodigy, 872.
Lip, *edge*, 230.
  beginning, 66.
  prominence, 250.
Lip-devotion, 989.
Lipogram, 565.
Lippitude, 443.
Lip-wisdom, 499.
Liquation, 384.
Liquefaction, 335, 384.
Liquescence, 384.
Liquescent, *soluble*, 335.
Liquid, *fluid*, 333.
  sound, 405.
Liquidate, *pay*, 807.
Liquor, *liquid*, 333.
  potable, 299.
Lisp, 583.
List, *catalogue*, 86.
  strip, 205.
  fringe, 230.
  to hear, 418.
  will, 600.
  choose, 609.
Lists, *arena*, 728.
Listed, 440.
Listen, 418.
Listless, *inattentive*, 458.
  inactive, 683.
  indifferent, 866.
Litany, 998.
Literal, *exact*, 19.
  meaning, 516.
*Literati, 492.
Literature, *learning*, 490.
  language, 560.
Lithe, 324.
Lithograph, 558.

Lithotint, 558.
Lithomancy, 511.
Litigant, 726.
Litigate, 713.
Litigious, 713.
Litter, *disorder*, 59.
  to derange, 61.
  trash, 643.
  useless, 645.
  vehicle, 272.
Little, *in degree*, 32.
  in size, 193.
Littoral, 342.
Liturgy, 998.
Live, *exist*, 1.
  continue, 142.
  dwell, 186.
  fame, 873.
Livelihood, 803.
Livelong, 110.
Lively, *sprightly*, 836.
  acute, 821.
  sensitive, 822.
  active, 682.
  style, 574.
Liver-coloured, 433.
Livery, *badge*, 550
  colour, 428.
  suit, 225.
Livid, *dark*, 431.
  purple, 437.
Living, *life*, 359.
  benefice, 995.
Lixiviate, 652.
Lixivium, 333.
Llama, 271.
Lo! *see*, 441.
  wonder, 870.
Load, *weight*, 319.
  cargo, 190.
  quantity, 31.
  redundance, 641.
  hindrance, 706.
  anxiety, 828.
  to oppress, 830.
Loadstar, *beacon*, 550.
  guide, 695.
Loadstone, 289, 615.
Lodge, *presence*, 186.
  dwelling, 189.
  receptacle, 191.
  place, 184.
Lodger, *inhabitant*, 188.
Loft, *garret*, 191.
Lofty, *high*, 206.
  proud, 878.
  magnanimous, 942.
Log, *measure*, 466.
  record, 551.
Log-book, 594.

Loggerhead, *fool*, 501.
Loggerheads, *quarrel*, 713.
Logic, 476.
Logogriph, 533.
Logomachy, *words*, 588.
   dispute, 720.
   reasoning, 476.
Logometer, 85.
Loin, 236.
Loiter, *slow*, 275.
   inactive, 683.
   tardy, 133.
   linger, 110.
Loll, *recline*, 215.
   lounge, 683.
   sprawl, 213.
Lollypop, 396.
Lone, 87.
Lonesome, 893.
Long, *in space*, 200.
   in time, 110.
Longanimity, 826.
Long-boat, 273.
Longeval, 110.
Long-headed, 498.
Longing, 865.
Longitude, 200.
Longitudinal, 200.
Longlived, 110.
Longsighted,   *sagacious*,
   498.
   presbyopic, 443.
Longsome, *long*, 200.
   in writing, 573.
Longsufferance, 826.
Long-winded, *diffuse*, 573.
   protracted, 110.
   loquacious, 584.
Looby, *clown*, 876.
   fool, 501.
Look, *see*, 441.
   appearance, 448.
Look after, 457.
Look for, *seek*, 461.
   expect, 507.
Look forward, *expect*, 507.
   foresee, 510.
Look into, 461.
Look out, *prospect*, 448.
Look out for, *expect*, 507.
Look over, 461.
Look upon, 484.
Looker on, 444.
Looking-glass, 445.
Loom, *dim*, 422.
   come in sight, 446.
   weaver's, 691.
Loon, *clown*, 876.
   fool, 501.
Loop, *curve*, 245.
336

Loop, *circle*, 247.
Loop-hole, *opening*, 260.
   vista, 441.
   plea, 617.
   refuge, 666.
   escape, 671.
   feint, 545.
Loose, *detach*, 44.
   free, 748.
   liberate, 750.
   incoherent, 47.
   vague, 519.
   style, 573.
   lax, 738.
   dissolute, 961.
Loosen, 47.
Lop, *retrench*, 38.
   shorten, 201.
Loquacity, 584.
Lord, *nobleman*, 875.
   ruler, 745.
   GOD, 976.
Lord it over, 885.
Lordling, 875.
Lordly, *proud*, 878.
   grand, 873.
Lordship, *title*, 877.
Lore, 490.
Lorication, 727.
Lorn, 893.
Loss, *privation*, 776.
   evil, 619.
Lost, *invisible*, 449.
   non-existing, 2.
   bewildered, 491.
   demoralized, 945.
Lot, *destiny*, 152.
   chance, 156, 621.
   group, 72.
   allotment, 786.
Lottery, 156, 621.
Loud, 404.
Lough, 343.
Lounge, *inactive*, 683.
   to loiter, 275.
Lout, *clown*, 876.
   fool, 501.
Love, *attachment*, 897.
   favourite, 899.
Lovelorn, *lovesick*, 897.
   rejected, 898.
Lovely, *dear*, 897.
   pleasing, 829.
   beautiful, 845.
Lover, 897.
Low, *depressed*, 207.
   debased, 940.
   vulgar, 876.
   cry, 412.
   price, 815.

Low, *sound*, 403.
Lower, *depress*, 308.
   decrease, 36.
   dim, 422.
   inferior, 34.
   sad, 837.
   discourteous, 895.
   irate, 900.
   predict, 511.
Lowlands, 207.
Lowly, 879.
Lown, 501.
Lowness, 207.   *See* Low.
Lowthoughted, 940.
Loyal, 939.
Lozenge, 244.
Lubber (*or* lubbard), *slow*,
   683.
   awkward, 699.
   fool, 501.
   big, 192.
Lubricate, *smooth*, 255.
Lubrication, 332.
Lubricity, *slippery*, 255.
   impurity, 961.
Lucid, *luminous*, 420.
   intelligible, 518.
   style, 570.
   sane, 502.
Lucifer, *Satan*, 978.
   match, 388.
Luck, *chance*, 621.
   good, 618.
   success, 731.
   prosperity, 734.
Luckless, *failure*, 732.
   adversity, 735.
   distressed, 828.
Lucky, 734.
Lucrative, 810.
Lucre, *gain*, 775.
   wealth, 803.
Luctation, 720.
Lucubration, 451.
Luculent, 420.
Ludicrous, *laughable*, 838.
   ridiculous, 853.
   witty, 842.
Lug, 285.
Luggage, *baggage*, 780.
   materials, 635.
Lugger, 273.
Lugubrious, 837.
Lukewarm, *temperate*, 382.
   indifferent, 866.
   torpid, 823.
Lull, *assuage*, 174.
   mitigate, 826.
   silence, 403.
   quiescence, 265.

Lullaby, *song*, 415.
  relief, 834.
Lumber, *useless*, 645.
  slow, 275.
  trash, 643.
  disorder, 59.
  hindrance, 706.
Luminary, *light*, 423.
  sage, 500.
Luminous, 420.
Lump, *mass*, 192.
  density, 321.
  concrete, 46.
  totality, 50.
  to amass, 72.
Lumpish, *heavy*, 319.
  massive, 192.
  sluggish, 683.
  awkward, 853.
Lunacy, 503.
Lunatic, 504.
Luncheon, 299.
Lunge, 276.
Lungs, *loudness*, 404.
Lunule, 244.
Lurch, *sink*, 306.
  difficulty, 704.
  failure, 732.
  deception, 545.
  oscillation, 314.
Lure, *entice*, 615.
  deception, 545.
Lurid, *dim*, 422.
  dark, 421.
  yellow, 436.
Lurk, *latent*, 526.
  concealed, 528.
  unseen, 447.
Luscious, *savoury*, 394.
  grateful, 829.
Lush, 428.
Lushy, 959.
Lusk, 683.
Lust, *desire*, 865.
  concupiscence, 961.
Lustration, *purification*, 652.
  atonement, 952.
Lustre, *brightness*, 420.
  chandelier, 423.
*Lustrum, 108.
Lusty, 192.
*Lusus naturæ, 83.
Lute, *cement*, 45.
  to cement, 46.
  guitar, 417.
Luxation, 44.
Luxuriant, 639.
Luxuriate, 827.
Luxurious, 829.
337

Luxury, *physical*, 377.
  enjoyment, 827.
  sensuality, 954.
Lying, *decumbent*, 213.
  deceptive, 546.
Ly-king, 986.
Lymph, 337.
Lynch, 972.
Lynch-law, 964.
Lynx-eyed, 441.
Lyre, 417.
Lyrics, 597.

M.

Mab, 979.
Macaroni, 854.
Macaronic, 597.
Mace, *club*, 633.
  weapon, 727.
  sceptre, 747.
Mace-bearer, 965.
Macerate, 337.
Maceration, *asceticism*, 955.
  atonement, 952.
Machiavelian, 544.
Machiavelism, 702.
Machination, 626.
Machine, 633.
Machinist, 690.
Macilent, *thin*, 193.
  narrow, 203.
Macrocosm, 318.
Macrology, 573.
Maculated, 440.
Maculation, 846.
Mad, *insane*, 503.
  violent, 173.
Mad-cap, 608.
Madden, *excite*, 824.
Madefaction, 339.
Made of, 54.
Madman, 504.
Madness, 503.
Madrigal, 597.
Magazine, 636.
Mage, 994.
Maggot, *whim*, 608.
  desire, 865.
Maggoty, 653.
Magi, *sage*, 500.
  saint, 948.
Magic, 992.
Magic-lantern, 445.
Magician, 994.
Magisterial, 878.
Magistery, 330.
Magistracy, *authority*, 737.

Magistracy, *jurisdiction*, 965.
Magistrate, *justiciary*, 967.
  ruler, 745.
Magistrature, 737.
Magnanimity, 942.
*Magnates, 875.
Magnet, 865.
Magnificent, *grand*, 882.
  fine, 845.
  magnanimous, 942.
*Magnifico, 875.
Magnifier, 445.
Magnify, *increase*, 35.
  enlarge, 194.
  praise, 990.
  approve, 931.
Magniloquent, 577, 582.
Magnitude, *quantity*, 25.
  size, 192.
Magpie, 584.
Maharajah, 745.
Mahogany colour, 433.
Mahomet, 986.
Mahometanism, 984.
Maid,   } *girl*, 129.
Maiden, } *servant*, 746.
  spinster, 904.
  guillotine, 975.
Mail, *letters*, 592.
  defence, 717.
  armoury, 727.
Maim, *injure*, 649.
  weaken, 160.
Main, *whole*, 50.
  tunnel, 260.
  conduit, 350.
  ocean, 341.
  principal, 642.
Main land, 342.
Mainpernor, 771.
Mainspring, *cause*, 153.
  motive, 615.
Mainstay, *instrument*, 631.
  refuge, 666.
Maintain, *continue*, 143.
  preserve, 670.
  sustain, 170.
  assert, 535.
Majestic, 873.
Majesty, *king*, 745.
  rank, 873.
  deity, 976.
Major, *greater*, 33.
  officer, 745.
Major-domo, *director*, 694.
  commissary, 746.
Majority, *age*, 131.
Make, *produce*, 161.
  constitute, 54.

Make, *form*, 240.
   arrive at, 293.
Make believe, 546.
Make fast, 43.
Make it up, 918.
Make known, 527.
Make out, *decypher*, 522.
   discover, 480.
Make over, 783.
Make up, *complete*, 52.
   compose, 54.
Make up for, 30.
Make up to, *accost*, 586.
   approach, 287.
Maker, *artificer*, 690.
   Deity, 976.
Makeshift, *substitute*, 147.
   plea, 617.
Make way, *progress*, 282.
   improve, 658.
Makeweight, 30.
Malachite, 435.
Maladministration, 699.
*Maladroit, 699.
Malady, 655.
*Malâ fide, 940.
*Malaise, 828.
Malapert, *jackanapes*, 887.
   insolent, 885.
*Malapropos, *irrelevant*,10.
   discordant, 24.
   inopportune, 135.
Malaria, 657.
Malcontent, 832.
Male, 159.
Malediction, 908.
Malefaction, 947.
Malefactor, 949.
Maleficent, 907.
Malevolent, 907.
Malformation, 846.
Malice, *spite*, 907.
Malign, 934.
Malignant, *malevolent*, 907.
   pernicious, 649.
Malignity, *violence*, 173.
Malinger, 544.
Mall, *club*, 633.
   street, 189.
Malleable, *soft*, 324.
   facile, 705.
Mallet, *hammer*, 276.
   instrument, 633.
Malpractice, 947.
Maltreat, *injure*, 649.
   aggrieve, 830.
   molest, 907.
Malversation, 818.
Mammal, 366.
Mammet, 554.

Mammiform, 250.
Mammilla, 250.
Mammon, 803.
Man, *mankind*, 372.
   person, 373.
   to arm, 673.
Man of war, 273.
Manacle, *shackle*, 752.
   to fetter, 43.
Manage, 693.
Manageable, 705.
Management, 698.
Manager, 694.
Mancipation, 751.
Mandamus, 741.
Mandarin, 745.
Mandate, 741.
Mandolin, 417.
Manducation, 297.
Mane, 256.
*Manes, 362.
Maneuvre. *See* Manœu-
   vre.
Manful, *strong*, 159.
   brave, 861.
Mangle, 44.
Mangy, 655.
Manhood, *virility*, 373.
   bravery, 861.
Mania, *insanity*, 503.
   desire, 865.
Maniac, 504.
Manicheism, 978.
Manifest, *visible*, 446.
   obvious, 518.
   to show, 525.
   to appear, 448.
Manifesto, 531.
Manifold, 102.
Manikin, *image*, 554.
   dwarf, 193.
Manipulate, *handle*, 379.
   conduct, 692.
Mankind, 372.
Manlike, 159.
Manly, *adolescent*, 131.
   resolute, 604.
   brave, 861.
Manna, 396.
Manner, *conduct*, 692.
   kind, 75.
Manners, *breeding*, 852.
   politeness, 894.
Mannerism, *singularity*,
   79.
   affectation, 855.
   vanity, 880.
Mannerly, 894.
Manœuvre, *scheme*, 626.
   operation, 680.

Manœuvre, *skill*, 698.
   stratagem, 545.
Manor, 780.
Manse, 1000.
Mansion, 189.
Mansuetude, 894.
Mantel, 215.
Mantilla, 225.
Mantle, *cloak*, 225.
   flash, 824.
   kindle, 900.
   spread, 194.
Mantology, 511.
Mantlet, 225.
Manual, 593.
Manufactory, 691.
Manufacture, 161.
Manufacturer, 690.
Manumit, 750.
Manure, 653.
Manuscript, 590.
Many, 102.
Many-coloured, 440.
Map, 554.
Mar, *spoil*, 649.
   obstruct, 706.
Marasmus, *atrophy*, 655.
   shrinking, 195.
Marauder, 792.
Marauding, 791.
Marble, *ball*, 249.
   hard, 323.
   sculpture, 557.
Marbled, *variegated*, 440.
Marble-hearted, 907.
March, 266.
Marches, 233.
*Marcor, 203.
Mare, 271.
Mare's nest, *absurdity*,
   497.
   failure, 732.
Mareschal, 745.
Margin, *edge*, 230.
   latitude, 748.
Margrave, 745.
Marine, *oceanic*, 341.
   fleet, 273.
   soldier, 726.
Marish, 345.
Marital, 903.
Maritime, 341.
Mark, *indication*, 550.
   record, 551.
   object, 620.
   degree, 26.
   observe, 441.
   attend to, 457.
Market, 799.
Marksman, 700.

Marl, 342.
Marplot, *bungler*, 701.
   obstacle, 706.
   malicious, 913.
Marqué, 792.
Marquetry, *mixture*, 41.
   variegation, 440.
Marquis, 875.
Marriage, 903.
Marrow, *essence*, 5.
   interior, 221.
   whole, 50.
   gist, 516.
   essential, 642.
Marsh, 345.
Marshal, *arrange*, 60.
   officer, 745.
   in law, 968.
   messenger, 534.
Mart, 799.
Martial, 720.
Martinet, *tyrant*, 739.
   teacher, 540.
Martingale, 752.
Martyr, 828.
Martyrdom, *torture*, 378.
   agony, 828.
   asceticism, 955.
Marvel, *wonder*, 870.
   prodigy, 872.
Marvellous, *great*, 31.
   impossible, 471.
Masculine, 159.
Mash, *mix*, 41.
   knead, 324.
Mask, *concealment*, 528.
   ambush, 530.
   untruth, 546.
   shade, 424.
   dress, 225.
Masked, *invisible*, 447.
Masorah, 985.
Masquerade, *frolic*, 840.
   concealment, 528.
   ambush, 530.
   deception, 546.
Mass, *quantity*, 25.
   degree, 31.
   whole, 50.
   heap, 72.
   size, 192.
   density, 321.
   rites, 998.
Massacre, 361.
Massive, *huge*, 192.
   heavy, 319.
   dense, 321.
Master, *ruler*, 745.
   director, 694.
   proficient, 700.

Master, *teacher*, 540.
   to succeed, 731.
   possessor, 779.
   to learn, 539.
   to understand, 518.
   to overpower, 824.
Mastered, 732.
Master hand, 700.
Master head, 698.
Master key, *explanation*, 462.
   instrumentality, 631.
Masterly, 698.
Masterpiece, 650.
Mastership, 737.
Mastery, *authority*, 737.
   success, 731.
Masticate, 297.
Mat, 219.
Match, *equal*, 27.
   similar, 17.
   to copy, 19.
   fuel, 388.
   marriage, 903.
Matchless, *good*, 648.
   perfect, 650.
   virtuous, 944.
Matchlock, 727.
Mate, *similar*, 17.
   equal, 27.
   wife, 903.
Materia medica, 662.
Material, *substance*, 3.
   important, 642.
Materialism, 450.
Materiality, 316.
Materials, 635.
Maternity, 166.
Mathematical, *exact*, 494.
Mathematics, 25.
Matins, 998.
Matress, 215.
Matriculation, 541.
Matrimony, *wedlock*, 903.
   mixture, 41.
*Matrix, *mould*, 22.
   workshop, 691.
Matron, *woman*, 374.
   old, 130.
   adolescent, 131.
Matted, 219.
Matter, *substance*, 3.
   material world, 316.
   topic, 453.
   meaning, 516.
   importance, 642.
Mattock, 633.
Mature, *ripe*, 673.
   scheme, 626.
   old, 124.

Mature, *adolescent*, 131.
Matutinal, 132.
Maudlin, *drunk*, 959.
   spurious sensibility, 823.
Maugre, 179.
Maul, 649.
Maunder, 839.
Mausoleum, 363.
Maw, 191.
Mawkish, *insipid*, 391.
   indifferent, 866.
Maxim, 496.
Maximum, 33.
May,   } *possible*, 470.
May be, } *chance*, 156.
Mayhap, } *supposition*, 514.
Mayor, 745.
Maypole, 206.
Maze, *convolution*, 248.
   bewilderment, 491.
   enigma, 533.
Mead, 344.
Meadow, 344.
Meagre, *thin*, 193.
   scanty, 640.
   style, 575.
Meal, *powder*, 330.
   repast, 299.
Mealy-mouthed, *false*, 544.
   servile, 886.
Mean, *average*, 29.
   middle, 68.
   small, 32.
   contemptible, 643.
   shabby, 874.
   base, 940.
   humble, 879.
   sneaking, 886.
   selfish, 943.
   stingy, 819.
   to intend, 620.
   to signify, 516.
Meander, *circuition*, 311.
   convolution, 248.
   river, 348.
Means, *appliances*, 632.
   fortune, 803.
Meantime, 120.
Measure, *extent*, 25.
   degree, 26.
   moderation, 639.
   to compute, 466.
   proceeding, 626.
   to apportion, 786.
   in music, 413.
   in poetry, 597.
Meat, 299.
Mechanic, 690.

Mechanical, *automatic*, 601.
Mechanism, 632.
Medal, *reward*, 973.
   palm, 733.
   decoration, 877.
Medallion, 557.
Meddle, *interpose*, 682.
   act, 680.
Meddlesome, 682.
Mediæval, 124.
Medial, 68.
Mediation, 724.
Mediator, *Saviour*, 976.
Medicament, 662.
Medicaster, 548.
Medicate, *heal*, 660.
   compound, 41.
Medicine, 662.
Mediety, *middle*, 68.
   central, 223.
Medieval, 124.
Mediocrity, *moderate*, 32.
   of fortune, 736.
   imperfect, 651.
Meditate, *think*, 451.
   purpose, 620.
Mediterranean, *middle*, 68.
   interjacent, 228.
Medium, *mean*, 29.
   instrument, 631.
Medley, 41.
Mead, *reward*, 973.
   gift, 784.
   praise, 931.
Meek, *humble*, 879.
   gentle, 826.
Meet, *contact*, 199.
   agreement, 23.
   converge, 291.
   assemble, 72.
   expedient, 646.
   proper, 926.
   fulfil, 772.
Meet with, *find*, 480.
   happen, 151.
Megascope, 445.
Megrims, 837.
Melancholy, *distressing*, 830.
   dejection, 837.
*Mélange, 41.
*Mêlée, 720.
Meliorate, 658.
Mellifluous, *sound*, 405.
   melody, 413.
   style, 578.
Mellow, *sound*, 413.
   mature, 673.
   soft, 324.

Mellow, *improved*, 658.
   tipsy, 959.
Melodrame, 599.
Melody, 413.
Melpomene, 599.
Melt, *liquefy*, 335.
   fuse, 384.
   disappear, 449.
   pity, 914.
Melt away, 2.
Member, *part*, 51.
   component, 56.
Membrane, 204.
Memento, 505.
*Memento mori, 363.
Memoir, 594, 595.
Memorable, 642.
Memorandum, 505.
Memorial, *record*, 551.
Memory, *reminiscence*, 505.
   fame, 873.
Menace, 908.
Menagery, *of animals*, 366.
   collection, 72.
   store, 636.
Mend, 658.
Mendacity, 544.
Mendicant, *beggar*, 767.
   monk, 996.
Mendicity, 804.
Menial, *servant*, 746.
   rustic, 876.
Mental, 450.
Mention, 527.
Menstrual, 108.
Mensuration, 466.
Mentor, *adviser*, 695.
   teacher, 540.
Mephistophiles, *Satan*, 978.
   miscreant, 949.
Mephitic, *fetid*, 401.
   pernicious, 649.
   deleterious, 657.
Mercantile, 794.
Mercenary, 819.
Merchandise, 798.
Merchant, 797.
Merchantman, 273.
Merciful, 914.
Merciless, 907.
Mercurial, *excitable*, 825.
   mobile, 264.
   quick, 274.
Mercury, *messenger*, 534.
Mercy, 914.
Mercy-seat, 966.
Mere, *simple*, 32.
   lake, 343.

Meretricious, *false*, 495.
   vulgar, 851.
   licentious, 961.
Merge, *plunge*, 337.
   insert, 301.
   include, 76.
   combine, 48.
   midst, 68.
Meridian, *summit*, 210.
   noon, 125.
Merit, *desert*, 944.
   usefulness, 644.
Mermaid, 979.
Merry, 836.
Merry-andrew, 844.
Merry-making, 840.
Merry-meeting, 892.
*Mésalliance, *ill-assorted*, 24.
   marriage, 903.
Meseems, 484.
Mesh, 219.
Mesmerism, 992.
Mess, *mixture*, 41.
   disorder, 59.
   failure, 732.
   meal, 299.
Message, *command*, 741.
   intelligence, 532.
Messalina, 962.
Messenger, 534.
Messiah, 976.
Messmate, 890.
Messuage, 189.
Metachronism, 115.
Metal, *material*, 635.
Metallurgy, 358.
Metamorphosis, 140.
Metaphor, *figure*, 521.
   comparison, 464.
   analogy, 17.
Metaphrase, 522.
Metaphysics, 450.
*Metastasis, *inversion*, 218.
   displacement, 270.
Mete, *measure*, 466.
   give, 784.
   distribute, 786.
Metempsychosis, 140.
Meteor, *luminary*, 423.
   light, 420.
Meteoric, 173.
Methinks, 484.
Method, *order*, 58.
   way, 627.
Methodize, 60.
Metonymy, 521.
Metoposcopy, 522.
Metre, 597.
Metropolis, 189.

Mettle, *spirit*, 820.
 courage, 861.
Mettlesome, *excitable*, 825.
 brave, 861.
Mew, *enclose*, 231.
 restrain, 751.
 complain, 839.
Mewl, 412.
*Mezzo termine, 68.
 mid-course, 628.
Mezzotint, 558.
Miasm, 663.
Microcosm, 193.
Microscope, 445.
Microscopic, 193.
Mid, 68.
Midas, 803.
Mid-course, 628.
Midden, 653.
Middle, *in order*, 68.
 in degree, 29.
 in space, 223.
Middleman, *director*, 694.
 salesman, 797.
Middling, 651.
Midland, 342.
Midnight, *evening*, 126.
 darkness, 421.
Midst, 223.
Midway, 68.
Mien, 448.
Miff, 900.
Might, *power*, 157.
 degree, 26.
 violence, 173.
Mighty, *much*, 31.
 large, 192.
 powerful, 159.
 haughty, 878.
Migrate, 266.
Milch-cow, 636.
Mild, *moderate*, 174.
 insipid, 391.
 lenient, 740.
 calm, 826.
 courteous, 894.
 warm, 382.
Mildew, 653.
Militant, 720.
Military, 726.
Militate, 708.
Militia, 726.
Milk, 174.
Milk and water, 651.
Milk-livered, 862.
Milk-sop, *coward*, 862.
 pampered, 954.
Milk-white, 430.
Milky, *semitransparent*, 427.
 emulsive, 352.
341

Milky-way, 318.
Mill, *machine*, 633.
 workshop, 691.
Millennium, *period*, 108.
 futurity, 121.
 utopia, 515.
 hope, 858.
Millesimal, 99.
Millet-seed, 193.
Million, 98.
*Millionnaire, 803.
Mill-pond, 636.
Mill-stone, *incubus*, 706.
 weight, 319.
Mime, *player*, 599.
 buffoon, 857.
Mimic, 19.
Minacity, 909.
Minaret, 206.
Minatory, *threatening*, 909.
 dangerous, 665.
*Minauderie, 855.
Mince, 44.
Mincing, *slow*, 275.
 affected, 855.
Mind, *intellect*, 450.
 will, 600.
 desire, 865.
 purpose, 620.
 to attend to, 457.
 believe, 484.
 remember, 505.
Minded, 602.
Mindful, *attentive*, 457.
 remembering, 505.
Mindless, *inattentive*, 458.
 forgetful, 506.
Mine, *store*, 636.
 abundance, 639.
 to hollow, 252.
 open, 260.
 sap, 162.
 damage, 659.
Mineral, 358.
Mineralogy, 358.
Mingle, 41.
Miniature, *portrait*, 556.
 small, 193.
Minikin, 193.
Minim, 193.
Minimum, 193.
Mining, 260.
Minion, 899.
Minister, *deputy*, 759.
 director, 694.
 to aid, 707.
 rites, 998.
Ministry, *direction*, 693.
 church, 995.
Minnow, 193.

Minor, *inferior*, 34.
 infant, 129.
Minotaur, 83.
Minster, 1000.
Minstrel, 416.
Minstrelsy, 415.
Mint, *workshop*, 691.
 mould, 22.
 wealth, 803.
Minuet, *dance*, 840.
*Minus, *less*, 38.
 in debt, 806.
 deficient, 304.
Minute, *in quantity*, 32.
 in size, 193.
 of time, 108.
 instant, 113.
 compendium, 596.
 record, 551.
Minutest, 34.
*Minutiæ, 32.
Minx, 962.
Miracle, 872.
Miraculous, 870.
*Mirage, 443.
Mire, 653.
Mirror, *reflector*, 445.
 perfection, 650.
 saint, 948.
 glory, 873.
Mirth, 836.
Misacceptation, 523.
Misadventure, *failure*, 732.
 misfortune, 830.
Misanthropy, 911.
Misapply, *misuse*, 679.
 misinterpret, 523.
 mismanage, 699.
Misapprehend, *mistake*, 495.
 misinterpret, 523.
Misappropriate, 679.
Misarrange, 61.
Misbecome, 945.
Misbegotten, 945.
Misbehaviour, *guilt*, 947.
Misbelief, 485.
Miscalculate, *sophistry*, 477.
 disappoint, 509.
Miscall, 565.
Miscarriage, 732.
Miscellany, *mixture*, 41.
 collection, 72.
Mischance, *misfortune*, 830.
 failure, 732.
Mischief, 619.
Mischievous, 649.
Miscible, 41.
Miscompute, 495.
Misconceive, *mistake*, 495.
 misinterpret, 523.

Misconduct, *guilt*, 947.
  bungling, 699.
Misconjecture, 495.
Misconstrue, 523.
Miscount, 495.
Miscreance, 485.
Miscreant, *wretch*, 949.
  apostate, 941.
Miscreated, 945.
Misdate, 115.
Misdeed, 947.
Misdemean, 945.
Misdevotion, 989.
Misdirect, 538.
Misdoing, 947.
Misemploy, 679.
Miser, 819.
Miserable, *contemptible*, 643.
  unhappy, 828.
  small, 32.
Miserly, 819.
Misery, 828.
Misestimate, 495.
Misfortune, *evil*, 619.
  failure, 732.
  unhappiness, 830.
Misgiving, *fear*, 860.
  doubt, 485.
Misgovern, 699.
Misguide, 538.
Mishap, *evil*, 619.
  failure, 732.
  disaster, 830.
Mishmash, 41.
Misinformation, 538.
Misinstruction, 538.
Misintelligence, 538.
Misinterpret, 523.
Misjudge, *err*, 495.
  sophistry, 477.
Mislay, *lose*, 776.
  derange, 61.
Mislead, *deceive*, 545.
  misteach, 538.
  error, 495.
Mislike, 867.
Mismanage, 699.
Mismatch, 15.
Misname, 565.
Misnomer, 565.
Misogamy, 904.
Mispersuasion, 538.
Misproportioned, 846.
Misquote, 523.
Misreckon, 495.
Misrelation, 10.
Misreport, *err*, 495.
  falsify, 544.
Misrepresent, 546.
Misrule, *misconduct*, 699.
842

Misrule, *laxity*, 738.
Miss, *lose*, 776.
  fail, 732.
  inattention, 458.
  want, 865.
Missal, 998.
Missay, 583.
  misnomer, 565.
Missend, 699.
Misshapen, 846.
Missile, 284.
  arms, 727.
Missing, 187.
Mission, *commission*, 755.
  business, 625.
Missive, 592.
Misspell, 523.
Misspend, 818.
Misstatement, *error*, 495.
  falsehood, 544.
  untruth, 546.
Mist, 422.
Mistake, *error*, 495.
  failure, 732.
  mismanagement, 699.
  misconstrue, 523.
Misstate, 523.
  falsify, 544.
Misteach, 538.
Misterm, 565.
Misthink, 495.
Mistime, 135.
Mistranslate, 523.
Mistress, *lady*, 374.
  concubine, 962.
Mistrust, 485.
Misty, *opaque*, 426.
  invisible, 447.
Misunderstanding, *error*,
  495.
  misinterpretation, 523.
  discord, 713.
Misuse, 679.
Mite, *small*, 192.
  bit, 32.
  money, 800.
Mitigate, *abate*, 174.
  relieve, 834.
  calm, 826.
  improve, 658.
Mitre, 999.
Mitten, 225.
Mittimus, 741.
Mix, 41.
Mixed, 59.
Mnemonics, 505.
Mnemosyne, 505.
Moan, 839.
Moat, *inclosure*, 232.
  ditch, 350.

Mob, *crowd*, 72.
  vulgar, 876.
  to scold, 932.
Mob-law, 964.
Mobile, *movable*, 264.
  sensible, 822.
  inconstant, 607
Mobility, 876.
Mobocracy, 737.
Moccasin, 225.
Mock, *imitate*, 17.
  repeat, 104.
  erroneous, 495.
  false, 544.
  to ridicule, 856.
  laugh at, 838.
Modal, 6, 7.
Mode, 852.
Model, *prototype*, 22.
  rule, 80.
  example, 82.
  to copy, 19.
  sculpture, 557.
  perfection, 650.
  saint, 948.
Modeller, 559.
Moderate, *small*, 32.
  to allay, 174.
  to assuage, 826.
  temperate, 953.
  cheap, 815.
Moderator, 745.
Modern, 123.
Modesty, *humility*, 881.
  purity, 960.
*Modicum, *little*, 33.
  allotment, 786.
Modification, *difference*, 15.
  variation, 20.
  change, 140.
  qualification, 469.
Modish, 852.
Modulation, 413.
Module, 22.
Moider, 458.
Moiety, 91.
Moil, 680.
Moist, *wet*, 337.
  humid, 339.
Molasses, 396.
Mold.   *See* Mould.
Mole, *mound*, 206.
  defence, 717.
  refuge, 666.
Molecule, 32.
Molehill, *lowness*, 207.
  trifling, 643.
Molestation, *evil*, 619.
  damage, 649.
  malevolence, 907.

Mollah, *judge*, 967.
  priest, 996.
Mollify, *allay*, 174.
  soften, 324.
  assuage, 826.
Mollusk, 366.
Moloch, *slaughter*, 361.
  Divinity, 979.
Molten, 333.
Moment, *of time*, 113.
  importance, 642.
Momentum, 276.
Momus, 838.
Monachism, 995.
Monad, 193.
Monarch, 745.
Monarchy, 737.
Monastery, 995.
Monastic, 995.
Monetary, 800.
Money, 800.
Money-bag, 802.
Moneyer, 801.
Moneyless, 804.
Monger, 797.
Mongrel, *mixture*, 41.
  anomalous, 83.
Moniliform, 247.
Monition, *advice*, 695.
  information, 527.
Monitor, *teacher*, 540.
  director, 694.
  oracle, 513.
  omen, 512.
Monitory, 511.
Monk, 996.
Monkey, *imitative*, 19.
  engine, 633.
  catapult, 276.
  ridiculous, 856.
  laughing-stock, 857.
Monkish, 995.
Monochord, 417.
Monody, 839.
Monogamy, 903.
Monogram, *word*, 562.
  cypher, 533.
  diagram, 554.
Monologue, 589.
Monomania, *insanity*, 503.
  error, 495.
  obstinacy, 606.
Monomaniac, 504.
Monopoly, 777.
Monosyllable, 561.
Monotheism, 983.
Monotony, *repetition*, 104.
  in style, 575.
Monsoon, 349.
Monster, *exception*, 83.
343

Monster, *prodigy*, 872.
  ugly, 846.
  evil doer, 913.
  ruffian, 949.
Monstrous, *excessive*, 31.
  huge, 192.
  wonderful, 870.
  ugly, 846.
  ridiculous, 853.
Montgolfier, 273.
Month, 108.
Monticle, 206.
Monument, *record*, 551.
  tallness, 206.
Mood, *nature*, 5.
  temper, 820.
  will, 600.
  variation, 20.
  change, 140.
Moody, *sullen*, 895.
  fretful, 900.
  furious, 825.
Mooncalf, 501.
Moon-eyed, 443.
Moonshine, *nonsense*, 497.
  excuse, 617.
  trumpery, 643.
Moonstruck, 503.
Moor, *open space*, 180.
  plain, 344.
  locate, 184.
  rest, 265.
Moorland, 344.
Moot, *inquire*, 461.
  argue, 476.
Moot point, 454.
Mop, 652.
Mope, 837.
Mope-eyed, 443.
Mopsy, 962.
Mopus, 800.
Moral, *right*, 922.
  duty, 926.
  virtuous, 944.
  maxim, 496.
Moralize, *reason*, 476.
  teach, 537.
Morass, 345.
Morbid, { *bad*, 649.
Morbific, { *diseased*, 655.
  { *noxious*, 657.
Mordacity, 907.
Mordant, *pungent*, 392.
  keen, 173.
More, 37.
Moreland, 206.
Moreover, 37.
Moribund, *dying*, 360.
  sick, 655.
Mormo, 860.

Morning, 125.
Morose, 895.
Morphology, 240.
Morrow, 121.
Morsel, *small quantity*, 32.
  portion, 51.
Mortal, *man*, 373.
  fatal, 361.
  bad, 649.
  wearisome, 841.
Mortality, *death*, 360.
  evanescence, 111.
  mankind, 372.
Mortar, *cement*, 45.
  artillery, 727.
  pulverization, 330.
Mortgage, *sale*, 796.
  lend, 787.
  security, 771.
Mortgagor, 805.
Mortiferous, *fatal*, 361.
  noxious, 657.
Mortify, *pain*, 828.
  to vex, 830.
  to discontent, 832.
  to humiliate, 874.
  asceticism, 955.
Mortoise, *unite*, 43.
  insert, 301.
  intersect, 219.
Mortuary, 363.
Mosaic, *mixture*, 41.
  variegation, 440.
  painting, 556.
Mosque, 1000.
Moss, *marsh*, 345.
  tuft, 256.
Moss-trooper, 792.
Mote, *particle*, 193.
  light, 320.
Moth, 659.
Mother, *parent*, 166.
  mould, 653.
Mother of pearl, 440.
Mother tongue, 560.
Mother wit, 498.
Motion, *change of place*, 264.
  proposition, 514.
  topic, 454.
  request, 765.
  offer, 763.
Motionless, 265.
Motive, 615.
Motley, *multiform*, 81.
  variegated, 440.
Mottled, 440.
Motto, *device*, 550.
  maxim, 496.
  phrase, 566.
Mould, *form*, 240.

Mould, *condition*, 7.
   earth, 342.
   to model, 554.
   carve, 557.
   matrix, 22.
Moulder, 659.
Moulding, 847.
Mouldy, *decayed*, 653.
   fetid, 401.
Moult, 226.
Mound, *defence*, 717.
   hillock, 206.
Mount, *to rise*, 305.
   hillock, 206.
Mountain, *hill*, 206.
   size, 192.
   weight, 319.
Mountebank, *quack*, 548.
   buffoon, 844, 857.
Mourn, *grieve*, 828.
   lament, 839.
Mournful, *sad*, 837.
   afflicting, 830.
Mouse, *little*, 193.
   to search, 461.
Mouse-coloured, 432.
Mouse-hole, 260.
Mouth, *entrance*, 66.
   opening, 260.
   brink, 230.
   voice, 580.
Mouthful, *portion*, 51.
   small part, 193.
Mouthpiece, *speaker*, 524.
   speech, 582.
Mouth-watering, 865.
Mouthy, 577.
Movable, 270.
Movables, 780.
Move, *be in motion*, 264.
   induce, 615.
   excite, 824.
   act, 680.
   propose, 514.
Move off, *recede*, 286.
   depart, 292.
Move on, 282.
Moveless, 265.
Movement, *motion*, 264.
   stir, 682.
Mow, 162.
Much, 31.
Mucilage, 354.
Muck, 653.
Muckworm, *miser*, 819.
   base-born, 876.
Mucus, 354.
Mud, 653.
Muddle, *derange*, 61.
Muddled, *confused*, 458.
344

Muddled, *tipsy*, 959.
   foolish, 499.
Muddy, *opaque*, 426.
   moist, 339.
Muffle, *silent*, 403.
   conceal, 528.
   taciturn, 585.
   stammer, 583.
   wrap, 225.
Mufti, 996.
Mug, 191.
Muggy, *dim*, 422.
   moist, 339.
Mulatto, 83.
Mulct, 974.
Mule, *beast*, 271.
   mongrel, 83.
   obstinate, 606.
   fool, 499.
Muliebrity, 374.
Multifarious, *multiform*, 81.
   various, 15.
Multifid, *divided*, 51.
Multifold, 81.
Multiform, 81.
Multigenerous, 81.
Multiple, *numerous*, 102.
   product, 84.
Multiplicand, 84.
Multiplicator, 84.
Multiplication, *arithmetical*, 85.
   reproduction, 163.
Multiplicity, 102.
Multiplier, 84.
Multitude, *number*, 102.
   assemblage, 72.
   mob, 876.
Multitudinous, 102.
Mum, *silence*, 403.
   aphony, 581.
   secrecy, 528.
Mumble, *eat*, 297.
   mutter, 583.
Mummer, 599.
Mummery, *absurdity*, 497.
   ridicule, 856.
   parade, 882.
   imposture, 545.
   masquerade, 840.
Mummy, *corpse*, 362.
   dryness, 340.
Mump, *mutter*, 583.
Mumps, *sullenness*, 895.
Munch, 297.
Munchausen, 549.
Mundane, *world*, 318.
   selfishness, 943.
   irreligion, 988.
Mundify, 652.

Municipal, 965.
Munificent, 816.
Muniment, *record*, 551.
   defence, 717.
   refuge, 666.
Munition, 635.
Murder, 361.
Muricated, 253.
Murky, 421.
Murmur, *sound*, 405.
   complaint, 839.
Murrain, 655.
Murrey, 434.
Muscadine, 400.
Muscle, 159.
Muscular, 159.
Muse, *to reflect*, 451.
   poetry, 597.
   language, 560.
Museum, *store*, 636.
   collection, 72.
   focus, 74.
Mushroom, *small*, 193.
   low-born, 876.
   upstart, 734.
Music, 415.
Musical, 413.
Musician, 416.
Musk, 400.
Musket, 727.
Musketeer, 726.
Musnud, *council*, 690.
   sceptre, 747.
   support, 215.
Mussulman, 984.
Must, *mucor*, 653.
   necessity, 152.
   obligation, 926.
   compulsion, 744.
Mustard, 393.
Mustard seed, 193.
Muster, *collect*, 72.
   numeration, 85.
   (to pass), 651.
Muster roll, *record*, 551.
   list, 86.
Musty, *foul*, 653.
   rank, 401.
Mutable, *changeable*, 149.
   irresolute, 605.
Mutation, 140.
Mute, *silent*, 403.
   speechless, 581.
   taciturn, 585.
Mutilate, *retrench*, 38.
   deform, 241.
   garble, 651.
   incomplete, 53.
   injure, 649.
   spoliation, 619.

Mutineer, 742.
Mutiny, 742.
　　revolt, 719.
Mutter, *speak*, 583.
　　threaten, 909.
Mutual, 12.
Muzzle, *opening*, 260.
　　edge, 230.
　　to silence, 403, 581.
　　taciturn, 585.
　　to incapacitate, 158.
　　restrain, 751.
　　imprison, 752.
Muzzy, *confused*, 458.
　　in liquor, 959.
Myomancy, 511.
Myopic, 443.
Myriad, 98.
Myrmidon, *troop*, 726.
　　swarm, 72.
Myrtle, 897.
Mysterious, *concealed*, 528.
　　obscure, 519.
Mystery, *secret*, 533.
　　concealment, 528.
　　craft, 625.
Mystic, *concealed*, 528.
　　obscure, 519.
Mystify, *to deceive*, 545.
　　hide, 528.
　　falsify, 477.
　　misteach, 538.
Myth, 515.
Mythological deities, 979.
Mythology, 984.

N.

Nab, *seize*, 789.
　　deceive, 545.
Nabob, 803.
Nacreous, 440.
Nadir, 211.
Nag, 271.
Nail, *to fasten*, 43.
　　fastening, 45.
*Naïveté, 703.
Naked, *denuded*, 226.
　　visible, 446.
Namby-pamby, 855.
Name, *appellation*, 564.
　　fame, 873.
　　to appoint, 755.
Nameless, *anonymous*, 565.
　　obscure, 874.
Namely, 82.
Namesake, 564.
Nap, *sleep*, 683.
　　down, 256.
345

Nap, *texture*, 329.
Napping, *inattentive*, 458.
Nappy, *frothy*, 353.
　　tipsy, 959.
Narcissus, 845.
Narcotic, 649.
Narrate, 594.
Narrator, 594.
Narrow, 203.
Narrow-minded,　*bigoted*, 499.
　　selfish, 943.
Nasal, *accent*, 583.
Nascent, 66.
Nasty, *foul*, 653.
　　unsavoury, 395.
　　offensive, 830.
　　ugly, 846.
Natation, 267.
Nathless, 179.
Nation, 372.
Nationality, 910.
Native, *inhabitant*, 188.
　　artless, 703.
Nativity, 511.
Natural, *intrinsic*, 5.
　　regular, 82.
　　true, 543.
　　artless, 703.
　　a fool, 501.
Natural history, 357.
Natural philosophy, 316.
Naturalized, *habitual*, 613.
　　established, 80.
Nature, *essence*, 5.
　　world, 318.
　　organization, 357.
　　affections, 820.
　　reality, 494.
　　rule, 82.
　　artlessness, 703.
　　unfashioned, 674.
　　spontaneous, 612.
　　style, 578.
Naught, *nothing*, 4.
　　zero, 101.
Naughty, 945.
*Naumachia, 720.
Nausea, *disgust*, 867.
　　weariness, 841.
　　hatred, 898.
　　unsavoury, 395.
Nautical, 267.
Nave, *middle*, 68.
　　centre, 223.
　　church, 1000.
Navel, 68.
Navigation, 267.
Navigator, 269.
Navy, 273.

Nay, 536.
Neap, 207.
Near, *in space*, 197.
　　in time, 121.
　　approach, 287.
　　stingy, 817.
　　likeness, 17.
Near-side, 239.
Near-sighted, 443.
Nearly, 32.
Neat, *spruce*, 845.
　　clean, 652.
　　in writing, 576.
Neb, 250.
Nebula,　⎱ *stars*, 318.
Nebulosity,　⎰ *dimness*, 422.
　　invisible, 447.
　　obscure, 519.
Necessity, *fate*, 601.
　　indigence, 804.
　　requirement, 630.
Neck, *contraction*, 195.
　　narrow, 203.
Necklace, 247.
Neckcloth, 225.
Necrology, 594.
Necromancer, 994.
Necromancy, 992.
Nectar, 396.
Need, *requirement*, 630.
　　insufficiency, 640.
　　indigence, 804.
　　desire, 865.
Needle, *sharpness*, 253.
　　perforator, 262.
Needless, 641.
Needs, 601.
Nefarious, 945.
Negation, 536.
Negative, *inexisting*, 2.
　　quantity, 84.
　　denial, 536.
　　refusal, 764.
Neglect, *disregard*, 460.
　　disuse, 678.
　　non-observance, 773.
　　to leave undone, 730.
　　to slight, 929.
　　to evade, 927.
Negotiate, *bargain*, 769.
　　traffic, 794.
　　mediate, 724.
Negro, 431.
Neigh, *cry*, 412.
　　boast, 884.
Neighbour, 890.
Neighbourhood, 197.
Neighbourly, *social*, 892.
　　friendly, 888.
Neither, 610.

*Nem. con. 488.
Nemesis, 922.
Neogamist, 903.
Neology, 563.
Neophyte, 541.
Neoteric, 123.
Nephelognosy, 353.
Nepotism, 892.
Neptune, 341.
Nerve, *strength*, 159.
  courage, 861.
Nerveless, 160.
Nervous, *weak*, 160.
  timid, 860.
  concise style, 572.
  vigorous style, 574.
Nescience, 491.
Nest, *lodging*, 189.
  cradle, 153.
Nestle, *lodge*, 186.
  safety, 664.
  endearment, 902.
Nestling, 129.
Net, *intersection*, 219.
  snare, 667.
  difficulty, 704.
Nether, 207.
Nettle, *to sting*, 830.
  incense, 900.
Network, 219.
Neutral, 29.
Neutralize, *counteract*, 179.
  compensate, 30.
Never, 107.
Nevertheless, 179.
New, 123.
Newaub, 745.
Newfangled, *new*, 123.
  strange, 83.
  barbarous, 851.
News, 532.
Newspaper, 551.
Next, *following*, 63.
  later, 117.
*Niaiserie, 497.
Nib, *point*, 253.
  summit, 210.
Nibble, *carp at*, 932.
  eat, 297.
Nice, *savoury*, 394.
  good, 648.
  exact, 494.
  pleasing, 829.
  honorable, 939.
  fastidious, 868.
Nicely, 31.
Nicety, *taste*, 850.
Niche, *recess*, 182.
  receptacle, 191.
Nick, *notch*, 257.
346

Nick, *mark*, 550.
  deceive, 545.
  of time, 134.
Nickname, 565.
Nictitate, 442, 443.
Nidget, 862.
Nidification, 189.
Nidor, 398.
Nidorous, 401.
Nidus, *nest*, 189.
  cradle, 153.
Niggard, 819.
Niggle, *trifle*, 643.
  depreciate, 483.
Nigh, 197.
Night, 421.
Nightfall, 126.
Nightingale, 416.
Night-mare, *pain*, 378.
  hindrance, 706.
Night-shade, 663.
Nigrification, 431.
Nihility, 4.
Nill, 764.
Nim, 791.
Nimble, *swift*, 274.
  active, 682.
  skilful, 698.
Nimiety, 641.
Nincompoop, 501.
Nine, 98.
Ninny, 501.
Ninnyhammer, 501.
Niobe, 839.
Nip, *cut*, 44.
  destroy, 162.
Nip up, 789.
Nipping, *cold*, 383.
Nipple, 250.
Nis, 980.
Nitency, 420.
Nizam, 745.
Nizy, 501.
No, 489, 536.
Noah's ark, 41.
Nob, 210.
Nobilitate, 873.
Nobility, 875.
Noble, *rank*, 873.
  generous, 942.
  virtue, 944.
Nobleman, 875.
Nobody, *absence*, 187.
  zero, 101.
  ignoble, 876.
Nocturnal, *dark*, 421.
  black, 431.
Nod, *sleep*, 683.
  signal, 550.
  assent, 488.

Nod, *order*, 741.
  information, 527.
  bow, 894.
Noddle, *head*, 450.
  summit, 210.
  to wag, 314.
Noddy, 501.
Node, 250.
Nodosity, *roughness*, 256.
  tuberosity, 250.
Nodule, 250.
Noggin, 191.
Noise, 402.
Noiseless, 403.
Noisome, 401.
Nolition, 603.
Nolleity, 603.
*Nom de guerre, 565.
Nomad, { *vagrant*, 264.
Nomadic, { *traveller*, 268.
  { *locomotive*,266.
Nomancy, 511.
Nomenclature, 564.
Nominate, 755.
Nominee, 758.
Nonage, 127.
Non-attendance, 187.
Non-appearance, 447.
Nonce, 118.
*Nonchalance, *neglect*, 460.
  indifference, 823.
Non-coincidence, 14.
Non-completion, 730.
Non-compliance, 742.
Nonconformity, *dissent*, 489.
  sectarianism, 984.
Nondescript, 83.
None, 101.
Nonentity, 2.
Non-essential, 643.
Nonesuch, 650.
Non-existence, 2.
Non-expectance, 508.
Nonny, 501.
Non-observance, 773.
*Nonpareil, 650.
Non-payment, 808.
Non-performance, 730.
Nonplus, 704.
Non-preparation, 674.
Non-resident, 187.
Non-resistance, *submission*, 725.
  obedience, 743.
Nonsense, *unmeaningness*, 517.
  absurdity, 497.
  folly, 499.

Nonsense, *trash*, 643.
Nonsuit, *to cast*, 731.
   to fail, 732.
Noodle, 501.
Nook, *place*, 182.
   receptacle, 191.
Noon,
Noonday, } *mid-day*, 125.
Noontide, } *light*, 420.
Nooscopic, 450.
Noose, *ligature*, 45.
   loop, 247.
   snare, 667.
Normal, *regular*, 82.
   vertical, 212.
Northern-lights, 420.
Nose, *smell*, 398.
   prominence, 250.
Nosegay, *fragrance*, 400.
   ornament, 847.
Nosology, 655.
Nostril, 351.
Nostrum, 662.
Not, 489.
Notable, *visible*, 446.
   important, 642.
   active, 682.
Notably, 31.
Notary, 553.
Notch, *nick*, 257.
   mark, 550.
Note, *sign*, 550.
   record, 551.
   letter, 592.
   music, 413.
   fame, 873.
   minute, 596.
   money, 800.
Note-book, 596.
Nothing, *nihility*, 4.
   zero, 101.
   trifle, 643.
Notice, *observe*, 457.
   mark, 550.
   warning, 668.
Notify, *inform*, 527.
   publish, 531.
Notion, *idea*, 453.
   belief, 484.
   knowledge, 490.
Notoriety, *fame*, 873.
   publication, 531.
Notorious, *known*, 490.
   seen, 446.
Notwithstanding, 179.
Noun, 564.
Nourish, 707.
Nous, *intellect*, 450.
   wisdom, 498.
Novel, *new*, 123.
347

Novel, *fiction*, 515.
   description, 594.
   unknown, 491.
   false, 546.
Novice, *learner*, 541.
   ignoramus, 493.
   bungler, 701.
   religious, 996.
Noviciate, *learner*, 541.
   training, 675.
Now, 118.
Now-a-days, 118.
Noways, 32.
Nowhere, 187.
Nowise, *in no degree*, 32.
   dissent, 489.
Noxious, 649.
Nozzle, *projection*, 250.
   air-pipe, 351.
   opening, 260.
*Nuance, 15.
Nucleus, *centre*, 223.
   middle, 68.
   cause, 153.
Nudge, 550.
Nudity, 226.
Nugatory, *inexistence*, 2.
   useless, 645.
Nuisance, *annoyance*, 830.
   evil, 619.
Null, 4.
Nullibiety, 187.
Nullify, *counteract*, 179.
   repudiate, 773.
Numb, *morally*, 823.
   physically, 381.
Number, *abstract*, 84.
   plurality, 100.
   to count, 85.
Numberless, 105.
Numbers, *poetry*, 597.
Numbness, *physical*, 381.
   moral, 823.
Numeral, 84.
Numeration, 85.
Numerator, 84.
Numerose, 578.
Numerous, 102.
Numismatics, 800.
Numpskull, 501.
Nun, 996.
Nuncio, *messenger*, 534.
   consignee, 758.
Nuncupatory,   *naming*, 564.
   informing, 527.
Nunnery, 1000.
Nuptials, 903.
Nurse, *servant*, 746.
   to help, 707.

Nurseling, 129.
Nursery, *school*, 542.
   workshop, 691.
Nurture, *food*, 299.
   to support, 707.
   prepare, 673.
Nutation, 314.
Nutbrown, 433.
Nutriment, 299.
Nutrition, 707.
Nutshell, 193.
Nymph, 374.

O.

Oaf, *fool*, 501.
   demon, 980.
Oak, 159.
Oar, *instrument*, 633.
   paddle, 266.
Oasis, 342.
Oath, *promise*, 768.
   assertion, 535.
Obedience, 743.
Obeisance, *bow*, 894.
   reverence, 928.
   worship, 990.
Obelisk, *monument*, 551.
   tall, 206.
Oberon, 980.
Obesity, 192.
Obey, 743.
Obfuscate, 426.
Obit, 360.
Obituary, 594.
Object, *thing*, 3.
   intention, 620.
   ugly, 846.
   to disapprove, 932.
Objective, *extrinsic*, 6.
Objurgate, 932.
Oblate, 201.
Oblation, *gift*, 789.
   proffer, 763.
   (religious), 990.
Oblectation, 827.
Obligation, *duty*, 926.
   promise, 768.
   debt, 806.
   gratitude, 916.
Oblige, *compel*, 744.
   benefit, 707.
Obliging, *kind*, 906.
   courteous, 894.
Oblique, 217.
Obliterate, *efface*, 552.
Oblivion, 506.
Oblong, 200.
Obloquy, *censure*, 932.

Obloquy, *disgrace*, 874.
Obmutescence, 581.
Obnoxious, *hateful*, 898.
  unpleasing, 830.
  pernicious, 649.
  liable, 177.
Oboe, 417.
Obscene, 961.
Obscure, *dark*, 421.
  unseen, 447.
  unintelligible, 519.
  style, 571.
  to eclipse, 874.
Obsecration, 765.
Obsequies, 363.
Obsequious, *respectful*, 928.
  courteous, 894.
  servile, 886.
Observe, *note*, 457.
  conform, 926.
  remark, 535.
Observance, *fulfilment*, 772.
  rule, 82.
  habit, 613.
  practice, 692.
  rites, 998.
Obsolete, *old*, 124.
  effete, 645.
  vulgar, 851.
Obstacle, *physical*, 179.
  moral, 706.
Obstinate, *stubborn*, 606.
  prejudiced, 481.
Obstreperous, *violent*, 173.
  loud, 404.
Obstruct, *hinder*, 706.
  close, 261.
Obtain, *exist*, 1.
  acquire, 775.
Obtainable, 470.
Obtestation, *entreaty*, 765.
  injunction, 695.
Obtrude, *intervene*, 228.
  insert, 301.
  obstruct, 706.
Obtund, *blunt*, 254.
  deaden, 376.
  paralyze, 826.
Obtuse, *blunt*, 254.
  stupid, 499.
  dull, 823.
Obumbrate, 421.
Obverse, 234.
Obviate, 706.
Obvious, *visible*, 446.
  clear, 518.
Occasion, *juncture*, 8.
  opportunity, 134.
348

Occasion, *cause*, 153.
Occasionally, 136.
Occlusion, 261.
Occult, *latent*, 526.
  hidden, 528.
Occupancy, *presence*, 186.
  property, 780.
  possession, 777.
Occupant, *dweller*, 188.
  proprietor, 779.
Occupation, *business*, 625.
  presence, 186.
Occupier, *dweller*, 188.
  possessor, 779.
Occur, *exist*, 1.
  happen, 151.
  be present, 186.
  to the mind, 451.
Ocean, 341.
Ochlocracy, 737.
Ocular, 441.
Odd, *exception*, 83.
  single, 87.
  remaining, 40.
  ludicrous, 853.
  vulgar, 851.
Oddity, *folly*, 499.
  laughing-stock, 857.
Oddments, 51.
Odds, *inequality*, 28.
  chance, 156.
  discord, 713.
Odds and ends, *portions*, 51.
  mixture, 41.
Ode, 597.
Odious, *ugly*, 846.
  hateful, 898.
Odium, *blame*, 932.
  disgrace, 874.
  hatred, 898.
Odour, 398.
Œcumenical, 78.
Œdematous, *soft*, 324.
  swollen, 192.
Œdipus, *expounder*, 524.
  answer, 462.
O'ertop, 194.
Off, 196.
Off-hand, *spontaneous*, 612.
  careless, 460.
Off-side, 238.
Offal, 653.
Offend, *affront*, 900.
Offence, *attack*, 716.
  guilt, 947.
Offensive, *unsavoury*, 395.
  fetid, 401.
  foul, 653.
  displeasing, 830.

Offensive, *distasteful*, 867.
  obnoxious, 898.
Offer, *proposal*, 763.
  gift, 784.
Offering, 990.
Office, *function*, 644.
  duty, 926.
  business, 625.
  mart, 799.
  room, 191.
Officer, *director*, 694.
  master, 745.
Official, *authoritative*, 737.
  business, 625.
Officiate, *conduct*, 692.
  act, 680.
  religious, 998.
Officious, 682.
Offing, 196.
Offscourings, *remains*, 40.
  dirt, 653.
  trash, 643.
Offset, 213.
Offshoot, 167.
Offspring, 167.
Offuscate, 421.
Often, 136.
Ogle, 441.
Oglio. *See* Olio.
Ogre, *demon*, 980.
  bugbear, 860.
Oil, } *unctuosity*, 355, 356.
Oily, } *smooth*, 255.
  flattery, 933.
  bland, 894.
  to assuage, 174.
Old, 124.
Old-fashioned, 851.
Oleaginous, 355.
Olfactory, 398.
Olid, 401.
Oligarchy, 737.
*Olio, 41.
Olive, 433.
Olive branch, 723.
Olive-green, 435.
*Olla podrida, 41.
Olympus, 981.
Omega, 67.
Omen, 512.
Ominous, 511.
Omission, *neglect*, 460.
  exclusion, 55.
  non-fulfilment, 773.
  guilt, 947.
Omnibus, 272.
Omnifarious, 81.
Omnipotence, 976.
Omnipresence, 186, 976.

Omniscience, 490.
   divine, 976.
Omnium gatherum, *mixture*, 41.
   confusion, 59.
On, *forwards*, 282.
*On dit, 531.
   news, 532.
On end, 212.
Once, 122.
One, 87.
Oneiromancy, 511.
Oneness, 87.
Onerous, 704.
One-sided, *prejudiced*, 481.
   partial, 940.
Onomancy, 511.
Onset, *attack*, 716.
   beginning, 66.
Onslaught, 716.
Ontology, 1.
*Onus, 926.
Onychomancy, 511.
Onward, 282.
Ooze, *distil*, 294.
   river, 348.
   sea, 341.
Opacity, 426.
Opalescent, 427.
Opaque, 426.
Open, *begin*, 66.
   expand, 194.
   unclose, 260.
   manifest, 525.
   reveal, 529.
   frank, 543.
   artless, 703.
Open-eyed, 457.
Openhearted, *sincere*, 543.
   frank, 703.
   honorable, 939.
Opening, *aperture*, 260.
   beginning, 66.
Openmouthed, *loud*, 404.
   loquacious, 584.
   gaping, 865.
Opera, *drama*, 599.
   music, 415.
   poetry, 597.
Operate, *incite*, 615.
   work, 680.
Operative, 690.
Operator, 690.
*Operculum, 222.
Operose, *difficult*, 704.
   active, 683.
Ophicleid, 417.
Opine, 484.
Opiniative, 606.
Opinion, 484.

Opinionative, 606.
Opium, 174, 823.
Oppilation, 706.
Opponent, *antagonist*, 710.
   enemy, 891.
Opportune, *well-timed*, 134.
   expedient, 646.
Opportunity, 134.
Oppose, *antagonize*, 179.
   clash, 708.
   evidence, 468.
Opposite, *contrary*, 14.
   anteposition, 237.
Oppress, *molest*, 649.
Oppression, *injury*, 619.
   dejection, 837.
Opprobrium, 874.
Oppugnation, 719.
Optative, 865.
Optics, *light*, 420.
   sight, 441.
Optimacy, 875.
*Optimates, 875.
Optimism, 858.
Option, 609.
Opulence, 803.
Opuscule, 593.
Oracle, *prophet*, 513.
   sage, 500.
Oracular, *wise*, 498.
   prophetic, 511.
Oral, 580.
Orange, 439.
Oration, 582.
Orator, *speaker*, 582.
   teacher, 540.
Oratorio, 415.
Oratory, 582.
Orb, *circle*, 247.
   region, 181.
   luminary, 423.
Orbicular, 247.
Orbit, *path*, 627.
Orchestra, 416.
Ordain, 741.
Ordained, *prescribed*, 924.
Ordeal, *experiment*, 463.
   sorcery, 992.
Order, *regularity*, 58.
   subordinate class, 75.
   law, 963.
   command, 741.
   rank, 877.
   quality, 875.
Orderless, 59.
Orderly, 82.
Orders (holy), 995.
Ordinance, *command*, 741.
   law, 963.
   rite, 998.

Ordinary, *usual*, 82.
   ugly, 846.
Ordination, 741.
Ordure, 653.
Ore, 635.
Organ, *instrument*, 633.
   music, 417.
Organist, 416.
Organization, *texture*, 329.
Organize, *arrange*, 60.
   plan, 626.
   prepare, 673.
   produce, 161.
Organized, 357.
Orgasm, 173.
Orgies, 954.
Orient, 420.
Orifice, 66.
Oriflamb, 550.
Origin, *cause*, 153.
   beginning, 66.
Original, *model*, 22.
   invented, 515.
Originate, *cause*, 153.
   begin, 66.
   invent, 515.
Originator, 164.
Orison, *request*, 765.
   prayer, 990.
Ormuzd, 979.
Ornament, 847.
   glory, 873.
   style, 577.
Ornate, 847.
Ornithomancy, 511.
Orphan, 160.
Orthodox, *true*, 494.
   in religion, 983.
Orthoepy, 580.
Orthography, 590.
Orthometry, 466.
Orts, *remnants*, 40.
   refuse, 643.
   useless, 645.
Oryctology, 368.
Oscillation, 314.
Oscitant, 260.
Oscitation, *sleepiness*, 683.
   fatigue, 688.
Osculate, 199.
Ossification, 323.
Ossuary, 363.
Ostensible, *visible*, 446.
   probable, 472.
   plea, 617.
Ostentation, 882.
Ostracise, *exclude*, 55.
   displace, 185.
   seclude, 893.
   censure, 932.

349

Other, 15.
Otherwise, 15.
O'Trigger, 887.
Ottar, 400.
Ottoman, 215.
*Oubliette, 752.
Ought, 926.
*Oui-dire, 532.
Oust, *displace*, 185.
    deprive, 789.
    dismiss, 756.
Out, 220.
Out and out, 31.
Outbalance, 33.
Outbid, 794.
Outbrave, 885.
Outbrazen, 885.
Outbreak, *violence*, 173.
    contest, 720.
Outcast, *secluded*, 893.
    sinner, 949.
    apostate, 941.
Outcry, *noise*, 411.
    complaint, 839.
    censure, 932.
Outdo, 682.
Outer, 220.
Outface, 885.
Outfit, 673.
Outgeneral, 731.
Outgo, *transgress*, 303.
    distance, 196.
Outgoings, 809.
Outgrow, 194.
Out-Herod, *bluster*, 173.
    exaggerate, 549.
Outhouse, 189.
Outlandish, *irregular*, 83.
    foreign, 10.
    barbarous, 851.
Outlast, 110.
Outlaw, *reprobate*, 949.
Outlawry, 964.
Outlay, 809.
Outleap, 303.
Outlet, *egress*, 294.
    opening, 260.
Outline, *contour*, 229.
    sketch, 554.
    features, 448.
    plan, 626.
Outlive, *survive*, 110.
    continue, 142.
Outlook, 885.
Outlying, 220.
Outmanœuvre, 731.
Outnumber, 102.
Outpost, *distance*, 196.
    circumjacent, 227.
    front, 234.
350

Outpouring, 527.
Outrage, *evil*, 619.
    grievance, 830.
Outrageous, *excessive*, 31.
    violence, 173.
*Outré, *ridiculous*, 853.
    exaggerated, 549.
Outreach, 545.
Outreckon, 482.
Outrider, 64.
Outright, 31.
Outrun, 274.
Outset, *beginning*, 66.
    departure, 292.
Outshine, *glory*, 873.
    eclipse, 874.
Outside, 220.
Outskirt, *environs*, 227.
    distance, 196.
Outspoken, 582.
Outspread, 202.
Outstanding, 40.
Outstep, *go beyond*, 303.
    distance, 196.
Outstretched, 200.
Outstrip, 274.
Out-talk, 584.
Outvie, *contend*, 720.
    shine, 873.
Outvote, 731.
Outward, 220.
Outweigh, *exceed*, 33.
    preponderate, 28.
    predominate, 175.
Outwit, *deceive*, 545.
    succeed, 731.
Outwork, *refuge*, 666.
    defence, 717.
Oval, 247.
Ovate, 247.
Ovation, *triumph*, 733.
    celebration, 883.
Oven, 388.
Over, *more*, 33.
    past time, 122.
    above, 220.
Over and above, 40.
Overabound, 641.
Over against, 237.
Over-act, *act*, 680.
    bustle, 682.
    affect, 855.
Overalls, 225.
Over-anxiety, 865.
Overawe, *intimidate*, 860.
    authority, 737.
Overbalance, *inequality*, 28.
    compensation, 30.
Overbearing, 885.
Overboard (to throw), 678.

Overburden, *fatigue*, 688.
    redundant, 641.
Overcast, *dark*, 421.
    dim, 422.
Overcharge, *exaggerate*, 549.
    redundance, 641.
    dearness, 814.
    style, 577.
Overcolour, 549.
Overcome, *conquer*, 732.
    shock, 824.
    tipsy, 959.
Overdate, 115.
Overdo, 682.
Overdose, 641.
Overestimate, 482.
Overflow, *stream*, 348.
    redundance, 641.
Overgo, 303.
Overgrown, 192.
Overhang, 206.
Overhaul, *inquire*, 461.
    attend to, 457.
    number, 85.
Overhead, 206.
Overhear, *hear*, 418.
    learn, 539.
Overjoyed, 827.
Overjump, 303.
Overlap, *cover*, 222.
    go beyond, 303.
Overlay, *excess*, 641.
    oppress, 649.
    hinder, 706.
    style, 577.
Overleap, 303.
Overload, *excess*, 641.
    obstruct, 706.
Overlook, *disregard*, 458.
    neglect, 460.
    superintend, 693.
    forgive, 918.
    slight, 929.
Overlooker, 694.
Overmatch, 28.
Overmuch, 641.
Overnight, 122.
Over-officious, 682.
Overpass, *exceed*, 33.
    transgress, 303.
Overplus, *excess*, 641.
    remainder, 40.
Overpower, *subdue*, 731.
    emotion, 824.
Overpowered, 732.
Overpowering, 825.
Overprize, 482.
Overrate, 482.
Overreach, *pass*, 303.

Overreach, *deceive*, 545.
  baffle, 731.
Over-ride, *pass*, 303.
  be superior, 33.
Over-righteous, 989.
Overrule, *control*, 737.
  cancel, 756.
Overrun, *ravage*, 649.
  excess, 641.
Overseer, 694.
Overset, *level*, 308.
  invert, 218.
  subvert, 731.
Overshadow, 421.
Overshoot, 303.
Oversight, *error*, 495.
  failure, 732.
Overspread, *cover*, 222.
  pervade, 186.
Overstate, 549.
Overstep, 303.
Overstrain, *overrate*, 482.
  fatigue, 688.
Overt, 446.
Overtake, *arrive*, 293.
Overtaken, *tipsy*, 959.
Overtask, 688.
Overtax, 688.
Overthrow, *destroy*, 162.
  level, 308.
  confute, 479.
  vanquish, 731, 732.
Overthwart, 708.
Overtop, *surpass*, 33.
  height, 206.
  perfection, 650.
Overture, *beginning*, 66.
  offer, 763.
  request, 765.
Overturn, *destroy*, 162.
  level, 308.
  invert, 218.
Overvalue, 482.
Overweening, *conceit*, 880.
  pride, 878.
Overweigh, *overrate*, 482.
  exceed, 33.
  influence, 175.
Overwhelm, *destroy*, 162.
  affect, 824.
Overwhelming, 825.
Overwise, 880.
Overwork, 688.
Overwrought, *excited*, 825.
  affected, 855.
Overzealous, 825.
Ovoid, 249.
Ovule, 247.
Owe, 806.
Owing to, 155.
351

Owl's light, 422.
Own, *assent*, 488.
  divulge, 529.
  possess, 777.
Owner, 779.
Ownership, 780.

P.

*Pabulum, 299.
Pace, *speed*, 274.
  step, 266.
  measure, 466.
Pacha, 745.
Pacific, 714.
Pacify, *allay*, 174.
  compose, 826.
  give peace, 723.
  forgive, 918.
Pachydermatous, 823.
Pack, *to join*, 43.
  arrange, 60.
  bring close, 197.
  locate, 184.
  assemblage, 72.
Pack off, *depart*, 292.
  recede, 286.
Pack up, 231.
Package, 72.
Packet, *parcel*, 72.
  ship, 273.
Packhorse, 271.
Packthread, 45.
Pact, 769.
Pactolus, 803.
Pad, 271.
Paddle, *oar*, 633.
  feet, 266.
  to row, 267.
Paddock, *region*, 181.
  prison, 752.
Padlock, *fastening*, 45.
  fetter, 752.
Pæan, *thanks*, 916.
  rejoicing, 836.
Paganism, 984.
Page, *attendant*, 746.
  of a book, 593.
Pageant, *spectacle*, 448.
  show, 882.
Pagoda, 1000.
Pail, 191.
Pain, *physical*, 378.
  moral, 828.
  penalty, 974.
Painful, 830.
Painim, 984.
Pains, 686.
Painstaking, *active*, 682.

Painstaking, *laborious*, 686.
Paint, *coat*, 222.
  colour, 428.
  delineate, 556.
  describe, 594.
Painter, 559.
Painting, 556.
Pair, *couple*, 89.
  similar, 17.
Palace, 189.
Palæontology, 368.
*Palæstra, *school*, 542.
  arena, 728.
  training, 673.
Palankeen, 272.
Palanquin, 272.
Palatable, *savory*, 394.
  pleasant, 829.
Palate, 390.
Palatine, 745.
Palaver, *speech*, 582.
  colloquy, 588.
  council, 696.
  nonsense, 497.
  loquacity, 584.
Pale, *dim*, 422.
  colourless, 429.
  inclosure, 232.
Paleography, 522.
Paleology, 122.
Palestric, 686.
Palfry, 271.
Palidoxy, 536.
Palimpsest, 147.
Palindrome, 563.
Palinody, *denial*, 536.
  recantation, 607.
Paling, } *prison*, 752.
Palisade, } *enclosure*, 232.
Pall, *funeral*, 363.
  satiate, 869.
Palladium, 717.
Pallet, 215.
Palliate, *mend*, 658.
  relieve, 834.
  extenuate, 937.
Pallid, 429.
Palling, 395.
Pallium, *dress*, 225.
  canonicals, 999.
Palm, *trophy*, 733.
  glory, 873.
  laurel, 877.
  deceive, 545.
  impose upon, 486.
Palmer, 268.
Palmistry, 511.
Palmy, *prosperous*, 734.
  joyous, 836.
Palpable, *tactile*, 379.

Palpable, *obvious*, 446.
  intelligible, 518.
Palpitate, *tremble*, 315.
  emotion, 821.
  fear, 860.
Palsy, *disease*, 655.
  weakness, 160.
  insensibility, 823.
Palter, *falsehood*, 544.
  shift, 605.
  elude, 773.
Paltry, *mean*, 940.
  despicable, 643.
  little, 32.
Paludal, 345.
Pampas, 344.
Pamper, *indulge*, 954.
  gorge, 957.
Pamphlet, 593.
Pamphleteer, 590.
Pan, 191.
*Panache, *plume*, 256.
  ornament, 847.
Pandect, *code*, 963.
  compendium, 596.
  erudition, 490.
Pandemonium, 982.
Pander (or pandar), *flatter*, 933.
  indulge, 954.
  help, 707.
Pandiculation, 260.
Pandora, 619.
Paned, 440.
Panegyric, 931.
Panel, 967.
Pang, *physical*, 378.
  moral, 828.
Panic, 860.
Pannel, 86.
Pannier, 191.
Panoply, 717.
Panopticon, 752.
Panorama, *view*, 448.
  painting, 556.
Pansophy, 490.
Pant, *breathless*, 688.
  desire, 865.
  agitation, 821.
Pantaloon, *buffoon*, 844.
  dress, 225.
Pantheism, 984.
Pantheon, 1000.
Pantomime, *sign*, 550.
  language, 560.
  drama, 599.
Pantry, 191.
Panurgy, 698.
Pap, *pulp*, 354.
  mamma, 250.
352

Paper, *writing*, 590.
  book, 593.
  record, 551.
  white, 430.
*Papilla, 250.
Pappy, 352.
Par, 27.
Parable, 594.
Parabolic, 521.
Parachronism, 115.
Parachute, 666.
Paraclete, 976.
Parade, *walk*, 189.
  ostentation, 882.
Paradigm, *prototype*, 22.
  example, 80.
Paradise, *heaven*, 981.
  bliss, 827.
Paradox, *obscurity*, 519.
  absurdity, 497.
  mystery, 528.
  enigma, 533.
Paragon, *perfection*, 650.
  saint, 948.
  glory, 873.
Paragram, 563.
Paragraph, *phrase*, 566.
  part, 51.
  article, 593.
Paralepsis, 460.
Parallax, 196.
Parallel, *position*, 216.
  similarity, 17.
  to imitate, 19.
  agreement, 23.
Paralogism, 477.
Paralyze, *weaken*, 160.
  deaden, 823.
  insensibility, *physical*, 376.
  moral, 823.
  disease, 655.
Paramount, *essential*, 642.
  in degree, 33.
Paramour, 897.
Parapet, 717.
Paraphernalia, *machinery*, 633.
  materials, 635.
  property, 780.
Paraphrase, *interpretation*, 522.
  phrase, 566.
  imitation, 19.
Parasite, *flatterer*, 935.
  servile, 886.
Parboil, 384.
Parcel, *group*, 72.
  portion, 51.
Parcel out, *arrange*, 60.

Parcel out, *allot*, 786.
Parch, *dry*, 340.
  bake, 384.
Parchment, *manuscript*, 590.
  record, 551.
Pardon, 918.
Pardonable, 937.
Pare, *scrape*, 38.
  shorten, 201.
  decrease, 36.
Paregoric, 656.
*Parenchyma, 329.
Parent, 166.
Parentage, *kindred*, 11.
Parenthesis, 228.
Parenthetically, 10.
Pariah, 876.
*Parietes, 224.
Paring, *part*, 51. See Pare.
Parishioner, 997.
Parity, 27.
Park, *plain*, 344.
  vegetation, 367.
  artillery, 727.
Parlance, 582.
*Parlementaire, 534.
Parley, *talk*, 588.
  mediation, 724.
Parliament, 696.
Parlour, 191.
Parody, *imitation*, 19.
  copy, 21.
  travestie, 856.
  misinterpret, 523.
Parole, 768.
Paronymous, 562.
Paroxysm, *violence*, 173.
  emotion, 825.
  anger, 900.
Parrot, *imitation*, 19.
  loquacity, 584.
Parry, *avert*, 623.
  defend, 717.
Parse, 567.
Parsee, 984.
Parsimony, 819.
Parson, 996.
Parsonage, 1000.
Part, *portion*, 51.
  component, 56.
  to diverge, 290.
  to divide, 44.
  business, 625.
  function, 644.
Part with, *relinquish*, 782.
  give, 784.
Partake, 778.
*Parterre, 367.

Partial, *unequal*, 28.
  special, 79.
  unjust, 923.
  love, 897.
  desire, 865.
  erroneous, 495.
Participation, 778.
Particle, *quantity*, 32.
  size, 193.
Particular, *special*, 79.
  event, 151.
  careful, 459.
  capricious, 608.
  odd, 851.
  item, 51.
  detail, 79.
Particularly, 31.
Parting, 44.
Partisan, 711.
Partition, *allot*, 786.
  wall, 228.
Partner, 711.
Partnership, *participation*,
  778.
  company, 797.
  companionship, 88.
Parts, *intellect*, 450.
  wisdom, 498.
  talents, 698.
Party, *assemblage*, 72
  association, 712.
  society, 892.
  special, 79.
Party-coloured, 440.
Party-wall, 228.
*Parvenu, *upstart*, 876.
  successful, 734.
Parvitude, 193.
*Pas, *rank*, 873.
  precedence, 62.
*Pasquinade, 932.
Pass, *move*, 264.
  move out, 294.
  move through, 302.
  exceed, 303.
  be superior, 33.
  happen, 151.
  lapse, 122.
  vanish, 449.
  passage, 260.
  defile, 203.
  way, 627.
  difficulty, 704.
  conjuncture, 8.
  forgive, 918.
  thrust, 716.
  passport, 760.
  time, 106.
Pass away, 2.
  cease, 141.

Pass by, 458.
Pass for, 544.
Pass in the mind, 451.
Pass over, *disregard*, 458.
  neglect, 460.
  exclude, 55.
  traverse, 302.
Pass the time, 106.
Passable, 651.
Passage, 264, 260, 151,
  302, 627. *See* Pass.
  transfer, 270.
  text, 593.
  act, 680.
  assault, 720.
Passenger, 268.
*Passepartout, 462, 631.
*Passetems, 840.
Passing, *exceeding*, 33.
  small, 32.
  transient, 111.
Passion, *emotion*, 820, 821.
  desire, 865.
  love, 897.
  anger, 900.
Passionate, *warm*, 825.
  irascible, 901.
Passionless, 823.
Passive, 172.
Passport, *permit*, 760.
  instrument, 631.
  order, 741.
Past, 122.
Paste, *cement*, 45.
  to cement, 46.
  pulp, 354.
*Pasticcio, 41.
Pastime, 840.
Pastor, 996.
Pastoral, *agricultural*, 371.
  poem, 597.
  religious, 995.
Pasturage, 344.
Pasture, *food*, 299.
  materials, 635.
Pasty, 352.
Pat, *expedient*, 646.
  pertinent, 9.
  to strike, 276.
Patagonian, 206.
Patch, *region*, 181.
  smallness, 193.
  blemish, 848.
  repair, 658.
Patchwork, *mixture*, 41.
  variegation, 440.
Pate, *head*, 450.
Patent, *open*, 260.
  visible, 446.
Patera, *plate*, 191.

Patera, *church*, 1000.
Paternity, 166.
Path, *way*, 627.
  direction, 278.
Pathetic, 830.
Pathless, *closure*, 261.
  difficult, 704.
  spacious, 180.
Pathognomonic, 550.
Pathology, 655.
Pathos, 821.
Pathway, 627.
Patience, *endurance*, 826.
  content, 831.
  perseverance, 682.
*Patois, 560.
Patriarch, 130.
Patrician, 875.
Patrimony, 780.
Patriot, 910.
Patrol, *safeguard*, 664.
  warning, 668.
Patronage, 707.
Patronize, 707.
Patronymic, 564.
Patter, 276.
Pattern, *model*, 22.
  type, 80.
  perfection, 650.
  saint, 948.
Patulous, 260.
Pauciloquy, 585.
Paucity, *fewness*, 103.
  scantiness, 640.
Paul Pry, 455.
Paunch, 191.
Pauperism, 804.
Pause, *stop*, 265.
  discontinuance, 141.
  rest, 687.
  disbelief, 485.
Pave, *prepare*, 673.
Pavement, 211.
Pavilion, 189.
Paving, 211.
Paw, *touch*, 379.
  finger, 633.
Pawn, 787.
Pay, *expend*, 809.
  defray, 807.
  paint, 222.
  condemn, 971.
  punish, 972.
Paymaster, 801.
Pea, 249.
Peace, *silence*, 403.
  amity, 721.
  concord, 714.
Peace-offering, *pacification*,
  723.

Peace-offering, *atonement*, 952.
Peach, 529.
Peach-colour, 434.
Peacock, *variegation*, 440.
  beauty, 845.
Pea-green, 435.
Peak, 210.
Peaked, 253.
Peal, *loudness*, 404.
  laughter, 838.
Pean. *See* Pæan.
Pearl, *gem*, 650.
  glory, 873.
Pearly, *nacreous*, 440.
  semitransparent, 427.
  white, 439.
Pear-shaped, 249.
Peasant, 876.
Peat, 388.
Pebble, *hardness*, 323.
  trifle, 643.
Peccability, 945.
*Peccadillo, 947.
Peccancy, *disease*, 655.
  imperfection, 651.
  badness, 649.
*Peccavi, 950.
Peck, *quantity*, 31.
  eat, 297.
Peckish, 865.
Pectinated, 253.
Peculate, 791.
Peculator, 792.
Peculiar, *special*, 79.
  exceptional, 83.
Peculiarly, 31.
Pecuniary, 800.
Pedagogue, *scholar*, 492.
  teacher, 540.
Pedant, *scholar*, 492.
  affected, 855.
  teacher, 540.
Pedantic, *affected*, 855.
  half-learned, 491.
  style, 577.
Peddle, *meddle*, 682.
  trifle, 643.
Pedestal, 215.
Pedestrian, 268.
Pedicle, 214.
Pedigree, *ancestry*, 166.
  continuity, 69.
Pediment, *capital*, 210.
  base, 215.
Pedlar, 797.
Peduncle, 214.
Peel, *skin*, 222.
  to uncover, 226.
Peep, 441.

Peep out, 446.
Peer, *equal*, 27.
  nobleman, 875.
  pry, 441.
  inquire, 461.
  appear, 446.
Peerless, *perfect*, 650.
  excellent, 648.
  virtuous, 944.
Peevish, *cross*, 895.
  irascible, 901.
Peg, *degree*, 26.
  project, 250.
  hang, 214.
  jog on, 266.
Pegomancy, 511.
Pelagic, 341.
Pelerine, 225.
Pelf, *money*, 803.
  materials, 635.
  gain, 775.
Pellet, 249.
Pellicle, *film*, 204.
  skin, 222.
Pell-mell, 59.
Pellucid, 425.
*Pelote, 249.
Pelt, *skin*, 222.
  throw, 276.
  attack, 716.
  beat, 972.
Pen, *surround*, 231.
  enclose, 232.
  restrain, 751.
  imprison, 752.
  write, 559.
Penalty, 974.
Penance, *atonement*, 952.
  penalty, 974.
*Penchant, *inclination*, 865.
  love, 897.
Pencil, *bundle*, 72.
  of light, 420.
  artist, 556, 559, 590.
Pencraft, 590.
Pendant, *flag*, 550.
*Pendant, *match*, 17.
Pendent, *during*, 106.
  hanging, 214.
Pending, 106.
Pendulous, 214.
Pendulum, *clock*, 114.
  oscillation, 314.
*Penetralia, 221.
Penetration, *ingress*, 295.
  passage, 302.
  discernment, 441.
  sagacity, 498.
  affection, 821, 824.
Penfold, 232.

Peninsula, 342.
Penitent, 950.
Penman, 590.
Penmanship, 590.
Penniless, 804.
Pennon, 550.
Pennyworth, 812.
Pensile, 214.
Pension, 803.
Pensioner, 746.
Pensive, *thoughtful*, 451.
  sad, 837.
Penumbra, 421.
Penurious, 819.
Penury, *poverty*, 804.
  scantiness, 640.
People, 373.
Pepper, *hot*, 171.
  pungent, 392.
  condiment, 393.
  attack, 716.
Peppercorn, 643.
Peppery, 901.
Peradventure, 156.
Perambulate, 266.
Percentage, 813.
Perception, *idea*, 453.
  of touch, 380.
Perceptible, 446.
Perceptivity, 375.
Perch, *support*, 215.
  to alight, 186.
  tall, 206.
Perchance, 156.
Percipience, 450.
Percolate, 294.
Percussion, 276.
Perdition, *ruin*, 732.
  loss, 776.
*Perdu, 528.
Peregrination, 266.
Peremptory, *assertion*, 535.
  denial, 536.
  firm, 604.
  rigorous, 739.
  authoritative, 737.
  compulsory, 744.
  order, 740.
Perennial, 110.
Perfect, *entire*, 52.
  complete, 729.
  excellent, 650.
Perfectly, 31.
Perfidy, 940.
Perflate, 349.
Perforate, 260.
Perforator, 262.
Perforce, 744.
Perform, *do*, 170.
  achieve, 729.

Perform, *produce*, 161.
  act, 599.
  fulfil, 772.
  duty, 926.
Performable, 705.
Performance, *effect*, 154.
Performer, *musician*, 416.
  actor, 599.
  workman, 164.
  agent, 690.
Perfume, 400.
Perfunctory, 460.
Perhaps, *possibly*, 470.
  chance, 156.
  supposition, 514.
Peri, 979.
Periapt, 993.
Pericranium, 450.
Perihelion, 197.
Peril, 665.
Perimeter, 229.
Period, *end*, 67.
  of time, 106, 108.
  point, 71.
  recurrence, 138.
Peripatetic, *traveller*, 268.
  ambulatory, 266.
Periphery, 229.
Periphrase, *phrase*, 566.
  diffuseness, 573.
Periscope, 441.
Periscopic, 445.
Perish, *vanish*, 2.
  die, 360.
  decay, 659.
Perissology, *diffuseness*, 573.
  loquacity, 584.
Perjury, *falsehood*, 544.
  untruth, 546.
Perked, *high*, 206.
  proud, 878.
  dressed up, 225.
Perlustration, 441.
Permanent, *unchanged*, 142.
  unchangeable, 150.
Permeable, 260.
Permeate, *pervade*, 186.
  insinuate, 228.
  pass through, 302.
Permission, 760.
Permit, 760.
Permutation, *change*, 140.
  numerical, 84.
Pernicious, 649.
Pernicity, 274.
Peroration, 67.
Perpend, 451.
Perpendicular, 212.
Perpetrate, 680.
355

Perpetual, 112.
  frequent, 136.
Perplex, *to derange*, 61.
  bewilder, 458.
  bother, 830.
  puzzle, 528.
Perplexity, *disorder*, 59.
  difficulty, 704.
  unintelligibility, 519.
  maze, 533.
Perquisite, 810.
Perquisition, 461.
Persecute, *worry*, 907.
  oppress, 619, 649.
Perseverance, *firmness*, 604.
  activity, 682.
  continuance, 143.
*Persiflage, 856.
Persist, 143.
Persistence, 142.
Person, 373.
Personable, 845.
Personage, 875.
Personal, *special*, 79.
Personate, *imitate*, 17.
  act, 554.
Personify, *metaphor*, 521.
Perspective, *view*, 448.
  futurity, 121.
  sagacity, 498.
  sight, 441.
Perspicacity, 518.
Perspicuity, 570.
Perspiration, 298.
Perstringe, 457.
Persuade, *induce*, 615.
  teach, 537.
  advise, 695.
Persuasible, 539.
Persuasion, *opinion*, 484.
  creed, 983.
Pert, *vain*, 880.
  saucy, 885.
  discourteous, 895.
Pertain, *belong*, 777.
  behove, 926.
Pertinacious, 606.
Pertinent, *relative*, 9.
  congruous, 23.
  applicable, 646.
Perturb, *derange*, 61.
  agitate, 315.
  emotion, 821.
  ferment, 171.
Pertusion, 260.
Peruse, 539.
Pervade, *extend*, 186.
  affect, 821.
Perverse, *crotchety*, 608.

Perverse, *difficult*, 704.
  wayward, 895.
Perversion, *injury*, 659.
  sophistry, 477.
  falsehood, 544.
  misinterpretation, 523
  misteaching, 538.
Pervicacious, 606.
Pervious, 260.
Pessomancy, 511.
Pest, 663.
Pester, 830.
Pesthouse, 662.
Pestiferous, 657.
Pestilence, 649.
Pestle, 330.
Pet, *plaything*, 840.
  favourite, 899.
  passion, 900.
  to love, 897.
  to fondle, 902.
Petard, 727.
Peterero, 727.
Petition, *ask*, 765.
  pray, 990.
Petitioner, 767.
*Petit-maître, 854.
*Pétri, 821.
Petrify, *dense*, 321.
  hard, 323.
  affright, 860.
  astonish, 870.
  thrill, 824.
Petronel, 727.
Petticoat, 225.
Pettifogging, 713.
Pettish, 901.
*Petto, 600, 620.
Petty, *in degree*, 32.
  in size, 193.
Petulant, *insolent*, 885.
  snappish, 895.
  angry, 900.
  irascible, 901.
Pew, 1000.
Phaeton, 272.
Phalanx, *army*, 726.
  party, 712.
  assemblage, 72.
Phantasm, *unreal*, 4.
  appearance, 448.
  delusion, 443.
Phantasmagoria, 445.
Phantasy, *imagination*, 515.
  idea, 453.
Phantom, *vision*, 448.
  unreal, 4.
  imaginary, 515.
Pharisaical, 544.

Pharisee, 548.
Pharmacology, 662.
Pharmacy, 662.
Pharos, 668.
Phase, *aspect*, 8.
    appearance, 448.
    form, 240.
Phasma, 448.
Phenix. *See* Phœnix.
Phenomenon, *appearance*, 448.
    event, 151.
    prodigy, 872.
Phial, 191.
Phidias, 559.
Philander, 902.
Philanthropy, 910.
Philippic, 932.
Philology, 567.
Philomath, *scholar*, 492.
    sage, 500.
Philomel, 416.
Philosopher, 492.
Philosophy, *calmness*, 826.
    knowledge, 490.
Philter, *charm*, 993.
    love, 897.
Phiz, 448.
Phlegm, 823.
Phœnix, *prodigy*, 872.
    exception, 83.
    paragon, 650.
    saint, 948.
Phonetics, ⎫ *sound*, 402.
Phonics, ⎭ *speech*, 582.
Phosphorescent, 420.
Photography, 556.
Photology, 420.
Photometer, 445.
Phrase, 566.
Phraseology, 569.
Phrensy, *madness*, 503.
    imagination, 515.
    passion, 825.
Phylacteric, 992.
Physic, *remedy*, 662.
    to cure, 660.
Physical, 316.
Physician, 695.
Physics, 316.
Physiognomy, *appearance*, 448.
    face, 234.
Physiology, 359.
Phytography, 369.
Phytology, 369.
Piacular, 952.
Pianist, 415.
*Piano, *slowly*, 275.
    faint sound, 405.
356

*Piano, *instrument*, 445.
Piazza, 189.
Pibroch, 415.
Picaroon, 792.
Pick, *select*, 609.
    extract, 300.
    eat, 297.
    clean, 652.
Pick up, *learn*, 539.
    acquire, 775.
Pickeer, 791.
Pickeerer, 792.
Picket, *join*, 43.
    tether, 265.
    fence, 231.
    guard, 664.
    imprison, 752.
    torture, 972.
Pickings, 775.
Pickle, *difficulty*, 704.
    condition, 8.
    preserve, 670.
    pungent, 392.
    macerate, 337.
Pickleherring, 844.
Pickpocket, 792.
Pickthank, 935.
Picnic, 299.
Picture, *painting*, 556.
    fancy, 515.
Picturesque, *beautiful*, 845.
    graphic, 556.
Piddling, *paltry*, 643.
Pie, *type*, 541.
Piebald, 440.
Piece, *bit*, 51.
    cannon, 727.
    drama, 599.
Piecemeal, 51.
Piece out, 52.
Pied, 440.
Pier, 666.
Pierglass, 445.
Pierce, *perforate*, 302.
    pain, 378, 830.
    affect, 824.
Piercing, *cold*, 383.
    sound, 404.
    sagacious, 498.
    feeling, 821.
    sight, 441.
Pietism, 989.
Piety, 987.
Pig, *sensual*, 954.
Pigeon-hearted, 862.
Pigeon-hole, *receptacle*, 191.
    aperture, 260.
Piggish, 954.

Pig-headed, *prejudiced*, 481.
    obstinate, 606.
    stupid, 499.
Pigment, 428.
Pigmy, 193.
Pignoration, 787.
Pig-stye, 653.
Pigwidgeon, *dwarf*, 193.
    fairy, 979.
Pike, *javelin*, 727.
    hill, 206.
Pikestaff, 206.
Pilaster, 206.
Pile, *heap*, 72.
    building, 189.
    store, 636.
Pilfer, 791.
Pilgarlic, 893.
Pilgrim, 268.
Pilgrimage, 266.
Pill, 249.
Pillage, *rob*, 971.
    rapine, 619.
    devastation, 649.
Pillar, *support*, 215.
    monument, 551.
    lofty, 206.
Pillion, 215.
Pillory, 975.
Pillow, *support*, 215.
    soft, 324.
    ease, 831.
Pilot, *director*, 694.
    to guide, 693.
    balloon, 273.
    trial, 463.
Pilous, 256.
Pimp, 962.
Pimple, *tumor*, 250.
    blemish, 848.
Pin, *fastening*, 45.
    to fasten, 43.
    axis, 312.
    sharp, 253.
    trifle, 643.
Pin down, *restrain*, 751.
    compel, 744.
Pinch, *emergency*, 8.
    to contract, 195.
    narrow, 203.
    chill, 385.
    pain, 378.
    to hurt, 830.
Pinching, *miserly*, 819.
Pine, *desire*, 865.
    grieve, 828.
    droop, 837.
Pinguid, 355.
Pin-hole, 260.

Pinion, *instrument*, 633.
  wing, 266.
  fetter, 752.
  to fasten, 43.
  to restrain, 751.
Pink, *colour*, 434.
  perfection, 650.
  beauty, 845.
  glory, 873.
  to pierce, 260.
Pinnace, 273.
Pinnacle, 210.
Pioneer, *prepare*, 673.
  teacher, 540.
Pious, 987.
Pipe, *conduit*, 350.
  vent, 351.
  tube, 260.
  sound, 410.
  cry, 411.
  music, 415.
  instrument, 417.
Piper, 416.
Piping, *sound*, 410.
  hot, 382.
Pipkin, 191.
Piquant, *pungent*, 392.
  style, 574.
Pique, *umbrage*, 889.
  hate, 898.
  anger, 900.
Pique oneself, 878.
Piquerer, 792.
Pirate, 792.
*Pirouette, 312.
*Pis-aller, 634.
  necessity, 601.
Piscatory, 366.
*Piste, 551.
Pistol, 727.
Piston, 263.
Pit, *hole*, 252.
  opening, 260.
  deep, 208.
  grave, 633.
  hell, 982.
Pit against, 708.
Pit-a-pat, 821.
Pitch, *degree*, 26.
  term, 51.
  height, 206.
  descent, 306.
  summit, 210.
  musical note, 413.
  dark, 421.
  black, 431.
  to throw, 284.
  to reel, 314.
  to place, 184.
Pitch tent, 265.

Pitch upon, *choose*, 609.
  reach, 293.
Pitch-pipe, 417.
Pitcher, 191.
Piteous, 830.
Pitfall, 667.
Pith, *gist*, 5.
  strength, 159.
  interior, 221.
  essential, 50.
  important, 642.
  meaning, 516.
Pithy, 572.
Pitiable, 643.
Pitiful, 643.
Pitiless, *malevolent*, 907.
  revengeful, 919.
Pittance, *allotment*, 786.
Pity, *compassion*, 914.
  regret, 833.
Pivot, *cause*, 153.
  axis, 312.
Pix, *assay*, 463.
  rites, 998.
Pixy, 980.
Placable, 918.
Placard, *notice*, 550.
  to publish, 531.
Place, *situation*, 182.
  circumstances, 8.
  rank, 873.
  term, 71.
  in order, 58.
  abode, 189.
  to locate, 184.
  substitution, 147.
  office, 625.
*Placebo, 933.
Placeman, 758.
Placid, *calm*, 826.
*Placit, 741.
Placket, 225.
Plagiarism, *stealing*, 791.
  borrowing, 788.
Plagiarist, 792.
Plague, *disease*, 655.
  pain, 828.
  to worry, 830.
  evil, 619.
Plaid, 225.
Plain, *horizontal*, 213.
  country, 344.
  obvious, 446.
  meaning, 518.
  simple, 849.
  artless, 703.
  ugly, 846.
  style, 576.
Plain-dealing, 543.
Plainsong, 990.

Plainspeaking, *veracity*,
  543.
  perspicuity, 570.
Plainspoken, 543.
Plaint, *cry*, 411.
  lamentation, 839.
Plaintiff, 967.
Plaintive, 839.
*Plaisanterie, 842.
Plait, *fold*, 258.
  to mat, 219.
Plan, *project*, 626.
  diagram, 554.
Plane, *flat*, 251.
  smooth, 255.
  horizontal, 213.
  to soar, 305.
Planet-struck, 732.
Plank, *board*, 204.
  safety, 666.
Plant, *vegetable*, 367.
  to insert, 301.
  place, 184.
  stop, 265.
Plantation, 367.
Plash, 343.
Plasm, 22.
Plasmic, 240.
Plaster, *cement*, 45.
  remedy, 662.
  mend, 658.
Plastic, *soft*, 324.
  form, 240.
Plat, 219.
Plate, *layer*, 204.
  engraving, 558.
Plateau, 213.
Platform, *support*, 215.
  stage, 542.
  horizontal, 213.
*Platitude, 497.
Platonic, *contemplative*,
  451.
  cold, 823.
  chaste, 960.
Platoon, *army*, 726.
  assemblage, 72.
Platter, *receptacle*, 191.
  layer, 204.
Plaudit, 931.
Plausible, *probable*, 472.
  sophistical, 477.
Play, *operation*, 170.
  scope, 180.
  chance, 186.
  drama, 599.
  amusement, 840.
  music, 415.
  oscillation, 314.
  to act, 680.

Play a part, 544.
Play of colours, 440.
Play upon, 545.
Play with, *deride*, 483.
Player, *actor*, 599.
   deceiver, 548.
   musician, 416.
Playfellow, 890.
Playful, 836.
Play-house, 599.
Playmate, 890.
Playsome, 836.
Plaything, *toy*, 840.
   trifle, 643.
   dependence, 749.
Plea, *excuse*, 617.
   vindication, 937.
   falsehood, 546.
   in law, 969.
Plead, *argue*, 467.
   encourage, 615.
   vindicate, 937.
Pleader, 968.
Pleasant, *agreeable*, 829.
   witty, 842.
   amusing, 840.
Please, 829.
Pleasing, 829.
Pleasure, *will*, 600.
   physical, 377.
   moral, 827.
Pleasurable, 829.
Plebeian, 876.
*Plébiciste, 969.
Pledge, *security*, 771.
   promise, 768.
   to borrow, 788.
   drink to, 894.
Plenary, *full*, 31.
   complete, 52.
   abundant, 639.
Plenipotentiary, 758.
Plenitude, 639.
Plenty, 639.
*Plenum, 3.
Pleonasm, 573.
Pleonastic, 573.
Plerophory, 484.
Plethora, 641.
*Plexus, 219.
Pliable, 324.
Pliant, *soft*, 324.
   facile, 705.
   irresolute, 605.
Plicature, 258.
Plight, *predicament*, 8.
   to promise, 768.
   security, 771.
Plinth, *base*, 211.
   rest, 215.
358

Plod, *trudge*, 275.
   work, 682.
Plodding, *dull*, 843.
Plot, *plan*, 626.
   of ground, 181.
Plough, 673.
Plough in 301.
Ploughman, 876.
Pluck, *take*, 789.
   cheat, 545.
   extract, 300.
   courage, 861.
   resolution, 604.
Plug, *stopper*, 263.
   to close, 261.
Plum, *sweetness*, 396.
   money, 800.
Plum-colour, 437.
Plumb, *close*, 261.
   measure, 466.
Plume, 256.
Plume oneself, 878.
Plummet, 466.
Plumose, 256.
Plump, 192.
Plump down, 306.
Plump upon, 293.
Plumper, 609.
Plunder, *booty*, 793.
   to steal, 791.
   ravage, 649.
   evil, 619.
Plunge, *dive*, 310.
   leap, 309.
   insert, 301.
   immerse, 337.
   precipitate, 308.
   adventure, 676.
   * *hurry*, 684.
Plurality, 100.
Plus, 37.
Plush, 256.
Plushy, 345.
Pluto, 982.
Pluvial, 348.
Ply, *use*, 677.
   work, 680.
   fold, 258.
Pneumatics, 333.
Pneumatology, 450.
Poach, 791.
Poachy, 345.
Pocket, *pouch*, 191.
   to place, 184.
   take, 789.
   receipts, 810.
   treasury, 802.
   diminutive, 193.
*Pococurante, 603, 823.
Poem, 597.

Poet, 597.
Poetry, 597.
Poignant, *physical*, 171.
   moral, 821.
Point, *condition*, 8.
   degree, 26.
   term, 71.
   place, 182.
   question, 461.
   topic, 454.
   prominence, 250.
   mark, 550.
   intention, 620.
   wit, 842.
   punctilio, 939.
   speck, 193.
   poignancy, 171.
   sharp, 253.
Point blank, 278.
Pointless, 843.
Point of view, *aspect*, 441.
   idea, 453.
   relation, 9.
Point to, *indicate*, 550.
   show, 525.
   mean, 516.
   predict, 511.
Pointer, *index*, 550.
Poise, *balance*, 27.
   measure, 466.
Poison, *bane*, 663.
   to injure, 659.
Poisonous, *deleterious*, 657.
   injurious, 649.
Poke, *push*, 276.
   project, 250.
   pocket, 191.
Poker, *stiff*, 323.
Polacca, 273.
Polacre, 273.
Polar, 210.
Polariscope, 445.
Polarity, *duality*, 89.
   antagonism, 179.
Pole, *lever*, 633.
   summit, 210.
   tallness, 206.
Poleaxe, 727.
Polecat, 401.
Polemics, *discussion*, 476.
   discord, 713.
Polemoscope, 445.
Polestar, *indication*, 550.
   guide, 695.
Police, *jurisdiction*, 965.
   constable, 968.
Policy, *plan*, 626.
   conduct, 692.
   skill, 698.

Polish, *smooth*, 255.
  to rub, 331.
  furbish, 658.
  beauty, 845.
  ornament, 847.
  taste, 850.
Polite, 894.
Politic, *wise*, 498.
  skilful, 698.
  cunning, 702.
Politician, *tactician*, 700.
  statesman, 745.
Polity, *plan*, 626.
  conduct, 692.
Poll, *count*, 85.
  parrot, 584.
Pollute, *corrupt*, 659.
  soil, 653.
  disgrace, 874.
  dishonour, 940.
Pollution, *vice*, 945.
  disease, 655.
Poltroon, 862.
Polychord, 417.
Polychromatic, 440.
Polyphonism, 580.
Polygamy, 903.
Polyglot, 562.
Polygon, *figure*, 244.
  buildings, 189.
Polygonal number, 84.
Polygraphy, 590.
Polylogy, 584.
Polyscope, 445.
Polysyllable, 561.
Polytheism, 984.
Pomatum, 356.
Pommel, 249.
Pomp, 882.
Pompous style, 577.
Pond, 343.
Ponder, 451.
Ponderation, 480.
Ponderous, 319.
Poney, 271.
Poniard, 727.
Pontiff, 996.
Pontifical, 995.
Pooh-pooh! 643, 930.
Pool, 343.
Poop, 235.
Poor, *indigent*, 804.
  weak, 160.
  insufficient, 640.
  trifling, 643.
  contemptible, 930.
  style, 575.
Poorly, 655.
Poor-spirited, 862.
Pop, *noise*, 406.

Pop, *unexpected*, 508.
Pop upon, *arrive*, 293.
  find, 480.
Pope, 996.
Pop-gun, 406.
Popinjay, 854.
Populace, 876.
Popular, *current*, 484.
  favourite, 897.
  celebrated, 873.
Population, *mankind*, 373.
  inhabitants, 188.
Populous, *crowded*, 72.
Porch, *entrance*, 66.
  opening, 260.
  mouth, 230.
  way, 627.
  receptacle, 191.
Porcupine, 253.
Pore, *opening*, 260.
  conduit, 350.
  look, 441.
  apply the mind, 457.
Porous, *foraminous*, 260.
  light, 322.
Porpoise (*or* porpus), 192.
Porringer, 191.
Port, *harbour*, 666.
  gait, 264.
  resting-place, 265.
  arrival, 293.
  carriage, 448.
  demeanour, 852.
Portable, *movable*, 268.
Portage, 270.
Portal, *entrance*, 66.
  mouth, 230.
  opening, 260.
  way, 627.
Portative, 268.
  small, 193.
Portcullis, 717.
Portend, 511.
Portent, 512.
Portentous, *prophetic*, 511.
  fearful, 860.
Porter, *carrier*, 271.
  janitor, 263.
Porterage, 270.
Portfolio, *record*, 551.
  miscellany, 72.
Porthole, 260.
Portico, *entrance*, 66.
  room, 191.
Portion, *piece*, 51.
  allotment, 786.
Portly, 192.
Portmanteau, 191.
Portrait, 556.
Portray, *describe*, 594.

Portray, *paint*, 556.
Pose, *puzzle*, 485.
  hide, 528.
  difficulty, 704.
  embarrassment, 491.
Position, *circumstances*, 8.
  situation, 183.
  assertion, 535.
Positive, *certain*, 474.
  real, 1.
  true, 494.
  unequivocal, 518.
  absolute, 739.
  obstinate, 606.
  assertion, 535.
  quantity, 84.
Positively, *great*, 31.
Posse, *collection*, 72.
  party, 712.
Possess, *have*, 777.
  feel, 821.
Possession, *property*, 780.
Possessor, 779.
Possible, *contingent*, 470.
  casual, 621.
Post, *support*, 215.
  place, 184.
  beacon, 550.
  swift, 274.
  employment, 625.
  office, 926.
  to record, 551.
  accounts, 811.
  mail, 592.
  to stigmatize, 874.
Post-date, 115.
Post-diluvian, 117.
Posterior, *in time*, 117.
  in order, 63.
  in space, 235.
Posterity, *in time*, 117.
  descendants, 167.
Postern, *back*, 235.
  portal, 66.
Post-existence, 121.
Post-haste, *fast*, 274.
  precipitate, 863.
Posthumous, *late*, 133.
  subsequent, 117.
Postillion, 694.
*Post-obit, 360.
Postpone, 133.
Postscript, *sequel*, 65.
  appendix, 39.
Postulant, 767.
Postulate, *supposition*, 514.
  evidence, 467.
  reasoning, 476.
Postulation, *request*, 765.
Posture, 8.

Posture-master, *buffoon*, 844.
  mountebank, 548.
Posy, *motto*, 550.
  poem, 597.
  flowers, 847.
Pot, *mug*, 191.
  ruin, 732.
Potable, 299.
Potation, 297.
Pot-companion, 890.
Potency, 157.
Potentate, 745.
Potential, *virtual*, 2.
  possible, 470.
  power, 157.
Pother, *to worry*, 830.
Pot-hooks, 590.
Pot-luck, 299.
Pottage, 299.
Potter, 682.
Pottle, 191.
Potulent, *drink*, 299.
  drunken, 959.
Pot-valiant, 959.
Pouch, 191.
Poultice, *soft*, 354.
  remedy, 662.
Pounce upon, 789.
Pound, *bruise*, 330.
  mix, 41.
  inclose, 232.
  imprison, 752.
Poundage, 813.
Pounds, 800.
Pour, 294.
Pour out, 296.
Pout, *sullen*, 895.
  sad, 837.
Poverty, *indigence*, 804.
  scantiness, 640.
  trifle, 643.
Powder, 330.
Power, *efficacy*, 157.
  authority, 737.
  much, 31.
  numerical, 84.
  of style, 574.
Powerful, 159.
Powerless, 160.
Pox, 655.
Praam, 273.
Practicable, *possible*, 470.
  easy, 705.
Practice, *act*, 680.
  conduct, 692.
  use, 677.
  habit, 613.
  rule, 80.
  proceeding, 626.
360

Practise, *deceive*, 645.
Practised, 698.
Practitioner, 690.
Pragmatical, *pedantic*, 855.
  vain, 880.
Prahu, 273.
Prairie, 344.
Praise, *commendation*, 931.
  thanks, 916.
  worship, 990.
Praiseworthy, *commendable*, 931.
  virtuous, 944.
Prance, *dance*, 315.
  move, 266.
Prank, *caprice*, 608.
  amusement, 840.
  vagary, 856.
  to adorn, 845.
Prate, *babble*, 584.
Prattle, *talk*, 582.
Praxiteles, 559.
Pray, 765.
Prayer, 765, 990.
Preach, *teach*, 537.
  predication, 998.
Preacher, 996.
Preadamite, 130.
Preamble, 64.
Preapprehension, 481.
Prebendary, 996.
Prebendaryship, 995.
Precarious, *uncertain*, 475.
  perilous, 665.
Precatory, 765.
Precaution, *care*, 459.
  safety, 664.
  expedient, 626.
  preparation, 673.
Precede, *in order*, 62.
  in time, 116.
Precedent, 80.
Precentor, 996.
Precept, *maxim*, 697.
  order, 741.
  permit, 760.
  decree, 963.
Preceptor, 540.
Precession, *in order*, 62.
  in motion, 280.
Precincts, *environs*, 227.
  boundary, 233.
  region, 181.
  place, 182.
Precious, *excellent*, 648.
  valuable, 814.
  beloved, 897.
Precipice, *slope*, 217.
  vertical, 212.
Precipitancy, 684.

Precipitate, *rash*, 863.
  early, 132.
  transient, 111.
  to sink, 308.
  refuse, 653.
  consolidate, 321.
  swift, 274.
Precipitous, 217.
*Précis, 596.
Precise, *exact*, 494.
  definite, 518.
Precisely, *assent*, 488.
Precisianism, 989.
Preclude, 706.
Precocious, *early*, 132.
  immature, 674.
Precognition, *foresight*, 510.
  knowledge, 490.
Preconception, 481.
Preconcert, 673.
Preconcerted, 600.
Precursor, *forerunner*, 64.
  harbinger, 512.
Precursory, *in order*, 62.
  in time, 116.
Predacious, 791.
Predatory, 791.
Predecessor, *in order*, 64.
  in time, 116.
Predeliberation, 459.
Predestination, *fate*, 152.
  necessity, 601.
  predetermination, 611.
Predetermination, 611.
Predetermined, 600, 611.
Predial, 780.
Predicament, *situation*, 8.
Predicate, 535.
Predication, 998.
Prediction, 511.
Predilection, *love*, 897.
  desire, 865.
  inclination, 602.
Predisposition, *proneness*, 602.
  motive, 615.
  affection, 820.
  preparation, 673.
Predominance, *influence*, 175.
  inequality, 28.
Pre-eminent, *celebrated*, 873.
  superior, 33.
Pre-emption, 795.
Pre-establish, 673.
Pre-examine, 461.
Pre-exist, *priority*, 116.
  past, 122.

Preface, 62, 64.
Prefatory, *in order*, 62.
   in time, 106.
Prefect, *ruler*, 745.
   deputy, 759.
Prefecture, 737.
Prefer, *choose*, 609.
   a petition, 765.
Preferment, *improvement*,
   658.
   ecclesiastical, 995.
Prefiguration, *indication*,
   550.
   prediction, 510.
Prefix, 62, 64.
Pregnant, *productive*, 168.
   predicting, 511.
   important, 642.
Prehension, 789.
Preinstruct, 537.
Prejudge, 481.
Prejudicate, 481.
Prejudice, *evil*, 619.
   detriment, 649.
Prelacy, 995.
Prelate, 996.
Prelection, 537.
Prelector, 540.
Preliminary, { *preceding*, 62.
Prelude, { *precursor*, 64.
Prelusory, { *priority*, 116
Premature, 132.
Premeditate, *intend*, 620.
   predetermine, 611.
Premeditated, 600.
Premier, 694.
Premise, *prefix*, 62.
   announce, 511.
Premises, *ground*, 182.
   evidence, 467.
Premium, *reward*, 973.
   receipt, 810.
Premonition, 668.
Premonstration, 511.
Prenomen, 564.
Prenotion, *prejudice*, 481.
   foresight, 510.
Prensation, 789.
Prenticeship, 673.
Preoccupy, *possess*, 777.
   the attention, 458.
Preoption, 609.
Preordain, 601.
Preordination, 152.
Prepare, *mature*, 673.
   plan, 626.
   instruct, 537.
Preparatory, 62.
361

Prepared, *ready*, 698.
Prepense, *advised*, 611.
   spontaneous, 600.
   intended, 620.
Prepollence, 157.
Preponderant, *unequal*, 28.
   important, 642.
Prepossessing, 829.
Prepossession, 481.
Preposterous, *in degree*, 31.
   in size, 192.
   ridiculous, 853.
   absurd, 499.
Prepotency, 157.
Prerequisite, 630.
Preresolve, 611.
Prerogative, *right*, 924.
   authority, 737.
Presage, *omen*, 512.
   to predict, 511.
Presbyopic, 443.
Prescient, 510.
Prescious, 511.
Prescribe, *order*, 741.
   entitle, 924.
Prescript, *decree*, 741.
   precept, 697.
   law, 963.
Prescription, *remedy*, 662.
Prescriptive, 924.
Presence, *in space*, 186.
   appearance, 448.
   carriage, 852.
Presence of mind, 864.
Present, *in time*, 118.
   in place, 186.
   in memory, 505.
   give, 784.
   offer, 763.
   introduce, 894.
   to the mind, 451.
Presentable, 852.
Presentation, *offer*, 763.
Presentiment, *prejudgment*,
   481.
   instinct, 477.
   foresight, 510.
Presently, 111.
Preservation, *continuance*,
   142.
   conservation, 670.
Preshow, 511.
Preside, 737.
Presidency, 737.
President, 745.
Press, *hasten*, 132.
   urge, 684.
   compel, 744.
   offer, 763.
   solicit, 615.

Press, *crowd*, 72.
   closet, 191.
   velocity, 274.
Press in, 301.
Pressing, *urgent*, 642.
Pressure, *weight*, 319.
   influence, 175.
   urgency, 642.
   affliction, 830.
Prestigation, 545.
*Prestige, *attractiveness*,
   829.
   motive, 615.
*Presto, 111.
Prestriction, 442.
Presume, *suppose*, 514.
   hope, 858.
Presumption, *probable*, 472.
   right, 924.
Presuppose, { *prejudge*, 481
Presurmise, { *conjecture*, 514.
Pretence, *untruth*, 546.
   excuse, 617.
Pretend, *simulate*, 544.
   assert, 535.
Pretender, *boaster*, 884.
   deceiver, 548.
Pretention, *claim*, 924.
   affectation, 855.
   vanity, 880.
Preterition, 122.
Preterlapsed, 122.
Pretermit, *omit*, 460.
Preternatural, *irregular*, 83.
Pretext, *excuse*, 617.
Pretty, 845.
Pretty well, *much*, 31.
   imperfect, 651.
Prevail, *influence*, 175.
   exist, 1.
Prevail upon, 615.
Prevailing, *preponderating*,
   28.
   usual, 82.
Prevalence, *influence*, 175.
   usage, 613.
Prevaricate, *falsehood*, 544.
   equivocate, 520.
Prevenient, 62.
Prevention, *hindrance*, 706.
   prejudice, 481.
Previous, *in order*, 62.
   in time, 116.
Prevision, 510.
Prewarn, 668.
Prey, *food*, 299.
   booty, 793.
   victim, 828.
Price, *money*, 812.

Price, *value*, 648.
Priceless, 643.
Prick, *sharpness*, 253.
  to incite, 615.
  to sting, 378.
  pain, 830.
Prickle, 253.
Pride, *loftiness*, 878.
  ornament, 847.
Priest, 996.
Priestcraft, 995.
Priesthood, 996.
Priestridden, 989.
Prig, *puppy*, 854.
  blusterer, 887.
  to steal, 791.
Priggish, 855.
Prim, 855.
Primacy, 995.
Primary, 642.
Primate, 996.
*Primates, 875.
Prime, *early*, 132.
  primeval, 124.
  excellent, 650.
  important, 642.
  skill, 698.
  to prepare, 673.
  teach, 537.
  number, 84.
Primeval, 124.
Primitive, 124.
Primogenial, 66.
Primogeniture, 167.
Primordial, 124.
Primrose-colour, 436.
Prince, 745.
Princely, *authoritative*, 737.
  liberal, 816.
  generous, 942.
Principal, 642.
Principality, 780.
Principle, *element*, 316.
  cause, 153.
  truth, 494.
  law, 80.
  tenet, 484.
  motive, 615.
Prink, *adorn*, 845.
  show off, 882.
Print, *mark*, 550.
  record, 551.
  engraving, 558.
  letter-press, 591.
Printless, 552.
Prior, *in order*, 62.
  in time, 116.
  religious, 996.
Prioress, 996.
Priory, 1000.

362

Prism, 445.
Prismatic, 428.
Prison, 752.
Prisoner, *captive*, 754.
  defendant, 967.
Pristine, 122.
Prithee, 765.
Prittle-prattle, 588.
Privacy, *secrecy*, 526.
  seclusion, 893.
Private, *special*, 79.
Privateer, 726.
Privation, *loss*, 776.
  poverty, 804.
Privilege, 924.
Privity, 490.
Prize, *booty*, 993.
  success, 731.
  palm, 733.
  good, 618.
Prizefighter, 726.
Probability, 472.
Probate, 467.
Probation, *trial*, 463.
  essay, 675.
  demonstration, 478.
Probationer, 541.
Probe, *stiletto*, 262.
  measure, 466.
  investigate, 461.
Probity, *virtue*, 944.
  integrity, 939.
Problem, *enigma*, 533.
  inquiry, 461.
Problematical, *uncertain*, 475.
  hidden, 528.
Proboscis, 250.
Procacity, *rudeness*, 895.
  insolence, 885.
  anger, 900.
Procedure, *conduct*, 692.
  action, 680.
  plan, 626.
Proceed, *advance*, 282.
  from, 154.
  happen, 151.
Proceeding, *action*, 680.
  event, 151.
  plan, 626.
Proceeds, *money*, 800.
  receipts, 810.
Procerity, 206.
Process, *projection*, 250.
  plan, 626.
  action, 680.
  conduct, 692.
  time, 109.
Procession, *train*, 69.
  ceremony, 882.

Prochronism, 115.
Proclaim, 531.
Proclivity, *disposition*, 602.
  proneness, 820.
Proconsul, 759.
Proconsulship, 737.
Procrastination, 683.
Procreant, 168.
Procreate, 161.
Procreator, 166.
Proctor, *officer*, 694.
  law, 968.
Proctorship, 693.
Procumbent, 213.
Procuration, 755.
Procurator, 694.
Procure, *get*, 775.
  cause, 153.
  buy, 795.
  pimp, 962.
Prodigal, *extravagant*, 818.
  lavish, 641.
Prodigious, *wonderful*, 870.
  much, 31.
Prodigy, 872.
*Prodromus, 596.
Produce, *cause*, 153.
  create, 161.
  prolong, 200.
  show, 525.
  evidence, 467.
  result, 154.
  fruit, 775.
Product, 154, 775.
  multiple, 84.
Productive, 168.
Proem, 64.
Proemial, *preceding in order*, 62.
  beginning, 66.
  in time, 106.
Profane, *impious*, 989.
  desecrate, 679.
  laical, 997.
Profess, 535.
Profession, 625.
Professor, 540.
Proffer, 763.
Proficience, 698.
Proficient, *adept*, 700.
  knowledge, 490.
  skilful, 698.
Profile, *lateral*, 236.
  outline, 229.
  appearance, 448.
Profit, *acquisition*, 775.
  advantage, 618.
Profitable, *useful*, 644.
  gainful, 810.
Profitless, 645.

Profligacy, 945.
Profluent, *advancing*, 282.
  flowing, 348.
Profound, *deep*, 208.
  knowledge, 490.
  sagacity, 702.
  feeling, 821.
Profoundly, 31.
Profuse, *prodigal*, 1 .
  lavish, 641.
Prog, *food*, 299.
  materials, 635.
Progenitor, 166.
Progeny, 167.
Prognostic, 512.
Prognosticate, 511.
*Programme, *catalogue*, 86.
  announcement, 510.
  plan, 626.
Progress, *advance*, 282.
  speed, 274.
  of time, 109.
  improvement, 658.
  success, 731.
Progression, *series*, 69.
  gradation, 58.
  numerical, 84.
  motion, 282.
Prohibit, 761.
Project, *bulge*, 250.
  propel, 284.
  plan, 626.
  intend, 620.
Projectile, *missile*, 284.
  weapon, 727.
Projection, *map*, 554.
Prolation, *voice*, 580.
  speech, 582.
*Prolegomena, 64.
*Prolepsis, 115.
Proletarian, 876.
Prolific, 168.
Prolix, 573.
Prolocutor, *teacher*, 540.
  speaker, 582.
Prologue, 64.
Prolong, *lengthen*, 200.
  protract, 110, 133.
Prolusion, *beginning*, 64.
  lesson, 537.
  dissertation, 595.
Promenade, 266.
Promethean, 359.
Prominent, *convex*, 252.
  conspicuous, 446.
  important, 642.
Prominently, 32.
Promiscuous, *irregular*, 59.
  casual, 621.
Promise, *engage*, 768.
363

Promise, *hope*, 858.
Premontory, *cape*, 342.
  projection, 250.
Promote, 707.
Promotion, 658.
Prompt, *in time*, 111.
  early, 132.
  quick, 274.
  suggest, 514.
  tell, 527.
  remind, 505.
  induce, 615.
  active, 682.
Promptuary, 636.
Promulgate, 531.
Pronation, 218.
Prone, *horizontal*, 213.
  tending, 176.
  inclined, 602.
  disposed, 820.
*Proner, 882.
*Proneur, 935.
Pronounce, *articulate*, 580.
  assert, 535.
  judge, 480.
  sentence, 969.
*Pronunciamento, 719.
Pronunciative,   *dogmatic*,
  536.
Proof, *demonstration*, 476.
  test, 463.
  copy, 21.
Prop, *support*, 215.
  help, 707.
  refuge, 666.
Propagable, 168.
Propagandism, 537.
Propagate, *produce*, 161.
  publish, 531.
Propel, 284.
Propensity, 602.
Proper, *special*, 79.
  right, 922, 926.
  expedient, 646.
  consonant, 23.
  handsome, 845.
Property, *possession*, 780.
  power, 157.
Prophecy, *prediction*, 511.
  scriptural, 985.
Prophet, 513.
Prophylactic, 662.
Prophylaxis, 670.
Propinquity, 197.
Propitiate, *forgive*, 918.
  atone, 952.
  pity, 914.
  religious, 976.
  worship, 990.
Propitious, *favouring*, 707.

Propitious, *opportune*, 134.
  prosperous, 734.
  auspicious, 858.
Proplasm, 22.
Proportion, *relation*, 9.
  mathematical, 84.
Proposal, 626.
Propose, *offer*, 763.
  intend, 620.
  suggest, 514.
  broach, 535.
  ask, 461.
Proposition, *reasoning*, 476.
  supposition, 454.
Propound, *broach*, 535.
  inquire, 461.
  suggest, 514.
Proprietary, 779.
Proprietor, 779.
Proprietorship, 777.
Propriety, *consonance*, 23.
  duty, 922, 926.
Propugn, *resist*, 717.
  vindicate, 937.
Propulsion, 284.
Prore, 234.
Prorogue, 133.
Proruption, 296.
Prosaic, *dull*, 843.
  style, 575.
Proscribe, *interdict*, 761.
  curse, 908.
  condemn, 971.
  denounce, 938.
  exclude, 77.
Prose, *not verse*, 598.
  to prate, 584.
  to weary, 841.
Prosecute, *pursue*, 622.
  arraign, 969.
Prosecutor, 967.
Proselyte, 541.
Proselytism, *teaching*, 537.
  belief, 484.
Prosody, 597.
Prosopopœia, 521.
Prospect, *view*, 448.
  futurity, 121.
Prospectus, *scheme*, 626.
  compendium, 596.
  programme, 86.
Prosperity, 731, 734.
Prosternation, 837.
Prostitute, *to corrupt*, 659.
  misuse, 679.
  dishonour, 962.
Prostrate, *low*, 207.
  level, 213.
  to depress, 308.
  weak, 160.

Prostrate, *exhausted*, 688.
  laid up, 655.
  dejected, 837.
  heart-broken, 830.
Prostration, *ruin*, 619.
  servility, 886.
  obeisance, 928.
  worship, 990.
Prosyllogism, 476.
*Protasis, *maxim*, 496.
  precursor, 64.
Protect, *shield*, 664.
  defend, 717.
Protector, 745.
Protectorate, 737.
*Protégé, 746.
Pro tempore, *temporarily*,
  111.
  occasion, 134.
Protervity, 901.
Protest, *dissent*, 489.
  denial, 536.
  refusal, 764.
  deprecate, 766.
  censure, 932.
  non-observance, 773.
  non-payment, 808.
Proteus, 149.
Prothonotary, 553.
Protocol, *document*, 551.
  warrant, 771.
Protoplast, 21, 22.
Protract, *time*, 110, 133.
  length, 200.
Protreptical, 615.
Protrude, 250.
Protuberance, 250.
Proud, *lofty*, 878.
  dignified, 873.
Prove, *demonstrate*, 478.
  try, 463.
  turn out, 151.
  affect, 821.
Provender, *food*, 299.
  materials, 635.
Proverb, 496.
Provide, *furnish*, 637.
  prepare, 673.
Provided, *qualification*, 469.
  condition, 770.
  conditionally, 8.
Providence, *foresight*, 510.
  divine government, 976.
Provident, *careful*, 459.
  wise, 498.
  prepared, 673.
Province, *region*, 181.
  department, 75.
  office, 625.
  duty, 926.
  364

Provincialism, 560.
Provision, *supply*, 637.
  materials, 635.
  preparation, 673.
  wealth, 803.
Provisional, *preparing*, 673.
  temporary, 111.
  conditional, 8.
Proviso, *qualification*, 469.
  condition, 770.
Provoke, *incite*, 615.
  excite, 824.
  vex, 830.
  hatred, 898.
  anger, 900.
Provost, 745.
Prow, 234.
Prowess, 861.
Prowl, 266.
Proximity, 199.
Proxy, 759.
Prudent, *cautious*, 864.
  wise, 498.
  discreet, 698.
Prudery, 855.
Prune, 201.
Prunello, 643.
Prurient, *desire*, 865.
  lust, 961.
Pry, *inquire*, 461.
  look, 441.
Psalm, 990.
Psalmody, 415.
Psephomancy, 511.
*Pseudo, *spurious*, 495.
  sham, 544.
Pseudo-revelation, 986.
Pseudoscope, 445.
Pshaw! 643.
Psychology, 450.
Psychomancy, 511.
Ptisan, 662.
Puberty, 127.
Public, 373.
Publication, *promulgation*,
  531.
  printing, 591.
  book, 593.
Publicity, 531.
Public-spirited, 910.
Puce-colour, 437.
Puck, 980.
Pucker, 828.
  fold, 258.
Pudder, 59.
Pudding, 299.
Puddle, 343.
Pudicity, 960.
Puerile, *boyish*, 127.
  trifling, 643.

Puerile, *foolish*, 499.
Puff, *wind*, 349.
  inflate, 194.
  boast, 884.
  pant, 688.
Puffed up, *vain*, 880.
  proud, 878.
Puffy, 192.
Pug, 201.
Pugh! 643.
Pugilism, 720.
Pugilist, 726.
Pugnacity, 901.
Puisné, 127.
Puissance, 157.
Puke, 296.
Pulchritude, 845.
Pule, *cry*, 411, 412.
  weep, 839.
Pull, *draw*, 285.
  attract, 289.
Pull down, *destroy*, 162.
  lay low, 308.
Pull out, *extract*, 300.
Pull up, *stop*, 265.
  accuse, 938.
Pullet, 129.
Pullulate, *grow*, 195.
  multiply, 168.
Pulp, 354.
Pulpiness, 352.
Pulpit, *rostrum*, 542.
  church, 1000.
Pulsate, { *oscillate*, 314.
Pulse,   { *agitate*, 315.
       { *periodically*, 138.
Pultaceous, 352.
Pulverulence, 330.
Pulvil, 400.
Pummel, *handle*, 633.
  beat, 276. 972.
Pump, *inquire*, 461.
  reservoir, 636.
Pun, *verbal*, 563.
  wit, 842.
Punch, *to perforate*, 260.
  perforator, 262.
  to strike, 276.
  punish, 972.
  buffoon, 857.
  humourist, 844.
  puncinello, 599.
  nag, 271.
Punctilio, 882.
Punctilious, *correct*, 494.
  observant, 772.
  scrupulous, 939.
Punctual, *early*, 132.
  periodical, 138.
  scrupulous, 939.

Punctuation, 567.
Puncture, 260.
Pundit, 492.
Pungent, *taste*, 392.
  caustic, 171.
  feeling, 821.
Punish, 972.
Punk, 962.
Punka, 349.
Punt, 273.
Puny, *in degree*, 32.
  in size, 193.
Pupil, 541.
Pupilage, 541.
Puppet, *subjection*, 749.
  effigy, 554.
  dupe, 547.
  little, 193.
Puppet-show, 599.
Puppy, *fop*, 854.
  blusterer, 887.
  braggart, 884.
Purana, 984.
Purblind, 442.
Purchase, *buy*, 795.
  leverage, 175.
Purgation, *cleansing*, 652.
  atonement, 952.
Purgatory, *suffering*, 828.
  atonement, 952.
  hell, 982.
Purge, *clean*, 652.
  improve, 658.
  atone, 952.
Pure, *simple*, 42.
  true, 494.
  clean, 652.
  truthful, 543.
  innocent, 946.
  virtuous, 944.
Purely, 32.
Purify, *cleanse*, 652.
  improve, 658.
Puritanical, *ascetic*, 955.
  pedantic, 855.
Purity, 960. See Pure.
  of style, 578.
Purl, *gurgle*, 405.
  music, 415.
Purlieu, 227.
Purloin, 791.
Purple, 437.
Purport, *meaning*, 516.
  intent, 620.
Purpose, 620.
Purposeless, 601.
Purposely, 600.
Purr, 412.
Purse, *money-bag*, 802.
  wealth, 803.
365

Purse, *to shrivel*, 195.
Purse-bearer, 801.
Purse-proud, 878.
Purser, 801.
Purse-strings, 802.
Pursuant to, 620.
Pursue, *follow*, 281.
  continue, 143.
  aim, 622.
  inquire, 461.
Pursuivant, 534.
Pursy, 192.
Purulent, 653.
Purvey, 637.
Push, *exigency*, 8.
  accelerate, 274.
  impel, 276.
  propel, 284.
  repel, 288.
  activity, 682.
Push on, 282.
Pushing, 682.
Pusillanimity, 862.
Pustule, *pimple*, 250.
  blemish, 848.
Put, *place*, 184.
  a question, 461.
  laughing-stock, 857.
  fool, 501.
Put about, *turn back*, 283.
  circuition, 311.
Put away, 624.
Put by, 817.
Put down, *destroy*, 162.
  baffle, 731.
  humiliate, 874.
Put forth, *assert*, 535.
  suppose, 514.
Put into, *insert*, 301.
  land, 293.
Put off, 133.
Put on, *clothe*, 225.
  deceive, 544.
Put out, *quench*, 385.
  darken, 421.
  perplex, 458.
  difficulty, 704.
Put up to, *teach*, 537.
Put up with, 821.
Put upon, 545.
Putative, 155.
Putid, 940.
Putrefy, 653.
Putrid, 653.
Putty, 45.
Puzzle, *enigma*, 533.
  mystify, 528.
  stagger, 485.
  bewilder, 491.
Puzzle-headed, 499.

Puzzling, *uncertain*, 475.
Pygmy, 193.
Pylades, 890.
Pyramid, *point*, 253.
  heap, 72.
Pyre, 363.
Pyromancy, 511.
Pyrometer, 389.
Pyrotechny, 382.
Pyrrhonism, 487.
Pythagorean, 953.
Python, 513.
Pyx, 191.
Pyxis, 1000.

Q.

Quack, *impostor*, 548.
  cry, 412.
Quacksalver, 548.
Quackery, 545, 855.
Quadrant, *measure*, 466.
Quadrate with, 23.
Quadratic, 95.
Quadrifid, 97.
Quadripartition, 97.
Quadrisection, 97.
Quadruped, 366.
Quadruple, 96.
Quaff, 297.
Quagmire, *bog*, 345.
  mire, 653.
  difficulty, 704.
Quail, 860.
Quaint, *odd*, 83.
  ridiculous, 853.
  pretty, 845.
  style, 572.
Quake, *shake*, 315.
  fear, 860.
  cold, 383.
Qualification, *modification*, 469.
  accomplishment, 698.
Qualify, *train*, 673.
  modify, 469.
  teach, 537.
Quality, *power*, 157.
  nature, 5.
  character, 820.
  nobility, 875.
Qualm, *fear*, 860.
  scruple, 616.
  disbelief, 485.
  penitence, 950.
Quandary, 704.
Quantity, 25.
*Quantum, *amount*, 25.
  allotment, 786.

*Quaquaversum, 278.
Quarantine, 664.
Quarrel, 713.
Quarrelsome, 901.
Quarry, *mine*, 636.
　object, 620.
Quartain, 597.
Quarter, *fourth*, 97.
　region, 181.
　side, 236.
　direction, 278.
　to place, 184.
　mercy, 914.
Quartering, 97.
Quartermaster, 637.
Quarters, 189.
Quartet, 95.
Quash, *destroy*, 162.
　annul, 756.
*Quasi, 17.
Quaternal, 94.
Quaternity, 95.
Quaver, *oscillate*, 314.
　shake, 315.
　sound, 407.
　music, 413.
　hesitate, 605.
　fear, 860.
　shiver, 383.
Quay, 189.
Quean, 962.
Queasiness, 867.
Queasy, 868.
Queen, 745.
Queer, 83.
Quell, *destroy*, 162.
　calm, 826.
　moderate, 174.
　subdue, 732.
Quench, *cool*, 385.
　dissuade, 616.
　satiate, 869.
*Quere, 461.
Querimonious, 839.
Querist, 461.
Querulous, 839.
Query, 461.
Quest, 461.
Question, *inquiry*, 461.
　topic, 454.
　to doubt, 485.
　to deny, 536.
Questionable, 475.
Questionless, 474.
Questor, 801.
*Queue, *appendix*, 39.
　sequel, 65.
Quib, 932.
Quibble, *sophistry*, 477.
　absurdity, 497.
366

Quibble, *wit*, 842.
Quick, *rapid*, 274.
　transient, 111.
　active, 682.
　skilful, 698.
　irascible, 901.
　feeling, 822.
Quicken, *hasten*, 132.
　animate, 163.
　urge, 615.
　excite, 824.
　promote, 707.
　violence, 173.
Quicksand, 667.
Quicksighted, *quickeyed*, 441.
　sagacious, 498.
Quicksilver, 274.
Quickwitted, 842.
Quiddity, *essence*, 5.
　quibble, 477.
Quidnunc, 455.
*Quid pro quo, *compensation*, 30.
　exchange, 794.
Quiescence, 265.
Quiet, *rest*, 265.
　silent, 403.
　calm, 174, 826.
　dissuade, 616.
　peace, 714.
*Quietus, 360.
Quill, 590.
Quill driver, 590.
Quinary, 98.
Quincunx, 98.
Quinquefid, 99.
Quinquesection, 99.
Quint, 98.
Quintain, 620.
Quintessence, *essence*, 5.
　importance, 642.
Quintuple, 98.
Quip, *wit*, 842.
　amusement, 840.
　ridicule, 856.
　satire, 932.
*Quiproquo, *joke*, 842.
　mistake, 495.
Quire, 415, 416.
Quirk, *caprice*, 608.
　evasion, 617.
　wit, 842.
Quit, *depart*, 292.
　relinquish, 624.
　pay, 807.
Quite, 31.
Quits, *equality*, 27.
　atonement, 952.
Quittance,*forgiveness*,918.

Quittance, *atonement*, 952.
　reward, 973.
Quiver, *agitate*, 315.
　shiver, 383.
　fear, 860.
　affect, 821.
　store, 636.
　arm, 727.
Quixotic, *imaginary*, 515.
　rash, 863.
　enthusiastic, 825.
Quiz, *to ridicule*, 856.
Quizzical, *ridiculous*, 853.
*Quodlibet, *sophism*, 477.
　subtle point, 454.
　wit, 842.
Quondam, 122.
Quorum, 72.
Quota, *contingent*, 786.
Quote, 467.
Quotidian, 108.
Quotient, 84.

R.

Rabbet, 43.
Rabbi, 996.
Rabble, *mob*, 876.
　assemblage, 72.
Rabid, 503.
Race, *to run*, 274.
　contest, 720.
　course, 622.
　career, 625.
　lineage, 69.
　kind, 75.
Racer, } *horse*, 271.
Racehorse, } *fleetness*, 274.
Raciness, } *strong*, 171.
Racy, } *pungent*, 392.
　style, 574.
Rack, *frame*, 215.
　physical pain, 378.
　moral pain, 828.
　to torture, 830.
　punish, 975.
　purify, 652.
　refine, 658.
　cloud, 353.
Racket, *noise*, 402.
　roll, 407.
Raddle, *weave*, 219.
　twist, 311.
Radiant, *diverging*, 290.
　light, 420.
　beauty, 845.
　glory, 873.
Radical, *cause*, 153.
　algebraic root, 84.

Radius, 200.
*Radix, 153.
*Radoter, 499.
Raff, *refuse*, 653.
   rabble, 876.
   miscreant, 949.
Raffle, 156, 621.
Raft, 273.
Rafter, 215.
Rag, *shred*, 51.
   clothes, 225.
Ragamuffin, 876.
Rage, *violence*, 173.
   fury, 825.
   desire, 865.
   wrath, 900.
Ragged, 846.
*Ragoût, 299.
Raid, 716.
Rail, *inclosure*, 232.
   fence, 666.
   imprison, 752.
Rail at, 932.
Rail in, 231.
Raillery, 856.
Railway, 627.
Raiment, 225.
Rain, 348.
Rainbow, 440.
Raise, *elevate*, 307.
   increase, 35.
   produce, 161.
   excite, 824.
Rajah, 745.
Rake up, *collect*, 72.
   extract, 300.
   recall, 504.
   excite, 824.
Rake-hell, 954.
Rakish, *intemperate*, 954.
   licentious, 961.
Rally, *ridicule*, 856.
   recover, 658.
   pluck up courage, 861.
Ram, *impel*, 276.
   press in, 261.
   insert, 301.
Ram down, *condense*, 321
   fill up, 261.
Ramadan, 956.
Ramble, *stroll*, 266.
   wander, 279.
   delirium, 503.
   folly, 499.
Rambler, 268.
Ramification, *branch*, 51.
   posterity, 167.
Rammer, *plug*, 263.
   impeller, 276.
Ramp, *ascend*, 305.
367

Rampant, *violent*, 173.
   vehement, 825.
   licentious, 961.
   free, 748.
Rampart, 717.
Ramrod, 263.
Rancid, 401.
Rancour, *malevolence*, 907.
   revenge, 919.
Random, *casual*, 156, 621.
   uncertain, 475.
Range, *space*, 180.
   extent, 26.
   to collocate, 60.
   series, 69.
   term, 71.
   class, 75.
   freedom, 748.
Rank, *degree*, 26.
   thorough, 31.
   collocate, 60.
   row, 69.
   term, 71.
   fetid, 401.
   bad, 649.
   to estimate, 480.
   nobility, 875.
   glory, 873.
Rankle, *animosity*, 900.
   to corrupt, 659.
Ransack, *seek*, 461.
   plunder, 791.
Ransom, *price*, 812.
   liberation, 750.
Rant, *nonsense*, 497.
   speech, 582.
   acting, 599.
   style, 573.
Rantipole, *fool*, 501.
   fanatical, 499.
Rap, *knock*, 276.
   beat, 972.
Rap out, 580.
Rapacious, *avaricious*, 819.
   greedy, 865.
   predatory, 791.
Raparee, 792.
Rape, *violation*, 961.
   seizure, 791.
Rapid, 274.
Rapids, 348.
Rapier, 727.
Rapine, *spoliation*, 791.
   evil, 619.
Rapscallion, 949.
Rapture, *emotion*, 821.
   bliss, 827.
Rare, *infrequent*, 137.
   light, 322.

Rare, *few*, 103.
Rare, *exceptional*, 83.
   excellent, 648.
Raree-show, *sight*, 448.
   amusement, 840.
Rarefy, *expand*, 194.
   render light, 322.
Rascal, 949.
Rascality, 945.
Rase, *obliterate*, 552.
Rash, *reckless*, 863.
   careless, 460.
Rasher, 204.
Rasp, 330.
Rasure, 552.
Rat, 607.
Ratan, 975.
Rat-a-tat, 407.
Ratchet, 253.
Rate, *degree*, 26.
   speed, 274.
   measure, 466.
   estimation, 480.
   price, 812.
   to abuse, 932.
Rather, 609.
Ratify, *consent*, 762.
   affirm, 488.
   compact, 769.
Ratio, *relation*, 9.
   proportion, 84.
Ratiocination, 476.
Ration, 786.
Rational, *sane*, 502.
   judicious, 498.
Rationale, *cause*, 153.
   attribution, 155.
   answer, 462.
   interpretation, 522.
Ratting, 607.
Rattle, *noise*, 407.
   prattle, 584.
Rattlesnake, 663.
Raucity, 581.
Ravage, *destroy*, 162.
   evil, 619.
   despoil, 649.
Rave, *madness*, 503.
   excitement, 825.
Ravel, *entangle*, 219.
   convolution, 248.
   difficulty, 704.
   untwist, 60.
Raven, *black*, 431.
   gorge, 297.
Ravenous, 865.
Raver, 504.
Ravine, *pass*, 203, 198.
   dyke, 259.
Raving, *mad*, 503.

Raving, *violent*, 825.
Ravish, *emotion*, 824.
  ecstasy, 829.
Raw, *immature*, 123.
  unprepared, 674.
  unskilful, 699.
  cold, 383.
  sensitive, 378.
Rawboned, *gaunt*, 203.
  ugly, 846.
Rawhead, 860.
Ray, 420.
Rayless, 421.
Raze, *level*, 308.
  demolish, 649.
Razor, 253.
Reabsorb, 297.
Reach, *length*, 200.
  degree, 26.
  distance, 196.
  fetch, 270.
  arrive at, 293.
  deceive, 545.
  grasp, 737.
React, *recoil*, 277.
  counteract, 179.
Read, *interpret*, 522.
  learn, 539.
Reader, 540.
Reading, 516.
Readjust, 27.
Readmit, 297.
Ready, *prepared*, 673.
  capable, 157.
  eager, 682.
  early, 132.
  cash, 800.
Ready money, 807.
Real, *existing*, 1.
  true, 494.
Realize, *attribute*, 155.
  produce, 161.
  substantiate, 494.
  imagine, 515.
Really, *very*, 31.
  indeed! 870.
Realm, *region*, 181.
  property, 780.
  land, 373.
Reanimate, *revivify*, 163.
  reinstate, 660.
Reap, *acquire*, 775.
  succeed, 731.
Reappear, *repetition*, 104.
  frequency, 136.
Rear, *back*, 235.
  erect, 161.
  sequel, 65.
Reason, *cause*, 153.
  motive, 615.

Reason, *intellect*, 450.
  wisdom, 498.
  moderation, 174.
Reasonable, *judicious*, 498.
  right, 922.
  equitable, 924.
  probable, 472.
  sane, 502.
  cheap, 815.
Reasoning, 476.
Reasonless, 499.
Reassemble, 72.
Reassure, 858.
Reasty, *foul*, 653.
  fetid, 401.
Rebate, 174.
Rebeck, 417.
Rebel, 742.
Rebellion, 719.
Rebellow, 412.
Reboation, 412.
Rebound, *recoil*, 277.
  react, 179.
*Rebours, 283.
Rebuff, *refuse*, 764.
  repulse, 732.
  resist, 719.
  recoil, 277.
Rebuke, 932.
Rebus, 533.
Rebut, *answer*, 462.
  confute, 479.
  deny, 536.
  counter-evidence, 468.
Recalcitrate, 719.
Recall, *recollect*, 505.
  cancel, 756.
Recant, *retract*, 607.
  deny, 536.
  resign, 757.
Recapitulate, *summary*, 596.
  describe, 594.
  enumerate, 85.
Recast, 626.
Recede, *move back*, 283.
  move from, 286.
  decline, 659.
Receipt, 810.
Receive, *admit*, 297.
  take in, 785.
  acquire, 775.
  learn, 539.
  welcome, 894.
  money, 810.
Received, *ordinary*, 82.
Recension, 85.
Recent, 123.
Receptacle, *recipient*, 191.
  magazine, 636.
Reception, *arrival*, 293.

Reception, *comprehension*,
  54.
  ingestion, 297.
Recess, *place*, 182.
  regression, 283.
  ambush, 530.
  holiday, 685.
  retirement, 893.
Recession, *motion from*, 286
*Réchauffé, 21, 658.
Recidivous, 283.
*Recipe, 662.
Recipient, *receptacle*, 191.
  receiving, 785.
Reciprocal, *mutual*, 12.
  quantity, 84.
Reciprocation, 718.
*Recitativo, 415.
Recite, *narrate*, 594.
  speak, 582.
  enumerate, 85.
Reckless, *rash*, 863.
  careless, 460.
Reckon, *count*, 85.
  measure, 466.
  believe, 484.
Reckoning, *accounts*, 811.
  price, 812.
Reckon upon, 507.
Reclaim, 660.
Recline, *lie flat*, 213.
  rest upon, 215.
  repose, 687.
  descend, 306.
Recluse, 893.
Recognizable, 446.
Recognizance, 771.
Recognize, *see*, 441.
  know, 490.
  assent, 488.
  remember, 505.
  discover, 480.
  acknowledge, 535.
Recognized, *received*, 82.
Recoil, *repercussion*, 277.
  shun, 623.
  reluctance, 603.
  dislike, 867.
  hate, 898.
  reaction, 179.
Recollect, 505.
Recommend, *advise*, 695.
  approve, 931.
  induce, 615.
Recompense, *reward*, 973.
  payment, 809.
Reconcile, *agree*, 23.
  content, 831.
  pacify, 723.
  forgive, 918.

Regard, *judge*, 480.
   conceive, 484.
   credit, 873.
Regarding, 9.
Regardless, 458.
Regatta, 840.
Regency, 755.
Regenerate, *reproduce*, 163.
   restore, 660.
   piety, 987.
Regent, *deputy*, 759.
   governor, 745.
*Régime, 737.
Regimen, *circumstances*, 8.
   diet, 299.
   remedy, 662.
Regiment, *army*, 726.
   assemblage, 72.
Regimentals, 225.
Region, 181.
Register, *record*, 551.
   list, 86.
   to arrange, 60.
Registrary, 553.
Regorge, 790.
Regrade, 283.
Regrater, 797.
Regress, 283.
Regression, 283.
Regret, *sorrow*, 833.
   penitence, 950.
Regular, *orderly*, 58.
   according to rule, 82.
   symmetric, 242.
   periodic, 138.
Regulation, *arrangement*, 60.
   direction, 693.
   usage, 80.
   order, 741.
   law, 963.
Regurgitate, *return*, 283.
   flow, 348.
   restore, 790.
Rehabilitate, *reinstate*, 660.
   restore, 790.
Rehearse, *repeat*, 104.
   describe, 594.
   dramatic, 599.
Reign, 737.
Reimburse, *restore*, 790.
   pay, 807.
Rein, *moderate*, 174.
   check, 179.
   slacken, 275.
   restrain, 616.
   hold, 737.
   curb, 747.
Reinforce, *strengthen*, 159.
   aid, 707.

Reinforcement, *supplies*, 635.
Reinless, 738.
Reinstate, 660.
Reis Effendi, 759.
Reiterate, *frequent*, 136.
   repeat, 104.
   multitude, 102.
Reject, *decline*, 610.
   refuse, 764.
   exclude, 55.
   eject, 296.
Rejoice, *exult*, 838.
   gratify, 829.
   cheer, 836.
   amuse, 840.
Rejoinder, *answer*, 462.
   evidence, 468.
Rejuvenescence, 660.
Rekindle, 615.
Relapse, 661.
Relate, *narrate*, 594.
   refer, 9.
Relation, 9.
Relative, 11.
Relax, *weaken*, 160.
   soften, 324.
   slacken, 275.
   unbend the mind, 452.
   repose, 687.
   amuse, 840.
   lounge, 683.
   loose, 47.
   misrule, 738.
   relent, 914.
Relay, 635.
Release, *liberate*, 750.
   discharge, 970.
   restore, 790.
   exempt, 927.
   repay, 807.
Relegate, *transfer*, 270.
   remove, 185.
   banish, 55.
Relent, *moderate*, 174.
   pity, 914.
Relentless, *malevolent*, 907.
   wrathful, 900.
   flagitious, 945.
   impenitent, 951.
Relevancy, *pertinence*, 9.
   congruity, 23.
Reliance, *confidence*, 484.
   hope, 858.
Relic, *remainder*, 40.
   reminiscence, 505.
   token, 551.
   sacred, 998.
Relief, } *comfort*, 834.
Relieve, } *refresh*, 689.

Relieve, *help*, 707.
   improve, 658.
*Relievo, 250.
Religion, *theology*, 983.
   piety, 987.
Religionist, 989.
Religious, *exact*, 494.
   pious, 987.
Relinquish, *a purpose*, 624.
   property, 782.
   to discontinue, 141.
Reliquary, 998.
Relish, *like*, 827.
   savoury, 394.
   desire, 865.
Relucent, *luminous*, 420.
   transparent, 425.
Reluctance, *dislike*, 867.
   unwillingness, 603.
   dissuasion, 616.
Reluctation, 719.
Rely, *confidence*, 484.
   expectation, 507.
   hope, 858.
Remain, *endure*, 106.
   to be left, 40.
   continue, 142.
Remainder, 40.
Remains, *corpse*, 362.
   vestige, 551.
Remark, *observe*, 457.
   assert, 535.
Remarkably, 31.
Remedy, *cure*, 662.
   salubrious, 656.
   to restore, 660.
Remember, 505.
Remembrancer, *recorder*, 553.
Rememoration, 505.
Remigration, 293.
Remind, 505.
Reminiscence, 505.
Remiss, *neglectful*, 460.
   idle, 683.
   reluctant, 603.
   laxity, 738.
Remission, } *forgive*, 918.
Remit, } *discontinuance*, 141.
Remnant, 40.
Remodel, 144.
Remonstrate, *dissuade*, 616.
   expostulate, 932.
Remorse, 950.
Remorseless, 900.
Remote, *distant*, 196.
   not related, 10.
Remotion, } *displace*, 185.
Remove, } *retrench*, 38.

Remove, *depart*, 292.
  recede, 286.
  transfer, 270.
  extract, 300.
  term, 71.
Remunerate, *reward*, 973.
  pay, 810.
Renascent, 163.
Rencounter, *fight*, 720.
  meeting, 293.
Rend, 44.
Render, *give*, 784.
  restore, 790.
  interpret, 522.
*Rendezvous, *focus*, 74.
  assemblage, 72.
Rending, 830.
Renegade, *apostate*, 941.
  turncoat, 607.
Renew, *repeat*, 104.
  frequent, 136.
  repair, 658.
Reniform, 245.
Renitent, *elastic*, 325.
  reluctant, 603.
  counteracting, 179.
Renounce, *relinquish*, 624.
  property, 782.
  recant, 607.
  resign, 757.
  deny, 536.
  repudiate, 927.
Renovate, *reproduce*, 163.
  restore, 660.
Renown, 873.
Renownless, 874.
Rent, *fissure*, 198.
  receipt, 810.
Rental, 810.
Renunciation. *See* Re-
  nounce.
Reorganize, 144.
Repair, *mend*, 658.
  refresh, 689.
  restore, 790.
  atone, 952.
  reward, 973.
Repair to, ᶜ66.
Repartee, *wit*, 842.
  answer, 462.
Repast, 299.
Repay, 807.
Repeal, 756.
Repeat, *iterate*, 104.
  copy, 21.
  imitate, 19.
  duplication, 90.
  frequent, 136.
  multiplied, 102.
Repel, *repulse*, 288.
371

Repel, *defend*, 717.
  resist, 719.
  disincline, 867.
  shock, 898.
  refuse, 764.
  deter, 616.
Repent, 950.
Repercussion, *recoil*, 277.
  counteraction, 179.
Repertory, 636.
Repetend, *iteration*, 104.
  arithmetical, 84.
Repetition, *iteration*, 104.
  copy, 21.
  imitation, 19.
Repine, *discontent*, 832.
  regret, 833.
  repent, 950.
Replace, 660.
Replenish, *fill*, 637.
  complete, 52.
Repletion, *filling*, 637.
  satiety, 869.
Replevin, *restore*, 790.
  borrow, 788.
Reply, 462.
Report, *noise*, 406.
  record, 551.
  inform, 527.
  publish, 531.
  rumour, 532.
  law, 969.
Repose, *quiescence*, 265.
  rest, 687.
Repose on, 215.
Reposit, 184.
Repository, *store*, 636.
  focus, 74.
Reprehend, 932.
Represent, *delineate*, 554.
  imitate, 19.
  simulate, 17.
  describe, 594.
  denote, 550.
  commission, 755.
Representative, 758.
Repress, *quiet*, 174.
  calm, 826.
  control, 179.
Reprieve, *pardon*, 918.
  deliverance, 671.
  respite, 970.
Reprimand, 932.
Reprint, 21.
Reprisal, *retaliation*, 718.
  resumption, 789.
Reproach, *blame*, 932.
  disgrace, 874.
Reprobate, *blame*, 932.
  sinner, 949.

Reprobate, *impious*, 989.
Reproduce, *repeat*, 104.
  copy, 19.
  renovate, 163.
Reprove, 932.
Reptile, *animal*, 366.
  servile, 886.
  base, 940.
  apostate, 941.
  miscreant, 949.
Republic, 373.
Repudiate, *exclude*, 55.
  reject, 610.
  violate, 773.
  evade, 927.
  non-payment, 808.
Repugn, 719.
Repugnance, *dislike*, 867.
  reluctance, 603.
  hate, 898.
  incongruity, 24.
Repulse. *See* Repel, 719.
Repulsive,   *disagreeable*,
  830.
Repurchase, 795.
Reputable, 873.
Repute, 873.
Request, 765.
Requiem, *funereal*, 363.
  dirge, 415.
Require, *need*, 630.
  insufficient, 640.
  to exact, 741.
Requisition, 741.
Requital, *reward*, 973.
  gratitude, 916.
Rescind, *cut off*, 44.
  abrogate, 756.
  refuse, 764.
Rescript, *order*, 741.
  letter, 592.
  answer, 462.
Rescue, *deliver*, 672.
  preserve, 670.
Research, 461.
Reseat, 660.
Resection, 44.
Resemblance, 17.
Resent, 901.
Reservation, ⎱ *concealment*,
Reserve,   ⎰   528.
  silence, 585.
  shyness, 881.
  store, 636.
Reservoir, 636.
Residence, *dwelling*, 186.
  abode, 189.
  location, 184.
Resident, *inhabitant*, 188.
Residentiary, 997.

Residue, 40.
Resign, *give up*, 757.
   relinquish, 782.
   submit, 743.
Resignation,   *endurance*,
826.
   content, 831.
   abdication, 757.
   humility, 879.
   renunciation, 782.
Resilient, 325.
Resist, *withstand*, 719.
   disobey, 742.
   refuse, 764.
   oppose, 179.
   tenacity, 327.
Resistless, 159.
Resolute, *determined*, 604.
   brave, 861.
Resolution, *decomposition*,
49.
   investigation, 461.
   solution, 462.
   topic, 454.
   determination, 604.
   courage, 861.
Resonant, *sonorous*, 402.
   ringing, 408.
Resorb, 297.
Resort, *employ*, 677.
   converge, 291.
   focus, 74.
   move, 266.
   dwell, 189.
Resound, *be loud*, 404.
   ring, 408.
   praises, 931.
Resources, *means*, 632.
   wealth, 803.
Respect, *deference*, 928.
   fame, 873.
   salutation, 894.
   reference, 9.
Respectable, 873.
Respecting, 9.
Respective, 79.
Respectless, 458.
Resperse, 73.
Respire, 687.
Respite, *pause*, 265.
   intermission, 106.
   escape, 671.
   reprieve, 970.
Resplendent,   *luminous*,
420.
   splendid, 845.
Respond, 23.
Response, *answer*, 462.
   verbal, 587.
   rites, 998.
372

Responsible, 926.
Responsive, 462.
Rest, *quiescence*, 265.
   repose, 687.
   remainder, 40.
   satisfaction, 831.
   recumbence, 215.
Rest on, 215.
Resting-place, *support*,215.
   quiescence, 265.
   arrival, 293.
Restitution, 790.
Restive, *obstinate*, 606.
   disobedient, 742.
Restless, *moving*, 264.
   agitated, 315.
   active, 682.
   excited, 825.
   fearful, 860.
Restorative, *remedial*, 662.
   salubrious, 656.
   relieving, 834.
Restore, *reinstate*, 660.
   improve, 658.
   refresh, 689.
   return, 790.
   meaning, 522.
Restrain, } *moderate*, 174.
Restrict, } *emotion*, 826.
   check, 706.
   curb, 751.
   prohibit, 761.
   circumscribe, 231.
   dissuade, 616.
Restringency, 751.
Result, *effect*, 154.
   remainder, 40.
Resume, 789.
*Résumé, 596.
Resurrection, 163.
Resuscitate,*reanimate*,163.
   reinstate, 660.
Retail, *sell*, 796.
   particularize, 594.
Retailer, 797.
Retain, 781.
Retainer, *servant*, 746.
Retaliate, *retort*, 718.
   revenge, 919.
Retard, *hinder*, 719.
   slacken, 275.
Retch, 296.
Retection, 525.
Retention, *keeping*, 781.
   in the memory, 505.
Retentive, 781.
Reticence, 526.
Reticle, 219.
Reticulated, 219.
Reticule, 191.

Retiform, 219.
Retinue, *followers*, 65.
   suite, 69.
   servants, 746.
Retire, *recede*, 286.
   depart, 292.
   resign, 757.
Retirement, *seclusion*, 893.
   privacy, 526.
   concavity, 252.
Retort, *answer*, 462.
   confutation, 479.
   retaliation, 718.
   wit, 842.
Retouch, 658.
Retrace, 505.
Retrace steps, 283.
Retract, *deny*, 536.
   recant, 607.
   abjure, 757.
   annul, 756.
   violate, 773.
Retreat, *recede*, 286.
   abode, 189.
   asylum, 666.
   escape, 671.
   concavity, 252.
Retrench, *subduct*, 38.
   shorten, 201.
   lose, 789.
   economize, 817.
Retribution,   *retaliation*,
718.
   payment, 807.
Retrieve, 660.
Retroaction, *recoil*, 277.
   regression, 283.
   counteraction, 179.
Retrocession, 286.
Retrograde, { *motion*, 283.
Retrogression, } *declension*, 659.
   relapse, 661.
Retrospect, *memory*, 505.
   thought, 451.
   past, 122.
Retroversion, 218.
Retrude, 288.
Return, *regression*, 283.
   arrival, 293.
   frequency, 136.
   to restore, 790.
   reward, 973.
   report, 551.
   profit, 775.
   proceeds, 810.
Reunion, *junction*, 43.
   assemblage, 72.
Reveal, 529.

Revel, *enjoy*, 827.
  amuse, 840.
  dissipation, 954.
Revelation, *disclosure*, 529.
  theological, 985.
Revelry, 836.
Revendicate, 765.
Revenge, 919.
Revenue, *wealth*, 803.
  receipts, 810.
Reverberate, *sound*, 408.
  recoil, 277.
Reverberatory, 386.
Reverence, *respect*, 928.
  salutation, 894.
  piety, 987.
  title, 877.
*Reverie, *train of thought*, 451.
  imagination, 515.
Reverse, *anteposition*, 237.
  contrary, 14.
  evolution, 313.
  inversion, 218.
  misfortune, 830.
  adversity, 735.
Revert, 136.
Review, *consider*, 457.
  judge, 480.
Revile, *abuse*, 932.
  blaspheme, 989.
Revise, 457.
Revisit, 186.
Revive, *live*, 359.
  restore, 660.
  refresh, 689.
Revivify, 163.
Revoke, *recant*, 607.
  deny, 536.
  cancel, 756.
  refuse, 764.
Revolt, *resist*, 719.
  disobey, 742.
  shock, 830.
Revolting, *vulgar*, 851.
Revolution, *rotation*, 312.
  change, 146.
  periodicity, 138.
Revolve, *meditate*, 451.
Revolver, 727.
Revulsion, 277.
Reward, 973.
Rhabdomancy, 511.
Rhapsody, *discontinuity*, 70.
  nonsense, 497.
  fancy, 515.
Rhetoric, 582.
Rheum, *humour*, 333.
  water, 337.
Rhino, 800.

Rhodomontade, *nonsense*, 497.
  unintelligible, 519.
  boasting, 884.
Rhomb, 244.
Rhumb, 278.
Rhyme, 597.
Rhymeless, 598.
Rhythm, 413.
Rib, *ridge*, 250.
  wife, 903.
Ribald, 961.
Ribbed, 259.
Ribbon, *filament*, 205.
  tie, 45.
  decoration, 877.
Rich, *wealthy*, 803.
  abundant, 639.
  savoury, 394.
Richly, 31.
Rick, *store*, 636.
  accumulation, 72.
Rickety, *imperfect*, 651.
  ugly, 846.
*Ricochet, 277.
Rid,   ⎫ *loss*, 776.
Riddance, ⎬ *relinquish*, 782.
  abandon, 624.
  deliver, 672.
Riddle, *enigma*, 533.
  question, 461.
  sieve, 260.
  arrange, 60.
Ride, *move*, 266.
  get above, 206.
Rider, *equestrian*, 268.
  appendix, 39.
Ridge, *narrowness*, 203.
  projection, 250.
Ridicule, 856.
  disrespect, 929.
Ridiculous, *grotesque*, 853.
  trifling, 643.
*Ridotto, *gala*, 840.
  rout, 892.
*Rifarcimento, 658.
Rife, 175.
Riff-raff, *vulgar*, 876.
  dirt, 653.
Rifle, *to plunder*, 791.
  musket, 726.
Rifleman, 727.
Rift, *separation*, 44.
  fissure, 198.
Rig, *dress*, 225.
  prepare, 673.
  frolic, 840.
Rigadoon, 840.
Rigging, *gear*, 225.
  cordage, 45.

Right, *just*, 922.
  privilege, 924.
  duty, 926.
  honor, 939.
  straight, 246.
Righteous, *virtuous*, 944.
  just, 922.
Rigid, *hard*, 323.
  exact, 494.
  severe, 739.
  stubborn, 606.
  regular, 82.
Rigmarole, *nonsense*, 497.
  unintelligible, 519.
Rigour, *severity*, 739.
  compulsion, 744.
  exactness, 494.
Rill, 348.
Rim, 230.
Rime, 383.
Rimple, 259.
Rind, 222.
Ring, *circle*, 247.
  sound, 408.
Ringleader, 745.
Ringlet, 247.
Rinse, 652.
Riot, *violence*, 173.
  revolt, 742, 719.
  confusion, 59.
  luxuriate, 827.
Rip up, *tear*, 44.
  recall to mind, 505.
Ripe, 673.
*Riposte, 462.
Ripple, *shake*, 315.
  murmur, 405.
Rise, *ascend*, 305.
  slope, 217.
  resist, 719.
  revolt, 742.
  spring, 154.
  grow, 35.
Risible, *laughable*, 828.
  ridiculous, 853.
  witty, 842.
Risk, 665.
Rite, *law*, 963.
  religious, 998.
*Ritornello, 136.
Ritual, 998.
Rival, *emulate*, 720.
  envy, 921.
  oppose, 708.
  competitor, 710, 726.
Rive, 44.
Rivel, 258.
River, 348.
Rivet, *to fasten*, 43.
  fastening, 45.

Rivulet, 348.
Road, *way*, 647.
   direction, 278.
Roadstead, *anchorage*, 189.
   refuge, 666.
Roadster, 271.
Roadway, 627.
Roam, 266.
Roan, 271.
Roar, *sound*, 404.
   cry, 411.
   weep, 839.
Roast, *heat*, 384.
   ridicule, 856.
   censure, 932.
Rob, *plunder*, 791.
   pulp, 354.
Robber, 792.
Robe, 225.
Robin Goodfellow, 980.
Robust, 159.
Rock, *hardness*, 323.
   land, 342.
   to oscillate, 314.
   pitfall, 667.
Rocket, *signal*, 550.
   arms, 727.
   light, 423.
   rise, 305.
   rapid, 274.
Rod, *sceptre*, 747.
   scourge, 975.
   bane, 663.
   measure, 466.
   divining, 992.
Rogation, 990.
Rogue, *cheat*, 548.
   scamp, 949.
Roguery, *vice*, 945.
   dishonor, 940.
Roguish, *sportive*, 842.
Roister, 885.
*Rôle, 625.
Roll, *rotate*, 312.
   move, 264.
   push, 284.
   flow, 348.
   sound, 407.
   cylinder, 249.
   fillet, 205.
   record, 551.
   list, 86.
Roll-call, 85.
Roller, 249.
Rollicking, *frolicsome*, 836.
   blustering, 885.
Rolling stone, 312.
Romance, *fiction*, 515.
   falsehood, 544.
   absurdity, 497.
574

Romance, *fable*, 594.
*Romanesque, 515.
Romantic, 822.
Romp, 840.
*Rondeau, *music*, 415.
   poem, 597.
Roof, *summit*, 210.
   ·*height*, 206.
   cover, 222.
   house, 189.
Roofless, 226.
Rook, 548.
Rookery, 189.
Room, *space*, 180.
   chamber, 191.
Roomy, 180.
Roost, 186.
Root, *cause*, 153.
   base, 211.
   algebraic, 84.
   to place, 184.
Rooted, *fixed*, 265.
   permanent, 142.
   old, 124.
Root out, *destroy*, 162.
   displace, 185.
   eject, 296.
   extract, 300.
   discover, 480.
Rope, *cord*, 205.
   fastening, 45.
Rope-dancer, 700.
Rope-dancing, 698.
Ropy, 352.
*Roquelaure, 225.
Roral, 339.
Rosary, 998.
Roscid, 339.
Roseate, 434.
Rose-colour, 434.
Roses, bed of, 377.
Rosicrucian, 548.
Rostrum, *beak*, 234.
   pulpit, 542.
Rot, *disease*, 655.
   decay, 659.
   putrefy, 653.
Rota, 138.
Rotation, 312.
Rote, by, 505.
Rotten, *foul*, 653.
   fetid, 401.
Rotunda, 189.
Rotundity, 249.
*Roturier, 876.
*Roué, *scoundrel*, 949.
   sensualist, 954.
Rouge, 434.
Rough, *uneven*, 256.
   shapeless, 241.

Rough, *sour*, 397.
   austere, 395.
   violent, 173.
   sound, 410.
   unprepared, 674.
   ugly, 846.
   churlish, 895.
   to fag, 686.
Rough-cast, 674.
Rough-grained, 329.
Rough-hewn, *rugged*, 256.
   unprepared, 674.
*Rouleau, *cylinder*, 249.
   money, 800.
Round, *circular*, 247.
   fight, 720.
   of a ladder, 215.
Round about, *circuitous*,
31.
   way, 629.
Roundelay, 597.
Roundhouse, 752.
Roundlet, 247.
Round-robin, 551.
Roup, 796.
Rouse, *stimulate*, 615.
   passion, 824.
Rout, *discomfit*, 732.
   assembly, 892.
   rabble, 876.
Rout out, 162.
Route, 627.
Routine, *order*, 58.
   rule, 60.
   custom, 613.
Rove, *wander*, 266.
   deviate, 279.
Rover, 268.
Row, *series*, 69.
   navigate, 267.
   riot, 720.
Rowel, *sharpness*, 253.
   stimulus, 615.
Royalty, 737.
*Ruade, 276.
Rub, *friction*, 331.
   difficulty, 703
Rub-a-dub, 407.
Rub down, 330.
Rub out, *disappear*, 449.
   efface, 552.
Rub up, 658.
Rubbish, 645.
Rubble, 643.
Rubicon, 303, 676.
Rubicund, 434.
Rubify, 434.
Rubric, *precept*, 697.
   liturgy, 998.
Ruby, *red*, 434.

Ruby, *gem*, 650.
Ruck, 258.
Rudder, 695.
Ruddy, 434.
Rude, *violent*, 173.
  vulgar, 851.
  uncivil, 895.
  ugly, 846.
  ignorant, 491.
  uncivilized, 876.
Rudiment, *beginning*, 66.
  cause, 153.
  smallness, 193.
Rudiments, *elementary knowledge*, 490.
  school, 542.
Rue, *regret*, 833.
  repent, 950.
Rueful, 837.
Ruffian, *maleficent*, 913.
  scoundrel, 949.
Ruffle, *derange*, 61.
  fold, 258.
  discompose, 821.
  excite, 824.
  anger, 900.
Rugged, *rough*, 256.
  ugly, 846.
  churlish, 895.
Rugose, 256.
Rugous, 256.
Ruin, *decay*, 659.
  failure, 732.
  evil, 619.
  adversity, 735.
Rule, *regularity*, 80.
  length, 200.
  measure, 466.
  government, 737.
  precept, 697.
  custom, 613.
  law, 963.
  to decide, 480.
Ruler, 745.
Rumble, 407.
Ruminate, 451.
Rummage, 461.
Rumour, *publicity*, 531.
  report, 532.
Rump, 235.
Rumple, *fold*, 258.
  derange, 61.
  rough, 256.
Rumpus, *confusion*, 59.
  violence, 173.
  contention, 720.
Run, *move quick*, 274.
  move out, 294.
  flow, 333.
  continue, 143.
375

Run, *smuggle*, 791.
Run after, 622.
Run away, *escape*, 671.
  avoid, 623.
  from fear, 862.
  recede, 286.
Run in, 301.
Run down, *censure*, 932.
  depreciate, 483.
Run high, 173.
Run on, *continue*, 143.¹
Run out, *elapse*, 122.
  waste, 638.
  spend, 818.
Run over, *redundant*, 641.
  describe, 594.
Run riot, 173.
Run up, *expend*, 809.
  increase, 35.
Rundle, *circle*, 247.
  convolution, 248.
  rotundity, 249.
Rundlet, 191.
Runnel, 348.
Runner, *courier*, 268.
  messenger, 534.
Running, *continuously*, 69.
Runt, 193.
Rupture, 713.
Rural, 367.
Ruralist, 893.
*Ruse, *cunning*, 702.
  deception, 545.
Rush, *rapidity*, 274.
  to pursue, 622.
  trifle, 643.
Rushlight, 423.
Russet, 433.
Rust, *decay*, 659.
  canker, 663.
Rustle, 409, 410.
Rustic, *clown*, 876.
  vulgar, 851.
Rusticate, 893.
Rusticity, 895.
Rusty, *sluggish*, 683.
  unserviceable, 645.
  dirty, 653.
Rut, 259.
Ruth, 914.
Ruthless, *savage*, 907.
  angry, 900.
Rutilant, 420.
Ruttish, 961.
Ryot, 876.

S.

Sabbatarian, 989.
Sabbatism, 989.

Sable, 431.
Sabre, *weapon*, 727.
  to kill, 361.
Sabulous, 330.
Sac, *bag*, 191.
  to take, 789.
Saccharine, 396.
Sacerdotal, 995.
Sachel, 191.
Sachem, 745.
Sack, *ravage*, 649.
  havoc, 619.
  plunder, 791.
Sackcloth, *asceticism*, 955.
  atonement, 952.
Sacrament, 998.
Sacred, *holy*, 976.
  pious, 987.
Sacrifice, *destroy*, 162.
  offering, 763.
  self-denial, 942.
  atonement, 952.
  worship, 990.
Sacrilege, 989.
Sacrilegist, 984.
Sacristan, 996.
Sacristy, 1000.
Sad, *dejected*, 837.
  bad, 649.
Saddle, *clog*, 706.
  add, 37.
Safe, *secure*, 664.
  cupboard, 191.
Safe-conduct, 664.
Safeguard, 664.
Safety valve, 666.
Saffron, 436.
Sag, 217.
Sagacious, *intelligent*, 498.
  skilful, 698.
Saic, 273.
Sail, *navigate*, 267.
  set out, 292.
  travel, 266.
Saint, 948.
  pious, 987.
Saintlike, } *virtuous*, 944.
Saintly, } *pious*, 987.
Sake, 615.
Salaam, *respect*, 928.
Salacity, 961.
Salad, 41.
Salamander, 386.
Salary, 809.
Sale, 796.
Salesman, 797.
Salient, *projecting*, 250.
  sharp, 253.
  important, 643.
Saline, 392.

Sallow, *yellow*, 436.
   pale, 429.
Sally, *issue*, 292.
   attack, 716.
   wit, 842.
Salmagundi, 41.
Saloon, 191.
Salt, *pungent*, 392.
   condiment, 393.
   wit, 842.
   preserve, 670.
Saltation, 309.
Saltatory, *rise*, 305.
   leap, 309.
   agitation, 315.
Salt-in-banco, 548.
Salubrity, 656.
Salutary, *salubrious*, 656.
   remedial, 662.
Salute, *compliment*, 894.
   kiss, 902.
   firing, 883, 882.
Salvage, *tax*, 812.
   discount, 813.
   reward, 973.
Salvation, *escape*, 671.
   religious, 976.
Salve, *to relieve*, 834.
   remedy, 662.
Salvo, *exception*, 83.
   condition, 770.
   excuse, 937.
   plea, 617.
   explosion, 406.
   salute, 882.
Samaritan, 912.
Same, 13.
Samiel, 349.
Sampan, 273.
Sample, 82.
Sanatory, 656, 662.
Sanctify, *authorize*, 924.
   piety, 987.
Sanctimony, 989.
Sanction, 924.
Sanctity, 987.
Sanctuary, *refuge*, 666.
   altar, 1000.
Sanctum, 1000.
Sand, 330.
Sandal, 225.
Sands, 667.
Sandy, 330.
*Sang froid, 823.
Sanguine, 858.
Sanhedrim, 696.
Sanies, 333.
Sanity, 502.
Santon, *hermit*, 893.
   priest, 996.
3476

Sap, *juice*, 333.
   to destroy, 162.
   damage, 659.
Sapid, 390.
Sapient, 498.
Sapless, 340.
Sapling, 129.
Saponaceous, 355.
Sapor, 390.
Sappy, *juicy*, 333.
   foolish, 499.
Saraband, 840.
Sarcasm, 932.
Sarcastic, 901.
Sarcophagus, 363.
Sardonic, 838.
Sash, 247.
Satan, 978.
Satanic, *evil*, 649.
   vicious, 945.
Satchel, 191.
Sate, 869.
Satellite, *follower*, 281.
   companion, 88.
Satiate, ⎱ *sufficient*, 639.
Satiety, ⎰ *redundant*, 641.
   cloy, 869.
Satire, *ridicule*, 856.
   censure, 932.
Satisfaction, *duel*, 720.
   atonement, 921.
Satisfy, *content*, 831.
   gratify, 827, 830.
   convince, 484.
   fulfil a duty, 926.
   an obligation, 772.
   reward, 973.
   pay, 807.
   satiate, 869.
   grant, 762.
Satrap, *ruler*, 745.
   deputy, 759.
Saturate, *fill*, 639.
   satiate, 869.
Saturnalia, 840.
Saturnian, 734.
Saturnine, 837.
Satyr, *ugly*, 846.
   demon, 980.
   rake, 961.
Sauce, *mixture*, 41.
   adjunct, 39.
   abuse, 832.
Saucebox, 887.
Saucer, 191.
Saucy, *insolent*, 885.
   flippant, 895.
Saunter, *ramble*, 266.
   dawdle, 275.
Savage, *violent*, 173.

Savage, *brutal*, 876.
   angry, 900.
   malevolent, 907.
   brave, 861.
   a wretch, 913.
Savanna, 344.
*Savant, 492, 500.
Save, *except*, 38, 83.
   to preserve, 670.
   deliver, 672.
   lay by, 636.
   economize, 817.
*Savoir faire, 698.
Saviour, 976.
   benefactor, 912.
Savour, 390.
Savouriness, 394.
Savourless, 391.
Savoury, 829.
Saw, *jagged*, 257.
   saying, 496.
Sawder (soft), 933.
Sawdust, 330.
Say, *speak*, 582.
   assert, 535.
Saying, *assertion*, 535.
   maxim, 496.
Sbirri, 965.
Scabbard, 191.
Scabby, 940.
Scabrous, 256.
Scaffold, *frame*, 215.
   preparation, 673.
   way, 627.
   execution, 975.
Scald, *burn*, 384.
   poet, 597.
Scale, *slice*, 204.
   portion, 51.
   skin, 222.
   order, 58.
   measure, 466.
   series, 69.
   gamut, 413.
   to mount, 305.
Scallop, 248.
Scalpel, 253.
Scamp, 949.
Scamper, 274.
Scan, 441.
Scandal, *disgrace*, 874.
   vice, 945.
   news, 532.
Scandalize, 932.
Scandent, 305.
Scant, *narrowness*, 203.
Scanty, *little*, 32.
   few, 103.
   insufficient, 640.
Scantling, *dimensions*, 192.

Scantling, *example*, 82.
  small quantity, 32.
  scrap, 51.
Scape, 671.
Scapegoat, 952.
Scape-grace, 949.
Scapulary, 999.
Scar, *blemish*, 848.
  seam, 43.
Scaramouch, *humorist*, 844.
  buffoon, 857.
Scarce, 640.
Scarcely, *little*, 32.
  rare, 137.
Scare, 860.
Scarecrow, *ugly*, 846.
  bugbear, 860.
Scarfskin, 222.
Scarify, *torment*, 830.
Scarlet, 434.
Scath, *evil*, 619.
  bane, 663.
  badness, 649.
Scathless, *secure*, 664.
  saved, 672.
Scatter, *disperse*, 73.
  diverge, 290.
  derange, 59.
Scavenger, 652.
Scene, *appearance*, 448.
  arena, 728.
  painting, 556.
  drama, 599.
Scenery, 448.
Scent, *smell*, 398.
  knowledge, 490.
  trail, 551.
Scent-bag, 400.
Scentless, 399.
Scepticism, *doubt*, 487.
  religious, 988.
Sceptre, 747.
Schedule, *list*, 86.
  record, 551.
  draft, 554.
Schematist, 626.
Scheme, *plan*, 626.
  draft, 554.
Schemer, 626.
Schesis, 7.
Schism, *discord*, 713.
  dissent, 489.
  heterodoxy, 984.
Schismless, 983.
Scholar, *learner*, 541.
  erudite, 492.
Scholarship, *school*, 490.
  learning, 539.
Scholastic, 490.
Scholiast, 522.

377

*Scholium, 522.
School, 542.
Schoolboy, 541.
Schoolfellow, 890.
Schoolman, *scholar*, 492.
  sage, 500.
Schoolmaster, 540.
Schooner, 273.
Sciography, 556.
Science, *knowledge*, 490.
  skill, 698.
Scientific, 494.
Scimitar, 727.
Scintillation, 420.
Sciolism, 491.
Sciolist, 493.
Sciomancy, 511.
Scion, *child*, 129.
  posterity, 167.
Scissile, 44.
Scission, 44.
Scobs, 330.
Scoff, *ridicule*, 856.
  deride, 929.
  impiety, 989.
Scold, *abuse*, 932.
  vixen, 936.
Scollop, 248.
Sconce, *summit*, 210.
  mulct, 974.
  defence, 717.
  candlestick, 423.
Scoop, *depth*, 208.
  depression, 252.
  perforator, 262.
Scope, *degree*, 23.
  extent, 180.
  intention, 620.
  freedom, 748.
Scorch, 384.
Score, *mark*, 550.
  motive, 615.
  price, 812.
  accounts, 811.
  twenty, 98.
  to count, 85.
*Scoriæ, 643.
Scorify, 384.
Scorn, 930.
Scorpion, *bane*, 663.
  painful, 830.
Scorse, 794.
Scotch, 649.
Scotomy, 443.
Scoundrel, 949.
Scour, *rub*, 331.
  clean, 652.
Scourge, *whip*, 942.
  bane, 663.
  painful, 830.

Scourge, *bad*, 649.
Scourings, 643.
Scout, *messenger*, 534.
  watch, 664.
  to disdain, 930.
  deride, 643.
Scowl, *frown*, 895.
  complain, 839.
  anger, 900.
Scraggy, *rough*, 256.
  narrow, 203.
  ugly, 846.
Scramble, *confusion*, 59.
  haste, 684.
  difficulty, 704.
  swift, 274.
  mount, 305.
Scranch, 330.
Scrannel, 643.
Scrap, *piece*, 51.
  bit, 32.
  small portion, 193.
Scrap-book, 596.
Scrape, *difficulty*, 704.
  mischance, 732.
  abrade, 331.
  bow, 894.
Scrape together, *collect*, 72.
  get, 775.
Scratch, *groove*, 259.
  mark, 550.
  write, 590.
  daub, 555.
  hurt, 619.
  to wound, 649.
Scratch out, 552.
Scrawl, 590.
Scream, 410, 411.
Screech, 410, 411.
  complain, 839.
Screech owl, 412.
Screen, *concealment*, 528.
  asylum, 666.
  ambush, 530.
  shade, 424.
Screened, *safe*, 664.
  invisible, 447.
Screw, *fasten*, 43.
  joining, 45.
  instrument, 633.
  rotation, 312.
  miser, 819.
Screw up, *strengthen*, 159.
  drunk, 959.
Scribble, 590.
Scribe, *writer*, 590.
  priest, 996.
Scrimp, 201.
Scrip, 191.
Scripture, *revelation*, 985.

Scripture, *certain,* 474.
Scrivener, 590.
Scroll, 551.
Scrub, 652.
Scrubby, *vulgar,* 876.
  shabby, 940.
  bad, 649.
  trifling, 643.
  small, 193.
Scruple, *doubt,* 485.
  dissuasion, 616.
Scrupulous, *careful,* 459.
  incredulous, 487.
  exact, 494.
  punctilious, 939.
  virtuous, 944.
Scrutiny, 461.
Scud, *speed,* 274.
  sail, 267.
  haze, 353.
Scuffle, 720.
Scull, 267.
Scullery, 191.
Scullion, 746.
Sculptor, 559.
Sculpture, *carving,* 557.
  form, 240.
Scum, 653.
Scupper, 350.
Scurf, 653.
Scurrility, *ridicule,* 856.
  detraction, 934.
Scurry, 274.
Scurvy, *bad,* 649.
  base, 940.
Scutcheon, *standard,* 550.
  honor, 877.
Scuttle, *tray,* 191.
  to destroy, 162.
Scythe, 244.
Sea, 341.
Sea-board, 342.
Sea-green, 435.
Seal, *to close,* 261.
  sigil, 550.
  evidence, 467.
  record, 551.
  compact, 769.
Seals, 747.
Seal up, *shut up,* 231.
Seam, 43.
Seaman, 269.
Seamanship, *conduct,* 693.
  skill, 698.
Sear, *burn,* 384.
  deaden, 823.
Search, 461.
Searchless, 519.
Seared, 951.
Sea-side, 342.

Season, *time,* 106.
  opportunity, 134.
  pungent, 392, 393.
  to preserve, 670.
  prepare, 673.
  accustom, 613.
Seasonable, *opportune,* 134.
  expedient, 646.
Seasoning, *mixture,* 41.
  pungency, 171.
Seat, *abode,* 189.
  to place, 184.
  support, 215.
Sea-worthy, 644.
Sebaceous, 355.
Secede, 489.
Seclude, 893.
Second, *of time,* 108.
  instant, 113.
  abet, 707.
Secondary, *following,* 63.
  consignee, 758.
  deputy, 759.
  inferior, 643.
  imperfect, 651.
Second-best, 651.
Second-fiddle, 651.
Second-hand, *borrowed,* 788
  indifferent, 651.
  imitated, 19.
Secondly, 91.
Second-rate, 651.
Second-sight, *prediction,* 510.
  witchcraft, 992.
Secret, *latent,* 526.
  hidden, 528.
  riddle, 533.
Secretary, *recorder,* 553.
  writer, 590.
Secrete, 528.
Sect, 75.
Sectarian, *adherent,* 711.
  dissenter, 984.
Sectator, 541.
Section, *part,* 51.
  class, 75.
  chapter, 593.
Sector, 51.
Secular, 99.
Secure, *fasten,* 43.
  safe, 663.
  engage, 768.
  gain, 775.
  confident, 858.
Security, *pledge,* 771.
  warranty, 924.
Sedan, 272.
Sedate, *thoughtful,* 451.
  calm, 826.

Sedate, *grave,* 837.
Sedative, *calming,* 174.
  remedy, 662.
Sedentary, 265.
Sediment, *dregs,* 653.
  remainder, 40.
Sedition, 742.
Seduce, *entice,* 615.
  love, 897.
Seducer, 962.
Seducing, 829.
Seduction, 961.
Sedulity, 682.
Sedulous, 682.
See, *view,* 441.
  look, 457.
  bishopric, 995.
Seed, *cause,* 153.
  posterity, 167.
Seedling, 129.
Seedy, *weak,* 160.
  exhausted, 688.
  worn, 651.
Seek, *inquire,* 461.
  pursue, 622.
Seem, 448.
Seeming, 448.
Seemless, 846.
Seemly, *expedient,* 646.
  proper, 926.
  handsome, 845.
Seer, *veteran,* 130.
  oracle, 513.
  sorcerer, 994.
See-saw, 314.
Seethe, 382, 384.
Segment, 51.
Segregate, *exclude,* 55.
  not related, 10.
  incoherent, 47.
Seignor, 745.
Seize, *take,* 789.
  rob, 791.
  possess, 777.
Sejunction, 44.
Seldom, 137.
Select, 609.
Self, 13.
Self-abasement, 879.
Self-admiration, 880.
Self-applause, 880.
Self-communing, 451.
Self-conceit, 880.
Self-conquest, 953.
Self-control, 942.
Self-deceit, 495.
Self-defence, 717.
Self-denial, *disinterested-ness,* 942.
  temperance, 953.

Self-evident, 478.
Self-existing, 1.
Self-indulgence, 943.
    intemperance, 954.
Selfish, 943.
Self-love, 943.
Self-opinionated, ⎱ foolish,
Self-opinioned, ⎰   499.
    obstinate, 606.
Self-possession, 864.
Self-praise, 880.
Self-reliance, 604.
Self-reproach, 950.
Self-reproof, 950.
Self-sacrifice, 942.
Self-satisfied, 880.
Self-sufficient, 880.
Self-taught, 490.
Self-tormenter, 837.
Self-willed, 606.
Sell, 796.
Selvedge, 230.
Semaphore, 550.
Semblance, likeness, 19.
    copy, 20.
Semi, 91.
Semicolon, 141.
Semidiaphanous, 427.
Semifluid, 352.
Semiliquid, 352.
Semilunar, 245.
Seminary, 542.
Semiopacous, 427.
Semipellucid, 427.
Semitransparent, 427.
Sempiternal, 112.
Senary, 98.
Senate, 696.
Senator, 695.
Senatorship, 693.
Send, propel, 284.
    transfer, 270.
    errand, 755.
Send out, 296.
Seneschal, 745.
Seneschalship, 737.
Senile, 128.
Seniority, 128.
Sensation, 375, 821.
Sense, intellect, 450.
    wisdom, 498.
    meaning, 516.
Senses, 375.
Senseless, foolish, 499.
    insensible, 376.
    unmeaning, 517.
Sensibility, physical, 375.
    moral, 822.
Sensible, material, 316.
    wise, 498.
379

Sensitive, physically, 375.
    morally, 822.
Sensorium, 450.
Sensual, 954.
Sensuous, 375.
Sentence, phrase, 566.
    maxim, 496.
    judgment, 969.
    decision, 480.
Sententious, 574.
Sentient, 375, 822.
Sentiment, opinion, 484.
    idea, 453.
Sentimental, 822.
Sentinel, ⎱ guardian, 664.
Sentry, ⎰ keeper, 753.
    watch, 668.
Separate, simple, 42.
    to disjoin, 44.
    divorce, 905.
Separatist, 984.
Sepose, divide, 44.
    exclude, 55.
Sepoy, 726.
Sept, 75.
Septic, 657.
Septuagint, 985.
*Septum, 228.
Sepulchre, 363.
Sepulchral sound, 408, 410.
Sepulture, 363.
Sequacity, softness, 324.
    tenacity, 327.
Sequarious, 63.
Sequel, following, 65.
    in time, 117.
    addition, 39.
Sequence, in order, 63.
    in time, 117.
    motion, 281.
Sequent, 63.
Sequester, ⎱ take, 789.
Sequestered, ⎰ hidden, 526.
    secluded, 893.
    confiscate, 974.
Seraglio, 961.
Seraph, angel, 977.
    saint, 948.
Seraphic, blissful, 829.
    virtuous, 944.
Seraskier, 745.
Serenade, music, 415.
    compliment, 902.
    social, 892.
Serene, calm, 826.
    content, 837.
Serf, clown, 876.
    slave, 746.
Serfdom, 749.
Sergeant, 745.

*Seriatim, 69.
Series, 69.
Serious, great, 31.
    important, 642.
    dejected, 837.
    resolved, 604.
Sermon, dissertation, 595.
    lesson, 537.
    speech, 582.
    pastoral, 998.
Serosity, 333.
Serpent, tortuous, 248.
    Satan, 978.
    deceiver, 548.
    evil, 663.
    guilt, 947.
Serpentine, 248.
Serrated, 244.
Serum, lymph, 333.
    water, 337.
Servant, 746.
Serve, aid, 707.
    obey, 743.
    work, 680.
Serve out, 972.
Service, good, 618.
    use, 677.
    utility, 644.
    worship, 990.
    servitude, 749.
    warfare, 722.
Serviceable, useful, 644.
    good, 648.
Servile, obsequious, 886.
    flattery, 933.
Servitor, 746.
Servitude, 749.
Sesqui, 87.
Sesquipedalian, long, 220.
    style, 577.
Sessions, legal, 966.
    council, 696.
Set, condition, 7.
    group, 72.
    class, 75.
    firm, 43.
    to place, 184.
    leaning, 278.
    gang, 712.
    lease, 796.
    difficulty, 704.
Set about, 676.
Set apart, 55.
Set aside, disregard, 460.
    annul, 756.
    release, 927.
Set down, humiliate, 879.
    censure, 932.
    slight, 929.
Set fast, 704.

Set fire to, 384.
Set foot in, 295.
Set forth, *publish*, 531.
    tell, 527.
    show, 525.
    assert, 535.
    describe, 594.
Set forward, 292.
Set in, *begin*, 66.
    tide, 348.
    approach, 287.
Set off, *depart*, 292.
    compensate, 30.
    adorn, 845.
Set on, 615.
Set out, *begin*, 66.
    depart, 292.
    decorate, 845.
Set right, *reinstate*, 660.
Set sail, 292.
Set to, 720.
Set to work, 676.
Set up, *raise*, 307.
    prosperous, 734.
Set upon, *attack*, 716.
    desire, 865.
    willing, 602.
Settee, 215.
Settle, *decide*, 480.
    fixed, 142.
    stationary, 265.
    dwell, 186.
    sink, 306.
    consent, 762.
    pay, 807.
    give, 784.
Settlement, *location*, 184.
    colony, 188.
    dregs, 653.
    compact, 769.
Settler, 188.
Sever, 44.
Several, 102.
Severalize, 465.
Severe, *harsh*, 739.
    energetic, 171.
    painful, 830.
    critical, 932.
Sew, 43.
Sewed up, 959.
Sewer, *drain*, 350.
    cloaca, 653.
Sex, *kind*, 75.
    women, 374.
Sexton, 996.
Sextuple, 98.
Shabby, *mean*, 874.
    bad, 649.
    disgraceful, 940.
    trifling, 643.

Shackle, *to tie*, 43.
    hinder, 706.
    restrain, 751.
    fetter, 752.
Shade, *darkness*, 421.
    shadow, 424.
    colour, 428.
    degree, 26.
    difference, 15.
    small quantity, 32.
    to paint, 556.
    screen, 530.
    manes, 362.
    ghost, 980.
Shaded, *invisible*, 447.
Shades below, 982.
Shadow, *darkness*, 421.
    shade, 424.
    error, 495.
    little, 193.
    small in degree, 32.
    part, 51.
    sequence, 281.
Shadow of doubt, 485.
Shadow forth, *show*, 525.
    indicate, 550.
    describe, 594.
Shadow out, 554.
Shadowy, *imaginary*, 2.
    invisible, 447.
    erroneous, 495.
Shaft, *pit*, 260.
    air-pipe, 351.
    deep, 208.
    frame, 215.
    missile, 284.
    weapon, 727.
Shag, 256.
Shaggy, 256.
Shah, 745.
Shake, *agitate*, 315.
    trill, 407.
    musical, 415.
    dissuade, 616.
    injure, 659.
    impress, 821.
    flutter, 824.
Shake off, 296.
Shake up, 315.
Shaken, 160.
Shaky, *in danger*, 665.
Shallop, 273.
Shallow, *not deep*, 209.
    foolish, 499.
Shallow-brained, 499.
Shallow-pated, 499.
Shallows, *dangers*, 667.
Sham, 544.
Shamble, 275.
Shambles, 361.

Shambling, *descending*, 306.
    shaking, 315.
Shame, 874.
Shamefaced, 881.
Shameful, *disgraceful*, 874.
    profligate, 945.
Shameless, *profligate*, 945.
    impudent, 885.
Shandredhan, 272.
Shank, 633.
Shape, *form*, 240.
    condition, 7.
    aspect, 448.
Shapeless, *amorphous*, 241.
    ugly, 846.
Shapely, *comely*, 845.
    symmetrical, 242.
Share, *part*, 51.
    participate, 778.
    allotted portion, 786.
Shark, *thief*, 792.
    cheat, 548.
Sharp, *acute*, 253.
    musical tone, 410.
    pungent, 392.
    energetic, 171.
    violent, 173.
    intelligent, 498.
    clever, 698.
    active, 682.
    rude, 895.
    censorious, 932.
Sharper, *cheat*, 548.
    thief, 792.
Sharpshooter, 726.
Sharpsighted, 441.
Shaster, 986.
Shatter, *destroy*, 162.
    weaken, 160.
Shatterbrained, 499.
Shave, 203.
Shaving, *layer*, 204.
    filament, 205.
    small part, 32, 51.
Shawl, 225.
Sheaf, 72.
Shear, 38.
Sheath, *receptacle*, 191.
    envelope, 222.
Sheathe, 174.
Sheathing, 222.
Shed, *building*, 189.
    to emit, 296.
    scatter, 73.
    diverge, 290.
Shed tears, 839.
Sheen, 420.
Sheepish, 881.
Sheer, *narrow*, 203.
    simple, 42.

Sheer off, 292.
Sheet, *layer*, 204.
  paper, 593.
Sheet anchor, 666.
Sheik, *ruler*, 745.
  priest, 996.
Shelf, *support*, 215.
  (on the), 678.
Shell, *cover*, 222.
  bomb, 727.
Shelter, *refuge*, 666.
  safety, 664.
Shelty, 271.
Shelve, *slope*, 217.
  locate, 184.
  disuse, 678.
Shend, 649.
Shepherd, *director*, 694.
  pastor, 996.
Sheriff, 965.
Shibboleth, 722.
Shield, *defend*, 717.
  safety, 664.
  buckler, 666.
Shift, *move*, 264.
  change, 140.
  transfer, 270.
  expedient, 626.
  evasion, 546.
  plea, 617.
  difficulty, 704.
Shiftless, *unprepared*, 674.
  inhabile, 699.
Shifting, *transient*, 111.
  moving, 270.
Shillelah, 727.
Shilly-shally, 605.
Shimmer, *lustre*, 420.
Shine, *to emit light*, 420.
  glory, 873.
  beauty, 845.
Ship, 273.
Ship-load, *cargo*, 31.
  abundance, 639.
Shipment, 270.
Shipwreck, 732.
Shire, 181.
Shirk, *avoid*, 623.
  disobey, 742.
Shirt, 225.
Shive, 51.
Shiver, *shake*, 315.
  cold, 385.
  layer, 204.
  fragment, 51.
  filament, 205.
  to divide, 44.
  destroy, 162.
Shivery, *brittle*, 328.
  pulverulent, 330.
381

Shoal, *shallow*, 209.
  assemblage, 72.
Shoals, 667.
Shock, *concussion*, 276.
  violence, 173.
  sheaf, 72.
  contest, 720.
  affect, 821.
  move, 824.
  pain, 830.
  dislike, 867.
  hate, 898.
  scandalize, 932.
Shocking, *bad*, 649.
  ugly, 846.
  vulgar, 851.
  fearful, 860.
  painful, 830.
  considerable, 31.
Shoe, 225.
Shoot, *propel*, 284.
  dart, 274.
  kill, 361.
  grow, 194.
  attack, 716.
  pain, 378.
  grieve, 828.
  offspring, 167.
Shoot up, *increase*, 35.
  ascend, 305.
  prominent, 250.
Shop, 799.
Shopkeeper, 797.
Shoplifting, 791.
Shopman, 797.
Shore, *support*, 215.
  land, 342.
  sewer, 653.
Shoreless, 180.
Shorn, *deprived*, 776.
  reduced, 36.
Short, *not long*, 201.
  concise, 572.
  incomplete, 53.
  unaccomplished, 730.
  insufficient, 640.
  brittle, 328.
  uncivil, 895.
Shortcoming, 304.
Short-hand, 590.
Short-lived, 111.
Short-sighted, *myopic*, 443.
  foolish, 499.
Short-witted, 499.
Shot, *missile*, 284.
  weapon, 727.
  variegated, 440.
Shot-free, 927.
Shoulder, *projection*, 250.
  support, 215.

Shoulder, *to shove*, 276.
Shout, *loudness*, 404.
  cry, 411.
  voice, 580.
Shove, 276.
Shovel, *vehicle*, 272.
  to transfer, 270.
  receptacle, 191.
Show, *manifest*, 525.
  appear, 448.
  evince, 467.
  demonstrate, 478.
  parade, 882.
Show up, *accuse*, 938.
Shower, *rain*, 348.
  abundance, 639.
  assemblage, 72.
Showy, *coloured*, 428.
  gawdy, 847.
Shrapnel, 727.
Shred, *bit*, 51.
  filament, 205.
Shrew, *vixen*, 901.
  scold, 932.
Shrewd, *intelligent*, 450.
  wise, 491.
  clever, 698.
  cunning, 702.
Shriek, 411.
Shrill, 410.
Shrimp, 193.
Shrine, *altar*, 1000.
  interment, 363.
Shrink, *shrivel*, 195.
  narrow, 203.
  decrease, 36.
  small, 32.
  recoil, 286.
  avoid, 623.
  unwilling, 603.
Shrive, 950.
Shrivel, *decrease*, 36.
  shrink, 195.
  small, 193.
Shroud, *funeral*, 363.
  shelter, 666.
  safety, 664.
  hide, 528.
Shrub, 367.
Shrug, *hint*, 527.
  dissent, 489.
Shrunk, 193.
Shudder, *tremble, fear*, 860.
  aversion, 867.
  hate, 898.
  cold, 383.
Shuffle, *mix*, 41.
  disorder, 59.
  derange, 61.
  agitate, 315.

Shuffle, *toddle*, 266, 275.
   evasion, 544, 546.
   irresolution, 604.
   disgrace, 940.
Shuffler, 548.
Shun, *avoid*, 623.
   dislike, 867.
Shut, 261.
Shut out, *exclude*, 55.
   prohibit, 761.
Shut up, *inclose*, 231.
   imprison, 751.
   close, 261.
Shuttlecock, 605.
Shy, *avoid*, 623.
   suspicious, 485.
   modest, 881.
   fearful, 862.
   propel, 284.
Sib, 111.
Sibilant, *hiss*, 409.
Sibilation, *decry*, 929.
Sibyl, *oracle*, 513.
   ugly, 846.
Sibylline, 511.
Siccity, 340.
Sick, 655.
Sicken, *weary*, 841.
   nauseate, 395.
   fall ill, 655.
   disgust, 830.
   hate, 898.
Sickle, 244.
Sickly, *ill*, 655.
   weak, 160.
Sickness, 655.
Side, *laterality*, 236.
   party, 712.
Side with, 707.
Sideboard, 191.
Sidle, *oblique*, 217.
   deviate, 279.
   diverge, 290.
   lateral, 236.
Sidelong, 236.
Sidereal, 318.
Sideromancy, 511.
Sideways, *oblique*, 217.
   lateral, 236.
Siege, 716.
Sieve, *perforation*, 260.
   to sort, 60.
Sift, *to sort*, 60.
   winnow, 42.
   clean, 652.
   inquire, 461.
Sigh, 839.
Sigh for, 865.
Sight, *vision*, 441.
   spectacle, 448.
382

Sight, *prodigy*, 872.
   large quantity, 31.
Sightless, *blind*, 442.
   invisible, 447.
   ugly, 846.
Sigil, *seal*, 550.
   evidence, 467.
Sigmoidal, 248.
Sign, *indication*, 550.
   omen, 512.
   record, 551.
   write, 590.
   prodigy, 872.
   evidence, 467.
   compact, 769.
Sign-manual, 550.
Signal, *sign*, 550.
   important, 642.
Signalize, *celebrate*, 883.
   glory, 873.
Signally, 31.
Signature, *mark*, 550.
   writing, 590.
Signet, *evidence*, 467.
   signature, 550.
   sign of authority, 747.
Significant, *meaning*, 516.
   clear, 518.
   foreboding, 511.
   important, 642.
Signify, *mean*, 516.
   inform, 527.
   forebode, 511.
Silence, *no sound*, 403.
   aphony, 581.
   taciturn, 585.
   to check, 731.
*Silhouette, *portrait*, 556.
   outline, 229.
Silken, 255.
Silky, 255.
Silly, 499.
Silt, *dirt*, 653.
   dregs, 40.
Silver, *money*, 800.
Silver-toned, 413.
Silvery, *colour*, 430.
*Simagrée, 856.
Similar,   ⎫ *resembling*,17
Simile,   ⎬ *comparison*,
Similitude, ⎭   464.
Simmer, 382.
Simony, 995.
Simoom, *blast*, 349.
   heat, 382.
Simper, *smile*, 838.
   affectation, 855.
Simple, *unmixed*, 42.
   unadorned, 849.
   small, 32.

Simple, *silly*, 499.
   true, 543.
Simpleton, 501.
Simplify, *meaning*, 518.
Simulate, *resemble*, 17.
   imitate, 19.
   cheat, 544.
Simultaneous, 120.
Sin, *guilt*, 947.
   vice, 945.
Since, *in order*, 63.
   in time, 117.
Sincere, *veracious*, 543.
   ingenuous, 703.
*Sine quâ non,*condition*,770
   requirement, 630.
Sinecure, 810.
Sinew, 159.
Sinewy, 159.
Sinful, 947.
Sing, *music*, 415.
   poetry, 597.
   cheerful, 836.
Singe, 384.
Singer, 416.
Single, *unit*, 87.
   unmixed, 42.
   secluded, 893.
   unmarried, 904.
Single out, 609.
Single-minded, 543.
Singular, *exceptional*, 83.
   one, 87.
   remarkable, 31.
Sinister, *left*, 239.
   bad, 649.
   discourtesy, 895.
   vicious, 945.
Sink, *descend*, 306.
   lower, 308.
   deep, 208.
   fail, 732.
   destroy, 162.
   decay, 659.
   fatigue, 688.
   cloaca, 653.
   depressed, 837.
   droop, 828.
   conceal, 528.
   in the memory, 505.
Sinless, 946.
Sinner, 949.
Sin-offering, 952.
Sinuous, *curved*, 245.
   convoluted, 248.
Sinus, 252.
Sip, 297.
Siphon, 350.
Sir, 877.
Sirdar, 745.

Sire, 166.
Siren, *musician*, 416.
  instrument, 417.
  seducing, 615.
  demon, 980.
Sirocco, *wind*, 349.
  heat, 382.
Sirrah! 949.
Sister, *kindred*, 11.
  likeness, 17.
Sisterhood, 72.
  party, 712.
Sit, *repose*, 215.
  lie, 213.
  descend, 306.
Site, 183.
Sitting, *consultation*, 696.
Situate, 184.
Situation, *circumstances*, 8.
  place, 183.
  business, 625.
Siva, 979.
Six, 98.
Size, *magnitude*, 192.
  glue, 45.
Sizy, 350.
Skean, 727.
Skein, *knot*, 219.
  disorder, 59.
Skeleton, *corpse*, 362.
  frame, 626.
  small, 193.
  imperfect, 651.
  essential part, 50.
Sketch, *painting*, 556.
  description, 594.
  plan, 626.
Sketcher, 559.
Skew, 217.
Skewer, 45.
Skiff, 273.
Skill, 698.
Skim, *move*, 266.
  rapid, 274.
  attend lightly, 458.
Skin, *tegument*, 222.
  to peel, 226.
Skin-deep, 220.
Skin-flint, 819.
Skinny, *small*, 193.
  slender, 203.
  tegumentary, 222.
Skip, *jump*, 309.
  ascend, 305.
  neglect, 460.
  dance, 840.
Skipjack, 876.
Skirmish, 720.
Skirt, *edge*, 230.
  appendix, 39.

Skirt, *pendent*, 214.
  circumjacent, 227.
Skit, 932.
Skittish, *capricious*, 608.
  bashful, 881.
  timid, 862.
Skulk, *hide*, 447, 528.
  coward, 860.
Skull, 450.
Skull-cap, 225.
Skunk, 401.
Sky, *world*, 318.
  air, 338.
  summit, 210.
Sky-blue, 438.
Sky-rocket, 305.
Slab, 204.
Slabber, 296.
Slack, *loose*, 47.
  weak, 160.
  slow, 275.
  inert, 172.
  unwilling, 603.
  laxity, 738.
  to moderate, 174.
  retard, 706.
  calm, 826.
Slag, *refuse*, 40.
  dirt, 653.
Slake, *quench*, 174.
  indulge, 954.
  satiate, 869.
Slam, 406.
  slap, 276.
Slander, 934.
Slanderer, 936.
Slang, *neology*, 563.
  language, 560.
Slant, 217.
Slap, *to strike*, 276.
  hit, 972.
  quick, 274.
  haste, 684.
Slash, 44.
Slashing style, 574.
Slate, 590.
Slate colour, 432.
Slating, 210.
Slattern, *negligent*, 460.
  awkward, 701.
Slatternly, *vulgar*, 851.
  unskilful, 699.
Slaughter, 361.
Slave, *servant*, 746.
  to toil, 686.
Slaver, *slobber*, 296.
  ship, 273.
Slavery, 749.
Slay, 361.
Sledge, 272.

Sledge-hammer, *impel*, 276.
  engine, 633.
Sleek, *smooth*, 255.
  pretty, 845.
Sleep, 683.
Sleeper, *support*, 215.
Sleepy, *inactive*, 823.
  slow, 275.
Sleet, 383.
Sleeveless, *mad*, 503.
  unreasonable, 608.
  foolish, 499.
Sleight, 698.
Sleight of hand, 545.
Slender, *narrow*, 203.
  small, 32.
  trifling, 643.
Slice, *layer*, 204.
  part, 51.
Slide, *pass*, 264.
  descend, 306.
  become, 144.
Slight, *small*, 32.
  trifle, 643.
  to neglect, 460.
  to dishonor, 929.
Slily, *craftily*, 702.
  surreptitiously, 544.
Slim, 203.
Slimy, *viscous*, 352.
  dirt, 653.
Sliness, *craft*, 702.
  deception, 545.
Sling, *hang*, 214.
  project, 284.
  weapon, 727.
Slink, *recede*, 286.
  escape, 671.
Slip, *descend*, 306.
  strip, 205.
  part, 51.
  transfer, 270.
  fail, 732.
  liberate, 750.
  workshop, 691.
  guilt, 947.
Slip away, 671.
Slip-cable, 292.
Slip of the tongue, *mistake*, 495.
  solecism, 568.
Slip on, 225.
Slip over, 460.
Slipper, 225.
Slippery, *smooth*, 255.
  uncertain, 475.
  dangerous, 665.
  not trustworthy, 940
Slipshod, 855.
Slipslop, *affected*, 855.

Slipslop, *absurd*, 497.
  style, 573.
Slit, *to divide*, 44.
  chink, 198.
Sliver, 51.
Slobber, *slop*, 337.
  emit, 296.
  soil, 653.
Sloe, *colour*, 431.
Sloop, 273.
Slop, *water*, 337.
  emit, 296.
  dirt, 653.
Slope, 217.
Sloppy, 337.
Slops, 225.
Sloth, 683.
Slouch, *oblique*, 217.
  low, 207.
  inactive, 683.
  ugly, 846.
Slough, *difficulty*, 704.
  quagmire, 345.
Sloven, *drab*, 653.
  careless, 460.
  awkward, 699.
  bungler, 701.
  vulgar, 851.
Slow, *sluggish*, 275.
  tardy, 133.
  inert, 172.
  inactive, 683.
Slubberdegullion, *apostate*,
  941.
  miscreant, 949.
Slug,   } *slow*, 275.
Sluggard, } *inert*, 172.
Sluggish, } *sleepy*, 683.
  callous, 823.
Sluice, *conduit*, 350.
  river, 348.
Slur, *stigma*, 874.
  gloss over, 937.
  reproach, 938.
Slur over, *neglect*, 460.
  inattention, 458.
  conceal, 528.
  exclude, 55.
Slush, 354.
Slut, 962.
Sluttish, 653.
Sly, *cunning*, 702.
  false, 544.
Smack, *ship*, 273.
  taste, 390.
  mixture, 41.
  small quantity, 32.
  kiss, 902.
Small, *in degree*, 32.
  in size, 193.

384

Smaller, 34.
Smallest, 34.
Smart, *pain*, 378.
  grief, 828.
  active, 682.
  clever, 698.
  to feel, 821.
  witty, 842.
  neat, 845.
Smash, 162.
Smatterer, 493.
Smattering, 491.
Smear, *daub*, 222.
  ugly, 846.
Smell, 398.
Smelt, 384.
Smicker, 838.
Smile, 838.
Smile upon, 894.
Smirk, 838.
Smite, *strike*, 276.
  afflict, 830.
  punish, 972.
  bad, 649.
Smith, 690.
Smitten, 897.
Smock, 225.
Smoke, *cloud*, 334.
  dimness, 422.
  heat, 382.
  trifle, 643.
  dirt, 653.
  to discover, 480.
  suspect, 485.
  (to end in), *disappoint*,
    932.
Smolder, *burn*, 382.
  inert, 172.
  latent, 526.
Smooth, *not rough*, 255.
  to calm, 174.
  rub, 331.
  easy, 705.
  to flatter, 933.
Smooth-faced, 544.
Smooth-spoken, 544.
Smooth-tongued, 544.
Smother, *kill*, 361.
  repress, 174.
  calm, 826.
  suppress, 528.
Smudge, *dirt*, 653.
  blemish, 848.
Smug, 855.
Smuggle, *contraband*, 791.
  introduce, 295.
Smuggler, 792.
Smut, *dirt*, 653.
  black, 431.
  blemish, 848.

Smut, *impurity*, 961.
Snacks, *part*, 51.
  participate, 778.
  food, 299.
Snaffle, 752.
Snag, *danger*, 667.
  sharp, 253.
  projection, 250.
Snail, 275.
Snake, *miscreant*, 913.
Snaky, *winding*, 248.
Snap, *noise*, 406.
  brittle, 328.
  break, 44.
  snarl, 895.
  angry, 900.
  seize, 789.
Snare, 667.
Snarl, *growl*, 412.
  angry, 900.
  rude, 895.
  threaten, 909.
Snatch, *to seize*, 789.
  part, 51.
Snatches (by), 139.
Sneak, *servility*, 886.
  baseness, 940.
  to hide, 528.
  retire, 286.
Sneer, *contempt*, 930.
  blame, 932.
  disparage, 929.
Sneeze, *snuffle*, 409.
  blow, 349.
Snick, 51.
Sniff, 398.
Sniffle, 349.
Snip, 44.
Snip-snap, 713.
Snivel, *cry*, 839.
  crouch, 886.
Snob, 876.
Snooze, 683.
Snore, } *noise*, 411.
Snort, } *sleep*, 683.
Snout, 250.
Snow, *ice*, 383.
  white, 430.
Snowball, 72.
Snub, *bluster*, 885.
  blame, 932.
Snuff, 398.
Snuff up, 297.
Snuffle, *hiss*, 409.
  blow, 349.
  stammer, 583.
Snug, *comfortable*, 831.
  safe, 664.
  latent, 526.
  secluded, 893.

Soak, *immerse*, 301.
    water, 337.
Soaker, 959.
Soap, *oil*, 356.
Soapy, *unctuous*, 355.
Soar, *rise*, 305.
    height, 206.
    great, 31.
    fly, 267.
Sob, 839.
Sober, *moderate*, 174.
    temperate, 953.
    abstinent, 958.
    sane, 502.
    wise, 498.
    calm, 826.
    grave, 837.
Sober-minded, *wise*, 502.
    calm, 826.
*Sobriquet, 565.
Sociable, 892.
Social, 892.
Society, 892.
    party, 712.
Sock, *stocking*, 225.
    drama, 599.
Socket, 191.
Socratic method, 461.
Sod, 344.
Sodality, *fraternity*, 712.
    association, 892.
    friendship, 888.
Sofa, 215.
Sofi, 996.
Soft, *not hard*, 324.
    moderate, 174.
    sound, 405.
    smooth, 255.
    weak, 160.
    silly, 499.
    irresolute, 605.
    timid, 862.
    lenient, 740.
    compassionate, 914.
    tender, 822.
    soothe, 826.
    mitigate, 834.
    to palliate, 937.
Soften, *overcome*, 824.
Soho! 265.
*Soi-disant, *pretender*, 548.
    misnomer, 565.
    boaster, 884.
Soil, *land*, 342.
    dirt, 653.
    spoil, 659.
    deface, 846.
    tarnish, 848.
*Soirée, 892.
Sojourn, *abode*, 189.

Sojourn, *inhabit*, 188.|
    settle, 265.
Solace, *relief*, 834.
    comfort, 827.
    recreation, 840.
Soldan, 745.
Solder, *cohere*, 46.
    cement, 45.
Soldier, 726.
Soldiery, 726.
Sole, *alone*, 87.
    base, 211.
Solecism, *ungrammatical*, 568.
    sophistry, 477.
Solemn, *awful*, 873.
    sacred, 987.
    grave, 837.
    important, 642.
Solemnity, *parade*, 882.
    rite, 998.
    dulness, 843.
Solemnize, 883.
*Solfeggio, 413.
Solicit, *induce*, 615.
    request, 765.
    desire, 865.
Solicitor, 968.
Solicitude, *anxiety*, 860.
    care, 459.
    desire, 865.
Solid, *complete*, 52.
    dense, 321.
    certain, 474.
    true, 494.
    firm, 604.
Solidify, 321.
Soliloquy, 589.
Solitary, } *alone*, 87.
Solitude, } *secluded*, 893.
Solo, 415.
Solon, *sage*, 500.
    wise, 498.
Soluble, 333.
Solution, *dissolving*, 333.
    explanation, 462.
Solvency, 803.
Somatics, 316.
*Sombre, *dark*, 421.
    gray, 432.
    black, 431.
    melancholy, 837.
Some, 100.
Somebody, *one*, 87.
    man, 373.
Somehow, 155.
Somerset, 218.
Something, *thing*, 3.
    small degree, 32.
Sometimes, 136.

Somewhat, 32.
Somewhere, 182.
Somnambulism, 515.
Somniferous, } *sleepy*, 683.
Somnolence, } *weary*, 841.
Somnolent, }
Son, 167.
Sonata, 415.
Song, 415.
Song (old), 643.
Songster, 416.
Soniferous, 402.
Sonnet, *music*, 415.
    poetry, 597.
Sonorous, 402.
Soon, *early*, 132.
    transient, 111.
Soot, *black*, 431.
    dirt, 653.
    blemish, 846.
Sooth, 511.
Soothe, *allay*, 174.
    calm, 826.
    relieve, 834.
Soothsay, 511.
Soothsayer, 513.
    magician, 994.
Sop, *bribe*, 615.
    reward, 973.
Sophi, 996.
Sophism, *bad logic*, 477.
    absurdity, 497.
Sophisticate, *mix*, 41.
    debase, 659.
Sophistry, 477.
Soporific, 841.
Soprano, 410, 413.
Sorcerer, 994.
Sorcery, 992.
*Sordes, 653.
Sordid, 819.
Sore, *pain*, 376.
    grievance, 828.
    painful, 830.
    angry, 900.
Sorely, 31.
Sorites, 476.
Sorrel, 434.
Sorrow, 828.
Sorry, *grieved*, 828.
    bad, 649.
    mean, 876.
    trifling, 643.
Sort, *kind*, 75.
    degree, 26.
    to arrange, 60.
Sortance, *agreement*, 23.
*Sortie, 716.
*Sortilege, 992.
Sortilegy, 621.

Sorting, 60.
So-so, 651.
Sot, *fool*, 501.
  drunkard, 959.
*Sotto voce, 405.
*Soubrette, 746.
Sough, *conduit*, 350.
  cloaca, 653.
Soul, *intellect*, 450.
  affections, 820.
  man, 373.
  important part, 50, 642.
Soul-sick, 837.
Sound, *noise*, 402.
  healthy, 654.
  perfect, 650.
  good, 648.
  to measure, 466.
  to investigate, 461.
  true, 494.
  wise, 498.
  bay, 343.
Soundings, 208.
Soundless, *deep*, 208.
  silent, 403.
Soundly, 31.
Soup, 354.
*Soupçon, 32.
Sour, *acid*, 397.
  uncivil, 895.
  misanthropic, 901.
  to embitter, 835.
Source, 153.
Souse, *immerse*, 301.
  water, 337.
Sovereign, *great*, 31.
  ruler, 754.
Sow, *scatter*, 73.
  prepare, 673.
Sow broadcast, 290.
Space, 180.
Spacious, 180.
Spahee, 726.
Span, *distance*, 196.
  nearness, 197.
  length, 200.
  measure, 466.
  time, 106.
Spangle, *spark*, 420.
  ornament, 847.
Spaniel, *servile*, 886.
  flatterer, 935.
Spanking, 192.
Spar, *discord*, 713.
  contention, 720.
Spare, *meagre*, 203.
  scanty, 642.
  to give, 784.
  relinquish, 782.
  disuse, 678.
386

Spare, *refrain*, 623.
  pity, 914.
  frugal, 953.
  economic, 817.
Spare time, 685.
Spargefaction, *dispersion*, 73.
  sprinkling, 37, 337.
Sparing, *temperate*, 953.
  economic, 817.
Spark, *light*, 420.
  fop, 854.
  humorist, 844.
Sparkle, *glisten*, 420.
  bubble, 353.
Sparse, 73.
*Sparsim, 73.
Spasm, *fit*, 173.
  pain, 378, 828.
Spatter, *dirt*, 653.
  damage, 659.
Spatula, 204.
Spawn, *dirt*, 653.
  offspring, 167.
Speak, 582.
Speak to, 585.
Speak out, 529.
Speaker, 582.
  teacher, 540.
  interpreter, 524.
  president, 745.
Spear, *lance*, 727.
  to pierce, 260.
  pass through, 302.
Spearman, 726.
Special, *particular*, 79,
  peculiar, 5.
Specie, 800.
Species, *kind*, 75.
  appearance, 448.
Specific, 79.
Specify, *name*, 564.
  tell, 527.
Specimen, 82.
Specious, *probable*, 472
  sophistical, 477.
Speck, *dot*, 193.
  small quantity, 32.
  blemish, 848.
Speckle, *variegated*, 400.
  blemish, 848.
Spectacle, *appearance*, 448.
  show, 882.
  prodigy, 872.
Spectacles, 445.
Spectator, 444.
Spectre, *vision*, 448.
  ugly, 846.
  ghost, 980.
Spectrum, *colour*, 428.

Spectrum, *appearance*, 448.
Speculate, *think*, 451.
  traffic, 794.
  view, 441.
Speculum, 445.
Speech, 582.
Speechify, 582.
Speechless, 581.
Speed, *velocity*, 274.
  activity, 682.
  to help, 707.
  succeed, 731.
Spell, *interpret*, 522.
  read, 539.
  period, 106.
  charm, 993.
  necessity, 601.
  motive, 615.
  exertion, 686.
Spell-bound, 615.
Spence, 636.
Spencer, 225.
Spend, *expend*, 809.
  waste, 638.
Spendthrift, 818.
Spent, *exhausted*, 688.
Spermaceti, 356.
Spew, 296.
Sphere, *ball*, 249.
  region, 181.
  rank, 26.
  business, 625.
Spheroid, 249.
Spherule, 249.
Sphinx, *oracle*, 513.
  monster, 83.
Spice, *small quantity*, 32.
  mixture, 41.
  pungent, 392.
  condiment, 393.
*Spicilegium, 72, 596.
Spick and span, 123.
Spiculum, 253.
Spike, *to pierce*, 260.
  plug, 263.
  pass through, 302.
  sharp, 253.
Spill, *filament*, 205.
  to shed, 296.
  waste, 638.
  splash, 348.
  lavish, 818.
  misuse, 679.
  a stopper, 263.
Spin, 312.
Spin out, *prolong*, 200.
  protract, 110.
  style, 573.
Spindle, 312.
Spindleshanks, 203.

Spine, 253.
Spinet, 417.
Spinster, 904.
Spiracle, 351.
Spiral, 248.
Spire, *peak*, 253.
   height, 206.
   soar, 305.
Spirit, *essence*, 5.
   immateriality, 317.
   intellect, 450.
   affections, 820.
   resolution, 604.
   courage, 861.
   ghost, 980.
   style, 574.
   activity, 682.
Spirited, *brave*, 861.
   generous, 942.
Spiritless, *torpid*, 823.
   dejected, 837.
   timid, 862.
Spirits, 836.
Spiritual, *immaterial*, 317.
   divine, 976.
*Spirituel, *witty*, 842.
Spissitude, 321.
Spit, *eject*, 296.
   pierce, 302.
   rain, 348.
   bar, 253.
Spite, *malevolence*, 907.
   notwithstanding, 179.
Splash, *affuse*, 337.
   spill, 348.
   spatter, 653.
   sully, 846.
   parade, 882.
Spleen, *melancholy*, 837.
   hatred, 898.
   anger, 900.
   discourteous, 895.
Spleenless, 906.
Splendid, *beautiful*, 845.
   glorious, 873.
Splenetic, *sad*, 837.
   irascible, 901.
Splice, 43.
Splinter, *divide*, 44.
   brittle, 328.
   bit, 51.
Split, *divide*, 44.
   quarrel, 713.
   fail, 732.
   laugh, 838.
Split hairs, 465, 477.
Splutter, *stammer*, 583.
   haste, 684.
   energy, 171.
   spitting, 296.
387

Spoil, *vitiate*, 659.
   hinder, 706.
   plunder, 791.
   booty, 793.
   injure, 649.
   satiate, 869.
Spoke, *tooth*, 253.
   radius, 200.
   obstruct, 706.
Spokesman, *interpreter*, 524.
   speaker, 582.
Spoliate, *plunder*, 791.
   evil, 619.
Sponge, *clean*, 652.
   obliterate, 552.
   despoil, 791.
   porous, 322.
   oblivion, 506.
Sponsion, 771.
Sponsor, *security*, 771.
   evidence, 467.
Spontaneous, *voluntary*,
600.
   impulsive, 612.
Spook, 980.
Spoon, *receptacle*, 191.
   ladle, 272.
Spoonful, 32.
Spoony, 499.
Sport, *amusement*, 840.
   gaiety, 836.
   wit, 842.
   enjoyment, 827.
   subjection, 749.
Sportulary, 785.
Sportule, 784.
Spot, *place*, 182.
   decoloration, 429.
   blemish, 848.
   to sully, 846.
   blot, 874.
   disgrace, 940.
Spotless, *innocent*, 946.
   clean, 652.
   good, 648.
   fair, 845.
Spotty, 440.
Spouse, *married*, 903.
   companion, 88.
Spousals, 903.
Spouseless, 904.
Spout, *conduit*, 350.
   egress, 294.
   flow out, 348.
   speak, 582.
   act, 599.
Sprain, 160.
Sprawl, *lie*, 213.
   leap, 309.
Spray, *sprig*, 51.

Spray, *foam*, 353.
Spread, *enlarge*, 35.
   expand, 194.
   disperse, 73.
   diverge, 290.
   expanse, 180.
   publish, 531.
Spree, 720.
Sprig, 51.
Sprightly, 836.
Spring, *early*, 125.
   cause, 153.
   arise from, 154.
   ensue, 151.
   strength, 159.
   velocity, 274.
   leap, 309.
   rivulet, 348.
   instrument, 633.
Spring back, *elastic*, 325.
   recoil, 277.
Spring tide, *flow*, 348.
   abundance, 639.
Spring up, *grow*, 194.
Springe, *snare*, 667.
   deception, 545.
Sprinkle, *add*, 37.
   mix, 41.
   disperse, 73.
   emit, 296.
   wet, 337.
Sprinkling, *small quantity*,
32.
   little, 193.
Sprite, 980.
Sprout, *grow*, 35.
   expand, 194.
   arise from, 154.
   offspring, 167.
Spruce, *neat*, 652.
   beautiful, 845.
Spry, *active*, 682.
   clever, 698.
Spume, 353.
Spunk, 861.
Spur, *sharp*, 253.
   incite, 615.
Spurious, *false*, 544.
   erroneous, 495.
   illegitimate, 925.
Spurn, *disdain*, 930.
Spurt, *impulse*, 612.
   haste, 684.
   swift, 274.
   gush, 348.
Sputter, *emit*, 296.
   stammer, 583.
Spy, *see*, 441.
   spectator, 444.
   emissary, 534.

Spy-glass, 445.
Squab, *large*, 192.
  broad, 202.
  recumbent, 215.
Squabble, 713.
Squad, 72.
Squadron, *navy*, 273.
  army, 726.
  assemblage, 72.
Squalid, 846.
Squall, *cry*, 411.
  wind, 349.
  violence, 173.
Squamous, 222.
Squander, 818.
Square, *number*, 95.
  buildings, 189.
  congruity, 23.
  expedience, 646.
  justice, 924.
  honor, 939.
  form, 244.
Square-toes, 857.
Squash, *destroy*, 162.
  throw, 276.
  leap, 309.
  soft, 324.
  water, 337.
Squashy, 352.
Squat, *to encamp*, 186.
  sit, 306.
  large, 192.
  broad, 202.
  flat, 213.
  ugly, 846.
Squatter, 188.
Squatting, 213.
Squeak,⎤ *cry*, 411, 412.
Squeal,⎦ *complain*, 839.
Squeamish, *fastidious*, 868.
  censorious, 932.
Squeasy, 868.
Squeeze, *contract*, 195.
  narrow, 203.
  condense, 321.
Squeeze out, 300.
Squib, *sound*, 406.
  lampoon, 932.
Squint, 443.
Squire, *gentry*, 875.
  attendant, 746.
Squirrel, 274.
Squirt, *eject*, 296.
  spurt, 348.
Stab, *pierce*, 260.
  kill, 361.
  injure, 649.
Stable, *house*, 139.
  at rest, 265.
  immutable, 150.
388

Stack, 72.
Stadtholder, 745.
Staff, *support*, 215.
  instrument, 633.
  weapon, 727.
  sceptre, 747.
  retinue, 746.
  party, 712.
  hope, 858.
Stage, *degree*, 26.
  term, 71.
  step, 58.
  layer, 204.
  forum, 542.
  vehicle, 272.
  arena, 728.
  drama, 599.
Stage-play, 599.
Stager, *agent*, 690.
  actor, 599.
Stagger, *totter*, 314.
  slow, 275.
  agitate, 315.
  doubt, 485.
  dissuade, 616.
  affect, 824.
  astonish, 870.
Stagnant, *quiescent*, 265.
  persistent, 142.
Staid, *steady*, 604.
  calm, 826.
  wise, 498.
  grave, 837.
Stain, *colour*, 428.
  deface, 846.
  blemish, 848.
  spoil, 659.
  disgrace, 874.
  dishonor, 940.
Stainless, *clean*, 652.
  innocent, 946.
Stair, *way*, 627.
Stake, *wager*, 621.
  danger, 665.
  security, 771.
  execution, 975.
Stalactite, 224.
Stalagmite, 224.
Stale, *old*, 124.
  vapid, 866.
Stale-mate, 732.
Stalk, 266.
Stalking-horse, *plea*, 617.
  deception, 545.
Stall, *lodge*, 189.
  mart, 799.
  cathedral, 1000.
Stallion, 271.
Stalwart, *strong*, 159.
  tall, 206.

Stalwart, *large*, 192.
Stamina, 159.
Stammel, 434.
Stammer, 583.
Stamp, *character*, 7.
  form, 240.
  to impress, 505.
  mark, 550.
  record, 551.
  complete, 729.
Stanchion, 215.
Stand, *to be*, 1.
  be present, 186.
  to continue, 142, 143.
  endure, 111.
  station, 58.
  rank, 71.
  support, 215.
  resistance, 719.
Stand against, *resist*, 719.
Stand by, *near*, 197.
  befriend, 707.
Stand for, 550.
Stand off, 196.
Stand on, 215.
Stand out, *project*, 250.
Stand up, 212.
Stand up for, 937.
Standard, *rule*, 80.
  measure, 466.
  degree, 26.
  colours, 550.
  good, 648.
Standard bearer, 726.
Standing, *footing*, 8.
  term, 71.
  degree, 26.
  note, 873.
  vertical, 212.
Stand-still, *stop*, 265.
  remain, 142.
Stanza, 597.
Staple, *whole*, 50
  pendent, 214.
  sharp, 253.
  mart, 799.
Star, *luminary*, 423.
  decoration, 877.
  glory, 873.
  actor, 599.
Starboard, 238.
Starch, *stiff*, 323.
  obstinate, 606.
  proud, 878.
  affected, 855.
Starchamber, 966.
Stare, *look*, 441.
  curiosity, 455.
  wonder, 870.
Stargazer, 318.

Staring, 446.
Stark, 31.
Stars, *celestial*, 318.
   necessity, 601.
Start, *depart*, 292.
   begin, 66.
   desultory, 139.
   arise, 151.
   suggest, 514.
   from fear, 860.
   from wonder, 870.
Start up, *project*, 250.
   arise, 305.
   appear, 446.
Starting point *or* post, 66.
Startle, *unexpected*, 508.
   wonder, 870.
   fear, 860.
Starve, *fast*, 956.
   with cold, 385.
Starved, *lean*, 193.
   insufficient, 640.
Starveling, *pinched*, 203.
   poor, 804.
State, *condition*, 7.
   nation, 373.
   ostentation, 882.
   property, 780.
   to inform, 527.
   describe, 594.
Stately, *pompous*, 882.
   proud, 878.
   grand, 873.
Statesman, 745.
Statesmanlike, 698.
Statesmanship, 693.
Statics, 319.
Station, *stage*, 58.
   term, 71.
   place, 182.
   to locate, 184.
   rank, 873.
Stationary, 265.
Statist, 745.
Statistics, 85.
Statue, 557.
Stature, 206.
*Status, 8.
   rank, 873.
Statute, 963.
Stave in, 260.
Stave off, 133.
Stay, *wait*, 133.
   continue, 142.
   support, 215.
   refuge, 666.
   prevent, 706.
   dissuade, 616.
   corset, 225.
Stead, 644.

Steadfast, *resolved*, 604.
   quiescent, 265.
Steady, *resolved*, 604.
   cautious, 864.
   constant, 150.
Steal, *rob*, 791.
   creep, 275.
Steal away, 671.
Stealth, 528.
Steam, *vapour*, 333.
   to sail, 267.
Steamboat, 273.
Steamer, 273.
Stearine, 356.
Steed, 271.
Steel, *strength*, 159.
   enure, 823.
Steeled, 604.
Steelyard, 466.
Steep, *slope*, 217.
   immerse, 301.
   soak, 337.
Steeple, *spire*, 253.
   high, 206.
Steeplechase, *race*, 274.
   advance, 282.
Steeps, 206.
Steer, 693.
Steerage, 278.
Steersman, 694.
Steganography, 590.
Stellar, 318.
Stelography, 590.
Stem, *origin*, 153.
   front, 234.
   to oppose, 708.
   to resist, 718.
Stench, 401.
Stencil, 556.
Stenography, 590.
Stentorian, 404.
Step, *degree*, 26.
   station, 58.
   term, 71.
   near, 197.
   support, 215.
   motion, 264, 266.
   measure, 466.
   expedient, 626.
   means, 632.
Steppe, 344.
Stepping-stone, *link*, 45.
   way, 627.
   resource, 666.
Stercoracious, 653.
Stereoscope, 445.
Stereotype, 550, 591.
Sterile, *unproductive*, 169.
   useless, 645.
Sterling, *true*, 494.

Sterling, *good*, 648.
   virtuous, 944.
Stern, *back*, 235.
   severe, 739.
   forbidding, 895.
Sternutation, 349.
   sound, 409.
Stew, *confusion*, 59.
   difficulty, 704.
   heat, 382.
   cook, 384.
   perplex, 828.
   bagnio, 961.
Steward, 694.
Stewardships, 693.
Stick, *adhere*, 46.
   staff, 215.
   to stab, 260.
   pierce, 302.
   difficulty, 704.
   to gravel, 830.
   fool, 501.
   scourge, 975.
Stick in, 301.
   locate, 184.
Stick out, } *project*, 250.
Stick up, } *erect*, 212.
Stickle, *haggle*, 769.
   barter, 794.
   contend, 720.
   reluctant, 603.
Sticky, *cohering*, 46.
   semiliquid, 352.
Stiff, *rigid*, 323.
   resolute, 604.
   severe, 739.
   affected, 855.
   haughty, 878.
   pompous, 882.
   ugly, 846.
   style, 572, 579.
Stiffnecked, *obstinate*, 606.
   resolute, 604.
Stifle, *silence*, 403.
   destroy, 162.
   kill, 361.
   sound, 405.
Stigma, *disgrace*, 874.
   blame, 932.
Stiletto, *piercer*, 262.
   dagger, 727.
Still, *ever*, 112.
   silent, 403.
   quiet, 174.
   quiescence, 265.
   calm, 826.
   notwithstanding, 179.
Still-born, 732.
Stillicidium, 348.
Stilts, *support*, 215.

Stilts, *height*, 206.
　　boasting, 884.
Stimulate, *incite*, 615.
　　violence, 173.
　　passion, 824.
Stimulus, 615.
Sting, *pain*, 378.
　　suffering, 824, 830.
　　provoke, 900.
Stingy, 817.
Stink, 401.
Stint, *degree*, 26.
　　limit, 233.
　　scanty, 640.
　　parsimony, 819.
Stipend, 809.
Stipendiary,　*receiving*,
　785.
　　subjected, 749.
Stippling, 558.
Stipulate, *conditions*, 770.
　　bargain, 769.
Stir, *move*, 264.
　　activity, 682.
　　energy, 171.
　　emotion, 824.
　　discuss, 476.
Stir up, *mix*, 41.
　　excite, 615.
　　violence, 173.
Stitch, *work*, 680.
　　to join, 43.
　　pain, 828.
Stiver, 800.
Stock, *cause*, 153.
　　store, 636.
　　materials, 635.
　　provision, 637.
　　property, 780.
　　money, 800.
　　merchandise, 798.
　　collar, 225.
　　offspring, 166.
Stockade, 717.
Stocking, 225.
Stocks, *funds*, 802.
　　punishment, 975.
　　restraint, 752.
Stock-still, 265.
Stoic, *insensible*, 823.
　　inexcitable, 826.
　　disinterested, 942.
Stole, 225.
Stolid, *dull*, 843.
　　stupid, 499.
Stomach, *pouch*, 191.
　　taste, 390.
　　liking, 865.
Stomacher, 225.
Stone, *dense*, 321.
390

Stone, *hard*, 323.
　　missile, 284.
　　weapon, 727.
Stone-blind, 442.
Stone-colour, 432.
Stone-hearted, 900.
Stool, 215.
Stoop, *lower*, 306.
　　slope, 217.
　　humble, 879.
　　servile, 886.
Stop, *close*, 261.
　　rest, 265.
　　prevent, 706.
　　continue, 142.
　　discontinue, 141.
Stopcock, 263.
Stopgap, *shift*, 626.
　　plug, 263.
Stopper, 263.
Stopple, 263.
Store, *magazine*, 636.
　　provision, 637.
　　shop, 799.
　　the memory, 505.
Storehouse, 636.
Stork, 792.
Storm, *wind*, 349.
　　violence, 173.
　　passion, 825.
　　anger, 900.
　　to attack, 716.
　　assemblage, 72.
Story, *history*, 594.
　　lie, 546.
　　rooms, 191.
Stound, 870.
Stout, *strong*, 159.
　　lusty, 192.
　　brave, 861.
Stove, 386.
Stow, 184.
Stowage, *space*, 180.
　　location, 184.
Strabism, 443.
Straggle, *stroll*, 266.
　　deviate, 279.
　　disjunction, 44.
　　disorder, 59.
Straggler, 268.
Straight, *rectilinear*, 246.
　　vertical, 212.
　　direction, 278.
Straightforward,　*artless*,
　703.
　　honest, 939.
　　true, 543.
　　mid-course, 628.
Straightway, 111.
Strain, *effort*, 686.

Strain, *violence*, 173.
　　fatigue, 688.
　　sound, 402.
　　melody, 413.
　　to clarify, 658.
　　percolate, 294.
　　transgress, 304.
　　poetry, 597.
　　voice, 580.
　　misinterpret, 523.
　　style, 569.
Strain the eyes, 441.
Strait, *maritime*, 343.
　　difficulty, 704.
Straitlaced, *severe*, 739.
　　censorious, 932.
　　haughty, 878.
　　fastidious, 868.
Strait-waistcoat, 752.
Strand, 342.
Stranded, 732.
Strange, *exceptional*, 83.
　　wonderful, 890.
　　ridiculous, 853.
Stranger, *extraneous*, 57.
　　ignorant, 491.
Strangle, 361.
Strap, *to tie*, 43.
　　ligature, 45.
Strappado, 972.
Strapping, *large*, 192.
Stratagem, *plan*, 626.
　　artifice, 702.
　　deception, 545.
Strategy, *conduct*, 692.
　　skill, 698.
　　warfare, 722.
　　plan, 626.
Stratification, 204.
Stratocracy, 737.
Stratum, 204.
Straw, *light*, 320.
　　trifling, 643.
Straw-colour, 436.
Stray, *wander*, 266.
　　deviate, 279.
　　exceptional, 83.
Streak, *colour*, 420.
　　stripe, 440.
　　intersection, 219.
Stream, *flow*, 347.
　　river, 348.
　　of light, 420.
　　of time, 109.
　　of events, 151.
　　abundance, 639.
Streamer, 550.
Streaming, *incoherent*, 47.
　　dispersed, 73.
Streamlet, 348.

Street, *buildings*, 189.
   way, 627.
Street-walker, 962.
Strength, *vigour*, 159.
   energy, 171.
Strengthen, *to increase*, 35.
Strenuous, *active*, 682.
   resolved, 604.
Stress, *weight*, 642.
   strain, 686.
Stretch, *increase*, 35.
   expand, 194.
   lengthen, 200.
   distance, 196.
   exertion, 686.
   encroachment, 925.
   exaggeration, 549.
Stretcher, 272.
Strew, 73.
*Striæ, 440.
Striated, 440.
Strict, *severe*, 739.
   exact, 494.
Stricture, 932.
Stride, 266.
Stridor, 410.
Strife, 713.
Strike, *hit*, 276.
   beat, 972.
   revolt, 719, 742.
   impress, 824.
   wonder, 870.
   operate, 170.
   music, 415.
Strike off, *exclude*, 55.
Strike out, *invent*, 515.
   plan, 626.
   efface, 552.
String, *continuity*, 69.
   to tie, 43.
   ligature, 45.
   to arrange, 60.
Stringy, 203.
Strip, *to divest*, 226.
   rob, 791.
   filament, 205.
Stripe, *length*, 200.
   blow, 972.
   mark, 550.
   variegation, 440.
Stripling, 129.
Stripped, *poor*, 804.
Strive, *exert*, 686.
   endeavour, 676.
Stroke, *impulse*, 276.
   mark, 550.
   work, 680.
   expedient, 626.
   success, 731.
Stroll, 266.

Strong, *powerful*, 159.
   energetic, 171.
   tenacious, 327.
   pungent, 392.
   feeling, 821.
Strong-box, 802.
Strong-hold, *defence*, 717.
   prison, 752.
Strongly, 31.
Strophe, 597.
Structure, *state*, 7.
   texture, 329.
   building, 189.
Struggle, *contend*, 720.
   exert, 686.
Strum, 415.
Strumpet, 962.
Strut, *parade*, 882.
   boast, 884.
   pride, 878.
Stubble, 40.
Stubborn, 606.
Stubby, *short*, 201.
   ugly, 846.
Stucco, *cement*, 45.
   covering, 222.
Stuck fast, *difficulty*, 704.
   stopped, 265.
Stud, *knob*, 250.
   point, 253.
   horses, 271.
Studded, 440.
Student, 541.
*Studio, 691.
Studious, *thoughtful*, 451.
   docile, 539.
Studiously, 600.
Study, *thought*, 451.
   learning, 539.
   research, 461.
   intention, 620.
Stuff, *substance*, 3.
   matter, 316.
   materials, 632.
   absurdity, 497.
   trifle, 643.
   to feed, 297.
   cram, 194.
Stultified, 732.
Stultify, *counteract*, 708.
Stultiloquy, 497.
Stumble, *fall*, 306.
   fail, 732.
   unskilful, 699.
   flounder, 315.
Stumble on, 480.
Stumbling-block, *difficulty*, 704.
   hindrance, 706.
Stump, *trunk*, 51.

Stump, *to step*, 266.
Stumpy, *short*, 201.
   ugly, 846.
Stun, *stupefy*, 823.
   affect, 824.
   deafen, 419.
   loud, 404.
Stung, 828.
Stunt, *small*, 193.
   contracted, 195.
Stupefy, *stun*, 823.
   wonder, 870.
Stupendous, *great*, 31.
   large, 192.
   wonderful, 870.
Stupid, *dull*, 843.
   foolish, 499.
Stupor, 823.
Stupration, 961.
Sturdy, 159.
Stutter, 583.
Stye, *dirt*, 653.
   pen, 189.
Stygian, *infernal*, 982.
   dark, 421.
   diabolic, 945.
Style, *state*, 7.
   time, 114.
   fashion, 852.
   taste, 850.
   to name, 564.
   diction, 569.
   pencil, 559.
Stylet, 727.
Styptic, 397.
Suasion, 615.
Suavity, 894.
Subacid, 397.
Subaction, 330.
Subahdar, 745.
Subaltern, *plebeian*, 876.
   inferior, 34.
   servant, 746.
   officer, 745.
Subaqueous, 208.
Subastral, 318.
Subcommittee, 696.
Subcontrary, 237.
Subcutaneous, 221.
Subdean, 996.
Subdititious, 147.
Subdivide, 44.
Subdivision, 51.
Subdolous, 702.
Subdual, 731.
Subduct, *retrench*, 38.
   take, 789.
Subdue, *calm*, 174.
   impress, 824.
   succeed, 731.

Subitaneous, 132.
*Subito, 113.
Subjacent, 207.
Subject, *topic*, 454.
   liable, 177.
   to enthral, 749.
Subjoin, 37.
Subjugate, *subject*, 749.
   conquer, 731, 732.
   impress, 824.
Subjunction, 37.
Sublation, 38.
Sublevation, 307.
Sublimate, *to elevate*, 307.
Sublimated, 320.
Sublimation, *vaporization*, 336.
   elevation, 307.
Sublime, *high*, 206.
   beauty, 845.
   glory, 873.
   magnanimous, 942.
Sublunary, 318.
Submarine, 208.
Submerge, *immerse*, 301.
   steep, 337.
   plunge, 310.
Submission, 725.
Submissive, *humble*, 879.
   enduring, 826.
Submit, 725.
   obey, 743.
Submonish, 695.
Subordinate, 34.
Subordination, 58.
Suborn, *hire*, 795.
   bribe, 784.
Subpœna, 741.
Subreption, *deceit*, 545.
   acquisition, 775.
Subscribe, *assent*, 488.
   agree to, 769.
   give, 784.
Subsequent, *in time*, 117.
   in order, 63.
Subservient, 644.
Subsidence, *sinking*, 306.
   decrease, 36.
Subsidiary, *tending*, 176.
   auxiliary, 708.
Subsidy, *pay*, 809.
   gift, 784.
Subsist, *existence*, 1.
   continuance, 142.
Subsistence, *food*, 299.
Subsoil, *earth*, 342.
   interior, 221.
Substance, *thing*, 3.
   matter, 316.
   interior, 221.
392

Substance, *texture*, 329.
   compendium, 596.
   meaning, 516.
   important part, 642.
   wealth, 803.
Substantial, *dense*, 321.
   true, 494.
Substantiate, 478.
Substantive, 3.
Substitute, *means*, 634.
   deputy, 759.
Substitution, *change*, 147.
*Substratum, *substance*, 3.
   interior, 221.
   layer, 204.
   base, 211.
   support, 215.
Subsultory, 315.
Subterfuge, *lie*, 546.
   sophistry, 477.
Subterranean, 208.
Subtile, *rare*, 322.
   light, 320.
Subtilize, *sophistry*, 477.
Subtle, *cunning*, 702.
   wise, 498.
   texture, 329.
Subtract, *retrench*, 38.
   arithmetical, 84.
   to take, 789.
Suburban, } *environs*, 227.
Suburbs, } *distance*, 197.
Subvert, *invert*, 218.
   depress, 308.
   destroy, 162.
*Succedaneum, 147, 634.
Succeed, *answer*, 731.
   follow, 63.
Success, 731.
Succession, *sequence*, 63.
   continuity, 69.
   of time, 109.
   luteness, 117.
Successless, 732.
Successor, *sequel*, 65.
   posterior, 117.
Succinct, 572.
Succour, 707.
Succubus, 980.
Succulent, *juicy*, 333.
   semi-liquid, 352.
Succumb, *yield*, 725.
   obey, 743.
   fatigue, 688.
Succussion, 315.
Such, 17.
Suck in, 297.
Suckle, 707.
Suckling, 129.
Suction, 297.

Sudation, 386.
Sudden, *early*, 132.
   transient, 111.
Suds, *difficulty*, 704.
   froth, 353.
Sue, *demand*, 765.
   at law, 969.
Suet, 356.
Suffer, *physical pain*, 378.
   moral pain, 828.
   to endure, 821.
   to allow, 760.
   disease, 655.
   experience, 151.
Sufficient, 639.
Suffix, *sequel*, 65.
   adjunct, 39.
Sufflation, 349.
Suffocate, 361.
Suffragan, 996.
Suffrage, *vote*, 609.
   prayer, 990.
Suffrance, 826.
Suffuse, *mix*, 41.
   feel, 821.
   blush, 874.
Sugar, 396.
Sugar-loaf, 250.
Suggest, *suppose*, 514.
   advise, 695.
   inform, 527.
   recall, 505.
   occur, 451.
Suicide, 361.
*Sui generis, *special*, 79.
   exceptional, 83.
Suit, *accord*, 23.
   class, 75.
   expedient, 646.
   clothes, 225.
   at law, 969.
Suite, *series*, 69.
   adjunct, 39.
Suiting, 23.
Suitor, 897.
Sulcated, 259.
Sulky, } *discourteous*, 895.
Sullen, } *gloomy*, 837.
Sully, *deface*, 846.
   dishonor, 874, 940.
Sulphur, *colour*, 436.
Sultan, 745.
Sultry, 382.
Sum, *total*, 50, 84.
   to reckon, 85.
   money, 800.
Sum up, 594.
Sumless, 105.
Summary, *transient*, 111.
   early, 132.

Suscitate, *produce*, 161.
  induce, 615.
  excite, 825.
  stir up, 173.
Suspect, 485.
Suspectless, 486.
Suspend, *hang*, 214.
  discontinue, 141.
  stop, 265.
Suspense, *doubt*, 485.
Suspicion, *doubt*, 485.
  incredulity, 487.
  uncertainty, 475.
Suspiration, 839.
Sustain, *support*, 215.
  aid, 707.
  operate, 170.
  preserve, 670.
Sustenance, 299.
Sutler, 797.
Suttee, 991.
Suture, 43.
Suzerainty, 737.
Swab, 652.
Swaddle, 225.
Swag, *hang*, 214.
  lean, 217.
  oscillation, 314.
  drop, 306.
Swagger, *boast*, 884.
  bluster, 885.
Swaggerer, 887.
Swain, 876.
Swallow, *gulp*, 297.
  believe, 484.
  destroy, 162.
Swamp, *marsh*, 345.
  destroy, 162.
Swamped, 732.
Swanpan, 85.
Swap, *blow*, 276.
  interchange, 148.
Sward, 344.
Swarm, *crowd*, 72.
  sufficiency, 639.
  multitude, 102.
Swarthy, 431.
Swash, *spurt*, 348.
  affuse, 337.
Swathe, *clothe*, 225.
  fasten, 43.
Sway, *power*, 157.
  influence, 175.
  authority, 737.
  induce, 615.
Swear, *promise*, 768.
  affirm, 535.
Sweat, *transude*, 348.
  heat, 382.
  labour, 686.
394

Sweep, *space*, 180.
  curve, 245.
  rapidity, 274.
  clean, 652.
  displace, 185.
  destroy, 162.
  devastation, 619, 649.
Sweeping, 50.
Sweepings, *refuse*, 653.
  trifle, 643.
Sweet, *saccharine*, 396.
  agreeable, 829.
  lovely, 897.
  melodious, 413.
Sweetheart, 897.
Sweetmeat, 396.
Swell, *increase*, 35.
  expand, 194, 202.
  bulge, 250.
  tide, 348.
  fop, 854.
  emotion, 821, 824.
  extol, 931.
  swagger, 885.
Swell-mob, 792.
Swelter, 282.
Swerve, *deviate*, 279.
  diverge, 290.
  irresolution, 605.
  tergiversation, 607.
Swift, 274.
Swig, } *drink*, 297.
Swill, } *tope*, 959.
Swim, *float*, 305.
  navigate, 267.
  vertigo, 503.
Swimming, *successful*, 731.
  buoyant, 320.
Swindle, *peculate*, 791.
  cheat, 545.
Swindler, *defrauder*, 792.
  sharper, 548.
Swine, 954.
Swing, *space*, 180.
  hang, 214.
  oscillate, 314.
  freedom, 748.
Swinging, 31.
Swinish, 954, 957.
Switch, 975.
Swivel, *hinge*, 312.
  cannon, 727.
Swollen, *proud*, 878.
Swoon, *fainting*, 160.
  fatigue, 688.
Swoop, *seizure*, 789.
  descent, 306.
Sword, 727.
Swordsman, 726.
Sybarite, 954.

Sycophant, *servility*, 885.
  adulation, 933.
  flatterer, 935.
Syllable, 561.
Syllabus, *list*, 86.
  compendium, 596.
Syllogism, 476.
Sylph, 979.
Sylvan, 367.
Symbol, *sign*, 550.
  mathematical, 84.
Symmetry, *form*, 242.
  order, 58.
  beauty, 845.
Sympathy, *kindness*, 906.
  love, 897.
  pity, 914.
Symphony, *music*, 415.
  overture, 66.
*Symposium, 299.
  festivity, 840.
Symptom, 550.
Synagogue, 1000.
Synchronism, 120.
Syncope, 160.
Syndic, 745.
Synecdoche, *metaphor*, 521.
  substitution, 147.
Synod, *council*, 696.
  church, 995.
  assemblage, 72.
Synonym, 564.
Synopsis, *arrangement*, 60.
  compendium, 596.
Syntax, 567.
Synthesis, 48.
Syrup, 396.
System, *order*, 58.
  plan, 626.
Syzygy, 199.

T.

Tabby, 440.
Tabernacle, 1000.
Tabid, *morbid*, 655.
  lean, 203.
  shrivelled, 195.
  noxious, 649.
Table, *stand*, 215.
  layer, 204.
  list, 86.
  record, 551.
  repast, 299.
Table land, *plain*, 344.
  flat, 213.
Table-talk, 588.
*Tableau, *list*, 86.
  painting, 556.

Tablet, *record,* 551.
  layer, 204.
Taboo, *spell,* 993.
  prohibition, 761.
Tabor, 417.
*Tabouret, 215.
Tabulate, *arrange,* 60.
  register, 86.
Tachygraphy, 590.
Tacit, 526.
Taciturn, 585.
Tack, *direction,* 278.
  to turn, 279.
  change course, 140.
Tack to, *add,* 37.
  join, 43.
Tackle, *gear,* 633.
  fastening, 45.
Tact, *touch,* 379.
  skill, 698.
  wisdom, 498.
  taste, 850.
  discrimination, 465.
Tactics, *conduct,* 692.
  plan, 626.
  skill, 698.
  warfare, 722.
Tactile, 379.
Taction, 379.
Tactitian, 700.
  clever, 698.
Tactual, 379.
Tadpole, 129.
*Tædium, 841.
Tag, *add,* 37.
  fastening, 45.
  part, 51.
  point, 253.
Tag-rag, 876.
Tail, *end,* 67.
  back, 235.
  adjunct, 37.
  sequel, 65.
Taint, *disease,* 655.
  decay, 659.
  dirt, 653.
  fault, 651.
  disgrace, 874.
Taintless, 652.
Take, *to appropriate,* 789.
  receive, 785.
  eat, 297.
  believe, 484.
  understand, 518.
  please, 769.
Take aback, 870.
Take away, *lose,* 776.
Take care, 864.
Take down, *swallow,* 297.
  note, 551.
395

Take down, *lower,* 308.
  humiliate, 879.
Take effect, 170.
Take heed, 457.
Take hold, 789.
Take in, *include,* 54.
  admit, 297.
  understand, 518.
  cheat, 545.
Take it, *believe,* 484.
  suppose, 514.
Take off, *remove,* 185.
  divest, 226.
  imitate, 19.
  personate, 554.
Take on, 837.
Take out, 300.
Take part with, 707.
Take place, 151.
Take root, *dwell,* 186.
Take ship, 267.
Take up, *inquire,* 461.
Take up with, *bear,* 826.
Take wing, 292.
Taking, *vexation,* 828.
  anger, 900.
Talbotype, 556.
Tale, *narrative,* 594.
  counting, 85.
Talebearer, 534.
Talent, 698.
Taleteller, 548.
Talisman, 993.
Talk, *speak,* 582.
  rumour, 532.
  conversation, 588.
Talkative, 584.
Tall, 206.
Tallage, 812.
Tallow, 356.
Tally, 23.
Talmud, 985.
Talons, *claw,* 633.
  authority, 737.
Tambourine, 417.
Tame, *inert,* 172.
  moderate, 174.
  calm, 826.
  teach, 537.
Tamper, *action,* 680.
  activity, 682.
Tan, 433.
Tandem, 272.
Tangible, *touch,* 379.
  material, 316.
Tangle, *derange,* 61.
Tangled, *disordered,* 59.
  matted, 219.
Tank, *recipient,* 191.
  reservoir, 636.

Tankard, 191.
Tantalize, *induce,* 615.
  desire, 865.
Tantamount, *equal,* 27.
  synonymous, 516.
Tantarum, 900.
*Tanti, 618, 644.
Tap, *hit,* 276.
  plug, 263.
  to let out, 296.
Tape, 45.
Taper, *narrow,* 203.
  sharp, 253.
  candle, 423.
Tapestry, 556.
*Tapinois, 528.
Tar, 269.
Tardy, *dilatory,* 133.
  slow, 275.
Tares, 643.
Target, 620.
Tariff, 812.
Tarn, 343.
Tarnish, *decoloration,* 429.
  deface, 846.
  spoil, 659.
  disgrace, 874.
  dishonor, 940.
Tarry, *remain,* 110.
  continue, 142.
  late, 133.
  expect, 507.
  rest, 265.
Tart, *acid,* 397.
  rude, 895.
  irascible, 901.
Tartan, 225.
Tartane, 273.
Tartar, 732.
Tartarus, 982.
Tartness, 901.
Tartuffe, *hypocrisy,* 544.
  impiety, 989.
Task, *business,* 625.
  to put to use, 677.
  function, 644.
  lesson, 537.
Taskmaster, 694.
Tassel, 847.
Taste, *sapidity,* 390.
  to experience, 821.
  discrimination, 850.
Tasteless, *vapid,* 391.
  unattractive, 866.
*Tâtonnement, *trial,* 463.
  essay, 675.
Tatter, 51.
Tatterdemalion, 876.
Tattle, 588.
Tattoo, 407.

Taunt, *reproach*, 938.
  ridicule, 856.
  hoot, 929.
Tautology, *repetition*, 104.
  diffuseness, 573.
Tavern, 189.
Tawdry, 851.
Tawny, 432, 433.
Tax, *impost*, 812.
  to accuse, 938.
  require, 765.
  employ, 677.
Teach, 537.
Teachable, 539.
Teacher, 540.
Team, 69.
Tear, *separate*, 44.
  destroy, 162.
  violence, 173.
  move rapidly, 274.
Tear out, 300.
Tease, 830.
Teat, 250.
Technical, 698.
Technology, 698.
Techy, 901.
*Te Deum, *gratitude*, 916.
  rejoicing, 836.
Tedium, 841.
Teem, *abound*, 639.
  numerous, 102.
Teemful, 168.
Teemless, 169.
Teeth, 708.
Teetotalism, 958.
Teetotum, 840.
Tegument, 222.
Telegraph, 550.
  velocity, 274.
Teleology, 620.
Telescope, 445.
Telesm, 993.
Tell, *inform*, 527.
  count, 85.
  speak, 582.
  describe, 594.
Tell off, 85.
Tell-tale, *evidence*, 467.
  divulge, 529.
Temerity, 863.
Temper, *nature*, 5.
  elasticity, 323.
  softness, 324.
  affections, 820.
  to moderate, 174.
  soften, 826.
  irascibility, 901.
Temperament, *nature*, 5.
  disposition, 820.
  music, 413.
396

Temperance, 953.
Temperate, *moderate*, 174.
  mild, 826.
Temperature, 382.
Tempest, *violence*, 173.
  wind, 349.
  excitement, 825.
Tempestivity, 134.
Temple, *church*, 1000.
  side, 236.
Temporal, *transient*, 111.
  laical, 997.
Temporary, 111.
Temporize, *cunning*, 702.
  policy, 698.
  opportunity, 134.
Tempt, *entice*, 615.
  desire, 865.
  attempt, 676.
Temulency, 959.
Ten, 98.
Tenacious, *retentive*, 781.
  avaricious, 819.
  resolved, 604.
  obstinate, 606.
  prejudiced, 481.
Tenacity, *toughness*, 327.
Tenant, *occupier*, 188.
  possessor, 779.
  present, 186.
Tenantless, 187.
Tend, *aid*, 107.
  contribute, 153.
  conduce, 176.
  direct to, 278.
Tender, *soft*, 324.
  susceptible, 822.
  compassionate, 914.
  to offer, 763.
Tendril, 129.
Tenebrious, 421.
Tenement, *house*, 189.
  property, 780.
Tenet, *belief*, 484.
  creed, 983.
Tenor, *course*, 7.
  degree, 26.
  direction, 278.
  meaning, 516.
  musical, 413.
Tense, *hard*, 323.
Tensile, 325.
Tension, *strength*, 159.
  length, 200.
  hardness, 323.
Tent, 189.
  covering, 222.
Tentacle, 633.
Tentative, *experimental*, 463.
  essaying, 675.

Tenterhook, *expectation*, 507.
Tenuity, *rarity*, 322.
  smallness, 32.
Tenure, 924.
Tephramancy, 511.
Tepid, 382.
Teratology, 855.
Terebration, *opening*, 260.
  piercing, 302.
Tergiversation, *change*, 607
  regress, 283.
Term, *place in series*, 71.
  end, 67.
  limit, 233.
  period of time, 106.
  word, 562.
  name, 564.
Termagant, 901.
Terminal, 67.
Terminate, 729.
Terminology, 562.
Terminus, 67.
Termless, 105.
Terms, *conditions*, 770.
  circumstances, 8.
  reasoning, 476.
Ternary, 93.
Ternion, 92.
Terpsichore, 415.
Terrace, *plain*, 344.
  level, 213.
  buildings, 189.
Terraqueous,   ⎱ *land*, 342.
Terrene,   ⎰ *world*, 318.
Terrestrial,
Terrible, *fearful*, 860.
  great, 31.
Terrier, *list*, 86.
  auger, 262.
Terrific, 830.
Terrify, 860.
Territory, 181.
Terror, 860.
Terse, 572.
Tertiary, 92.
Tesselated, 440.
Test, 463.
Testament, 985.
Tester, 215.
Testify, 467.
Testimonial, 551.
Testimony, 467.
Testy, *irascible*, 901.
  rude, 895.
*Tête-à-tête, 89.
Tether, *fasten*, 43.
  moor, 265.
  restrain, 751.
Tetractic, 95.

Tetrad, 95.
Tetrarch, 745.
Text, *meaning*, 516.
   prototype, 22.
   printing, 591.
Text-book, *lesson*, 537.
   synopsis, 596.
Texture, *condition*, 7.
   fabric, 329.
Thalia, 599.
Thane, 745.
Thankful, 916.
Thankless, 917.
   painful, 830.
Thanks, *gratitude*, 916.
   worship, 990.
Thatch, 210.
Thaumatrope, 445.
Thaumaturgy, 992.
Thaw, *melt*, 333.
   heat, 384.
Theatre, *drama*, 599.
   arena, 728.
   school, 542.
   spectacle, 441.
Theatrical, *ostentatious*, 882.
Theft, 791.
Theism, 987.
Theme, 454.
Then, 121.
Thence, *cause*, 155.
   departure, 292.
Thenceforth, 121.
Thenceforwards, 121.
Theocracy, 976.
Theopathy, 987.
Theorem, 535.
Theorize, 514.
Theory, *knowledge*, 490.
   attribution, 155.
Therapeutics, 662.
There, 186.
Thereabouts, *nearly*, 32.
   near, 197.
Thereafter, 117.
Thereby, 631.
Therefore, *reasoning*, 476.
   attribution, 155.
Therein, 221.
Thereof, 9.
Thereupon, 117.
Therewith, 88.
Theriac, 662.
Thermal, 382.
Thermometer, 389.
Thesaurus, *store*, 636.
   words, 562.
Thesis, *theme*, 454.
   affirmation, 535.
Thetis, 341.
397

Theurgy, 992.
Thew, 159.
Thick, *broad*, 302.
   dense, 321.
   semi-liquid, 352.
   turbid, 426.
   dirty, 653.
   numerous, 102.
Thickcoming, 136.
Thicket, 367.
Thick-skinned, 823.
Thickskull, 499, 501.
Thief, 792.
Thievery, 791.
Thimble, 191.
Thimbleful, 193.
Thimblerig, 545.
Thin, *small*, 193.
   narrow, 203.
   rare, 322.
   scanty, 640.
   few, 103.
   to subduct, 38.
Thing, 3.
Things, *events*, 151.
Think, *cogitate*, 451.
   believe, 484.
Think of, *intend*, 620.
Think upon, *remember*, 505.
Thin-skinned, 822.
Third part, 94.
Thirdly, 93.
Thirst, 865.
Thistle, 253.
Thistledown, 320.
Thither, 278.
Thong, 45.
Thorn, *sharp*, 253.
   painful, 830.
   pain, 378.
Thorny, 704.
Thorough, 52.
Thorough-bass, 413.
Thoroughbred, 852.
Thoroughly, 31.
Thoroughpaced, 31.
Thorp, 189.
Though, *notwithstanding*, 179, 708.
   evidence, 468.
Thought, *reflection*, 451.
   maxim, 496.
   small quantity, 32, 193.
   idea, 453.
Thoughtful, *reflecting*, 451.
   wise, 498.
Thoughtless, *incogitant*, 452.
   careless, 460.
   foolish, 499.
   improvident, 674.

Thoughtless, *unskilful*, 699.
Thousand, 98
Thraldrom, 749.
Thrash, 972.
Thread, *tie*, 45.
   filament, 205.
   continuity, 69.
   to pass through, 302.
Thread one's way, 266.
Threadbare, *bare*, 226.
   imperfect, 651.
Threat, 909.
Threaten, *future*, 121.
   alarm, 669.
   danger, 665.
Three, 90.
Threefold, 93.
Threnody, 839.
Thresh, 972.
Threshold, 66.
Thrice, 93.
Thrid, 302.
Thrift, *success*, 731.
   prosperity, 734.
   economy, 817.
Thriftless, 818.
Thrill, *touch*, 379.
   affect, 821, 824.
Thrive, *succeed*, 731.
   prosper, 734.
Throat, *opening*, 260.
   air-pipe, 351.
Throb, *agitate*, 315.
   emotion, 821.
Throe, *violence*, 173.
   agitation, 315.
   pain, 378, 828.
Throne, *seat*, 215.
   abode, 189.
   authority, 747.
Throng, 72.
Throttle, *seize*, 789.
   occlude, 261.
   suffocate, 361.
Through, *passage*, 302.
   instrument, 631.
   owing to, 154.
   (go), *effect*, 729.
Throughout, *totality*, 50.
   time, 106.
Throw, *propel*, 284.
   exertion, 686.
Throw away, *lose*, 776.
   relinquish, 782.
Throw down, 162.
Throw in, 301.
Throw off, 296.
Throw up, 757.
Thrum, 415.
Thrush, 416.

Tompion, 263.
*Ton, 852.
Tone, *state*, 7.
   strength, 159.
   melody, 413.
   minstrelsy, 415.
   colour, 428.
Tongue, 560.
Tongue of land, 342.
Tongueless, 581.
Tonguetied, 581.
Tonic, 656.
Tonnage, 192.
Tonsure, 999.
Tony, *fool*, 501.
   silly, 499.
Too, 37.
Tool, 633.
Tooth, *projection*, 250.
   notch, 257.
   sharp, 253.
   link, 45.
   taste, 390.
Toothsome, *savoury*, 394.
   agreeable, 829.
Top, *summit*, 210.
   good, 648.
   to surpass, 33.
Topaz-colour, 436.
Tope, 959.
Toper, 959.
Topfull, 639.
Topheavy, *inverted*, 218.
   dangerous, 665.
   tipsy, 959.
Tophet, 982.
Topic, 454.
Topical, 183.
Topmast, 206.
Topmost, 33.
Topography, 183.
Topple, *fall*, 306.
   ruin, 659.
Topple over, 218.
Topsawyer, 700.
Topsy-turvy, 218.
Torch, 423.
Torchlight, 420.
Torment, *physical*, 378.
   moral, 828, 830.
Tornado, *violence*, 173.
   wind, 349.
Torpedo, 683.
Torpid, *inert*, 172.
   insensible, 823.
   inactive, 683.
Torrefy, 384.
Torrent, *flow*, 348.
   violence, 173.
Torrid, 382.
399

Torsion, 311.
Tortoise, 275.
Tortoise-shell, 440.
Tortuous, 248.
Torture, *physical*, 378.
   moral, 828, 830.
Toss, *throw*, 284.
   oscillate, 314.
   agitate, 315.
   derange, 61.
Toss up, 156, 621.
Toss-pot, 959.
Total, 50.
Totter, *limp*, 275.
   oscillate, 314.
   agitate, 315.
   decay, 659.
Tottering, *dangerous*, 665.
   imperfect, 651.
Touch, *tact*, 379.
   contiguity, 199.
   to relate to, 9.
   music, 415.
   mix, 41.
   small quantity, 32, 39.
   act, 680.
   treat on, 595.
   excite, 824.
   pity, 914.
   test, 463.
Touch up, 658.
Touching, 9.
Touchstone, 467.
Touchwood, 388.
Touchy, 901.
Tough, *strong*, 327.
   difficult, 704.
Tour, 266.
Tourist, 268.
Tournament, 720.
Tournay, 720.
*Tournure, *outline*, 229.
   beauty, 845.
Touse, 285.
*Tout ensemble, 50.
Touter, *eulogist*, 935.
   solicitor, 767.
Tow, 285.
Towards, 278.
Tower, *height*, 206.
   building, 189.
   defence, 717.
   to soar, 305.
Towering, *great*, 31.
   passion, 900.
Town, *city*, 189.
   fashion, 852.
Townsman, 188.
Toxicology, 663.
Toy, *amusement*, 840.

Toy, *trifle*, 643.
*Tracasserie, 713.
Trace, *inquire*, 461.
   discover, 480.
   vestige, 551.
Trace to, 155.
Tracery, *lattice*, 219.
   ornament, 847.
Traces, *harness*, 45.
Trachea, 351.
Track, *way*, 627.
   to trace, 461.
Trackless, *difficult*, 704.
   space, 180.
Tract, *region*, 181.
   dissertation, 595.
Tract of time, 109.
Tractable, } *easy*, 705.
Tractile, } *malleable*, 324.
Traction, 285.
Trade, *business*, 625.
   traffic, 794.
Trade wind, 349.
Trader, 797.
Tradesman, 797.
Tradition, *record*, 551.
   description, 594.
Traduce, 932.
Traffic, 794.
Tragedy, *drama*, 599.
   disaster, 830.
Tragic, *distressing*, 830.
Tragi-comic, 599.
Tragi-comedy, 856.
Trail, *sequel*, 65.
   pendent, 214.
   slow, 275.
   odour, 398.
   indication, 551.
   to track, 461.
Train, *series*, 69.
   sequel, 65.
   appendix, 39.
   traction, 285.
   teach, 537.
   accustom, 613.
   drill, 673.
Trainbearer, 746.
Trained, 698.
*Trait, *appearance*, 448.
   lineament, 550.
Traitor, 941.
   disobedient, 742.
Trajection, 296.
Trajectory, 627.
Tralatitious, 521
Tralineate, 279.
Tralucent, 425.
Trammel, *fetter*, 752.
   restrain, 751.

Trammel, *hinder*, 706.
Tramontane, *distant*, 196.
  outlandish, 851.
Tramp, *to stroll*, 266.
  stroller, 268.
Trample, *violate*, 927.
  bully, 885.
  spurn, 930.
Tramway, 627.
Trance, *lethargy*, 823.
  inactivity, 683.
Tranquil, *calm*, 174, 826.
  peaceful, 721.
  quiet, 265.
  to pacify, 723.
Transact, *conduct*, 692.
  traffic, 794.
Transaction, 151.
Transalpine, 196.
Transanimation, 140.
Transcalency, 384.
Transcend, *go beyond*, 303.
Transcendent, *great*, 31, 33.
  perfect, 650.
  good, 648.
  glorious, 873.
  incomprehensible, 519.
Transcolate, 348.
Transcribe, } *write*, 590.
Transcript, } *copy*, 21.
Transcursion, 303.
Transept, *of church*, 1000.
  crossing, 219.
Transfer, *things*, 270.
  property, 783.
  remove, 185.
Transfiguration, 140.
  divine, 998.
Transfix, *perforate*, 260.
Transform, 140.
Transfuse, *transfer*, 270.
  mix, 41.
  translate, 522.
Transgress, *go beyond*, 303.
  infringe, 773.
  violate, 927.
  sin, 947.
Transient, 111.
Transilient, 303.
Transit, 264.
Transition, 264.
Transitive, 111.
Transitory, 111.
Translate, *interpret*, 522.
  transfer, 270.
  promote, 995.
Translocation, 270.
Translucent, 425.
Transmigration, 140, 144.
Transmission, *moving*, 270.
400

Transmission, *of property*, 783.
  passage, 302.
Transmogrify, 140.
Transmute, 140, 144.
Transparent, 425.
  obvious, 518.
Transpicuous, 425.
Transpierce, 260.
Transpire, *appear*, 525.
  disclose, 529.
Transplant, 270.
Transplendent, 420.
Transport, *transfer*, 270.
  emotion, 821, 824.
  pleasure, 827, 829.
Transpose, *displace*, 185.
  invert, 218.
  transfer, 270.
  exchange, 148.
Transubstantiation, 998.
Transude, *ooze*, 294.
  exude, 348.
Transumption, 270.
Transverse, 217.
Trap, 667.
Trap-door, *escape*, 671
  pitfall, 667.
Trapping, *clothes*, 225.
  ornament, 847.
  instrument, 633.
  property, 780.
Trash, *absurdity*, 497.
  trifle, 643.
Travail, 686.
Travel, 266.
Traveller, 268.
Traverse, *move*, 266.
  pass, 302.
  obstruct, 706.
*Travestie, *copy*, 21.
  to imitate, 19.
  misinterpret, 523.
  burlesque, 856.
Travis, 215.
Tray, 191.
Treachery, 940.
Treacle, 396.
Tread, 266.
Treadle, 633.
Treason, *revolt*, 742.
  treachery, 940.
Treasure, *money*, 800.
  perfection, 650.
Treasure up in the me-
  mory, 505.
Treasurer, 801.
Treasury, 802.
  store, 636.
Treat, *manage*, 692.

Treat, *bargain*, 769.
  amuse, 840.
  please, 827.
Treatise, 595.
Treatment, 692.
Treaty, 769.
Treble, *number*, 93.
  music, 413.
Tree, *plant*, 367.
  execution, 975.
Trellis, 219.
Tremble, *agitate*, 315.
  with cold, 385.
  with fear, 860.
  with emotion, 821.
Tremendous, *great*, 31.
  fearful, 860.
Tremor, } *agitation*, 315
Tremulous, } *fear*, 860.
Trench, *furrow*, 259.
Trench on, 197.
Trencher, *plate*, 191.
  layer, 204.
Trend, *bend*, 278.
  curve, 245.
Trennel, 45.
Trepan, *deceive*, 545.
  perforator, 262.
Trepidation, *agitation*, 315.
  emotion, 821.
  fear, 860.
Trespass, *go beyond*, 303.
  sin, 947.
Tress, 256.
Trevit, 215.
Trey, 92.
Triad, 92.
Trial, *experiment*, 463.
  essay, 675.
  difficulty, 704.
  suffering, 828.
  lawsuit, 969.
Triality, 92.
Triangle, 417.
Tribe, *class*, 75.
  assemblage, 72.
Tribulatio., 828.
Tribunal, 966.
Tribune, 966.
Tributary, 784.
Tribute, *donation*, 784.
  reward, 973.
  approbation, 931.
Trice, 113.
Trichotomy, 94.
Trick, *deception*, 545.
  contrivance, 626.
  to dress, 225.
  adorn, 845.
Trickle, *ooze*, 294.

Tumbler, *glass*, 191.
　　buffoon, 844.
Tumbling, 856.
Tumbrel, 272.
Tumefaction, 194.
Tumid, 192.
Tumor, 250.
Tumult, *disorder*, 59.
　　agitation, 315.
　　resistance, 719.
　　revolt, 742.
　　emotion, 825.
Tumultuous, 59.
Tumulus, 363.
Tun, *large*, 192.
　　drunkard, 959.
Tune, *music*, 415.
　　to prepare, 673.
Tuneable, 413.
Tuneful, 413.
Tuneless, 414.
Tunic, ⎱ *cover*, 222.
Tunicle, ⎰ *dress*, 225.
Tuning-fork, 417.
Tunnage, 192.
Tunnel, 260.
Turban, 225.
Turbid, *opaque*, 426.
　　foul, 653.
Turbinated, 248.
Turbulence, *disorder*, 59.
　　violence, 173.
　　agitation, 315.
　　excitation, 825.
Turcism, 984.
Tureen, 191.
Turf, 344.
Turgescent, *expanded*, 194.
　　redundant, 641.
　　exaggerated, 549.
*Turlupinade, 842.
Turmoil, *confusion*, 59.
　　agitation, 315.
　　violence, 173.
Turn, *state*, 7.
　　form, 240.
　　period of time, 138.
　　curvature, 245.
　　deviation, 279.
　　circuition, 311.
　　rotation, 312.
　　change, 140.
　　translate, 522.
　　purpose, 620.
　　aptitude, 698.
　　emotion, 820.
　　nausea, 867.
Turn away, *diverge*, 290.
　　dismiss, 756.
Turn-coat, 607, 941.
402

Turn off, *dismiss*, 756.
　　execute, 361.
Turn out, *happen*, 151.
　　eject, 296.
　　strike, 742.
　　equipage, 852.
Turn over, *invert*, 218.
　　reflect, 451.
Turn round, 312.
Turn tail, 282.
Turn up, *happen*, 151.
　　chance, 621.
Turnpike, 706.
Turnpike road, 627.
Turns, 138.
Turpitude, *dishonor*, 940.
　　disgrace, 874.
Turret, 206.
Turtle dove, 897.
Tush, *silence*, 403.
　　taciturn, 585.
Tusk, 253.
Tussle, 720.
Tutelage, 664.
Tutelary, 664.
Tutor, 540.
　　to teach, 537.
Twaddle, *absurdity*, 497.
　　loquacity, 584.
Twain, 90.
Twang, *taste*, 390.
　　sound, 402, 410.
　　voice, 583.
Twattle, *talk*, 584.
　　jargon, 497.
Tweak, *squeeze*, 195, 203.
　　punish, 972.
Twelfth, 99.
Twelve, 98.
Twenty, 98.
Twice, 90.
Twiddle, 312.
Twig, 51.
Twilight, *morning*, 125.
　　evening, 126.
　　gray, 432.
Twill, 258.
Twilled, 219.
Twin, *duplicate*, 90.
　　accompaniment, 88.
　　similar, 17.
Twine, *thread*, 45.
　　intersect, 219.
　　convolution, 248.
　　cling, 46.
Twinge, *bodily pain*, 378.
　　mental pain, 828, 830.
Twinkle, 420.
Twinkling, *moment*, 113.
Twirl, 315.

Twirl, *convolute*, 248.
　　turn, 311, 312.
Twist, *cord*, 45.
　　distort, 243.
　　obliquity, 217.
　　convolution, 248.
　　bend, 311.
　　prejudice, 481.
Twit, 932.
Twitch, *pull*, 285.
　　pain, 378.
　　mental, 828.
Twitter, *agitation*, 315.
　　cry, 412.
　　music, 415.
　　emotion, 821.
Two, 89.
Two-fold, 91.
Tyke, 876.
Tymbal, 417.
Tympanum, 418.
Tympany, 194.
Type, *pattern*, 22.
　　rule, 80.
　　indication, 550.
　　printing, 591.
Typhoon, 173.
Typify, 550.
Typography, 591.
Tyranny, 739.
Tyrant, 745.
Tyro, 541.

U.

Uberty, 639.
Ubiety, 186.
Ubiquity, 186.
Ugly, 846.
Ukase, *order*, 741.
　　law, 963.
Ulcer, *disease*, 655.
　　care, 830.
Ulema, *judge*, 967.
　　priest, 996.
Ulterior, *in space*, 196.
　　in time, 121.
Ultima Thule, 196.
Ultimate, 67.
Ultimatum, 770.
Ultra, 33.
Ultramarine, 438.
Ultramontane, 196.
Ululation, 412.
Ulysses, 702.
Umbilicus, 223.
Umbrage, *shade*, 424.
　　darkness, 421.
　　offense, 900.

Umbrella, 666.
Umpire, 967.
Unabashed, *bold*, 861.
 haughty, 873.
 insolent, 885.
Unabated, 31.
Unable, 158.
Unacceptable, 830.
Unaccommodating, *disagreeing*, 24.
 uncivil, 895.
Unaccompanied, 87.
Unaccomplished, 730.
Unaccountable, *obscure*, 519.
 wonderful, 870.
 arbitrary, 964.
 irresponsible, 927.
Unaccustomed, *unused*, 614.
 unusual, 83.
Unachievable, *difficult*, 704.
 impossible, 471.
Unacknowledged, *ignored*, 489.
 unrequited, 917.
Unacquainted, 491.
Unactuated, 616.
Unadmonished, 665.
Unadorned, *simple*, 849.
 style, 575.
Unadulterated, *simple*, 42.
 genuine, 494.
Unadventurous, 864.
Unadvisable, 647.
Unadvised, 665.
Unaffected, *callous*, 376.
 genuine, 494.
 sincere, 543.
 in good taste, 850.
Unafflicted, 831.
Unaided, *weak*, 160.
 unsupported, 708.
Unalarmed, 861.
Unalienable, 924.
Unallayed, 159.
Unallied, 10.
Unallowable, 923.
Unalluring, 866.
Unalterable, ⎰ *identical*, 13.
Unaltered, ⎱ *unchanged*, 142.
 unchangeable, 150.
Unamazed, 871.
Unambiguous, 518.
Unambitious, 866.
Unamiable, 907.
Unanimity, *accord*, 714.
 assent, 488.
Unannexed, 44.
403

Unanswerable, *demonstrative*, 478.
 certain, 474.
 irresponsible, 927.
 arbitrary, 964.
Unappalled, 861.
Unapparent, *invisible*, 447.
 latent, 526.
Unappeasable, 173.
Unapplied, 678.
Unapprehended, 491.
Unapprehensive, 861.
Unapprized, 491.
Unapproachable, ⎰ *distant*, 196.
Unapproached, ⎱ *great*, 31.
Unapproved, 932.
Unapt, *incongruous*, 24.
 inexpedient, 647.
 unskilful, 699.
Unarmed, 160.
Unarranged, *in disorder*, 59.
 unprepared, 674.
Unarrayed, 849.
Unascertained, 491.
Unasked, *voluntary*, 602.
Unaspiring, *indifferent*, 866
 modest, 881.
Unassailable, 664.
Unassailed, 748.
Unassembled, 73.
Unassisted, 708.
Unassociated, 44.
Unassuming, 881.
Unatoned, 951.
Unattached, 44.
Unattackable, 664.
Unattainable, *difficult*, 704.
 impossible, 471.
Unattained, 732.
Unattempted, 623.
Unattended, 87.
Unattended to, 460.
Unattested, *counter-evidence*, 468.
 unrecorded, 552.
Unattracted, 616.
Unattractive, 866.
Unauthentic, 475.
Unauthorized, *undue*, 925.
 wrong, 923.
 lawless, 964.
Unavailing, *useless*, 645.
 failure, 732.
Unavoidable, *necessary*, 601.
 certain, 474.
Unavowed, 489.

Unawakened, 683.
Unaware, *ignorant*, 491.
 unexpecting, 508.
 impulsive, 601.
Unawed, 861.
Unbalanced, 28.
Unbar, 750.
Unbearable, 830.
Unbeaten, 731.
Unbecoming, ⎰
Unbefitting, ⎱ *undue*, 925.
 disgraceful, 940.
 incongruous, 24.
Unbefriended, 708.
Unbegotten, 2.
Unbeguile, 529.
Unbegun, 674.
Unbeheld, 447.
Unbelief, 485.
 infidelity, 988.
 incredulity, 487.
Unbeloved, 898.
Unbend, *straighten*, 246.
 repose, 687.
 the mind, 452.
Unbending, *hard*, 323.
 resolute, 604.
Unbenevolent, 907.
Unbenighted, 490.
Unbenign, 907.
Unbent, 246, 452.
Unbeseeming, 940.
Unbesought, 602, 766.
Unbestowed, 785.
Unbewailed, 932.
Unbiassed, *wise*, 498.
 spontaneous, 602.
Unbidden, *spontaneous*, 600.
 disobedient, 742.
Unbigoted, 490.
Unbind, *detach*, 44.
 release,
Unblamabl 750e,4
Unblemished, 946.
Unblenching, 861.
Unblended, 42.
Unblest, 932.
Unblown, 674.
Unblushing, *impudent*, 885.
 proud, 878.
Unboastful, 881.
Unbodied, 317.
Unbolt, 750.
Unborn, *future*, 121.
 not existing, 2.
Unborrowed, 787.
Unbosom, 529.
Unbought, 942.
Unbound, *free*, 748.
 exempt, 927.

Undated, *time,* 115.
Undaunted, 861.
Undazzled, 498.
Undebauched, 946.
Undecayed, 648.
Undeceive, 527.
Undeceived, 490.
Undecided, 605.
Undecipherable, 519.
Undecked, 849.
Undecomposed, 42.
Undefaced, 845.
Undefended, 725.
Undefiled, 946.
Undefinable, ⎫ *unmeaning,*
Undefined, ⎰   517.
   obscure, 519.
   uncertain, 475.
Undeformed, 845.
Undemolished, *entire,* 50.
   good, 648.
Undemonstrable, 475.
Undeniable, 474.
Undeplored, 898.
Undepraved, 946.
Undeprived, 781.
Under, *below,* 207.
   less, 34.
Underbreath, 405.
Underbred, 851.
Undercurrent, 347.
Underestimate, 483.
Underfoot, 207.
Undergo, 821.
Underground, *low,* 207.
   deep, 208.
Underhand, 528.
Underline, *mark,* 550.
   emphatic, 642.
Underling, *servant,* 746.
   clown, 876.
Underlying, 207.
Undermine, *burrow,* 262.
   counteract, 706.
   damage, 659.
Undermost, 211.
Underneath, 207.
Underpin, 215.
Underplot, 626.
Underprop, 215.
Underrate, 483.
Under-reckon, 483.
Undersell, 796.
Undersized, 193.
Understand, *know,* 490.
   meaning, 516.
   intelligible, 518.
Understanding, *intellect,*
450.
   agreement, 714.

Understood, *implied,* 516.
   metaphorical, 521.
Understrapper, 746.
Undertake, *promise,* 768.
   pursue, 622.
   endeavour, 676.
Undertaking,   *enterprize,*
676.
   business, 625.
Undertone, 405.
Undervalue, 483.
Underwood, 367.
Underwrite, 769.
Undescribed, 83.
Undeserved, 925.
Undesigned, 601.
Undesigning, 703.
Undesirable, 830.
Undesired, 830.
Undesirous, 866.
Undespairing, 858.
Undestroyed, *whole,* 50.
   persisting, 142.
   existing, 1.
Undetermined,   *irresolute,*
605.
   obscure, 519.
   chance, 156.
Undeveloped, *latent,* 526.
Undeviating,   *progression,*
282.
   straight, 246.
   mid-course, 628.
   unchanged, 150.
Undevout, 988.
Undigested, *unarranged,* 59.
   crude, 674.
Undiminished, *whole,* 50.
   great, 31, 35.
Undirected, *deviating,* 279.
   casual, 621.
Undiscerned, 447.
Undiscerning, *blind,* 442.
   stupid, 499.
Undisciplined, 699.
Undisclosed, 528.
Undisguised, *explicit,* 516.
   sincere, 543.
   true, 494.
Undismayed, 861.
Undisposed of, 678, 781.
Undisputed, 474.
Undissolved, *entire,* 50.
   dense, 321.
Undistinguished, 465 *a.*
Undistorted, *straight,* 246.
   true, 494.
Undistracted, 457.
Undisturbed, *quiet,* 265.
   calm, 826.

Undisturbed, *orderly,* 58.
Undiverted, 604.
Undivided, 50.
Undivulged, 528.
Undo, *untie,* 44.
   take down, 681.
   counteract, 706.
   reverse, 145.
Undoing, *ruin,* 735.
Undone, 73.
   incomplete, 730.
   foiled, 732.
   hapless, 828.
Undoubted, 474.
Undreaded, 861.
Undreamed, 452.
Undress, *nudity,* 226.
   morning dress, 225.
Undressed,   *unprepared,*
674.
   unadorned, 849.
Undried, 339.
Undrilled, 674.
Undriven, 602.
Undrooping, 682.
Undue, 923.
Undulate, *oscillate,* 314.
   wave, 248.
Unduteous, 945.
Undyed, 429.
Undying, *perpetual,* 112.
   immutable, 150.
Unearthly, *immaterial,* 317.
   heavenly, 981.
   pious, 987.
Uneasy, 828.
Unedifying,   *misteaching,*
538.
Uneducated, *ignorant,* 491.
   unprepared, 674.
Unembarrassed, 852.
Unemployed, *inactive,* 683.
   not used, 678.
Unencumbered, *easy,* 705.
   exempt, 927.
Unendeared, 898.
Unendowed, 158.
Unendurable, 830.
Unenjoyed, *weary,* 841.
Unenlarged, 203.
Unenlightened, *dark,* 421.
   ignorant, 491.
   foolish, 499.
Unenslaved, 748.
Unenterprizing, 864.
Unentertaining, 843.
Unenthralled, 748.
Unentitled, 925.
Unequal, 28.
   unable, 158.

Unequalled, 33.
Unequipped, 674.
Unequivocal, *sure*, 474.
 clear, 518.
Unequivocally, 31.
Unerring, *certain*, 474.
 true, 494.
 innocent, 946.
Unessayed, 678.
Unessential, 643.
Uneven, *rough*, 256.
 unequal, 28.
Unexact, 495.
Unexaggerated, 494.
Unexamined, 460.
Unexceptionable, *good*,648
 legitimate, 924.
 innocent, 946.
Unexcited, 826.
Unexecuted, 730.
Unexempt, 177.
Unexercised, *unused*, 678.
 unprepared, 674.
 unskilled, 699.
Unexerted, 172.
Unexhausted, *vigorous*,
 159.
 abundant, 639.
Unexpanded, 195.
Unexpected, 508.
 wonderful, 870.
Unexpensive, 815.
Unexplained, { *latent*,526.
Unexplored, { *unknown*,
    491.
Unexposed, *unseen*, 526.
Unexpressed, *hid*, 526.
Unextended, 317.
Unextinguished, *violent*,
 173.
 burning, 382.
Unfaded, *colour*, 428.
 fresh, 648.
Unfading, 112.
Unfailing, *constant*, 142.
Unfair, *unjust*, 923.
 dishonorable, 940.
 false, 544.
Unfaithful, 940.
Unfaltering, 604.
Unfamiliar, 83.
Unfashionable, 851.
Unfashioned, *formless*,241.
 unwrought, 674.
Unfasten, 44.
Unfathomable, *deep*, 208.
 infinite, 105.
Unfavourable, *obstructive*,
 708.
 out of season, 135.
405

Unfeared, 861.
Unfeasible, 471.
Unfed, *fasting*, 956.
 deficient, 640.
Unfeeling, 823.
Unfeigned, 543.
Unfelt, 823.
Unfeminine, 851.
Unfertile, 169.
Unfetter, *unfasten*, 44.
 release, 750.
Unfettered, *spontaneous*,
 600.
Unfinished, 730.
Unfit, *inappropriate*, 24.
 inexpedient, 647.
Unfix, *disjoin*, 44.
 mutable, 149.
Unfixed, *irresolute*, 605.
Unflagging, 682.
Unflattering, *sincere*, 543.
Unfledged, 674.
 young, 129.
Unflinching, *resolute*, 604.
 bravery, 861.
 persevering, 682.
Unfoiled, 731.
Unfold, *evolve*, 313.
 straighten, 246.
 disclose, 529.
 interpret, 522.
Unforbidden, 760.
Unforced, *free*, 748.
 willing, 602.
Unforeseen, 508.
Unforfeited, 781.
Unforgiving, 919.
Unforgotten, 505.
Unformed, 674.
Unfortified, 160.
Unfortunate, *failure*, 732.
 adversity, 735.
 unhappy, 828.
Unfounded, 544.
Unfrequent, 137.
Unfrequented, 893.
Unfriended, *weak*, 160.
 enmity, 889.
Unfriendly, 889.
 malevolent, 907.
Unfruitful, 169.
Unfulfilled, 773, 923.
Unfurl, 313.
Unfurnished, *unprepared*,
 674.
 insufficient, 640.
Ungainly, *ugly*, 846.
 rude, 895.
Ungarnished, *plain*, 849.
 ugly, 846.

Ungathered, 678.
Ungenerous, *stingy*, 819.
 selfish, 943.
Ungenial, 657.
Ungenteel, *vulgar*, 851.
 rude, 895.
Ungentle, *rude*, 895.
 violent, 173.
Ungentlemanlike, *vulgar*,
 851.
 rude, 895.
 dishonorable, 940.
Ungifted, 499.
Ungird, 44.
Unglue, 44, 47.
Ungodly, 988.
Ungovernable, *violent*, 173.
 passion, 825.
Ungoverned, 748.
Ungraceful, *ugly*, 846.
 vulgar, 851.
Ungracious, *uncivil*, 895.
 unfriendly, 907.
Ungrammatical, 568.
Ungrateful, 917.
Ungratified, 828.
Ungrounded, 495.
Ungrudging, 816.
Unguarded, *neglected*, 460.
 dangerous, 665.
 spontaneous, 612.
Unguent, 356.
Unguided, 491.
Unguilty, 946.
Unhabitable, 187.
Unhabituated, 614.
Unhackneyed, 614.
Unhallowed, *irreligion*,988.
 profane, 989.
Unhand, 750.
Unhandsome, 940.
Unhandy, 699.
Unhappy, 828.
Unhardened, *tender*, 914.
 penitent, 950.
 innocent, 946.
Unharmed, 664.
Unharmonious,*discord*,414.
 incongruous, 24.
Unharness, *disjoin*, 44.
 liberate, 750.
Unhatched, 674.
Unhazarded, 664.
Unhealthy, *ill*, 655.
 unwholesome, 657.
Unheard of, *ignorant*, 491.
 exceptional, 83.
 impossible, 471.
 wonderful, 870.
Unheeded, 460.

Unhelped, 708.
Unhesitating, 604.
Unhewn, *formless*, 241.
   unprepared, 674.
Unhindered, *free*, 748.
Unhinge, *weaken*, 169.
   derange, 61.
Unhinged, 732.
Unholy, 988.
Unhonoured, 874.
Unhook, 44.
Unhoped, 508.
Unhorse, 732.
Unhostile, 888.
Unhoused, 185.
Unhurt, 670.
Unicorn, *monster*, 83.
   prodigy, 872.
Unideal, *true*, 494.
   existing, 1.
Unintellectual, 452.
Uniform, *homogeneous*, 16.
   simple, 42.
   orderly, 58.
   regular, 82.
   symmetrical, 242.
   livery, 225.
Unilluminated, 421.
Unimagined, 494.
Unimitated, 20.
Unimpaired, *preserved*, 670.
   sound, 648.
Unimpassioned, 826.
Unimpeached, *innocent*, 946.
Unimpelled, 616.
Unimportant, 643.
Unimpressed, 823.
Unimpressible, 823.
Unimproved, 659.
Unincited, 616.
Unincreased, 36.
Unincumbered, *easy*, 705.
   exempt, 927.
Uninduced, 616.
Uninfectious, 656.
Uninfluenced, 616.
   obstinate, 606.
Uninfluential, 172.
Uninformed, 491.
Uninhabited, 187.
Uninitiated, 699.
Uninjured, *good*, 648.
   preserved, 670.
   healthy, 644.
Uninquisitive, 456.
Uninspired, *unexcited*, 823.
   unactuated, 616.
Uninstructed, 491.
Unintellectual, 452.
   imbecile, 499.
407

Unintelligent, 499.
Unintelligible, 519.
   style, 571.
Unintentional, 621.
Uninterested, 841.
Unintermitting, *unbroken*, 69.
   durable, 110.
   continuing, 143.
   active, 682.
Uninterrupted, *continuous*, 69.
   unremitting, 143.
Uninured, 674.
Uninvented, 526.
Uninvestigated, 491.
Uninvited, 893.
Union, *junction*, 43.
   combination, 48.
   concord, 23, 714.
   concurrence, 178.
   marriage, 903.
*Unique, *alone*, 87.
   exceptional, 83.
Unirritating, 174.
Unison, *agreement*, 23.
   concord, 714.
   uniformity, 16.
   melody, 413.
Unisonant, 413.
Unit, 87.
Unite, *join*, 43.
   agree, 23.
   concur, 178.
   assemble, 72.
   converge, 291.
Unity, *singleness*, 87.
   integrity, 50.
Universal, 78.
Universe, 318.
University, 542.
Unjust, 923, 925.
Unjustifiable, 923, 925.
Unjustified, 923, 925.
Unkempt, 653.
   slovenly, 851.
Unkennel, *turn out*, 185.
   disclose, 529.
Unkind, 907.
Unknit, 44.
Unknown, *ignorant*, 491.
   latent, 526.
   to fame, 874.
Unlaboured, *unprepared*, 674.
   style, 578.
Unlace, 44.
Unlade, 296.
Unladylike, *vulgar*, 851.
   rude, 895.

Unlamented, 898.
Unlatch, 44.
Unlawful, *undue*, 925.
   illegal, 964.
Unlearn, 506.
Unlearned, 491.
Unleavened, 674.
Unless, *circumstances*, 8.
   qualification, 469.
   condition, 770.
Unlettered, 491.
Unlicenced, 761.
Unlicked, *clownish*, 876.
   vulgar, 851.
   unprepared, 674.
Unlike, 18.
Unlikely, 473.
Unlimited, *infinite*, 105.
   space, 180.
   great, 31.
Unlink, 44.
Unliquefied, 321.
Unlively, *dull*, 843.
   grave, 837.
Unload, *unpack*, 296.
   disencumber, 705.
Unlock, *unfasten*, 44.
   explain, 462.
Unlooked for, 508.
Unloose, *unfasten*, 44.
   liberate, 750.
Unloved, 898.
Unlucky, *inopportune*, 135.
   failing, 732.
   unfortunate, 735.
   luckless, 828.
   bad, 649.
Unmaimed, 654.
Unmake, 145.
Unmanageable, *perverse*, 704.
   unwieldy, 647.
Unmanly, 940.
Unmanned, *weak*, 160.
   sad, 837.
Unmannered, 895.
Unmarked, 460.
Unmarred, *sound*, 654.
   preserved, 670.
Unmarried, 904.
Unmask, *show*, 525.
   disclose, 529.
Unmatched, *unparalleled*, 20.
   dissimilar, 18.
Unmeaning, 517.
Unmeant, 517.
Unmeasured, *abundant*, 639.
   infinite, 105.
   ndistinguished, 465 *a*.

Unmeditated,*impulsive*, 612.
   casual, 621.
Unmeet, 925.
Unmellowed, 674.
Unmelodious, 414.
Unmelted, 321.
Unmentioned, 526.
Unmerciful, 907.
Unmerited, 925.
Unmethodical, 59.
Unmindful, 458, 460.
   ungrateful, 917.
Unmingled, 42.
Unmissed, 460.
Unmistakeable, *clear*, 518.
   visible, 446.
Unmitigable, 173.
Unmixed, 42.
Unmodified, 142.
Unmolested, 831.
   safe, 664.
Unmonied, 804.
Unmourned, 898.
Unmoved, *quiescent*, 265.
   resolute, 604.
   obstinate, 606.
   torpid, 823.
   uninduced, 616.
Unmusical, 414.
Unmuzzled, 748.
Unnamed, 565.
Unnatural, 83.
Unnecessary, 645.
Unneeded, 645.
Unnerved, 158, 160.
Unnoted, } *neglected*, 460.
Unnoticed, } *ignoble*, 874.
Unnumbered, 105.
Unnurtured, 674.
Unobeyed, 742.
Unobnoxious, 648.
Unobscured, 420.
Unobserved, 460.
Unobservant, 458.
Unobstructed, *free*, 709, 748.
   clear, 705.
   nobtainable, 471.
Unobtained, 776.
Unobtrusive, 881.
Unoccupied, *vacant*, 187.
   unthinking, 452.
   inactive, 683.
Unoffended, *humble*, 879.
   enduring, 826.
Unoften, 137.
Unopened, 261.
Unopposed, 709.
Unorganized, *mineral*, 358.
   unprepared, 674.

Unornamented, 849.
   style, 576.
Unorthodox, 984.
Unostentatious, 881.
Unowed, 807.
Unpacified, 713.
Unpack, 296.
Unpaid, 806.
Unpalatable, *unsavoury*, 395.
   disagreeable, 830, 867.
Unparagoned, 650.
Unparalleled, *great*, 31.
   exceptional, 83.
   unmatched, 20.
Unpardonable, 945.
Unpassionate, 826.
Unpathetic, 826.
Unpatriotic, 911.
Unpeaceful, 722.
Unpeople, 185.
Unperceived, *latent*, 526.
   neglected, 460.
   unknown, 491.
Unperformed, 730.
Unperjured, 939.
Unperplexed, 498.
Unpersuadable, 606, 616.
Unphilosophical, 499.
Unpierced, 261.
Unpin, 44.
Unpitying, *ruthless*, 907.
   angry, 900.
Unplagued, 831.
Unpleasant, 830.
Unpoetical, 598.
Unpolished, *rude*, 895.
   vulgar, 851.
Unpolite, 895.
Unpolluted, 648.
Unpopular, 867.
Unpossessed, 776.
Unpractised, 699.
Unprecedented, 83.
Unprejudiced, 498.
Unpremeditated, *impulsive*, 612.
   unprepared, 674.
Unprepared, 674.
Unprepossessed, 498.
Unpresentable, 851.
Unpretending, 881.
Unprincipled, 945.
Unprivileged, 925.
Unproclaimed, 526.
Unproduced, 162.
Unproductive, *barren*, 169.
   useless, 645.
Unproficiency, 699.
Unprofitable, *useless*, 645.

Unprofitable, *bad*, 649.
   unproductive, 169.
Unprolific, 169.
Unpromising, 859.
Unprompted, 612.
Unpronounced, 526.
Unpropitious, 859.
   inauspicious, 135.
Unproportioned, 24.
Unprosperous, 735.
Unprotected, 665.
Unproved, 477.
Unprovided, *scanty*, 640.
   unprepared, 674.
Unprovoked, 616.
Unpublished, 526.
Unpunctual, *tardy*, 133.
   untimely, 135.
   irregular, 139.
Unpunished, 970.
Unpurchased, 796.
Unpurified, 653.
Unpurposed, 621.
Unpursued, 624.
Unqualified, *inexpert*, 699.
   unentitled, 925.
Unquelled, 173.
Unquenched, 173.
   burning, 382.
Unquestionable, 474.
Unquestioned, 474.
   assent, 488.
Unquiet, 825.
Unravel, *untie*, 44.
   straighten, 246.
   solve, 462.
   discover, 482.
   interpret, 522.
   to disembarrass, 705.
   to arrange, 60.
   arranged, 58.
Unreached, 304.
Unread, 491.
Unready, 674.
Unreal, *non-existing*, 2.
   erroneous, 495.
   imaginary, 515.
Unreasonable, *foolish*, 499.
   unjust, 923.
   impossible, 471.
   erroneous, 495.
Unreclaimed, 951.
Unreconciled, 713.
Unrecorded, 552.
Unrecounted, 55.
Unrecovered, 659.
Unreduced, 31.
Unrefined, 851.
Unreformed, 951.
Unrefreshed, 688.

Unrefuted, 494.
Unregarded, *neglected*, 460.
 unrespected, 929.
Unregistered, 552.
Unrelated, 10.
Unrelenting, *malevolent*, 907.
 revengeful, 919.
Unrelieved, 835.
Unremarked, 460.
Unremedied, 651.
Unremembered, 506.
Unremitting, *continuing*, 110.
 industrious, 682.
Unremoved, 184.
Unrenewed, 142.
Unrepaid, 806.
Unrepealed, 142.
Unrepeated, *fewness*, 103.
 unity, 87.
Unrepentant, 951.
Unrepining, 831.
Unreplenished, 640.
Unreported, 526.
Unrepressed, 173.
Unreproached, 946.
Unreproved, 946.
Unrequited, *owing*, 806.
 ingratitude, 917.
Unresented, *forgiven*, 918.
 enduring, 826.
Unreserved, 543.
Unresisting, 743.
Unresolved, 605.
Unrespected, 929.
Unrest, *moving*, 264.
 change, 140.
 changeable, 149.
Unrestrained, *free*, 748.
 unencumbered, 705.
Unrestricted, *undiminished*, 31.
 free, 748.
Unretracted, 535.
Unrevealed, 528.
Unrevenged, 920.
Unreversed, 142, 143.
Unrevoked, 143.
Unrewarded, 806, 917.
Unriddle, *solve*, 462.
 interpret, 522.
 disclose, 529.
Unrighteous, 945.
Unrip, 260.
Unripe, 674.
Unrivalled, 648.
Unrivet, 44.
Unrobe, 226.
Unroll, *straighten*, 246.
409

Unroll, *evolve*, 313.
 display, 525.
 unravel, 47.
Unromantic, 494.
Unroof, 226.
Unroot, 162.
Unruffled, *calm*, 174.
 placid, 826.
 unaffected, 823.
 quiet, 265.
 orderly, 58.
Unruly, *disobedient*, 742.
 obstinate, 606.
Unsaddle, 756.
Unsafe, 665.
Unsaluted, 929.
Unsanctified, 988, 989.
Unsanctioned, 925.
Unsated, 865.
Unsatisfactory, 832.
 displeasing, 830.
Unsatisfied, 832.
Unsavoury, 395.
Unscanned, 460.
Unscathed, 654.
Unscattered, 72.
Unschooled, *illiterate*, 491.
 uneducated, 699.
Unscientific, 495.
Unscoured, 653.
Unscreened, 665.
Unscrew, 44.
Unscriptural, 984.
Unscrupulous, 940.
Unseal, 529.
Unsearched, 460.
Unseasonable, 135.
 inexpedient, 647.
 inappropriate, 24.
Unseasoned, *unprepared*, 674.
 unaccustomed, 614.
Unseat, 756.
Unseconded, 708.
Unseemly, *undue*, 925.
 vicious, 945.
 vulgar, 851.
 ugly, 846.
 inexpedient, 647.
Unseen, *invisible*, 447.
 neglected, 460.
Unselfish, 942.
Unserviceable, 645.
Unsettle, *derange*, 61.
 irresolute, 605.
 mutable, 149.
 insane, 503.
Unsevered, 50.
Unshackle, *free*, 748.
 liberate, 750.

Unshackle, *untie*, 44.
Unshaken, *strong*, 159.
 resolute, 604.
Unshapen, *amorphous*, 241.
 ugly, 846.
Unshared, 777.
Unsheathe, 720.
Unsheltered, 665.
Unshifting, 143.
Unshocked, 823.
Unshorn, 50.
Unshrinking, 604.
 courage, 861.
Unsifted, 460.
Unsightly, 846.
Unsinged, 670.
Unskilful, 699.
Unslacked, 865.
Unsmooth, 256.
Unsociable, 893.
Unsocial, 893.
Unsoiled, 652.
Unsold, 777.
Unsolder, 47.
Unsolicited, 602.
Unsolicitous, 866.
Unsolved, 526.
Unsophisticated, *genuine*, 494.
 simple, 42.
 good, 648.
Unsorted, 59.
Unsought, *avoided*, 623.
 unrequested, 766.
Unsound, *imperfect*, 651.
 unhealthy, 655.
 sophistical, 477.
Unsown, 674.
Unsparing, 639.
Unspeakable, *great*, 31.
 stammering, 583.
Unspecified, 78.
Unspent, 678.
Unspied, 526.
Unspoiled, 648.
Unspoken, 581.
Unspotted, *clean*, 652.
 innocent, 946.
 beautiful, 845.
Unstable, 149.
Unstained, 652.
 honorable, 939.
Unstatesmanlike, 699.
Unsteadfast, 605.
Unsteady, *mutable*, 149.
 irresolute, 605, 607.
 dangerous, 665.
Unstinted, 639.
Unstirred, 826.
Unstopped, *open*, 260.

Unstopped, *continuing*, 143.
Unstored, 640.
Unstrained, *unexerted*, 172.
  relaxed, 687.
  turbid, 653.
  simple, 516.
Unstrengthened, 160.
Unstruck, 823.
Unstrung, 160.
Unsubject, 748.
Unsubmissive, 742.
Unsubservient, *useless*,645
  inexpedient, 647.
Unsubstantial, 4.
  rare, 322.
  texture, 329.
  erroneous, 495.
Unsuccessful, 732.
Unsuccessive, 70.
Unsuitable, } *incongruous*,
Unsuited, }   24.
  inexpedient, 647.
  time, 135.
Unsullied, *clean*, 652.
  honorable, 939.
  guiltless, 946.
Unsung, 526.
Unsupplied, 640.
Unsupported, *weak*, 160.
  opposed, 708.
Unsuppressed, 142.
Unsusceptible, 823.
Unsuspected, 526.
Unsuspicious,   *credulous*,
  486.
  hopeful, 858.
Unsustained, *weak*, 160.
  opposed, 708.
Unswayed, 616.
Unsweet, 395.
Unswept, 653.
Unswerving, *straight*, 246.
Unsymmetric, 59, 243.
Unsystematic, 59.
Untack, 44.
Untainted, *healthy*, 654.
  pure, 652.
  honorable, 939.
Untalented, 699.
Untalked of, 526.
Untamed, *rude*, 851.
  ferocious, 907.
Untangled, 58.
Untarnished, 939, 946.
Untasted, 391.
Untaught, 491.
Untaxed, 815.
Unteach, 538.
Unteachable, 699.
Untempted, 616.

Untenable, *weak*, 160.
  undefended, 725.
  sophistical, 477.
Untenanted, 187.
Unthanked, 917.
Unthankful, 917.
Unthawed, *solid*, 321.
  cold, 383.
Unthinking, 452.
Unthought of, *neglected*,
  460.
  unconsidered, 452.
Unthreatened, 664.
Unthrifty, *prodigal*, 818.
  unprepared, 674.
Unthrone, 756.
Untidy, *in disorder*, 59.
  slovenly, 653.
Untie, *loose*, 44.
  liberate, 750.
Until, 106, 108.
Untilled, 674.
Untimely, 135.
Untinged, *simple*, 42.
  uncoloured, 429.
Untired, 689.
Untiring, 682.
Untitled, 876.
Untold, *secret*, 526, 528.
  countless, 105.
Untouched, *disused*, 678.
  insensible, 376, 823.
Untoward, *bad*, 649.
  unprosperous, 735.
  unpleasant, 830.
Untraced, 526.
Untracked, 526.
Untrained, *unskilled*, 699.
  unprepared, 674.
  unaccustomed, 614.
Untranslated, 523.
Untravelled, 265.
Untreasured, 640.
Untried, 461.
Untrimmed, *simple*, 849.
  unprepared, 674.
Untrodden, *new*, 123.
  not used, 678.
  impervious, 261.
Untroubled, 721.
  calm, 174.
Untrue, 544.
Untruth, 546.
Untunable, 414.
Unturned, 246.
Untutored, 491.
Untwist, *straighten*, 246.
  evolve, 313.
  separate, 44, 47.
Unused, 614, 699.

Unusual, 83.
Unutterable,*wonderful*,870
  great, 31.
Unvalued,*depreciated*,483.
  undesired, 866.
  disliked, 398.
Unvanquished, 748.
Unvaried, 142, 143.
Unvarnished, 494.
Unveil, *manifest*, 525.
  disclose, 529.
Unventilated, 261.
Unversed,*unconversant*,491
  unskilled, 699.
Unvexed, 831.
Unviolated, 939.
Unvisited, 893.
Unvitiated, 648.
Unwakened, 683.
Unwarlike, 862.
Unwarmed, 383.
Unwarned, 665.
Unwarped, 480.
Unwarranted, 923, 925.
  inconclusive, 477.
Unwary, 460.
Unwashed, *unclean*, 653.
  vulgar, 851.
Unwasted, 639.
Unwatchful, 458.
Unwavering, 604.
Unweakened, 159.
Unwearied,   *indefatigable*,
  682.
  refreshed, 689.
Unwedded, 904.
Unweeting, 491.
Unweighed, 460.
Unwelcome, 830.
Unwell, 655.
Unwholesome, 657.
Unwieldy, *large*, 192.
  heavy, 319.
  difficult, 704.
  cumbersome, 647.
Unwilling, 603, 489.
Unwind, *evolve*, 313.
  straighten, 246.
Unwiped, 653.
Unwise, 499.
Unwished, 866.
Unwithered, *sound*, 159.
Unwitnessed, 526.
Unwitting, *ignorant*, 491.
  involuntary, 601.
Unwonted,   *unaccustomed*,
  614.
  unusual, 83.
Unworn, 159.
Unworthy, *vicious*, 945.

Unworthy, *shameful*, 874.
Unwrap, 246.
Unwreathe, 246.
Unwrinkled, 255.
Unwrought, 674.
Unyielding, *tough*, 323.
   resolute, 604.
   obstinate, 606.
   resisting, 719.
Unyoke, 44.
Upbear, *support*, 215.
   raise, 807.
Upbraid, 932.
Upcast, 307.
Upgrow, 206.
Upgrowth, 305.
Upheave, 307.
Uphill, *acclivity*, 217.
   ascent, 305.
   difficult, 704.
Uphoist, 307.
Uphold, *support*, 215.
   aid, 707.
   continue, 143.
Uplands, 206.
Uplift, 307.
Upper, 206.
Upperhand, *authority*, 737.
   success, 731.
Uppermost, 206.
Upraise, 307.
Uprear, 307.
Upright, *vertical*, 212.
   honest, 939.
Uprise, 305.
Uproar, *noise*, 405.
   turmoil, 173.
Uproot, 162.
Upset, *throw down*, 308.
   invert, 218.
   destroy, 162.
Upside-down, 218.
Upshot, *end*, 66.
   total, 50.
Upstart, *plebeian*, 876.
   prosperous, 734.
Upturn, 218.
Upwards, 206.
Uranology, 318.
Urbane, 894.
Urchin, *demon*, 980.
   small, 193.
   child, 129.
   wretch, 949.
Urge, *impel*, 276.
   incite, 615.
   hasten, 684.
   accelerate, 274.
   violence, 173.
Urgent, *important*, 642.

Urgent, *required*, 630.
Urn, *vase*, 191.
   funereal, 363.
Usage, *custom*, 613.
   rule, 80.
Usance, 806.
Use, *employment*, 677.
   waste, 638.
   utility, 644.
   habit, 613.
   rule, 80.
Used up, *worn*, 651.
   surfeited, 869.
Useful, 644.
Useless, 645.
Usher, *teacher*, 540.
   servant, 746.
   announce, 511.
   precede, 62.
   prior, 116.
Usual, *ordinary*, 82.
   customary, 613.
Usurp, *assume*, 739.
   seize, 789.
   illegality, 925.
Usury, 806.
Utensil, *recipient*, 191.
   instrument, 633.
Utilitarian, 910.
Utility, 644.
Utilize, 677.
Utmost, 33.
Utopia, *visionary*, 515.
   hopeful, 858.
Utricle, 191.
Utter, *extreme*, 31.
   to speak, 580.
   disclose, 529.
   distribute, 73.
Uxorious, 897.

V.

Vacant, *void*, 4.
   absent, 187.
   thoughtless, 452.
   foolish, 499.
   scanty, 640.
Vacate, 187.
Vacation, 685.
Vacillate, *undulate*, 314.
   waver, 605.
Vacuity,   ⎱ *void*, 4.
Vacuous, ⎰ *absence*, 187.
*Vacuum,
*Vade-mecum, 537, 542.
Vagabond, *rogue*, 949.
   wanderer, 268.
Vagary, *whim*, 608.

Vagary, *absurdity*, 497.
   imagination, 515.
   antic, 856.
Vagrant, *moving*, 264.
   roving, 266.
   traveller, 268.
Vague, *uncertain*, 475.
   obscure, 519.
   style, 571.
Vails, 809.
Vain, *unreal*, 2.
   unprofitable, 645.
   conceited, 880.
   unvalued, 866.
Vain-glorious,   *haughty*,
878.
   boasting, 884.
   vain, 880.
Vaivode, 745.
Vale, 252.
Valediction, *departure*, 292.
   courtesy, 894.
Valentine, *courtship*, 902.
Valet, 746.
Valetudinarian, 655.
Valiant, 861.
Valid, *strong*, 159.
   powerful, 157.
   influential, 175.
*Valise, 191.
Valley, 252.
Vallum, 717.
Valour, 861.
Valuable, 648.
Value, *price*, 812.
   goodness, 648.
   importance, 642.
   to measure, 466.
   estimate, 480.
Valueless, 645.
Valve, *stop*, 263.
   conduit, 350.
Vamp, 658.
Vampire, *bane*, 663.
   demon, 980.
Van, *front*, 234.
   beginning, 66.
   waggon, 272.
Vandal, 876.
Vandalism, 851.
Vane, 550.
Vanguard, *front*, 234.
   beginning, 66.
Vanish, *disappear*, 449.
   perish, 2.
   transient, 111.
Vanity, *conceit*, 880.
   worthlessness, 645.
Vanquish, 731.
Vanquished, 732.

Vantage ground, 175.
Vapid, *insipid*, 391.
   unattractive, 866.
   style, 575.
Vaporization, 336.
Vapour, *gas*, 334.
   bubble, 353.
   insolence, 885.
   boasting, 884.
   chimera, 515.
   rare, 322.
Vapours, *megrims*, 837.
Variable, *changeable*, 149.
   irresolute, 605.
Variance, *difference*, 15.
   disagreement, 24.
   discord, 713.
Variation, *non-imitation*, 20.
   irrelation, 10.
Varied, 15.
Variegation, 440.
Variety, 15.
   exception, 83.
Various, 15.
   many, 102.
Varlet, 949.
Varnish, *coat*, 222.
   decorate, 845, 847.
   sophistry, 477.
   falsehood, 544.
   excuse, 937.
Varying, 15.
Vase, 191.
Vassal, 746.
Vassalage, 749.
Vast, *in quantity*, 31.
   in size, 192.
Vat, 191.
Vaticination, 511.
*Vaudeville, 599.
Vault, *cellar*, 191.
   sepulchre, 363.
   to leap, 305, 309.
Vaulting, *superiority*, 33.
   aspiring, 865.
Vaunt, 884.
*Vaurien, 949.
Vection, 270.
Vectitation, 270.
Veda, 986.
Vedette, 664, 668.
Veer, *regression*, 283.
   deviate, 279.
   change intention, 607.
Vegetable, 365, 367.
Vegetarian, 953.
Vegetate, *grow*, 194.
   insensibility, 823.
Vehemence, *violence*, 173.
412

Vehemence, *emotion*, 825.
Vehicle, 272.
Veil, *mask*, 530.
   to conceal, 528.
   shade, 424.
   covering, 225.
Veiled, 447.
   latent, 526.
Vein, *humour*, 602.
   affections, 820.
   mine, 636.
Veined, 440.
Velitation, 720.
Velleity, 600.
Vellicating, 392.
Vellum, 590.
Velocity, 274.
Velvet, *soft*, 255.
   ease, 705.
   physical pleasure, 277.
   moral pleasure, 827.
Venal, 819.
Vend, 796.
Vender, 797.
Vendible, 796.
Vendidad, 986.
Venditation, 884.
Veneer, 222.
Venemous, 649.
Veneration, *respect*, 928.
   piety, 987.
Vengeance, 919.
   (with a), 31.
Vengeful, 919.
Venial, 937.
Venom, *bane*, 663.
   malignity, 907.
Vent, *air-pipe*, 351.
   emit, 294.
   sale, 796.
Ventiduct, 351.
Ventilate, *perflate*, 349.
   clean, 652.
Ventilator, 349.
Ventosity, 349.
Ventricle, 191.
Ventriloquism, 580.
Venture, *chance*, 156.
   to try, 675.
   danger, 665.
   courage, 861.
Venturous, 861.
Venue, 182.
Venus, *beauty*, 845.
   love, 897.
Veracious, 543.
Veracity, 543.
Veranda, 191.
Verbal, 562.
*Verbatim, 19, 562.

*Verbiage, *diffuse*, 573.
   nonsense, 497.
Verbose, 573.
Verdant, *green*, 435.
   vegetation, 367.
Verdantique, 435.
Verdict, *opinion*, 480.
   sentence, 969.
Verdigris, 435.
Verdure, 435.
Verecundity, *modesty*, 881.
   humility, 879.
Verge, *brink*, 230.
   to tend, 278.
   contribute, 176.
Verger, 996.
Verify, *test*, 463.
   demonstrate, 478.
   judge, 480.
   warrant, 771.
Verily, *positively*, 32.
Verisimilitude, 472.
Veritable, 494.
Verity, 494.
Verjuice, 397.
Vermicular, 248.
Vermiform, 248.
Vermilion, 434.
Vermin, *base*, 876.
   unclean, 653.
Vernacular, 560.
Vernal, *early*, 123.
   spring, 125.
Versatile, 605.
Verse, 597.
Versed, 698.
Versicolor, 440.
Versifier, 597.
Version, 522.
Vertex, 210.
Vertical, 212.
Verticity, 312.
Vertigo, 503.
*Verve, 515, 820.
Very, 31.
Vesicle, *cell*, 191.
   globe, 249.
Vespers, 998.
Vessel, *recipient*, 191.
   ship, 273.
   tube, 260.
Vest, *dress*, 225.
   give, 784.
Vestal, 960.
Vestibule, *entrance*, 66.
   room, 191.
Vestige, 551.
Vestry, *conclave*, 995.
   church, 1000.
Vesture, 225.

Veteran, *old*, 130.
   adept, 700.
*Veto, 761.
*Vetturino, 694.
Vex, 830.
Vexation, 828.
Vexatious, 830.
Viability, 359.
Vial, *bottle*, 191.
   wrath, 900.
Viands, 299.
Viaticum, 998.
Vibrate, 314.
Vicar, 996.
Vicarage, *office*, 995.
   house, 1000.
Vicarious, 755.
Vice, *guiltiness*, 945.
   deputy, 759.
Vicegerency, 755.
Vicegerent, 758, 759.
Vice-president, 745.
Viceroy, 759.
*Vice versâ, 148.
Vicinity, 197.
Vicissitude, 140, 149.
Victim, *injured*, 732.
   dupe, 547.
   sufferer, 828.
Victimize, *deceive*, 545.
   baffle, 731.
Victualling, 637.
Victuals, 299.
*Videlicet, *example*, 82.
   namely, 522.
   specification, 79.
Vie, 720.
*Vielle, 417.
View, *sight*, 441.
   appearance, 448.
   to attend to, 457.
   landscape, 556.
   opinion, 484.
   intention, 620.
Viewless, 447.
Vigilance, 457, 459.
Vignette, 558.
Vigour, *strong*, 149.
   healthy, 654.
   activity, 683.
   energy, 171.
   style, 574.
Vile, *bad*, 649.
   valueless, 643.
   disgraceful, 874.
   dishonorable, 940.
   plebeian, 876.
Vilify,   } *censure*, 932.
Vilipend, } *shame*, 874.
   disrespect, 929, 930.

Villa, 189.
Village, 189.
Villager, 188.
Villain, 945.
Villany, 945.
Villenage, 749.
Villous, 256.
Vincible, 160.
Vinculum, 45.
Vindicate, *justify*, 937.
   a claim, 924.
Vindictive,   *revengeful*,
   919.
   irascible, 901.
Vinegar, 397.
Vineyard, 371.
Vintage, 371.
Viol, 417.
Violate, *disobey*, 742.
   engagement, 773.
   right, 925.
   duty, 927.
   a usage, 614.
Violence, 173.
   arbitrariness, 964.
Violently, 31.
Violet, 437.
Violin, 417.
Violincello, 417.
Violinist, 416.
Viper, *bane*, 663.
   miscreant, 949.
Virago, 901.
Virent, 435.
Virgin, *girl*, 129.
   celibacy, 904.
Virginal, 417.
Viridescent, 435.
Virile, *manly*, 373.
   adolescent, 131.
   strong, 159.
*Virtu, 850.
Virtual, 2.
Virtually, 494.
Virtue, *goodness*, 944.
   power, 157.
   courage, 861.
Virtueless, 945.
*Virtuoso, 850.
Virulence, *energy*, 171.
   insalubrity, 657.
Virus, *poison*, 663.
   disease, 655.
Visage, *front*, 234.
   appearance, 448.
*Vis-à-vis, 234.
Viscera, 221.
Viscid, 352.
Viscount, 875.
Viscous, 352.

Vishnu, 979.
Visible, 446.
Vision, *sight*, 441.
   apparition, 980.
Visionary, *erroneous*, 495.
   imaginary, 515.
   heterodox, 984.
Visit, *sociality*, 892.
   arrival, 293.
Visitation, *pain*, 828.
   calamity, 830.
Visitor, *director*, 694.
Visor, 528.
Vista, *point of view*, 441.
   prospect, 448.
Visual, 441.
Vital, 642.
Vitality, 359.
Vitals, 221.
Vitiate, 659.
Vitrefy, 321.
Vitreous, 321.
Vituperate, 932.
*Vivâ voce, 582.
Vivacious, *active*, 682.
   sensitive, 822.
   cheerful, 836.
Vivid, *light*, 420.
   colour, 428.
   energetic, 171.
Vivify, 359.
Vixen, 901.
Vizier, 759.
Vizor, 528, 546.
Vocable, 562.
Vocabulary, 562.
Vocal, *voice*, 580.
   music, 415.
Vocalist, 416.
Vocalize, 580.
Vocation, 625.
Vociferate, *cry*, 411.
   loudness, 404.
   voice, 580.
Vogue, *fashion*, 852.
   custom, 613.
Voice, 580.
   sound, 402.
   cry, 411.
   choice, 609.
   opinion, 484.
Void, *vacuum*, 2, 4.
   absence, 187.
   to emit, 296.
Volant, 267.
Volatile, *vaporizable*, 336.
   irresolute, 605.
Volatility, 608.
Volcanic, 173.
Volition, 267.

Volition, 600.
Volley, *impulse*, 276.
   attack, 716.
   violence, 173.
   collection, 72.
*Voltigeur, 726.
Voluble, 584.
Volume, *bulk*, 192.
   book, 593.
Voluntary, *willing*, 602.
   music, 415.
Volunteer, *endeavour*, 676.
   offer, 763.
Voluptuary, 962.
Voluptuous, *sensual*, 954.
   pleasure, 377, 827, 829.
Volutation, 312.
Volute, 248.
Vomit, 296.
Voracious, 865.
Vote, 609.
Votive, 768.
Vouch, *testify*, 467.
   assert, 535.
Voucher, *evidence*, 467.
   record, 551.
Vouchsafe, *permit*, 760.
   consent, 762.
   ask, 765.
Vow, *promise*, 768.
   assert, 535.
   worship, 990.
Voyage, 267.
Vulgar, *unrefined*, 851.
   commonalty, 876.
Vulgate, 985.
Vulnerable, 665.
Vulnerary, 662.
Vulpine, 702.
Vulture, 663.

W.

Wabble, 314.
Wadding, 263.
Waddle, 275.
Wade, 267.
Wafer, 204.
Waft, *transfer*, 270.
   blow, 267.
Wag, *oscillate*, 314.
   agitate, 315.
   wit, 844.
Wage war, 720.
Wager, 621.
Wages, 809.
Waggery, 842.
Waggle, 314, 315.
Waggon (*or* wagon), 272.
414

Wail, 839.
Wain, 272.
Wainscot, 224.
Waist, 203.
Waistcoat, 225.
Wait, *tarry*, 133.
   expect, 121, 507.
   inaction, 681.
Wait on, *accompany*, 88.
   help, 707.
   call on, 894.
Waiter, 746.
Waits, 416.
Wake, *sequel*, 65.
   back, 235.
   trace, 551.
   to excite, 824.
   funeral, 363.
Walk, *move*, 266.
   region, 181.
   business, 625.
   way, 627.
   conduct, 692.
   arena, 728.
Wall, *lining*, 224.
   inclosure, 231, 232.
   prison, 752.
   asylum, 666.
   defence, 717.
   obstacle, 705.
   (take the), 878.
Wallet, 191.
Wallop, 315.
Wallow, 312.
Wamble, 867.
Wan, 429.
Wand, 747.
Wander, *roam*, 266.
   deviate, 279.
   circuit, 629.
   delirium, 503.
Wanderer, 268.
Wane, *decay*, 659.
   contract, 195.
Want, *desire*, 865.
   require, 630.
   scant, 640.
   poverty, 804.
   incomplete, 53.
Wantless, 639.
Wanton, *unrestrained*, 748.
   impure, 961.
War, 722.
War cry, 550.
War whoop, 550.
Warble, 415.
Ward, *restraint*, 751.
   safety, 664.
   asylum, 666.
Ward off, *defend*, 717.

Ward off, *avert*, 706.
Warden, *guardian*, 664.
   deputy, 759.
   master, 745.
Wardmote, 966.
Wardrobe, 225.
Wardship, 664.
Ware, 798.
Warehouse, *store*, 636.
   mart, 799.
Warfare, 722.
Warlike, 720.
Warlock, *spirit*, 980.
   sorcerer, 994.
Warm, *hot*, 382.
   ardent, 821, 824.
   angry, 900.
   irascible, 901.
Warming pan, *heater*, 386.
   preparation, 673.
Warmth, *heat*, 382.
   emotion, 821.
   passion, 900.
Warn, *admonish*, 695.
   forebode, 511.
Warning, 668.
   omen, 512.
   alarm, 669.
Warp, *narrow*, 203.
   deviate, 279.
   prejudice, 481.
   imperfect, 651.
   sail, 267.
Warrant, *evidence*, 467.
   order, 741.
   permit, 760.
   protest, 535.
   money order, 800.
   security, 771.
   to authorize, 737.
Warranty, *surety*, 771.
   sanction, 924.
Warren, 168.
Warrior, 726.
Wart, 250.
Wary, *cautious*, 864.
   careful, 459.
Wash, *cleanse*, 652.
   colour, 428.
   water, 337.
   marsh, 345.
Wash out, 552.
Washy, *watery*, 337.
   weak, 160.
   valueless, 645.
   style, 573.
Waspish, 901.
Wassail, *feast*, 840.
Waste, *decrease*, 36.
   contract, 195.

Waste, *expend*, 638.
  destroy, 162.
  vacant space, 180.
  plain, 344.
  misuse, 679.
  useless, 645.
  prodigality, 818.
  refuse, 643.
  loss, 776.
Wasted, 160.
Wasteful, 818.
Waste-pipe, 350.
Watch, *observe*, 441.
  attend to, 457.
  expect, 507.
  sentinel, 753.
  clock, 114.
Watchet, 438.
Watchfire, 550.
Watchful, 459.
Watchman, 664.
Watch-tower, 668.
Watchword, 550.
Water, 337.
Watercourse, 350.
Waterfall, 348.
Watergate, 350.
Waterlogged, *danger*, 665.
  difficulty, 704.
Waterspout, 348.
Wave, *of water*, 348.
  the sea, 341.
  sinuous, 248.
  oscillate, 314.
  hint, 527.
Waver, 603, 605.
Wavy, 248.
Wax, *become*, 144.
  soft, 324.
  unctuous, 355.
  substance, 356.
Way, *road*, 627.
  space, 180.
  passage, 302.
  conduct, 692.
  habit, 613.
Ways and means, 632.
Wayfarer, 268.
Waylay, 545.
Wayward, *obstinate*, 606.
  capricious, 608.
  discourteous, 895.
Wayworn, 688.
Weak, *feeble*, 160.
  small in degree, 32.
  foolish, 499.
  irresolute, 605.
  compassionate, 914.
  vicious, 945.
Weak-headed, 499.

Weak-hearted, 862.
Weaken, 160.
  decrease, 36.
Weak side, 945.
Weal, 618.
Weald, 367.
Wealth, 803.
Wean, *change habit*, 614.
  change opinion, 484.
Weapon, 633, 727.
Wear, *decrease*, 36.
  decay, 659.
  use, 677.
  clothe, 225.
Wear and tear, *waste*, 638.
  injury, 619.
Wear off, *diminish*, 36.
  cease, 141.
  habit, 614.
Wear out, *damage*, 659.
  fatigue, 688.
Wearisome, ⎱ *fatigue*, 688.
Weary, ⎰ *ennui*, 841.
  uneasy, 828.
Weasand, 351.
Weather, 338.
  succeed, 731.
Weatherbeaten, 160.
Weathercock, *irresolute*, 605.
  mutable, 149.
Weatherglass, 466.
Weatherwise, 511.
Weave, 219.
  produce, 161.
Web, *texture*, 329.
  intersection, 219.
Wed, 903.
Wedded to, *habit*, 613.
  opinion, 484.
  obstinate, 606.
Wedge, *sharp*, 253.
  intervention, 228.
  instrument, 633.
  to insert, 301.
  locate, 184.
  join, 43.
  ingress, 295.
Wedlock, 903.
Weetless, 491.
Weigh, *heavy*, 319.
  ponder, 451.
  measure, 466.
  lift, 307.
Weigh (under), 282.
Weigh anchor, 292.
Weigh down, *aggrieve*, 649.
Weigh with, 615.
Weight, *influence*, 175.
  gravity, 319.

Weight, *importance*, 642.
Weightless, 320.
Weir, 706.
Weird, 994.
Welcome, *grateful*, 829.
  sociality, 892.
  reception, 894.
  arrival, 293.
  friendly, 888.
Weld, 46.
Welfare, 734.
Welkin, 318.
Well, *water*, 343.
  to flow, 348.
  much, 31.
  healthy, 654.
  deep, 208.
  assent, 488.
  origin, 153.
Well to do, 734.
Well-a-day, 839.
Well-a-way, 839.
Well-being, *prosperity*, 734.
  gratification, 827.
Well-born, *patrician*, 875.
Well-bred, *courteous*, 894.
  genteel, 852.
Well-doing, 944.
Well done ! 932.
Well enough, 651.
Well-favoured, 845.
Well-founded, *probable*, 472.
Well-grounded, 490.
Well-informed, 490.
Well-intended, 944.
Well-mannered, 894.
Well-meant, 906.
Well-met, 892.
Well-nigh, 32.
Well off, 734.
Well-spent, 731.
Well-tasted, 394.
Well-timed, 134.
Well-wisher, 890.
Welt, 230.
Welter, 312.
Wem, 848.
Wen, 250.
Wench, *girl*, 129, 374.
  impure, 961, 962.
Wend, 266.
Wet, *water*, 337.
  moisture, 339.
Whack, 276.
Whale, 192.
Whaler, 273.
Whallop, 972.
Wharf, 189.
Wheal, 250.

Wrapper, *dress*, 225.
Wraprascal, 225.
Wrapt, 451.
Wrench, *extract*, 300.
   seize, 789.
   draw, 285.
Wrest, *seize*, 789.
   distort, 523.
Wrestle, 720.
Wrestler, 726.
Wretch, *sinner*, 949.
   apostate, 941.
Wretched, *unhappy*, 828.
   bad, 649.
   contemptible, 643.
Wriggle, 314, 315.
Wright, 690.
Wring, *pain*, 378.
   to torment, 830.
Wring from, 789.
Wrinkle, 258.
Writ, *order*, 741.
   in law, 969.
Write, 590.
Writhe, *agitate*, 315.
   pain, 378, 828.
Writing (act of), 590.
   book, 593.
Wrong, *evil*, 619.
   badness, 649.
   vice, 945.
   immoral, 923.
Wrong-doer, 949.
Wrong-headed, 499.
Wrought up, 824.
Wry, *oblique*, 217.
   distorted, 243.
Wynd, 189.

X.

Xebec, 273.
Xylography, 558.

Y.

Yacht, 273.
Yahoo, 876.
Yap, 412.
Yard, *workshop*, 691.
   abode, 189.
Yarn, *filament*, 205.
   exaggeration, 549.
Yawl, 273.
Yawn, *open*, 260.
   fatigue, 688.
   sluggish, 683.
   insensible, 823.
Yclept, 564.
Yea, 488.
Year, 108.
Yearn, *desire*, 865.
   pity, 914.
   love, 897.
   sad, 837.
Yeast, 353.
Yell, *cry*, 411.
   complain, 839.
Yellow, 436.
Yelp, 412.
Yeoman, 373.
Yerk, *kick*, 276.
   attack, 716.
Yes, *affirmation*, 488.
   consent, 762.
Yesterday, 122.
Yet, *exception*, 83.
   time, 106.
   counteraction, 179.
Yield, *submit*, 725.
   obey, 743.
   consent, 762.
   furnish, 784.
   gain, 810.
   price, 812.
   facility, 705.
Yoke, *join*, 43.
   vinculum, 45.

Yoke, *couple*, 89.
   subjection, 749.
Yonder, 196.
Yonker, 129.
Yore, 122.
Young, 127.
Youngster, 129.
Youth, *age*, 127.
   lad, 129.

Z.

Zany, 501.
Zeal, *activity*, 682.
   feeling, 821.
Zealot, *active*, 682.
   resolute, 604.
Zealotry, 606.
Zebra, 440.
Zendavesta, 986.
Zenith, *summit*, 210.
   climax, 33.
Zephyr, 349.
Zest, *relish*, 394.
- *enjoyment*, 827.
Zero, *nothing*, 4.
   naught, 101.
Zig-zag, *angle*, 244.
   obliquity, 217.
   oscillation, 314.
   circuit, 629.
Zodiac, 229.
Zohygiastics, 370.
Zoilus, 921.
*Zollverein, 769.
Zone, *circle*, 247.
   belt, 229.
   layer, 204.
Zoography, 368.
Zoology, 368.
Zoophyte, 366.
Zootomy, 368.
Zoroaster, 986.
Zymotic, 657.

THE END.

LONDON:
SPOTTISWOODES and SHAW,
New-street-Square.